Crusader Institutions

JOSHUA PRAWER

Clarendon Press · Oxford

1980

Oxford University Press, Walton Street, Oxford OX2 6DP

OXFORD LONDON GLASGOW
NEW YORK TORONTO MELBOURNE WELLINGTON
KUALA LUMPUR SINGAPORE JAKARTA HONG KONG TOKYO
DELHI BOMBAY CALCUTTA MADRAS KARACHI
NAIROBI DAR ES SALAAM CAPE TOWN

Published in the United States by Oxford University Press, New York

British Library Cataloguing in Publication Data

Prawer, Joshua
    Crusader institutions.
      1. Jerusalem – History – Latin Kingdom, 1099–1244
    I. Title
    956.9   D182   79-40296

ISBN 0–19–822536–9

Typeset by CCC and printed and bound at William Clowes (Beccles)
Limited, Beccles and London

For my wife, Hadassa

Contents

List of Abbreviations

AOL	*Archives de l'Orient Latin*, 2 vols. (Paris, 1881–4).
Benvenisti, *Crusaders*	M. Benvenisti, *The Crusaders in the Holy Land* (Jerusalem, 1970).
Delaborde	H. F. Delaborde, *Chartes de la Terre Sainte provenant de l'abbaye de Notre-Dame de Josaphat* (Paris, 1880).
Delaville	J. Delaville le Roulx, *Cartulaire générale de l'ordre des Hospitaliers de Saint-Jean de Jérusalem, 1100–1310*, 4 vols. (Paris, 1894–1906).
Delaville, *Archives*	J. Delaville le Roulx, *Les Archives, la bibliothèque et le trésor de l'ordre de Saint-Jean de Jérusalem à Malte* (Paris, 1883).
Eracles	*L'Estoire d'Eracles Empereur* (*RHC Occ.*).
John of Ibelin	*Livre de Jean d'Ibelin* (*Lois* i. 7–423).
Kohler	C. Kohler, *Chartes de l'abbaye de Notre-Dame de la vallée de Josaphat. Analyses et extraits* (Paris, 1900), previously published in *ROL* 7.
La Monte, *Feudal Monarchy*	J. L. La Monte, *Feudal Monarchy in the Latin Kingdom of Jerusalem* (Cambridge, Mass., 1932).
LdAdB	*Livres des Assises des Bourgeois*, ed. H. Kausler, in *Les Livres des Assises et des usages dou reaume de Jérusalem* i (Stuttgart, 1839).
Livre au Roi	ed. Beugnot, *Lois* i. 601–44.
Livre du plédéant	*Livre du plédéant et du plaidoyer* in *Assises du royaume de Jérusalem* ii, ed. V. Foucher (Rennes, 1840) or Beugnot, *Lois* ii.
Lois	*RHC Lois*, ed. Beugnot, 2 vols. (Paris, 1841–3).
MGH SS	*Monumenta Germaniae Historica. Scriptores*, 1826 ff.
Müller	G. Müller, *Documenti sulle relazioni delle città toscane coll' Oriente* (Florence, 1879).
Phillip of Novara	*Livre de Philippe de Navarre, Lois* i. 469–571.
PPTS	*Palestine Pilgrims' Text Society*, 13 vols. (London, 1896–1907).
Prawer, *Histoire*	J. Prawer, *Histoire du royaume latin de Jérusalem*, 2 vols. (Paris, 1869–70, 2nd edn. 1975).
Prawer, *Latin Kingdom*	J. Prawer, *The Latin Kingdom of Jerusalem. European Colonialism in the Middle Ages* (London, 1972).
Regesta	R. Röhricht, *Regesta Regni Hierosolymitani* and *Additamentum* (Innsbruck, 1893–1904).
RHC	*Recueil des Historiens des Croisades*.
HOcc.	*Historiens occidentaux*. 5 vols. (Paris, 1844–95).
HOr.	*Historiens orientaux*. 5 vols. (Paris, 1872–1906).
HArm.	*Documents arméniens*. 2 vols. (Paris, 1869–1906).
HGr.	*Historiens grecs*. 2 vols. (Paris, 1875–81).

RHDFE	*Revue historique de droit français et étranger.*
Richard, *Royaume latin*	J. Richard, *Le Royaume latin de Jérusalem* (Paris, 1953).
Riley-Smith,	J. Riley-Smith, *The Feudal Nobility and the Kingdom of*
Feudal Nobility	*Jerusalem, 1174–1277* (London, 1973).
Riley-Smith, *Knights*	J. Riley-Smith, *The Knights of St. John of Jerusalem and*
of St. John	*Cyprus, 1050–1310* (London, 1967).
Röhricht, *GKJ*	R. Röhricht, *Geschichte des Königreichs Jerusalem* (Innsbruck, 1898).
ROL	*Revue de l'Orient Latin,* 13 vols.
Rozière	E. de Rozière, *Cartulaire de l'église du Saint-Sépulcre de Jérusalem (Paris, 1849).*
Smail, *Crusading Warfare*	R.C. Smail, *Crusading Warfare (Cambridge, 1956).*
Strehlke	E. Strehlke, *Tabulae Ordinis Theutonici* (Berlin, 1869); phot. reprint with an introduction by H. E. Mayer (Toronto, 1975).
Tafel–Thomas	G. L. F. Tafel and G. M. Thomas, *Urkunden aur älteren Handels- und Staatsgeschichte der Republik Venedig,* 3 vols. (Vienna, 1856–7).
W. T.	Willelmus Tyrensis, *Historia rerum in partibus transmarinis gestarum.* RHC HOcc. I 1–2.
ZDPV	*Zeitschrift des Deutschen Palästina-Vereins.*

Introduction

In the past generation there has been a remarkable revival of interest, within the field of medieval studies, in the Crusades, marked by a pronounced shift in emphasis from the Crusades as a movement to the history of Crusader establishments in the East, and attracting a steadily increasing number of scholars and students. This is not to imply that the more traditional lines of inquiry are being abandoned. Current studies of the Crusades continue to contribute to a better understanding of the ever-fascinating questions of their origins, motives, and their many-sided political and ideological facets, as well as to what might be described as their 'posthumous' existence well into the later Middle Ages. Yet, paralleling this more traditional approach, there is an ever-growing interest in the tangible results of the movement, the European colonies on the eastern shores of the Mediterranean.

A growing number of scholars are now exploring problems which, although they have been the subject of research in the field of European medieval history for more than a century, have only recently begun to engage the interest of those involved in Crusader studies—the constitutional and legal, cultural, social, and economic history of the Crusader establishments in the East. Though not entirely new (some excellent work in the field was done even before the First World War), the recent approach has combined a better knowledge of sources with a more rigorous method of research and a better understanding of the problems and mechanisms of society and economy. The new focus of interest, the concentration on particular subjects, has resulted in a large and growing number of monographs, which are a constant feature of Crusader studies today. The fruits of these studies, which have substantially contributed to a new image of the Latin establishments in the East and the first encounter of Christian Europe and the Muslim Near East, have already begun to be integrated into new histories of the Crusades and of the Crusader Kingdom. The validity, however, of any such synthesis must in the last resort be based on monographic studies of the specific aspects of Crusader society. This is the reason for, and justification of, the following study, which in its five parts deals with the major aspects of Crusader existence in Outremer. The division into parts might be found schematic and even somewhat arbitrary, as the various sections bear in one way or another, though from different perspectives, on problems of social stratification, social classes, and the economic foundations of their existence. Even legal and constitutional history is, in a sense, social history conceived in legal terms, and cultural history expressed in social *mores* transferred from Europe to the Crusader colonies. Still, this division seemed convenient to promote the organization of the material in a coherent manner.

The first section deals with the feudal aristocracy of the Latin Kingdom, its emergence, evolution, and impact on Crusader constitutional history. Taken together as a whole, the chapters of this section provide a description of what seem to me the major trends in the evolution of the Frankish nobility and its shaping of the political regime of the kingdom.

The following section treats the Syro-Palestinian rural regime and the Crusaders' attempts to colonize the conquered country and exploit its agricultural resources. The attempts to colonize the country by the European immigrant population are studied from two aspects: urban settlement in Jerusalem and rural settlements in the countryside, where, paralleling and imitating European practices, particular *consuetudines* of colonization developed.

The study of agriculture is based on the Syro-Palestinian villages of the coastal plain of ancient Phoenicia around Tyre. The available statistical data bear on demography and on countryside and city conditions as well as on aspects of economy and possessory relations. In addition, the existing documentation permits a reconstruction of agricultural techniques, crops, crop rotation, and Crusader taxation of the countryside—that is, of the native peasant population. In this context some basic questions, such as that of the permanency of patterns of settlement in this area, are broached. The relevance of this aspect of Outremer study transcends the period under discussion, because Crusader documentation supplies data almost entirely lacking for rural relations in the previous Arab period and very scarce even in the following period of Mameluk domination.

In the closing part in this section the legal standing of the native population, both rural and nomad, is discussed. Here we encounter the serfs, a class which did not legally exist during the previous Arab period and arose in the wake of the Crusader conquest. But this was serfdom of a particular type because it was not only occupation but also religion and habitat that were decisive in fixing the legal status of the native population of the kingdom.

The third section deals with the two major non-noble components of Crusader society: the members of the Italian communes and the Frankish burgesses. The Italians, far better known of the two as a result of many economic studies, are envisaged from the point of view of the Crusader Orient. I have concentrated on the Venetians partly because of the relative wealth of documentation, but mainly because I feel that they succeeded, where the other communes did less, in creating a state within a state. A comparison of Crusader documentation of the two largest Italian emporia in the Latin Kingdom—Acre (for which we also make use of a recent archaeological survey) and Tyre—give us a very detailed picture of their physical features in terms of territorial space, number of houses, and even of rooms and rents. The changing type of Italian, from wandering and trafficking merchants to permanent settlers, as well as their colonial administration, can be seen in these reconstructed Levantine surroundings, where they tried to colonize the Crusader colonizers.

The bulk of this section, however, deals with Crusader cities and their non-noble Frankish inhabitants. Despite the fact that the overwhelming majority of European colonists were 'burgesses'—that is, according to Crusader definitions, non-nobles, commoners—they are only now beginning to be studied in detail. A primary factor, legal as well as economic, in defining this class of Frankish commoners is linked to the property-type identified with them—the burgage-tenure or *borgesie*. It was the *borgesies* that furnished the overwhelming bulk of business that came before the most important institution of Frankish city administration and burgess jurisdiction, the very famous, but little-studied, Court of Burgesses. I have endeavoured to follow the emergence, evolution, and functioning of this court, which became an integral part of royal and seignorial administration, as well as the only institution that could on occasion express the sentiments of the burgesses of the city or of the kingdom.

The study of the royal Court of Burgesses in Jerusalem has brought to light the existence of an ecclesiastical lordship in the Crusader capital city, the 'Quarter of the Patriarch', a transformed remnant of the previous period, but also a vestige of a once vigorous territorial and theocratic claim of the ecclesiastical hierarchy in the kingdom. The study of city lordships and administration brings to light the existence of an urban patriciate of the capital. This upper stratum of the burgesses of Jerusalem seems to have differed in function and composition from its counterpart in Acre, the economic and, later, official capital of the Second Kingdom.

City properties were often either *francalmoigns* held by ecclesiastical establishments or quasi-burgage-tenures held by the Italian communes. This created complicated problems of jurisdiction, since both types of property tended to become immunities with claims transcending landownership and emerging as overlordships. The possessory relations exhibit the same centrifugal tendencies that mark the constitutional evolution of the kingdom. The last chapter of this section attempts, in the light of this earlier evidence, to reconsider the standing of the burgesses in the kingdom, particularly in regard to their relations with the Crown.

The following section, on the legal sources and legal history, deals with several problems which, although they have been studied relatively little, are of paramount importance for understanding almost every aspect of life in Outremer. The analysis of the basic notions connected with feudal property and, in particular, allodial property, shows peculiarities of Crusader feudo-vassalic relations unsuspected in a kingdom described as the 'Paradise of feudalism'. The following chapters deal with legal sources, the most important being the *Livre des Assises des Bourgeois*. The proof that a twelfth-century Provençal manual of Roman law served as a model for the *Livre des Assises des Bourgeois* and the study of how it was used a century later by the anonymous Crusader jurist of Acre contribute to the understanding of Crusader legal realities. Whereas literary legal influences lead to Provence and perhaps to Italy, a study of the actual legislation points to what might be called the 'Reception of Roman law' on the one hand, and to direct contacts with the heart of France, the royal Capetian domain, on the other. The latter can be illustrated by Crusader penal law, which survived the kingdom and remained in force in later centuries in Cyprus.

The final section, on military history, deals with an outline of Crusader political and strategic thinking, and with a case study of the disastrous battle of Hattin, one of the most famous of medieval and Crusader battles.

Of the nineteen chapters that comprise this book, four have already been published in English, and five in other languages. Because they appeared over a long stretch of time and in diverse periodicals which are not all acccessible, it seemed useful to gather them together, along with the ten new studies, in a single volume. The earlier studies have been changed to correct obvious errors, some have been enlarged, others slightly shortened to prevent redundancies or overlappings. In all cases I have indicated studies that have appeared since the original publication and that bear on the subject. As pioneering studies, they are characterized by the shortcomings, but also the challenge, of research in a newly opened field. I hope that they will contribute to our knowledge of the Middle Ages in general and of the Crusader Kingdom in particular, and will act as a stimulant for continued research in these areas.

My debt to scholars is amply attested in the notes, but I owe a great deal to friends and colleagues who have encouraged and stimulated my studies at different times and places. I happily take this occasion to acknowledge my debt and gratitude to some of them. It will be only proper to state here my debt to my own teachers, the late R. Koebner of Breslau and later of Jerusalem; to Ch.-E. Perrin and R. Fawtier of Paris, as well as to Y. Baer of Jerusalem. I owe a great deal to the late Ch. Wirszubski, a classicist turned Kabbala and Renaissance scholar, whose untimely death deprived me of a lifelong friend and mentor. The generosity and unsparing interest of my friends R. C. Smail of Sidney Sussex College, Cambridge, J. Richard of the University of Dijon, and H. E. Mayer of Kiel University, in whose company I travelled many a Crusader road, were always a source of stimulation and encouragement. My warmest thanks are due to Mme M. Mulon of the Archives Nationales in Paris and to my former students and colleagues E. Sivan and B. Kedar of the Hebrew University of Jerusalem. Their critical reading and help were invaluable. Miss S. Schein, presently of Haifa University, facilitated the arduous task of writing and annotating the text, and Mrs. S. Argyle was instrumental in editing and giving it its final form. I owe a great debt to P. Lemerle of the Collège de France whose solicitude and interest in the progress of my work accompanied me for many years. Last but not least, my thanks to M. Wallace-Hadrill for his courtesy in helping me to find my way at All Souls College, Oxford. The matchless hospitality of its warden and fellows enabled me to finish this book in its august precincts.

Hebrew University, Jerusalem,   J. P.
1978

The Feudal System
and Constitutional History

1 The Earliest Period of Crusader Feudalism: A Reconsideration[1]

Among the many myths of history denounced today, the feudal system is one of the historian's favourites. What is attacked is not so much the notion of the feudal system or feudal society but the definite article—*the* feudal system, *the* feudal society. These expressions, which still exist in general histories and manuals of the history of law, are disappearing from the vocabulary of research. Time and again we have been taught that there was nothing that could be identified with a European feudal system; at a given period the social and political structure of Europe revealed characteristics that could be found almost everywhere in Western Europe, more marked in some places, diversely nuanced, changing in time and space. As many species of the same genus, these characteristics adapted themselves to the land, climate, and mentality of given societies. Strangely enough, at a time when even legal historians are ceasing to use the expression without adding a qualitative adjective, the sociologists are using it voluntarily, unfortunately without all the painstaking precautions of a Max Weber.[2]

But although the term 'feudalism' is being used cautiously, there is one exception to the rule: the states founded by the Crusaders in the Orient. One has the impression that European erudition, which has succeeded in considering feudalism in a more realistic light, somehow wants to preserve a kind of *monumentum aere perennius* of that notion for the states founded by the Crusaders. The feudal system of the Latin establishments in the Near East have remained feudalism pure and simple.[3] It was labelled as such, and so distinguished a scholar as the late J. L. La Monte devoted his

---

[1] This chapter was previously published as 'Les premiers temps de la féodalité dans le royaume latin de Jérusalem: une reconsidération', *Revue d'histoire du droit* 22 (1954), 401–24.

[2] For a select bibliography see 'Feudalism' by J. Prawer and S. Eisenstadt in the *International Encyclopaedia of Social Sciences* (1968). An iconoclastic and lively discussion was started by my friend E. A. R. Brown, 'The tyranny of a construct: Feudalism and the historians of medieval Europe', *American Historical Review* 79 (1974), 1063–88.

[3] Cf. M. Grandclaude, *Étude critique sur les Livres des Assises de Jérusalem* (Paris, 1923).

last study to the defence of this purity in the states founded by the Crusaders—even in comparison with Anglo-Norman England.[4] In the following study we propose to reconsider the problem of Crusader feudalism. As it is a reconsideration, no new sources will be discussed. Our aim is to envisage the problem of the political regime of the Latin establishments in the Near East, and more especially that of the Latin Kingdom of Jerusalem, from a point of view which, we believe, merits more attention than it has attracted up to now.

Once the Crusader states have been declared a kind of *sauveté* of 'pure' feudalism in the Orient, it becomes difficult to define its essence. In particular cases historians have appealed to negative characteristics—for example the most allegedly evident, the weakness of the royal power in the face of a hereditary aristocracy which held the reins of government. This situation, it is argued, was easily realized in the Near East because the Latin Kingdom was able to create a monolithic building on a homogeneous plan, by the wholesale importation of a system which prevailed in northern France in the eleventh century. M. Bloch even decried Crusader feudalism as 'féodalité d'importation'.[5]

Moreover, whereas in northern France—that is France between the Seine and the Loire—this Gothic edifice was spanned and intersected by marble columns, remnants of older, imperial, and royal constructions, nothing of the kind influenced the structure of the Latin states. They were erected, so goes the argument, on a kind of *terra rasa* and there was nothing to prevent or impair their homogeneous architecture. The kingdom was the creation of the barons, the knights and nobles of the first Crusade; the *Advocatus Sancti Sepulcri* as well as his royal successors owed their throne to them. The structure of the kingdom thus reflects the circumstances of its creation. What the nobles wanted to create was a feudal Paradise, the realization of an ideal of the noble class, indifferent to the hopes and memories of a monarchy.

The homogeneity of the system was apparent in all parts of the body politic. The weakness of the royal power had its counterpart in the omnipotence of the aristocracy which ruled the country and its destinies from the summit of the *Haute Cour* or High Court. Jurisdiction, the most sensitive indicator of royal power, was entirely in the hands of the nobility. The lordships were autonomous principalities where the king's writ did

---

[4] J. L. La Monte, 'Three Questions concerning the Assizes of Jerusalem', *Byzantina—Metabyzantina* i (New York, 1949), 201–12.

[5] M. Bloch, *La Société féodale* i (Paris, 1939), 289.

not run. The whole framework of organization, all the services of the state, were feudalized. The vassalic relations assured the working of the administrative machinery and feudal law cemented the cohesion of the upper class of the Frankish population. This is the traditional picture of the Latin Kingdom and prima facie it is a plausible conjecture. With the exception of England, there were very few states for which one could muster such a large number of sources to support this thesis. It is precisely the question of proofs and evidence that we would like to analyse. The elements at the disposal of the historian are of two kinds:

1. Some actual premises as to the political heritage the Crusaders brought with them from Europe: to a large extent these premises, as well as the analysis of the events of the first Crusade, determine the answer to the question: what kind of state was created by the Crusaders?

2. A large number of sources and extracts almost entirely drawn from the treatises of jurisprudence written in the Latin Kingdom and in the Kingdom of Cyprus.

Before analysing and discussing the available material, we should realize how they affect and influence the whole picture. What we have termed premises are taken from eleventh-century France. The treatises of jurisprudence, with the exception of the *Livre au Roi*, which was composed in the last years of the twelfth century, belong to the middle and the second half of the thirteenth century. This means that these sources were written 150 years after the events. Unless we assume that during that period nothing, or almost nothing, changed, we are dangerously projecting to *c.* 1100 a situation which might have existed *c.* 1250. In fact, the historians of the Latin Kingdom too often present us with a static picture, as if almost no change at all took place in its 200-year-long existence. Here and there, to be exact, our attention is drawn to some changes, but they are hardly more than variations on the main theme.[6] Thus a strange illusion has been created—that of a frozen state and social structure. In no other place can one find, so to speak, such a fossilized situation. This is all the more improbable in view of the exceptional military and political vigour of the Latin Kingdom, at least during the first 100 years of its history.

Hypothesis, Right or Wrong?

The premises to which we have alluded tend to explain the organization of the Latin Kingdom by the wholesale importation of political practices

---

[6] The only change was triggered off by the famous *Assises sur la ligece* of King Amalric. Its importance and influence is discussed below, Ch. 2, pp. 36 ff.

common in northern France at the end of the eleventh century. But in the process of transplantation the remnants of the ancient royal institutions that survived until the eleventh century were consciously put aside and disregarded; only the essence of feudalism, so to speak, was infused into the embryonic political body of the newly created states in the Levant.

The transplanting of these institutions, customs, and practices has to take into account the media of transfer. In the final analysis it was the knowledge and consciousness of these customs and practices, the knowledge of these institutions, that made the transfer from one place to another possible. Consequently, we have to establish: (a) which institutions, customs, and practices could have been imported from France to the Orient; (b) what sort of men were the depositaries or the carriers of these traditions? These two problems can be summarized in one question: what were the political traditions of the French noble and knightly class that established itself in the Latin Kingdom?

It is well known that no member of the highest French aristocracy, with very few exceptions, remained in the Latin Kingdom after the first Crusade. Excluding the princely houses of Bohemond in Antioch, Raymond of St. Gilles in Tripoli, Godfrey of Bouillon in Jerusalem, and his brother Baldwin in Edessa, the nobility which survived the First Crusade returned to Europe. We can conclude from this that the Crusader nobility, the aristocracy which settled in the Latin Kingdom, did not belong to the European social élite. On the contrary, if at the end of the twelfth century Crusader nobility was regarded as belonging to the highest aristocracy in Christendom—a fact illustrated by their intermarriage with European princely families and even with the imperial dynasty of Byzantium—we have here a process whereby people of somewhat obscure origins rose to the highest steps of the social ladder in a few generations because they had installed themselves on the frontiers of Christendom. Henceforth they were regarded as champions of the faith, crowned with a halo of glory. A look at the *Familles d'Outremer* makes it clear that, with very few exceptions, it is impossible to link the great Crusader families to eleventh-century European aristocracy. The year 1095 seems to have been an impassable barrier. This is no pure coincidence. It is more plausible to account for the absence of famous ancestors and ancestral geneologies by the simple fact that they were unknown. Here and there, Du Cange found a *châtelain* or a viscount who might have had some connection with a Crusader family, but even this is unusual, if not impossible. A *Who's Who* of the twelfth century would have comprised names for which we would have looked in vain in the eleventh century. In the eleventh century we shall not find among the great feudal European dynasties the future ancestors of the great tenants-in-chief of Jerusalem. Rather, they would be from obscure families, which very rarely left traces, let alone influenced history.[7] It is true that during the twelfth century there was an immigration of noble families from Europe to the Holy Land, but very few definitely established themselves there. The overwhelming majority of Crusader nobility were products of the Holy Land itself. Their rise was conditioned by the general political and religious framework of Christendom. The fact that even the most important tenants-in-chief of the Crown and principalities originated in a third-class European aristocracy seems to us to be of the highest importance in evaluating the type of tradition that these knights could have brought with them from Europe.

Was their tradition really that of independence, turbulence, and anarchy? There is certainly more than one answer to this question. The *Regnum Francorum* was a vast territory of different traditions. The reigns of Philip I and Louis VI, it is true, show turbulent aristocracy in the Capetian domain. At the same time, that agitated period was ending. In certain territories such as Normandy, Anjou, Flanders, the local princely authorities had the upper hand over their adversaries. In other principalities, from the dawn of the eleventh century they were beginning to establish their sovereignty solidly. Everywhere one witnesses the process of internal consolidation in which public offices begin to function in a coherent and hierarchic framework. It is slow but steady labour, one which laid the foundations of solidly constituted local entities which later facilitated the great work of the Capetians—a work termed by a great historian a 'concentration concentrique'.

How do these facts influence our picture? It is true that France, regarded as a whole, was still a prey to centrifugal tendencies; royal power was more nominal than real. Yet the important political entity, the unit of everyday political life, was not the kingdom but the principality. And it is precisely on that level that the period of anarchy was approaching its

---

[7] Even the origins of the most illustrious noble family of Outremer, the Ibelins, are obscure. A semi-legendary genealogy linked them with the viscounts of Chartres. It has been suggested that they were of Sardinian, Pisan, or south-Italian origin. Cf. La Monte, 'The Lords of Le Puiset on the Crusades', *Speculum* 17 (1942), 110–18; J. Richard, 'Guy d'Ibelin, évêque de Limassol', *Bulletin de correspondance hellénique* 1950, pp. 98–133; N. H. Rüdt de Collenberg, 'Les premiers Ibelins', *Moyen-Âge* 71 (1965), 433–74.

end. Tenants-in-chief and vassals were taught obedience on the level of lordships. The general situation of the Kingdom of France had little or no influence on the simple knight. In everyday life the cohesion of the kingdom was of little importance to a lord's vassals. Their needs and aspirations were on the level not of the state but of the principality. Consequently, their political tradition could not have been that of a feudal anarchy. At the end of the eleventh century the contrary is true for the vast majority of the knights of northern France.

These considerations on the general situation in France and the origin of the Crusader nobility on the eve of the First Crusade lead us to conclusions diametrically opposed to those current for the Latin Kingdom. If the kingdom had been founded by the high aristocracy of France, it would perhaps have been admissible to consider it a weak creation, where a nominal Crown reigned, but did not rule. This would have been justified by the particularistic tendencies of the French high nobility and its secular traditions of independence *vis-à-vis* the royal power. But this, as we have noted, was not the case. Those who carried the political European traditions to the Orient were, on the one hand, the future rulers of the Crusader principalities and, on the other, the simple knights who belonged to the low nobility. Their traditions were generally those of feudal submission to a territorial ruler whose growing power kept them in line and to whom they were bound by an oath of homage and fidelity. Consequently, the feudal tradition which might have been transmitted was that of a hierarchical feudal organization, revolving round a territorial ruler whose control was already accepted, or in the process of being accepted. It is true that centrifugal tendencies could have been found among knights and nobles, but only among those who had what the French call a sufficient *assiette foncière*. At the end of the eleventh century the turbulent barons of our text were usually (barring exceptions) not the simple knights, the *pauvres sires*, who constituted the majority of the noble class of the Crusaders. We still have to wait for a study of the composition of the royal *curia* of the Latin Kingdom to clarify the personal relations that existed in the *curia* itself. But, as Jean Richard has pointed out, the court of Godfrey of Bouillon was overwhelmingly composed of people who were his vassals in Lower Lotharingia.[8] The political tradition of these vassals could not have been that of strong aristocratic opposition against the *Advocatus* who was their sovereign as duke of Lotharingia.

[8] Private communication from Professor J. Richard.

The Primitive Feudal Organization

It is generally suggested that from the beginning the Latin Kingdom was a full-fledged body with all the essential features, all its organs defined and articulated. It is reminiscent of the goddess who leaped out in full armour from the head of Zeus. Brought to life without pain, there was no evolution of its adult body. The origin of this view has to be partially sought in the current opinion that the whole state organization was simply imported from Europe, but it is also due to the fact that historians were unhesitatingly following the descriptions of the Latin Kingdom penned by Philip of Novara and John of Ibelin. Here, we would like to challenge the legitimacy of this method. How can one describe a kingdom founded in 1099 by using legal treatises written in the middle of the thirteenth century? It is true that anyone who has dipped into these treatises—especially that of John of Ibelin—may sympathize with historians unable to resist the temptation to use these monumental sources. A historian once called the legal treatise of John of Ibelin the 'Bible of Feudalism'—without exaggeration. There is no similar source for contemporary Europe. Only the very erudite treatises of Roman law at the time of Azo could possibly compare with the treatise of John of Ibelin; but medieval Roman law had the resplendent edifice of Justinian behind it. The temptation to use these Crusader treatises of jurisprudence is very strong and it is almost too much to ask historians not to use them. But is their use justified without any qualification? We have serious doubts for two reasons.

John of Ibelin and his precursor Philip of Novara reflect the practice of the mid-thirteenth century, in the best of cases, although they do preserve certain traditions of the previous century. Both jurists—and this is also true for all others except the anonymous author of the *Livre au Roi*—were outspokenly biased towards the social class to which they belonged. This has been rightly observed by Jean Richard.[9] In addition to presenting the danger of anachronisms, because they project thirteenth-century realities (even if they are faithfully reproduced), into the twelfth century, the use of legal treatises as the principal sources for the constitutional history of the Latin Kingdom creates the illusion of a fossilized constitution.

Starting from the premises to which we have referred and the legal sources of the thirteenth century, historians have assigned characteristics

[9] J. Richard, 'Pairie d'Orient latin', *RHDFE* 28 (1950), 67–8, and see below, Ch. 14, *passim*, and Ch. 17, p. 461.

to the beginnings of the kingdom which not only were uncertain, but in our opinion are impossible to relate to its earliest period. Take as a case in point the constitutional activities of Godfrey of Bouillon. Although his role in the first Crusade has already been brought back to more realistic proportions, many more points remain to be revised.

Godfrey of Bouillon was the founder of the kingdom. This fact, seen through the legal sources of the thirteenth century, implied two events of prime importance: the establishment of the constitutional basis and the creation of the feudal map of the kingdom. These two phenomena were directly related and influenced each other.

Though some legislative or constitutional work may have been accomplished in the period before Godfrey's death and in the period immediately following it, the question is what was actually accomplished and in what manner. Somehow the *Advocatus Sancti Sepulcri* came to combine Moses and Joshua the son of Nun in one person. It was he who was the lawgiver and it was he who divided the Holy Land between his companions, assigning a heritage to each according to his rank or merit. As the lawgiver, he was the creator of the *Assises*, the code of law continued and developed by his successors. The original *Assises*, or rather the *Lettres du Saint-Sépulcre*, remain a mystery, though individual *assises* have been preserved in more recent texts and can be assigned to the time of Godfrey or his immediate successors. But what was the general character of this legislation? One historian has spoken of a constitutional charter, which fixed the power and the respective competences of the man who ruled, the *primus inter pares*, and the aristocracy who chose him. Such a division of power naturally had to be conceived in feudal terms; it had to translate into practical terms what was regarded by the feudal aristocracy as the essentials of an ideal state. This was the 'Paradise of feudalism' to which we have already referred.

Godfrey also appears as the man who divided and distributed the land—Godfrey the creator of baronies and fiefs. This picture would not significantly change, if part of this work, which must have been enormous, were brought forward to the next period, that is, to the time of Baldwin I or even Baldwin II.

Again, we would like to challenge this picture. Did it really happen this way? Was there ever an actual division of land to create a territorial framework for a feudal state? Once such a division of fiefs is admitted, one is led to a far-reaching general conclusion, namely, the homogeneity of the feudal organization. Godfrey's chiefs or companions received fiefs in exchange for military service and they proceeded in their turn to enfeoffments. Lordships were created, and with them, the whole hierarchical edifice of the feudal society. On every level, feudal relations fixed military and administrative services; all the aspects of political and personal relations bore the stamp of feudalism. At this point we touch upon the real essence of a feudal state.

To begin with, is it correct to assume that only feudal links were known in the Latin Kingdom? For the sake of simplification, let us disregard the Italian communes and the burgesses of the kingdom and limit our question to the Frankish knights and an analysis of the legal status of land.

In two European states, England and Normandy, which G. B. Adams has asserted to be 'more feudal' than others, land held by nobles was of one type—fiefs. This was expressed in the French legal maxim: *nulle terre sans seigneur*. The hierarchy of lands reflects the hierarchy of persons. Disregarding embarrassing cases such as land held of two lords, we face two parallel structures, a hierarchy of lands and a hierarchy of people. All land was cut up into fiefs—a fact explained by the military conquest. England, it was once said, suffered two conquests, that of Rollo the Norman, and later on, that of William the Conqueror. Other countries did not know this type of homogeneity. Consequently, we find elsewhere two types of land existing side by side—*allodia* and fiefs, each representing a different tradition, a different stratum of historic evolution in the pre-feudal and feudal periods.

In many respects the Latin Kingdom was reminiscent of Normandy and England. There was a conquest; no former aristocracy could intervene in the creation of the systematic structure of new states. Moreover, the Crusaders had to conceive all relationships of rule and dependence in their language and vocabulary, and in the framework of their vision of a 'feudal Paradise'. If there was one country in which one would not expect to find *allodia*, the enclaves of non-feudal property, this would naturally be the Latin Kingdom of Jerusalem.

The reality, however, was different. We have proved elsewhere the existence of allods in the Latin Kingdom.[10] What is the significance of this phenomenon in our context? The existence of allods is reason enough to reconsider the total feudalization which is alleged of the Kingdom. For one reason or another allodial islets appeared here and there on its map. As

---

[10] See below, Ch. 14, pp. 350 ff.

no research has been done in this area, their number and relative importance is not known; but this is beside the point. What is important is the proof of an eminently non-feudal element in the organization of the kingdom.

How can the existence of these allodial lands be explained? Conscious imitation of European customs is out of the question. Allodial property in fact was rending the feudal tissue, and the Crusader nobles would certainly have opposed the creation of allods in their own lands. This was not only a fiscal problem but foremost a problem of relations between individuals. Anyone who had allodial lands acquired a certain autonomy *vis-à-vis* his lord. We explain the existence of Crusader allods by the process of conquest and arrive at the conclusion that the distribution of land and fiefs by Godfrey of Bouillon is purely legendary. The Crusader conquest had a character of its own, which permitted and conditioned the creation of allodial lands.

Take an analogous case, that of the Latin conquest of the Empire of Constantinople. The difference between the two is quite clear. In the Latin Empire of Constantinople there was a division of spoils between Venice and the future Emperor; each parcel of land was held by one or the other. They in turn enfeoffed their parts to their dependants. Nothing like this took place in the Latin Kingdom. The conquest lasted for more than ten years (without taking into account the late conquests of Tyre, 1124, Banyas, 1131, and Ascalon, 1153). The conquest was not accomplished by one chief; an actual period of *conquistadores* was known in the kingdom— Tancred in Galilee, Raymond of St. Gilles, Hugh of St. Omer, and others. It was only later that some sort of integration took place, a period during which the conquered lands were grouped under common denominators of royal or seignorial fiefs. But under twelfth-century conditions this process could not have been carried out in a systematic way. There were lands that somehow escaped the feudal mesh. In the thirteenth century these lands still remained allods.

The existence of allodial lands is therefore of twofold importance in our context: because it undermines the notion of 'pure feudalism' by the existence of an eminently non-feudal element; because it proves that the idea of a rigid constitution in the kingdom requires revision. If our hypothesis is correct, we have to consider three different periods within the twelfth century: (a) the period of conquest which also included the second decade of the history of the kingdom; (b) a period of reorganization which coincided with the times of Baldwin II and perhaps also of Fulk of

Anjou; (c) the last period which coincided with the second half of the twelfth century.

Let us try to picture the Latin Kingdom at its beginning. Although the division of land by Godfrey and his legislation are pure legend, the importance of his rule for the future organization of the kingdom should not be underestimated. Somehow we seem to pass too easily from the First Crusade to the creation of the kingdom. By so doing we by-pass a phase which might have been of great importance, the transformation of those personal relationships common during the last three years of the First Crusade, to relationships based on fiefs.

The First Crusade was undertaken by different armies commanded by military chiefs and princely leaders. Each of these groups represented a kind of *levée en masse* in the framework of territorial principalities, such as Normandy, Flanders, Provence, and Lotharingia. Around these local nuclei we find large groups of external followers, knights and lords who came from neighbouring lands but who were not vassals of the leader of the army. During the Crusade we often witness a process of accelerated cohesion in the different groups—a cohesion brought about by accidents of the military enterprise but also, no doubt, due to financial considerations. Apart from Raymond of Toulouse, the Crusader chiefs in Constantinople found themselves financially hard pressed. In such, or similar, circumstances the independence of smaller nobles can hardly be argued. They entered the service of the *principes* and *potentes*, joined larger groups, and were absorbed by them. Some simply became salaried warriors. Such a man as Tancred comes to mind, and he certainly did not belong to the smaller fry among the nobility: nevertheless he served Bohemond of Otranto, later Raymond of Toulouse who proposed better terms, and finally Godfrey of Bouillon. During the three-year-long march to the East, we witness, so to speak, a regression in feudal relations to the original vassalic relationships. Salaries and spoils replaced non-existent fiefs. This did not change vassalic links essentially. On the contrary, personal relationships and personal dependencies became stricter. They developed in the favourable climate of a band of warriors on a military expedition.

Then came the conquest. The personal relationships of loyalty which bound the companions-in-arms now had to find their expression in a new framework. The land was now conquered and the former links of cohesion had to be territorialized. The hierarchy of persons had to be reflected and find its expression in the hierarchy of possessions. It is precisely this transformation that had to take place at the time of Godfrey of Bouillon and his immediate successor. We know that in the group of knights that remained with Godfrey in the kingdom, there was a strong contingent of vassals from his native Lotharingia. Even a decade later under Baldwin I there was still a *familia Godefridi*, almost reminiscent of the *nurriti* of Carolingian times. This in itself did not assure the future of government. These knightly followers had to be integrated into the new realities of the conquered country. If they had to remain vassals of Godfrey, their former dependence was of little avail. They had to receive fiefs. And what was true for the former Lotharingian vassals was *a fortiori* true for knights who belonged to other contingents now disbanded. But here, a historical factor intervened—the impossibility of proceeding to a distribution of fiefs because of the smallness of the kingdom. Our documentation for this period proves that Godfrey did not readily enfeoff land but rather used revenues from some of his landed property to maintain his companions. We are even inclined to believe that he proceeded in this way on purpose. However, some lands were captured without Godfrey's intervention. Nablus, Bethsan and Tiberias, Bethlehem, and perhaps also Tibnin, to quote particular examples, were conquered by individual lords without royal intervention. This was a period of transition and incubation. The organization of the kingdom, far from being imported *en gros* was put together piece by piece in terms of European experience and local conditions.

It seems to us that the period of transition, accompanied by growing expansion, coincided with the rule of Baldwin I, that is, until *c.* 1118. With the progress of conquest a *modus vivendi*, the framework of government, the land, and personal relations became better defined and stabilized. We would suggest that by the time of Baldwin II a definite integration had taken place. This is indicated by a new aspect of our documentation: one can see principles of feudal hierarchy being strongly expressed in the royal confirmations (these are almost the only ones to survive) of ecclesiastical property. A church received land from a lord, this donation was confirmed by an overlord, and this in its turn received the King's confirmation. The first confirmation[11] of this type appeared under Baldwin I (1100–18), and was hardly a coincidence, but rather a reflection of stabilization. Not only did the feudal pyramid become solidified, but state power also had a strong, or a stronger, grip on the feudal machinery. The erstwhile warriors of the Crusade became vassals, took an oath of

[11] Cf. charter of 1110, *Regesta*, no. 57.

fealty and homage to the lord of the place, and became his men. Land and property, which they previously held on different titles—more often than not by the law of conquest—were subjected to the machinery of state and society. But in the process some lands escaped the regularization and remained allods, souvenirs of the heroic time of conquest. This process of integration presumes the existence of a power capable of ruling the country, namely the power of the Crown.

Royal Power—Illusion or Reality?

We thus arrive at a particularly important problem in the history of the feudal organization of the kingdom. 'Ideal feudalism', by definition, presumes a weak royal power. It is not always an indispensable part of the system, but is almost always implied when we speak of Crusader feudalism. In fact, John of Ibelin hardly left any position for the Crown. The king, as chief seignor, had an honourable standing but it was the High Court that was vested with power and the source of authority. Some historians have observed that a strong royal personality could keep the High Court in line, but with reference to occasional events and not to constitutional elements. However, if it is true that no medieval constitution was coherent enough to exclude royal action completely, the domination of the aristocracy in the Latin Kingdom, according to the jurists, was guaranteed by the written laws and unwritten customs of the constitution.

Jurisdiction was certainly one of the main attributes of medieval rulers. Yet, according to Crusader jurists, the courts of the lordships were entirely autonomous and enjoyed full rights of jurisdiction. They judged and rendered verdicts in all cases and there was no redress from their decisions. Thus, what the Latin Kingdom had in common with a number of European principalities was that there was no appeal or no instance of appeal above the level of lordship. Certainly, there was no place for royal interference in the seignorial courts. The exclusive seignorial jurisdiction was probably the most conspicuous characteristic of feudal autonomy and particularism.

But do we have to accept these affirmations of thirteenth-century jurists as reflecting the realities of 150 years earlier? Since there are no court registers of the kingdom extant it is difficult to confront the opinion of the jurists with reality. But there is at least one document which, as far as we know, has not been used in our context, namely the decrees of the Council, or rather of the *parlement*, of Nablus (1120). The decrees concerning

morals and ecclesiastical discipline have often been invoked, but there are
other important decrees which have attracted little attention:

Ch. xxiv: Si quis furtum fecerit, et infra annos fuerit, custodiatur, donec in curia
regis provideatur quid de eo sit agendum.

Ch. xxv: Si quis baronum hominem sui comparis in latrocinio cepit, membris non
comminatur, sed in curiam regis ad judicandum mittatur.[12]

The first of these decrees can be variously interpreted. However the
presence of the *curia regis,* considered according to the rules laid down by
the jurists of the thirteenth century, is absolutely out of place here. Why
should a thief be judged by the *curia regis*? If he committed the crime in
the territory of a lord, then by all accepted rules should he not be judged
in the court of the lordship? What seems to be decisive in this decree is the
criminal's age: viz. the fact that he is a minor. In such a case instead of
being judged by the seignorial court for a crime which no doubt involved
corporal punishment, he was kept in the prison of the local lord until he
appeared before the royal court. The latter thus performed the royal duty
expressed in biblical terms in the coronation oath to defend widows,
orphans, and all the oppressed of this world. There was nothing feudal in
it, it was the spirit of monarchy which drew its inspiration from the oldest
source of Christian morality—the Bible. The constitutional bearing of
this decree is important. It proves that for the nobles of 1120 there was
nothing exceptional in seeing the Crown enjoying a legal prerogative,
namely the right of intervention in dealing with a case that was the
preserve of the seignorial court.

The second decree quoted above (ch. xxv) brings us into the usual
complexity of feudal justice. Its main purpose seems to have been to
reserve to the royal court, on one hand the right of *haute justice* following
larceny, and on the other, the right of intervention in cases that provoked
a conflict of jurisdictions (for example when a vassal, thieving in another
lordship, was caught *in flagrante delicto*). However, in addition to these
considerations, it seems to us that the basic aim of this decree was different.
A cruel punishment for theft was announced in ch. xxiii of the same
council: 'Si furtum fuerit ultra bisantios tres, membris comminatur, manu
et pede et oculis. Si vero infra bisantium furtum fuerit, cauterio in facie
coquatur, et per villam ductus flagellis caedetur.' The punishment seems to
have been valid for noble and non-noble Franks alike. Therefore it appears

---

[12] J. D. Mansi, *Sacrorum Conciliorum . . . Collectio* xxi. 266 ff.

that ch. xxv restricted the application of the law by reserving judgment of vassals to the royal court alone. One thing is clear: it was the royal and not the seignorial court that was competent to judge such cases. Whether the reason was the right of *haute justice* or the judgment of a noble (which were royal prerogatives), or a kind of compromise between the territorial law of jurisdiction (the right to judge cases because a criminal act was committed in territory over which the lord had the right of jurisdiction) on the one hand and personal law (the lord's justice over his vassals) on the other, all this leads to the same conclusion: the existence of royal rights of jurisdiction, which, according to more recent, mid-thirteenth-century legal sources, would have been entirely in the hands of the *seigneurs justiciers*, that is the holders of lordships in the kingdom. Thus in 1120, at least in the realm of jurisdiction, the Crown was not entirely limited in its action by the barons.

Legislation was the prerogative of the High Court, and even the *Assises* which bear the name of a king have to be considered, at least formally, as the work of the High Court.[13] But there is an aspect that sheds a particular light on the Latin Kingdom if we compare it with contemporary France— the fact that in the Crusader Kingdom there was *one* legislation for *all* the nobles of the kingdom. Nothing similar existed in France until the second half of the twelfth century, practically up to the time of Philip Augustus or even St. Louis. We do not stress this phenomenon as indicative of royal prerogative but of political cohesion. Rather, in this aspect the Crusader Kingdom should be compared with England of the Plantagenets or with Norman Sicily.

This political cohesion, which was well marked by a legislation valid for the whole country, also found expression in the political and economic domains. A long list of agreements was concluded between the kingdom and the Italian communes.[14] All were concluded by the kings. However, these treaties assured the enjoyment of their privileges to the Italian communes in *all* the cities of the kingdom, even in cities which by then belonged to particular lords, tenants-in-chief of the Crown. This would have been absolutely unthinkable if the lordships had been entirely autonomous. In fact, in the thirteenth century such agreements granting privileges to the communes were concluded by the lords of the cities and

---

[13] Cf. M. Grandclaude, op. cit., *passim*, and 'Liste d'assises remontant au premier royaume de Jérusalem', *Mélanges Paul Fournier* (Paris, 1929), pp. 329–47.

[14] A convenient list is to be found in La Monte, *Feudal Monarchy*, Appendix D, pp. 261 ff.

not by the Crown. Again, from this point of view, there was nothing comparable in France at the time of Louis VI or Louis VII. The agreements of the kings of Jerusalem surpassed the boundaries of the royal domain and were binding on the vassals of the kingdom. The kings acted as sovereigns of the state—a state well centralized.

If one had to judge by the treatises of jurisprudence, the royal prerogatives were purely honorary. But what was true for the thirteenth century was certainly not true for the beginning of the twelfth. The anonymous author of the *Livre au Roi*, written at the end of the twelfth century, still listed cases in which a vassal could lose his fiefs. Among them: 'se aucun home lige . . . faiset faire et labourer et batre monée en sa terre . . . *por ce que nul hom ne deit aver port, euvreneour ne monée labourant, fors li rois.*' Also: 'se aucun hom lige . . . faiseit faire port en sa terre de naves et des vaisseaus, et chemin en paienime *por amender sa terre et por amermer les droitures dou roi.*'[15] Here the royal prerogatives were neatly listed. These were simply *regalia*: the right to mint money and open a port, which also implied the right to impose customs. It is the same idea expressed in the prohibition against 'opening a road to paynim', meaning the imposition of customs on merchandise going to and from the Muslim world.

These *regalia* were certainly no longer to be found in the thirteenth century. Numismatics reveal a large number of seignorial coins, and the right to mint money was, as expressed by Schlumberger, one of the means of pronouncing local sovereignty *urbi et orbi*. The same can be said of the right to impose customs which were later on in the hands of particular lords—for example in maritime Tyre or in the desert castle of Montreal in Transjordan, which commanded the caravan routes in the East. It is clear that some time before the beginning of the thirteenth century the notion of *regalia* disappeared. Their existence in the twelfth century was another non-feudal element in the Latin Kingdom. No such institution could have existed if the Crusaders had structured their kingdom according to the principles of 'pure feudalism'. The royal prerogatives could have been the result of a pre-feudal evolution, as in Germany, or the result of the establishment of a strong territorial power, as in Normandy, England, or Sicily, over the whole country. Their existence bears witness to real royal authority.

The existence of *regalia* in the Latin Kingdom raises the problem of their origin—a problem of little significance during the short reign of

[15] ch. xvi (*Lois* i. 616–17).

Godfrey of Bouillon. It has more relevance to the time of Baldwin I (1100–18) when the feudal map of the kingdom was etched on the conquered land. Although we do not know if Baldwin I acted according to any set of laws or customs, the decrees of Nablus may perhaps show an attempt to affirm the preponderance of royal power over possible centrifugal tendencies. In all probability the notion of *regalia*[16] also came into being at that time, though its sanction by law was somewhat later, under the rule of Baldwin II or even of Baldwin III.[17]

The different elements of royal power in the first half of the twelfth century point to the conclusion that they were quite different from the royal power of a Louis VI or even of a Louis VII in France. In the Crusader Kingdom royal power was a reality which did not depend upon the personality of the ruler, but on the royal institution itself.

[16] There were also the rights of the kings of Jerusalem to intervene in ecclesiastical elections.

[17] See below, Ch. 17, p. 435.

2 Crusader Nobility and the Feudal System[1]

The purpose of this chapter is to bring out the main lines in the development of the nobility of the Latin Kingdom of Jerusalem—a nobility which changed profoundly during the first hundred years of its existence—and to outline the relationship of that class to the political order of the Crusader Kingdom. We have tried to show[2] that the commonly held notion of the Crusaders' society as a pure form of feudalism stems from an anachronistic use of historical sources and that the royal power of the first kings of Jerusalem in no way resembles that of their Capetian contemporaries. An analogy might be found more easily and with more justification in the power of the princely houses of Normandy, Anjou, and Flanders.

On what social base was the royal power of the kingdom erected? What determined its evolution during the first century of its history? These questions immediately bring us to the social structure of the nobility of Jerusalem[3] and to the study of changes in the constitutional life of the kingdom.

1. The Formation of the Nobility and the Dominance of the Royal Power

Two main factors determined the character of the oldest nobility of the kingdom: the chronic state of war against Islam and the continual wave of immigrants to the Holy Land during the first three decades of its existence. Obviously, the kingdom could not sustain itself against Islam without a large number of immigrants to replace the losses on the battlefield.

---

[1] This chapter was first published in a longer version as 'La noblesse et le régime féodal du royaume latin de Jérusalem', *Moyen-Âge* 65 (1959), 41–74. The translation was by F. Cheyette who published it in *Lordship and Community in Mediaeval Europe* (New York, 1968). Some of the material appears in Ch. 3 below. I wish to thank Professor Cheyette for his permission to reprint his translation.

[2] See above, Ch. 1, pp. 3–19.

[3] See C. Cahen, 'La féodalité et les institutions politiques de l'Orient latin', Accad. naz. dei Lincei, Fond. Alessandro Volta, *Atti dei Convegni* 12 (1957), 167–91. H. Prutz, *Kulturgeschichte der Kreuzzüge* (Berlin, 1883), and La Monte, *Feudal Monarchy*, explain many important points.

The First Crusade left only a thin deposit of settlers. Chronicles inform us that in 1100 there were no more than 300 knights and 1,200 sergeants. Who were these knights? Certainly not the members of the great families of the West, since these left the country after the conquest. The majority were either European vassals of the house of Bouillon[4] or men who had entered the service of that family during the First Crusade. Fed by the stream of new immigrants, this original seed grew with time. It is unfortunately impossible to know these new colonists any better. We know, it is true, that several great lords of the West sailed to the East. But we should not be misled: these lords, with very rare exception, did not stay in the Holy Land but, after touring the holy places and taking part in a few skirmishes against the Muslims, returned home. We are sometimes told that the younger sons of great families left for the Middle East. This would appear logical, but we have insufficient proof that it was true.[5] On the contrary, that the surnames of the immigrants, as the documents of the kingdom attest, are Syrian or Palestinian (a fact that greatly astonished their contemporary, the chronicler Fulk of Chartres)[6] seems to prove that these settlers were of modest origin and had no reason to retain surnames drawn from their European possessions.[7]

The first concern of the kings was to use these knights in the arduous task of securing the country from the Muslims. They therefore took them into their service as royal vassals. Some of the great lords who remained in the East after the First Crusade, such as Tancred, did the same. But the flood of newcomers had to be supported. The 'normal' method would have been to give the conquered territories as fiefs. The kings acted otherwise, however; Godfrey of Bouillon, for example, preferred to give town and city revenues as fiefs. Furthermore, many knights were simply retained directly in the service of the royal house.[8] It is impossible to say

[4] On the vassals of Godfrey of Bouillon, see J. C. Andressohn, *The Ancestry and Life of Godfrey of Bouillon* (Bloomington, 1947), and C. Moeller, 'Les Flamands du Ternois au royaume latin de Jérusalem', *Mélanges P. Frédéricq* (Brussels, 1904), pp. 189–203.

[5] Cf. R. Fawtier, *Les Capétiens et la France* (Paris, 1942), pp. 193–6. Is it not suprising that in Flanders, one of the greatest centres of the Crusading movement, no noble family disappeared during the 200 years of the Crusades? See P. Feuchère, 'La noblesse du Nord de la France', *Annales, E.S.C.* 6 (1951), 311 n. 4.

[6] Fulk of Chartres, *Historia Hierosolymitana* III.37 (*RHC HOcc.* iii. 467–8).

[7] Ibid. 468: 'Nos nostri sequuntur de die in diem propinqui et parentes, quaecumque possederant omnino relinquentes, nec etiam volentes. Qui enim illic erant inopes, hic facit eos Deus locupletes … qui non habuerat villam, hic … jam possidet urbem. Quare ergo reverteretur in Occidentem, qui hic taliter invenit Orientem?'

[8] Cf. above, p. 14. On the infeudation of town revenues by Godfrey of Bouillon, see

whether the princes' hesitation to enfeoff their land was a consequence of the small size of the royal domain at the beginning of the conquest or the result of a far-seeing policy aimed at putting a tight rein on the knights, at restraining their freedom of action.[9] The Normans, conquering England, did the same thing; and forty years after the conquest, the kings of England preferred to pay salaries or to grant sources of revenue to their knights rather than to enfeoff them with lands.[10] However, the inevitable process of infeudation could not be arrested; and under Baldwin I, with the expansion of the frontiers and the integration of the lands of independent lords into the kingdom, the land began to be granted in fief. These grants drew the first lines of the future feudal map of the kingdom and at the same time formed the basis of its political organization.

The origins of the feudal seignory are extremely obscure. Thus we do not know the principle by which a simple fief, destined to remain such in the royal domain, was distinguished from the fief that would become a barony or an independent seignory. Was it the size of the fief? We have no way of telling, since the earliest acts of investiture have disappeared. In the thirteenth century jurists would maintain that any lord having enough vassals to make up a court could have his own justice.[11] Did they mean that every lord having the three vassals necessary to make up a court became *ipso facto* a justicer lord (*seigneur justicier*)? If this was the jurists' intention, the explanation does not fit the first enfeoffments very well. We should prefer to imagine that the creation of a seignory in the Latin Kingdom was expressly accompanied by the grant of feudal rights of justice and that elsewhere, where lands were conquered independently of the king (such as the principality of Galilee), feudal justice was automatically retained when the land was integrated into the kingdom. Yet others probably won these rights through *de facto* evolution. In 1120,

---

Albertus Aquensis, *Historia Hierosolymitana* VII. 37 (*RHC HOcc.* iv. 532), and below, Ch. 14, p. 350 n. 19.

[9] A conqueror who was independent of the king, such as Tancred, assured himself of the services of knights by distributing tithes of ecclesiastical establishments in Galilee: *Cartulaire du Mt. Thabor*, in Delaville ii. 898 and i. 826, no. 2837.

[10] A. L. Poole, *From Domesday Book to Magna Carta* (Oxford, 1951), p. 13.

[11] *La Clef des Assises de la Haute Cour* 60 (*Lois* i. 584): 'Partout là où le seignor et trois de ces houmes ou plus est, si sont le court.' See John of Ibelin, ch. 164 (*Lois* i. 254). Feudal jurisdiction is defined in the kingdom by the expression 'droit de court, coins et justice'. On the meaning of this expression see Chandon de Briailles, 'Le droit de coins dans le royaume de Jérusalem', *Syria* 23 (1943), 244–57. See J. Richard, 'Les listes des seigneuries dans le Livre de Jean d'Ibelin', *RHDFE* 32 (1954), 566 ff., and *Royaume latin*, p. 85.

however, the king continued to possess the right to interfere in seignorial justice.[12]

While the feudal regime was crystallizing during the first two or three decades of the kingdom's history (1100–30), the noble class was taking shape.

If continual immigration and colonization explain the creation of baronies and seignories, it was the continual state of war that accounted for the most characteristic trait of the knightly class: the instability of its families and of their possessions. It is astonishing to note the small number of possessors of lordships who succeeded in handing their estates on to their descendants between 1100 and 1130. Hebron, for example, conquered in 1099, had its revenues enfeoffed to Gerard of Avesne. By the middle of 1100 it was again in the hands of King Baldwin I, who enfeoffed it to Gaudemar Carpinel (whose descendants remain unknown); the city later belonged to Roger of Haifa (1102), Hugh of Rebecq (1104), and Gautier Mahomet (1107–15), persons apparently unrelated. Only in 1115 did a seignorial family of Hebron appear.[13] This case is extreme, but not exceptional, as the history of Haifa proves. First promised by Godfrey of Bouillon to Gaudemar Carpinel, the city was taken away from him by Tancred in 1100, then given back to Baldwin I after Tancred's departure. The king then gave it to Rohart (who died in 1107). In 1109 it was again in Tancred's hands for a short time, then returned to the royal domain. Only under Baldwin II was Haifa linked to the name of Vivien, the father of Payen II (*c.* 1138) who became lord of the city.[14] The history of the principality of Galilee had no fewer ups and downs. After its conquest the territory was turned into a principality by Tancred (1099); then enfeoffed by Baldwin I to Hugh of St. Omer (1100). Upon Hugh's death (1106), Baldwin gave it to Gervais of Basoches, who was captured by the Muslims in 1108; given to Tancred in 1109, Galilee soon returned to the royal domain and was then enfeoffed to Jocelin of Courtenay in 1113. The three next lords of the principality belonged, apparently (but it is not certain), to the family of Bures (until 1168). The principality then went back to the

---

[12] See Ch. 1 above, pp. 16 ff. This right to intervene in the independent jurisdiction of baronies and seignories represented a transitional phase in the growth of absolute seignorial independence.

[13] G. Bayer, 'Die Kreuzfahrergebiete von Jerusalem und S. Abraham', *ZDPV* 65 (1942), 165 ff. It appears that St. Abraham did not leave the royal domain until 1161 when the Milly family acquired it.

[14] Du Cange, *Les Familles d'Outremer*, ed. E. Rey (Paris, 1869), s.v. *Haifa*.

family of St. Omer until in 1173 it came into the domain of the famous Raymond of Tripoli.[15]

These incessant changes of seignorial families explain the obscurity that surrounds the early history of the seignories. The later possessors, who were not related to their predecessors, did not bother to keep a record of their genealogies. For proof one need only look at the case of Beirut, which fell to the Christians in 1110 and was enfeoffed to Fulk of Guines. Beirut's lord is not cited in any text before 1125—Gautier I Brisebarre, who was no relation to Fulk of Guines. Gautier's brother, who succeded him in 1127, was the true founder of the seignorial family.[16] Sometimes these seignorial changes were the result of fights with the king, as was the case with the lord of Jaffa from the family of Le Puiset,[17] or the lords of Transjordan from the family of Le Puy.[18] Under these conditions, it was the family that took solid root—such as the Garniers of Caesarea-Sidon (appearing around 1108), both of whose branches continued for nearly a century—that was the exception.[19]

Warfare, which took its heavy toll of prisoners and dead, was the main cause of these changes. But one should not neglect the character of the immigration itself, the work of younger sons or of young men, very few of whom were married when they left for the East. Economic motives not being among the main reasons for immigration, the immediate departure of entire families from their European homes was not necessary. It was only when the married knight was well established in the Latin Kingdom that he thought of bringing over his family.[20]

It was to this society, formed by successive waves of immigrants, that the earliest legislation applied. Its purpose seems to have been to help the

---

[15] R. Grousset, *Histoire des Croisades* 2 (Paris, 1936), appendix, 837 ff.

[16] E. Rey, 'Les seigneurs de Barut', *ROL* 4 (1896), 12 ff.; M. E. Nickerson, 'The seigneurie of Beirut in the 12th century and the Brisebarre family of Beirut-Blanchegarde', *Byzantion* 19 (1949), 141 ff.

[17] J. L. La Monte, 'The Lords of Le Puiset on the Crusades', *Speculum* 17 (1942), 100 ff.

[18] E. Rey, 'Les seigneurs de Montréal et la Terre d'Outre-le-Jourdain', *ROL* 4 (1896), 19 ff.

[19] Even Caesarea was not originally a fief of the Garnier family, but of one Harpin, or Arpin, viscount of Bourges (d. 1102), who sold his fief to Philip I of France and came with the first Crusade to the Holy Land (Quantin, 'Les Croisés dans la Basse Bourgogne', *Annuaire de l'Yonne* (1854), p. 223). See Röhricht, *GKJ*, p. 23 n. 3, p. 32 n. 8, and pp. 37–9. Eustace Garnier appeared only six years later. See J. L. La Monte, 'The Lords of Caesarea in the Period of the Crusades', *Speculum* 22 (1947), 145 ff., and 'The Lords of Sidon in the 12th and 13th centuries', *Byzantion* 17 (1944–5), 183 ff.

[20] This explains the severe and frequently repeated legislation against bigamy in the Holy Land.

knightly class put down roots in the conquered country. An analysis of this legislation will allow us to delimit more clearly the shape of the noble class and the problems created by its existence.

The earliest legislation chiefly concerned rights of succession and infeudation.[21] An early *assise* allowed women to inherit land in the absence of male heirs.[22] This decision moved in a direction opposite to contemporary tendencies in Europe, but suited the conditions and demands of life in the Latin Kingdom. The knight who had devoted his life to the service of king and country was assured that if chance did not grant him a male heir, he could leave to his daughter the fief he had acquired through hardship and danger. He was thus more strongly attached to his new country.

Another *assise* (an early one, although we cannot fix its date precisely) established the terms and conditions of infeudation. According to John of Ibelin, 'ancient fiefs descend to all heirs';[23] in other words, investiture assured possession of a fief to the knight who received it and to all his descendants, direct and collateral.[24] This was of the greatest importance, for it enlarged the right of succession at a time when such tendencies were not common[25] and by this, again, helped the knightly class to establish itself. Since many of the new immigrants were not married and death and captivity took their toll, nothing was more natural than to compensate those who fought by guaranteeing that their family, even their distant family, might enjoy the fruits of their bravery. At the same time the *assise* induced relatives both near and distant to join the immigrant in the hope of inheriting his fief.

Still another *assise* fixing the rules of succession to fiefs had the same object: no knight who already possessed a fief could enter into possession of another one due to him by the common law of succession. The second fief went to his younger brother if the brother had as yet no fief, or even—

---

[21] It is not possible to date this legislation exactly. However, as M. Grandclaude has proved, these *assises* belong to the oldest legislation of the kingdom—M. Grandclaude, 'Liste d'assises remontant au premier royaume de Jérusalem', *Mélanges Paul Fournier*, pp. 329 ff.

[22] Philip of Novara, ch. 71 (*Lois* i. 542). M. Grandclaude, 'Liste d'assises', p. 335, thinks that this *assise* goes back to Godfrey of Bouillon.

[23] John of Ibelin, ch. 150 (*Lois* i. 233, 235); Philip of Novara, ch. 66 (ibid. 537).

[24] Philip of Novara, ch. 66 (ibid.): 'celui don de tous heirs peut venir et escheir à toz ceaus qui sont heirs de ses biens, soit frere ou seur ou parent, jà ne soit il descendu de la souche dou conqueror, mais qu'il seit de cele part dont le fié muet.'

[25] Collateral succession was not accepted in Germany until the end of the twelfth century under Henry VI. See P. Guilhiermoz, *Essai sur l'origine de la noblesse en France au moyen-âge* (Paris, 1902), p. 199.

as a result of the enlargement of the group who could inherit—to any other relation who did not yet have a fief.[26] Evidently, the concern here was that as large a number of knights as possible should establish themselves within the confines of the small kingdom. This *assise* prevented the accumulation of fiefs in the hands of a small number of noble families; it facilitated the establishment of a large number of knights, especially of those belonging to the same line. Another one with the same intent prohibited the subinfeudation of parts of fiefs unless the lord retained more than the total of the land subinfeudated;[27] thus the lords were obliged to support a large number of household knights without weakening the economic potential of their fief.

The oldest legislation of the kingdom thus throws some light on the formation of the noble class. It was, furthermore, the work of a strong central power, which found its most complete expression in the *Assise* on the dispossession of vassals by the king, promulgated under Baldwin III (1143–63).[28] As yet there was nothing to limit that power. The knights were gradually establishing themselves as a class; they undoubtedly had some kind of class-consciousness, but not enough to form the basis for a baronial opposition. Its members changed too often, their roots in the country were too weak, and new waves of immigration shook the weakly cemented structure too often for any noble opposition party to have a chance against the king.

In contrast to this weak and heterogeneous class, the king drew strength from his position as commander in time of war and as the source of honour and favour in time of peace. His domain at the time was quite large: the great ports and the revenues from commerce belonged to him, as well as vast territories (all of Judaea and Samaria). The principality of Galilee, the only one that could compare with his domain, cut a poor figure next to Jaffa, Tyre, and Acre.[29] The king therefore had at his disposal both land and money, not to speak of the fiefs that so often returned to him on the failure of seignorial lines. Nor ought we to forget that feudal wardship of minors and widows gave the king still other

---

[26] Philip of Novara, chs. 68, 71 (*Lois* i. 538, 542); John of Ibelin, chs. 148, 187 (ibid. 223–4, 297–9). And see E. Meynial, 'De quelques particularités des successions féodales dans les Assises de Jérusalem', *RHDFE* 16 (1892), 408–26.

[27] Philip of Novara, ch. 81 (*Lois* i. 553–4); John of Ibelin, chs. 142, 143, 148, 150, 182 (ibid. 216–17, 223–7, 284–5); *Livre au Roi*, chs. 38, 46 (ibid. 633–4, 640).

[28] On the royal power in this period, see below, Ch. 17.

[29] On the royal domain see Richard, *Royaume latin*, p. 72.

means to reward his vassals' services. Philip of Novara[30] informs us that the rule allowing noble women to choose their husbands freely, the rule in force immediately after the conquest, was replaced by arbitrary royal choice, imposing on noble widows the knights chosen by the king. This change, which probably occurred under Baldwin II or shortly thereafter,[31] still further enlarged the king's power and his grip on the knightly class, whose fortunes depended almost entirely upon him.

ii. *The Period of Transition: The Growing Importance of the Nobility*

The moment at which this primitive structure began to change, when a greater social cohesion began to turn the political regime in a new direction, is impossible to fix with any certainty. We think that some time during the reigns of Fulk of Anjou (1131–43) and Baldwin III (1143–63), the change took place that brought about a lessening of royal power; the period of Amalric (1163–74) opened a new period in the constitutional life of the kingdom.

About 1130 one can discover the first signs of opposition to royal power and at the same time a new stability among seignorial families. Almost immediately after Fulk of Anjou came to power, two great revolts broke out: one led by Hugh of Le Puiset, count of Jaffa, and the other by Romain of Le Puy, lord of Transjordan.[32] Twenty years later the country was again in the throes of civil war; the support of aristocratic factions decided the disputed succession between Queen Melissenda and her son Baldwin III. To be sure, royal power was not completely shaken; the king was still the head of the kingdom, but the revolts, a phenomenon unknown at an earlier period, marked a change in the balance of power between king and vassals.

This change will be shown by an analysis of the development of the noble class during the thirty years that separate the beginning of Fulk's reign from the beginning of that of Amalric.

The first impression one receives is that of stability. In startling contrast to the preceding period, we see the noble families now firmly established in their seignories. Succession has become regular; genealogies are

---

[30] Philip of Novara, ch. 85 (*Lois* i. 588).

[31] See Ch. 17 below.

[32] Like Richard, *Royaume latin*, p. 90, we think that there were really two revolts, probably contemporaneous and related to each other, and not one as the chronicle of William of Tyre would have one believe. For further discussion see H. E. Mayer, 'Studies in the History of Queen Melisende', *Dumbarton Oaks Papers* 26 (1972). See below, p. 438.

continuous and clear—proof that the seignorial families have become rooted in their patrimonies. There remains no trace of any important line becoming extinct and thereby escheating an important fief back to the royal domain. On the contrary, fiefs were passed to related families when there was no male heir, or at the time of a marriage.

New seignorial lines came into being as new seignories were created: Casal Imbert (*c.* 1123), the fief of Joffroi le Tort (*c* 1125), Caymont (*c.* 1139), Ibelin (1141), Scandalion (*c.* 1148), the fief of the Chamberlain (*c.* 1149), Blanchegarde (1166), and so on. Colonization by the knightly class became more dense. To settle the knights, means of support had to be found. These means were the royal domain, handed out in large slices. Under Amalric this came to an end (unless one considers his Egyptian expeditions to be colonizing movements); the creation of the seignory of Jocelin of Courtenay, formed by bringing together fiefs of different origins (*c.* 1179–92), was a late and altogether exceptional case. By 1150 the feudal map of the kingdom had been fixed and would hardly vary until the end of the First Kingdom.

New problems now had to be faced. The kingdom had reached saturation point. New arrivals found it difficult to place themselves in a now rigid feudal hierarchy. The only way for the Crown to win the allegiance of the new members of the noble class was to grant yet more fragments of the royal domain, which was becoming too small for comfort. From time to time the king managed to reconstitute a reserve, as when he bought the seignory of Beirut from its impoverished possessor, giving in return the unimportant fief of Blanchegarde (1166).[33] But the gradual impoverishment of the royal domain was not noticeably slowed— think only of Nablus, given in dowry to Queen Mary, Amalric's wife, which passed in 1176 into the hands of the Ibelins,[34] or of the rich fief of Transjordan, which had left the royal domain and belonged since 1160 to the Millys.[35] This shrinkage of the royal domain meant the weakening of the Crown, which could strengthen itself against the great lords only by acquiring new vassals; and this could be done only by cutting yet more fiefs from the royal domain. The king's means of action became dangerously reduced.

At the same time a caste spirit began to form among nobility and knights while the noble class, socially more and more differentiated, split

---

[33] See Bayer, 'Die Kreuzfahrergebiete', *ZDPV* 65 (1942), 165 ff.

[34] G. Bayer, 'Neapolis und sein Gebiet', *ZDPV* 63 (1940), 155 ff.

[35] Bayer, 'Die Kreuzfahrergebiete', 165 ff.

into two distinct groups. A spirit of class-consciousness had already existed in latent form among the nobles and knights of the First Crusade; one may see it in the first efforts to organize the kingdom. Godfrey of Bouillon[36] or Baldwin I had established a special court for the nobility, distinguished from the Court of the Burgesses by its clientele, procedure, and penalties. But the conscious formulation of this class spirit appeared only with the rise of aristocratic dynasties around which it could crystallize.

Two *assises* expressed this new spirit. First, 'an *assize* that a lord may arrest neither knight nor lady for debt'[37]—probably promulgated on the occasion of a general discussion of debts—which made a characteristic distinction: whereas neither a knight nor a noble lady nor anyone who had pledged faith and rendered homage could be imprisoned for debt, a burgess could be imprisoned and even forced to work until his debt was completely paid. This double standard was a legal recognition of the class spirit. This *assise*, which goes back to the twelfth century, was undoubtedly promulgated after 1146 (for at this date nobles were still being arrested for debt).[38] It probably dates from the reign of Baldwin III or Amalric.

The same spirit inspired the so-called *assise* of Bilbais (1168), which distinguished nobles from non-nobles serving on horseback; the former were not required to dismount during an attack on a besieged city.[39] The *chevauchée*, the aristocratic form of combat, became the monopoly of a class, even if it immobilized the cavalry beneath the walls of a besieged fortress. Such was the behaviour required by the knightly code.

The formation of a new class of great lords—a class whose rise was marked by rebellions at the beginning of this period and by intervention in a disputed succession to the Crown at its end—reinforced this spirit. Everywhere that it existed, this upper stratum of the nobility manifested itself by similar signs, by rules tending to favour the accumulation of land in its hands. In Europe this was achieved by several means: by the *Leihezwang*, which forced the prince to grant out immediately any fief

---

[36] Following the famous prologue of John of Ibelin and all the sources that derive from it. See the peculiar discovery of G. Recoura in *Mélanges d'histoire et d'archéologie de L'École française de Rome* 42 (1925), 147–66, and our review of the study of P. W. Topping in *RHDFE* 1954, fasc. 1, pp. 129–33.

[37] John of Ibelin, ch. 188 (*Lois* i. 300–1).

[38] M. Grandclaude, 'Liste d'assises', recognized that the *assise* belonged to the twelfth century. Our dating is based on a charter of 1146 which states that Walter of Caesarea sold part of his possessions to the Knights of St. John 'pro liberatione mea et hominum meorum qui pro debitis meis apud Acon sepissime tenebantur capti' (Delaville i. 133).

[39] Richard, *Royaume latin*, p. 78; *Lois* i. 455 n. c.

that fell into his hands by the disappearance of a noble line; by restricting marriages of the nobility to a narrow circle of families; by rules of succession favouring the concentration of landed wealth in a few hands. The Latin Kingdom was no exception, for special legislation facilitated the same development. These various *assises* following the first period of conquest all belong to the twelfth century, although they cannot be dated exactly. We are inclined to place them about the middle of the century, an estimate that seems to be corroborated by the general direction of developments as well as by indications drawn from independent sources.

Accumulation of fiefs in the hands of the high nobility had been restricted by old legislation whose intent was contrary to noble interests. These acts had sought to colonize the country densely and had opposed concentration of fiefs all the more, since as immigration continued unabated, the pool of available fiefs slowly evaporated. In this first conflict between the interests of the nobility and that of the kingdom, the nobility came out on top. Abrogating the earliest legislation, a new *assise* allowed a vassal already holding a fief to succeed to another as long as he hired a fighting-man to do military service for it.[40] This reform served the interests of eldest sons who, usually already fief-holders, could inherit other lands, accumulate several fiefs, and thus establish a foundation for a growing family fortune.

Rules concerning the wardship of widows were modified in the same sense. Although the power of the king to choose a second husband for a noble widow might often have wounded the sensibilities of the woman concerned, it was the noble houses themselves that led the opposition. The widow's 'friends' (that is, family), says Philip of Novara, were wronged because the king asked neither their counsel nor their consent. Under their pressure a new rule was introduced: the king was to propose three barons to the widow, from among whom she was obliged to choose her husband.[41] A small concession, to be sure, but one that left the widow's family a limited choice and undoubtedly presupposed their advice and consent. Meanwhile the nobility prepared a new weapon. Although obliged to choose her husband from the three candidates proposed by the king, under pain of losing her fief by *commise*, the widow (adds Philip of Novara) could refuse all of them on the grounds of disparagement or misalliance. The king thus found himself forced to propose to the heiress

---

[40] Philip of Novara, chs. 67–70 (*Lois* i. 538–41).
[41] Philip of Novara, ch. 86 (ibid. 558–60).

candidates of her own social rank and of similar wealth, or else the widow, with the advice of her family, might refuse the marriage.[42]

The results were clear. Not only did the king lose control of wealthy heiresses and thus of one means of rewarding his followers; the new rules also favoured the confining of noble marriages to a very small number of families and helped a few houses of high nobility to accumulate great wealth. The upper stratum of the nobility closed itself off. The knights, legally members of the same class, became a lower order.

These high nobles, who could be described—in the words of Gislebert of Mons—as 'potentes parentela et turribus fortes' began to lay claim to power in the kingdom, made themselves the guardians of a kind of Palestino-Syrian national feeling, and looked upon all newcomers as intruders and foreigners. Their xenophobia was the common factor connecting the opposition to Manasses of Hierges, constable and favourite of Queen Melissenda; the opposition to Thierry of Flanders, the eternal crusader who never succeeded in carving out a seignory for himself in the East; and the opposition to Renaud of Châtillon, Miles of Plancy, and the two Lusignans—one of whom nevertheless became the Tragic King. To the nobles these newcomers were nothing but rivals who could find a place for themselves in the eastern sun only by marrying a rich heiress. And royal support was not always enough to assure their success. Some, like Châtillon and Lusignan, achieved their object; others, like Manasses of Hierges, were forced to leave the country, even after marrying an heiress and receiving her dowry; others, such as Miles of Plancy, were simply assassinated.

Beneath this choice aristocracy crowded the mass of small knights, 'noble' by birth—an anonymous mass about whom the chroniclers tell very little and the documents nothing at all. The kingdom's service list (unfortunately twenty or thirty years later than the period with which we are here concerned)[43] only half reveals them, but it can be of some use if we correct it in matters of detail. In any event, an analysis of this list is indispensable for an understanding of the reign of Amalric, during which

---

[42] The date of this *assise* is unknown. M. Grandclaude, 'Liste d'assises', shows that the king offered a widow a single candidate in 1177, but Grandclaude rightly refused to draw any conclusions. The case was perhaps an exception, and we would prefer to place this *assise* in the middle of the twelfth century. The promulgation of the new *assise* must have occurred at the time when the great seignorial families, such as the Ibelins, were contracting marriages with the royal families of Jerusalem and even with the imperial family of Byzantium.

[43] For the date of this list see J. Richard, 'Les listes de fiefs dans Jean d'Ibelin', *RHDFE* 32 (1954), 566 ff., and his bibliography. The problem does not seem to have been resolved;

these ordinary knights played an important role in the constitutional life of the kingdom.

From the viewpoint of feudal ties the knights can be divided into royal vassals and seignorial vassals, the latter being rear-vassals of the king. Toward 1170, 257 knights were attached to the royal domain, 402 to the lay seignories, and sixteen to ecclesiastical seignories. Thus, about 40 per cent were connected to the royal domain and 60 per cent to seignorial domains.[44] The information available concerning the knights of the royal domain allows us to define with some precision the structure of this social class, a class which was not perfectly homogeneous.[45] We may generalize these conclusions to cover the seignorial domains; for there is no reason to suppose a different social structure there and, furthermore, we have a few additional pieces of information which allow us to verify these conclusions.

Of the 213 knights of the royal domain,[46] fifty-nine owed only their own service; sixteen owed, in addition, the service of one vassal; eight owed their own service and that of two vassals; six their own and that of three vassals; two their own and that of four vassals; two their own and that of six vassals; one his own and that of seven vassals. The fief of the Chamberlain, serving with six knights, was exceptional, as were the Constable's fief, serving with seven, and the fiefs of the viscount of Nablus and of Balian of Ibelin at Nablus, which served with fourteen knights.

The preponderance of those holding 'fiefs of one knight' and of knights serving with only one or two vassals (who hardly differ from the first) is striking. Thus, to sense the reality of this feudal hierarchy we must know what this 'fief of one knight' was and what was the economic situation of these knights who served 'with their own body'.

Very few of the knights mentioned in these service lists actually held landed fiefs.[47] Most had only *fiefs en besant*, fief-rents assigned on royal revenues, markets, customs, or maritime ports. This type of fief must have

---

Smail, *Crusading Warfare*, p. 89, suggests 1170–86. Richard, pp. 565–77, suggests 1185–7; cf. below, p. 152 n. 31.

[44] John of Ibelin, ch. 271 (*Lois* i. 422–6).

[45] In John of Ibelin's list the descriptions of seignorial contingents give no details but simply the total number of knights due from each seignory; the lists from the royal domain, on the other hand, are detailed and give the names of the knights from each locality.

[46] Subtracting the contingents of Haifa, Scandalion, and Blanchegarde (twenty-one knights altogether) from the sum of 257 knights in the royal domain. These seignories no longer belonged to the royal domain when the lists were drawn up and, as a result, we have for them only the total size of their contingents—insufficient information for detailed analysis. We do not know the details of the contingent from Beirut (twenty-three knights).

[47] For the seignories of Tyre and Arsuf see below, Ch. 6, pp. 148 ff.

been more common in the seignories and parts of the royal domain near the coast than in those of the interior. For it was in the maritime cities that economic life offered the best conditions for the creation of money-fiefs, even though in the cities of the interior, such as Tiberias in Galilee and Nablus in Samaria, commerce was developing because of international trade-routes and the traffic in rural products on their way to the markets of the maritime cities.

Unfortunately, it is impossible to know the percentage of fiefs that were money-fiefs. Only the frequency with which they appear in the texts and the place they hold in the works of the jurists (who consider them the equals of landed fiefs, treating them, so to speak, as 'normal' fiefs)[48] indicate their great diffusion. Saladin's attacks and the loss of territory that followed meant that money-fiefs became preponderant in the thirteenth century. One has only to compare the number of knights recruited in the Latin Kingdom with that raised at the same time in France. The *milites regni Franciae*[49] who owed service to the king in 1216 numbered about 800; the French army that took part in the battle of Bouvines, three-fifths of the total contingent, counted the same number of knights and some fewer sergeants than the Latin Kingdom threw into the battle of Hattin.[50] To be sure, France recruited three or four times the number of knights who owed service to the king. But how could the arid earth of Palestine, whose area was no greater than that of a French province, support some 675 knights[51] if it had disposed of only its landed revenues?

The average value of the money-fief seems to have been an income of 400 to 500 besants.[52] What was this worth? According to a source

---

[48] See e.g. John of Ibelin, ch. 182 (*Lois* i. 284–5): 'Que qui a II. M. besanz, et il doive servise de son cors et de un autre chevalier ou de deus sanz son cors.' See also Philip of Novara, ch. 46 (*Lois* i. 521).

[49] F. Lot, *L'Art militaire et les armées au moyen-âge* i (Paris, 1946), 219.

[50] E. Audouin, *Essai sur l'armée royale au temps de Philippe Auguste* (Paris, 1913), p. 3, and cf. below, Ch. 18, p. 487.

[51] This is the estimate calculated by Smail, *Crusading Warfare*, p. 89.

[52] La Monte, *Feudal Monarchy*, p. 150. Fiefs of 600 besants and more, apparently, were to be found. But La Monte's calculations on the fluctuations in value of these fiefs are not well founded. The fact that a lord received 1,200 or 2,000 besants annually for the service of two knights (see above, n. 48) does not prove that a simple fief was worth 600 or 1,000 because some allowance must be made for the lord's profit. In direct investiture the fief was from 400 to 500 besants (see Philip of Novara, ch. 67). Furthermore, there is an irrefutable proof in the colonization of Cyprus by the Lusignans at the end of the twelfth century. According to the *Continuation de Guillaume de Tyr* 26. 12 (*RHC HOcc.* ii. 192), 'Et furent establi le fié à quatre cens besanz blanz le chevalier, et à trois cenz besanz blanz li Turquoples, à II. chevaucheures et hauberjon.'

published (and forgotten) long ago,[53] the daily wage of a knight in the mid-thirteenth century amounted to approximately 7*s*. 6*d*., an amount about equivalent to a gold besant of the Latin Kingdom.[54] The annual upkeep of a knight thus cost about 350 besants, not counting such extraordinary expenses as the costly replacement of a sick or dead horse. The margin between the revenue of a 400-besant fief and a knight's expenses was therefore minimal, if it existed at all.

The noble class in the third quarter of the twelfth century was thus composed of an exclusive circle of barons and magnates at the summit. There existed hardly more than twenty-four important seignories, which as a result of marriage and inheritance within a small group were held by no more than ten lords, of whom many possessed several seignories. Thus, fewer than ten families held these twenty-four seignories, since several lords belonged to the same houses (not counting family alliances, close or distant). Between this small number of great lords and the mass of knights there existed no intermediate class, no well-off knights in possession of large enough fiefs to be able to enfeoff, in turn, a number of their own vassals. The feudal hierarchy in the Latin Kingdom was thus greatly simplified: there existed scarcely more than one degree of vassalage. The royal domain at Jerusalem consisted of twenty vassals and twenty-one rear-vassals; at Acre, apart from the fiefs of the officers of the kingdom, of twenty-three vassals and nine rear-vassals; at Tyre it comprised fourteen vassals and fourteen rear-vassals; at Nablus, not counting the fief of an Ibelin, thirty-five vassals and thirty-five rear-vassals. On the lay seignories, whose extent was less than that of the royal domain, subinfeudation must have been even rarer.

The populous class of simple knights reinforced by mercenaries recruited for the great campaigns, occupied a social and economic position which was manifestly inferior. A few of them held landed fiefs; most had only their money-fiefs. For one and another, income barely exceeded expenses. Their outlook and their conduct must, as a result, have been profoundly marked. Enjoying the prestige their rank conferred among the conquered population and the bourgeoisie, they did not have the means to lead an aristocratic way of life. Furthermore, their fief-rents

---

[53] R. Röhricht, 'Der Kreuzzug d. König Jacob I von Aragonien (1269)', *Mitt. des österreichischen Instituts für Geschichtsforschung* 11 (1890), 384 ff.

[54] Practically the same wages as were customary in the army of Philip Augustus and St. Louis. See E. Audouin, *Essai sur l'armée royale*, pp. 51 ff. Our source is contemporary with St. Louis.

denied them the privilege of true nobility which Marc Bloch called 'the right to command'. The slenderness of their means made them strictly dependent on their immediate lords and thus in no way comparable to the English squire, the lord of the manor, pillar and foundation of Plantagenet administration.

iii. *The Period of Amalric and the Predominance of the Great Families*

Under Amalric the Latin Kingdom achieved its political apogee, while feudal legislation continued to adjust to the new social and economic realities. During his reign the most famous statute of the Latin Kingdom, the so-called 'Assize concerning liege homage' (*Assise sur la ligece*), was enacted. Probably at the same time far-reaching changes in the rules of infeudation were taking place.

The first fiefs of the kingdom had been conferred on vassals and their entire family lines both direct and collateral. Later, as both Philip of Novara and John of Ibelin inform us,[55] infeudation was restricted to a vassal and his direct descendants born of his legitimate wife. (The jurists give no date for this change, but we may date it approximately, for an act of infeudation of 1152 already contains the formula[56] which treatises of jurisprudence will later reproduce.)

Whom did this change profit? The king, now able to take back fiefs from those lines that disappeared? But what advantage could the king possibly have from the return to his domain of a simple knight's fief? He needed knights more than land and rents. He would have to infeudate the escheated land immediately, in order to ensure military service. The advantage would be clearer if one of the great seignorial houses were extinguished. But this was not a very probable occurrence. The old families, deeply rooted in the country, whose wealth eased the way to marriage alliances, did not expire so easily. And even if a direct line did disappear, the king could not profit because the great families remained enfeoffed according to the old law rather than the new: their fiefs descended to all possible heirs or heiresses. If anyone profited from the change in the law, it was the possessors of the great seignories, within

---

[55] Philip of Novara, ch. 66 (*Lois* i. 536–7); John of Ibelin, ch. 150 (ibid. 225–7).

[56] Pons, abbot of Mt. Tabor, enfeoffed Hugh of Bethsan (1152) with the formula 'do et concedo Hugoni de Bethsa . . . heredibusque suis legitimis legitime de eo natis' (Delaville ii. 903, no. 11). In an act of enfeoffment by Amalric in 1169 'confirmo tibi . . . et heredibus, quos de filia Jozelini Peselli habebis' (Strehlke, no. 5). In another act by the same king from 1174 is to be found, in all probability, the original phrase of the *assise*: 'Confirmo tibi . . . et heredibus tuis quos de uxore tua legitime desponsata genueris' (Strehlke, no. 7).

which a single knight's fief counted more than in the royal domain. But still the real object of this new *assise* remains unclear.

Another *assise* of Amalric, conceding important privileges to the class of great lords, testifies to the way their relations were developing. Maritime affairs held a particular interest for the king; it was he, in all probability, who gave the kingdom the *Cour de la chaîne*, a special commercial and maritime court. Among the chapters of the *Livre des Assises des Bourgeois* on maritime questions, the following statement appears: 'Whenever a ship may be wrecked, the lord of the land must have the mainsail and tiller of a ship broken up on the sea or on land, for King Amalric gives this liberty to all the Kingdom of Jerusalem.'[57] This is irrefutable evidence that the Crown had retained until the mid-twelfth century the right to wrecks on the entire coast, as it had, until 1130, a monopoly of the ports. Infeudation of large coastal stretches had certainly reduced the king's powers, but baronies and great seignories had not been closed to royal intervention—at least in cases of shipwreck. Now, faced with the increasing power of the high nobility, Amalric was forced to give up this last vestige of his rights. One recalls the *Charte aux Normands*, which Louis X granted in 1315 to the coastal lords of Normandy.

It is our argument that the *Assise sur la ligece* is another expression of the changing balance of power between Crown and nobility. The circumstances of its promulgation remain obscure, and the manner in which it was applied, even more so. Nevertheless, in the light of the social climate we have described, we may reach some conclusions that are quite different from those usually accepted.

According to all the sources, the *assise* concerning liege homage was issued after a war between Amalric and Gerard, lord of Sidon, a war whose apparent cause was the arbitrary dispossession by Gerard of one of his vassals.[58] Can we accept this explanation?

We must remember first that when Amalric came to the throne, he had to face violent opposition. Even the chronicler William of Tyre, usually so discreet when it comes to anything that might embarrass the court of Jerusalem[59] does not hide the fact that only a few barons, backed by the clergy and people, supported the king against all the rest of the nobility.[60]

[57] *LdAdB*, ch. 49 (*Lois* ii. 47).
[58] See the sources cited by Grandclaude, 'Liste d'assises', p. 339 n. 44, and Richard, *Royaume latin*, pp. 78, 81.
[59] William of Tyre wrote his chronicle at the request of King Amalric.
[60] W.T. xix.1.

The nobility was contesting Amalric's right to succeed to the throne: a characteristic feature of the social evolution that had taken place, a result of the shift in the balance of power in favour of the noble families. Even the support of the clergy and people had its price: Amalric was forced to repudiate his wife.[61] In these circumstances, did the king have the means to promulgate an *assise* that, as a matter of course, required the consent of the great men of the kingdom and that, at the same time, had the diminution of their power as its object?

Another difficulty: Amalric carried on his war against Gerard with the aid of a feudal army. Would the nobility have fought one of the most powerful of its members in order to put a minor rear-vassal back into his fief? Furthermore, it is rather difficult to imagine the hard-headed, greedy Amalric going to war for some abstract notion of justice.[62]

In reality, although it was the avowed aim of the war, neither the king nor the nobility was fighting for the rights of a minor rear-vassal. The nobility certainly expected some profit from the venture. (E. Meynial suggested that, to gain their support, the king had agreed that fiefs falling to noblemen already enfeoffed might be served by a paid warrior,[63] a change we prefer to ascribe to an earlier period.)

If the nobility took part in the war against Gerard of Sidon, it was rather because this war meant a tacit abrogation of the ancient *assise* of Baldwin II (or Baldwin III) which allowed the king to dispossess his vassals at will.[64] The war punished a lord who had dispossessed his own vassal without judgment. It followed that the rule ought *a fortiori* to apply to the king's vassals, to his noble tenants-in-chief. In fact Gerard, a lord who had gone so far as to make Sidon a nest of pirates[65] lost little. The nobles finally stepped between the combatants; peace was re-established, the lord of Sidon made his due show of humility, and the rear-vassal was restored his rights. More important, the judicial precedent was immediately confirmed by an *assise* which was pledged to long life.

The *assise* concerning liege homage had many facets and many ramifications. Historians, however, have paid little attention to anything but the oath of liege homage it required from all rear-vassals of the Crown. To be sure, the liege homage now given by all fief-holders created

[61] W.T. xix.4; xxiv.1 (ibid. 888–90, 1004).

[62] W.T. xix.2 (ibid. 886): 'Interventu munerum auferebat saepe, differebat saepius, aliter quam censurae rigor et juris modestia pateretur.'

[63] Meynial, 'De quelques particularités' (above, n. 26).

[64] See Ch. 17, p. 456.

[65] Richard, *Royaume latin*, p. 81.

a direct link between the mass of knights and the king. The 'vavassours des riches homes'[66] became 'ses homes liges qui tienent de ses homes.' All of them are, therefore, summoned: 'Que il li viengent aidier ou consellier ou servir à armes, se il en a besoing',[67] to give customary *consilium et auxilium*. One should not forget, however, that the primary object of this oath was to make all rear-vassals members of the royal High Court and to allow them to demand justice there if their immediate lord did not give it to them. This new link, we are told, was directed, or could have been directed, against the great nobility. But we never see it applied in this fashion: the explanation that it could strengthen a strong king and weaken a weak one is insufficient.

To a certain degree, it is the superficial analogy between the oath of liege homage in the Latin Kingdom and the famous Oath of Salisbury taken by the English and Normans to William the Conqueror in 1086, that has influenced historians' commentaries. If the English oath was the foundation of Anglo-Norman royal power, then it is plausible to believe that the oath of liege homage played an analogous role in the Kingdom of Jerusalem. But this was not so.

The *assise* concerning liege homage is known to us almost uniquely through thirteenth-century sources. At this time its influence was felt throughout the judicial and constitutional life of the kingdom.

1. In the area of politics: all fief-holders, being the king's liege men, could take part in the deliberations of the High Court, whose competence extended to political as well as administrative and judicial questions.

2. In the judicial field: a lord's vassal dispossessed without judgment of the court of his seignory had the right to proceed against his lord before the king.

3. In the field of feudal relations: every vassal, doing liege homage to the king, from now on owed him fealty against all. Liege homage could be rendered only to the king; it became a royal monopoly.[68]

But the oath of *ligece* not only forged vertical links, meeting at the ideal apex of the feudal pyramid, in the Crown, as the suzerain *par excellence*, it also forged horizontal links, embracing all nobles, which had not previously existed. To quote Philip of Novara: 'Le rei otroia... que tous ses homes liges qui tenoient de li ou de ses homes, queis qu'il fussent, grans ou petis, fussent tenu de fei l'un à l'autre de ce que est dessus escrit, et que

---

[66] Philip of Novara, ch. 40 (*Lois* i. 517).

[67] Philip of Novara, ch. 51 (ibid. 526).

[68] In glaring contrast to European usage; see John of Ibelin, ch. 195 (*Lois* i. 313–14).

chascun d'eaus peust requerre les autres come ses peirs en teil endreit.'[69] This meant that henceforth new and formal links would firmly hold together the internal fabric of the class. These new links would give rise to reciprocal legal obligations of all members to each other. They will all be 'peers' of each other. The class becomes an 'estate' with identical duties and privileges of all members towards each other and in its external relations to the Crown.[70]

1. As to real political influences the *assise* made little, if any, impression at all. All we know of the Kingdom of Jerusalem and of every other medieval state allows us to affirm with certainty that neither the king nor the great lords could draw any advantage from having the knights join in the deliberations of the royal court. A medieval *parlamentum* was not an anticipation of a modern national assembly; even in the East votes were weighed rather than counted. Although the numerous knights of the royal domain, all tenants-in-chief of the Crown, had a right to participate in the meeting of the High Court, it was only the barons, tenants of seignories held from the Crown, who had an actual voice in its deliberation. From time to time simple knights might play a more decisive role. During certain military expeditions, the *populus*, knights and non-nobles, could force a decision on their leaders. But the 'people in arms' had already played this role during the First Crusade, and its force was not augmented by the *assise* concerning liege homage.

2. The judicial aspect of the problem is quite different. The war won by Amalric over his vassal did not result in a constitutional victory for the monarchy: quite the contrary. Victory signified the safeguarding of a vassal's rights against his lord's arbitrary proceedings and, as an explicit or tacit corollary, an identical guarantee to the tenants-in-chief against their own lord, the king. As a further consequence, a rear-vassal, if wronged, could in principle call all the fief-holders from his seignory to sit in judgment with his lord on the case and ask his fellow vassals to refuse their service to their common lord, if he did not do justice. Furthermore, the rear-vassal could now call on the king, his liege lord, to force his immediate

[69] Philip of Novara, p. 527: 'The king granted . . . that all his liegemen, who hold from him or from his men, whoever they are, great and small, should be held to fealty one to another in regard to what was written above and that each of them could require others as his peers in such a place [= such circumstances].' See also John of Ibelin, ch. 140 (*Lois* i. 214–15).

[70] On the general problem of 'estates' see E. Lousse, 'La Formation des ordres dans la société médiévale', *L'Organisation corporative du moyen-âge à la fin de l'Ancien Régime* (Louvain, 1937), pp. 63–90; idem, 'Parlementarisme ou corporatisme', *RHDFE* xiv (1935), 638 f.

lord to do justice or to execute the judgment of the court. If the immediate lord refused, he lost for life his rights of jurisdiction. In principle, then, this was a victory for the rear-vassals. But was not this victory more apparent than real? To decide this we must first discover the men concerned and how they acted.

In the first place a rear-vassal could not present his complaint before the High Court except in two well-defined situations: when his immediate lord refused to do justice, or when his lord condemned him without judgment. The High Court was never a 'court of appeal' in the modern sense. Its doors opened to rear-vassals only when the doors of their own lord's court had remained closed. If the seignorial court gave a judgment the vassal thought wrong, he could not carry this case before the High Court but could only accuse his judges of 'false judgment'—and engage in single combat with each of them before the seignorial court, to prove his accusation. In other words, a lord could easily prevent a vassal from appealing to the king's court by judging the case himself.

In this seignorial court—composed of knights largely without independent means, whose fiefs were usually money payments from the lord's treasury—the lord enjoyed unequalled prestige. His vassals had neither the power nor the ability to resist strong pressure on his part. Of course it does not follow that the lord could openly dictate the sentence of his court or openly disregard the prescriptions of custom. In everyday affairs, however, the lord's opinion must have weighed heavily. Against his lord's opinion, a rear-vassal had hardly any recourse. Calling his peers to sit in judgment was no help, and he could neither appeal to the High Court nor call the vassals of another lord to sit in judgment. Here is the most important effect of the *assise* concerning liege homage: the knights of the kingdom did not become peers at all times or everywhere; their 'peerage' was neither absolute nor universal; they became peers only *vis-à-vis* the king. They received no right to involve themselves in the business of any seignorial court other than their own; seignorial affairs remained the business of the lord and his own vassals.

It is obvious that the *assise* concerning liege homage was not a general remedy for the difficulties of rear-vassals; it did not correct, and probably was not issued with the intention of correcting, anything but the most crying abuses. It had preventive value—no lord would have liked to be cited before the High Court by one of his own vassals who would have then had the right to call the vassals of other seignories. It was a salutary threat hanging over the heads of the great lords, but not a dangerous one.

The king, however, had more immediate vassals than the nobles had; the menace that was partially effective against them must have been much more effective against him. His immediate vassals, the *seigneurs justiciers*, could call all the members of their class, of their 'estate', to take part in giving judgment—against him. For all noble tenants-in-chief were peers in relation to the king. And in all the known cases in which the *assise* concerning liege homage was invoked, it was invoked not against a justicer lord but against the king. Raoul of Tiberias, dispossessed for treason by King Aimery (the so-called Amalric II) without judgment of the High Court, called the nobles of the kingdom to sit in judgment (then, faced with the obstinate refusal of the king, renounced his case and quit the kingdom).[71] It was different with the famous lord of Beirut, who, dispossessed by order of Frederick II, called on his peers and succeeded in depriving the Emperor of his vassals' service.[72] The same Emperor's *bailli*, Balian of Sidon, having received an order not to execute a judgment of the High Court in favour of the Princess Alice against the Teutonic Order, found himself deprived of the service of the nobility and knights, who had been called upon to aid the princess. Even in this case, however, the princess found herself obliged to absolve her 'peers' of their obligation.[73] Again, Henry II, king of Cyprus and Jerusalem, saw his knights withhold their service until his vassal, Philip of Gibelet, received the fief-rent due him.[74] On another occasion, led by a certain Guillaume Raymond, Henry's vassals—described as 'a great mass of men, most of whom were sergeants, more than there were of knights'—demanded their pay which had been long delayed and threatened to renounce their service. Only the aged John of Ibelin, the finest jurist of his age, rid the king of this menace by finding that the vassals' procedure had been faulty.[75] In all these cases, the only ones we know, it was always the king who was threatened; it was his immediate vassals, justicer lords, knights of his house and domain, who used the *assise* concerning liege homage through which every knight became 'peer' of his lord and his fellow knights, but only with respect to the king.[76]

[71] Philip of Novara, ch. 42 (*Lois* i. 518); John of Ibelin, ch. 203 (ibid. 325).
[72] Philip of Novara, ch. 52 (*Lois* i. 528); John of Ibelin, ch. 203 (ibid. 325).
[73] John of Ibelin, ch. 203 (ibid. 436).
[74] Ibid.
[75] John of Ibelin, ch. 239 (ibid. 384); see also chs. 236–7 (ibid. 376–82).
[76] From a strictly legal point of view, anyone who possessed a fief in the kingdom had the right to intervene in cases before the High Court, even if it concerned only a knight of the royal domain (for the seignorial court of the king was the High Court). However it appears

3. The importance of the *assise* for feudal relations came from the obligation it imposed on vassals to quit the service of their immediate lord if he refused to be judged by the High Court (if the lord rebelled), and to join the king's service. This royal 'advantage' (as it was called), while important, remained limited—as the interpretation of its content by contemporary jurists demonstrates. Those vassals who left their lord's service to join the king were within forty days to be paid a recompense equal to the revenues they lost. If the king could not pay this indemnity, they could return to their lord and the king thus lost their support. What this meant in practice, since the royal treasury was usually empty during the thirteenth century, was that the king had to suppress a rebellious vassal within forty days or lose the support of his rear-vassals. Neither chronicles nor jurists, however, mention any case that would allow us to gauge the real import of this clause. Its true value must have resided less in its judicial contents than in its moral force: it was a means of prevention, giving a prospective rebellious lord a subject for reflection before he dared defy the king and his High Court.

The *assise* concerning liege homage contains another clause that has never attracted historians' attention. If the king has reason to suspect one of his men of possible rebellion 'all the people of the towns and castles of the king's vassal must, at the king's request or command, swear fealty to the king.'[77] Thus, after the war against Gerard of Sidon the inhabitants of Sidon and Beaufort (another castle of the seignory) swore fealty to the king. Although we know of no other example of this oath after the promulgation of the *assise* concerning liege homage, one is to be found— curiously enough—in 1155, about ten years before the *assise* appeared: the settlers of the canons of the Holy Sepulchre swore fealty to the canons, but reserved the *fidelitas regis*, their fealty to the king.[78]

We can probably detect an even older example of this kind of oath in a text of 1142 in which Count Raymond of Tripoli gave Rafaniyah to the Knights of St. John, 'in peace, freely in alms and dominion and liege fealty

---

to us to be highly improbable that the jurists of the kingdom drew these consequences from the *assise*.

[77] Philip of Novara, ch. 51 (*Lois* i. 527); John of Ibelin, ch. 140 (ibid. 215), ch. 199 (ibid. 320); James of Ibelin, ch. 10 (ibid. 457).

[78] The formula of the oath is conserved in Rozière, no. 131: 'ego . . . juro fidelitatem Deo et sanctissimo Sepulcro et conventui eiusdem S. Sepulcri ad custodiendum et manutenendum vitam et membra eorum et omnia quae ad S. Sepulcrum et ad predictum conventum pertinent, salva fidelitate regis Jerusalem. Sic Deus me adiuvet et istud sanctum evangelium.' See below, Ch. 5, pp. 126 f.

of all men, both knights and burgesses, holding lands and possessions there'.[79] Thus the oath of liege homage, obligatory on all possessors of land, whether vassals, rear-vassals, or burgesses, existed in the county of Tripoli nearly twenty years before the *assise* concerning liege homage. Was this a usage peculiar to Rafaniyah or to the county of Tripoli? It is impossible to say. However, the oaths of fealty taken by the colonists of Mahomeria[80] in 1155 show that an analogous usage existed in the Latin Kingdom in the days of Baldwin III, the predecessor of King Amalric.

Another document emanating from the court of Baldwin III (1161) shows that the oath of liege homage to the king was already being taken by a rear-vassal. When Philip of Milly acquired the great fief of Transjordan from the king, he was required to safeguard the possessions of John Gothman, who until this time had been vassal of the king. The king, furthermore, stipulated 'that the aforesaid John, for the land he holds beyond the Jordan, will do homage to me the aforesaid king and service to Lord Philip.'[81] Since this newly created seignory of Transjordan was autonomous, like all the great seignories, and since its lord became a justicer lord, it is possible that this was a special case in which liege homage was given the king to protect a former vassal, now 'mediatized', against any possible injury from his new lord.

These facts lead us to the conclusion that the most striking clauses of the *assise*—liege homage from rear-vassals and oaths of fealty from the burgesses of the great seignories to the king—were not so revolutionary as some would like to think. At most, the *assise* now generalized and rendered obligatory for the entire kingdom a technique used in exceptional circumstances during the previous twenty years.

To sum up, the *assise* concerning liege homage appears to have a different import from that ordinarily ascribed to it. It did not strengthen the king nor the position of the knights and rear-vassals. Its only beneficiaries were the members of the high nobility, the lords holding the rights of justice. An alliance between the king and the mass of simple knights was conceivable only if the king were a Machiavellian prince and the knights were lords of the manor, like the English gentry. The knights

---

[79] '... quiete, libere in elemosinam et dominationem, et ligietatem omnium hominum, tam militum quam burgensium, ibidem terras habentium et possessiones.' Delaville i. 117, no. 144.

[80] Now al-Bira, east of Ramallah, to the north of Jerusalem.

[81] Strehlke, no. 3: 'quod praefatus Iohannes pro terra, quam ultra Iordanem tenet, michi, predicto regi faciat hominium et domino Philippo servicium.'

of the Latin Kingdom had poor fiefs or modest rents, however, and therefore could not form a serious opposition to the high nobility.

The heroic but sad reign of Baldwin IV (1174–85) marked the final collapse of royal power. From then on, the fight for power was not between king and nobility, but between two parties, two factions of the nobility, one of which received the support of a few members of the royal court.[82] It was the great rich and powerful families who disputed the Crown. A historical accident, the succession of a child to the throne (Baldwin V), and the worsening of the political situation put the future of the country into the hands of the nobility. The respective places of Crown and baronage at the end of the First Kingdom are pithily described in the defiant answer of one of the great barons. The fabulous Reynald of Châtillon, entreated (1186) by the king, Guy of Lusignan, to stop pillaging Muslim caravans in his Transjordan principality, sent back word 'que aussi estoit il sires de sa terre, come il [Guy] de la soe et que il n'avoit point de trive as Sarrasinz.'[83] It was a rejoinder that not only proclaimed the weakness of the Crown but announced the virtual disruption of the unity of the kingdom. A *grand seigneur* did not acknowledge a truce contracted by the state with a foreign power but resolved to pursue an independent policy. And Reynald of Châtillon was not the only one to do so. At the end of 1186, Raymond, prince of Galilee, entered into a private agreement with Saladin which verged on treason against the state. This was within a twelve-month of the disastrous battle of Hattin (1187).

Saladin did not allow the royal power any time to reconstitute itself; and the battle of Hattin simultaneously marked the end of the First Kingdom and the complete annihilation of royal power. The vicissitudes of the Crown after that battle may be succinctly told in the language of the agreement concluded between Richard of England and Philip II of France on the eve of the Third Crusade. They divide, in advance, all future conquests of the Crusade, and virtually imply that the state and the Crown of Jerusalem are vacant or have ceased to exist. The future conquerors will decide their fate after the expected victory.[84] The brisk business of offering the Crown to Guy of Lusignan, Conrad of Montferrat, and Henry of

[82] M. W. Baldwin, *Raymond III of Tripoli* (Princeton, 1936), and Richard, *Royaume latin*, pp. 134 ff., give excellent accounts of these fights, taking into consideration the family ties among the noble factions.

[83] *Eracles, RHC HOcc.* ii. 34.

[84] *Itinerarium Regis Ricardi*, ed. W. Stubbs (London, 1864), vol. i. 1. II, ch. 9, p. 150; *L'Estoire de la Guerre Sainte par Ambroise*, ed. G. Paris, vers. 365 ff. For further discussion see S. Runciman, *The Families of Outremer. The Feudal Nobility of the Crusader Kingdom of Jerusalem*, Creighton Lecture (London, 1959); and J. Riley-Smith, *Feudal Nobility*.

Champagne (who never accepted it) shows the lamentable depths to which the throne of Jerusalem had sunk.

This once more explains that, during the Fifth Crusade, Pelagius not only displayed little ability and less knowledge in his command of the armies bogged down on the muddy banks of the Nile, but even raised doubts whether captured Egypt belonged at all to the Kingdom of Jerusalem. These doubts subsequently prompted King John of Brienne to press the Pope for a promise that the newly envisaged Crusade would assign to the kingdom all its conquests to come.

3 Estates, Communities, and the Constitution of the Latin Kingdom[1]

Studies dealing with the political and social structure of the Crusader Kingdom tend more and more to modify the image hitherto accepted of the Latin establishments in the East. It was an image designed by the great Crusader jurists of the thirteenth century, and, in the main, it has been unquestioned by historians and by students of law and constitution in particular, until our own times.[2] The so-called 'Paradise of feudalism', a figment of the imagination of that biased jurist of the nobility, John of Ibelin, is giving place to the more balanced and more nuanced description of the political system of the kingdom based on contemporary chronicles, acts, and deeds, and not on juridical treatises. We turn now to what seems to us to be a significant development in the Second Kingdom during the thirteenth century.

i. The Assise sur la ligece and the Second Kingdom

The *Assise sur la ligece*, the most famous single piece of Crusader legislation, was born in obscure circumstances. Its apparent purpose, the strengthening of royal power, was scarcely accomplished. Owing to the particular structure of Crusader nobility, as well as to the political circumstances of a royal minority, a foreign invasion which almost annihilated the

---

[1] This chapter is an enlarged version of a lecture read before the Israel Academy of Sciences and Humanities and published in the *Proceedings of the Israel Academy of Sciences and Humanities* 2, no. 6 (Jerusalem, 1969). A number of studies and a lively discussion of the problem followed this publication: H. E. Mayer, 'On the beginnings of the Communal Movement in the Holy Land. The Commune of Tyre', *Traditio* 24 (1968), 443–57; idem, 'Zwei Kommunen in Akkon?', *Deut. Archiv für Erforschung d. Mittelalters* 25 (1970), 434–53; J. Riley-Smith, 'The assise sur la ligece and Commune of Acre', *Traditio* 27 (1971), 179–204; idem, 'A Note on Confraternities in the Latin Kingdom', *Bull. of the Inst. of Hist. Research* 44 (1971), 301–8; cf. idem, *Feudal Nobility*, pp. 194 ff.; J. Prawer, 'The Earliest Commune of Tripoli', *Studies in Memory of Gaston Wiet*, ed. M. Rosen-Ayalon (Jerusalem, 1977), pp. 171–9.

[2] On research in the field of the history of institutions see C. Cahen, 'La féodalité et les institutions politiques de l'Orient latin', XII Convegno 'Volta', *Accad. Naz. dei Lincei* (Rome, 1956), pp. 167–94; H. E. Mayer, 'Probleme moderner Kreuzzugforschung', *Vierteljahresschrift für Sozial- und Wirtschaftsgeschichte* 50 (1964), 505–13; J. A. Brundage, 'Recent Crusade Historiography—Some Observations and Suggestions', *Catholic Historical Review* 49 (1964), 493–507.

kingdom, and finally a succession of short reigns, it was the upper class of
nobility, the narrow circle of magnates, that emerged in the last quarter
of the century as a powerful, in fact the decisive, factor in the kingdom.

What remained of the *assise* as a permanent feature destined to influence
in some measure its constitutional history was the formation of a legal
notion of an 'estate'—and this rather earlier than it happened in Europe.
The creation of the 'estate' of nobility was the result of a legislative act,
which bound all members of the class by an oath to a party outside their
own ranks, the Crown.

Yet the emergence of an estate did not immediately result in any
noteworthy constitutional changes. Somehow, the legal 'estate of nobles',
although stabilized very early in the history of the kingdom, never went
a step further. The kingdom did take one stride beyond the stage of a
magnum consilium composed of all the tenants-in-chief by adding *all* fief-
holders to its meetings, but it never evolved a system of representation
which would have assured the simple knights a permanent standing in the
High Court. The reason for this arrested evolution should be sought not
only in the lack of experience, but in the realities of life in the kingdom.
The main purpose of the *Assise sur la ligece* was to prevent arbitrary
confiscation of fiefs without a legal judgment of a court. Denial of justice
was dealt with in all feudal systems by the right of appeal to the jurisdiction
of the overlord. The Crusader Kingdom underpinned this procedure by
a system of common petitioning of nobles, barons, and knights in the
High Court. In such cases, it was in the interest of the petitioners not only
to be represented, but to be present in person. The sheer weight of
numbers was of the utmost importance in impressing accused and court.
Thus the main purpose of the *Assise sur la ligece* stultified its potentialities
and cut short the development of a representative system. Only such a
system could have made certain of the permanent attendance of the simple
knights at the meetings of the High Court. Without it, the High Court
remained a monopoly of the *grands seigneurs*. Nothing could be more
illuminating than the decision of 1182, to levy a general tax on the
kingdom, virtually taken by the higher nobility acting alone, although, in
fact, the simple knights, possessing land-fiefs or money fiefs, were taxed as
well.[3]

---

[3] W.T. xxii. 23: 'Convenerunt regni principes universi . . . de rerum statu . . . consilium
habituri.' And in the official document: 'Haec est forma colligendi census, qui de communi
omnium principum, tam ecclesiasticorum quam secularium, et de assensu universae plebis
regni Hierosolymorum, pro communi utilitate ejusdem regni, contra imminentes necessitates,

(continued)

It needed a different kind of cause and stimulus to start the wheels of the machinery turning and put it beyond the bounds of a *magnum consilium*. We see its operation on the occasions when a *coniuratio* of nobles was used against the Crown.[4] The petition of the knights of Cyprus against their king, Henry II, after the siege of Cérines, is significant as evidence of the shortcomings of the *coniuratio* in common petitioning: 'la court fu pleniere et que grant partie de ciaus à qui le rei deveit lors vindrent devant le rei en las presence de sa court. Un d'iaus por toz conjura le rei et semonst por lui et por toz les autres.'[5] This seemed to be a perfect setting for a common petition, but things turned out differently. After eulogizing the loyal service rendered by the knights, John of Ibelin took pleasure in pointing out their defects as laymen: 'car sauve seit vos honors, il semble que vos ne savés mie bien les uz et les assises dou reiaume de Jerusalem.' They should have put their demand forward in the customary way of summons, requests, and delays, each claimant demanding individually what was due to him and then threatening the lord legally with relinquishment of service ('gagier de son service') and then of fealty. In lieu,[6] the guileless men mustered their courage, chose one of their number to speak in their name, and put their demand in common to their overlord. But this, said John of Ibelin, was precisely contrary to the customs and *assises*.

No doubt this answer was in strict accordance with prevailing practice, namely, that a claim to a vassal's salary or to a fief should follow the mode of conjuring the lord to fulfil his obligations towards the vassal. In the true spirit of vassalic relations, with their insistence on the direct nexus between lord and vassal, such a claim has to be presented individually and not through a common petition of the vassals. Thus John of Ibelin narrowly circumvented a possible use and development of the *Assise sur la ligece*. He must have argued that the competence of the *Assise sur la ligece* was restricted to its primary cause: unlawful confiscation of a fief. Although the *assise* branched out, and one ramification was the right of all fief-holders to attend the High Court, a common petitioning in respect of fiefs

---

colligi debet.' In the French translation even the implied assent of *universa plebs* disappeared: 'Ce est la forme de cueillir la cense qui est estàblie par l'otroi des prelaz et des autres barons por le besoign du roiaume de Jherusalem' (*Guillaume de Tyr et ses continuateurs*, ed. P. Paris, 1880, xxii. 22 (ii. 450).

[4] See above, Ch. 2, p. 41.

[5] John of Ibelin, ch. 239 (*Lois* i. 384); see also chs. 236–7 (ibid. 376–82).

[6] This interminable procedure is described minutely by John of Ibelin in ch. 237 (*Lois* i. 381–2).

seemed to John of Ibelin unlawful, or, to put it otherwise, such a case should be determined by the traditional customs obtaining in that regard.

Confined in jurisdiction to confiscation of fiefs, the *Assise sur la ligece* could still play a part even in politics because of the connection, ingrained in the feudal system, between fief-holding and the favoured status of the class of fief-holders. Thus it was invoked and activated during the struggle between the representatives of Frederick II and the baronial party led by the Ibelins,[7] in a clash which may illustrate a point in the institutional evolution of the kingdom.

ii. *Classes and Corporative Bodies*

Around 1231 the central institution of the kingdom was still the High Court, the undifferentiated *curia regis*, cutting a rather poor figure compared, for example, with the contemporary *curia* of Henry III of England. Court of justice, advisory council, legislature, and political assembly, the High Court, despite its undeveloped character, acquired more and more power in direct ratio to the weakening of the Crown. The great offices of the state, the executive organs of the kingdom, never became powerful in the East, and this is probably the main reason, as far as we can see, why the High Court never really sought to control their appointment or functioning. The High Court was itself dominated by some half a dozen families and their feudal dependants. The simple knights, the *vavassours*, although theoretically members of the High Court according to the *Assise sur la ligece*, were in effect denied all influence.

Their position in the kingdom was at no time especially flourishing. Dependence on their lords, hardly mitigated by the *Assise sur la ligece*, was stringent. A great many of them, living on rent-fiefs, were very often hardly anything but salaried retainers. If there was a small group of knights who held more than a fief *unius militis* (*fief de son corps* in Crusader terminology), its numbers were always few. Moreover, Crusader legislation of the middle of the twelfth century, which allowed accumulation of fiefs (thereby reversing earlier canon), paved the way for the magnates to swallow up fiefs and replace land-fiefs by rent-fiefs. Both sides, lord and vassal, may well have regarded this arrangement as a convenient answer to their problems. Consequently, the never numerous intermediate class of knights, somewhere between barons and simple knights, was probably disappearing rapidly at the end of the twelfth

[7] Prawer, *Histoire* ii. 175 ff.

century. The 'estate of nobility' tended to become polarized and clearly split between highest and lowest levels.

Forfeiture of the kingdom at Hattin and its reconstruction after the Third Crusade did not better the standing of the simple knights. It would be truer to say that the Second Kingdom, which comprised no more than a fifth of the former territory, drastically diminished the number of land-fiefs in their possession. Seignorial dynasties that survived, but had lost their fiefs east of the narrow strip along the sea-shore which was the Second Kingdom, must surely, if they still kept knights, have done so on a basis of salary or rent-fief. And the same will apply to seignorial families that settled in Cyprus and derived their incomes from the island, quite often as a means of allowing them to hold on to their continental possessions.[8]

In these circumstances, the simple knight, just a paid warrior—although all appearances of genuinely vassalic relations were preserved by jurists and legislation—was in no position to act independently either inside his class or in political life. He might have been proud to be a cut above the Frankish burgesses, and his feelings of superiority might have been bolstered by his so immensely transcending a conquered and contemptible population. But such subjective emotions could not alter the fact that the kingdom was ruled by the magnates, whereas he, as a part of the *maisnie* of a *lignage,* was completely dependent and could be manipulated by his superiors for their own purposes.

At the time when the magnates, barons, and knights were becoming an 'estate' in the juridical sense of the word as a result of the *Assises sur la ligece,* other strata of society took on greater importance in the life of the kingdom. They did not form 'estates', but their cohesion and corporative structure made them a factor of consequence in a society where the fabric of state was crumbling. Roughly speaking, there were two types of corporations: the Military Orders, in a steadily rising ascendancy, and the communes of the great Italian cities. Constituted as they were, the Orders were, in a sense, out of the mainstream of circumstance: their power and resources were chiefly recruited from outside the kingdom from their chapters and priories, their fiefs and domains, all over Europe. Their great number (Hospitallers, Templars, the Teutonic Order, St. Lazar, St. Thomas, and Montjoie) and their authority should, in theory, have assured

---

[8] See the speech of John of Beirut before Frederick II in *Les Gestes des Chiprois*, ed. G. Raynaud, (Geneva, 1887), § 127, pp. 41–2. Beirut was fortified and garrisoned out of John's income from Cyprus.

them the standing of an 'estate', and their chronic quarrels and quick partisanry made them redoubtable adversaries or staunch supporters. But these were not the cohesive qualities that led to the emergence of an 'estate'. Socially, as their members did by birth, they belonged to nobility.

On a different level, the communes, that is, the colonies of the Italian cities, and to a smaller degree of the Provençal, were corporative bodies. They can scarcely be classified as belonging to one of the traditional social classes, let alone as an 'estate'. Their standing in the kingdom was not ordained by tradition, by the origin of their members, or—except to a small degree—by their social function. It was fixed once and for all, and statutorily, by the privileges accorded to them by the rulers of the kingdom in the early history of the conquest. Governed by their own local establishments and judged by their own codes of law, differing from those of noble and burgess alike, the communes were corporations of which the members, bound by oath to their magistrates, wielded a preponderant influence on the affairs and destiny of the kingdom. The famous 'War of the Communes', raging on the high seas and bringing havoc to Acre, was among the most unedifying episodes of thirteenth-century Christendom. In a way, the state came to a halt when Venice, Pisa, and Genoa, seesawing from alliance to alliance, supported by baronial factions and Military Orders, gave vent to their Italian jealousies inside the walls of that city. They behaved and acted, each like an independent political entity, with no regard for the law and order of the state to which they belonged. It was a kind of foretaste of wars to be fought, in centuries to come, between colonial powers on soil not their own.

In the history of the kingdom in the thirteenth century, one group of corporations is conspicuous by its absence: the cities and their burgesses. It is, indeed, a strange phenomenon. There were Crusader cities, populous, rich, and, with few exceptions, surpassing in size their counterparts in Europe, and yet they never became corporative bodies. Stranger still, urban environment, fertile in producing corporative organizations such as guilds, for example, seems to have been entirely sterile in the Latin East. It was pointed out long ago that one of the reasons for this complete lack of communal city developments might have been the chronic warfare of the Latin East. It will be impossible to prove or disprove this explanation, but it appears to us that, in the best of cases, it is only a partial one. A city's autonomy is not necessarily a handicap to its fighting power.

The major cause should be sought elsewhere. The most characteristic trait of Crusader society is its complete urbanization. We doubt if there was any other area in Christendom where the entire Christian population lived in cities, and in cities only.[9] This intriguing and significant social feature is explained by the exigencies of a minority faced with a permanently hostile majority. To assure its military striking power, the minority gathered itself in walled cities and in castles, and from those centres it kept the countryside in thrall.

The Crusader cities were, consequently, almost the only habitat of the conquerors. And this is probably the principal reason for the absence of urban autonomy. Magnates, knights, Italian communes, Latin clergy—all lived together in the same cities. So did the burgesses, but the cities were not burgess cities. It was that composition of the urban population, where the burgesses were only one component and surely not the most important, that prevented the rise of any communal movement. No city in the kingdom or in the principalities enjoyed any privileges. None had even the most elementary charter. Jerusalem, alone, enjoyed two special privileges for some time: lower duties on imported foodstuffs, and abolition of the property or possession rights of absentee landlords.[10] But it was not only the burgesses of Jerusalem who enjoyed these favours; all the townspeople enjoyed them. The grants were not part of any 'city' policy, they were a part of a royal policy to make sure of a stable population in the capital.

This state of things did not preclude the existence of a well-defined class of burgesses, but it never attained the stage of real corporative organization. Burgesses of a given city were a corporation only to the extent that they were subject to a special code of customary law and that a competent jurisdiction operated, following the general pattern of judgment by peers. The Court of Burgesses, with an appointed viscount as its president, was composed of burgess jurors, also appointed by the city lord. On occasion, this tribunal could submit demands or complaints to the city lord or even take part in administration.[11]

---

[9] By 'Christian' we mean European Christians, i.e. the Frankish population. The only exceptions were Crusader castles, some of them as large as cities (e.g. Crac des Chevaliers, Safad) and a few villages which the Crusaders tried to colonize. The process of colonization was never very successful and in the thirteenth century, it seems, was halted entirely. Cf. below, Ch. 5.

[10] Cf. Ch. 4, pp. 91 and 94.

[11] When we find military service due to the Crown listed according to cities (John of Ibelin, ch. 271), it is not the corporate body of a city that owes it, but the lord of the city. A good indication of the non-corporative character of the cities is furnished by the taxation experiment of 1182. It is not the Court of Burgesses that is responsible for imposing and collecting the tax, but four specially selected citizens in each city (W.T. xxii. 23).

Although, then, the class boundaries were clear, the burgesses nowhere succeeded, not even inside particular cities, in organizing themselves corporately. This goes far to show why no 'estate of burgesses' ever came into being. There was a consciousness of belonging to a common class, but a meeting of delegates of corporate city bodies was needed to engender the attitudes of an 'estate' and develop the institutions suited to represent one.

If the presence and overwhelming influence of non-burgess elements are the answer to the question why the cities themselves never became autonomous, it is even more surprising, and puzzling why no corporate urban bodies, such as guilds, were ever established. The nearest we get to them are streets or quarters settled by men pursuing the same trade, or, more often, by men of common ethnic origin. But there were no guilds, and no guild organizations. The fact that Muslim, Jewish, or local Christian artisans would never have been admitted into a Frankish guild, if there ever had been one, so that no joint craft organization was possible, might be part of the reason. But the main reason, we think, was different. Any guild organization presupposes the possibility of monopolizing the pursuit of a given craft, and it becomes an exclusive and excluding body. Such an organization might fit well into a settled society with its ideal of *standesmässiger Unterhalt*, but it would hardly do in the Latin Kingdom. We are dealing with a foreign colony, constantly fed and living by and through new contingents. In that set-up, any monopolistic agency would hamper the integration of newcomers in the economy. A guild in the Latin East would be detrimental to further intake and harmful to the interests of state and society. The only exception was medicine. Examination by the bishop and the *confrères* was a prerequisite to the exercise of that profession:[12] solicitude for public health (or perhaps for the salvation of souls) prevailed over the interest of absorbing more colonists.

In the absence of guilds, the only other comparable form of social cohesion were the fraternities. The earliest to be found is of foreign origin and, as far as we can see, it was very short lived: it was the *Societas Vermiliorum* of Pisan origin, a product of the Third Crusade.[13] The existence of other fraternities is well attested for the middle and the second half of the thirteenth century. But is is only one of them that furnishes us with any details as to the nature and functions of a fraternity. And it is

---

[12] *LdAdB*, ch. 298 (*Lois* ii. 169).

[13] For more details see J. Prawer, 'Social Classes in the Latin Kingdom—The Franks', to be published in *The History of the Crusades*, ed. K. M. Setton, vol. v.

precisely this one that became a pivot of politics during one of the severest crises that the kingdom underwent.

iii. *The Community of Acre*

There was no power or factor in the Second Kingdom that could consciously will and direct the evolution of its political regime. In the period of Henry III, Louis IX, and Frederick II, it had no captain to chart is fateful courses. After the Crusade of Frederick II, formal sovereignty was vested in an absentee Crown, the government was run by the Emperor's appointees from among the local baronage, and supreme authority exercised by Richard Filangieri, nominated as the Emperor's *bailli* for the kingdom. Frederick II not only left insecure boundaries and a provisional government, he left a climate of permanent resentment and rebellion.

Filangieri's first act was to seize the city (but not the castle) of Beirut (1231), the honour, that is, the main fief, of John Ibelin, acknowledged chief of the baronial opposition. It was at this stage that there were new constitutional developments, both new theory and new practice. In themselves, they mark an important chapter in the constitutional history of the kingdom, one which not only denoted a new phase in the general history of the thirteenth century, but, in a sense, more than any other happening, crystallized the image of the kingdom in historiography and, in the process, obscured its earlier annals. On the other hand, an understanding of these developments can contribute to the study of a basic problem, that of transition from a feudal monarchy to a *Ständestaat*. It is a transition of utmost interest, as it exemplifies a special case conditioned by the social and political framework of the Latin Kingdom.

After seizing Beirut, Filangieri went on to Acre, the true capital of the kingdom, with letters from the Emperor. The ordinary procedure for proclaiming the government's policy and announcing the new appointments of state would have been to summon the High Court. But Filangieri and the Emperor were not only interested in legal technicality: they wanted to make certain of the loyalty of the population and sway public opinion. Here, Filangieri had recourse to a novel and revolutionary method. Instead of convening the High Court, which legally could have been done by Balian of Sidon, till then the *bailli* of the kingdom, he called a special and extraordinary meeting in the Great Palace of the castle of Acre: 'il assembla tos les chevaliers et les borgeis.'[14] As far as we can see, no

---

[14] *Eracles* xxxiii. 23 (*RHC HOcc.* ii. 388).

institution in the kingdom was composed of nobles and burgesses. Some burgesses might attend the judicial meetings of the High Court, but as individuals, owing the privilege to their knowledge of the law of the realm. Naturally, the two classes would have found themselves together in a military expedition or at a coronation, but never for joint deliberations.

From the institutional aspect, it is hard to classify the gathering. There cannot be the slightest doubt that it was neither a spontaneous occasion nor just a fortuitous rendezvous. Filangieri bore imperial rescripts addressed to the ruling and responsible class of the kingdom. The theatre was the Great Palace of Acre, the customary venue for meetings of the royal court. The barons were in attendance, the powers that be, the nobility and the knights. This could have been brought about within the ambit of state forms: a general session of the High Court with the knights taking part according to the *Assise sur la ligece*. What was truly unprecedented was the inclusion of burgesses. They had, till then, no *locus standi* in the High Court: inviting them, possibly not altogether formally, served Filangieri's purpose of making the imperial proclamation public and gaining their support. Yet one wonders if the originator of the change was Filangieri himself, or whether he was following the instructions of Frederick II. In this connection one may recall the summoning of burgesses to the meeting of the *curia regis* in Frederick's Italian kingdom (1232), which is almost contemporary with the events in Acre. Even more indicative is one of the last acts of the Emperor before quitting the Holy Land (May 1229) which was to accord privileges (perhaps tax remissions) to the burgesses of Acre and to support the Syrian Christians against the Latin clergy.[15] In the light of this policy, is it not natural to suppose that he expected backing from the popular element and so instructed Filangieri to summon the burgesses to the extraordinary meeting? It is a plausible hypothesis, at least.

It seems to us that there is reason enough to regard the assembly as a meeting of an enlarged High Court with addition of popular elements. But whereas the whole nobility of the kingdom could have taken part— a fairish number were at the time in Cyprus—it was only the burgesses of Acre and not of all the cities who came. No unusual significance need be attached to this. Filangieri, still preoccupied with the siege of the castle of Beirut, had little leisure to order other burgesses to come, and, anyway, politics had always been debated and decided in Acre. The imperial

[15] J. L. A. Huillard-Bréholles (ed.), *Historia Diplomatica Friderici II*, iii (Paris, 1852), 137 and 140 n. 1.

proclamation may be characterized as a royal decree reminiscent of similar decrees in the contemporary England of Henry III. What Frederick told his hearers was what every gathering or any assembly of estates would have liked to hear. The government will strive: 'por maintenir dreit et justice, et por garder en lor raisons les granz et les petiz et les riches et les povres.' And Filangieri added: 'Et je sui prest dou faire par le conseil des prodes homes de la terre.'[16] No wonder that our anonymous chronicler, the author of a *Continuation of William of Tyre*, remarks: 'If the behaviour and activities had been as the words in his [the Emperor's] letter, the people of the country would have been appeased and would have accepted him as *bailli*.'

While Filiangieri was mouthing anew traditional sentiments and well-worn clichés, the Frankish nobility was expounding a theory of government conceived in terms of historical development, which not only distorted but in a sense falsified all the early history of the kingdom. The theory was unfolded by Balian of Sidon, the *bailli* in office before Filangieri's arrival:

I have been charged to tell you in their name and my own [says Balian] that they let you know that, when this land was captured, it was not done by any *chef seignor*.[17] It was conquered by a Crusade and a movement of pilgrims and people foregathered. And when they had conquered it, they made a seignor by accord and by election and they gave him the seignorship of the kingdom; and then, by accord and recognition of *preudes homes*, they made *establissemens* and *assises*, which they willed that they be held and used in the kingdom to safeguard the seignor and other people and to maintain reason[18] and then they swore to hold it and they made the seignor swear it. And thenceforth all the seignors of the kingdom had sworn it until now, and likewise swore it the emperor also.[19]

Three points were underlined by Balian: the popular (or noble, but opposed to royal) origin of the kingdom; the inviolability of laws sworn by the king and people; a *contrat social* binding king and people, confirmed and systematically renewed in the coronation oath. What was said so succinctly by Balian was to be set forth at length, a generation later, by John of Ibelin. The three introductory chapters of his *Livre* repeat the *exposé* of Balian, but the whole work, as far as it deals with feudal theory of government, is wittingly based on those assumptions and draws far-

---

[16] *Eracles* xxxiii. 23 (*RHC HOcc*. ii. 389).

[17] *Chef seignor* is the normal designation of the king in the jurists' treatises. It stresses the element of suzerainty in the competences of the Crown.

[18] *Raison*, meaning: 'to each his reason, that is, his rights'.

[19] *Eracles* xxxiii. 24 (*RHC HOcc*. ii. 389–90).

reaching conclusions from them.[20] A hereditary monarchy notwithstanding, it is the original constitutional act of election of a lord by peers that for ever engages the consciousness of the nobility. John, spokesman of the nobility, sees its era, with power balanced between Crown and itself, as a natural outcome of this primary election; moreover, the theory postulates an uninterrupted continuity of that state of affairs during the century and a half that elapsed between the first election and its own time. The election taken out of context and the oversight of four generations of history thus confound the true historical evolution. The establishment of a strong kingly power and its centralistic tendencies, the ample means at the disposal of the Crown and the favourable circumstances which facilitated centralization—all this was thrust into oblivion.[21] It needs all the acumen of a historian to extract evidence in proof of a situation different from that described by the *Livre de Jean d'Ibelin*. A comparison of the juridical treatise of Philip of Novara, which served as its basis, with the larger and more elaborate work of John of Ibelin, will demonstrate how a political theory and a prejudiced concept of the kingdom's history enabled John to conjure up a coherence, an abstraction and symmetry which only a complete detachment from reality could have fashioned. In the light of his concepts, an earlier juridical treatise, the *Livre au Roi*,[22] appears to belong not only to another period but to a completely different state, and yet it was written at the end of the twelfth century in the Kingdom of Jerusalem.

Filangieri's attempt to generate a favourable public opinion did not succeed. But the institutional machinery which he set in motion, although it failed him, was to figure prominently in the history of the kingdom. The events that followed are known to us from a unique source, the *Eracles*, and we shall let the chronicler tell the story.

The people having heard Filangieri's refusal to abandon the siege of the castle of Beirut as required by the barons and to bring the case against John of Beirut to the High Court—

The wisest among them and the most far-sighted held counsel together and saw

[20] It is of importance and interest that James of Ibelin, pleading against Hugh III of Cyprus before Prince Edward of England in Acre in 1271, took a far more historical view of the origin of the Crusader laws and institutions. What he says should really guide modern research, if it finally cuts loose from John of Ibelin: 'Cest reaume fu conquis par Latins et par genz espessiaument qui esteient de la corone de France et de pluisors provinces d'outre les mons; donc deit on creire que il n'establirent mie usages ne divers ne estranges: on deit miaus creire qu'ils pristrent les usages de leur pays ou de leur veisins.'—'Document relatif au service militaire', *Lois* ii. 431.

[21] See above, Ch. 1.   [22] *Livre au Roi* (*Lois* i. 607–44).

that there was no salvation for them save that they be bound together by oath to guard and to maintain their reasons, their rights, and the franchises of the kingdom. Then they remembered that there was in the country a fraternity, the Fraternity of St. Andrew, which had its grant from King Baldwin and was confirmed by his privilege. And, later on, it was confirmed by Count Henry [of Champagne] and he made of it a privilege. And this fraternity had *establissemens* devised and fixed in the privileges, and among other *establissemens* was this, that all those who wanted to enter the fraternity were free to do so and that those of the fraternity were free to receive them. Then assembled 'li riche home et li chevalier et li borgeis' and, when they were assembled, they ordered the councillors of the fraternity to be found and the privileges. And when they came, they caused the two privileges to be read and then swore the fraternity and then swore most [? many] of the people, who did it right willingly because of the fear of the malice of Marshal Richard [Filangieri]; and thus they were all bound to each other.[23]

The events thus described are well known, but in their interpretation we must differ from the accepted views. The starting-point is Filangieri's assembly of magnates, knights, and burgesses, which declined to accept the imperial policy of administration. This is not yet an assembly of 'estates', but it is an assembly in which 'estates' take part. Under the real or seeming threat of arbitrary rule, and under the unmistakable threat to rescind, or control the franchises of the kingdom, which included institutions in the sphere of public law and privileges in the sphere of private, it became a revolutionary assembly. Its first thought was to find a formula which would enable the participants to form a legal united front against the imperial menace. It was in perfect compatibility with the incredibly legalistic minds of the Crusader nobility, and in a sense was implied in the feudal system, that even a revolutionary movement should have a legal basis and should be able to pursue its aims within the confines of existing canon and custom.

The result of this deliberation was that the insurgents swore a common oath, which served a dual end: it established a united front against an external danger and, by mutual alliance, assured the safety of each individual inside the new institution. Historians have linked this oath with similar phenomena known in Europe in the context of urban communal movements. *Coniuratio* would be the right technical expression; it was a *coniuratio* that underlay such movements. The plausibility of this connection seemed all the stronger, seeing that the new institution

---

[23] *Eracles* xxxiii. 26 (*RHC HOcc.* ii. 391–2). The chapter is to be found translated into English by J. L. La Monte, *The Wars of Frederick II against the Ibelins in Syria and Cyprus by Phillip de Novare* (New York, 1936), pp. 122–3 n. Our translation differs in some details.

was, indeed, called *commune* and was staged in the city of Acre.[24] But this interpretation hardly fits the data at our disposal, nor can it clarify some of the major developments. In our opinion, the right interpretation must be sought in the compass of the customs and institutions of the kingdom.

The oath taken by the revolutionary movement had nothing to do with a 'communal oath'. The nearest parallel would be one taken by the insurgent English barons a generation later, during the crisis of the Provisions of Oxford. The commonalty at Oxford swore thus: 'Ceo jura le commun de Engleterre a Oxenford. Nus... fesum a saver a tute genz, ke nus avum jure sur seintes Evangeles, e sumus tenuz ensemble par tel serment, e promettuns en bone fei, ke chescun de nus e tuz ensemble nus entre eiderums, e nus e les nos cuntre tute genz.'[25] In definition and aims, this matches what we are told by our Crusader source: 'que il fussent toz tenus ensemble par seerement de garder et de maintenir les raisons et lor dreitures et les franchises dou reiaume.' One is almost tempted to look for straightforward links between the two events, and it might prove not to be beyond the bounds of reasonable possibility to discover them.

The question arises why the barons of the Latin Kingdom had recourse to this extra-constitutional procedure at all. They had to hand an institution which was not to be found, in similar form, in England—the High Court with its conjuration of 'peers'; in the given circumstances, this would have suited their needs and attitudes admirably. We believe that it is only by understanding this overt side-stepping of a traditional institution, which the barons always fought to preserve in all its integrity of power, that we can explain events and interpret them aright.

A twofold difficulty faced the insurgents. The High Court might have been legally convoked either by the new *bailli*, Marshal Richard Filangieri, or by the 'sitting' *bailli*, Balian of Sidon. It goes without saying that Filangieri would not bestow upon an insurrection the favour of legal status. On the other hand, Balian's legal standing was obscure. With the

---

[24] This was the line of thought of J. L. La Monte, 'The Communal Movement in Syria in the Thirteenth Century', *Charles Haskins Anniversary Essays in Mediaeval History* (Boston–New York, 1929), pp. 117–31, which is in the main accepted by C. Cahen (see below) and unanimously followed in all general histories of the Crusades. A different interpretation was suggested by J. Colson, 'Aux origines des assemblées d'états — l'exemple de l'Orient latin', *Revue des études byzantines* 12 (1954), 114–28. This interpretation comes near to our own, but we think that the author tried to read more into the events than our sources warrant. Moreover, the machinery of the movement cannot be described without due regard to the infrastructure of the state and society and these were entirely neglected by the author.

[25] W. H. Stubbs (ed.), *Select Charters . . . Eng. Const. Hist.*[7] (Oxford, 1890), p. 388.

arrival of the new *bailli* appointed by the Emperor, his tenure of office should have come to an end. True, the legal minds of the Ibelins argued that the Emperor had no right to undo by script what was done viva voce in the High Court. Still, the position was doubtful. And there was a further difficulty, not legal but actual, which the Ibelins could not surmount. As it turned out, Balian, expounder of the constitution of the kingdom to the imperial envoy, did not join the extreme faction of baronial resistance. He belonged to a small group of nobles who co-operated with the the Military Orders and the Communes of Venice and Genoa in mediating between the rival parties. Even assuming that a meeting of the High Court convoked by Balian had been legal, Balian himself was, then, by no means a certain bet.[26]

There was yet another problem of the utmost moment, the problem of the burgesses. Granted, for the sake of argument, that the High Court could have been convened, it would still have been no more than a meeting of barons and knights, at most the 'estate of nobles', duly constituted as a body sworn in through the *Assise sur la ligece*. But, at this juncture, the baronial opposition urgently needed a far larger popular backing than the upper 'estate' alone could assure. At its zenith, the 'estates of nobles' hardly exceeded a count of some thousands,[27] whereas Acre by itself probably exceeded 40,000, and perhaps had as many as 60,000 inhabitants, and Filangieri, like Frederick II before him, was apparently wooing the populace.

How to gain the allegiance of that element and at the same time mould it institutionally—this was the main problem of the baronial opposition. It was not just a problem of engineering a declaration of allegiance, which could have been done spectacularly by vociferous acclamation. What was wanted, and by those members of the baronial faction who had a legal training, was an institution, parallel to the High Court, which would bring solidly together people of different classes. The barons and knights already formed an 'estate'; the popular element did not, and could not, so long as the kingdom had failed, as the first step, to evolve an 'estate of burgesses', or a corporative urban organization, which might be put forward as its popular, non noble sector. Consequently, the barons could not simply add 'representatives' of the burgesses to the 'estate of nobility'.

---

[26] Balian was ready to execute an imperial order against a decision of the High Court. See above, p. 41 n. 73.

[27] The number of knights serving the Crown was around 600. Cf. Smail, *Crusading Warfare*, pp. 88 ff.

Moreover, for reasons already given, they could not use the High Court for such a purpose, because it was not 'constitutionally' possible to convene it. The way out was found in the Fraternity of St. Andrew. By taking the common oath of the fraternity, every man was bound by its rule and also each to the other, as our chronicler explicitly says—after taking the oath: 'et lors furent toz tenus les unz as autres.' This could not have been put more neatly.

Before analysing the institutional results of the 'oath of St. Andrew', it will pay us to look more closely into what is known about the fraternity. It clearly belongs to the First Kingdom, as its rule, or its foundation, was confirmed by a privilege of one of the Baldwins. Of the five Baldwins known, it is scarcely possible that either the first or the last can have been the author of the privilege, and we are inclined, although lacking proof, to infer that the fraternity was established by Baldwin IV (1174–85) or perhaps earlier, and confirmed by Henry I of Champagne (1192–7). The seal of the fraternity, fortunately extant, adds some details to our knowledge.[28] On one side are depicted two figures, marked by the letters: S.P[etrus]—S.A[ndreas] and surrounded by an inscription: ELEMOSINA. FR[ater]NITATIS. ACCO[nensis]. St. Peter holds the traditional keys and a volumen, and St. Andrew the Gospel. The reverse includes the conventional design of the church of the Holy Sepulchre with its conical open roof and, beneath it, the Holy Sepulchre itself. The sun and the moon flank the design. On the rim is the inscription: IN. HONOR [em]. D[e]I. ET XR[istia]NITATIS.

The connection with Jerusalem or the Holy Sepulchre is enigmatic. Allowing that the fraternity was established with Jerusalem still in Crusader hands, during the First Kingdom, it is difficult to explain the conjunction of a reproduction of the Holy Sepulchre with a Fraternity of Acre. We prefer to conclude that the image pertains to the king of Jerusalem. As a matter of fact, pieces of money struck by two kings of Jerusalem bear it.[29] The two saints, Peter and Andrew, are a riddle in themselves. We know the name of the fraternity, from written sources, as eponymous of St. Andrew alone.[30] Remarkably enough, neither of the

---

[28] Published by G. Schlumberger, 'Neuf sceaux de l'Orient latin', *ROL* 2 (1894), 177 and pl. I : 1.

[29] See G. Schlumberger, *Numismatique de l'Orient latin* (Paris, 1878), pl. III, 19, 20, 30.

[30] *Eracles* xxxiii. 29 (*RHC HOcc.* ii. 395); Marino Sanudo, *Secreta Fidelium Crucis*, in Bongars (ed.), *Gesta Dei per Francos* (Hanover 1611), p. 214, calls it *Fraternitas Sancti Iacobi*, evidently a mistake.

two saints had a church dedicated to him in Jerusalem, whereas St. Andrew had one in Acre. But in all probability we should not link the fraternity with any contemporary church. On the other hand, these two fishermen saints would have a special appeal for a sea-faring city such as Acre and its citizens. The official name, according to the seal, was 'The Charity of the Fraternity of Acre—to the Honour of God and of Christendom'. Unless we surmise that the seal belongs to a different fraternity, which is rather improbable, we must take it that 'Fraternity of St. Andrew' was the name in vogue or that the seal belongs to our period and that the name, while it stresses the fraternity's new institutional status as the 'Fraternity of Acre', is still joined with an image reflective of the fraternity's first patrons.

The primary aim of the fraternity, as of many others, must have been charity and social welfare. If it was chosen by the leaders of the revolution for their remoter purposes, that might have been because of its popularity, but, more likely, because of the character of its privileges, that whoever wished might enter it. The royal privilege it enjoyed is further proof of the general attitude of misgiving on the part of the authorities, lay and ecclesiastic, towards any sworn corporation. The subsequent confirmation by Henry of Champagne might have been one of property, if the fraternity had any, or, more probably, followed the line taken by the Italian communes, which eagerly sought confirmation of their ancient privileges on the establishment of the Second Kingdom as the upshot of the Third Crusade. What was, doubtless, extraordinary in the rules of the fraternity was that everybody (which presumably meant every Frank) could be admitted to membership. The Venetian Marino Sanudo, a contemporary of the fall of Acre (1291) and for some time resident in the city, was already struck by the liberality of that privilege.[31] And it was precisely this rule that the insurgent Frankish nobles found so meet for their purpose. It enabled nobles, knights, and burgesses to form a legal body, bound together by a common oath, assuring mutual security and competent to act as a *persona iuris*. If we were to look for a technical term to describe the body thus created, we would, in accordance with contemporary usage, employ the expression *communitas* or *universitas*. There is no need to add that the *communitas* has nothing to do with any 'communal movement', despite the noun *communitas* which it shared with many other corporative bodies.

It is a purely academic speculation whether, following the oath, the

---

[31] Loc. cit.: 'Cui [i.e. Fraternitati] regali privilegio, ut cuncti intrare volentes libenter possint recipi, concessum erat de gratia singulari.'

Fraternity of St. Andrew was still a fraternity. If the seal described was engraved in 1232, then the name 'Fraternitas Acconensis' is living testimony to a change from the archaic organization. Our written sources do not mention the fraternity again; the name *commune* takes its place and this should be translated into contemporary French as *le commun* as in the Provisions of Oxford, and as 'commonalty' in English.[32] It is only in this context that we can rightly understand Philip of Novara, who tells how John of Beirut, in Cyprus during the rebellion in Acre, wrote letters to certain nobles and to his kinfolk in Acre 'et envoia unes letres au comun des homes de la terre'.[33] Had he written Latin, he would in all probability have employed the expression *communitas hominum terrae*, as that was the exact institutional meaning of the corporative body brought into existence by the oath to the Fraternity of St. Andrew. No wonder that the ambassador Godfrey de la Tor sent to Pope Gregory IX is described: 'et por ce se mist li roi Henris en la communauté des gens do roiaume de Jerusalem.'[34]

Not long afterwards, the same pope, in an effort to establish peace between Frederick II and the barons, addressed a letter (8 August 1234) thus: 'Nobilibus viris baronibus et civibus Acconensibus,' but a few lines later the double addressee becomes 'Universitas Vestra'.[35] In a second letter, in 1235, he calls the new revolutionary body 'Universitas Acconensis'.[36] If additional proof is required that *Acconensis* in the two texts has no special urban or 'communal' attribution, it is furnished by the rebellious movement itself. In a letter written in 1241, the senders describe themselves as 'barons et chevaliers et citeens del reaume de Jérusalem'.[37] The *cives Acconenses* are simply replaced by *cives regni Hierosolymitani*, as the French title would have been put in Latin. In the letter itself, the trinity of senders became *gens de la terre*, meaning the 'commonalty of the land'.

Let us now attempt to review what is known about the organization of the rebellious 'community'. For it is in the details of organization that we can trace some truly urban or 'communal' influences, explained, simply, by the fact that the new institution was established inside the walls of Acre and confronted day by day with the practical example of the Italian cities. Unfortunately, only a few glimpses into its inner organization are possible.

[32] See G. Post, 'The Two Laws and the Statute of York', *Speculum*, 29 (1954), 417–32, with bibliography.
[33] *Eracles* xxxiii. 28 (*RHC HOcc.* ii. 393).
[34] *Eracles* xxxiii. 40 (*RHC HOcc.* ii. 406).
[35] *MGH, Epistolae saeculi XIII e regestis pontificum Romanorum selectae*, i, no. 594.
[36] *MGH, Epistolae*, i, no. 656, p. 554.   [37] *AOL* i. 402.

The most spectacular feature is the *campanae*, the bells of the 'community', sounding the tocsin of alarm when need arose, and perhaps as a summons to assembly. It does not appear that a special *campanile* was built. In all likelihood, it was the bells of the cathedral, the *Sainte Croix*, that were rung. At the time Frederick II sent the bishop of Sidon in 1234 to Acre to mediate peace, the bishop persuaded Balian of Sidon and the *connétable*, Montbéliard, to make peace on the basis of a division of the bailliship between Filangieri in Tyre and a local baron, Philip of Maugastel, in Acre. When all was ready for renewal of the oath of fealty to the Emperor in the cathedral, it was the irruption of the Ibelin lord of Caesarea that turned the tables. 'He entered', Philip of Novara recounts, 'into the cathedral church of the Holy Cross and ordered the bell of the commune to be pealed. When they heard this in the Fraternity of St. Andrew, they took to their arms and all shouted: "Death [to the bishop of Sidon, Balian of Sidon, and the *connétable*]!"'[38] It was this *campana* that the barons, knights, and citizens of Acre proposed to demolish if they came to agreement with the Emperor.[39] Our quotation might, perhaps, prove that a special bell was hung in the belfry of the cathedral for the use of the 'commune', so as not to confuse the bells tolled for religious purposes with those used by the 'community'.

As long as the fraternity existed, it may be supposed that a man who entered it after taking the oath became a member for life. This was hardly enough for the revolutionary community. Two years after its establishment, there was a general renewal of the oath and, at the same time, a new election of the community's head, the mayor.[40] Some further data on inner organization can be extracted from the peace proposals offered by the barons to Frederick II in 1243, in which *les conseles et les cheuetaines de la commune* are mentioned, and from a more itemized enumeration of offices in a letter of Pope Gregory IX of 1235. Here we find the phrase: 'Communiam dissolvant, campanam deponant et amoveant consules et capitaneos ab eis post ortam discordiam ordinatos... In civitatem Acconensem interdicti et in sindicos praedictorum civium et nobilium et

---

[38] *Gestes des Chiprois*, § 205, p. 113: 'il entra dedens la mere yglize de Sainte Cruis, et comanda à souner la campane de la commune. Quant à frarie de saint André ler sot, il furent as armes et crierent tuit: "Muire! Muire!".' John of Ibelin (*Lois* ii. 399) has a different expression: 'si que y ot si grant remor que la campane dou comun sona.' Attention should be paid to the parallel expressions: 'la campane de la commune' and 'la campane dou comun.'

[39] In 1241, in a letter to the Emperor: 'et osterons la campane', *AOL* i. 403.

[40] *Gestes des Chiprois*, § 206, p. 113: 'Le seignor de Baruth ala à Acre, et tant ordena et fist que les sairemens des Poulains furent tous refreichis, et qu'il fu maire de nouveau.'

maiorum consulum universitatis Acconensis ac eorum fautores et consiliarios excommunicationis sententias promulgavit.'[41] Unhappily, the text is not easy to interpret. If we take *consiliarii* in the proper technical sense of 'counsellors', we may detect in it an earlier layer of organization from the first days of the fraternity, which, as we saw, had its own 'counsellors', and these were possibly carried over into the later 'community'. But as the noun appears in the conjuncture of *fautores et consiliarii*, adherents and counsellors, we hesitate to assign a precise technical meaning to it. Nor are other names of office exact. Gregory IX mentions 'syndics', which in this case, can only mean 'representatives'. But whom do they represent? Plainly enough the non-noble *cives*, but, according to our text, also the nobles. Then the phrase degenerates into obscurity. Whereas we understand the phrase: 'sindici praedictorum civium et nobilium', we do not grasp: 'sindici . . . maiorum consulum'. The latter suggests *maiores consules*, which means at least two major consuls and presupposes minor consuls, which would point to a somewhat elaborate machinery if we add the 'captains' and 'counsellors'. Besides, John of Beirut is called *maire* and not 'consul', and he was definitely the chief man in the organization. It might be held that the *capitanei* = *cheuetaines* are military officers, but the *maiores consules* are really baffling. Did Gregory IX, Italian that he was, mix up northern *maiores* with southern consuls? It is possible, but we are now in the realm of conjecture.

For ten or, maybe, even twelve years (1231–43), the period of the 'Wars of Frederick II against the Ibelins', the 'commonalty of Acre', or the 'commonalty of the Kingdom of Jerusalem', abided as an institutional reality and a legal personality in the political history of the kingdom. As far as we can ascertain, it is referred to for the last time in our sources by Marsiglio Zorzi (Marsilius Georgius), the famous Venetian *bailli*, who reports to his metropolis on the wresting of Tyre from imperial hands. Among the participants in that engagement he lists the Military Orders, the Commune of Acre, the Communes of Venice and Genoa.[42] This happened in 1243. The year is not an accident, but fits perfectly into the institutional history of the kingdom. It coincides with the revival of the High Court, which heard the claimants to the Crown of Jerusalem[43] and accepted the Princess Alice and her husband, Ralph of Soisson, as the rulers of the kingdom. It was, therefore, the year that signalled a return to

---

[41] *MGH, Epistolae saeculi xiii*, no. 656, p. 554; cf. a letter of 1236, ibid., no. 674, p. 571.
[42] Tafel–Thomas, ii. 354–5.
[43] 'Documents relatifs à la successibilité au trône et à la régence', in *Lois* ii. 397–422.

normal working of the kingdom's institutions. In this context, there was, from the baronial point of view, neither place nor need for the 'commonalty of Acre' nor any special need for the popular support given by the burgesses to the government.

The last official act of the 'community' is the offer of peace drawn up by John of Ibelin on 7 May 1241, and sent, it seems, to Richard of Cornwall, brother of Henry III of England, asking for his mediation.[44] The Ibelins there suggested the appointment of Simon of Montfort, earl of Leicester, as *bailli* of the Emperor. Being the Emperor's brother-in-law and well connected with the local nobility—the great local baron Philip of Montfort was his nephew—Leicester was an excellent choice. It is not unreasonable to suppose that the barons had approached him, and got his agreement to the nomination, during his Crusade to the Holy Land (1241) with Richard of Cornwall. There was no imperial answer. In this offer of peace (*forme de las pais*), there is one phrase that draws our special attention: 'Et nos gens de la terre... osterons la campane et les conseles et les cheuetaines de la commune, sauf ceaux qui esteient auant que l'emperere fuist seignor des païs.' This is not a sentence from a chronicle, it is from a legal document written by the finest jurist of the Latin East, John of Ibelin. Consequently we can assume very circumspect phraseology, where nothing was left to chance. Even so, the words are astonishing. Frederick II became king of Jerusalem by his marriage to Isabella of Jerusalem in 1225. He had been regent of the kingdom since the birth of his son Conrad in 1228. He was crowned in 1229. But the *commune* was not established before 1231! What, then, did John of Ibelin imply by saying that they would abolish the heads of the *commune*[45] excepting those who existed before the emperor became lord of the land'? The only explanation we can suggest is that, in John's mind, a *communitas regni* existed long before the establishment of the 'community of Acre' as a legal personality, before the inception of the oath of that 'community'. As a matter of fact, it had existed since the founding of the First Kingdom and the election of Godfrey by the warriors of the First Crusade, or, to use John's own words in the introductory chapter to his legal treatise: 'when the princes and barons who captured it [the city of Jerusalem] elected as king and lord of

---

[44] Published by R. Röhricht in *AOL* i. 402–3.

[45] It is impossible to argue that John referred to the restitution of the 'Fraternity of St. Andrew' to its erstwhile position. Frederick II could not have cared less about the whereabouts of a welfare fraternity.

the Kingdom of Jerusalem the Duke Godfrey'. This line of thought would not be out of place in the middle of the thirteenth century,[46] although it certainly was amiss in 1099. But it was conceivable and even logical for a John of Ibelin, who shaped a political theory and insinuated into it a changelessness of political practice in the Latin Kingdom from the day of its birth down to his own generation.

It is very tempting to ask if the events of the Latin East had any actual, and not only theoretical, impact beyond its frontiers. The late M. Powicke suggested that Simon of Montfort might have taken the idea of a government-by-council, as proposed by the Provisions of Oxford, from his own Crusade.[47] We would subscribe to Powicke's hesitancy, as the Latin Kingdom was never ruled by barons in permanent attendance on the king, nor was there a permanent council in the sense of the 'Provisions' or any direct appointment of officers of the Crown by a council, not even the High Court. The institutional patterns of the two states were too divergent for a practice evolved in the East to have been imported into, and applied in, the West. But it is not impossible that another event influenced Montfort. We refer, as already hinted, to the common oath taken by the rebellious barons in Acre and the oath taken by their equivalents in Oxford. Such a mutual oath of security, giving rise to a corporative body in opposition to an authority which was deemed to have overreached itself and perverted justice, could have been applied successfully even to an institutionally different political make-up.

Furthermore, the famous summons of the burgesses of 'York, Lincoln, and other boroughs of England' to the parliament to be held in January 1265 might have reflected another of Simon's experiences on the Crusade. He had then witnessed the organization of a baronial opposition to established authority. As a royalist, but at the same time an ardent legitimist, he might have identified himself with the Syrian barons' 'offer of peace' to Frederick II, and perhaps agreed, on the spur of the moment, to be the agent of establishment of peace in the tottering Latin Kingdom. It might have been the memory of the united *communitas regni* of that kingdom, consisting of barons, knights, and burgesses, which, in the hour of crisis, precipitated his famous decision to summon burgesses to a *commune consilium* and assure his party of a popular backing.

---

[46] See G. Post, 'The Two Laws and the Statute of York', *Speculum*, 29 (1954), 417–32.

[47] M. Powicke, *The Thirteenth Century, 1216–1307, The Oxford History of England* iv (Oxford, 1953), 134 and n. 1. There is a slight contradiction between the text and the note.

iv. The 'Community of Antioch'

So far, we have dealt exclusively with the Latin Kingdom proper. We turn now to two other developments, one preceding the ominous happenings of Acre and the other a generation after them, when 'communities' came into being again.

In 1193 or 1194, Bohemond III, prince of Antioch, was treacherously taken prisoner by Leo II of Armenia and, under duress, consented to cede the principality to him. The Armenian commander, Hetoum of Sasoun, accompanied by certain knights from Bohemond's entourage, was dispatched to occupy Antioch, but found himself faced with an insurrection of the populace led by Aimery, the Latin Patriarch, or by Richier, one of the knights sent by Bohemond. Our only relevant source tells how Armenian soldiers, entering Antioch, derided the chapel dedicated to St. Hilaire of Poitiers. They scoffed: 'We do not know what "St. Hilaire" means, but we shall baptize it and it will be called St. Sarquis'.[48] This provoked a general outcry against the rule of 'so vile a people as the Armenians'. The offending soldiers were seized.

> Immediately they assembled together in the cathedral church of Antioch, and the Patriarch Amalric was with them and they ordered among themselves and made a *commune*, which they had not had at all before, and it lasted thence onward until today. And they came to Raymond, the eldest son of the prince, and told him that they would hold him as lord in place of his father, until his father were freed.[49]

This extract from one of the French Continuations of William of Tyre is as obscure as can be. One gets the impression that, at the time when the chronicle was written, the *commune* was a well-established institution known to everybody in the East, which, as a matter of fact, it never was. Not a word is said about its composition, but at least we know it aims, and, by using sources which tell of events that occurred some years afterwards, we can partially retrace the general outline of the movement.[50]

[48] *Eracles*, in *RHC HOcc.* ii. 209, variant.

[49] Loc. cit.: 'Tantost furent assembles comunaument en la maistre yglise d'Antioche, et le patriarche Aymeri avec iaus, et ordenerent entr'iaus et firent comune, la quele devant n'avoient point eu, qui des puis a duré jusques au jor de hui, et vindrent a Raymont l'ains né fis dou devant dit prince, et dirent que il le tendreient por seignor en leu dou pere, tant que le pere fust delivres.'

[50] An unreliable account is given by E. Rey, 'Les Dignitaires de la principauté d' Antioche, grands-officiers et patriarches, XIe–XIIIe s.', *ROL* 8 (1900/1), 116–57, and 'Résumé chronologique de l'histoire des princes d'Antioche', *ROL* 4 (1896), 383 f. Cf. also Mas Latrie, 'Les Patriarches latins d'Antioche', *ROL* 2 (1894), 193–4. The narrative of events was somewhat corrected by J. L. La Monte, 'The Communal Movement in Syria in the Thirteenth Century', *Charles Haskins Anniversary Essays*, pp. 122–4, who was not in a

The commune, then, was organized by Patriarch Aimery, or by the knight Richier, and was designed at the outset mainly to prevent Armenian domination in Antioch. The establishment of an Armenian dynasty, however strongly 'gallicized', would have meant the intrusion of another ruling aristocracy into the principality; it is barely possible that it would also have meant an end to the privileged standing of the Frankish aristocracy and burgesses. On the other hand, it would certainly have meant a privileged, not to say predominant, status for the autocephalous Armenian Church, which, despite its flirtation with Rome, had not ceased to be a national church. Both aspects of the revolutionary movement are visible in its origin. There is the anathema to 'so vile a people as the Armenians', and there is the affront to St. Hilaire and the threat of St. Sarquis. The close relationship between the two facets seems to hold the key to the problem. A change of dynasty might have concerned the ruling aristocracy, but it was the religious implication that was strongly felt by the unsophisticated Frankish burgesses of the city. The Patriarch had summoned the faithful into the cathedral, and Frankish clergy, knights, and burgesses flocked to it. But they were not the only ones. If the commune was to succeed in holding its own, it needed a firmer foundation than the Frankish citizens alone. Antioch was never Frankish in the sense that Jerusalem or Acre was. The majority were still Greek and Jacobite, as on the eve of the Frankish conquest.[51] But whereas the Jacobites at no time became a political factor in the life of the Frankish capital, the Greeks, enjoying the protectorate of Byzantium and its timely interventions, could even see a Hellene in the Chair of St. Peter in Antioch. It was the Greeks who would be the greatest losers if the Armenians ruled. Relations between Greeks and Armenians had worsened during the eleventh and twelfth centuries, and in matters of faith their contacts were hate-ridden. It was natural, then, that the local Christians should join an uprising aimed against Armenian supremacy. And although the sole surviving chronicle of events does not explicitly tell us that the Greeks took part in the establishment of the commune, their share in it and their importance are beyond doubt and are disclosed in sources that treat of the developments some years afterwards.

position to profit from the first complete study by C. Cahen, *La Syrie du Nord à l'époque des Croisades* (Paris, 1940) iv, ch. 5: 'La Commune', pp. 598, 652–9, and *passim*. Cf. S. Runciman, *A History of the Crusades* (Cambridge, 1954), iii. 87 f. Our interpretation differs from that of these two eminent scholars.

[51] See C. Karalevskij, 'Antioche', *Dictionnaire d'histoire et de géographie écclésiastique*, iii (1924), cols. 563–703, esp. col. 613.

The organization of the commune thwarted the cession of Antioch to Leo II of Armenia, and he finally freed Bohemond. But, at the same time, he made sure of his own freedom from Antiochene vassalage and might reasonably expect to see Antioch one day in the hands of Raymond husband of his niece Alice, and heir-apparent to Bohemond. But Raymond predeceased his father, and the outlook for his infant son, the Franco-Armenian Raymond-Roupen, was not too bright. The anti-Armenian faction in Antioch produced a rival claimant to the principality in Bohemond IV, count of Tripoli.

The relations of Bohemond IV with the Latin Church were far from amicable. They were punctuated by constant clashes with the bishop of Tripoli, Peter of Angoulême, who, in the meantime, had become Patriarch of Antioch. This state of things did not displease either the Greeks or the Jacobites of Antioch. Bohemond first gained the favour of the Templars and Hospitallers and secured his frontiers with Aleppo, whose ruler preferred an Antioch independent to an Antioch allied to the Cilician Armenians. Next he won the commune over to his side. After taking counsel with the commune, the nobles decided (at the end of 1198) to exclude Raymond-Roupen from the succession. 'Through bribery, they poisoned the minds of the Antiochenes, who decided that the count [that is, Bohemond] was the lawful successor of the prince.'[52] The reigning prince, Bohemond III, even found it possible to associate his name with those of the commune, the Patriarch, and Bohemond IV in protesting to Pope Innocent III against the refusal of Leo II to restore the castle of Baghras to the Templars.[53] Bohemond IV, whose right of succession was not unarguably convincing, had, of course, to identify himself with the commune, which accepted his claim and proclaimed him prince-designate of Antioch. But the Greek element was a factor of major importance in the commune, and to safeguard this alliance with the local citizenry even the

[52] The letter of complaint sent by Leo II to Innocent III and Innocent's answer of December 1198 repeating the former almost verbatim: 'habito concilio cum communia dominum principem R. (proh dolor!) exclusere et tam contumeliis minarum quam iniuriis detractorum exasperaverunt. Exsulato itaque principe, quidam ficti amici comitis, et pretio et precibus ipsi comiti alligati, populum Antiochiae venenoso instinctu suo subverterunt, dicentes comitem esse legitimum haeredem principis, quod nefas est praedicare.'—J. P. Migne (ed.), *Patrologia Latina* (= *PL*), ccxiv, cols. 810–13. *Innocentii III Epistolae*, Lib. ii, nos. cclii–ccliii. Text quoted: ibid., col. 812.

[53] From a letter of Innocent III to Leo II of Armenia (Dec. 1199), reasserting the demand of the Templars to the Castle Gaston: 'Cumque dilecti filii magister et fratres militiae Templi cum nuntiis . . . patriarchae et . . . principis Antiochensis, Tripolitanensis comitis, et totius Antiochensis communia supplicassent ut castrum ipsum Templariis resignares . . .'—*PL* ccxv, col. 819. *Epistolae*, Lib. ii, no. cclix.

Latin clergy had to suffer. 'The communes of the city', wrote Innocent III in January 1199, 'burden churches, clerks, and their men of whatever standing or nation by taking tallages contrary to the old customs.' What was more serious, the Antiochene clergy was being forced to answer to lay accusations by coercion of a *iuramentum*. And, the Pope adds, 'trying to deal with church possessions according to the judgments and customs of the Greeks, they pervert abusively the privileges of the Church of the Latins.'[54] As all our knowledge of events is one-sided, it is impossible to say how many of these grievances were real. Still, the general picture seems to be quite clear. The *iuramentum* created a *communitas*, a 'community' or commune, to which the Latin clergy gave their adherence. But the plaint of Innocent III also proves that the Greeks took the oath of the commune and, by sheer numbers, became a cardinal, if not a determinant, part of it. It is the *iudicia et consuetudines Graecorum* that are forced upon the city; even the sacred privileges of the Latin Church were being infringed. Only the overwhelming weight of the Greek element can explain such an eventuality. The resultant situation was almost paradoxical. A movement which aimed, in its beginnings, at blocking the establishment of an Armenian dynasty and government underwent modification in the course of time as its divergent components gave expression to their will and stamped that will on its evolution.

The official adherence of the ruler of Armenia, Leo II, to the Church of Rome since 1194–5 made him a person of consequence in the eyes of Pope Innocent III, if it did not endear him to the Greeks of Antioch. This *rapprochement* between Armenia and Rome certainly had some bearing on the attitude of the Latin clergy. The Patriarch, Peter of Angoulême, executed a volte-face in 1206 and began openly to support Raymond-Roupen. Some of the Latin nobility started to foment an insurrection. But, by a strange coincidence, at this inopportune moment the Patriarch was suspended by the zeal of a papal legate for the sin of glaring nepotism. It was in such circumstances that the alliance with the Greeks in Antioch came to matter so greatly to the ruling Prince Bohemond IV. He repaid by installing Greek Patriarch, Simeon II, with the Arabic sobriquet of Ibn

[54] From a letter of Innocent III to the Patriarch of Antioch, Lib. i, no. 512, *PL*, ccxiv, col. 474. See *Acta Innocentii Papae III, 1198–1216*, ed. Th. Haluscynskij (Vatican, 1944), no. 6: 'communia ipsius civitatis ecclesias, clericos et eorum homines cuiuscunque condicionis vel linguae sint, in exactione talliae contra antiquam consuetudinem aggravant … Praeterea … omnes clericos Antiochenos ad iustitiam cuilibet laico exhibendam nituntur sub praetextu sui compellere iuramenti. Possessiones etiam ecclesiasticas per iudicium et consuetudines Graecorum tractare conantes, iura Ecclesiae Latinorum consuetudinibus abusive pervertunt.'

Abu Shaiba, the 'white-haired one'. This was the crowning victory of the Greeks in Antioch. True, a Greek Patriarch had previously officiated in Antioch under Frankish rule, and the princes of Antioch had more than once promised to accept one.[55] But, till now, such ordinations had been made under the pressure, and through the intervention, of the Byzantine Empire. This time it was the revolutionary movement and purely local forces that scored a resounding triumph over Frankish authority. This is correctly perceived by Innocent III, who wrote on 9 January 1208 to John, cardinal of Santa Maria in Via Lata and charged to inquire into the situation in Antioch:

> And because the prince and the citizens of Antioch, who already revolted against the Church, seized the occasion to riot in the things which brought damage to the Patriarch and the Chapter, so that they devastated the possessions of the Church and, through the Syrians, chose someone else as Patriarch, thanks to the favour of the prince, it is apparent that great danger is imminent by reason of which it seems that Antioch will entirely fall away from the Latin communion.[56]

The Syrians, namely the Greeks of Antioch, were threatening to make Antioch Byzantine. And again: 'Through the assent and will of Bohemond, count of Tripoli, and some of the citizens of Antioch, the people and a part of the Greek clergy, having thrown away the fear of God, dare to foist a Greek Patriarch on to the province of Antioch.' Moreover, excommunicated Latins are admitted by the Greeks to divine services.[57] It is at this point of time that the Pope instructs the Patriarch of Jerusalem—

> definitely to depose the said intruder and to remove him from the province, and to curb, without appeal, through ecclesiastical censure, any who oppose that step. You should stop the count, also the Antiochene mayor and consuls, under threat of excommunication, so that they dare not maintain the said intruder and the Greek clerics in such a state of rebellion.[58]

---

[55] In the treaties of Bohemond I in 1108, Raymond of Antioch in 1137, Renaud in 1141. Cf. F. Chalandon, *Les Comnènes*, ii (Paris, 1912), 132, 445, 449. In 1165 Bohemond accepted the Greek Athanasius, whereupon the city was laid under interdict by Patriarch Amalric, who retired to Qosair. He came back to Antioch only after Athanasius' departure; cf. ibid. 470, 531. In 1178 Pope Alexander III prevented the enthronement of a Greek Patriarch. Cf. C. Karalevskij, op. cit., cols. 616 f.

[56] *Innocentii III Epistolae*, lib. x, no. 186 (*PL* ccxv, col. 1280; Baluze, pp. 104 f.): 'Quia vero Princeps et cives Antiocheni, qui jam ante contra Ecclesiam se erexerant, ex his quae in injuriam Patriarchae Capitulique fiebant, occasionem sumpserunt in eos enormius debachandi, ita quod possessionibus Ecclesiae devastatis, et alio quodam in Patriarcham per favorem ejusdem Principis a Syrianis electo, grave periculum sibi cernebat imminere, per quod Antiochia totius Latinitatis communionis subtrahi videbatur.'

[57] Lib. xi, no. 9 (*PL* ccxv, col. 1345).

[58] Ibid., letter of 4 Mar. 1208: 'memoratum intrusum omnino deponas, et a tota provincia

Once restored by the papal legate, Peter of Angoulême, whose suspension from patriarchal office had opened the way to the enthronement of a Greek successor, sought to lay the city under interdict, but the working of the Greek churches frustrated his attempt. At the end of 1207 or the beginning of 1208, he instigated a revolt of the commune against Bohemond. Knights were brought into the city, but Bohemond, in a sally from the citadel, crushed the rising,[59] and Peter died in prison.

Some years after this we find, for the last time, tangible proof of the existence of the commune in Antioch. That the Greek Patriarch officiated until 1213, despite papal pressure,[60] sufficiently demonstrates its continuity. In 1216 the city was finally taken over by Leo II and Raymond-Roupen. According to a letter of Leo to Innocent III, the induction of Raymond-Roupen meant a true restoration.[61] The prime mover of it seems to have been the Patriarch, who 'cum universo clero, maiori parte milicie et universo populo' invited Raymond-Roupen. As Leo gave back their possessions to the Templars, the full support of that Order was forthcoming. The letter does not mention the commune in terms, but it may be suggested that 'the greater part of the militia' represents a (perhaps non-Greek) section of it. The induction of Raymond-Roupen also bespoke the repatriation of those banished by the will of Bohemond IV, possibly after he had put down the insurrection of the nobility in 1207. 'De hinc', writes Leo II, 'barones, milites, burgentes [*sic*] eliminati de civitate introducuntur et restituuntur eis iusto ordine domus, haereditates, possessiones et legitima tenimenta sua.' This was followed by an oath of *ligece*, taken by knights and *clientes belligeri* and one of fealty taken by everybody else not bound to *ligece* (which might mean the burgesses). Pope Honorius III recommended Raymond-Roupen to the legate, the Military Orders, and the commune. It is at this time (1216) that

facias removeri, et contradictores per censuram ecclesiasticam sublato appellationis impediment compescens, eidem Comiti necnon Majori et Consulibus Antiochensis sub poena excommunicationis inhibeas ne dictum intrusum aut clericos Graecos in tali rebellione temere manutenere praesumant.'

[59] *Annales de Terre Sainte, ad annum 1208*, in *AOL* ii (1883), 436 in both versions. Both stress: 'desconfist la commugne'. The mention of the knights in Version B is rather obscure. *Chronique de Terre Sainte*, A.D. 1208, § 65, in *Les Gestes des Chiprois* is clearer: ' A. M.CC.VIII, desconfist le prince Baymont d'Antioche les chevaliers et la coumune qu'il avéent faite, et prist le patriarche quy estoit lor consentant, et le mist en sa prizon où il morut, et vindrent les chevaliers à sa mercy.'

[60] *Innocentii III Epistolae*, lib. ix, no. 214 (*PL* ccxv, col. 1321); lib. xi, no. 110 (ibid., cols. 1428–9).

[61] *Acta Innocentii III* (ed. T. Haluscynskij), Appendix i, no. 21, pp. 588–91. The editor assigns this letter, with some hesitation, to 1207, but it seems to belong to 1216.

one act of Raymond-Roupen is signed by Acharie of Sermin, seneschal of the principality as *maios communie*,[62] and another by Robert Mansel (1219), the constable, as *maior Antiochie*.[63] Here we lose all track of the Antiochene commune.

As we have shown, the history of that commune is fragmentary and it is difficult to fill in the canvas of its rise and development. But certain salient points can be assembled and interpreted. There is no reason to suppose that this revolutionary movement had anything to do with a communal movement or that it was a 'communal movement' in the urban sense. The insurgents did not aim at city privileges or city autonomy. The commune which they formed is a *communitas*, a corporative body to govern the capital and, through it, the entire principality. It does not necessarily follow that, to accomplish this task, the movement did not borrow city formulae for its organization; but there is nothing intrinsically urban about it. Clearly, problems and institutions of state were its primary inspiration.

The main problem was the succession to the princely title of Antioch. Normally it should have been resolved in the High Court of the principality. In ordinary circumstances the suzerain from Jerusalem or Constantinople might intervene. But the circumstances were certainly not normal. The ruling prince, Bohemond III, was in captivity. Even if free, he could not by himself decide an issue of succession and an order given under duress was decidedly invalid. A meeting of the High Court, with Armenian soldiers streaming into the city, was equally out of the question. The attitude of some of the nobility, for generations intermarried with the Armenian aristocracy, was at least doubtful, although others were undoubtedly loyal to the ruling dynasty. Whether the prompting came from a noble of the prince's entourage or from the Patriarch is not clear, but that knights and clergy and burgesses co-operated from the beginning seems evident. And yet all three together were only a minority in Antioch. The Greeks and Jacobites, if not an actual majority, were at any rate very numerous. The conundrum was how to find an institutional formula that would permit them to join in a movement which appealed to them emotionally, for Armenian rule would, it goes without saying, be less tolerant than the Latin with which they had established a *modus vivendi*. Neither the High Court nor the Court of Burgesses could furnish the formula: their doors were shut to the Greeks. The *communitas*, an

[62] *Liber Iurium Reipublicae Genuensis*, i (1854), 578; Regesta, no. 885.
[63] Strehlke, no. 51, p. 42.

institution out of the ordinary, transcending the existing organs and class-structure of the principality, was the right answer.

The cohesiveness of the new institution lay in the *iuramentum* taken by all, an oath of mutual security, and possibly an oath to a common political programme: namely to hand the regency over to Raymond, son of the imprisoned Bohemond III, and prevent Armenian rule from establishing itself in the principality.

It was now in the logic of things that the non-Frankish element, the Greeks, should prove the staunchest supporters of the commune. The nobility, although vacillating during the first crisis, must have regarded with horror the proceedings at Gaston, when Bohemond III was forced into promising to cede Antioch to Leo II, and there was nothing to change their loyalty to him. But the reopening of the issue of succession with Raymond's death generated a new atmosphere. The nobility were party to the marriage agreements of Raymond and Alice of Armenia; there was a legitimate successor, the infant Raymond-Roupen. Their feudal conscience felt pangs concerning the rights of Bohemond IV. Their loyalties were divided, probably inclining to Raymond-Roupen. His long minority was not likely to distress them much. As the upper stratum of society was thus ambivalent in its attitude, it was only natural that the burgesses and Greeks should become the dominant party in the movement, and all the more so once the posture of the Latin clergy became uncertain. The Patriarch, who supported the Military Orders, had no other ally to fall back upon once their claims were satisfied (1198) save for Bohemond IV, a doubtful ally at best. That prince, denied a unanimous vote of the nobility, asserted his claim not through the High Court, but through the commune. The inferior strata of society became his automatic allies, which gave them greater audacity: they imposed their *iudicia* and *consuetudines* and found an opportune moment to settle accounts with the Latin clergy. The canonical but non-political views of the papal legate destroyed the authority of the Patriarch, and Bohemond IV availed himself of the occasion to introduce a Greek, perhaps of Syrian origin (his nickname, we saw, was Arabic), whose interests, no less than those of his community, made his submissiveness sure.

The last attempt to overthrow the government was essayed by Peter of Angoulême: with a Greek Patriarch in the See of Saint Peter, he was fighting for his own survival. It may well be that the nobility from outside the city joined forces with the Latin Patriarch. It is less clear how and why the commune followed suit. Did the Latin Patriarch have such a hold over it? This would seem to be a far-fetched explanation. The only other possibility is that Latin burgesses clung to the Latin Patriarch, as they probably did at the restoration of 1216.

As to the organization of the commune, we know that it used the *campana,* which was, in all probability, a set of bells in the cathedral church. The cathedral church of Antioch, in which, its seems, Latins and Greeks normally attended, was being used as a meeting-place. The commune tried to levy taxes—tallage, to which all were liable, and it appears to have established even a court with its own customs, or to have imported Greek procedures which might mean Byzantine legislation, into the existing courts. The head of the commune was a 'mayor' and its council consisted of 'consuls'. It is not impossible that the 'consuls' were militia commanders of the city quarters, or, if we accept the establishment of an independent jurisdiction, the court jurors.

vi *The Community of Tripoli*

The last case of a revolutionary movement is the shortlived experiment of Tripoli. As in the case of Antioch, the sources at our disposal are meagre: a few paragraphs in the chronicle of the so-called Templar of Tyre. And yet, in some ways, they yield a great deal of information.

The revolt broke out on the heirless death of Bohemond VII. As the city was menaced by Muslim troops, the citizens asked the mother of the deceased prince, the Armenian Sibylla, to appoint a regent until the arrival of her daughter Luciana, wife of the admiral of Charles of Anjou. Sibylla inauspiciously nominated Bartholomew, bishop of Tortosa, as regent; Bartholomew's regency during the minority of Bohemond VII had already provoked civil war in the county. The choice set the city in an uproar. The knights came to Sibylla 'and told her that this bishop was their enemy, and will never be their ruler; and they parted and went to a counsel and then organized a commune to the honour of the Holy Virgin Mary, mother of God, ordered captains and a *prévôt* and what they thought fit to do, and maintained themselves through them.'[64] A new government was formed, led by Bartholomew Embriaco, prominent in the baronial opposition. Luciana, who came to Syria and was recognized

[64] *Le Templier de Tyr ad annum 1288,* § 467, in: *Les Gestes des Chiprois,* p. 231: 'li distrent que ce vesque estoit lor henemy, et quy ne seroit ja lor governeor, et se partirent et alerent à conseill, et adons ordenerent une coumune à l'henor de la beate Virge Marye, mere de Dieu, et ordenerent chevetaines et prevost, et se qu'il lor sembla à faire, et se maintindrent par yaus.'

On an earlier Commune of Tripoli created in the 1260s see J. Prawer, 'The Earliest Commune of Tripoli' (above, p. 46, n. 1, *sub fin.*).

by the Hospitallers as the legitimate ruler of the county, took up residence in the castle of Nefin. But Hospitaller attempts to bring her into the capital failed, and there were already bloody collisions between the besiegers and the commune, which closed the city gates. The leaders of the commune sent a letter to Luciana, specifying their aims and demands.

They let her know that this thing was not hidden from her, how she needs to know the outrages which her brother, the prince, did to them, and moreover they let her know that her father, the prince, and her grandfather always did them much damage, many outrages, and much violence, to knights, to burgesses, and to other people; that they will not tolerate what they and their ancestors, who were at the conquest of the land of Tripoli, had suffered; and so as not to come to such a situation they had organized and established a community among them to the honour of God and Notre Dame in whose name their community was called. And they did not do it to disinherit any soul, nor against the Holy Church; they did it to maintain everybody in his rights and privileges and they are ready to receive her as ruler but so that she should swear to the *commune* to sustain and maintain it.[65]

Luciana did not accept the conditions, and the commune endeavoured to strengthen its position by allying itself with Genoa, a natural move for an Embriaco. Genoa was ready to conclude the alliance and sent the legendary Benedetto Zaccaria to Tripoli. Zaccaria was not only granted additional possessions in the city, but, more than likely, suggested an entirely new concept of relations between Tripoli and Genoa: not just an autonomous Genoese quarter in the city, but to turn Tripoli into a Genoese colony and part of the Republic.[66] This was perhaps too much for a 'frenchified'

[65] Ibid., § 468, p. 232: 'yaus li faissoient saver que à elle n'estoit mye chose selée, coment elle devoit bien saver les outrages que son frere le prince lor avoit fait, et encores ly faiseent saver que son pere le prince et son ayol lor aveent tous jours fait mout de maus et d'outrages, et de force à chevaliers et as bourgois et as autres gens, que il ne voleent plus soufrir à ce que yaus et lor ansestres, qui furent au conquest de la terre de Triple, aveent soufert et pacé, et pour non venir plus à celle condecion aveent ordené et fait j. coumun entr'iaus à l'enor de Dieu et de Nostre Dame à quy nom lor comun est noumé, et que il ne l'ont fait pour dezeriter nule arme ny contre sainte yglisc, ains estoit fait por maintenir chascun en son droit et en sa raison, et que il sont aparaillés de reserver la come dame, par enssi qu'elle jurast à la coumune de souslenir et maintenir la dite coumune . . .'

[66] The difference between the original treaty and that of Benedetto Zaccaria is obscurely indicated in the inimical *Iacobi Aurie Annales Ianuenses*, *MGH*, *Scriptores*, ed. G. H. Pertz (Hanover, 1863), xviii. 322. It is clear that the Genoese were to send to Tripoli not a consul or viscount, who usually ruled the local colony, but a 'potestas', that is a *podestà* of Genoa— ibid., p. 326. The new concepts of relations were hinted at by G. Caro, *Genua und die Mächte am Mittelmeer, 1257–1311*, ii. (Halle, 1899), 126, and developed by R. Lopez, *Genova marinara nel ducento—Benedetto Zaccaria, ammiraglio e mercante* (Messina–Milan, 1932), 137. For some reasons not accepted or else neglected by later scholars, their views seem to me convincing. Cf. Prawer, *Histoire*, ii. 534.

Embariaco to carry through. He fortified himself by pledging the town of Gibelet to his daughter and then to his son, and, particularly, by liberal concessions to the inhabitants of Tripoli. 'Many other franchises were conceded to knights and burgesses, which will be too long to put in writing.'[67] Embriaco then sent a letter to Luciana saying that if she was ready to ratify the changes and not enlarge the Genoese concessions they would accept her: he was by then ready to sell out the commune. Luciana decided that she could strike a better bargain by dealing directly with Benedetto Zaccaria. She might in that event forfeit her standing in the principality, but would not have to ratify class privileges, which probably included a remission of taxes. The new prestige of Genoa persuaded its antagonists (possibly Venetians or Pisans) to an act of treachery. A Christian delegation went to Cairo, representing to the Sultan the dangers of a Genoese foothold in Tripoli, which, allegedly, would put Genoa in virtual control of Egyptian commerce. On 17 March 1289 Kalaun appeared before the walls of Tripoli and on 26 April he captured the city. City and commune alike vanished. Among the dead was Barthelmé of Giblet, *maire et chevetaine*[68] of the commune.

Again, as in Acre and Antioch, to call the revolutionary movement in Tripoli a 'communal' or 'urban' movement would be a misnomer. Except that the events took place within the walls of a city, there was nothing urban in it. What was at issue was the form of government of the county. The baronial faction, which led the rebellion, has left us its official programme. Topping a long list of grievances against authority, a list going back to the two previous reigns, the prospect of the hated bishop of Tortosa acting as regent, or of Luciana continuing the dynastic rule as countess, precipitated a rising. The revolting barons demanded the establishment of a 'constitutional' government in the medieval sense of the term, a government guaranteeing every person his position in his own class and the different classes a position in the state according to their collective standing. Such a slogan was good enough to rouse the burgesses and unite them with the nobles. It is less clear what happened to the non-Frankish population, most likely the bulk of the citizenry. James of Vitry, who visited Tripoli, noted with dismay: 'As the common language of the city was Arabic, I preached often and received confession through

---

[67] *Le Templier de Tyr*, § 470, in: *Les Gestes des Chiprois*, p. 233: 'plusors autres franchises fusent octreées à chevaliers et à bourgés, que trop seroit lonc à metre par escrit.'

[68] Ibid., § 477.

interpreters.'[69] In their letter to the countess, the barons do in fact complain of violence done 'to knights, to burgesses, and *to other people*', which may have meant the non-Frankish townspeople. There is, then, a possibility that the townspeople joined in the movement. The oath taken in common, an oath of security and of a united front, made the whole population into the corporative body of a *communitas* with its own extraordinary offices. The *prévôt*, as seen above, is identical with the mayor of the commune, having at his side *capitanei = chevetaines*, possibly the military officers of the *communitas*. As might be expected, the ruler of the commune, heading a popular movement, accorded privileges to the classes of knights and burgesses, as the new government had to give proof of its constitutional intentions. The fall of the commune was imminent on the eve of the Mameluke conquest, for its ruler was on the point of betraying it. As things turned out, it was the fall of the city that ended the revolutionary interlude.

vi. *The Aftermath*

Was there any tangible change in the regime of the states in the aftermath of the *communitates* movement? Tripoli is naturally out of the question. Antioch's internal history is not known enough for us to draw conclusions. It is only in the Latin Kingdom that such results can be sought.

The virtual disappearance of the royal power and the paralysis of the kingdom's institutions, generally speaking, induced a dislocation of the social framework.[70] One marked outcome, to our way of thinking, was a widespread urge to find protection in small corporative bodies which could, on occasion, wield influence even in politics. This development, as might have been foreseen, is especially conspicuous among the burgesses of the Crusader Kingdom, and, under their influence, in their emulation by the Syrian Christians.

It was only in exceptional circumstances that burgesses came into direct contact with the Crown, barring the cases when the king was also lord of a city.[71] But in the middle of the thirteenth century we observe an entirely new trend. It is the sudden flourishing of *fraternitates*. Until about

[69] *Lettres de Jacques de Vitry*, ed. R. B. C. Huygens (Leiden, 1960), ii. 344–6: 'et quia communis lingua civitatis erat lingua sarracena, per interpretes frequenter praedicabam et confessiones audiebam.'

[70] See J. Prawer, 'Social classes in the Latin Kingdom', cit. p. 53 n. 13 above.

[71] The *Assise sur la ligece* stipulated that the king could require an oath from burgesses in cities not belonging to the Crown, if he had doubts as to the loyalty of their lord. Cf. above, pp. 42 f.

1240, we know of the actual existence of only two, but after that they figure frequently in our sources.

In 1261, after the death of Plaisance, when Hugh (the future Hugh III of Cyprus and Jerusalem, 1267–84) and Hugh of Brienne claimed the *bailliage* of the kingdom in one of the most remarkable feats of oratory before the High Court:

Godfrey of Sargines and the legate and the masters [of the Military Orders] and the [European] communes and fraternities agreed that the *bail* [Hugh of Cyprus] should have the *bailliage* of the kingdom before the count of Brienne; and all the knights who were liegemen were on one side, and recognized through the *Assise* of Jerusalem that the *bailliage* belonged to the *bail*, as he was older than the count of Brienne. And then Godfrey of Sargines [who had been *bail*] laid down his office and was the first to do homage to the *bail*, and then all the men and burgesses and fraternities.[72]

This text is explicit enough to show that the kingdom really entered a new phase of evolution. Juridically speaking, the meeting described is that of the High Court. But is no longer the High Court of the First Kingdom, nor even that following the *Assise sur la ligece*. Since about 1240, if not earlier, the representatives of the corporative bodies, of the Military Orders and Italian and other communes had been present. But now we have also the presence of the fraternities, spokesmen of the corporative bodies of the burgesses. *Pari passu* with that presence a new custom emerged: an oath of homage of the fraternities and of the burgesses to the *bailli*, an oath unknown, or at least not generalized, in the First Kingdom.

Seven years afterwards, in 1287, when the same Hugh of Lusignan, now already Hugh III of Cyprus, came to the High Court of Jerusalem, sitting in Acre, to claim the crown of the kingdom and was opposed by 'Damoiselle Marie', daughter of Bohemond VI of Antioch, the same evolution is once more exemplified, and the terms in which it is described vividly illustrate the general direction of evolution. After donning the crown of Cyprus, Hugh appeared in Acre—

to claim the Kingdom of Jerusalem from the men and people of Acre, the legate, and members of the orders [or monasteries], and the Master of the Temple, and the

---

[72] 'Documents relatifs à la successibilité au trône et à la régence', ch. 11 (*Lois* ii. 414–15): 'Messire Joffroy de Saugine, et le legat, et les maistres, et les comunes, et les frairies s'accorderent que le baill ost le bailliage dou royaume avant que le conte de Braine; et tous les chevaliers homes liges furent d'une part, et coneurent, par l'assise dou royaume de Jerusalem, que le bailliage montoit audit baill, pour ce que il estoit ainsné dou conte de Braine. Et lors messire Joffroi de Saugines se depouilla et ala premier faire homage au baill, et puis tous les homes et borjois et frairies.'

Teutonic Order, the 'consul' [or council] of Pisa, and the *bailli* of Venice and the fraternities, and all the people of Acre who were there. And the said king spoke to the men of the High Court of Jerusalem who were gathered there in the presence of those named above.[73]

The last phrase proves that, in fact, it is still the 'estate of nobility' that composes the High Court. Representatives of the corporative bodies are present but take no part in the proceedings. It seems patent that their presence added nothing to the legality of the meeting, though it certainly gave force to the deliberations. And yet something is already changing. After hearing the claims of Hugh III and Mary—

the said men of the kingdom went to one part and after a short while returned and made say for the commonalty and with the consent of all, by one of them, that is, Sire James Vidan, that, following the clear request made by the king, they were all ready to give him their homage and their taxes and services as was the custom to do to the lord of the kingdom.[74]

The 'commonalty' (= *la comunauté*) mentioned in the text is still the 'commonalty' of the nobility, as is clear from the rest of the text.[75] But a notable modification is seen in the composition of the bodies that owe homage or perhaps an oath of fealty to the king. Our source goes on to say that, after the king's coronation oath, administered to him by James Vidan—

the liegemen of the kingdom who were there of the said kingdom of Jerusalem made their homage, and first of all Godfrey, and the lord of Tyre and he of Toron, and all the rest of the men who were there; and after that he received the homage of others who were obliged to offer it, and after he received the oaths of the fraternities and of all the others who were obliged to give him oaths.[76]

[73] Ibid., ch. 12 (*Lois* ii. 415): 'A requerre le royaume de Jerusalem as homes et à la gent de Acre, le legat et les gens de religion, et le maistre du Temple, et l'Ospital des Alemans, et le concile de Pise, et le baill de Venise et les frairies, et tous les homes d'Acre que là se troverent. Et le dessus nomé roy dit as homes de la Haute Court de Jerusalem que là estoient assemblés en la presence des dessus només.' The speech is quoted in ch. 13.

[74] Ibid., ch. 13 (*Lois* ii. 416): 'Les devant dis homes dou royaume alerent d'une part, et au chief d'une presse se retournerent, et firent dire par la comunauté et par l'otroy d'eaus tous, par l'un d'eaus, ce est assavoir par sire Jacque Vidan, que selon clere requeste que le roy lor avoit fait, il estoient tous apareillés de faire li lors homages et lors redevances et services si com l'on estoit usé de faire à seignor dou royaume.'

[75] Ibid., ch. 16 (*Lois* ii. 418): 'Adonc les homes liges revindrent devant le roy, et parla por la communauté de tous sire Jacques Vidan . . .'

[76] Ibid., ch. 17 (*Lois* ii. 419): 'les homes liges qui là estoient doudit royaume de Jerusalem li firent homage et tout premierement messire Joffroy, et le sire de Sur, et celui dou Touron, et tout le remanant des homes que là se troverent; et puis aprez receut les homages des autres qui li estoient tenus à faire, et aprez receut les seremens des frairies et de tous les autres qui serement li devoient.'

Only this new development can explain the fact that a king of Jerusalem left the country because of his quarrels with the nobility and the fraternities.[77] The fraternities[78] became a normal part of the kingdom's 'estate'-building apparatus and a new factor in its political life.

Taken, then, as a whole, the evolution of the thirteenth century did not bring the Crusader state down to the common denominator of 'communal movements'. For that, it lacked primary urban and social premises, but it brought the state to the common denominator of formation of 'estates' and *communitates*, the normal transition from feudal monarchies to *Ständestaaten*. Still, the Latin states never reached the point of a full-fledged variation in their constitutional history. Perhaps a hundred years more of existence were needed to produce one.

[77] *RHC HOcc.* ii. 474.

[78] The existence of fraternities was not limited to Acre. In 1264 Philip of Montfort, lord of Tyre, had to promise to the Genoese that property in their quarter in Tyre will not be given: 'comunitatibus nec frareriis pro hospitando, neque pro alia re facere'—*AOL* ii B. 227.

Colonization and Economy

4 The Latin Settlement of Jerusalem[1]

The economic and social history of European cities long ago became a fruitful field of research in medieval history. Their foundation, settlement, and development have been described and explained. The study of Crusader cities in Palestine, however, is still in its infancy. The problem here is different, owing to the special set of political circumstances, and all the more interesting, as a great many Crusader cities started life on a *tabula rasa* after the destruction of the former population.

A distinction can be made between cities captured before Sidon (1110) and cities captured later on. Until 1110 the capture of cities was usually accompanied by the annihilation of the former population. From that time on the population of a captured city was generally spared. This can be attributed to two factors: (a) a change in Crusaders' policy; (b) a change in Crusaders' mentality.

In the earlier period occupation of a city was preceded by its conquest by force. Even in cases where surrender was negotiated the conditions offered by the Crusaders were unacceptable to the Muslim population,[2] or if accepted they were violated by the besieging host.[3] But from about 1110—witness the cases of Sidon, Tyre, and Banias—occupation followed

---

[1] This chapter was first published in *Speculum*, 27 (1952), 490–503. Since then several studies have appeared dealing with different aspects of urban problems of the Latin Kingdom. M. Benvenisti, *The Crusaders in the Holy Land* (Jerusalem, 1970), pp. 25–207. J. Riley-Smith, 'The survival in Latin Palestine of Muslim administration' in *The Eastern Mediterranean Lands in the Period of the Crusades*, ed. P. M. Holt (Warminster, 1977), pp. 9–23. J. Prawer, 'Crusader Cities' in *The Medieval City*, in honour of R. S. Lopez, ed. H. A. Miskimin, O. Herlihy, A. L. Udovitch (Yale Univ. Press, 1977) pp. 179–201. And cf. below, Chs. 8–13.

[2] Typical are the conditions offered by the bishop of Venice to besieged Haifa: enslavement of the whole Muslim population or evacuation of the city, or conversion to Christianity and degradation to the status of second-class citizens. The reported conditions may be historically untrue, but I believe they reflect fairly the general opinion of the time. Cf. Monachus Littorensis in *RHC HOcc.* v. 276.

[3] e.g. in Acre (1104), cf. *Gesta Francorum*, 63 (*RHC HOcc.* iii. 567); Beirut (1110), cf. Albertus Aquensis, xi. 17.

capitulation.[4] In each case part of the native population stayed on to become the lowest stratum of the new city community.[5]

We may look on this change as a sign of maturer statesmanship on the part of the Frankish newcomers. At the same time, it should not be forgotten that the conquest was not always caused by an actual necessity. In some measure it also reflected the aspirations of the rank and file of the army. Conquest meant spoils for everybody; capitulation meant conservation of riches for the benefit—almost unique benefit—of the future ruler of the city. This explains the too often violated capitulations and the opposition of the common people (e.g. during the siege of Tyre) to the capitulation of the city.[6] That such opposition (probably more chronic than could be gathered from our sources) was overcome about 1110, is a sign of the strengthening of discipline and state organization of the Latin Kingdom.[7]

Jerusalem, the first city captured in the Holy Land by the Crusaders, was occupied following conquest by force; its new life grew up from ruins.

To get a clear view of the situation we need to start our inquiry in the middle of the eleventh century. The year 1063 seems decisive in more aspects than one. The treaties of 1026 and 1037 permitted the ruler of Constantinople to repair the church of the Holy Sepulchre, damaged by the insane Al-Hakim. But an earthquake in 1036 destroyed part of the city walls and their repair was ordered by the Caliph of Egypt.[8] The Christians'

---

[4] Ascalon, captured in 1153, is an exception. Ascalon's strategic importance necessitated evacuation of its Muslim inhabitants.

[5] In any case, according to an Arab historian, only the poor and the sick remained. Ibn al-Athir, *A.H.* 518 in *RHC HOr.* i. 359.

[6] W. T. xiii. 13. In this connection it is important to quote the interpretation given to these events by the French translator of William of Tyre, not to be found in the original: 'disoient [sc. menue gent] tout apertement que li Baron estoient traiteur qui avoient pris granz loiers por fere la pais et li povre home, qui avoient toute la douleur souferte, n'alegeroient leur povretez de nule rien en cele conqueste. Tant monterent les paroles qu'il dut avoir grant mellée entre les povres et les riches.' P. Paris, *Guillaume de Tyr et ses continuateurs* (Paris, 1879) p. 492.

[7] Beugnot's hypothesis (cf. *LdAdb, Lois* ii, preface, p. xvii) that the Crusaders were able to expel the Muslim population as they could colonize the cities immediately from their own resources, does not seem justified by our sources. See also below, Ch. 5, pp. 116 f.

[8] The earthquake and the repairs of the walls are mentioned by Yahia of Antioch. *Corp. Script. Or. Arab.*, ser. 3, vii. 27, quoted by H. Vincent and F. M. Abel, *Recherches de topographie, d'archéologie et d'histoire*, ii: *Jérusalem nouvelle* (Paris, 1926), 942b. This earthquake is probably identical with the great earthquake in Syria and Palestine at the end of 1033. According to a Hebrew letter from Jerusalem, the earthquake started on 5 Dec. 1033 (J. Mann, *The Jews in Egypt and in Palestine under the Fatimids* (Oxford, 1922), ii. 176–8).

share in the reconstruction was to rebuild the walls of their own quarter. Lacking the necessary funds, they turned for help to Byzantium. The Emperor agreed to assign money for the repair of the walls of the Christian quarter in Jerusalem on condition that all Christians should henceforth live only in their own fortified quarter of the city. This was the area around the Holy Sepulchre, which even before the middle of the eleventh century was considered the Christian quarter *par excellence*. The novelty consisted in the fact that, according to this treaty between the Caliph and the Emperor, all Christians had to live exclusively in their quarter. This new arrangement may have appeared a means of safeguarding the security of the Christian population. But at the same time the Christian quarter became a kind of shut-in ghetto subject to discrimination, servitude, and humiliation. It was in 1063, according to William of Tyre,[9] that the transfer of the Christian population and the repair of the walls came to an end.

At the same time the Jews were concentrated to the east of the Christian quarter, i.e. in the north-eastern quarter of the city, which even in the twelfth century was known as *Juiverie*.[10] Consequently, the Muslim population occupied the remaining, southern quarter of the city. Some places remained in the hands of their former possessors even if the

---

[9] W. T. ix. 17–18 (*RHC HOcc.* i. 390 f.). William of Tyre missed the point when he wrote: 'Habitaverunt sane usque ad illum diem promiscue cum fidelibus Sarraceni, sed ab ea hora, audita jussione principali ad alias civitati partes de necessitate se contulerunt, quarta praedicta fidelibus sine contradictione relicta.' He comes nearer the truth in another place (xviii. 5, *HOcc.* i. 824–5): 'Erat autem civitas, sicut et hodie est, in quatuor partes pene divisa aequaliter, ex quibus sole quarta in qua Sepulcrum Dominicum situm est, fidelibus concessa erat ad habitandum, reliquas autem cum Templo Domini, soli infideles habebant domesticas.' This is repeated but not very faithfully, by James of Vitry in the beginning of the thirteenth century: 'Princeps autem Aegyptius, qui universas regiones a Laodicia Syriae usque ad extremam Aegypti civitatem Alexandriam possidebat, quartam civitatis Hierosolymitanae portionem ex parte Dominici Sepulchri Surianis et Patriarchae eorum sub annuo tributo ad habitandum concesserat; alias autem tres portiones inhabitabant Saraceni' (*Historia Orientalis*, ed. Bongars, *Gesta Dei per Francos* (Hanover, 1611), p. 1082). For the fate of the earlier Carolingian foundations cf. Dom Gariador, 'Monastères bénédictins antérieurs aux croisades', *Jérusalem* (1905), pp. 328 f., and P. Riant in *AOL* i (1881), 56. See also S. Runciman, 'The Byzantine "Protectorate" in the Holy Land,' *Byzantion* (1949), 207–15. The whole quarter was not surrounded by the wall, but only its exterior part, where the walls of the city were the walls of the quarter. Cf. below, Ch. 11.

[10] See J. Prawer, 'The Vicissitudes of the Jewish and Karaitic Quarters in Jerusalem during the Arab Period (640–1099)', *Zion Quarterly for Research in Jewish History*, N.S. 12 (1947), 136–48, and 'The Jews in the Latin Kingdom of Jerusalem', ibid., N.S. 11 (1945–6), 38–82 (both in Hebrew with short English summaries). The Christians are naturally the native, oriental Christians. It is at the southern limits of their quarter that the Amalfitans received a place for their famous hospice. The number of European Christians was negligible and the

(continued)

population abandoned the quarter as a whole, e.g. the rebuilt church of St. Mary Magdalen of the Jacobites on the outskirts of the Christian quarter.[11]

During the fifty years between the time of these topographic changes and the Crusaders' conquest, the city suffered greatly from earthquakes and predatory invasions of Arab and Seldjuq tribes, although its population probably reached the substantial number of 30,000 souls. These disastrous events, although affecting all parts of the population, no doubt had more ruinous effects on the Christians and the Jews.[12]

During the last three years before the actual conquest, the situation of the Christians in Jerusalem became desperate. The Muslim authorities, suspecting them of a friendly attitude towards the advancing Crusaders, had many of them killed; others escaped from the city and the Muslim terror with their bare lives.[13] It would, therefore, be reasonable to assume that after the capture of the city there was no Christian population left worth reckoning with. On the other hand, almost the whole Jewish and Muslim population was massacred by the conquerors. The awesome descriptions of the blood-bath in the city are too well known to be repeated. They leave no doubt about the complete annihilation of the non-Christian population. Those who escaped the sword were sold into captivity.[14] It seems that the only survivors were a group of Saracen fighters who capitulated to Raymond of Toulouse and withdrew from the

---

splendid Carolingian establishments did not survive al-Hakim's persecutions (W. T. xvii. 4–5). See P. Riant, 'La donation de Hugues, marquis de Toscane, au Saint Sépulcre et les établissements latins de Jérusalem au Xe siècle', *Mém. de l'Acad. des Inscriptions et Belles Lettres*, 31, 2 (1884), 151–95; Riley-Smith, *Knights of St. John*, pp. 32 ff.; Prawer, *Latin Kingdom*, pp. 170 ff. (with bibl.). There is little unanimity as to the fate of these early foundations.

[11] On the church of Mary Magdalen see E. Cerulli, *Etiopi in Palestina, storia della comunità etiopica de Gerusalemme* (Rome, 1943), i. 10–12. See Prawer, *Latin Kingdom*, pp. 227–9, and p. 94 n. 35 below.

[12] There are no statistics available for this period but it is remarkable that of thirty Jewish communities known to have existed in Palestine between the sixth and the eleventh century only twelve are mentioned in the sources after 1071, the year of the Seljuq conquest.

[13] W. T. xi. 27: 'Suriani autem qui ab initio urbis cives extiterant, tempore hostilitatis per multas tribulationes et infinitas molestias adeo rari erant, ut quasi nullus eorum esset numerus. Ab introitu siquidem Latinorum in Syriam, maxime autem postquam Antiochia capta, versus Hierosolymam tendere coepit exercitus adeo praedictos Dei famulos concives eorum coeperunt affligere, ut pro quolibet levi verbo multos ex eis occiderunt.' Cf. vii. 23.

[14] The sale of Jews into captivity became part of the Christian anti-Jewish polemic. See Prawer, 'The Jews in the Latin Kingdom', pp. 11 ff. Cf. S. D. Goitein, 'Contemporary letters on the capture of Jerusalem by the Crusaders', *Journal of Jewish Studies* 3 (1952), 162–77.

city. We have, then, to imagine Jerusalem on the morrow of the conquest as a city of complete desolation and death.

In view of this, some questions arise: How did the Crusaders start their life in the city? Who were its inhabitants? How did the Crusaders turn Jerusalem, the goal of their long journey and fighting, into a place not only venerable but also habitable?

It is in the conquering Crusaders' army that we must look for the nucleus of the new population. We know that this army, at the time of the siege of Jerusalem, comprised no more than 60,000 men. Some of these were already settled in other cities captured before; therefore, only a portion of the army remained in Jerusalem. In the two months between the conquest of the city and the battle of Ascalon the greater part returned home, either to Syria or to Europe.[15] Consequently, the city's population must have been very small, numbering perhaps no more than a few hundred souls.[16]

The once flourishing and populous city became a small town in the Latin Kingdom of Jerusalem. True, it was the capital, and was described in itineraries and documents as 'gloriosa' and 'inclita', but such descriptions were no doubt prompted by reminiscences of the glorious biblical past. The coastal towns of Jaffa, Acre, Tyre, and Beirut bustled with new life, and the newcomer was there attracted by the possibilities of earning a livelihood, but Jerusalem was only a place to be visited and revered. The devoted pilgrim or European colonist made the perilous journey through Ramle and the Judaean mountains only to return hastily to the coast.

William of Tyre states explicitly that only one quarter of the city was inhabited, and even this inadequately. When the Latin Kingdom called on the population in its life-and-death struggle, the inhabitants leaving the

---

[15] The following numbers are instructive. From about 60,000 people at the time of the conquest of the city, only 10,000 took part in the battle of Ascalon two months later (August 1099). In the autumn of the same year there were only 3,000 at the battle of Arsuf. In the spring of 1100 and September of 1101 there were only 1,200 and 1,300 combatants respectively. These combatants were drawn from the whole kingdom. This gives us some idea about the population of Jerusalem (see next note). The quoted numbers are taken from W. B. Stevenson, *The Crusaders in the East* (Cambridge, 1907), pp. 33, 35, 39, 44.

[16] Fulk of Chartres, *Historia Hierosolymitana*, ed. H. Hagenmeyer (Heidelberg, 1913), ii. 10): 'Non enim tunc habemus (1100) plusquam CCC milites et tantum de peditibus qui Hierusalem et Joppem et Ramulam [Ramle], Caypham etiam castrum custodiebant.' W. T. ix. 19: 'tam modicae erant nostrorum facultates et militantium copiae, ut omnibus convocatis et certatim concurrentibus, vix invenirentur equites trecentos et peditum duo milia.' To these numbers we have to add the non-combatant members of the families and the relatively large number of clergy.

city risked losing it altogether because there were not enough persons to guard the towers, walls, and city gates.[17]

The newly created population, doubtless settled in the north-western quarter of the city, round the Holy Sepulchre, taking the place of the former Syrian-Christian inhabitants who had left the city before its capture by the Crusaders. Even those who remained seem to have migrated, as the Latins distrusted them and suspected them of being in league with the Muslims.[18] In this way the former Christian quarter inhabited by the Syrians became a European quarter. This contained a wider area than before, including the vicinity of the citadel (David's Tower) and further to the south the area of the so-called Mt. Zion inside the walls, where a group of the followers of Raymond of Toulouse, who hailed from Beaucaire in southern France took possession of the area, as would appear from the name of a postern in this quarter: 'Porta Belcayre'.[19] Another outlying quarter was the Temple area, with the *Templum Salomonis* (mosque of al-Aqsa) serving as the king's palace (later the headquarters of the Knights Templar) and the *Templum Domini* in charge of secular (later Augustinian) canons.[20] Within not less than twenty years this was the whole population of the city and only the Christian quarter was inhabited.

The Crusaders prevented Muslims and Jews from coming back to settle in the city. An official edict banished them forever from the place in order that their presence might not pollute its holiness.[21] If we later find Jews or Muslims there, they are usually pilgrims,[22] or people who have obtained

[17] W. T. xi. 27: 'Nostrates vero adeo pauci erant et inopes, ut vix unum de vicis possent incolere.'

[18] Matthew of Edessa, ch. 21, *RHC HArm.* i. 54–5. Cf. E. Cerulli, *Etiopi in Palestina*, p. 13.

[19] This is the ingenious explanation of the place-name by F. M. Abel, *Jérusalem nouvelle* ii. 945. It ought, however, to be remarked that the postern is called as late as 1178 'Porta Nova que vocatur Belcayra.' Delaville, no. 537.

[20] H. E. Mayer, *Bistümer, Klöster und Stifte im Königreich Jerusalem, MGH Schriften*, 26. 222–30.

[21] W. T. xi. 27: 'iis non est datus locus intra urbem ad manendum. Instar enim sacrilegii videbatur Deo devotis principibus, si aliquos qui in Christiana non censerentur professione in tam venerabili loco esse permitterent habitatores.' Cf. Achard d'Arrouaise, *Tractatus super Templo Domini*, vv. 408–10: 'Interfectus est ab eis pro nostris excessibus, qui sine peccato natus est in terra Dominus. Et dispersa gens Judea loco caret hactenus', *AOL* i. 567. This is also confirmed by later Jewish sources. R. Abraham bar Hiyya (fl. early twelfth cent.) *Megillath ha-Megalleh*, ed. J. Guttmann, p. 99: 'Since these sinners [Crusaders] became lords of the Temple, they have not allowed any Jew to enter it. There are no Jews at this our time in Jerusalem.' This is confirmed 100 years later (*c.* 1218) by the Jewish-Spanish poet Juda Alḥarizi, *Tahkemoni*, ed. Kaminka, ch. 28.

[22] e.g. the Arab traveller Ali al-Harevy, *AOL* i. 593 f. The number of Jewish travellers and pilgrims is rather large. A complete list will be found in *Sefer hayishuv: Sources of Jewish*

a special permit to settle for some business purpose, paying a special tax for this favour.[23]

The Christian population did not show any tendency to grow. On the contrary, we have clear evidence of re-emigration from Jerusalem to other cities or even to Europe. The inadequate economic basis of a pre-eminently consumers' centre without any important productive enterprises, would itself warrant the assumption of emigration rather than immigration, and the testimony of William of Tyre corroborates this assertion. He mentions a special law granting possession of a house to a man who lived in it a year and a day. It was directed, says William, against those who left estates when conditions were difficult, and returned when conditions improved. This law invalidated their claims.[24] It seems likely that a law preserved in the writings of thirteenth-century jurists, whereby an estate was forfeited to the benefit of its tenant if the owner failed to get from it the 'census' during a year,[25] is a remnant of the twelfth-century law described by the contemporary historian.

Living conditions in Jerusalem at this period were difficult. Witness again the historian, who, although writing some seventy years later, is reliable, as he had undoubtedly used for his history the abundant correspondence of this period. At night, he says, thieves broke into empty and sparsely populated cities. Even in the homes within the city walls it was difficult to find security because of the scarcity of the inhabitants.[26] As we have seen, the king tried to prevent the flight from the country—which virtually means from the cities, as they were the centres of the Crusaders' settlement—by the law of an annual prescriptive right. Laws like this could not have been very effective, as they lacked the force of persuasion or coercion. Those who had something to lose in Europe left the country. This state of affairs lasted well into the second decade of the

---

History in Palestine iii (Crusader and Mameluk periods), ed. J. Baer and J. Prawer, (forthcoming).

[23] *The Itinerary of Benjamin of Tudela* (Eng. trans.) ed. Asher (New York, 1900), p. 69, mentions four Jewish families in Jerusalem. The reading 'two hundred families,' found in some manuscripts is erroneous. See B. Dinaburg in *Zion. Quarterly for Research in Jewish History* ii (1927), 54.

[24] W. T. ix. 19. *RHC HOcc.* i. 394: 'Hi [sc. possessiones deserentes] causam edicto dederunt, ut annua praescriptio locum haberet, et eorum foveret partes, qui in tribulatione perseverantes, per annum et diem tranquille et sine quaestione aliquid possederunt. Quod introductum est . . . odio illorum qui timoris causa suas reliquerant possessiones, ne, post annum redeuntes ad earum admitterentur vendicationem.' As the law was issued about 1100 it could have applied only to a small number of cities, the most prominent being Jerusalem.

[25] See below, Ch. 14, p. 344.   [26] W. T. ix. 19.

century in the whole kingdom (the maritime cities excepted), and especially in Jerusalem. The usual description of a period of bliss almost immediately following the conquest has no foundation in contemporary documents. The famous description of the development of the kingdom taken from Fulk's account[27] and quoted to prove the prodigious progress of the young establishment was written specially for the third redaction of the *Historia Hierosolymitana* which was not composed until 1124. Even then it is more than doubtful if it depicted the real situation. Hagenmeyer[28] calls it straight *Schönfarberei*. Another no less famous description is to be found in Ekkehard's *Hierosolymita*, ch. xxxvi.[29] But here again this optimistic description does not appear in the first three redactions of the book. It belongs to the fourth redaction, written between 1114 and 1117. Moreover, its was written as an encouraging exhortation for Erkembart, abbot of Corvey, and should be appreciated accordingly. Historians of the thirteenth century describing the early history of the kingdom projected this kind of description to that period. We cannot, therefore, take seriously James of Vitry's description: 'Ex omni natione, tribu et lingua, post Terrae Sanctae liberationem, Christi fideles Sepulchrum Domini visitaturi Hierosolymis confluebant, largitione principum et eleemosynis fidelium modico tempore adeo ditati sunt, quod ab unversis occidentalibus provinciis redditus copiosos colligentes, casalia sibi et oppida tamquam terrae princepes comparantes ditioni suae subjecerunt.'[30]

This situation needed redress, and Baldwin I, second ruler of Jerusalem, undertook the difficult task. Men had to be found to settle in the capital and means had to be found for their livelihood. The European population, as has been said, was not attracted to Jerusalem; therefore people had to be found elsewhere. The solution was found in the Christian Syrians from Transjordan. The king came across them during his campaign in 1115 or 1116 and decided to turn these peasants and villagers into city dwellers. A migration scheme on a grand scale was organized. A Christian exodus started from Transjordan. 'Cum uxoribus et liberis cum gregibus et armentis et universa familia', as the historian puts it, these settlers came to Jerusalem.[31] They had good reasons to migrate and co-operate. The resettlement meant, first of all, an escape from the ever impending threat

---

[27] Ed. H. Hagenmeyer, iii. 37.   [28] Ed. *Historia Hierosolymitana*, p. 746 n. 1.
[29] Ed. H. Hagenmeyer (1876).
[30] *Hist. Jherosol.*, Ch. lxiv, in Bongars, *Gesta Dei per Francos*, p. 1083.
[31] W. T. xi. 27. The date is fixed by Röhricht, *GKJ*, p. 113.

of Muslim anger. Secondly, there was the attraction of the Holy Places. Last but not least, they received privileges from the king of Jerusalem. Unfortunately, we have no evidence as to their exact nature.[32] William of Tyre is vague about it, but his French translator, interpreting rather than translating, says: 'Franchement leur fist li roi tenir leur teneurs que il leur asena, si come il estoit bien droiz en si franche ville et en si noble come estoit la cité de Jerusalem.' They doubtless received houses ('eis domicilia replevit') and, it seems some land tenures in the vicinity of the city, which would account for the agricultural occupation of the newcomers. It is hard to say what is the meaning of 'franchement'. It could describe tenure without any feudal obligations or fiscal burden, but we cannot insist on this meaning of the word.

The Syrian settlement of Jerusalem is attested not only by William of Tyre. We have in the topographical disposition of the city, some fifty years later, a silent testimony of the event and its success. All descriptions of Jerusalem connected with the *L'estat de la cité de Jherusalem* mention a special quarter called *Juiverie*. Paradoxically enough, 'la manoient li plus des Suriiens de Iherusalem', says the French author of the description.[33] This fact may well be explained by the above-mentioned colonization. As has been seen, the *Juiverie* was inhabited by the Jews until their massacre in 1099. Then it remained uninhabited. When the wave of Syrian colonization reached Jerusalem, their former quarter, the Christian quarter round the Holy Sepulchre, was already occupied by the European Christians. Having no other choice, they settled in the neighbourhood and so repopulated the former Jewish but now completely empty quarter.[34] Here they erected their churches—St. Abraham near St. Stephen's Gate (now Damascus Gate), St. Mary Magdalen, and St. Elias. Perhaps some churches in their former quarter— St. Jacob of the Jacobites near the Holy Sepulchre, St. Cariton, St. George in the Market Place, and St. Saba near

[32] W. T. xi 27. *RHC HOcc.* i. 500: 'Hos evocans Dominus rex, et meliores promittens conditiones, tractos tum locorum reverentia, tum nostrorum dilectione et amore libertatis, infra modicum tempus multos cum uxoribus et liberis, cum gregibus et armentis et universa familia recepit.'

[33] *Itinéraires à Jérusalem et descriptions de la Terre Sainte rédigés en français aux XIe, XIIe et XIIIe siècles*, ed. H. Michelant and G. Raynaud (Geneva, 1882), p. 49. This quarter, called in Latin *Judearia*, is also mentioned in charters from the abbey of Notre-Dame de Josaphat and the church of the Holy Sepulchre. Delaborde, pp. 43–5, and Rozière, pp. 329–31.

[34] The best maps of the Crusaders' Jerusalem are F. M. Abel, 'L'estat de la Cité de Jérusalem', *Jerusalem, Records of the Pro-Jerusalem Council* i. (Jerusalem, 1918–20), ed. C. R. Ashbee; F. M. Abel, 'Jérusalem au temps du Royaume latin, XIIe siècle', *Jérusalem nouvelle*, planche lxxxvi; C. N. Johns, *Palestine of the Crusaders* (Jerusalem, 1936).

David's Tower, probably belonging to the Greeks—were renovated for the use of the newcomers pouring in.[35] It is also safe to assume that at this period a part of the northern wall encircling the new Syrian quarter was built. This new wall, just behind the church of Mary Magdalen, connected the eastern and the northern walls of the city, creating a 'between the walls' space in the north-eastern corner. It encompassed the Syrian quarter and provided for its safety. Becoming smaller, the quarter was more easily protected from robbers and in times of siege a double wall in the most vulnerable part of the city was of special importance for its defence.[36]

Only a few years after the first attempt to develop the city we see the clergy of Jerusalem take the initiative in the same direction. Their interest is obvious. Beside natural spiritual considerations there existed mundane interests. The Patriarch of Jerusalem claimed the whole city as his own property. In fact, Godfrey of Bouillon granted him the possession, and only owing to circumstances did the city remain in the royal domain. The wealth of the clergy in the city was remarkable. Let us only mention that the monopoly of the city bakeries belonged to them. It is on their initiative that King Baldwin II passed a law in 1120 exempting all food-stuffs from custom payments exacted at the entrance to the city. So also the extra 'weights and measures' were abolished.[37] The French translator of William

---

[35] The names are taken from the twelfth-century map of MS. Cambrai, published by R. Röhricht, 'Karten und Pläne zur Palästinakunde aus dem VII bis XVI Jahrhundert', *Zeitschrift des deutschen Palästinavereins* 14 (1891), 134–5. The remains of the church of St. Abraham, it seems, have been found during excavations near the Damascus Gate. J. B. Henessy, 'Preliminary Report on the Excavations at the Damascus Gate 1964–6', *Levant* 2 (1970), 2–7. These churches are not mentioned in sources of earlier periods. The only exception is the church of Mary Magdalen. A church of this name is mentioned in the beginning of the ninth century, but its topographical position at this time is unknown. In 1092 took place the consecration of a Syrian church in Jerusalem, which is identified—although the text of the 'History of the Jacobite Patriarchs of Alexandria' does not warrant it—with Mary Magdalen. See the explanation given by E. Cerulli, *Etiopi in Palestina* i. 11, and ibid., n. 3, the Arabic text. On churches in Byzantine Jerusalem see F. M. Abel, 'Jérusalem' in *Dictionnaire d'archéologie chrétienne et de liturgie*, ed. Dom Cabrol and Dom Leclercq. The Armenian church of St. James, opposite David's Tower, was also built in the first half of the twelfth century (probably after 1142). Cf. Prawer, *Latin Kingdom*, p. 228.

[36] It was at this place that the Crusaders forced their way into the city. The spot is marked on the map of MS. Cambrai by a cross and an inscription: 'Hic capta est civitas a Francis.'

[37] Rozière, pp. 83–5: 'Ego Balduinus secundus ... condescendens precibus patris nostri domini Guarmundi patriarche, cleri quoque ac capituli sancte civitatis Jherusalem, consuetudinem, que actenus exigebatur et dabatur in porta ab his, qui frumentum et ordeum et legumina inferebant, amodo et deinceps, assentientibus optimatibus meis, remitto. ... Consuetudo etenim illa dura valde et dampnosa tam peregrinis Sepulcrum Domini invisentibus, quam eiusdem sancte civitatis habitatoribus videbatur. Absolvo itaque ab omni exactione omnes, qui per portas Jherusalem frumentum aut ordeum, fabas, lenticulas et cicer

of Tyre, again interpreting rather than translating his original text, describes vividly the circumstances of passing this law and its importance:

... tandis come li Rois fu à sejor en Jherusalem, si com il estoit piteus et large de fere bonté à sa gent, il dona une grant franchise au borjois de Jherusalem et leur conferma par sa charte seelée de son seel. Il avoit costume en la cité que l'en prenoit tonlius et paages trop griés des marcheandises et des gens qui venoient en la ville; et il leur otroia la franchise que nus latins ne nule marcheandise, queue qu'ele fust, ne paiast nule rien à l'entrer en Jherusalem ne à l'issir; ainçois vendist chascuns et achatast tout franchement quan qu'il vodroit en la cité. Et si otroia aus Suriens, aus Greus, et aus Ermins, aus Sarazins meismes, que il poissent en la cité aporter froment, orge et toute maniere de leun, sanz paier nule costume. De la mine à quoi l'en measure la blé, et des balances à quoi l'on poise l'avoir de pois, quita tout et pardona quanque l'on en soloit prendre. Li peuples et li grant home de la ville l'en sorent mout bon gré et mereierent de bons cuers, et bien entendirent tuit que li Rois leur avoit fet mout grant bonté en ces choses, et que la cité en amenderoit en deus manieres; car il i viendroit plus gent por la franchise, et marcheandises i aporteroit l'en plus volentiers, por ce que l'en n'en rendroit paages ne costumes.[38]

This description makes additional comments superfluous; by encouraging imports of cheap food-stuffs and by lowering the cost of living the king tried to ameliorate the situation of the city. Through these measures Baldwin I and Baldwin II deserve the title of colonizers of Jerusalem. Both are praised by William of Tyre: 'tam ipse [rex] quam ejus predecessor tota diligentia procurabat, ut urbs Deo amabilis multiplicatis et frequentibus habitationibus incoloretur.'[39]

Comparing Jerusalem with other cities at the same period we are struck by the complete absence of the Italian 'communes'. The merchants of Italy and southern France were of paramount importance in the colonization of Palestinian cities at this period, and their conspicuous absence in Jerusalem is significant. They received privileges in Jerusalem equalling those granted in the other cities.[40] Even if we take into account the

inferre voluerint: habeantque liberam facultatem ingrediendi et egrediendi atque vendendi ubi et quibus voluerint absque molestia tam Sarraceni quam Christiani .... Remitto quoque mercedem modii consuetudinariam.' Cf. W. T. xii. 15. *RHC HOcc.* i. 534 f. The text is summarized in Fulk of Chartres, iii. 8.

[38] Paris, *Guillaume de Tyr et ses continuateurs*, p. 456. The text in the *Recueil* edition is corrupt in this place.

[39] W. T. xii. 15.

[40] Even the general privileges of the 'communes' granting them special rights in all the towns of the kingdom could be understood as including Jerusalem. But there are special privileges explicitly mentioning Jerusalem. The Venetians received a privilege in 1123 granting them a quarter in Jerusalem as large as that of the king. Tafel–Thomas, no. 40: 'Verum in plathea Jerusalem tantum ad proprium habeant quantum rex habere solitus est.' As late as 1104 the Genoese received a quarter in Jerusalem. *Liber Iurium Reipublicae*

(continued)

economic unimportance of Jerusalem, the absence of the communes' quarters remains a puzzle. We could suggest one solution. The merchants of the Italian communes in the East were generally wholesale traders and therefore had no business in Jerusalem. They were never established in any inland city; they preferred the coastal towns. They did not traffic in souvenirs or relics and their merchandise could more easily be bought or sold in the ports of embarkation for Europe. On the other hand, the inland retailer could more easily buy his multifarious merchandise in the ports, the established exchange centres of oriental and occidental products.

The fact that the Italian communes did not establish themselves in the city gave Jerusalem some special economic, administrative, and even topographical features. Instead of the several market and warehouse complexes in Acre and Tyre, with a market and a warehouse in each Italian quarter, Jerusalem had only one market, composed of three covered streets, partly built and maintained by royal bounty in the middle of the twelfth century. If there were special streets, the basis of differentiation was strictly economic, never national. Various kinds of handicrafts or merchandise had special stands; sometimes Franks and Syrians carrying on the same trade, occupied opposite sides of the same street. But that is the whole extent of the national differentiation. From this point of view Jerusalem was more like the normally homogenous European city than the nationally heterogenous city of the East; it was unique in this amongst the bigger cities of the kingdom of Jerusalem.[41]

The important economic and colonizing role of the communes, which did not deign to put up their *fondachi* in Jerusalem, fell to other bodies in the kingdom. The double aspect of Jerusalem as capital of the kingdom and the religious centre of Christendom made up for the loss suffered through the absence of the Italians. It was first of all the king and his court, his small standing army and governmental machinery, whose presence injected new life into the veins of the old city. Next, the numerous clergy of all denominations, orders, and congregations, and especially the canons of the Holy Sepulchre, the possessors of great wealth, developed the city

---

Genuensis i (Genoa, 1854), ed. E. Ricotti, no. 8: 'trado ianuensi ecclesiae beati laurentii plateam unam in civitate sancta iheruzalem.' In 1152 the commune of Marseilles received a quarter and a church in Jerusalem. Méry and Guindon, *Histoire analytique des actes et des délibérations da la municipalité de Marseille* i (Marseilles, 1841), 183: 'communis Marcellia habeat in Hierusalem . . . unam ecclesiam, unum furnum et unam viam.' Only Pisa, it seems, did not enjoy such privileges in Jerusalem.

[41] See Prawer, 'Crusader Cities', cit. above, p. 85 n. 1; *Latin Kingdom*, p. 412.

by concentrating in it their administration. Then there was the wealthy Patriarch of Jerusalem (sometimes quarrelling with the clergy), and, last but not least, the two powerful religious Orders. On these the city depended for its economic existence. Compared with them even the pilgrimages must have been only of secondary importance as far as the whole of the city was concerned.[42] All these institutions, economically typical rent-receiving establishments, their servants and clients, needed food and clothing, and even the most autarchic policy of these institutions had to compromise with the local market.

The absence of the Italian quarters had its repercussion in the administrative organization of the city. We look in vain in Jerusalem for quarters enjoying special lay immunity.[43] There are no special lay jurisdictions but the king's; no other taxes but the king's. As no autonomous city organization developed, it was the king who ordered the cleaning of the streets, which almost led to a general 'passive resistance' movement among the population.[44] The public establishments remained *regalia*. So the twenty-seven bakeries in the city (twenty-four of which were granted to the clergy of the Holy Sepulchre, two to the Knights of St. John, and one to Sancta Maria Latina), and possibly also the slaughter-house which remained in his hands, not to mention customs paid at the city-entrance and taxes paid in the markets.

We have already said that the Italian communes did not make use of the privileges granted to them and so no *immunitates* divided the city into special national areas. The same is true also for other *linguae* or nationalities. Besides the rough religious division between Frank and Syrian (which could not be thought of as a national division), the national components of the Frankish population are only very slightly marked. The only evidence for these semi-national subdivisions is preserved in the street names of the city. The Teutonic order of St. Mary had already in the twelfth century an *ecclesia Sancti Thomae Alemannorum* and in all probability the *Rue des Alemans* in which the church was situated belongs

---

[42] There were rich pilgrims, but the great majority were extremely poor. The Hospital's munificence in distributing alms, praised in the 'itineraries,' is an indication of the condition of the pilgrims, and so is the special cemetery for poor pilgrims in Aceldama, outside the city walls.

[43] On the ecclesiastical lordship inside the city see below, Ch. 11.

[44] This interesting and amusing anecdote about street cleaning, which has even some constitutional bearing, is preserved in the *LdAdB*, ch. ccciii, (*Lois* ii. 225) cf. below, Ch. 16, p. 425. If not cleaned by order, Jerusalem enjoyed natural cleaning. Fulk of Chartres, i. 26: 'Non desunt etiam civitati per vicos aquaeductus, per quos imbrium tempore omnes spurcitiae diluuntur.'

to the same period.[45] This would be in accord with the national spirit of this order, as opposed to the cosmopolitan Hospitallers and Templars. But how inconspicuous this national German colony was, may be gathered from a German pilgrim, John of Würzburg, who wrote about 1165: 'nulla pars civitatis etiam in minima platea esset alemannis distributa.'[46] The Spanish Street, leading from St. Stephen's Gate to the Temple area, no doubt was called after some immigrants from the Iberian peninsula, but nothing more specific can be said about them. We may assume that the *vicus Gerardi de Lissbonetta* is identical with the Spanish Street. Perhaps we have to look to this street as the birthplace of some Spanish religious order, but this is pure conjecture.[47] Except for a Hungarian church, and probably hospital, in the north-western part of the city,[48] and a fair number of Frenchmen living near the Temple area, nothing can be said about national agglomerations in Jerusalem.

Almost all European countries had representatives in the city. Our German pilgrim says: 'tota civitas occupata est ab ... francis, lotharingis, normannis, provincialibus, alvernis, italis et hispanis et burgundionibus.' This list could be enlarged by more names from contemporary documents. But the point is, that these nationals were never organized so as to form particular political bodies. As the Italian communes did not become a colonizing factor, so also the different racial groups did not become active colonizing centres.

The unimportance of national groups in Jerusalem (as contrasted, e.g., with Acre and Tyre), the absence of Italian quarters, and the lack of any lay seignoral *burgi* whose owners enjoyed some kind of *immunitas*[49] are the clue to the understanding of a most interesting document of King Amalric confirming the possession of the canons of the Holy Sepulchre:

[45] The church of the German branch of the Order of St. John (later the Teutonic Order) was excavated in 1968–9 in the Jewish quarter of the Old City of Jerusalem. See A. Obadiah, 'A Crusader church in the Jewish Quarter of Jerusalem' (Heb.), *Eretz Israel* 11 (1973), 208–12.

[46] Johannes Wirzburgensis, ch. 13 in *Descriptiones Terrae Sanctae ex saeculo VIII, IX, XII et XV*, ed. T. Tobler (Leipzig, 1874), p. 155.

[47] The *vicus Gerardi de Lissbonetta* is mentioned in Rozière, no. 185.

[48] The Hungarian hospice of the twelfth century is no doubt a new foundation, but a Hungarian hospice in Jerusalem was allegedly built by Géza I of Hungary between 1075 and 1077. Cf. P. Riant in *AOL* i (1881), 28, and n. 10. Is there any connection between the two?

[49] Exceptional are the rights of jurisdiction possessed by the Patriarch and clergy and those rights which arise in the Middle Ages from the possession of special kinds of property. See below, Chs. 11–12. Colonization *per burgi* can be proved for several places in the kingdom, among them Acre. Prawer, op. cit. below (p. 142 n. 166), pp. 181–3.

infra septa Jerusalem sitas, et domos et stationes suas ad faciendum in eis quicquid illis libuerit, eo solummodo excepto quod nulli alii nisi soli regi in predicta urbe facere licet, prefatis canonicis adeo liberas confirmo, ut quicumque sive cambiatores, sive mercatores, sive cuiuscumque operis aut artificii actores, easdem a prefatis canonicis conduxerunt aut conducere voluerunt, libere, quiete et sine omni disturbatione vel impedimento officium suum ibi peragant.[50]

This document has a bearing on certain aspects of the royal prerogative. According to it, some rights will even in future be reserved for the king alone; these are, no doubt, some kind of *regalia* or *ban* privileges. On the other hand, the king renounces certain rights for the benefit of the clergy. The canons of the Holy Sepulchre are allowed to lease their houses to moneylenders, merchants, and artisans, who will be able to practise their trades without let or hindrance. This last concession cannot be considered a usual property grant. The king points out explicitly ('adeo liberas confirmo') that it is a special privilege. These houses will be 'free' in a special and exclusive manner.

What is the meaning of this special freedom? Specific limitation on the lease of houses[51] is not known in Jerusalem; why then, should a special privilege be necessary? A clue to the answer is perhaps to be found in the tenants' professions specified in the privilege. All belong to the merchant and artisan class. As such, we can imagine, they needed special authorization to exercise their trades, an authorization to be bought for ready money, or otherwise paid for through duties and customs levied on their produce or transactions.

In the second case the collection of taxes was simple enough, if these men were established in the market place. The king's representative, the *vicecomes*, or his official, would see to it in the market. But should their shops not be concentrated in one place, collecting the king's income becomes a very difficult matter. We can look to Acre for an analogy. A decision of the king's court (where, significantly enough, the *burgenses* were represented) held that the non-Catholic population, paying customs and duties to the king, should live in a special quarter of the city 'porce que le seignor ne poiroit prendre jà bien autrement sa raison de ce qui est estably de prendre sur iaus.'[52] The same might have happened in Jerusalem.

[50] Rozière, p. 265.
[51] The only limitation on lease of houses could derive from the tenure of *borgesie*. See below, Ch. 9, p. 251.
[52] *LdAdb*, ch. ccxliii (*Lois* ii. 178). See also J. Prawer, 'L'établissement des coutumes du marché à Saint-Jean d'Acre,' *RHDFE* 1951, pp. 329–51.

This is, presumably, why artisans and merchants had to exercise their crafts in a specially assigned area, and this is the explanation of the exemption granted to the clergy of the Holy Sepulchre. The king authorizes them to lease their houses, no matter where situated, to merchants and artisans.

If this explanation is correct, another question arises: what is the theoretical or practical foundation of the king's right in this matter? There are two possible answers. In our case the king is also the lord of the city, and as such he collects the customs and the duties of the place. We could, therefore, presume that as lord of the city he has the right of intervention in property and lease relations, as far as they are connected with his income. But there is also another explanation. As already pointed out, Jerusalem is peculiar among the bigger cities of the kingdom, because there was in it no other lay jurisdiction, seignoral or 'communal,' than the king's; therefore the king's grip on the population was stronger than in other places. We would rather explain the king's right of intervention as the consequence of his colonizing activities. Colonization is always a lucrative business; opening markets, fairs, and money exchanges is always an income-bearing enterprise. European cities of the same period furnish innumerable examples. We assume that the king, who colonized the city and furthered its development, kept for himself as late as 1164 the right to intervene wherever the city's progress and his own interest may have been concerned. Fixing the establishments of merchants, moneylenders, and artisans, the destination of city areas and buildings, and, perhaps, even the sole right of drawing the productive strata of society into the city, remained the colonizer's prerogative.

This description may be summarized as follows: The settlement of the Crusaders in the Holy City starts *a nihilo*. The nucleus of the new population is to be sought for in the conquering army, whose religious ardour prohibited any settlement of non-Christians in the place. The king (also feudal lord of the place) and the clergy were the chief factors in promoting the development of the city. To attain their aims the king took a very active part in the process of colonization. The first step was the settlement of oriental Christian peasants from Transjordan, followed by the promotion of cheap food-stuff imports and lowering of the cost of living by the abolition or reduction of taxes and customs on imported goods. Other attempts aiming at settling traders of international standing, the Italian communes, and thereby making Jerusalem a trading centre, failed completely. Its geographic position, out of the way of the great trade-routes, and its economic structure, a city of consumers, did not warrant such development.

For purely sentimental reasons Jerusalem remained the capital of the kingdom. Its well-being depended first of all on the rent-receiving strata of population: the king and his court, the clergy of all denominations, and the religious orders, though the population doubtless derived some income from the fluctuating stream of pilgrims and from alms sent from Europe.

The absence of the Italian communes and other specially privileged groups, whether national or social, gave Jerusalem a unique homogenity of administration, to be seen even in its economic establishments, despite its international (European and Syrian) population.

Jerusalem cannot be thought of as a typical Crusaders' city. It is an exception to the rule. Its existence was preserved artificially for emotional reasons; the development of other cities depended entirely on economic and administrative foundations and institutions.

5 Colonization Activities in the Latin Kingdom[1]

An important feature of the social and economic aspect of the Crusader conquest and of the creation of the Latin Kingdom of Jerusalem were the attempts to colonize the conquered territories. Such efforts took place in the cities, as we have seen in the case of Jerusalem, as well as in the countryside. We now turn to the Crusader settlement and colonization efforts in the countryside in the period of the First Kingdom—that is, during the greater part of the twelfth century.

Let it be stated from the beginning: the Crusaders' society was predominantly, almost exclusively, an urban society, an exceptional phenomenon in twelfth-century feudal Europe (excepting, and even this in small degree, Italy). This urban society expanded outside the city for political and economic reasons but only a small part of its total population was affected by this movement. Nevertheless the movement is interesting and important in itself. The creation of the Crusaders' city-settlement and city population was conditioned and defined by the intrusion of a mainly agricultural and village-dwelling society into a country where the city had been for centuries an established and central institution. On the other hand, the non-city settlement was shaped by other factors.[2]

Two reasons decided the Crusaders to leave the cities, their mainstay in the kingdom, and to venture into the open country: (a) the all-important question of defence; (b) the economic necessity of creating or safeguarding their sources of income in the agricultural produce of the land. They could not possibly defend the land from their cities only, since these lay mostly along the coast and their hinterland was open to any razzia by an armed band of Muslims. Boundaries had to be defended and this could be done only by settling in fortresses along the frontier. But settling in fortresses far

---

[1] This chapter was first published in *Revue belge de philologie et d'histoire* 29 (1951), 1063–1118. It was inspired by the classical study of the late Professor R. Koebner, 'The Settlement and Colonization of Europe', *Cambridge Economic History of Europe* i (Cambridge, 1941), 1–88. Help and encouragement also came from Professor I. Baer, the late Professor L. A. Mayer of Jerusalem, and C. E. Perrin of the Sorbonne, as well as Mr. C. N. Johns (then at the Dept. of Antiquities of Palestine).

[2] See Ch. 6 below, pp. 180 ff.

from the kingdom's centres raised questions of a standing army and its logistics, a problem that could be solved only by a special way of settlement. Besides the question of defence there was that of administration, of ruling the land and of gathering its income in the face of open hostility and hatred on the part of the subjugated Muslim population. To this effect the Crusaders had to strike roots in the rural areas. Parallel to their establishment in the chain of fortresses along the frontiers they had to settle in fixed centres in the open land.[3]

Additionally, there was a purely economic reason for settlement. Palestine had witnessed during the last fifty years before the First Crusade a long series of calamities, of earthquakes, revolts, and Seljuq invasions. The Crusaders added the new horrors of a Holy War against the Crescent. The outcome was a ravaged land, sacked cities, and a decimated population. What happened to escape complete destruction had to be restored. But restoration, or to use a more modern phrase, the task of reconstruction, needed, besides rulers and administrators, peasants.

A Frankish agricultural society, a sane peasant class rooted in the soil of the country, had to be created if the new invaders wanted to become Palestine's permanent inhabitants and not only its ephemeral conquerors. The creation of a Frankish agricultural population, concentrated in villages dispersed in the country, very often beyond the reach of help from its co-religionists, living on the coast or in the very few cities inland, was not an easy task. These settlements had to be specially adapted, and this involved the creation of a special type of settlement.

The whole question boiled down to creating a *modus* of settlement appropriate to its strategic or economic purposes.

Where could the Crusaders look for a suitable solution to their problem? We can suggest several possibilities. First there was the important factor of local conditions; secondly, the possibility of local precedents which could help or inspire the new enterprisers; and thirdly, there was obviously their European background. They could look back to Spain, to north-western or southern France, to find a pattern for settlement. All these lands had had their invaders of Saracenic or Norman origin; all had had a period of *Reconquista*; all had to solve for themselves problems of colonizing ruined lands, or of putting to the plough virgin soil in the

---

[3] R. C. Smail in his article 'Crusaders' Castles of the Twelfth Century', *Cambridge Historical Journal*, 10 (1951), 133–49, pointed out rightly that the usual appreciation of castles as defence establishments only, is too one-sided.

midst of a wilderness. So we might expect that the Crusaders brought with them some knowledge and experience from Europe.

It is true that the Crusaders' achievements were only temporary. Saladin's zeal blotted out the whole enterprise, and so far as we can see, it left no trace of lasting imprint on Palestinian soil. But its importance as a chapter in Palestinian and Crusader history remains. It is still significant as an offshoot of Europe's war against calamities wrought by heaven and men upon earth. In point of time it coincides with the early phases of the European colonization movement.

1. *Colonization around Strongpoints*

The coastal cities fell one by one before the Crusaders, and gradually there grew up in them new communities, essentially Frankish, with an ever-increasing population of Syrian Christians, and later on, even Muslims. Nevertheless, throughout this period, a period of half a century, the danger of a Muslim counter-attack continually threatened the kingdom, and in order to meet such an emergency, settlements, or fortresses, were erected with the express purpose of defence.[4] Several of these places eventually developed into cities; others became villages mushrooming around fortresses; and some remained primitive fortresses as originally constructed. To a large degree, the character of the colonization, and indeed the original purpose of their construction, was responsible for their ultimate status, but there were important economic and social factors that tended to encourage development along urban or rural lines in some places and not in others.

Very few entirely new settlements were founded by the Crusaders. There was a tendency, which can be explained on technical and geographical grounds, to build in places where there were traces of previous habitation. In the first place it solved the very serious problem of building materials. Amongst ruins there always remains enough debris from which reconstruction can be accomplished. The French translator of William of Tyre seems to be quoting a popular dictum of his time, saying: 'si comme l'en dist Chastel abatuz est demi refez'.[5] Secondly, from the military and strategic points of view, these old places now satisfied the requirements of the Crusaders no less than they had previously satisfied

---

[4] These fortresses seldom secured any function but administration or military. See P. Deschamps, *Les Châteaux des croisés en Terre Sainte*: i. *Le Crac des chevaliers* (Paris, 1934); ii. *La Défense du royaume de Jérusalem* (Paris, 1939).

[5] *Eracles, RHC HOcc.* i. 697.

those of the Jews, Byzantines, and Arabs. Thirdly, water was then as before one of the chief determinants of settlements. This fact explains the continuity of Palestinian place-names in the Crusaders' period, though distorted in the French or Latin spelling, not to mention faulty identification.

A. FRONTIER COLONIZATION (SOUTH-WEST)

We begin our survey of frontier colonization in what proved to be the most dangerous district, the south. The threat from Ascalon and Egypt continued there till the fall of Ascalon in 1153. During this period the Crusaders were busy surrounding Ascalon with a chain of fortresses, whose attacks harassed its population and undermined its economic well-being, and which with ever-increasing efficiency prevented raids and overrunnings from the city north-east and east, in the direction of Jerusalem and Hebron. Three forts: Ibelin, Blanchegarde, and Beit-Jibrin, founded between 1134 and 1143, illustrate the special stereotype in fortress construction. A slight elevation or a hill was chosen as the site for a small fort (*praesidium*). This consisted simply of four walls arranged in a square, at whose angles stood towers, and which was surrounded by a moat.[6] It was usually granted either to one of the nobles, or to one of the Orders.

These fortresses filled more than a military function. They were responsible for the reconstruction and renewed cultivation of a large area in the south, where they afforded protection and assured the security of the farmers. The lands, on which stood Muslim or Syrian villages, were administratively and legally dependent on the fortresses; these in turn were economically dependent on the land, whose agricultural produce, collected as taxes, they absorbed. In the course of time, the fortresses evolve from mere rent-collectors to centres of further settlement and reconstruction. We hear for instance, that in Blanchegarde

from then on, those who owned land in the surrounding country placed reliance on this fortress . . . and they constructed a large number of villages which contained many families and tillers of the soil. And because of their settlement, the whole area was made more secure, and there was an abundance of food for the whole region.[7]

It may be said that in this case the settler's plough followed the horse of the conqueror.

[6] On Ibelin, see W. T. xv. 24; on Blanchegarde, ibid. xv. 25; on Beit-Jibrin, ibid. xiv 22. Cf. Deschamps, *Le Crac*, pp. 52–6.

[7] W. T. xv. 25. The meaning is not absolutely clear and there is a difference between the
(continued)

But not only is it true that independent agricultural settlements followed in the wake of the erection of fortresses; these fortresses themselves became sites of settlements of an unmilitary character. One of the small fortresses set up at that time was 'Gath' i.e. Ibelin. When completed in 1141, it was given over to the Ibelin family of future fame. For forty years we hear nothing whatsoever of it. But on the eve of Saladin's conquest, it reappears. Now however it is not merely a fortress, but a Frankish settlement; if not absolutely autonomous, at least it has achieved a certain degree of self-government through its *cour des bourgeois*, or Court of Burgesses which is also a conclusive indication of the presence of a Frankish non-military (i.e. feudal) urban community.[8] As there are no direct sources concerning the Ibelin fortress, we lack any familiarity with the subject. We shall have an opportunity, however, to study a similar development in other localities, and this will give us insight into the growth of Ibelin.

In 1149 Baldwin III decided to set up a fortress in Gaza to cut the lines of communication between Egypt and its last remaining outpost in Palestine, Ascalon. On the agreed day, a large gathering of people assembled for the task. Sufficient building materials remaining from the old city were found on the spot, as were many wells. They chose for their site a hill, upon which rose the first Crusaders' settlement.

And when our men saw that it was not proper and that their energies would not suffice for the present to build over the entire area, they took only a part of the hill; and after they had laid the foundations, they erected a wall and towers ... and when they finished, in accordance with a previous agreement, the entire construction was committed to the Knights of the Temple, to be kept by them, along the remaining area, for ever.[9]

It is interesting to note the contraction of the enclosure in comparison to the previous city. The necessity for a large urban area lost its cogency, and the individual settlement, either new or else a survivor of that great

---

Latin text and the French translation. In all probability it is not a faulty translation, but an additional explanation which the Frenchman, as usual, thought worthy to interpolate: 'Porro qui circumcirca possidebant regionem ... suburbana loca aedificaverunt quam plurima, habentes in eis familias multas et agrorum cultores; de quorum inhabitatione facta est regio tota securior et alimentorum multa locis finitimis accessit copia.' The translation runs: 'Li gaengnor des terres gaengnierent les terres d'entor le chastel qui mout grant bien fist; il i venoit assez blé. Ne demora guieres qu'il i firent bones viles qui rendoient granz rentes.' In the first case the villages have been founded by the noble landowners; in the second case, the villages sprang up spontaneously, although even in this case the fortress-people, being the landed-proprietors, would have had to decide.

[8] *Lois* i. 419. John of Ibelin, ch. 270.   [9] W. T. xvii. 12 (*RHC HOcc.* i. 778).

change, 'contracted its line of defence' by building a wall around itself, sometimes in the midst of the former city.

Four years after the founding of Gaza, it lost its original *raison d'être*: Ascalon fell. There follows a period whose major characteristics parallel those of similiar *villes* foundations in Europe. Around the fortress, a new settlement blossoms. Desirable permanent elements are attracted: ordinary people seeking a measure of security, farmers possibly from the vicinity, but also traders and artisans to supply the needs of the castle, the new settlement and the neighbouring villages. To protect themselves, the newcomers built, by their own effort, a second wall around the fortress, which enclosed the castle and the homes of the new settlement. This wall, equipped with gates and towers, was low and weak, but succeeded in affording a measure of security from assault.[10]

When in 1170 Saladin attacked Gaza on his way from Egypt northwards, the inhabitants abandoned their homes, situated between the two walls, and took refuge in the fortress. Meanwhile their unprotected homes were razed. William of Tyre comments: 'homines inermes, talibus inassueti', but the fortress held out, and the inhabitants themselves were saved.[11] The Arab chronicler Ibn al-Athir calls the ruined settlement 'rabad' i.e. 'suburb'.[12]

In the development of Gaza, we see all the characteristics typical of European urban growth: the fortress, surrounded by a semi-agricultural, semi-urban community. This is the *burgus* of western Europe, that eventually enclosed itself with a wall and started along the path of internal urban expansion. It may be worth while pointing out the fact that *c.* 1180 Gaza appears as the seat of a bishopric, though probably a Greek one.[13]

A similar process can be seen in a fortress that was erected at Darum in 1170. The motives for erecting this fortress were, according to William of Tyre, twofold: to expand the boundaries of the kingdom southward (previously, the boundary had been at Gaza) and to establish political and

---

[10] W. T. xx. 20 (*RCH HOcc.* i. 977): 'sed convenientes quidam ad loci illius habitationem, ut tutius ibi morarentur, reliquam partem collis, portis et muro, sed humili et infirmo, tentaverant munire.' Eracles, ibid: 'mès povres gent gaengneor et marcheant vindrent après qui se herbergierent entor ce chastel et clostrent ce leu où il estoient de murs bas et des portes.'

[11] W. T. xx. 20 (*RCH HOcc.* i. 977).

[12] Ibn al-Athir, *A. H.* 566 (*RCH HOcc.* i. 577); cf. Lane's *Lexicon*, s.v. Part I, 3, p. 1012, col. 2.

[13] *Patriarcats de Jérusalem et d'Antioche (1168–1187)*, ed. H.-V. Michélant et G. Raynaud, *Itinér. de Jérusalem et descript. de T. S. rédigés en français aux XIe, XIIe et XIIIe siècles* (Geneva, 1882), p. 14.

economic hegemony which would carry with it the right to collect taxes
from the agricultural settlements in this area and duties from caravans
plodding northward from Egypt on the *Via maris*, which crossed the
Frankish border.

First of all, according to the description of the erection of Darum by
William of Tyre,[14] a small fortification ('castrum') was erected covering
an area whose radius was approximately a stone's throw. This construction
was square, had towers at its angles, but lacked both a moat ('vallum') and
forewall ('antemurale'). And to this place there came from round about
farmers, traders, and artisans ('negotiationibus quidam operam dantes'),
who became its permanent inhabitants, and built there a *suburbium* and a
church near the castle.[15] Here in even greater detail than in Gaza, we find
all the elements of a primitive city: a community, a mixture of both city
and country folk, which surrounds itself with a wall and builds itself a
church, a true facsimile of the European *suburbium*.[16] From the social
point of view it is interesting to quote William of Tyre's comment on the
population: 'Erat enim locum commodum, ubi tenuiores homines facilius
proficerent quam in urbibus.'

This *suburbium* also achieved a certain degree of urban development,
characterized by a Court of Burgesses.[17]

A contributing factor to this development was the fact that Darum was
the last stopping-place in the land of the Franks before embarking upon
the desert route to Egypt. Moreover it was an administrative centre in the
kingdom.[18]

This settlement was captured by Saladin, but nevertheless succeeded in
surviving well into the thirteenth century because of its geographical
importance and its economic functions in that area. When Richard the
Lion Heart advanced southward, the fortifications of the city were
destroyed[19] at Saladin's command, but a garrison was left in the castle.[20]

---

[14] W. T. xx. 19 (*RHC HOcc.* i. 975): 'Condiderat autem rex ea intentione praedictum
municipium ut et fines suas diletaret, et suburbanorum adjacentium, quae nostri casalia
dicunt, et annuos redditus et de transeuntibus, statutas consuetudines plenius et facilius sibi
posset habere.'

[15] This church was directly dependent on the Patriarch of Jerusalem. It was once the
residence of a bishop (*Regesta*, no. 439).

[16] The French translation of the word *suburbium* is 'une vile i avoient fete'.

[17] John of Ibelin, ch. 270.

[18] *Eracles, RHC HOcc.* i. 975: 'l'en conduisoit iluecques les trespassanz, li marcheant i
donnoient paage.'

[19] *Itinerarium Ricardi I*, ed. W. Stubbs (London, 1864), iv. 34.

[20] Ibid. v. 7. This garrison guarded the passage from Egypt to Jerusalem.

A contemporary description of Darum says: 'It has seventeen towers, tall and close together, one of which rises above the others. On the outside, it is surrounded by a deep moat, on the one side revetted with stone, and the other characterized by a precipitous drop carved in the natural rock.'[21] It was captured by Richard and given to Henry of Champagne, but Richard himself ordered it to be destroyed when in the peace negotiations he was forced to cede Ascalon to Saladin.[22] About thirty years later it is described by James of Vitry as 'praesidium quoddam seu oppidum', by which he probably meant something more than a fortress, something less than a city,[23] although it was at that time no more a Frankish possession.

B. FRONTIER COLONIZATION (SOUTH-EAST)

In the broad southern region, a region permanently threatened, the Crusading *conquistadores* had a free hand to try their fortunes. In the wild district, south-east of the Dead Sea, in Transjordan, there sprang up fortresses and settlements, the motives for their erection being as in former cases military and economic. Fortresses to the east of the Dead Sea and the Jordan meant the disruption of the last feasible line of communication between Egypt and Damascus, a vital artery in the body of Muslim domination. The most prominent points in this expansion are the erection of Montreal (1115) and Kerak (1143). In both instances we see the same phenomena; the erecting of the fortress results in two closely related kinds of settlement: embryonic urban activities at the site of the fortress; reconstruction, and renewed cultivation of the surrounding lands, lying waste after having been ravaged by wars or abandoned by its former proprietors.

William of Tyre describes the founding of Montreal thus:

Inasmuch as until that time there had been no Christian fortress east of the Jordan, and he [i.e. the king] wanted to expand the boundaries of the kingdom in that direction [into the 'third Arabia' known as 'Syria Sobal'], the king decided to build a fortress whose inhabitants would defend the conquered lands and those tributary to the kingdom against the inroads of enemies.[24]

It was reinforced with the strongest fortifications of which they were

[21] Ibid. v. 39.
[22] Ibid. vi. 11.
[23] James of Vitry, ch. xl, ed. J. Bongars, *Gesta Dei per Francos* (Hanover, 1611), p. 1070. This description must refer to the First Kingdom.
[24] W. T. xi. 26 (*RHC HOcc.* i. 499): 'Per idem tempus, cum adhuc christianus populus ultra Jordanem non haberet ullum praesidium, cupiens rex in partibus illis regni fines dilatare, prosposuit . . . in tertia Arabia castrum aedificare, cujus habitatores terram subjectam et regno tributariam ab hostium irruptionibus possent protegere.'

capable. It had the advantage of natural strategic position, and was further strengthened by a wall, moat, and bulwark; it was well stocked with provisions and arms. In regards to the population the historian sums up: 'Tam equites quam pedites ampla illis conferens praedia habitatores locat',[25] i.e. the king sent to the fortress as its regular inhabitants knights and foot soldiers, and gave them large tracts of land. The expression 'habitatores locat', classical in the settlement of Europe, is not accidentally employed. The king had to give these men land to tie them down. They were not mere knights composing a garrison with their armour-bearers, not mere receivers of fiefs. We have before us a clear picture of the establishment of an urban nucleus on the king's initiative. For who are the *pedites* of William of Tyre? The French translator and interpreter removes all doubts. He adds commenting the event: 'Il [i.e. rei] i fist remanoir de sa gent chevaliers, sergens, villains gaengneors, et à toz douna granz teneures en la terre selonc ce que chascun estoit.'[26] So among the *pedites* are peasants, and it is of importance to note that they are not the indigenous inhabitants of the area, they are 'de sa gent', i.e. men whom the king has brought along in his campaign in the south.

After a time, there appear in this southern region lords who wanted to follow the king's example of creating for themselves new sources of income from the land. One of them is Baldwin, son of Hulricus,[27] viscount of Nablus in the sixth decade of the twelfth century.[28] His lands were eventually bought by King Baldwin III, who, in turn sold them to Philip of Nablus. But Viscount Baldwin did not sell all his possessions to the king. He kept for himself those lands which had been brought under cultivation by his own efforts, through organized colonization. When the king sold the lands in 1161, this reservation clause was preserved. The settlers brought into the place by Baldwin were Christians and Muslims. On his initiative these men founded farms on his land, farms paying taxes to the organizer and settler. The king described them as: 'Suriani, Sarraceni sive villani..., quos Baldwinus ... in terra sua ad ignem et focum hospitatos, locatos et manentes in die concambii retinuit.' Attention should be called to the expression 'ad ignem et focum hospitare, locare et manere'. The words *ignis* and *focus* are familiar to us in European history and in Palestine we meet them in connection with the collection of certain

[25] Ibid.   [26] *Eracles, RHC HOcc.* i. 500.

[27] Strehlke, pp. 2–3; *Regesta*, no. 366.

[28] Cf. J. L. La Monte, 'The Viscounts of Naplouse in the XIIth century', *Syria* (1933), 272–8. Du Cange, *Les Familles d'Outremer*, p. 412.

taxes.[29] But here we can take them to connote the farm 'hearths', built on the initiative of the lord and constituting a unit of taxation. The whole phrase designates the process of settling known from Europe.[30] Even the *termini* of settling are the same, as a comparison with contemporary French documents will prove beyond all doubt.[31]

Our information about the urban development of Montreal is dated after Saladin's attempted conquest. We have already seen that the settlers, at least at the beginning, were not natives of this region, and had been brought here by the king. We may presume, therefore, that they took the obvious precaution of building their settlement on a site unexposed to attack, and this means in the castle, or at least in its vicinity. Later information corroborates this presumption. The settlers created a *burgus* similar to those we have seen at Gaza and elsewhere. The innovation is that here, unlike other Palestinian or European settlements, the *burgus*, it seems, was created simultaneously with the fortress.

In 1171, the year Saladin began his siege,[32] the castle is described as a very strong fortress, defended by towers and walls. It played an important part in the defence of the neighbouring villages, and later in the administration of the area.[33] Below the fortress, on the slope of the hill, stood the *suburbium* out of range of the crossbowmen and archers. All the inhabitants of this *suburbium* were Christians.[34]

Another stronghold in this area was Kerak, similar to Montreal in purpose and built by the king's butler, Pagan, in 1143.[35] Between then and the eighties of the twelfth century, a heterogeneous group of men gravitated to this fortress in the desert. They had left their homes for various reasons, chiefly economic. Of these men, the French chronicler says: 'Avoient fet un bourc où meintes genz s'etoient recetées et herbeergiées';[36] and around this *bourc* they built a wall.

The lord of the region, the ill-famed Renaud of Châtillon, had so much

---

[29] W. T. xxii. 23.

[30] R. Koebner, 'The Settlement of Europe', *Camb. Econ. Hist.*, vol. i, pp. 69 ff.

[31] Cf. C. Lamprecht, *Étude sur l'état économique de la France pendant la première partie du moyen-âge* (Paris, 1889), p. 235, nn. 1 and 2; p. 237. The common designations of colonization are: *manere, habitare, inhabitare, demorari, ponere, mittere hospites*. Usually *manere*, as in our text. *Hospitare* is in all probability equivalent to *hospites mittere*. On *locare*, connected with *locatio*, see below.

[32] For the date see Roehricht, *GKJ*, p. 351 n. 2.

[33] W. T. xx. 27: 'universae regionis caput ... et singulare praesidium', *Eracles* (ibid.): 'garantissoit touz ceuls de la terre.'

[34] *Eracles* (ibid.): 'Cil dedenz estoient tuit crestien.'

[35] W. T. xii. 21.   [36] *Eracles*, xxii. 28.

faith in its fortifications that he deemed it unnecessary, on the approach of Saladin, to gather the inhabitants into the fortress. The result was catastrophic. The enemy penetrated into the *bourc*, which the settlers abandoned at the last minute. They withdrew into the fortress and lost all their possessions. This was the end of the urban nucleus of Kerak.[37]

Up to this point we have examined the founding and development of Crusaders' settlements, whose primary *raisons d'être* were political and in a far lesser degree economic, the latter being rather a contributing cause. But as time marched on, the settlements fulfilled an economic function, which, though perhaps not conceived at the time of their founding, was nevertheless of the greatest importance to the well-being of the kingdom. From what we have seen, there is no doubt that this colonization parallels, in appearance at least, the urban developments of the *bourg* or *suburbium* in western Europe, and in central eastern Europe, if we consider the frontiers which faced the Normans and Arabs in the north and south and the Slavs in the east. Objectives were similar and so, *mutatis mutandis*, was the historical background. On the other hand, we cannot point to a single analogy with eastern, Muslim forms of settlement, and in any case there is none in Palestine.[38]

Before we continue with the description of agricultural colonization that sometimes leads also to quasi-urban concentrations, we shall briefly describe the refounding of one urban community, destroyed by the Frankish conquest. We are dealing with it exceptionally, because of its later importance in non-urban colonization.

C. THE COLONIZATION OF RAMLE AND ITS IMPORTANCE

Ramle, midway between Jerusalem and the port of Jaffa, played an important military role in the history of the Kingdom. Here a system of colonization was perfected which not only founded Frankish Ramle, but also created a model which served similar enterprises throughout the country. The point of departure was the Crusader capture of the city.

There are three sources describing the entry of the Crusaders into the

---

[37] *Eracles*, xxii. 28. For topographical details and a map, see Prawer, *Histoire* i. 624 ff.

[38] The more important texts have been collected by E. v. Reitemeyer, *Die Städtegründungen der Araber im Islam* (Munich, 1912). The chief difficulty in finding analogous processes in Palestine during the Muslim period probably lies also in the scarcity of Muslim new-founded settlements in the country. Only one city, Ramle, was founded by the Muslims, who generally occupied the cities of the previous Byzantine period.

For the Near East see *The Islamic City*, ed. A. H. Hourani and S. M. Stern (Oxford, 1970); I. M. Lapidus, *Muslim Cities in the Later Middle Ages* (Cambridge, Mass., 1969); *Middle Eastern Cities*, ed. I. M. Lapidus (Berkeley and Los Angeles, 1969).

city. They differ in quantity of detail but are on the whole complementary.[39] From them we get the following picture. Ramle was deserted.

> We came to the city [the *Anonymus* says] which the Saracens abandoned before the Franks. Near by stood a church in which lay the precious body of St. George ... here the nobles gathered to choose a bishop to occupy and re-establish the church; and they gave him tithes and enriched him with gold and silver, horses, and some cattle, so that he might live in righteousness and honour amongst his followers.

William of Tyre relates that as a result of a Frankish ambush near the city, the count of Flanders found it completely deserted. He summons the Crusaders to the city. 'And they chose a bishop for the church, Robert, a native of Normandy ... and granted him Ramle and Lydda and the neighbouring villages,[40] to be his for ever; and thus they brought the first fruits of their labours, a token of their adoration for the Holy Martyr.' In a later chapter William of Tyre adds the finishing touches to this story: 'Our men, as we have said, finding the city empty, constructed in one part a fortress complete with walls and moat, considering it would be difficult to occupy the space encompassed by walls, with so few people.'[41]

From these two stories we can learn how the Crusaders approached the problem of the occupation and settlement of the city. First of all, as was fitting to a Christian army, a bishop was chosen whose task it was to re-establish the church, and guard two places: Lydda, which apparently was uninhabited[42] but contained a church, and the city of Ramle. The bishop received the two places and the surrounding lands as fiefs and in addition he received horses and cattle as livestock besides gold and silver. On the other hand, we read also of the settling of the city by the Crusaders. They built a wall surrounding only the fortress, whose area satisfied their

---

[39] *Anonymi Gesta Francorum*, ch. 36 (pp. 446–8), ed. H. Hagenmeyer (Heidelberg, 1890) (*Tudebodus abbreviatus* of *RHC HOcc*. iii. 158); Albertus Aquensis v. 42; W. T. vii. 22.

[40] The Latin text has 'suburbana loca' and the French translation 'et les villes d'entor'. The word *ville* had already in the twelfth century the modern meaning of 'city'. Cf. C. Lamprecht, *Étude* etc., p. 143 n. 1. A. Dauzat, *Les Noms de lieux, origine et évolution* (Paris, 1937), p. 157. But this is not the case in the twelfth-century translation of William of Tyre. Cf. 'Les viles entor leur citez que l'en cleime casiaux', W. T. ix. 19.

[41] W. T. x. 17: 'Nostri vero urbe, ut prediximus, reperta vacua, in quadam parte eius, castrum muris et vallo communierunt, difficile arbitrantes tantum murorum ambitum cum paucis habitatoribus occupare.'

[42] Ramle developed at the expense of Lydda. After the foundation of Ramle the inhabitants of Lydda migrated there. Cf. *Encyc. of Islam*, s. v. *Ramle*. Muslim geographers such as Muqaddasi (985) and Nasir-I-Khusrau (1047) do not mention Lydda as being inhabited. In the thirteenth century Lydda is called a village. Cf. G. Le Strange, *Palestine under the Moslems* (Yakut's description) (London, 1890), p. 494. On the foundation of Ramle, see E. v. Reitemeyer, op. cit., p. 73.

needs.[43] These arrangements permitted an adequate defence even with a small number of men. Our anonymous source describes those left behind at Ramle as: 'qui cum eo [sc. episcopo] essent'. William of Tyre calls these men 'habitatores', which usually designates inhabitants, and not a garrison. And indeed one of the chroniclers, Albert of Aix-la-Chapelle, dispels all doubts; the correctness and exactness of his words are corroborated by later facts from other sources. He says that the Crusaders encamped in the city three days, drawing food from its store-houses. 'And there they anointed a bishop, Robert, leaving there Christians who would till the soil, organize justice, and bring of the fruits of the field and orchard.'[44] So it is clear that not only was a garrison stationed there, but actual inhabitants, farmers, and husbandmen, paying taxes from their crops.

The story of Ramle two years later, described by Fulk of Chartres, confirms these facts. In 1102, the Muslims counter-attacked. The scene of battle was, as usual, the plain around Ramle.

> In the fortress stood a garrison of fifteen knights placed here by the king, outside of which lived Syrian farmers. The Saracens, who had often attacked these farmers, wanted to destroy them once and for all, and to raze the fortress which hindered their free passage over the plain. Besides which, they wanted to capture the bishop and his subordinates ('de clientala sua'), who occupied the church of St. George.

The outcome of the battle was catastrophic for the Christians. After an unsuccessful attack on the monastery, the Muslims turned to Ramle, and burned it to the ground. 'This resulted', says Albert of Aix-la-Chapelle, 'in the destruction of the crops, the work of the pilgrims, and the hopes of a whole year'.

The settlement of Ramle–Lydda could be reconstructed as follows: The bishop, Robert of Rouen, built and fortified a monastery at Lydda. Within the monastery settled the bishop, the clergy, and men connected with the administration of the property ('clientala sua'). A short distance away stood Ramle, as yet inadequately fortified. Around its main defence, its fortress, we find a colony of Christian Syrians and Franks. Most of these Syrians[45] were probably the previous inhabitants of the city having returned when the situation stabilized. Some were certainly new. Links of dependence must have been moulded between the Franks and Syrians on

---

[43] Cf. on Europe J. Flach, *Les Origines de l'ancienne France* (Paris, 1886–1917), ii. 238.

[44] Alb. Aqu., v. 42: 'Episcopum etiam illic quendam Robertum constituerunt, christianos incolas in ea relinquentes, qui terras colerent et justitias facerent, agrorum vinearumque fructus redderent.'

[45] Fulk of Chartres, ii. 15. The Syrians are described as 'Syri agricolae loci ipsius suburbani'; another version 'quasi suburbani' seems to be faulty.

the one hand, and Bishop Robert, on the other. There was a need for negotiations to fix the terms on which the lands would be divided and the bishop would receive the expected contributions, like the tithe, and his feudal income as the lord of the lands. Whether a formal contract was drawn up or just a verbal agreement, we do not know. Albert summarizes the principal conditions accepted by the settlers: 'ut terras colerent et justitias facerent, agrorum vinearumque fructus redderent.' These remarks, perfunctory though they necessarily are, remind us of negotiations connected with new settlements in Europe at the end of the eleventh and during the twelfth century, wherever there was colonization, be it Spain, Flanders, France, or the Slavic countries east of the Elbe. They remind us of the *ville neuve*. Some families are assembled; the soil is divided up between them. In return for the fields and vineyards which provide for their maintenance they pay dues in crops and wine to the owner of the land, in this case, the bishop. The framework of rights and obligations basic to their relations to the landlord, being fixed in advance, contrasts advantageously with the older system, where the not fixed, often arbitrary demands of a *seigneur* are checked only by the force of tradition, the customs of the place.

The *habitatores* are what would be called in a French contemporary document *hospites*. They are also usually entrusted to a certain extent with the administration of justice in the new settlement. The distribution of justice covers of course a wide field of regulations, concerning the relations between the settlers themselves as well as those existing between them and the lord of the place. These regulations could not, all of them, be fixed beforehand; they were bound to develop out of the conditions in which the settlement grew up. The embryonic *justicia* grew up to become a *consuetudo*. And indeed fifty years after the settlement of Ramle, a charter given to another settlement, Beit-Jibrin, refers to a 'consuetudo of Ramle', which will be discussed below.

The Ramle settlement was dealt a severe blow by being set on fire in 1102. The settlement was, however, resuscitated and in 1107 we find it well fortified and resisting attacks from the Saracens of Ascalon,[46] whose usual battlefield was the plain of Ramle.[47] The city became on such occasions a refuge for all those in the vicinity who managed to escape. The fields were ruined, but the fortress remained intact. In 1113 a Russian

[46] Alb. Aqu., ix. 5–6; x. 9–19.
[47] Idem, x. 10: 'Si forte aliqui prodirent ex ea [sc. urbe Ramnes], prout solitum semper eorum audacia habebat.'

traveller, the Abbot Daniel, writes that Ramle was always in danger of attack, but still served as a station for pilgrims going from Jaffa to Jerusalem.[48] Obviously the peculiar conditions of chronic warfare surrounding Ramle impressed their stamp on the pattern of its settlement.

In summarizing the process of the Crusader settlement, which we have taken so far, we may isolate one phenomenon as basically characteristic: the strong point, the fortress or the fortified city, becomes the centre of a double colonization, urban and rural.

In the space encompassed by the walls a group of Franks would seek security and means of sustenance, either as artisans, merchants, or husbandmen, tilling the surrounding fields. Or in the shade of the fortress, there would gather a new kind of population, neither military nor of officials, usually Frankish, but sometimes Syrian, giving birth to a *suburbium* or *bourc* outside the walls.

On the other hand the fortresses would put under cultivation lands until now lying untilled or abandoned in the wake of the Conquest, by affording them its military protection, and so creating in their vicinity new villages or hamlets. It was like dropping a stone into still water. From the point of entry concentric ripples spread over the surface. The area of the circle is dependent on the radius, which in our analogy is the protecting hand of the fortress.

ii. *The Task of Reconstruction and the Problem of Manpower Shortage*

Parallel to this process of settlement accompanying a fortress, there is a process of agricultural settlement that serves an independent purpose. It may happen that there is a fortress in the vicinity, but this fortress does not necessarily determine the location of the settlement. Often there is no fortress whatsoever, rather an administrative centre of some sort and a 'tower' (*turris*) built for the express purpose of defending the settlement. The object of this colonization is to enrich the owners of the land by cultivation of the soil and expansion of the population. The outcome of these concentrations of people, despite their apparent preoccupation for the most part with agriculture, was the formation of centres, which could hardly be called rural. They differ basically from the existing Palestinian village, by their size, population, and administrative arrangements. The settlements should be qualified as a species in themselves, on the verge of city and village, if such a classification be needed at all. They have no

[48] *ZDPV* vii. (1884), 22.

relatives in the East, but belong to quite a big family in the West, in the native lands of the Franks.

The difficult problem which faced the Crusaders was not scarcity of land, but shortage of manpower. A large part of the Muslim population was killed during the Conquest or in the chronic clashes in the course of subduing the country. Others preferred emigration to Egypt, Muslim Syria, or Iraq to subjugation to the yoke of despised Frankish domination. The much quoted sentences of the Arab traveller, Ibn Jubair, describing the tolerant attitude adopted by the Franks toward the local population, was not the result, as some historians would like to have it, of humanitarianism, or other lofty sentiments.[49] If this were true, how are we to account for the fact, that the dukes of Lorraine and *seigneurs* of other French counties were indulgent to their Muslim subjects in Palestine, but forgot their Christian love for the co-religionist subjects in Europe? There is a different answer. The noble who in Europe had no problem of manpower, found himself in Palestine dependent for his income largely on the shrinking population of Muslim peasants, whose unwillingness, and even open obstruction, had to be overcome.[50]

This phenomenon is not new in Palestine. Eastern countries are not only conservative in their pattern of living, but also in regards to the problems of conquerors and conquered. If we go back 400 years to the Muslim conquest, we see the same situation with minor variations. The historian Diehl writes:

It has been correctly observed that the thorough consolidation of a Christian society in the West has no parallel in the countries overrun by Islam. Here the existence of non-Muslim masses within Muslim society was natural and almost necessary. The sources of income of the true believers depended on the work of conquered populations, tenaciously keeping the faith of their fathers. This explains in part the growth of practical toleration enjoyed by the 'protected' (*Dhimmi*), and the lack of serious attempts on the part of the Muslims to convert the conquered.[51]

[49] Ibn Djobeir, *RHC HOr.* iii. 448. Such apologetic idealization is to be found in the otherwise fine tableau of L. Madelin, 'La Syrie franque', *Revue des deux mondes* 1917; A. Hatem, *Les Poèmes épiques des Croisades* (Paris, 1932); F. Duncalf, 'Some influences of oriental environment in the Kingdom of Jerusalem' (*Annual Report of the Amer. Hist. Assoc.* (1901), i. 510 ff.) and in almost everything written by E. Rey, G. Dodu, R. Grousset, and in some measure J. Longnon. C. Cahen in *Bullet de la Faculté des Lettres de Strasbourg*, xxix. 7 (April 1951) and R. C. Smail (above, p. 103 n. 1) are rightly reluctant to accept this view.

[50] W. T. ix. 19: 'Hi [sc. infideles] non solum nostros incaute gradientes viis publicis obtruncabant et hostium mancipabant servituti; verum etiam et agrorum culturae operam denegabant, ut fame nostros affligerent, malentes ipsi esuriem pati, quam nostris, quos hostes reputabant, aliquam ministrare commoditatem.'

[51] Ch. Diehl and G. Marçais, *Le Monde oriental de 359 à 1081* (Paris, 1936), p. 360.

We do not know to what extent the Crusaders attempted to convert the Muslims in the period following the conquest, when their religious enthusiasm was still at its peak. We do know of attempts to convert Muslim princes and rulers because of political considerations. Attempts were made, indeed, by popes and monks in the thirteenth century, and limited success was achieved by zealous individuals like James of Vitry, bishop of Acre, but we know nothing of the attempts by the Frankish lords towards their subjects, the Muslim farmers.[52]

The other agricultural class, the Christian Syrians, could not make up for the labour shortage. Moreover, the development of urban commerce and the opportunities for livelihood afforded to them as middlemen between the Crusaders and Muslim countries, for which they were particularly suited because of their religion on the one side and language on the other, attracted the Christian Syrians to the cities. There were prospects there for a more comfortable living than on farms. And if there was any influx of Syrians from beyond the borders of the kingdom, it certainly was directed and absorbed by the cities.[53] The Franks were faced with the problem, therefore, of settling the land with any available manpower, either foreign or Frank. The country was desolate. This desolation was keenly felt in the contracted areas of Frankish farms. The word *gastina* appears so often in documents, that we might consider it an integral part of the village. The wastes, the arabic 'khirbet', were spreading throughout the land and the only way to stop this degeneration was by fresh colonization.

This situation, though for different reasons, was current in certain parts of Europe in the eleventh and twelfth centuries. Large stretches of northern, north-eastern, and southern France were laid waste by the Arab and Norman invasions. Other areas were covered by thick forests. The Church, monasteries, king, and seignors tried to redeem these wastelands, variously called *warest, woestinen, moeran*.[54] To attract independent and resourceful men to these lands, it was necessary to guarantee them rights and privileges not enjoyed by the ordinary farmer.

---

[52] On the whole not only Crusader authorities but even Military Orders were reluctant and even opposed to the conversion of their Muslim subjects. See Prawer, *Latin Kingdom*, pp. 504 ff.

[53] It should be borne in mind that a Syrian holding landed property was *de iure* a serf. Cf. below, Ch. 7, pp. 203 f.

[54] Cf. H. Pirenne, *Histoire de Belgique*, i (Brussels, 1909), 297. Other names are *solitudo* and *wastina*, from which comes *gastina*, found in almost every Crusader document dealing with land (see below, Ch. 6, pp. 161 f.).

But though the problem was the same, the causes not always were. In France, for example, a reason not less important than the financial desires of landowners, was the demographic change, the unexplained but none the less real, increase of population.[55] Clearing and colonization of wastes have been not only a financial investment of the rich but also a refuge for the increasing number of the poor.

In Palestine on the other hand there was no overpopulation; on the contrary there was a shortage of man-power in relation to the quantity of land, threatening an economic crisis or even a political one. There is no better illustration of this situation than the well-known attempt to colonize Palestine by Armenian immigration in the sixties of the twelfth century. The king of Armenia, Thoros, visiting Amalric, was amazed to find almost all the land in the hands of Military Orders and all the villages settled by Muslims (both remarks are rather exaggerated), a situation dangerous from financial and strategic points of view. Thoros proposed then to send from Armenia 30,000 people to defend and colonize the country and expel the Muslims from it. This interesting project was abandoned because of the clergy. The barons of the kingdom agreed to accept the newcomers and give them land on the same conditions as those of the Muslims, adding military service. But the clergy insisted on collecting the tithe from these Christians, which was not being collected from the Muslims. This demand was not accepted by the king of Armenia, and the whole project miscarried.[56]

This large-scale attempt to colonize Palestine was not the only one. The Crusaders colonized Palestine by other means and other resources.

A. COLONIZATION THROUGH THE 'CUSTOM OF RAMLE–LYDDA'

In 1136 King Fulk built a fortress at Beit-Jibrin to prevent an attack by Ascalon on Jerusalem.[57] This place, the Beith Govrin of the Talmud and the Eleutheropolis of the Romans, was not naturally fortified. It was located on a slope facing north-west.[58] Its fortifications consisted of a wall, a forewall, a moat, and towers. It was given to the Order of St. John. For

---

[55] M. Bloch, *Les Caractères originaux de l'histoire rurale française* (Oslo, 1931), p. 17. But cf. R. Koebner in *Camb. Econ. Hist.* i. 69, n. 1. The importance of this phenomenon is underlined by L. Verriest, *Institutions médiévales* i (Mons–Framerie, 1947), *passim*.

[56] *Chronique d'Ernoul et de Bernard le Trésorier*, ed. M. L. de Mas-Latrie (Paris, 1871), pp. 27–30. Cf. *Guillaume de Tyr et ses continuateurs*, ii. 289 ff.

[57] W. T. xiv. 22. A Jacobite source mentions also the event in 1138. Martin, 'Les Premiers Princes croisés et les syriens jacobites de Jérusalem', *Journ. Asiat.* xii (1889), 35.

[58] V. Guérin, *Description géographique, historique et archéologique de la Palestine*: 'Judée' ii. 307 ff. Survey of Western Palestine, iii. 268 ff.

fifteen years we hear nothing of it. Its condition was probably the same as that of the other frontier fortresses. A garrison was stationed there dependent, during the few peaceful years, on the more secure areas of the kingdom in the rear, the economic arrangements being cared for by the administration of the Hospitallers. But around 1153, before the fall of Ascalon, a colony of new settlers was organized in the village.[59] At the same time, the Arab traveller Idrisi tells us that the fortress was a stopping-place for caravans.[60] After the fall of Ascalon and re-establishment of peace, the Hospitallers organized a new settlement here. Master Raymond took the initiative in granting special rights and privileges to the settlers, old and new. The number of the first settlers already reached thirty-two families, i.e. between 100 and 150 people. The lands of the settlement stretched to the valley called Tamarin.[61]

This interesting document connected with the new colony has been published several times,[62] and was analysed by Beugnot and Prutz.[63] Their analysis however is open to discussion. They both think the settlement dependent for jurisdiction on the Court of Burgesses at Jerusalem and the viscount there. According to Beugnot it was founded by settlers from Jerusalem, and it is an example of a *commune rurale*, like those founded in France.

This is not a case of a 'military settlement' nor a *commune rurale*. We have before us a document that describes a process we have already seen from the chronicles, at Darum and Kerak. It is not a 'military settlement', because thirty families would but slightly increase the military strength of the place. It is an attempt by the inhabitants and possessors of the fortress to strike roots, to establish a settlement with agriculture as the base of its economy. The settlers, like their European prototypes, are farmers and artisans.[64] We have before us a 'bourc', and since the settlement was not

---

[59] These first settlers are mentioned in a document of 1168. See below.

[60] Idrisi in *ZDPV* viii (1885), 123.

[61] Identified by Conder in *Quarterly Statement (Pal. Exp. Fund)*, 1890, p. 39. This place is to be found on the detailed map of Beit-Jibrin district villages of the Palest. Dept. of Antiquities (not printed) less than a mile north-west of Beit-Jibrin.

[62] S. Paoli, *Codice diplomatico del sacro militare ordine gerosolimitano* (Lucca, 1723), i. 46–7. Beugnot, *Lois* ii. 528; Delaville, no. 399, p. 273.

[63] *Lois* ii, Préface, pp. xviii–xxix. H. Prutz, *Kulturgeschichte der Kreuzzüge* (Berlin, 1883), p. 246. Idem in *ZDPV* iv. 173–4. R. C. Smail, loc. cit., p. 145, analysed this grant briefly and his conclusions are, in outline, identical with our own.

[64] There are mentioned in the charter: Lambertus sutor; Stephanus carpentarius; Poncius camelarius. Some twenty years later Benjamin of Tudela found three Jews here, who in all probability were dyers, like their co-religionists in other parts of the country.

spontaneous but organized, we may even call it justly a *ville neuve* and the charter of Master Raymond not less than a *carte de peuplement*, a real *carta puebla*.[65] The purpose of the settlement is clearly stated in the document: 'ut terra melius populetur', that the lands be populated and redeemed, undoubtedly taking into consideration the economic needs of the fortress. Let us examine the settlers, their rights and duties. They are all 'Franks', gathered from the four corners of the Christian world, many of them already assimilated by Palestine, as shown by their surnames. Not all are Jerusalemites, as held by Beugnot. There are only two Jerusalemites: 'Bernardus de Josaphat', i.e. Bernard from the Valley of Josaphat in Jerusalem and 'Petrus de Jerusalem'. On the other hand, there is one from Edessa ('de Rohas'), one from Hebron ('St Abraham'), and two from Ramle or ar-Ram, near Jerusalem ('de Ramis'). Besides these, there were people from Auvergne, Gascogne, Lombardy, Poitou, Catalonia, Burgundy, Flanders, Carcassonne, thus mostly from France and its southern and northern neighbours.[66] These must have been newcomers, their unaltered European names betraying their origin.

Every settler received a stretch of land of two *carrucae*, i.e. about 62·5 ha[67] for cultivation and upon which to build a house, and settle. In return he was obliged to pay an annual tax (*terragium*), the tithe of his crops and fruits, except olives, and certain customary payments,[68] besides

---

[65] On these kinds of charters in Europe, see R. Koebner, op. cit., p. 65; J. Flach, *Les Origines etc.* ii. 206 f.

[66] We have not identified the following places: Johannes de *Corseniana;* Petrus de *Lesmeses;* Helyas de *Milac;* Johannes de *Corozana;* Helyas de *Burdel;* Bernardus *Pictagoricensis;* Petrus de *Fabrica.*

[67] The *carruca* is the usual land measure. It is estimated by Guérard (re: Chartres) in the twelfth century at 42·8 ha (B. Guérard, *Cartulaire de l'abbaye de S. Père de Chartres* (Paris, 1840), 'Prolégomènes', p. 169). In a *glossa* to a Palestinian document of 1195 the following description is found: 'Chascun charue dot havoir XXIV cordes du longe et XVI du large; et la corde dot havoir XVIII toise du home mezaine.' Strehlke, no. 31, p. 27. E. G. Rey estimates a Crusaders' *carruca* at 31·25 ha (*Les Colonies franques*, pp. 242–3). The land plots given to settlers were therefore quite large and in accordance with the extensive cultivation system of twelfth-century Palestine. It seems that Rey rather underestimated the *carruca*. The *toise* is 6 feet. We do not know which foot was taken as measure-unit. The *pied* in France is usually bigger than the Roman *pes*. Cf. P. Guilhiermoz, 'De l'équivalence des anciennes mesures', *BEC* lxxiv (1913), 267–328. But even taking the Roman foot of 0·295 m a *carruca* will equal *c*. 39 ha. According to this calculation every settler received *c*. 78 ha. See Ch. 6 below, pp. 158 f.

[68] 'atque justitiam et consuetudinem servabunt'. 'Justitiam servare' is quite clear; it means that the Hospitallers will profit from the amends of the culpable or the litigants. The *consuetudo* must have had a very definite meaning, but it escapes us now. We could think, for example, in this instance of repairs of the fortress, Cf. e.g. A.D. 1102 in the province of Chartres: 'sit ipse locus liberrimus ab omni exactione et consuetudine, preter unam rem, id

(continued)

a percentage of what he squeezed from the Saracens.[69] In case he should want to sell his house or land, first he had to offer them to the officer of the Order at one *robuinus* less than he asked from the others. If the officer of the Order did not want to buy them, he could sell them, with the approval of the officer, to someone else on condition that the rights of the Order were preserved. These were the rights of the settlers as set forth in the original charter. In a confirmation of these rights, in 1168 several new ones were added which shed light on the development of the settlement. The Order relinquished its right of pre-emption. The settlers could now sell their property to whomever they wished, except clergy and knights. One besant must be paid to the Order from the sale of each *carruca* or a part of a besant in proportion to the size of the plot. Sale of the house or orchard involves the payment of a *robuinus* only.[70]

Two special laws are also mentioned. Adultery was punishable by lashing and expulsion: theft, by confiscation of property by the Order, and the thief put at its mercy. Beugnot and Prutz were of the opinion that the laws of Jerusalem governed the settlement, and Beugnot goes further, saying that the jurisdiction lay with the Court of Burgesses of Jerusalem. This hypothesis has no support in the text and poses difficult questions that Beugnot himself admitted. Why give them two very unpolished laws when the advanced legal code in Jerusalem covered the two crimes from every point of view? It is illogical, too, that the founder of the settlement, guarding jealously all his rights, should give up one of his most lucrative sources of income to the viscounts of Jerusalem. If this were the case, how can we account for the fact that the property of the thief is given to the Hospitallers?[71]

These explanations seem inadmissible. Take the sentence: 'Judicia Jerusalem et de omnibus lucris quae fecerint super paganos reddent nobis juxta consuetudinem Lithde quam alio nomine vocamus Ramas.' The bone of contention here is 'Judicia Jerusalem ... reddent.' The word *reddere* cannot possibly have the meaning Beugnot assigns it. It always means 'to return', 'to give', 'to repay'. We would translate: 'The fines

---

est munitionem prefati castri; atque, cum tempus exigerit, incolae . . . muniant ostensum sibi locum in predicto castro' (*Cart. de S. Père*, p. 230). In any case *consuetudo* is a fixed or defined rent or service in opposition to rents or services *à merci*.

[69] See below, n. 73.

[70] A *robuinus* is a third or a quarter of a besant. J. L. La Monte, *Feudal Latin Kingdom of Jerusalem*, p. 181 n. 1; G. Schlumberger, *Numismatique de l'Orient latin*, p. 492.

[71] Besides, the charter states clearly that every change in ownership is conditioned 'salva per omnia Hospitalis justicia'.

known and customary in Jerusalem' for certain offences[72] will also be paid in the new settlement.

Let us now turn to the second part of the quoted sentence. It deals with the division of the *lucrum* taken from the Saracens. *Lucrum* is indubitably booty.[73] On the basis of this sentence it was suggested that Beit-Jibrin was a military settlement. This is not convincing nor conclusive. One need only read a chronicle of the period to realize that the booty taken from the Saracens was one of the sources of income for the kingdom.[74] Clashes with the Saracens on the borders of the kingdom and the looting of their caravans were daily occurrences; the Hospitallers considered that booty, made possible ultimately by the strength of their fortress, was a justified source of income, and they stipulated their share: 'de omnibus lucris que fecerint super paganos reddent nobis iuxta consuetudinem Lithde quam alio nomine vocamus Ramas'. Now, how are we to understand this sentence? Ramle is not Lydda. How did the two get confused?

The confusion of names can be explained in several ways. It is no wonder, considering their proximity, that contemporary chronicles and *itineraria* confused them.[75] But how did it happen that in official documents it became 'the custom of Ramle otherwise called Lydda'? It obviously arose in the first two decades following the conquest, since they were both captured on the same day, and both cities constituted one fief. We do not know exactly when the bishop's lordship was split into two; probably between 1115 and 1120, Ramle already belonged to a seignor called Baldwin, who took part in the council of Nablus.[76] For the first fifteen to twenty years, therefore, both cities were under one seignor, and their names became confused. To add to this process was the fact that Ramle was the centre of colonization, while Lydda contained only the

---

[72] *Judicia*, like a great number of other words e.g. *justitia, districtura, leges* (cf. the interesting text quoted by J. Flach, *Les Origines*, ii. 152, n. 1), denotes not only the object, but also the profit coming from it. For *judicium* with this meaning cf: 'Et ad dictum Guarinum judicium scu punimentum forefacti pertineat' (A.D. 1279). Du Cange, s. v. *Judicium*.

[73] Cf. W. T. iv. 17: 'Colligebantur, ergo ad invicem, praebitis iuramentis, quod aequis portionibus et bona fide, cuncta quae lucro cederent dividerentur.' In the agreement between John, king of Jerusalem and the Teutonic Order it is stated (1221): 'partem quam habeo in lucro, quod faciunt in armis predicti fratres cum homines mei cum signo regali cum eis sunt me absente' (Strehlke, no. 55).

[74] Cf. Alb. Aqu. x. 47 or x. 36: 'Quorum [sc. caravannae spoliarum] abundantia tota regio peregrinorum relevata et confortata est.'

[75] Cf. E. Robinson, *Biblical Researches in Palestine, Mt. Sinai and Arabia Petraea* iii (Boston, 1841), 34 n. 4.

[76] *Regesta*, nos. 80, 87, 89. He may be identified as the same Baldwin known to have had property in Ramle in 1115, although at that time he did not have the title.

church.[77] Since the bishop was lord of both places, and supervised the colonization which lay between the two, it was a short step to call the 'custom of Ramle' the 'custom of Lydda'.[78] It is also obvious why this custom of Ramle was transplanted to Beit-Jibrin; during the twenty-year period following the conquest, Ramle was in a constant state of war, as pointed out above. During this period of warfare the 'Ramle–Lydda-customs' were created. In the years 1153–68 (the years of development of the settlement at Beit-Jibrin) Ramle was already the geographical centre of the kingdom, strongly fortified on all sides, and enjoying complete peace. This custom then had been created earlier and applied wherever useful, i.e. in areas whose conditions approached those of Ramle in the first two decades of Crusaders' rule.

The *consuetudo* spread throughout the kingdom. An example is Beit-Jibrin, which undoubtedly was not the only place to use this model of settlement. The use of undefined expressions such as 'judicium et consuetudinem reddent' in documents, which otherwise excel in leaving nothing to the tight-fisted judgments of the owner of the lands, shows that these expressions were well known and in common usage—unlikely to be interpreted as a *taille*—a usage established by a colonizing practice in the country.

How far was this colonizing practice original, and how far was it successful? Neither question is easy to answer. The colonization of Ramle, about the year 1100, is in any case rather early in comparison with French colonization by charter (and taking into account the origin of the Crusaders we have to look to French influences). The whole of the Beit-Jibrin document reflects French influence. First of all there is a *charte de peuplement*. Secondly the settlers are free men, their liberty being guaranteed by the right to leave the place whenever they want. Moreover the lands they receive are not on conditions of feudal tenure; these are tenures of a special kind. They are their hereditary possessions, which they have the right to sell or mortgage at will, although paying rent for them. The *dominium* rests with the Hospitallers who have jurisdiction over

[77] Beha ed-Din says that Saladin ordered the burning of the church at Lydda and the castle at Ramle, which proves that after eighty years of Crusader rule Lydda remained in the same condition as at the time of the conquest (*PPTS* xiii. 300).

[78] Professor R. Koebner suggested the reading: 'iuxta consuetudinam Lithde quam [sc. consuetudinem] alio nomine vocamus Rames', meaning the 'customs of Lydda' also called the 'customs of Ramle'. This double name would be accounted for by the colonization in the area between these two centres of the bishop's fief.

them.[79] For all these facts we could easily find French analogies in the beginning of the twelfth century. Furthermore, and this fact is instructive, those settlers are paying a *terraticum*, the typical rent paid in French *villes neuves*, the *champart*,[80] which is paid in proportion to the crops, and not rigidly fixed by the amount of land. Moreover the granting of a *consuetudo* reminds us that we are in the period of the famous *consuetudines Lauriacenses*, the *coutumes de Lorris en Gâtinais*, or the *Recht* or *fuero* given to the new creations of ecclesiastical or lay enterprise.[81]

Did the enterprise succeed? In Beugnot's opinion it was a failure. Beit-Jibrin did not become a city with municipal rights, nor could it possibly have in such a short period, remembering especially that in 1158 it was sacked.[82] But the renewal of the charter in 1168 proves the vitality of the charter. Moreover it was confirmed again in 1177.[83] Taking into account that these confirmations did not come *sponte sua* on the part of the Hospitallers, we have to conclude that they were given on the demand of the settlers, a positive proof of the continuation of the settlement and its satisfactory conditions. Eventually the settlement also got its autonomous Court of Burgesses at the end of the century,[84] which could not have

---

[79] The settlers are doubtless *burgenses* and their holdings burgage-tenures. On this complex problem see below in Chs. 9 ff.

[80] Cf. Lamprecht, *Étude* etc., pp. 187–9; p. 236. Guérard, *Cartulaire de S. Père*, Prolégomènes, p. 153.

[81] Cf. R. Koebner, op. cit., p. 65. Cf. below, Ch. 16, pp. 420 ff.

[82] Ibn Moyesser in *RHC HOr.* iii. 472.

[83] This confirmation was unknown to Beugnot. Delaville, no. 509, p. 350; *Regesta*, no. 554a.

[84] It is listed as belonging to the lord of Hebron (John of Ibelin, ch. 270) (*Lois.* i. 420). If such connection existed at all, it must have been created between 1177, when it still belonged to the Order, and 1187, when it was conquered by Saladin. Beit-Jibrin was again in Christian hands in 1192 and 1240–4 (Roehricht, *GKJ*, p. 621 n. 7, and p. 886), but it is unthinkable that the Court of Burgesses was only then created. It is to be noted that Arabic chronicles assign it at the time of Saladin's conquest to the Templars and not the Hospitallers ('Imad al-Dīn in *RHC HOr.* iv. 313 and possibly also Ibn al-Athir in *RHC HOr.* i. 697). Beit-Jibrin appears also as a bishopric (*Itin. franç.*, ed. H.-V. Michélant and Reynaud, p. 14) but we have to presume it is the Greek or Syrian bishopric. See the list of Nilus Doxapatrius in F. M. Abel, *Géographie politique de la Palestine* (Paris, 1938), pp. 202–5. On the Syrian monastery in Beit-Jibrin see *AOL* i. 413–15, and cf. *ZDPV* vii. 215 ff. That proves that it was not completely deserted when first settled by the Franks, but that there was already a Syrian community, and that the newcomers added to the already existing institutions a Frankish *bourc*. In February 1179 the Templars complain against the *Turcoples* of Beit-Jibrin, who have allegedly robbed a Bedouin tribe, under the Templars' protection (Delaville, i. 378–9, no. 558; *Regesta*, no. 572). The *turcoples*, the light cavalry of the Hospitallers, were probably a part of the garrison stationed in the place. It is a plausible guess that our settlers took also part in this depredation, which will exemplify a case of dividing the *lucrum*.

happened had it not already become a semi-urban settlement, which it was from the beginning, according to the status of its inhabitants and their possessions.[85]

iii. *Colonization Activities of the Church*

However, not only the Knights of St. John and the lords of fortresses busied themselves with colonization. Perhaps with even greater assiduity the Church and the monasteries participated in this activity. Perhaps even, as in Europe, the religious institutions blazed the trail in which the secular lords followed. Through each attempt new experience was gained, and this was laid down in *consuetudines*.[86]

A. THE HOLY SEPULCHRE'S MAHUMERIA ESTATES AND THE 'CUSTOM OF MAHUMERIA'

A very wealthy church, the church of the Holy Sepulchre, did much to further colonization in the vicinity of Jerusalem. Here we can observe more intensely than at Ramle the emergence of a *consuetudo* connected with the new colonization enterprise, which influenced other places later, and especially those where the same church possessed estates.

The story begins early in the conquest with Godfrey of Bouillon. At that time[87] the clergy of the Holy Sepulchre received many estates, amongst which were the villages Beit-Lige, Kalendria, and al-Bira, on the road leading from Jerusalem to Nablus.[88] In 1114 Baldwin I confirmed these lands at the request of Arnulf, Patriarch of Jerusalem.[89] A tower was built at al-Bira[90]—where the canons first took possession of the land. Besides the clergy, there were other landlords in this area, such as the king, the Hospitallers, and other churches and individuals. The 'tower' in the meantime became a stronger fortification, a 'castle'.[91] Around this new

---

[85] On the possible existence of a Court of Burgesses in Beit-Jibrin in the thirteenth century see J. Prawer, 'L'établissement des coutumes du marché à S. Jean d'Acre et la date de composition du Livre des Assises des Bourgeois', *RHDFE* 1951, pp. 347–8.

[86] The real meaning of this word is usually misunderstood and interpreted (following Beugnot) as customary law ruling certain areas of the kingdom and differing from the *Assises de Jérusalem*. M. Grandclaude justly rejected this interpretation, but supposed it denotes customary payments. Cf. M. Grandclaude, *Étude critique sur les livres des Assises de Jérusalem* (Paris, 1923), p. 24 n. 2.

[87] Rozière, no. 29.

[88] Cf. *ZDPV* x. 24. A good historical resume was given by F. M. Abel in *Revue Biblique*, 1926, pp. 272 ff.

[89] Rozière, no. 29; Delaborde, no. 6.

[90] The fortification is called 'turris' by Fulk of Chartres, iii. 33.

[91] Fulk of Chartres describes the place in the beginning, as: 'turris tempore nostro illic [sc.

fortification a new settlement took root, surrounding itself with a wall and so creating a double settlement area: a smaller one within the 'castle' and a larger one between the fortification and the walls of the outlying settlement.[92] Clergy of the Holy Sepulchre who were sent from Jerusalem to build a church here[93] organized from this centre a lively colonization movement distinguished by careful planning and based on tested principles.

Like Beit-Jibrin, the village of al-Bira was not found completely deserted. In it and its vicinity we find Muslim and Christian Syrian peasants, bound to the soil and obliged to give their service. But the new creation was purely Frankish and we can safely assume that this population was, at least in the beginning, securely entrenched within the outer walls of the place.

In the middle of the twelfth century, around 1155, they numbered about ninety families, some 350 persons, and later on fifty new families arrived, making a total of about 500 souls, a number enlarging the village into a township of considerable prominence. Their origins may be traced to every country and province which participated in the Crusades, but chiefly to France and southern Europe: Auvergne, Provence, Burgundy, Gascogne, Limoges, Poitou, Tours, St. Gautier, Bourges, Catalonia, Valencia, Lombardy, Venice, Barletta, 'de Balneis' perhaps Bagnols in southern France (Rhône, or B.-sur-Cèze, Gard), 'de Sancto Albino' which corresponds probably to one of the numerous Saint-Aubin in France. From Palestine there were people from in and around Jerusalem ('de Josaphat') Nablus, Sinjil, ('casale Sti Egidii'), Nebi Samuel, al-Ram, ('Ramatha' here is apparently not Ramle), and Jaffa.[94]

Most of the new settlers were laymen. But here and there we see 'fratres'

in viculo Birrum] aedificata'. Later it is described as 'castrum'. See the next note. At the time of the *turris* the village was sacked. In addition to 'Birra' the Crusaders called the place 'Magna Mahomeria' (or 'Mahumeria'), 'Great Mosque', to distinguish it from a near-by village Qubeiba ('Little Dome'), named 'Parva Mahomeria'.

[92] Delaborde, p. 30: 'in castro domum unam et infra muros Mahumerie [= al-Bira] aliam et ante castrum terram arabilem quatuor carruciis sufficientem.' A *lapsus* is to be found in the masterly book of L. Bréhier, *L'Église et l'orient au moyen âge: Les Croisades* (Paris, 1928), p. 391, where we read: 'Non seulement Marseille et Narbonne avaient des comptoirs en Syrie, mais dans la communauté marchande ou "mahomerie" installé à Jérusalem, on voit figurer dès 1155 des bourgeois venus d'Auvergne, etc.'

[93] Rozière, p. 37: 'castrum Mahomarie cum ecclesia et omnibus pertinentiis eius.' Cf. *Regesta*, no. 124. The church was finished in 1146. Cf. C. Enlart, *Les Monuments des Croisés dans le royaume de Jérusalem. Architecture religieuse et civile*, ii (Paris, 1928), 474.

[94] The list of the older and new settlers is preserved in the juridically most important document described as: *De sacramento burgensium Mahumerie*. Rozière, no. 131, pp. 242–4.

and 'sorores'. These people gave themselves and their property to the Church. The Church however let them run their own households for the rest of their lives.[95] This is not a simple act of commendation, because the commendators became 'brothers' and 'sisters'. We have before us a kind of *fratres conversi* which the Augustinian canons of the Holy Sepulchre brought from their colonization experience in European countries.[96]

The economic arrangements of settlements of this kind are well known from France and there is no doubt about their origin and purpose.

This agricultural community organized by the Church undertook as its main occupation vine-growing, but we must imagine that most of the settlers had besides vineyards arable land and cattle, although it is almost only the vineyards that are mentioned in our documents. Besides, a number of settlers specialized in professions, as smiths, carpenters, builders, gardeners, shoemakers.[97] The great concern of the canons with regard to wine is obvious: the Church needed wine for its ritual, and wine was one of the items of Palestinian export. Vinyard culture was of two types: either the vineyards were scattered individually around the church,[98] or there was one large vineyard parcelled out amongst the inhabitants.[99] This latter shows a definite pattern and technique. The settlers gave up their individual holdings for a share in the larger vineyard. The individual holdings in close proximity were probably combined to form a new vineyard which was then parcelled out again, taking into consideration not the rights of property, but the most advantageous method of cultivating the larger unit.

In the matter of payments, the administration of the whole area was more or less the same. Ordinarily, the payments included the tithe belonging to the canons, the *terraticum*, a land tax in shares of the crop, involving as much as a third or even a half.[100] Sometimes a parcel of the

---

[95] See below, Ch. 12, pp. 312 ff.

[96] On the different *fratres conversi*, see R. Koebner, *Cambridge Economic History*, pp. 74, 85, and F.-L. Ganshof, ibid., pp. 314–15. E. Levasseur, *Histoire des classes ouvrières*, i. 194 f. On *donati*, ibid., p. 191.

[97] *Fabri; carpentarius; cortiliarius; corveser; cementarius; aurifaber.*

[98] The vineyards of Stephan Pastina or Pontius Faverius who exchanged his land in Kalendria for land in Mahumeria (Rozière, p. 140).

[99] Gilbert Papasius, Walter Carpentarius, Ainard Cavallon, each of whom received 'quandam partem magne vinee' (Rozière, p. 293); and cf. the interesting grant of a vineyard to the whole community (ibid., pp. 249–50). See below.

[100] Rozière, p. 240. Pontius Faverius pays 'tertiam partem et decimam'; Stephan Pastina pays 'medietatem et decimam'.

vineyard was given away with a parcel of waste under the condition 'ut incultam terram praescripte vinee pertinentem plantaret'.[101]

But beside these *champart*-contracts which we saw at Beit-Jibrin, we have here a different kind of contract, pointing indubitably to French influence, and especially to the customs of southern France. This new kind of contract was introduced here for the same reasons as in France. The *champart*-grants which were in France almost always hereditary,[102] were used almost exclusively for arable lands, whereas the vine-growing areas evolved another kind of contract on the *champart* line but more adapted to this kind of plantation.

In a general grant of two big vineyards to the inhabitants of Mahumeria, the prior provided the land 'ipsis et heredibus eorum habendas in perpetuum ... tali tenore ut unusquisque ex parte sua mediam partem frugum, tam in racemis quam in fructibus arborum, tam in seminibus quam in complantationibus, et decimam ... deferat'.[103] This is neither the usual *champart* nor *complant* evolved in the vine- or olive-growing areas.[104] It is a peculiar kind of contract *à part de fruits*, the so-called *medietaria*, described as a 'customary holding in perpetuity with a rent equal to half the produce, apparently a variety of *champart*'.[105] But even the *medietaria* was on a fixed-term lease or, as in the west and south of France, a holding in perpetuity of the *whole* planted area, while in our case there is a slight trace of another arrangement. The colonizer, the prior Arnald, goes on to say: 'si aliquis vineam suam vendere voluerit ... mediam partem precii nobis persolvet.' The payment is therefore not of a fixed sum, but exactly half of the price of the land, undoubtedly an outgrowth of the *complant*. But whereas the *complanteur* 'at the end of five years would return one-half of the received piece of land, planted ... retaining the other half in tenure at a quitrent or produce-rent', in our case he pays half of its value when selling his land only. On the other hand we know that during the thirteenth and fourteenth centuries the returning of the half disappeared almost completely.[106] Our case, where not land is returned but money—and only when quitting the holding—seems to be

---

[101] Rozière, ibid. This method was also known in Europe. Cf. *Cart. Grenoble* (*c.* 1105), p. 103: 'Dederunt vineam quandam, et que erat hedificata et non edificata, ad medium plantum', quoted by Lamprecht, *Étude* etc., p. 192 n. 3.

[102] Cf. on non-hereditary *champart* in the vicinity of Paris, F. L. Ganshof, *Cambridge Economic History* i. 299.

[103] Rozière, no. 135, pp. 249–50.

[104] On the *complant* see Lamprecht, *Étude* etc., p. 192, and F. L. Ganshof, op. cit., p. 132.

[105] F. L. Ganshof, op. cit., p. 307.   [106] Ibid., p. 312.

an intermediate phase in this development, all the more important because it is in use already in the middle of the twelfth century.[107]

A uniform system of administration was the rule in the colony. There were cases of men who could not bear the intensification, and left.[108] There was also a system of supervision. The representative of the Church, the *dispensator*, supervised the work, and collected the rents due to the Church. If a farmer's work did not satisfy him, he warned him before witnesses from among his fellow-farmers; and if the warning did not avail, the farmer was forced to pay a half mark of silver, and his holding was given to someone else.[109] The lordship of the land and the organization of the settlement involved certain rights, amongst which was the legal and economic dependence of the inhabitants on the lord, however weak these may have been in comparison with the feudal rights enjoyed by lords in Europe and over the Muslim and Syrian population in Palestine. The canons of the Holy Sepulchre obtained monopoly rights on manpower at al-Bira. As a rule it was accepted: 'Si aliquis autem virorum . . . terram ad plantandam vineam accipere voluerit, nisi [= non ei] licebit plantare, nisi in terra Sancti Sepulchri.'[110] In another place, the canons gave the local inhabitants permission to cultivate the lands of a local lord: 'non solum in frumento et oleo et legumina verum etiam in vineis et in arboribus et omnibus, que terra reddere potest'.[111]

Thus a landlord received from the Church the right to have his field and vineyards cultivated by the local inhabitants. He then owed the Church the tithe and had to negotiate with the farmers the terms on which they would work his vineyards. But in this case, the canons feared that they were establishing an undesirable precedent in the formation of

[107] In this connection, note that Lamprecht, *Étude*, etc., p. 192, maintains that the *complant* was the usual form under which the colonization progressed in south-eastern France.

[108] Rozière, p. 241: 'Umbertus . . . qui quoniam terram predictam secundum statutum morem colere non poterat, et terram, et villam desererat.' There were also cases of people who had not found enough sustenance: 'Ainardus . . . nimia paupertate compulsus, nec habens unde uxorem suam et liberos sustentare et educare posset, ad eorundem sustentationem et nutrimentum . . . [vineam] pro XXVI bisantios vendidit' (ibid., p. 239).

[109] Rozière, p. 250; cf. a similar case in colonization in central France (*Cart. de S. Père*, p. 437).

[110] Ibid. The same provision is to be found in a charter dealing with new settlers in central France at the end of the eleventh century. *Cart. S. Père*, p. 402: 'qui scilicet hospites ita terras militum ab eis excolendas habebunt, ut . . . neque quandiu militum terre inculte remanebunt ab aliis alias accipere possint.' On the other hand, the knights would give their lands as far as possible to the *hospites* only.

[111] This special favour was granted, because: 'Robertus [the local seigneur] benignum se erga dominos exhibuit.' Rozière, p. 245.

new privileges. To remove the possibility that economic dependence would turn into a legal one, creating a seignorial jurisdiction, they provided: 'Super burgenses prefatos nullam dederunt neque sibi neque heredibus suis potestatem vel dominium exercere, nec violentiam inferre, aut forifactum vel exactionem exigere.'[112]

The Frankish settler, the *burgensis*, apparently enjoyed an institution similar to the Court of Burgesses. Here is the basis for a quasi-autonomy; for instance, the settlers had the right to express their opinion in the sale of land in the village. The sale was completed: 'consensu etiam domini [priori] iustoque iuditio et intuitu curie.'[113]

This may be further understood from the natural right of the inhabitants to determine their neighbours, especially since there was the possibility that they be held responsible collectively for common obligations—those proceeding, for example, from their individual holdings in the large vineyard. As a rule, the Church had the last word in matters of property. A sale must be made, they said, 'cum nostro consilio'.[114] In one place, the Church forbade the inhabitants to interfere in these matters at all, as far as they were concerned with colonization: 'Si canonici predicti villam suam amplificare voluerint, in vineis supradictis sine interdictione et restauratione mansiones dabunt cuicumque voluerint', a very important clause, because cheap housing and property rights had been a special attraction to the settlers.[115]

Whether the right of the community to announce its *desiderata* in matters of new neighbours had any other value is not known. It appears once when lands were given over to the Church, as this is done in the presence of 'plenaria curia pretaxate ville burgensibus'.[116]

Our impression is that here the *curia* is actually an assembly of the community. In special cases the assembly could serve a legal body, as we have seen in European town or village assemblies. In time of need there could be drafted from it a body of judge-witnesses, like the *jury* in European countries, whose members were called *jurati*. In fact, we can identify one such person, called in 1151, 'Arnulfus juratus de Mahumeria'.[117] At the head of this court undoubtedly stood the representative of the Church, the *dispensator*.

[112] Rozière, p. 245.   [113] Ibid., p. 239.   [114] Ibid., p. 249.
[115] In 1160 three settlers received houses *iure perpetue hereditatis habendas* for 5, 6, and 8 besants as an annual rent. The only property restriction was the pre-emption right of the canons and 'suo consimili burgensi ibi manere debenti vendere liceat. salvo prenominato censu et nostra donatione [iure]'. Rozière, nos. 137–9.   [116] Rozière, no. 129, p. 240.
[117] Rozière, p. 247. On the jurors and Court of Burgesses see below, Ch. 10.

From this centre, Mahumeria, the process of settlement undertaken by the Church spread to the surrounding areas. The canons put to good advantage the broad experience gathered here and in other places. In 1169 the Patriarch Amalric confirmed to the canons of the Holy Sepulchre: 'villas etiam quas edificastis, ut Magnam Mahumeriam et Parvam et Bethsuri, et alias omnes quas edificaturi estis, ubi Latini habitabunt cum integritate iustitie et iuris parrochialis'.[118] F. M. Abel has proved that the references are to al-Bira, Qubeiba, and Beth Surik,[119] the last two near Mahumeria, and all of which the canons populated with Latin (i.e. Frankish) inhabitants as may be deduced from this document.

The village of Ramathes lies in the same area. Once it appears in a list with the names Calandria, Aithara, and Bethlegel.[120] In another place, with Calandria and Bethsurie.[121] A third reference places it on the boundary of the lands belonging to the church of Mary Magdalene of the Jacobites in Hadessa.[122] We may then safely identify it with one of the places called al-Ram today,[123] which are situated in between Calandria, Bethlegel, Aithara, and Hadessa.[124] At Ramathes, that is at al-Ram, the canons organized a new settlement. We learn about it in a late document of 1160,[125] when it is already solidly established.

Nevertheless, we can clearly reconstruct the process of settlement. As in many other cases the settlement was not started in an uninhabited place. There was already a village Ramathes, whose inhabitants were Syrian Christians, when the place came into the clergy's possession. Some twenty of them we know by name.[126] It is to be supposed that the base of the older village's economy was grain, besides the growing of vegetables or olives, always elements of Palestinian farming.

The cultivation of vineyards was either much restricted or did not exist at all during the period of Muslim domination. The market, restricted by

[118] Rozière, p. 303.

[119] *Revue biblique*, 35 (1926), 272 f. Cf. L. H. Vincent, 'Les monuments de Qoubeibeh', ibid. 40 (1931), and Benvenisti, *Crusaders*, pp. 224–7 (with plan and photo); B. Bagatti, *I monumenti di Emmaus, el Qubeibeh e dei dintorni* (Jerusalem, 1947).

[120] Rozière, p. 109.   [121] Rozière, pp. 87–9.   [122] Rozière, p. 221.

[123] Two places having the same name are to be found in *Survey Map of Palestine, Sheet 8*. One is south-east of Calendria, 'Adassa and 'Atharot, to the east of the Jerusalem–Nablus road; the second is Kh. al-Ram more to the west, west of the above-mentioned road.

[124] There are three possibilities: (1) Kh. 'Adassa directly north-west of Jerusalem; (2) to the east of the former; (3) near Hebron, cf. Roehricht, *ZDPV*. xviii. 92–3. It is very hard to decide which of the two first is our Hadessa, because of the proximity of both al-Ram and 'Adassa. 'Adassa is mentioned in connection with the Jacobites (M. F. Nau, 'Croisé Lorrain Godefroy de Asha', *Journ. asiat.* 1899, pp. 421–31).

[125] Rozière, no. 136, p. 251.   [126] Rozière, pp. 88, 108.

a religious precept, did not offer much scope for restoring the glory of the ancient Palestinian wine culture. This changed with the Crusaders' conquest. As already mentioned, wine had the largest possible market in the Latin Church and among the Frankish city-dwellers. So vine-growing became lucrative and the *cellarii* of the monasteries were probably the first to grasp its importance. No wonder therefore, that the Church took the lead in planting vineyards. The colonization of Ramathes seems to have had no other purpose than of establishing a vine-growing settlement.

This Frankish settlement was built outside the older village and was rightly baptized with the European name *Villa nova*.[127] Though we have only one document dealing with the establishment of three new settlers in this place, we can safely outline its economic organization.

One part of the clergy's estate was under the direct supervision of the Church and a big vineyard was planted; the other part was put aside for colonization purposes. In this second part the new settlers received land, to be used partly for corn-growing and partly for planting fruit-trees and vineyards, the all-present olive-tree being a complementary crop with a restricted allotment of land.[128] Besides, the settlers received allotments in the new village to build their houses.[129]

The settlers were obliged to pay a quarter of the crop of the corn and vegetables and a fifth of the crop from the newly planted olive-trees and vineyards (besides the tithe). The houses were free from any rent. Moreover they also received plots in the clergy's vineyard paying from it the tithe and half the produce. All their possessions were hereditary with full disposition rights, but in case of sale the clergy had the right of pre-emption, and there is the usual restriction on the sale of the property to anybody but Frankish *burgenses*. The new settlers were thus holding their own lands under a hereditary *champart*-contract, which together with their rent-free houses formed probably the main attraction to live in the place.

Special attention should be called to the clergy's vineyards. With few

[127] '. . . damus . . . venientibus ad manendum infra casale nostrum de Ramathes, in loco qui dicitur Nova Villa' (Rozière, no. 136, p. 251). All the following quotations are from this charter.

[128] In one case three settlers received 1, 1, 2, *carrucae* respectively. They received: 'terram ad plantandum vineas et arbores' and later are mentioned 'fructus segetum et leguminum' and 'fructus vinearum et olivarum'. It is interesting to note that in the village were not only isolated olive trees but real olive groves: 'damus magnam partem oliveti quod Willelmus Beritensis sibi plantare fecit', which suggests an advanced plantation system. On the *carruca* see below, Ch. 6, pp. 157 ff.

[129] '. . . damus . . . plateas ad aedificandum domos libere sine quolibet censu possidendas.'

exceptions, there was no *terra dominicata* in the rural regime of the Latin Kingdom.[130] The clergy's vineyard was a kind of substitute for this European institution. It was cultivated under a real *medietaria* contract of the southern-French type and replaced the villeins' *corvées* on the lord's demesne.

The canons profited not only from the agricultural produce of the settled area, but also from that new social creation, the village community. Though it is not stated, we can safely presume that the canons for example, as owners of the place, had some right of jurisdiction over the Frankish settlers. The canons introduced also the European *ban*, a monopoly of the bakery and flour-mill and in all probability several other monopolies which are unfortunately only generally stated in a sentence: 'Furnum vero et molendinum et alias consuetudines secundum Mahumerie usum illis predictis et aliis venientibus ad manendum concedimus.' So we have here a new *consuetudo*, the 'custom of Mahumeria' the first centre of the canon's colonization activity, whose experiences were laid down in terms of a *consuetudo* and propagated throughout the area of the Jerusalem region owned and colonized by the canons. Owing to its local fame, the canons and settlers thought it quite unnecessary to give any detailed description.

There are several examples which go to show how intensively the environs of Jerusalem were colonized and cultivated. For instance the future king of Hungary, Bela III, sent the Hospitallers 10,000 besants to buy him lands, pending his arrival in Palestine. It was agreed that after his return the lands were to pass into the hands of the Hospital. But when they went in search of lands—this in 1168, almost the same period as that of the settlements of the canons—it transpired that 'prope urbem Hierosolymitanam terrae venales inveniri non potuissent.' They therefore suggested to him lands in other areas.[131]

The Greek traveller Phocas, passing from Jerusalem to Jericho in 1185, gives us a good picture of the great change brought by the canons and possibly by other churches.

Today [he writes] all the neighbouring country abounds with springs of water for the use of the monasteries which have been founded in the wilderness, for the land having been divided and parcelled out among these holy monasteries has become well wooded and full of vines; so that the monks have built towers upon their fields, and reap rich harvest from them.[132]

---

[130] See below, Ch. 6, pp. 160, 196–7, 207.   [131] Delaville, no. 309.
[132] Phocas in *PPTS* v. 26.

In closing the description of colonization activity by the Ausgustinian canons of the Holy Sepulchre in the vicinity of Jerusalem we have to add that even the general base of the whole organization was taken over from similar experiences in Europe. The *curiae* and *voltae* of places such as Mahumeria or the 'Ville Neuve' of Ramathes are replicas of the European *curiae* or *grangiae*,[133] i.e. the administrative centres and crop-collection barns created in the wake of new colonization.[134]

Probably a special Palestinian tinge were the *turres* mentioned in documents and recorded by the Greek traveller Phocas as a characteristic landmark of Jerusalem's vicinity. If these *turres* turned into *castra* and the *Villae Novae* included a population of half a thousand souls, it serves only as proof of the successful enterprise and a confirmation of the similarity of processes in European and Palestinian settlement. Naturally some variations like the intermediate *medietaria-complant* system could have been a Palestinian innovation.

B. THE CLUNIAC COLONIZATION AND THE 'CUSTOM OF BURIA'

As the canons of the Holy Sepulchre settled the outlying districts of Jerusalem, so did other monastic orders in other areas. In the north, round Mt. Tabor, monks were busy cultivating lands received as gifts from feudal lords. Here, too, the work was carried out under an explicit organization and according to a specific pattern, and a distinct *consuetudo* emerged.

In 1100, a year after the fall of Jerusalem, the prince of Galilee, Tancred, conferred some estates on Mt. Tabor and stretching to the Jordan, to the old monastery situated on that mountain, called St. Salvator. The villages on these lands, were partly still in the hands of the Saracens and some were destroyed during the conquest. Amongst the latter was a place called Buria, which was then uninhabited.[135]

---

[133] The Cistercian *grangia* is not envisaged; it was a part of a very special kind of settlement based on the *fratres conversi*.

[134] Cf. on the European system F. L. Ganshof in the *Cambridge Economic History* i. 314. In the case of Mahumeria a *curia* is mentioned several times but probably means a court. But in one sentence at least there is no doubt about its meaning: 'mediam partem frugum ... et decimam, quantum ad ipsum pertinet, curie S. Sepulcri de Mahumeria, vel in quocumque loco in Mahumeria dispensator Mahumerie iusserit, deferat.' Rozière, no. 135; and cf. on Ramathes: 'Predictam vero nostram partem scil. quartam, quintam et decimam, ad voltas nostras de Nova Villa deportabunt.'

[135] Delaville ii. Appendix, no. 1, p. 897. These villages allegedly belonged to the monastery in the previous Muslim period. The document has some strange features and we suspect it to be a partial falsification.

We hear very little of the place during the period of the First Kingdom. But six years before Saladin's conquest, William of Tyre gives us a description of a Muslim attack. There we can learn of several details concerning the settlement. The men in this area incautiously placed too much trust in the truce concluded with the Saracens. The Muslims, having surrounded them, attacked suddenly. The men in the village could not flee up the mountain. That retreat had been cut off. When the inhabitants saw the large horde attacking them, they fled 'in turrim quae suburbio praeerat'.[136]

Obviously a settlement (*suburbium*) had grown in the meantime, which had built for defence against a sudden attack, a *turris* to which the inhabitants could flee in time of danger. This *turris* was probably of the same type as those mentioned by Phocas in the vicinity of Jerusalem, which served the same purpose. In case of a prolonged attack, the inhabitants took refuge in the fortress on Mt. Tabor.[137] What was the pattern of their living? We can learn little from these scraps of information, but a source concerning a different place casts light on this question.

In 1165 Vivian, lord of Haifa, gave the clergy of the Holy Sepulchre a ruined site in the vicinity of Haifa. The place is designated as *villa deserta*, located between Haifa and a place called Palmarea.[138] This deserted and ruined village was surrounded by a wall in which the gate still stood.[139] The boundaries were defined: the area extended to the middle of the ancient village and included a hill, caves, carob trees, and bordered an old

[136] W. T. xix. 14.

[137] A. Battista and B. Bagatti, *La fortezza saracena del Monte Tabor* (Jerusalem, 1976); B. Meistermann, *La Montagne de la Galilée où le Seigneur apparut* (Jerusalem, 1901).

[138] Such names were quite common in Crusader Palestine. There was one near the Dead Sea (cf. Roehricht, *ZDPV* x. 207 n. 2) and probably another one near Ascalon (*ROL* i. 52–4 and Alb. Aqu. x. 16). Benjamin of Tudela mentions 'Palmis' near Ashod. Schumacher identifies our Palmarea with today's downtown Haifa, the Crusader Haifa being at Ras al-Krūm, now called Haifa al-'Atiqa (*QS* 1888, pp. 138–40). This identification is not convincing, because the document describing Palmarea's borders does not mention such a splendid designation as the sea-beach. We are therefore inclined to look for the place more inland, south-west of Ras al-Krūm. A place in this vicinity is mentioned several times in chronicles (cf. *HOcc.* i. index s.v.) usually in connection with grazing horses from Acre. On the other hand we have a description of this pasture, near Acre, from the thirteenth-century traveller Thietmar: 'Ad montem istum [sc. Carmelum], sive montana, quando sunt treuge, Christiani ... annuantim in mense Februario cum equis vel mulis solent convenire' (*Mag. Thietmari Peregrinatio*, ed. J. C. M. Laurent, ch. cviii, 2.28 ff.). Our charter mentions explicitly 'ad radicem montis' and 'usque ad superiora cacumina montium', which would point to Mt. Carmel, but we cannot be certain of the position. The place is marked on a thirteenth-century map (MS. Oxford, *ZDPV* xviii. Table VI).

[139] Rozière, no. 127: 'ab antiqua porta ville'.

cemetery or scattered graves. It included also a part of a valley. Besides, the canons received custom-free rights of commerce with Palmarea.

In the absence of any other information concerning the deserted place between Palmarea and Haifa, we have to assume that the canons of the Holy Sepulchre failed to colonize this place. But if their attempt was a failure, it was not a complete one. Their place was taken over by another group of clergy, which introduced its own pattern of colonization and succeeded. These monks came from Palmarea and we have to turn there for further elucidation.

Our information is scanty, but we know of the existence of a monastery[140] because of an exchange of letters on this subject between Pope Alexander III, and the bishops of Nazareth, Bethlehem, Acre, and Lydda. The Pope demanded that the place be committed to the monastic order of Cluny.[141] Negotiations were held in this regard about 1172 between the Pope and King Amalric.[142] The king assented to the Pope's request and asked him to send monks for that purpose.[143]

A source dated 1180 sheds some light on the condition of Palmarea. This source mentions 'Palmerium quod et Solinum dicitur'. It is our Palmarea,[144] as the place mentioned in our document as being near to *Palmerium* is *Cayre*, doubtless a mis-spelling for 'Cayfe', i.e. Haifa.[145]

In this document, Ahuhisa, lady of Palmarea, gave Johannes, abbot of the monastery on Mt. Tabor, estates and privileges in Palmarea. The area between Haifa and Palmarea no longer depended on Haifa, but belonged to a new lordship, the lordship of Palmarea.

From previous documents we know that there existed a Cluniac monastery in Palmarea, which was in a state of decline through the negligence of its former abbot.[146] The monks dispersed and a revival was brought about by a new influx of monks from Mt. Tabor.[147]

[140] In 1138 the abbot was Elijah (Helyas), *Regesta*, no. 33.

[141] Jaffé-Loewenfeld, *Regesta Pontif. Roman.*, no. 13516; Roehricht, *Regesta*, no. 484. Cf. U. Berlière, 'Les anciens monastères bénédictins de Terre Sainte', *Rev. bénédictine* 5 (1888), 559.

[142] Du Cange, *Familles d'Outremer*, p. 837; Roehricht, *Regesta*, no. 495.

[143] At this time, not only the former deserted village lay in ruins, but even 'locus ille . . . Palmareae . . . desolatus erat', says King Amalric.

[144] The place was called in the spoken French 'Les Palmiers' or 'Paumiers', from which could be taken a double Latin transcription in the feminine and neuter.

[145] Delaville, ii. 908–9 (*Chartes du Mont Thabor*, no. xix). The correction of spelling is the editor's. All following quotations are from this document. See *Regesta*, no. 594.

[146] Du Cange, *Familles d'Outremer*, p. 837.

[147] 'Trado tibi, Johannes . . . Montis Tabor . . . abbas quandam domum novam, quam ibi [in Palmeria] fieri fecistis, cum prior ibidem eratis.'

The monks of Palmarea had some houses at the place before the new donation of 1180. Moreover, there was already at this time a group of Frankish inhabitants there, dependent on and linked with them in a special way. They are described as the *familia* of the monks.[148]

Consequently, there were two groups of inhabitants at Palmarea. Those connected with the monks, and those connected with the lay overlord of the place. The question arises, how did it happen that the population was dual? And there is only one answer: because the monks created one of these groups by settling Franks in Palmarea, a fact not only to be deduced logically, but confirmed by the analysis of the new privileges granted to the monks.

The territorial acquisitions of the monks, as enumerated in our document, seem to have been considerable; besides the houses and lands already belonging to them in Palmarea, they received: 'totam possessionem, que interjacet contigua, usque ad portam Cayre'. This territory is therefore our former *villa deserta*, which had the same limits. We can conclude therefore, that the canons of the Holy Sepulchre had not succeeded in settling this area, and their task now fell to the Cluniacs.

The most interesting clauses in the privilege are the provisions regarding the inhabitants of the place. There are three clauses regarding the population: (1) All *burgenses* of Palmarea have the right to dispose at will of their property, 'selling, mortgaging, or alienating it in any other way', except to Military Orders and clergy, and this was to be done 'ad usum et consuetudinem Burie' safeguarding the rights of the lord of the place; (2) The bakery of the place belonging to the monks should be used by the *familia* of the priory only; (3) Members of the *familia* should be judged by the bailiff of the church, the right of coercion remaining with him, but the amends going to the lord of the place.[149]

First let us remark that the two last points confirm our assumption

---

[148] The monks of the monastery could not be referred to by this term. The organization of justice (described below) would have no meaning, if *familia* meant 'monks of the convent'.

[149] 'Praeterea dono et concedo in perpetuum libertatem omnibus burgensibus Palmerii, hoc modo, ut ab hac die in antea, liberam potestatem habeant possessiones suas, quas ibi nunc tenent vel amodo tenuerunt, tam foris quam intus, vendendi, inguadiandi, et quomodo libet alienandi, exceptis militibus et cujuscumque religionis fratribus, salvo iure mei dominii ad usum et consuetudinem Burie . . . quendam furnum ibidem, in quo nullus burgensium panes coquat nisi vestra familia; si quis ex familiaribus ecclesie . . . forfecerit, vel aliquod incommodum violenter intulerit, unde clamor oriatur, sub iure domini Palmerii non erit coercendus, sed a baiulo ecclesie, qui steterit ibi, ad rationem et iustitiam observandam erit constringendus; ceterum si ex casu vel forfacto ipsius culpabilis, aliquod juris acciderit domino Palmerii erat tribuendum.'

about the two groups of inhabitants of the place. Remembering what we have seen so far of Palestinian colonization we could easily imagine not only two groups of Frankish settlers at the place, but even a territorial division of the place into two *bourcs*: the seignorial and the monastic. It is superfluous to look for analogies which are to be found almost everywhere in western and central Europe. The first difficult question arising from the privilege is, why should the rights of the *burgenses* of the place, and very important rights too, dealing with land alienation, why should they be mentioned in a privilege granted to the monks? Should this provision concern the *familia* only, it would be clear, but this is not the case; these rights are granted to all *burgenses*.

There are two explanations in this case of the word *burgenses*. It is possible that all inhabitants of Palmarea (meaning the *familia* and the *manants* of the *seigneur*) are brought under this common denominator, or that only the men of the lay-lord are meant by it. We are inclined to accept the second possibility. The free alienation privilege is described as 'ad usum et consuetudinem Burie'. Now this Buria is the ruined village which we met near Mt. Tabor amongst the estates of the Cluniac monks. The above-mentioned sentence proves, that there was a colonization movement near Mt. Tabor, conducted by the monks, and its customs have been known, from the place of their origin as 'the usages and customs of Buria'. It is only logical to assume, that these usages, as in the case of the usages of the clergy of the Holy Sepulchre, accompanied the Cluniac monks wherever they tried their hand at settlement. And so they came with them and their settlers to Palmarea. But they found here other settlers already living under other rules, probably harsher ones. The living example of more lenient rules at the same place could cause friction, or in any case it could have a deteriorating effect on the lord's income. His men, being free men, could leave him and settle on the lands of the monks. To forestall this possibility, the lord of the place thought it wiser to pass an Act of Uniformity in matters of land-holding in his whole little dominion for all its Frankish inhabitants. This is the way by which a remote usage of Galilee came to the shores of Haifa Bay.

The provision concerning the monks' bakery should not be regarded as a *ban*. It is just the opposite. Its purpose was to prevent the lord's men from using it, and so diminish the income of his bakery. Only the *familia* of the monks was allowed to use it.

The last provision concerning the judicial organization of the place was an outcome of two divergent tendencies. The settlers of the Church, the *familia,* were as a matter of course under the jurisdiction of the settling authorities, i.e. the monks. This dependence could not be averted. The lord thought then, that if their *justicia* must inevitably infringe upon his rights, it could at least feed his purse. The two divergent tendencies brought about a *pariage* compromise: judging and coercing belonged to the monks, the *emolumentum* to the lay-lord.

iv. *The King's Colonization Enterprise*

We now turn to colonization enterprises by secular authorities. Unfortunately, there is only one source of this type. Undoubtedly there were many others, but they have been lost, and a single document remains a lone witness to the work of settlement undertaken by secular lords (apart from the testimonies of the chronicles which we examined above). The administrative arrangements and the phrasing of the rules offer proof of a well-known colonization technique. This allows us to assume that there was an abundance of similar documents which have not been preserved.[150]

The name of the place we shall deal with is 'casale Huberti de Paci' sometimes called 'casal Imbert'.[151] This is the Akhzib of the Bible, north of Acre, on the road leading to Tyre.[152] This place was acquired by a knight called Hubert of Paceo, between 1104 and 1108.[153] We do not know much about him. It seems that he was one of the knights at the court of Baldwin of Edessa, later Baldwin I, king of Jerusalem. Once he signed a document of Baldwin's.[154] After the king's death, in 1118, he returned to Edessa where we meet him at the court of Joscelin, prince of Edessa.[155]

In 1123, the monks of the abbey of St. Mary in the Valley of Josaphat possessed already land in that area[156] as a gift from Letardus, apparently the viscount of Acre. This estate contained many olive groves, a house in the village, and a garden near by.[157]

[150] This fact is easily explained if we keep in mind that only the archives of Church institutions have been preserved.

[151] E. G. Rey, *Recherches géographiques et historiques sur la domination des Latins en Orient* (Paris, 1877), p. 39; cf. *Regesta,* nos. 733, 1208.

[152] *Regesta,* no. 134: 'casale Huberti de Pazi, Siph vocato'. *Survey of West. Pal.* i. 155; *ZDPV* x. 213, n. 6. Benvenisti, *Crusaders,* pp. 221–3 (with plan).

[153] This village between Muslim Acre and Tyre could not have come into Christian hands before the fall of Acre in 1104. The name 'casale Huberti de Patci' appears for the first time in 1123, *Regesta,* no. 101.

[154] In 1108. *Regesta,* no. 52.

[155] In 1129. *Regesta,* no. 113a.

[156] Delaborde, no. 12. This estate is mentioned in a confirmation of privileges to the abbey by Stephan, the Patriarch of Jerusalem, in 1129. Kohler, no. xvii.

[157] Delaborde, no. 18.

We do not know who the lord of the village was after Hubert, but it seems logical that it reverted to the king. The king then tried to concentrate all the lands of the village in his own hands. He exploited for this purpose a dispute with the monks of the abbey of St. Mary in the Valley of Josaphat over the lands in Thaeresibena in the vicinity of Tibnin,[158] and the lands bordering on the village Bathfella. The outcome of the dispute was as follows: the monks received the lands over which the dispute began; in return for these they resigned all their property in Akhzib: the fields, olive groves, and garden near the town.[159] This was in 1146. During the time in which the monks of the abbey of St. Mary possessed the place these lands were undoubtedly exploited. Now when, as a result of the agreement, the lands were transferred to the king, the work of settling Franks in the village began. The approximate date of this settlement falls probably between 1146 and 1153.[160]

The actual settlement was supervised by an otherwise unknown Gerard of Valencia, who performed the task of the European *locator*. Authorized by the proprietor, the king, he entered into negotiations with those wishing to become settlers[161] and concluded the terms of the agreement with them.[162] The inhabitants received houses as hereditary possessions without paying rent or duty. The basis of the village's economy was not only vine-growing, but mixed agriculture. Each peasant received a plot of land for tilling and additional land for a vineyard or a garden. Complementary income was the fruit of existing olive trees. The men who worked the land received three-quarters of the crops, the king one-quarter. We hear of an interesting method of cultivation of the olive groves, which stretched between two streams and along their banks. Every inhabitant received a share in the olive groves. The olives were gathered by the collective effort of all the inhabitants. Of the produce, two-thirds belonged to the king, one-third to the inhabitants.

[158] *ZDPV* x. 216, no. 1.

[159] Delaborde, no. 26.

[160] In 1146 the king received the lands of the church. The confirmation of the rights of the settlers (see below) was granted in 1153.

[161] Strehlke, no. 1. All following quotations are from this document.

[162] 'dona sive conventiones quas Giraldus de Valencia Latinis in casali Huberti de Paci ab eodem locatis iussu meo habuit.' The phrase 'dona sive conventiones' seems to be connected with Spanish usages. Cf. *Fueros of Jaca* (1084): 'Haec est carta conventionis, quam ego . . . cum burgensibus nostris fecimus de furno' quoted by E. Mayer, *Hist. de las institut. soc. y polit. de España y Portugal* i. 51 n. 2. *Cartas pueblas* of Asin (1132) and Artasona (1134), quoted by J. Flach, *Les Origines* ii. 206–7, start: 'Ego Alfonsus . . . rex facio hanc cartem donationis'. It is possible that the wording of the phrase is connected with the place of origin of the king's *locator*: Gerard of *Valencia*.

Parcels of arable land were allotted to the inhabitants by the king's agent. The terms were tempting. The workers received six-sevenths of the produce, the king one-seventh. In the village there were several royal monopolies. One was a bakery (*furnus*), for the use of which the inhabitants paid every fifteenth loaf. Non-inhabitants paid every tenth loaf. Another establishment was the communal bath (*balneum*) whose use cost half a dinar at a time. There was a flour-mill outside the village, at a place called *Ferge*. The inhabitants had the use of it three days and nights a week.[163] For commercial purpose, there was a set of scales. The buyer paid for its use from each quantity of grain worth a besant 1 dinar.[164] In addition the inhabitants were exempt from customs on foodstuffs then sold in Acre.

The conditions for alienating the land and houses were stipulated. They are as usual: The new owner was responsible for the same payments as the previous one. If there are houses on the land, the new owner must pay, when buying the house, *caroubel* from every besant, i.e. one-twenty-fourth of the whole sum.[165] The same conditions of the settlement of 1153 were also promised to all future settlers.

All these enterprises disappeared when Saladin conquered the Holy Land. The newly reconstructed kingdom of the thirteenth century was a rump state clinging tenaciously to the Mediterranean shore. Was there any colonization movement in the thirteenth century attested at least by such scraps of information as we found in the twelfth century? Some colonization activity there was in the dying kingdom, but it went in another direction. No new settlements were founded and no new areas put to the plough. The colonization effort was concentrated in the extension of the cities, whose importance in the thirteenth century became paramount in the kingdom. The problems of colonization in the new kingdom are connected with urban development and compose an interesting chapter in themselves.[166]

[163] We do not suppose that the use of the flour-mill was duty-free, because the use was restricted by *salvo iure regio*. In all probability it is a case of a special priority privilege.

[164] 'de unaquaque bisantiata pro mensuratione, denarium dabit.' This expression has an analogy in the following sentence: '150 bisanciatas frumenti vel olei aut vini seu cujuslibet fructus terre', *ROL* xi (A.D. 1134).

[165] It is strange that no sale-tax on land property is mentioned. Possibly the word *domus* means here: house and land attached to it, something like the European *mansura*. In this case the tax of one-twenty-fourth of the whole sum means of the price of house and land.

[166] For additional material on the subject cf. Riley-Smith, *Feudal Nobility*, pp. 49 ff. and 254. See also idem, *Knights of St. John*, pp. 421 ff. Cf. H. E. Mayer, *The Crusades* (Oxford, 1972), pp. 148–51 and 176 f. Another aspect of the problem is that of colonizing the cities. See above, Ch. 4, and J. Prawer, 'Crusader Cities', *The Medieval City* in honour of R. S. Lopez (Yale Univ., 1977), pp. 179–209.

6 Palestinian Agriculture and the Crusader Rural System[1]

Despite the large amount of literature dealing with Crusader history, the study of the social, economic, and institutional problems of the Latin Kingdom is only in its infancy. The following chapter is an attempt to describe the rural regime of the kingdom and to analyse several of its social and economic problems. The study is conducted in the framework of one Crusader lordship for which we are fortunate to have a relatively rich documentation—Tyre.[2]

We have limited our study to the lordship of Tyre, since the great differences in climate and soil, despite the smallness of the country, preclude conclusions which are too general. Moreover, the specific structure of the lordship, namely the existence of a large urban centre and the small area of its countryside, make generalizations somewhat hazardous. The results obtained from a monograph on a restricted area can, we hope, be used for future comparative studies of other areas of the kingdom. Yet the study of this single lordship has brought to light some general problems which apply to the Latin Kingdom as a whole and in some cases to the place of the Crusader period in the social and agricultural history of the country. These problems are dealt with in the second part of this chapter.

I. The Lordship of Tyre

The city of Tyre was one of the last to be captured by the Crusaders. After a long siege it was taken in 1124 by the forces of the kingdom in alliance with a Venetian fleet. Two earlier attempts to capture the city, in 1107

---

[1] This chapter was first published in Hebrew in a shortened form in *Mélanges Moshé Schwabé* (Jerusalem, 1950). This is an enlarged version of 'Étude de quelques problèmes agraires et sociaux d'une seigneurie croisée au XIIIe siécle', *Byzantion* 22 (1952), 1–61, 23 (1953), 143–70.

[2] The study of C. Cahen, 'Le régime rural au temps de la domination franque', *Bulletin de la Faculté des Lettres de Strasbourg* (April 1951), deals with similar questions in a larger framework and is consequently less detailed.

and in 1111, failed by virtue of the resistance of the citizens and the outside help of the Muslim powers, Egypt and Damascus. Yet using their Galilean bases, first at Tiberias and later at Toron (= Tibnin), the Crusaders succeeded, if not in dominating, at least in imposing their authority on the countryside long before the actual capture of the city.

Five years after its capture the lordship was given to Fulk of Anjou (1129), but two years later, in 1131, when he ascended the throne of Jerusalem, it reverted to the royal domain where it remained until the conquests of Saladin. It was at this point that Tyre was to play a leading role in the history of the Latin establishments in the East, since it remained the only city in the kingdom to escape Muslim conquest. As such, it became, together with the impoverished camp of the unhappy king of Jerusalem, Guy of Lusignan, the bridgehead for the armies of the Third Crusade.

The city, together with the neighbouring lordships of Sidon and Beirut (1190), passed into the hands of Conrad of Montferrat, who saved it from Saladin. Conrad, subsequently elected king of Jerusalem, was assassinated on the day of his coronation. Henceforth the city remained in the royal domain until the arrival of Frederick II Hohenstaufen and the protracted 'War of the Lombards' (1230–43). During this fratricidal war the city was in the hands of the 'Lombards', that is the imperial contingent and its local allies; after their defeat it was handed over to a noble who represented the local aristocracy, Philip of Montfort, lord of Toron (1246). Tyre remained in his family until the fall of the kingdom when the city was abandoned without a fight and captured by the Mameluke Sultan al-Malik al-Ashraf Halil (June 1291).

During 200 years of Crusader rule, the city and its countryside were an independent lordship, and not part of the royal domain, for only forty-five years. During that period, the second half of the thirteenth century, the title *Dominus Tyri* appears in acts and on seals.[3] The boundaries of the lordship were fixed by the Crusaders immediately after the capture of the city, or more exactly, were adapted to the already existing situation. By

[3] The literature on the city of Tyre is abundant, but it deals mainly with ancient history. A good bibliography is printed by A. Poidebard, *Un Grand Port disparu: Tyr* (Paris, 1939), pp. ix–x. The medieval city was studied by L. Lucas, *Geschichte der Stadt Tyrus zur Zeit der Kreuzzüge* (Marburg, 1895). The most important study is that of H. Prutz, *Aus Phönizien* (Leipzig, 1896), pp. 205–302, written after the excavations of G. N. Sepp (1874) to find the tomb of Frederick Barbarossa. Cf. H. E. Mayer, 'Life and Works of Ernst Strehlke' in the introduction to *Tabulae Ordinis Theutonici* (repr. Toronto University Press, 1975), pp. 13–15. Specifically dealing with the territory of Tyre are the studies of J. Richard, 'Un partage de seigneurie entre Francs et Mamelouks, Les "casaux de Sur"', *Syria*, 30 (1953), 72–82.

then a large part of the former Arab emirate was already in Crusader hands. Sidon in the north, Tibnin and Tiberias in the east, and Scandalion and Acre in the south circumscribed the new lordship, whose frontiers remained, it seems, unchanged until the slow disintegration of the kingdom. Only the eastern border fluctuated when, in the thirteenth century, the lordship was united with that of Tibnin. But such unions had no influence on Crusader administration and each lordship preserved its identity whether or not it was united with another, even a neighbouring, lordship.

It was only between 1269 and 1289 that three treaties between the lordship and the encroaching Mameluke power cut increasingly into its territory, until at the end only the city remained in Crusader hands.[4]

The Lordship: Size and Boundaries

The southern boundary of the lordship began at the coast, at Ras al-ʿAbyad, and continued east to Matfana. From here it turned northeast along Wadi al-ʿAzziye and then east to Zabaqine. At this point the boundary is unclear, but in all probability it passed near Yaʿatar and al-Tairi. Here it turned north and, leaving the centre of the neighbouring lordship of Tibnin to the east, it continued to Khan Islin. The frontier continued to the Qassimiye river leaving Qalʿat Marun and Olmane inside the frontiers of the lordship. Then, following the river, the frontier turned westwards until it reached the Mediterranean.[5]

The lordship was by European and even Crusader standards very small; in fact, it was one of the smallest. Its maritime border did not exceed 24 km, some 15 km to the south and about 9 km to the north of the city. Its eastern border was not more than 17 to 21 km from its western seaboard. The whole lordship covered a rectangular area of some 450 square kilometres.[6]

---

[4] Medieval historical geography of the lordship has been studied by R. Röhricht, 'Studien zur mittelalterlichen Geographie und Topographie Syriens', *ZDPV*, 10 (1887), 282–90; H. Prutz, op. cit.; C. Ritter, *Die Erdkunde*, vols. xv–xvii (Berlin, 1854), esp. vol. xvii, pp. 332–46; E. G. Rey, *Les Colonies franques de Syrie aux XIIᵉ et XIIIᵉ siècles* (Paris, 1883); R. Dussaud, *Topographie historique de la Syrie antique et médiévale* (Paris, 1927); cf. J. Prawer and M. Benvenisti, 'Crusader Palestine', *Atlas Israel*, IX/12 (Jerusalem, 1960). See now also P. M. Holt, 'Qalāwūn's treaty with Acre 1283', *English Historical Review* 91 (1970), 802–12; cf. M. L. Favreau, 'Die Kreuzfahrerherrschaft Scandalion', *ZDPV* 93 (1977), 12–29; M. H. Chehab, *Tyr à l'époque des Croisades, hist. militaire et diplomatique*, i (Paris, 1975).

[5] We quote the names as indicated on the French maps: *Levant* (1:50,000), Flle N1-36-xxi, I, a–b.

[6] W.T. xiii. 3 gives the following description: 'Protenditur ... in austrum versus
(*continued*)

This rectangle fell into two parts: (a) a narrow band of land along the coast, with the city of Tyre linked to it by the famous isthmus built by Alexander the Great; (b) the countryside, a plain area and rising hills in the east. The coastal plain was not more than 3 to 5 km wide, which probably caused the Crusader historian, William of Tyre, to assign to the lordship an area even smaller than it actually comprised. This maritime band was cut by several valleys: the river Qassimiye, in the north, the wadis al-Hubeshiye and Uqab to the south, and the Wadi al-ʿAzziye more to the south, all of which poured their waters from east to west into the sea. In addition a number of sources watered the maritime plain—the most important among them being the famous spring of Ras al-ʿAin.[7]

The hilly area rose in the vicinity of Tibnin (Jebel Gamle) to 800 m above sea level and 715 m south-west of Tibnin. The boundary between the lordships of Tyre and Tibnin cut between 500 and 700 m across this hilly or mountainous area and it is difficult to trace it by following any natural features. This probably results from the fact that Tibnin was in Crusader hands before Tyre and the future boundaries were largely artificial. The highest part of the country was to be found east of Tibnin, just above the great depression of Marj ʿAyun, but this was already outside the lordship of Tyre.

Density of Population

The number of villages in Tyre is better known to us than that of any other lordship. Venice, which took part in the capture of the city (1124), stipulated in advance that one-third of the city and one-third of the lordship should be handed over to the commune as recompense for her part in the siege. The promise was kept, but during the thirteenth century the whole picture changed. The source from which we draw our most

Ptolemaidam, usque ad eum locum qui hodie vulgo dicitur Districtum Scandarionis, milliaribus quatuor aut quinque; e regione in septentrionem, versus Sareptam et Sydonem iterum porrigitur totidem milliaribus; in latitudinem vero, ubi minimum, ad duo, ubi plurimum, ad tria habens milliaria.' This is correct for the southern and northern boundaries, but we have to keep in mind that the *milliarium* of William of Tyre is not the Roman one but roughly corresponds to 2·5 km. Cf. Propst, 'Die geographischen Verhältnisse Syriens und Palästinas nach Wilhelm von Tyrus', *Das Land der Bibel*, iv, fasc. 5–6, p. 82. The oriental boundary which according to William of Tyre was between 5 and 8 km from the seashore, was actually 17–21 km distant. In another place William of Tyre seems to evaluate the distance as between 10 and 12 km (W.T. xiii. 13).

[7] On the physical structure of the area, cf. F. M. Abel, *Géographie de la Palestine*, i (Paris, 1933), 94 ff. and map III. On the *Survey of Western Palestine* map, Palestine, sheet 1, *Metulla*, we find the following wadis: W. Aabbasiya joining W. Hammadiye and in the southern part: Biane el-Borj, Achour, Maliyé, Aazziye, Sam, Chamaa.

precious information is a document written during that most critical period in the history of the kingdom. The 'Lombards' of Frederick II were expelled (1243) by the native aristocracy with the help of the Venetians from the city of Tyre, but the Frankish barons decided to limit the power of the Venetians and not to fulfil the engagements they had undertaken as a condition of the commune's alliance. At this point a memorandum was written by the Venetian *bailli* in Syria, Marsiglio Zorzi, to be sent to the government of the Republic. After relating the story of the war against the 'Lombards' and the history of the conflict between the Venetians and the magnates of the kingdom, the memorandum continues with an inventory of the properties of the commune and its claims to privileges and other possessions.[8]

The information derived from this document, as well as from some additional data from other sources, allows us to conclude that the total number of villages in the lordship came to about 120. As other studies have reached different conclusions, we shall present the method by which we arrived at our conclusions.

The basic text for the understanding of the division of landed property in the lordship is the agreement known as *Pactum Warmundi*, a treaty signed in 1123 between the Patriarch Warmund on behalf of the kingdom and the Venetians.[9] By the terms of the treaty one-third of the city and one-third of the countryside were promised to the Commune of Venice. But how was the treaty actually executed? Marsiglio's inventory proves that the Franks kept their promise according to the letter if not always according to the spirit of the agreement.

The Venetians received twenty-one (or at least sixteen) villages in full.[10] In 1243, according to our memorandum, no more than four villages remained in their full possession, whereas the remaining eleven

---

[8] This important text was printed by Tafel–Thomas ii. 351–89 from the manuscript 'Liber Albus', fos. 172–92. We collated all the passages quoted below with MS. *Querini, Stampalia*. Cl. iv, cod. 3. There is no difference between the texts. The summary given in *Regesta*, no. 1114, pp. 289–97, is unsatisfactory. Marsiglio Zorzi's inventory was doubtless based on documents or registers in the archives of the Venetian colony, whether in Tyre or in Acre. This explains a number of repetitions and in some cases it is even possible to distinguish between the different sources of the inventory.

[9] W.T. xii. 25 and Tafel–Thomas i. 85–9.

[10] The numbers in brackets show the difficulty of identification of place-names. Some names are repeated under different headings; some villages are mentioned as entirely belonging to the Venetians, and again as belonging to them in a third only. This confusion was probably caused by a variety of documents of different periods at the disposal of the *bailli*.

(or at least eight) were enfeoffed to a noble Venetian, Rolando Contarini, and six other villages (or at least four) were given as fiefs to other nobles from Venice. If we multiply this number by three, counting two royal to one Venetian village, we total sixty-three (or at least forty-eight) villages. To this we must add fifty-one villages known by name (five are mentioned twice) in which the Venetians received one-third of the land. We can thus evaluate the total number of villages in the lordship at 114 (21 × 3 + 51).[11] By listing the names of villages known to have existed in the lordship of Tyre, we arrive at almost the same number. In reality the number of villages was probably slightly higher, because a band of land, almost at the city walls, had no villages but was certainly cultivated. We do not know by what principle this fertile land was partitioned, but the Venetians possessed land in this area, which must have been calculated as equivalent to a definite number of villages. We can thus conclude that about 120 villages or hamlets existed in an area of *c.* 450 square kilometres. The density of settlement was consequently, on average, one village for each 4 square kilometres. If we remember that there were very few villages near the seaboard, the density of settlement was even higher. Theoretically, the average distance from one village to another was 2 km only.

Strangely enough, the number of villages in this region is almost identical at the beginning of our own century. Turkish statistics before 1914 and more recent statistics from Lebanon, though probably still based on the earlier Turkish estimate, indicate that in the three *nahiés* (districts) of Sour, that is Tyre, there were 133 villages. The Turkish district of Sour did not differ very much from the Crusader lordship of Tyre. In the east, the Turkish district included Tibnin, and in the north and in the south the limits were slightly different.[12]

Lords, Fiefs, and Military Service

The small area of the lordship was divided among a large number of

---

[11] W. Heyd, *Histoire du commerce du Levant*, i. (Leipzig, 1885) 155, assigns almost all the ninety villages to the Venetians alone. L. Lucas counted 100 villages. G. Schlumberger, *Numismatique de l'Orient latin*, p. 128, counted ninety-seven villages in the lordships of Tyre and Toron in 1277.

[12] G. Samné, *La Syrie* (Paris, 1920), pp. 279–80: 'District de Sour. Ce district est limité au Nord par celui de Saida, à l'Est par le district de Merj ʿAyoun [instead of Tibnin–Toron at the time of the Crusaders], au Sud par l'arrondissement de Saint-Jean d'Acre [instead of Iskanderune–Scandalion] . . . Il comprend trois cantons et 133 villes, bourgs, villages et hameaux.' Cf. ibid., p. 259.

Frankish lords. The most important landlords were the king and the Venetians. Both had a large number of villages, which, it is worth noting, did not create continuous territories. The primary division according to the principle of one-third to Venice and two-thirds to the king, split a large number of villages, almost 50 per cent, between the two contracting parties. This in itself prevented the formation of continuous landed possession. But even the villages that remained in the full possession of king or of Venice did not form continuous areas.

As we have seen, the Venetians had twenty-one villages in full possession and one-third of the territory in fifty-one villages. The commune did not administer all its villages directly. A relatively important part was enfeoffed to three families: the Pantaleons, the Jourdains, and the Contareni. It seems that in the twelfth century only two families were prominent, the Pantaleons and the Contareni. John Pantaleon, father of Vitalis, received a fief from the commune. Through marriage William Jourdain acquired part of the possessions of the Pantaleons, viz. three villages, whereas three other villages remained with the Pantaleons.[13] Other possessions were enfeoffed by the Venetians immediately after the capture of Tyre (1124) to one Roland Contarenus. His widow, Dame Guide, played a rather nasty trick on the commune by recommending herself and her possessions to the king who, in this way, claimed rights to former Venetian property.[14]

Another Roland Contarenus, whom Marsiglio Zorzi distinguishes by the adjective 'minor', lived in the middle of the thirteenth century in Tyre, near the Greek church of St. Mary. Roland the Elder, fully possessed twelve (or ten) villages and additionally one-third in four (or six) villages.[15] Roland the Younger possessed five entire villages.

[13] William Jourdain held his fief in the name of his wife. Tafel–Thomas ii. 372 and 373: 'quod habet in feudum a Venecia Guillielmus Jordanis pro uxore sua'; ibid. 377: 'feudo tenet nunc Guilielmus Jordanis pro uxore sua, quae fuit de domo Pantalei'.

[14] The chronological problems and the genealogy of this family create some difficulties. We know that a Roland Contarenus received his fief after the conquest of the city (ibid. ii. 387). He was a personality of some standing under King Fulk of Anjou (1131–43), ibid. i. 141; when the Venetians lost their annual rent of 300 besants (1164), Roland was already dead. Consequently we should fix the date of the recommendation of his widow, Lady Guide, in the second half of the twelfth century, but before the reign of Henry of Champagne, (ibid. ii. 375 and 379). We are inclined to see in the Roland Contarenus *minor* mentioned below as living in 1243, a grandson or great-grandson of Roland *maior*. His *avus* is mentioned as a contemporary of Pantaleon Barbo at the time of Henry of Champagne and Roland was still a minor under Stephan Justinian, successor of Barbo as Venetian *bailli* in Syria (ibid. ii. 379). But Marsiglio says explicitly: 'Est sciendum quod . . . Rolandus . . . maior decessit nullo herede derelicto.' ibid. ii. 387.   [15] Tafel–Thomas ii. 387.

Thus the enfeoffments of the commune included almost 50 per cent of its possessions and, generally speaking, were practised in villages that the commune possessed in full. No doubt this was prompted by the vassals of the commune who were not anxious to risk a future clash with their powerful neighbour, the king. The conditions of enfeoffment are only known as far as the Contareni are concerned. The fief of Roland the Elder is described as given 'tempore captionis Tyri. . . pro tribus militijs'[16] and this is confirmed by the roll of the military services of the kingdom preserved in John of Ibelin's treatise: 'La seignorie de Sur doit xxviij chevaliers, la devise: Les Venitiens III chevaliers.'[17] As this enfeoffment took place at the beginning of the twelfth century, it seems that the amount of land was disproportionately large in relation to the limited military service exacted from the family and it must have been the standing of Roland Contarenus or the position of his family in the metropolis that influenced such an advantageous enfeoffment.

Compared with the Venetians, other proprietors seem insignificant. This is particularly true of the Military Orders. They were somewhat inconspicuous even in the middle of the thirteenth century at the time that they were acquiring large possessions abandoned by the local aristocracy[18] all over the kingdom. This was probably due to the relative security and fertility of the region, which made it worth while for the Frankish nobility to hold on to their possessions.

Hospitallers, in the twelfth century, possessed only some orchards in the vicinity of the city and, it was not until the middle of the next century that they acquired three villages in the lordship. One of them, 'La Tor de l'Ospital', was in all probability, a military observation point.[19] To that we should add some scattered property which came with the merger of the Order of St. Lazarus with the Hospital in 1259.

The Templars possessed even less: two-thirds of a village belonged to them from the middle of the twelfth century.[20] The Teutonic Order, at

---

[16] Ibid.

[17] John of Ibelin, *Lois* i. 425.

[18] H. Prutz, 'Die Besitzungen des Johanniterordens in Palästina und Syrien', *ZDPV*, 4 (1881), p. 171; G. Beyer in *Palästina–Jahrbuch* 32 (1936), 101 ff.; Riley-Smith, *Knights of St. John*, p. 484, map 4.

[19] In the following list we do not indicate the names of villages. The references to sources indicate only the fact of acquisition or possession. The Knights of St. John acquired their possessions between 1243 and 1271. Cf. *Regesta*, nos. 1366, 1374b; Delaville ii. 238.

[20] *Regesta*, no. 442a. The other third belonged to the Venetians. King Amalric promised them the whole village: 'si quandoque venerit in manu mea vel successorum meorum'.

the end of the twelfth century, possessed one village and, in the middle of the thirteenth century, the same village and an additional one-third of another.[21]

The scarcity of ecclesiastical possessions is somewhat surprising. Apart from Italian clergy (from St. Mark in Venice or St. Lawrence in Genoa etc.), who held their property from the communes, the native clergy had very little. The Archbishop of Tyre held three villages and part of a fourth;[22] the canons of the Holy Sepulchre held two villages;[23] the prior of Mt. Zion held scattered land in two villages;[24] the monks of St. Mary of Josaphat held two villages in addition to some scattered land;[25] the monastery of Mt. Tabor held two villages.[26]

The possessions of other Italian communes, compared with those of Venice, were very modest. The Pisans had four villages which they received before Saladin's conquest. The *Societas Vermiliorum* of the Pisans later (in 1188) acquired nine villages taken from the Venetians.[27] The Genoese did not have more than one village in addition to some scattered land.[28] The Commune of the Provençals had one village only.

As to individual Frankish lords, we have found only nine of them: their possessions totalled fourteen villages, the most important property not exceeding three villages.[29] We do not take into account small areas, gardens or orchards, dispersed in the immediate vicinity of the city.

---

[21] *Regesta*, nos. 722, 1086.

[22] The report of Marsiglio Zorzi *passim* and *Regesta*, no. 1458.

[23] *Regesta*, nos. 109, 370, 375.

[24] *Regesta*, no. 576.

[25] *Regesta*, no. 137a.

[26] Delaville ii. 826.

[27] *Regesta*, nos. 665, 675.

[28] *Regesta*, no. 659.

[29] The following knights or nobles held villages or lands in the lordship: Joscelin of Edessa (after 1182), *Regesta*, no. 614; Jacques Cayme, the owner of city properties who seems to have given his name to hills or mountains near the city: *montana Jacobi Caime, AOL* ii. 222; the lord of Sidon (probably Julian) held two villages; Jean Dasce held one village and city real estate; Bartholomew Caime (d. 1266) held two villages. His tombstone was discovered by H. Prutz (he was probably a relative of Jacques Caime). (Raymond?) son of Guido de Scandalion is the only one to have held three villages in the lordship; a son of Gautier Morellus (identical with *magister Morellus, Regesta*, no. 609); Hugh l'Amiral (*Amiratus*) held one village. His wife was the daughter of Zunzulicus Gazellus (to be identified with Gazellus Tyrensis, *Regesta*, nos. 579, 684, 693, 702, see below, p. 153 n. 32); Lord d'Engarrand: a village bearing this name is printed on the map published in *PPTS* xiii, south-east of Rasal-Naqura, but the village he held in the lordship of Tyre was to the north of Femon, that is to say, to the east of Tyre.

Thus, the distribution of landed property can be summed up as follows.

The king: 36 per cent—10 villages and two-thirds in 49.
Venice: 31 per cent—21 villages and one-third in 51.
Other communes: 5 per cent—6 villages.
Orders and clergy: 13 per cent—15 villages.
Individual lords: 12 per cent—14 villages.
Total: 97 per cent—115 villages (for a total of *c.* 120 villages).

From these data we can draw several general conclusions: The remarkable feature of the lordship is the insignificant number of possessions belonging to clergy and the Military Orders. Our data show that the generally held view about the encroachment or the preponderance of ecclesiastical possessions, as compared with lay possessions, cannot be accepted for the whole of the kingdom.

The importance of landed property should be re-examined by a comparison with other data.[30] Let us begin with military services due from the clergy. According to the list preserved by John of Ibelin, the Archbishop of Tyre owed the service of 150 sergeants to the Crown, whereas the burgesses of the city owed him 100 sergeants. Clearly there is little relation between the landed property of the archbishop and his military obligations. This disproportion between the large quota of sergeants owed by the Archbishop and the exiguity of his landed property poses a question for which we can perhaps find a solution by discussing another problem.

Looking at the list of services preserved by John of Ibelin, we find that the lordship of Tyre owed the Crown the service of twenty-eight knights. This, it seems, was the situation *c.* 1180–7.[31] Thirteen lords were obliged

---

[30] G. Bayer's studies on the lordship of Caesarea, *ZDPV* 59 (1939), and on the other lordships of the kingdom: 'Neapolis und sein Gebiet', *ZDPV* 63 (1940), 155–209; 'Die Kreuzfahrergebiete von Jerusalem und S. Abraham', *ZDPV* 65 (1942), 165–211; 'Die Kreuzfahrergebiete Akko und Galilaea', *ZDPV* 67 (1944/5), 183–260, greatly facilitate monographs on the Latin Kingdom. His conclusions seem, with very few exceptions, to be definitive. Comparing the lordship of Tyre with that of Nablus, we find in the latter the following: the king: 25 per cent; knights: 41 per cent; clergy: 24 per cent; Military Orders: 10 per cent. Unfortunately these data refer to about seventy villages, whereas in reality there were about 300.

[31] John of Ibelin, ch. 271. A similar list (which does not differ except for some details from that of John of Ibelin, leaving out the names of possessors of fiefs) is given by Marino Sanuto, *Liber Secretorum Fidelium Crucis* iii. 7, ch. 50, in Bongars, *Gesta Dei per Francos* ii (Hanover, 1611), and cf. *Gestes des Chiprois,* §§ 520–1. La Monte, *Feudal Monarchy*, p. 139 n. 3, assigned the list to the time of King Baldwin IV or Baldwin V and more exactly to the years 1182–91, ibid., p. 148 and see above, p. 31 n. 43; cf. J. Richard, 'Les listes de fiefs de Jean d'Ibelin. Recherches sur l'Assebèbe et Mimars', *RHDFE* 32 (1954), 565–77.

to render military service. Only one of them owed the service of seven knights, others owed two or three knights. But almost half of the Frankish nobles owed no more than their own service.

We know some of these lords. Besides the Venetians, who owed the service of three knights, we find one Girart Gazel—two knights;[32] the widow of William le Grant—two knights;[33] and Fulk of Falaise—two knights.[34] It is remarkable that the possession of land in the lordship can be proved only for the Gazel family. True, there is a gap of two generations between the time of the composition of the list of military services and the inventory drawn up by Marsiglio Zorzi but he mentions the ancient possessors of fiefs in the lordship also. On the other hand, according to John of Ibelin, of the thirteen lords who owed military service, none, excluding Gazel, held any land in the kingdom, as far as we know. It seems inadmissible to see this as pure coincidence or due to insufficient documentation. There is also the question of the large contingent of the sergeants' services owed by the Archbishop of Tyre as compared with the smallness of his feudal possessions. We think that there is a link between these two phenomena. We suggest that the military services owed by the lordship had little relation to the possession of ordinary fiefs, if by fiefs we mean landed property. The lords who owed military service in their overwhelming majority did not hold landed property as fiefs proper, but as what was known as 'besant fiefs'.[35] The crux of the problem was the smallness of the lordship and its particular economic structures. To put the question in better relief let us compare our lordship with that of the lordship of Caesarea. In the latter,[36] a territory of around 1,200 sq. km, the lordship owed the service of twenty-five knights to the Crown; the average was then, one knight per 50 sq. km. Keeping the same proportions, the lordship of Tyre, with its 450 sq. km, should have owed the service of

---

[32] Gazellus Tyrensis signed various charters between 1189 and 1191 (*Regesta*, nos. 684, 693, 702); cf. above, p. 151 n. 29.

[33] To be identified with Wilhelmus Magnus who signed charters in 1158 and 1186 (*ROL* ix. 181; *Regesta*, no. 656).

[34] He held a house in Tyre near the bath of the Genoese in 1190 (*Regesta*, no. 691); he signed a charter of Baldwin IV in 1181 (*Regesta*, no. 608).

[35] The question of money-fiefs in the Latin Kingdom was dealt with rather superficially by G. Dodu, *Histoire des institutions monarchiques dans le royaume latin de Jérusalem* (Paris, 1894), pp. 192 ff.; La Monte, *Feudal Monarchy*, pp. 143 ff.; H. Prutz, *Kulturgeschichte der Kreuzzüge* (Berlin, 1883), pp. 182 ff. We still need a study paralleling those of M. Szczaniecki (*Essai sur les fiefs-rentes*, 1946) for France, and B. D. Lyon ('The Money Fief, under the English kings', *English Historical Review*, 1951) for England. The importance of this type of fief was seen by H. Prutz; cf. Riley–Smith, *Feudal Nobility*, see index, s.v. 'fiefs'.

[36] G. Beyer, *ZDPV* 59 (1939), 15.

nine instead of the twenty-eight knights it actually owed the Crown. Though our knowledge of the lordship Caesarea is not as detailed as that of Tyre, we have an impression of a relatively well-settled territory, as it comprises no less than 100 villages—almost the same number as the lordship of Tyre. The only peculiarity, which could have made the difference between the two lordships, was the existence of an opulent city as the capital of the lordship of Tyre.

Because of the revenues from the port and the income from the markets, taxes, and customs and royal monopolies, the king could command the service of knights by distributing fiefs in money or in income instead of giving away land property. It was the riches of the capital city that made possible the creation of a large number of 'besant fiefs', from which he could claim military service. If the average 'besant fief ', assuring the service of one knight, is evaluated at *c.* 400–500 besants per annum,[37] then 12,000 besants was sufficient to assure the service of twenty-four knights (in addition to the three Venetian ones) for the defence of the kingdom.[38]

Here we touch upon one of the most characteristic features of the Crusader feudal system—the use of money instead of land to create the scaffolding of feudo-vassalic relations. One example will suffice to illustrate the situation, the small lordship of Arsuf on the coast between Caesarea and Jaffa. It belonged to the famous Ibelins. The military service of the lordship is hardly mentioned in the inventories of John of Ibelin or Marino Sanuto. John of Ibelin lists the service of the burgesses of Arsuf, which amounted to fifty sergeants.

It is obvious however, that the lords of the city had a number of knightly vassals as well as administrative officers. Balian of Ibelin, selling his lordship in 1261 to the Order of St. John, stipulated the rights of his vassals and of his sergeants as well as their possessions with the Order. According to the deed of sale, Balian had six knights and twenty-one sergeants in the lordship; their fiefs and their services are described in detail. Each knight owed the service of four *chevaucheures* besides his own

---

[37] La Monte, *Feudal Monarchy*, p. 150.

[38] The urban revenues from the Venetian third of Tyre were *c.* 4,200 besants according to Marsiglio Zorzi's inventory, but actually they were higher. The revenue from the port (*catena*), theoretically one-third of its income, is indicated as 480 besants; this must be a misprint or a misreading, seeing that a simple *fondicum* brought in 500 besants annually (Tafel–Thomas ii. 384–5). When, after the death of John of Montfort in 1283, King Hugh III of Cyprus gave Tyre to Humphrey of Beirut, he reserved to himself the right to buy back the lordship for 150,000 besants. *Gestes des Chiprois*, § 421 and cf. G. Hill, *A History of Cyprus*, ii (Cambridge, 1948), 177.

personal service. The services of the sergeants are partly military but there are also administrative offices—*escrivanage* and *durgemanage*. It seems that even the vicomte, the butler, and the chaplain held sergeantry fiefs. The list of fiefs shows that in all probability there is only one that actually consisted of landed property. All the others are besant fiefs, which come near to comprising simple salaries. The 'fiefs' are composed of a given amount of money and a quantity of agricultural products. The annual amount of money and agricultural products spent by the lord of Arsur for the maintenance of his household and his administration was as follows: 2,448 besants (for knights: 1,500 besants), 137 *modii* of wheat (knights: 100 *modii*), 145 *modii* of oats (knights: 120 *modii*), 22 *modii* of vegetables (knights: 16 *modii*), 127 litres of oil (knights: 100 litres), in addition to rations for the beasts and the *restor* obligation.[39]

We have portrayed the administrative organization of a Crusader lordship almost entirely based on payments in money and agricultural products. The document cited above was written in 1261 and is therefore contemporary with the stabilization of Mameluke rule in Egypt. The similarity between the Crusader fiefs we have analysed and a type of Mameluke fiefs composed of an amount of money (*jāmakīya*) and a quantity of wheat (*ghillat al-anbār*) is very curious. Is it pure coincidence? It is not in our competence to answer this question. Perhaps specialists of the Mameluke period will provide a solution.

Comparing Tyre with Caesarea we have tried to prove that it was the relative position of the great urban centre that made for the basic difference between the two lordships. Perhaps an even more general conclusion transcending the two lordships can be drawn. In Syria and in Palestine during the twelfth and thirteenth centuries the military potential of any given area cannot be based, as it can for Europe in the early Middle Ages, on the value of land alone.[40] The decisive factor here, which influences the military structure and the general organization of the kingdom, is the urban monetary economy. A comparison of the medieval lordship and its great urban centre, with the modern district and city of Sour (see below), will lead to similar conclusions.

---

[39] Delaville, no. 2985 (iii. 6–7). It is not beside the point to note that this lordship was sold for an annual rent of 4,000 besants (*Regesta*, no. 1313).

[40] The evaluation of the military potential of the Carolingian Empire was thus established by F. Lot, *L'Art militaire et les armées au moyen âge*, i. 91 ff. As already mentioned, this method, even if acceptable for Europe, cannot be applied to the Latin Kingdom because of its particular economic structure.

We should also note, among the peculiarities of the Crusader Kingdom the rarity of subinfeudation below the third and second degrees, that is to say, the king and the great lords, his tenants-in-chief. The scarcity of the land in general, the smallness and barrenness in particular, and the possibilities of enfeoffment of monetary revenues instead of land, seem to explain this phenomenon. The great tenants-in-chief were the lords of major urban centres and consequently they were the only ones who had the power to enfeoff and to create a clientele. If our conclusions are correct, the kingdom had a particular feudal and social structure. With few exceptions the feudal hierarchy was made up of the great tenants-in-chief and their immediate vassals only. The latter included a large class of people of different social positions, but all of them at the same level in the feudal hierarchy. Since the rents were regarded as fiefs, even the legislation of the kingdom (*Assise sur la ligece*) has to be interpreted in this light. All contributed to a general levelling of that large class composed of knights, soldiers, and *ministeriales*—all of them vassals or linked by quasi-vassalic bonds to the lord. This, no doubt, had repercussions on their mentality and behaviour.[41]

The Village and its Territory

The villages in the lordship of Tyre were not grouped in any larger distinct administrative units. Each village constituted an autonomous cell. The sole centre of administration, and indeed the concentration point of all the landlords, was the city of Tyre. One of the reasons is obviously the fact that only 20 or 30 kilometres separated any village in the lordship from the capital. Consequently, the landlords had no difficulty in transporting their share of the agricultural products, without any intermediary centres, to the capital.

The village territory was composed economically of different parts, which were differently taxed. The nucleus was the *casale*, that is the village, a small area in which we find the peasants' dwellings.[42] The number of houses varies but, it seems, we never find isolated farms.

[41] See above, Ch. 2.

[42] It seems that the Crusaders sometimes distinguished the *casale* (in a French charter of 1243: *le chasel*, Delaville, no. 2296, ii. 603) from its acreage; cf. 'In casali Huberti de Pazi [i.e. in the Biblical Akhzib, north of Acre] Letardus vicecomes dedit quatuor carrucatas terre et olivetum et infra casale unam domum et extra ortum unum' (Delaborde, no. 18, p. 46). At the end of the twelfth century the noun *villa* begins to be applied to a city. This explains the comment of the French continuation of William of Tyre: 'les villes champestres que l'en apele casiaus', ed. P. Paris, ii. 451 (xxii, ch. 22). The noun *villa* does not appear in the Latin original.

The arable of the village was measured in *carrucae* or *charrués* considered as economic units, but basically they were administrative and fiscal ones. The *carruca, carruga,* or *charrué* is the technical term most frequently used in Palestine as a land measure. Another measure, less frequently used, is the *aratrum,*[43] which similarly denotes an area which can be laboured by one team or plough during a year.

In addition to these measures, which in a sense are ideal or abstract measures, the Crusaders used a real measure of local or Arab origin. It can be clearly deduced from a phrase of strange construction and written in a somewhat barbarous Latin: 'Que pecia terre potest laborari et est sufficiens duobus paribus bouum in Sarraceno dictam peciam duarum carucarum per unam diem,'[44] that is, an area worked during one day by two teams, each composed of a pair of oxen. The unit is therefore a stretch of land worked by one team of oxen in one day. This, as our text indicates, is the local Arab *carruca.* We know its European equivalent well—it is the *journée* or the *journal.* In fact we also find in the Latin Kingdom the name *jornatae* as distinct from the *carruca.*[45] The question is, to what kind of actual local measures do our documents refer? We do not hesitate to identify it with the Arab *faddān* of Palestine and Syria which is precisely defined in the same way.[46]

Among measures employed by the Crusaders we also find the *carrucata graeca,*[47] which seems to be the Greek equivalent of the *faddān,* a name which will survive the Crusaders and Mameluks and reappear under the Ottomans as *faddān rūmī,*[48] the Byzantine *faddān.*[49] Other measures were

---

[43] Delaborde, no. 4, p. 27: 'duo aratra terre'; ibid., no. 8, p. 34: 'terra duobus aratris sufficiens'; ibid., no. 6, p. 30 and Kohler, no. 4, p. 8: 'terra unius aratri'.

[44] Tafel–Thomas ii. 380: 'et est tanta terra, que per unam diem potest laborari a duobus paribus bouum'; 'potest laborari per unam diem per unum par bouum'; ibid. ii. 369: 'pecia terre que laboratur in die una paribus bouum tribus'; ibid. ii. 381: 'potest laborari a duobus paribus bouum per unam diem.' We do not believe that teams of two or three pairs of oxen were actually used. The text refers to an acreage worked by two or three teams, each using one pair of oxen. The basic unit is an acreage worked by a pair of oxen during one day.

[45] Two villages were sold 'cum duabus carrucatis et quinque iornatas terrae', Rozière, no. 64, p. 131. We do not find the European distinction between *carruca* and *carrucata* in the Crusader sources. Cf. R. Grand and R. Delatouche, *L'Agriculture au moyen âge* (Paris, 1950), p. 79.

[46] G. Dalman, *Arbeit und Sitte in Palästina,* ii. 47: 'Der faddān ist das Land bei den Bauern das das Joch (Ochsen) an einem Tage pflügt.'

[47] *Regesta,* no. 971.

[48] See C. Cahen, 'Aperçu' (next note), p. 295 n. 3.

[49] Cf. C. Cahen, 'Aperçu sur les impôts du sol en Syrie au moyen âge', *Journal of the Economic and Social History of the Orient,* 18 (1976), 239. In fact the *carrucata graeca* could be

(continued)

the *caballaria* and the *paraillée* or *pariliata*.[50] The *paraillée*, of Provençal origin, also found in Catalonia, was peculiar to the country of Tripoli, ruled by a Provençal dynasty. Its juxtaposition in one of our texts with *iugerum* leads us to think that it describes a local measure rather more like the *journal* than the *carruca*. Finally, arable was measured as it is still in the country, by the quantity of grain used to sow a given surface.[51]

Let us now try to evaluate the different measures. Fortunately, we possess a *glossa* appended to a document of 1195, which furnishes the following definition: 'Chascun charue dot havoir xxiiii cordes du longe et xvi du large, et la corde dot havoir xviii toise du home mezaine, et insi le tout [probably corr. *on le tient*] en la Secrète du reame de Ierusalem par l'asise du reame duvant dit.'[52] E. Rey has empirically evaluated this measure as 31·25 ha,[53] but even if we use the Roman foot and count 6 feet to one *toise*,[54] we arrive at 39 ha.

This official *carruca* (we evaluate it at an average of 35 ha) is basically a unit of taxation. This explains why it (or rather its component measures) was preserved in the *Secrète*, the Exchequer of the kingdom. The *carruca*, as a concept, corresponds to the European *mansus*: an ideal unit of tenure belonging to a family. In fact, Marsiglio Zorzi describes a given area in his

---

regarded as an official Byzantine measure. But it seems to us more plausible that it refers to a local measure paralleling the *carruca in saraceno dicta*, which is the Syrian *journée*. Still it is not impossible that this is actually the Greek *zeugaria*.

[50] The *pariliatae* indicated by J. Richard, 'Le chartier de Sainte-Marie Latine et l'établissement de Raymond de Saint Gilles au Mont Pèlerin', *Mélanges L. Halphen*, p. 612. The texts are not precise enough to determine if *caballaria* was actually a measure. It is possible that it is a kind of fief, like the *pheon kavalleriou henos* in Norman Sicily, see H. Mitteis, *Der Staat des hohen Mittelalters*[2] (Weimar, 1948), p. 280 n. 4. In addition there are *carrucae liberae*, which perhaps correspond to *charrués françoises*, which are 'mesurées à la mesure selon l'usage dou reaiume de Jerusalem' (Strehlke, no. 120, p. 110).

[51] For the period of the Mishna and Talmud, i.e. the Roman and Byzantine period, see S. Krauss, *Talmudische Archäologie*, ii (Leipzig, 1911), 175; G. Dalman, 'Pflügelänge, Saatstreifen und Ernteretiefen in Bibel und Mishna', *ZDPV* 28 (1905), 37; idem, *Arbeit und Sitte*, p. 48. Tafel–Thomas ii. 369: 'Est [pecia terre] adeo magna que pro semine vult modia regalia XXVI'. Cf. C. Cahen, 'Le régime rural', p. 295: 4 *ghirara* used for 1 *carruca*. A measure we have found only once is the *modiata*; the Order of St. John received: 'duas modiatas de terra laborativa et duas modiatas de vineis' (Delaville, no. 7).

[52] Strehlke, no. 31, p. 27.

[53] E. Rey, *Les Colonies franques*, pp. 242–3.

[54] For the twelfth century the French *carruca* of Chartres has been estimated at 42·8 ha (*Cartulaire de l'abbaye de Saint Père de Chartres*, ed. B. Guérard (Paris, 1840), Prologomènes, p. 169). The French *pied* was longer than the Roman *pes*. But even using the Roman foot of 0·295 m, the *toise* of 6 feet was 1·77 m; the *corde*: 1·77 × 18 = 31·85 m; the *carruca* thus (764·6 m × 509·7 m): 389·717 m², that is almost 39 ha. Cf. P. Guilhiermoz, 'De l'équivalence des anciennes mesures', *Bibl. de l'École des Chartes*, 74 (1913), 267 ff.

inventory as follows: 'Dicta [terra] est caruge, quem nos apellamus Masos, infra viii.'[55]

It is more difficult to evaluate the local *carruca*, which we identify with the *journal* or the Arab *faddàn*. As a local unit, the *faddàn*, even today, does not have the same value everywhere. In mountainous regions like Jerusalem, for example, it is evaluated at 734 square metres; but, in the valleys and plains it is almost twice as large.[56] For the lordship of Tyre, as we do not have any detailed data, we can evaluate it only approximately. In three areas planted with olives, each evaluated at two local *carrucae*— one has forty olive trees, another twenty-five, and the third forty again. Olive trees need a given amount of space for their growth and in the first case mentioned above the olive trees were newly planted, which implies that such needs were calculated. At the beginning of our century it was usual to plant ten trees on a *dunam* of land[57] (a *dunam* corresponded to slightly less than 0·1 ha). Consequently one needed four *dunams* for forty trees,[58] or about 0·37 ha.[59] This Arab *carruca*, which, to prevent any confusion, we shall call *faddàn*, differs from the official *carruca* not only in surface measure but probably also in its technical use. In all three cases in which the *faddàn* was used, special cultivation was involved; as far as we have been able to ascertain, it was never used for simple arable. The same is true for the *paraillée* which, like the *faddàn*, is a measure of specially cultivated land in the vicinity of Tripoli. On the other hand, the official *carruca* is used for arable only.

Let us now try to evaluate the size of the arable belonging to the villages. The areas mentioned in our documents show a great variety: 6, 12, 14, 20, and 30 *carrucae*[60] respectively: that is to say, approximately

[55] Tafel–Thomas ii. 368. The term *mansus* appears only once more in Delaville, no. 7. The charter under consideration has many peculiarities from the point of view of Crusader diplomacy.

[56] Dalman, *Arbeit und Sitte*, ii. 48. As the *faddàn* represents the area ploughed during one day it is obviously smaller in rough mountain soil than in the plain.

[57] A. Rupin, *Syrien als Wirtschaftsgebiet* (Berlin, 1917), p. 45.

[58] This is a hypothetical evaluation. If we suppose that in the thirteenth century more olive trees were planted to a *dunam*, we shall have to reduce our evaluation.

[59] P. Guérard evaluated the Carolingian *jornalis* at 34·13 *ares*, i.e. approximately the same area we propose for the local *carruca* of Tyre. Cf. *Polyptique de l'abbaye de Saint-Germain des Prés*, ed. A. Longnon (Paris, 1895), pp. 22–3. Grand and Delatouche, op. cit., evaluate it at one-half or one-third of a ha.

[60] We follow the order of the Venetian inventory: Homeire, Tafel–Thomas, p. 374; Mahallie, p. 327; Hanosie, Tollifit, p. 378. In the last case the Venetians possessed four *carrucae* which corresponded to one-third of the arable. Supposing that there was no difference in the quality of soil, the total acreage was of 12 *carrucae*. The same is true for Betheron, pp. 383–4,

(continued)

from 190 ha to 1120 ha. These data do not represent the total amount of land belonging to a village: lands with specially cultivated crops were excluded. This was done because the taxation of particular cultivated land was not calculated in relation to the area but in relation to the amount of products or to the number of trees; secondly, the cultivated land did not belong to the household's *mansus*. If the *carruca* is a hereditary tenure, the cultivated lands are part of the demesne land and farmed out for a given price or worked on the basis of a division of crops (*champart* or *complant*). Three types of cultivation belong to this special category: olives, vineyards, and sugar-canes. Perhaps we should also add the *zardini*, which included orchards, vegetable gardens, and gardens in which plants peculiar to the region were grown—for example tinctorial plants.

Sugar plantations are never mentioned as being part of the territory of a village. In fact they demanded special conditions of irrigation, which could be found only near the ancient aqueduct of Ras al-'Ain (some 5 km to the south of Tyre and 800 m from the coast).[61] Similarly, we find plantations of olives and vineyards *in sabulo*. The area of special plantations in the lordship can be quite well defined. In the west, along the seashore, was one of the most important plantations of sugar-cane, which belonged partly to the Venetians and partly to the king.[62] Its surface was of 8 local *carrucae* or 3½ ha limited on the east by the famous aqueduct. If we assume that it began some 200–300 m from the coastline, that is to say just beyond the line of dunes and sand, we can imagine the plantation extending to the north in a narrow band of land almost 1 km long. But plantations of sugar-cane were also found more to the north, almost up to the gates of the city.

Vineyards are found in the immediate vicinity of the city, where they were being worked on the basis of *complant*,[63] but they were also dispersed in some villages. We shall not enter into detail about the 'gardens' of the city. They belonged to different proprietors and were very small. Although their general economic importance was probably not very high, they may have played an important role in the consumer market of the city.

Besides arable and special cultures, we find another type of land in our

---

Soafin, p. 378, Theiretenne, p. 373, and probably also Femon, if we use the same method of calculation as for Tollifit.

[61] All *Itineraria* describe the famous place, which was identified with the *puteus aquarum viventium* of the Song of Songs 4: 4.

[62] Tafel–Thomas ii. 368.

[63] Kohler, no. 78, p. 79.

villages which is described as *gastina*. The name was derived from the Latin *vastus*, ancient French *guaste*, Germanic *waste*. Consequently scholars were inclined to see in it deserted lands, corresponding to the Arab *khirbet*, which has such an eminent place in the toponomy of Palestine and Syria.

Beugnot gave the word its etymological meaning of 'desert' and remarks that sometimes it also describes non-built-up city areas.[64] H. Prutz and G. Beyer defined it almost in the same terms as Beugnot.[65] The word was restricted to its specific Palestinian and Syrian meaning by R. Röhricht who considered the *gastina* as equivalent to *khirbet*.[66] More recently C. Cahen has given a wider definition: 'sometimes abandoned land more often places which, as one text explicitly states, were once villages and consequently corresponding, as was already remarked by Röhricht, to the innumerable modern places called *khirbet*, that is ruin, where naturally some houses may exist, but which differ from the *casale* which is the centre of life and administration.'[67] The large number of these places does not denote the desolation of the country, 'their abundance signifies less agriculture regression as the small and frequent replacement necessitated by primitive (agricultural) technique inside the same territory.' Leaving the explanation given by Conder, which for no known reason compares *gastina* with the *carrucata* of Domesday Book as a 'unit of a village or of an estate which equals 80 acres',[68] let us also mention the definition of E. Rey whereby the village area was divided into *carrucae* and *gastinae*, on whose number the taxation and revenue of the lord was based.[69]

All these definitions, which actually do not differ very much from each other, are no doubt correct. It is possible that here and there lands were temporarily occupied and later abandoned. Certainly these are uninhabited sites.[70] Frequent small displacements at that level of agriculture cannot be doubted.[71] Yet all these definitions, mainly based on the etymological

---

[64] *Lois* ii in the glossary, s.v. *gastine*.
[65] G. Beyer in *ZDPV* 54 (1939), 18; H. Prutz, *Kulturgeschichte*, p. 330.
[66] *Regesta*, glossary, s.v. *gastina*.
[67] C. Cahen, 'Lé régime rural', p. 294.
[68] 'The city of Jerusalem', translated by R. R. Conder in *PPTS* iv. 58.
[69] *Colonies franques*, p. 241.
[70] E. Rey, *Recherches géographiques et historiques sur la domination des latins en Orient* (Paris, 1877), pp. 38–40: 'IV gastinae non habitatae'.
[71] Explicitly proved by John of Ibelin, ch. 247, and Philip of Novara, ch. 62. A committee visiting a given area to decide on its boundaries, has to 'regarder la tenure des deux parties et enquere des leus habités qui les parties tienent, qués il furent ancienement et que il soleient tenir, et sil sont translaté et remué d'une place en autre' etc.

meaning of the expression, are insufficient to evaluate the term as it is employed in the documentation of Frankish Syria.

In principle the *gastina* was a part of the village, of the *casale*. Sometimes it carried a special name, such as that of a man or of a characteristic feature, or again (we know at least one case) the name derived from the Arab root *khirbet*,[72] but it seems that more often the *gastina* was indicated by its belonging to a *casale*. The boundaries of the *gastina* were inside the boundaries of the *casale*[73] and the *gastina* appeared as an appurtenance and appendage of the village. The decisive question is: what were its functions? To us this seems to be the decisive point. Basically, we find two types of *gastinae*: (a) those detached from *casalia* and their number relatively small; (b) those that preserved their original status. The former, once detached from the *casale*, became simply arable lands. Henceforth they are measured for fiscal purposes in *carrucae*, the official *carrucae*, as much as all the rest of the arable of the *casale*. Sometimes they are even, as much as the *casale*, autonomous administrative unit.[74] Sometimes, despite the change in their legal status and their economic functions, they preserved their former name of *gastina*.

The *gastinae* of the second category, *gastinae* properly speaking, are uncultivated and seldom inhabited areas. Yet they fill an important economic function in the life of the village, that of meadows and pasture. We recall what was once said by F. W. Maitland: 'Arable implies pasture. This is not a legal theory: it is a physical fact. A householder can not have arable land unless he has pasture rights.'[75] We look in vain in the very detailed inventory of Marsiglio Zorzi for pasture. Consequently, how did the beasts of the village live? We do not find any mention of meadows in his inventory. Moreover, meadows, properly speaking, were almost unknown in the Orient before modern times.[76] It is in this context that

[72] Delaville, *Archives*, no. 87, p. 193: one *gastina* is called Karbet el-Ezairac.

[73] Tafel–Thomas ii. 371: 'Casale Batiole cum suis gastinis et pertinencijs omnibus; de quibus gastinis que dicto casali pertinent, una vocatur Mensara, que est in montana versus orientem; quae uuastina et casale firmat in summitate montane.' Ibid.: 'Firmat versus austrum [casale Gaifitha] in una guastina que nominatur Mensore et est casalis Batiole.'

[74] e.g. Delaville, *Archives*, no. 32, p. 117: 'Dono eciam eidem Hospitali gastinam de Meois cum suis pertinentiis omnibus'. Ibid., no. 28, p. 111: 'Hec collis est de pertinentia Gastine Putei [near Antioch].'

[75] *Domesday Book and Beyond* (Cambridge, 1921), p. 388.

[76] We shall find them in the Mameluke royal lands in Iraq and Egypt, where they were used for breeding the horses of the Sultan and his emirs. We are obliged to our colleague D. Ayalon for this information. We find limited areas of this nature near Margat and Tripoli, but they are certainly exceptions (Delaville, nos. 457–8; i. 313 and 315).

we have to envisage the major role of the *gastina*. It perfectly corresponded to the European waste and commons, defined as 'uncultivated and waste lands where the animals found their nutrition.'[77] They were of particular importance in our region where no forest could have served as pasture. Because the *gastinae* are pastures, there is nothing extraordinary in the fact that neighbouring villages can have, and use, common *gastinae*.[78] It is not extraordinary to find traces of habitation and even temporary cultivation of plants or vegetables in the *gastinae*, as witnessed by the recorded toponymy.[79] The particular function of *gastinae* as pasture can also be deduced from the fact that in the enumeration of appurtenances of *casalia* we find either *pascua* or *gastinae*. It is exceptional to find both together.[80] For the clerks of the Crusader chanceries *gastinae* and *pascua* were synonomous. In a document unfortunately preserved in register form only, we read: 'Vente faite... d'une gastine ou paturage nommé Daudenit'.[81] No doubt the writer of the register read: *gastina vel pascuum* in the original.

What was the legal status assigned to this village appurtenance? In our opinion the *gastinae*, as much as their European counterpart, were commons. This does not mean that a legal theory assigned collective possession to the peasants over their pastures. It simply implied the right to use pasture collectively; a right reserved to the possessors of arable in

---

[77] R. Grand and R. Delatouche, op. cit., pp. 298 ff.

[78] Delaborde, nos. 15 and 32.

[79] So the *gastinae* of the village Maharone are called: Mezarha—*mazra'a*, i.e. sown land; Mezara de zote—an olive grove; Bisilie—*bazilia*, peas (Tafel–Thomas ii. 371).

[80] We have found it once only (Delaville ii. 673), but may have missed some others.

[81] Delaville, no. 1473; ii. 190. An apparently different view is taken by my friend Riley-Smith, *Feudal Nobility*, pp. 43–4 and 250 ff. He does in fact agree to all these uses of *gastinae*, but insists: 'we can first of all establish that they were not usually the pasture lands which lay round many villages'. The charters in Strehlke, nos. 117–20, use a standard legal formula including every imaginable type of land, and can hardly give proof one way or the other. In some cases in which the *gastina* is resettled and laboured it will obviously have its own pasture land—e.g. in the donation of the village of 'Araba by Isabella of Bethsan, sold to the Teutonic Order with its three *gastinae* 'cum omnibus terris laboratis et non laboratis, montibus, vallibus, planis, nemoribus, aquis et pascuis predicti casalis et gastinarum ipsarum' etc. (Strehlke, no. 77, p. 62); no. 78, p. 62, is a confirmation of the above and uses the same formulas. It is significant that some of the *gastinae* bear names of tribes or *hamulas* as is still the custom in the country, usually signifying their grazing grounds: e.g. in the donation of Julian of Sidon in the mountainous al-Shuf area, 'une autre gastine, qui est en la devise de Maassar Beni Elhon [near the 'casau Massar Beni Elhon']... le casau Deir Eleamar et ses gastines, la gastine Beni Belmene et la gastine de Beni Nemre'. The same charter also mentions the *gastinae* of Beni Eleczem, Beni Rages, Beni Ougih. Strehlke, no. 117, p. 103. And see above, nn. 64 and 72.

the village only.[82] The situation could not have been very different from that existing in contemporary Europe. No doubt a *dominium eminens* was claimed by the lords of the village. In fact we see the kings and the Venetians dividing *gastinae* which belonged to a *casale* between them, in their co-property (in the usual proportions of two-thirds for the king and one-third for the Venetians).[83] As the *gastina* was free from direct taxation it cannot mean anything else than a legal recognition or proclamation of sovereignty. But below this *dominium eminens* it was the peasants who enjoyed the right of pasture. This right of use, if not the right of possession, is not legally divided either by tenants and lords, or by tenants themselves. The same is, generally speaking, also true for thirteenth-century Europe, where we would look in vain for a legal theory, defining the legal status of pasture as commons. It is only later when litigations come to courts, that problems of rights to property will emerge.

To sum up: the *gastina* was pasture and as such an integral part of the village. Without meadows and pasture it would be impossible to imagine an agriculture community leading a normal life. It is the community of the village as such that has the right of use of the untilled land. No document indicates whether the right to pasture was limited by the quantity of the arable held by a family. This was probably so but these are questions to which we have not found any definite answer.

It is natural to ask here if commons existed in the Near East. Their existence would corroborate our interpretations of the functions and the status of the *gastina*; because it is far more plausible to see the commons as an institution which antedated the Crusaders and was perpetuated by them after the conquests, than to suppose a Frankish innovation.

In Islamic law the notion of commons is in some way linked to the notion of uncultivated or abandoned land. The law distinguishes two principal types of such lands: commons, *stricto sensu*, include all types of land in public usage, roads, thoroughfares, and threshing floors. These are called *matrūka*, a word which signifies 'abandoned land'.[84] One can also include, in this category, land that is not fit for cultivation and called

---

[82] Cf. L. Verriest, *Institutions médiévales* i. 47.

[83] Tafel–Thomas ii. 376: 'Est aliud casale ... eius feudi, quod vocatur Maharona cum guastinis ... Et de dicto casali habet terciam partem cum dictis vastinis; et due partes sunt regis.'

[84] The noun *tarīka* is defined in Lane's *Lexicon*, s.v. (p. 305) as: 'a meadow the depasturing of which has been neglected, or pasture where people have pastured their beasts, either in the desert or upon a mountain, and of which the beasts have eaten until there remain (only) some relics of wood'. The *matrūka* seems to correspond to the European *Warechaix*.

kharāb (which has the same root as *khirba*) and in some cases forests (*his* or *hirs*).[85] The second category includes uncultivated land, abandoned land, and consequently a land without proprietor. These are called *mauat* or 'dead land', which can be converted into property by a process similar to the European *adprisio*.[86] But land near neighbouring villages (like our *gastina*) cannot become private property, either by being cultivated or by the authorization of any public authority. They have to remain commons, domains of public usage.[87]

That our *gastina* can be classified with one or the other category of Islamic commons is obvious. The Crusaders, in all probability, found the *gastinae* in collective usage and simply sanctioned the situation. There is, however, some difference. In the Muslim state the sovereignty over land which was not enfeoffed remained with the state or with the prince[88] even when it was limited by the rights of usage of the peasants. Where feudal relations intervened, these rights would come into the hands of the new possessors of sovereign rights. We do not know the extent of feudalization in Syria and Palestine on the eve of the Crusades, but we can surmise that the introduction of feudal institutions by the Crusaders meant that such rights automatically became part of the privileges of the lords of the kingdom who became the legal successors of this public sovereignty. This can be proved by a legal text of the thirteenth century. In the juridical treatise of Philip of Novara and a corresponding chapter in the treatise of John of Ibelin[89] there is a question as to the division of land between two lords. Because the original division of property was forgotten or perhaps never put into practice, the question was how to find the

---

[85] Dalman ii. 38.

[86] There are differences among the Muslim schools of law if one needs a formal gift or formal confirmation of the state or ruler for this kind of *adprisio*. The process is called *ḥiya*, i.e. the reclamation (lit. revivication) of dead land. Cf. Abou l'Hassan al-Mauardi, 'Livre des préceptes de gouvernement' (eleventh century) in Worms, *Recherches sur la constitution de la propriété territoriale dans les pays musulmans* (Paris, 1846), p. 184; cf. p. 197.

[87] Ibrahim al-Halabi, *Moultaqà al-Abhour* ('Les confluents des mers'), ch. V, transl. D'Ohson, *Tableau général de l'empire ottoman* iv. 122 ff., repr. by Worms, op. cit., p. 91: 'it is forbidden to cultivate empty lots of land in the immediate neighbourhood of productive lands, seeing that space should be left for the use of herds or a place for collecting the harvest of other proprietors.' Cf. Khalil ibn Ishak, *Précis de jurisprudence musulmane, selon le rite malékite*, transl. M. Perron, v (Paris, 1852), 23. Cf. L. Cardon, *Le Régime de la propriété foncière en Syrie et au Liban* (Paris, 1923), p. 82; H. A. R. Gibb and H. Bowen, *Islamic Society and the West*, i. (Oxford, 1950), 236.

[88] C. Cahen, 'Les liens de dépendance et les société en Europe orientale, à Byzance et en pays musulmans', *Rapports du IXe Congrès international des sciences historiques* (Paris, 1950), pp. 464 ff.

[89] Philip of Novara, ch. 62, *Lois* i. 533, and John of Ibelin, ch. 247, *Lois* i. 395.

boundaries of the property. 'Mais tout avant', writes Philip of Novara, 'deivent estre les devisors certefiés que les parties marchissent ensemble; car s'il y a leu gaste, ou terre que l'on apele *vaselico*, qui est dou seignor, la doit sauver au seignor tout premier.' John of Ibelin repeats the phrase, but changes the end of phrase. 'Car', he says, 'ce il y a leuc gasté que l'on appelle *chemin reau* qui est dou seignor l'on le deit sauver au seignor tot premierement.' Beugnot interpreted this paragraph in the following way: 'we think that to have the right version one has to compare both texts and to read: "leuc gaste (terre inculte), chemin reau ou terre que l'on appelle *vaselico*, qui est dou seignor".' Understandably, he thought that the three types of land defined boundaries by themselves.[90] Yet this interpretation is doubtful. It was not a question of fixing the boundaries of the properties but of safeguarding the rights of the lord because all uncultivated land was his property or in his sovereignty. In fact, the two jurists point to the source from which the Crusaders drew this notion. They describe a situation which certainly antedates the Crusaders' arrival. 'Chemin reau... qui est dou seignor' is a significant juxtaposition. The notion of a 'royal road' was not a creation of Crusader feudalism and could have been a legacy of the Muslim, if not of an earlier period. However, comparing Philip of Novara with John of Ibelin we arrive at another conclusion. Beugnot assumed three different types of land, but actually Philip of Novara and John of Ibelin mention two types only: places that are *gastes* and another type which is called by John of Ibelin 'royal road' and by Philip of Novara *vaselico*. The expressions must be synonymous and we suggest that *vaselico*, is no other than the Greek *basilikos* or rather *basilike ge*, that is Crown land, exactly translated into French as *chemin reau*. Consequently we are dealing here with a Byzantine concept which survived Arab domination because it was acceptable and easily adopted by the Muslim tradition. It could be suggested that *vaselico* specially refers to Cyprus, where Byzantine traditions were of more recent origins. This is quite possible, but the expression *chemin reau* is also used by the author of the *Livre des Assises des Bourgeois*[91] which was composed in Acre and refers to the Crusader kingdom only and does not refer to the island of the Lusignans.

This then is the picture of the villages in the lordship of Tyre: always very small, the *casale*, the inhabited area, surrounded by cultivated fields,

[90] *Lois* i. 533.
[91] Ch. 261, *Lois* ii. 197. Note also that Philip of Novara calls public places such as streets and markets 'chambre dou roi', ch. 77 (*Lois* i. 549).

the arable. The olive groves, the vineyards, the gardens and orchards were planted wherever the soil permitted. Only a small part of the cultivated area was demesne land: the olives, vineyards, and the plantations of sugar-cane. The latter were nowhere a part of the village *tenurae*. On the other hand there was no trace of ordinary arable as belonging to the demesne. This fact in itself suffices to explain the character of commons inherent in the uncultivated areas which like satellites surround the villages—the *gastinae*.

Peasants and their Possessions

The differences in the quantity of land that belonged to the villages corresponded to the differences in the size of their population. The data at our disposal show 3, 5, 8, 18, and 38 families in different villages.[92] These numbers are based on the assumption that the names of the peasants represent heads of families.

How large was a peasant family? There is little information on the subject, but what is available shows a marked difference between the thirteenth century and the modern Arab family with its numerous children. In the village of Hobdelemen[93] there were three children in the family; in Maharona one family had one child; two families two sons each, and another had five children.[94] In Bethoron one family had two children and two other families two children each.[95] Obviously, the peasant families were small, but we have to assume that our documents mention only the youngest children, or perhaps even grown-up children, which, for some reason, had not yet left the parental household. Children who had left the household are not mentioned[96] and consequently we cannot reach any conclusion as to the absolute size of the biological family.[97] What tangible knowledge at our disposal refers to actual households.

---

[92] The data are supplied from the following villages: Homeire, Tafel–Thomas ii. 374; Dairram, p. 375, where we find a father, his three sons, and his brother. We assume that the sons already had families of their own. Soafin, p. 375; Bethoron, pp. 383–4; Theiretenne, p. 373, where in the Venetian third we find twelve families, we assume then thirty-six families for the whole village.

[93] Ibid., p. 375.   [94] Ibid., p. 373.   [95] Ibid., pp. 383–4.

[96] This may perhaps explain the apparent difference between the ancient Arab family and the traditional Arab family of our times. There is however a difficulty—the serfs' right to leave a village. See below, Ch. 7, esp. p 207.

[97] The same problem exists for Europe. For the Carolingian period see M. Bloch, 'Les invasions, occupation du sol et peuplement', *Annales*, 1945, pp. 13–28. Cf. C. Cipolla,

(continued)

It is worth noting that sometimes after the death of their parents children not only remained on the farm but continued to maintain it jointly. Thus we read of a peasant 'and his brother' in a given household.[98] They may have held it jointly, performing duties and services as one administrative unit.

The relation between the family and its land possession is implied in the notion of *carruca*, which, as we saw before, corresponded to the European *mansus*, in theory an amount of land sufficient to nourish a family.

In the village of Bethoron there were 15 *carrucae* belonging to the Archbishop of Tyre. Each family held 1 *carruca*, the only exception being that of the *praepositus*, who held 2 *carrucae*. In the Venetian third of the village 5 *carrucae* were in the hands of three families.[99] In Theireitenne thirty-six families held 30 *carrucae*, that is *c.* 29 ha per family,[100] an evaluation based on the assumption that the division of peasant families between Crown and Venetians corresponded to the division of land: one-third to Venice and two-thirds to the Crown. In the Venetian part of the village Femon, each family held *c.* 57 ha.[101] In Homeire there were 2 *carrucae*, that is *c.* 70 ha, per family.[102] In Soafin *c.* 100 ha per family.[103]

As we see, the amount of land held by a household varied from village to village. Whereas in Theiretenne we can see the ideal proportion of 1 *carruca* per family, in other villages the *carruca* did not remain the family unit. On average a family possessed more than 1 *carruca*. It would be hazardous to draw more conclusions. What we can prove is the theoretical relation between the number of families and the amount of cultivated land in the village.

It is only for the village of Bethoron that we know exactly how much land was actually held by a household. Bethoron is also important from another point of view. When a redistribution of land took place, following the taking over of Venetian possessions by the Archbishop of Tyre, the operation was accomplished on the basis of 1 *carruca* to each family. This demonstrates that the variations we found in the different families are not the result of economic changes or differences in soil quality but in all probability of demographic changes.[104]

J. Dhont, M. Postan, and P. Wolff, 'Anthropologie et démographie', *Rapports du IXe Congrès international des sciences historiques* (Paris, 1950), pp. 56 ff.

[98] Tafel–Thomas ii. 375.   [99] Ibid. ii. 383.   [100] Ibid. ii. 373.

[101] Ibid. ii. 378.   [102] Ibid. ii. 374.   [103] Ibid. ii. 378.

[104] See below, pp. 180–4.

The Agricultural Year

The principal object of cultivation was, and is, the production of cereals, the base of economy and subsistence. Our documentation proves a uniform system of cultivation, common to the whole lordship. The methods of cultivation are described in three different passages in Marsiglio Zorzi's *memorandum*. His terminology is somewhat obscure but its elucidation can give us a picture of the agricultural technique of the period.

In the description of the village of Bathiole, we read: 'Seminantur annuatim inter granum et ordeum nouem modijs et insuper est tanta terra sufficiens que remanet pro sequenti anno seminanda quam appellant garet; in qua seminant in parte legumina iusta modium unum pro qualibet carruca.'[105] In the village of Mahallie: 'Et quelibet caruca seminatur IX modijs inter frumentum et ordeum et postquam seminauerunt, habent tanta terra, quam appellant garet, que efficitur mazaticha pro sequenti anno; in qua seminant legumina iusta modium unum pro qualibet caruca.'[106] And in the village of Theiretenne: 'Et seminatur quelibet carruca IX modijs. Et de terra, que efficitur Mazadica pro alio anno, quod ipsi appellant garet, seminant in parte huius garetti cum legumina quasi modium pro qualibet caruca.'[107]

Rey and Prutz read a triennial crop rotation into these passages [108] and have been followed by other historians. We doubt the correctness of this interpretation and suggest that the alleged triennial crop rotation is the result of Marsiglio Zorzi's clumsy Latin. Starting from the three descriptions above, we suggest the following system of cultivation. The land was divided into two fields. One was destined for winter crops, wheat and barley, the other remained fallow. A portion of the fallow, however, was planted with leguminous plants and the rest remained completely fallow.

Two baffling expressions, *garet* and *mazatica*, are key expressions to the understanding of our text. *Garet* is found in medieval Latin as well as in several Romance dialects. It means: land without vegetation, virginal

---

[105] Tafel–Thomas ii. 371.

[106] Ibid. ii. 372.

[107] Ibid. ii. 373.

[108] E. Rey, *Les Colonies franques*, p. 240: 'L'assolement parait avoir été triennal; la première année la terre était semée en grains, la seconde elle était garet et la troisième mazaticha ou mazadica et cultivée alors en plantes légumineuse.' Only C. Cahen, 'Le régime rural', p. 292, whose study was published at the same time as ours, has interpreted the texts as pointing to a biennial system of rotation.

land, field after harvest, uncultivated land, and finally fallow. Its root is the Latin *vervactum*—fallow.[109] Referring to the above texts we note that although part of the land is described as *garet*, a portion is cultivated and planted with leguminous plants. Marsiglio Zorzi stresses that *garet* is the expression used in the country: it is French (as distinct from Italian). On the other hand *mazadica* (in the third quotation) is an Italian word, the meaning of which is near that of *garet*.

We suggest that *mazaticha* or *mazadica* is the Italian *maggiatica*, which is defined as: 'terreno lasciato a maggese'. The adjective *maggese* has two meanings: (a) agricultural products of the month of May: hay and certain fruits; (b) lands left fallow or tilled in May to be sown during the forthcoming season in November or the next year. In the latter sense Du Cange quotes the Latin form *magisia*[110] from Monte Cassino. *Maggiatica* being fallow is used by Marsiglio Zorzi as synonymous with *garet*. But, as we shall try to prove, the analogy is only partly valid.

Let us now reconstruct the chronology and the system of cultivation following our text but comparing it with methods of cultivation still surviving in the country. The whole economy was based on winter crops. Ploughing began in mid-November, just before the rains. This tillage was called *ḥerat shitani*[111]—'rain tillage'. This was followed, as indicated in the text and in accordance with the actual practice, by a part of the land being sown first with wheat and then with barley. The other half, or rather the other part (as unfortunately we do not know the relation between the

---

[109] Du Cange, s.v. *garricae, garricus, garratum, garachium*, and in his French *Glossarium*, s.v. *garatier, gareg, garrigue*, Godefroy, *Lexique*, s.v. *garet, garete*. Cf. Isidore of Seville, *Etymologiae* (Oxford, 1911 edn.), xvii. 2, 5: 'Vervactum dictum quasi vere actum id est verno aratum', where he seems to mean land worked in the spring after lying fallow during the winter. Du Cange, s.v. *garricus*: 'ager pascuus ab Occitano garric ilex'. Note that in Arabic *jarid* or *jirad* means land without vegetation. Cf. Lane's *Lexicon*, s.v. This word is also to be found in Hebrew in the form of *gríd*, parched field, arid land, unbroken or untilled ground, cf. M. Yastrow, *Dictionary*, s.v.

[110] *Vocab. degl. Acad. della Crusca*[5] (1905), s.vv. *maggiatica, maggiatico, maggese*. N. Tommaseo–B. Bellini, *Dizionario della lingua Italiana*, s.v. *maggese*: 'Campo o terreno, che si lavora nel maggio, e talora anche prima, e si lascia senza seminarlo sino a novembre o all'anno prossimo, per dar riposo alla terra, distruggese le male erbe, etc.' Cf. Du Cange, s.v. *novale* and *magisca*. For France see B. Guérard in his introduction to the *Polyptyque de l'abbaye de Saint-Germain des Prés*, pp. 175–6.

[111] From the many studies dealing with the economy of the fellahin the most important is still the monumental work of G. Dalman, *Arbeit and Sitte in Palästina*, i (Gütersloh, 1928), 261 ff. and 400 ff. The most detailed description is that of A. Rupin, *Syrien als Wirtschaftsgebiet* (Berlin, 1917), pp. 67 ff. Cf. a short summary of J. Eleazari-Volcani, *The Fellah's Farm*, transl. from Hebrew (Tel-Aviv, 1930), and a detailed study by Z. Abramowicz and J. Gelfat, *The Arab Farm in Palestine and the Near East* (Heb., Tel-Aviv, 1944).

two), was ploughed and prepared for the leguminous plants. This the Arabs call *kutani*. The plants were probably the same as today: beans, chickpeas, lentils, vetches (*kirsenne*), green peas (*galbena*).[112]

According to our text the whole field was ploughed. Part of it was kept aside as absolute fallow, *garet*, until the next spring. The fields sown with winter crops and leguminous plants would have no other crop during the current agricultural year, because the harvest came later than the sowing of the summer crops. Consequently after the harvest of the winter crops these fields would remain fallow until the sowing of the next year.

The part of the field which remained fallow would be ploughed, as the name *maggiatica* indicates, in the spring, around March. Marsiglio Zorzi, at home with Italian practice, used the expression 'May ploughing', but in our climate it is done two months earlier. This is the tillage known in Arabic as *kerab rabi'*, the 'labour of spring'.

Is the aim of ploughing simply to prepare the land for the November sowing or is it also sown for a summer harvest? There is nothing in our text or in the list of peasant payments to answer our question one way or another, but there is no doubt that there was a summer harvest. Its income was small, but it was necessary for the good maintenance of land for the winter harvest. It kept the humidity of the soil and above all destroyed the weeds. The land was then ready to produce grain.[113] It would be quite surprising if there were no summer crop in the region of Tyre, which did not suffer from excessive dryness.

There is perhaps even an indication of the fact in our text, with reference to a Venetian monopoly in Tyre: 'Item ex oleo Sussimani recipitur pro eius appalto CLX bis'.[114] But sesame seeds, from which oil is derived, were a summer crop—in fact, one of the most important. Today, in addition to sesame,[115] the summer crops also include chickpeas (*hummus*) and two kinds of *dhurā* (*beda* and *safra*), that is, sorghum and corn. We have no direct proof for it in the thirteenth century but the cultivation seems traditional. This can further be corroborated by the enumeration of crops in an agreement of 1257 between Florence, bishop of Acre, and the Teutonic Order,[116] dealing with tithes in the villages of Galilee. The tithe had to be paid: 'de frumento, ordeo, ciceribus, lenticulis, fabis, avena,

---

[112] G. Dalman, op. cit., pp. 401 ff.

[113] Eleazari-Volcani, op. cit., p. 29.

[114] Tafel–Thomas ii. 385.

[115] L. Anderlind, 'Ackerbau und Thierzucht in Syrien, insbesondere in Palästina', *ZDPV* 9 (1866), 9.

[116] Strehlke, no. 112, p. 93.

melique, coctono, milio, mais, pisau, gerbains [perhaps Arab *galbena*]'. A number of these plants are typical summer crops.

It is possible that this practice was not followed every year, but it certainly was not entirely absent. Thus the *maggiatica* could have been, in certain places in certain years, a single spring ploughing, and in other years, a tillage followed by sowing of summer crops.[117] Today both practices exist in the fellah's agriculture. The first is known as *kerab barad*, the 'rain ploughing'[118] (black fallow or sun fallow); the other followed by sowing: *kerab sefi*.

The following table gives a rough indication of the whole system:

Year	Season	First field	Second field
1st	winter:	winter crops	leguminous plants; Fallow
	spring–summer:	fallow	Fallow; summer crops
2nd	winter	leguminous plants; Fallow	winter crops
	spring–summer:	Fallow; summer crops	Fallow

We end this section with an analyis of an obscure passage in the memorandum of Marsiglio Zorzi. In the description of the village of Betheron we read: 'Habemus etiam de terra Gariti, quam Manzancam seu Terram fratam appellamus, in qua seminantur annuatim tria modia leguminum.'[119] *Terra gariti* is obviously *terra garetti*, because we know now that leguminous plants were planted in the *garets*. *Manzanca* is certainly *manzatica* ($ti = n$) and corresponds consequently to *terra fracta*, broken, laboured land.[120] This is no doubt a *terminus technicus* and explains why in the same description of Bethoron we have: 'in terra de gareto quam frangunt'.[121]

---

[117] Thus in the description of the village of Theiretenne, the expression: 'Terra ... que efficitur mazadica pro alio anno' may possibly indicate a full year's fallow. On the other hand in the village of Mahallia: 'que efficitur mazaticha pro sequenti anno' suggests the next year, that is the spring of next year.

[118] A. Ruppin, op. cit., p. 67: *Schwarzbrache*. The 'kerab barad' is described as follows: 'half the field is sown with cereals while of the second part a portion is reserved to the leguminous "kerabs" and a part of the field is left fallow, that is ploughed at the end of the winter, and then left fallow for a year' (Eleazari-Volcani, op. cit., p. 38). This system seems also to be corroborated by a Hospitaller charter regarding the village of Qaqun: 'quatuor carrugas terre in Chaco ad serendum et garetandum' (Delaville, no. 94 (i. 84)) and in Kafr Salem: 'duas carugas terre ... et serendum et garetandum' (ibid., no. 97 (i. 87)). Hugh, lord of Jaffa, gave them: 'decem terre carrucatas ad seminandum et garettandum' (ibid., no. 97 (i. 87)). The biennial rotation is also indicated in the fourteenth century by Nuwayri, viii. 256, see p. 173 and n. 122.

[119] Tafel–Thomas ii. 383.

[120] Marsiglio Zorzi wrote *frata* instead of *fracta* probably influenced by the Italian *fratturare*.   [121] Tafel–Thomas ii. 383.

This reconstruction of the agricultural year based on Crusader documentation and the system of cultivation still current in the fellah's farm in Palestine before the introduction of modern techniques is well corroborated by Nuwayri's description of Mameluke taxation at the beginning of the fourteenth century. Although mainly interested in fiscal matters, its importance cannot be ovestimated, as it seems to be a unique Arabic source regarding Syria and Palestine.[122] We quote here the paragraphs dealing with the system of cultivation:

The regime (*qānūn*) of the land of al-Sham [Syria and Palestine] is based on rains and precipitations taking place at the right time and at the time of need. One of these rains is called the autumn rain (*wasmi*), and this is the rain which falls in autumn, and when this rain falls, one tills the land with plough and this is followed by sowing the grain. Then the ploughing is repeated to hide grain from birds, out of fear that they will collect it. When the second rain comes, the grain germinates and shows up on the surface of the earth. At that stage this grain is called 'dark green' (*aḥwā*). Afterwards the rains do not stop to drench the land and so do the precipitations until they create muddy torrents (*ghūṭa*). Afterwards comes the rain, which is called the 'weaning one' (*fāṭim*), generally in Nīsān (April), when the grain ripens and this ends the normal cycle. This is the method of labour of autumn crops (*wasmi*).

There are lands in Syria in which the autumn rain comes late and which the inhabitants sow when they are (still) dry, and that means, that they sow the seeds in the earth before the time of sowing, and wait for the rain to drench them. It is a remarkable fact that in some years they put the grain in the earth as usual, but afterwards the rain does not fall on it, and the seeds remain in the earth until the next year. The inhabitants of the land give this planting up, sow in the next year half of the land which was fallow (*kerāb*) and not sown. As a matter of fact, it is the custom in other parts of Syria that each *fellah* divides the land in two parts, one to sow and the other to be left fallow. Yet, the latter they still plough, so that the warmth of the sun should penetrate the earth. [This part] they sow in the next year and leave fallow the part sown the year earlier. This is their custom in contrast to Egypt, where they sow every year when the rain comes and where both halves yield simultaneously and the harvest is bountiful and double. This is a rare and remarkable phenomenon.

There are also lands in Syria that are irrigated by running water from rivers and sources. These bring more revenue than the lands watered by rain, and the value of this type of land is higher. The majority of these lands lie in the plain. Allah knows better.

[122] Nuwayri, *Nihāya* viii. 255 ff. The importance of the text has been noted by A. N. Poliak, *A History of Landed Property in Egypt, Syria, and Palestine* (Heb., Jerusalem, 1940), p. 15, but misinterpreted as describing a triennial system of cultivation. We pointed out in *Byzantion* 22 (1952), 48 n. 2, that it was actually a biennial system of rotation. A translation of the text was printed by C. Cahen in *Journal of Economic and Social History of the Orient* 18 (1976), 233–44. The text is difficult and the translation printed here was rechecked by my colleague Professor D. Ayalon, to whom I would like to express my thanks. As to the Arabic names of plants, see G. Dalman, *Arbeit und Sitte*, ii, Arabic index.

As to the task of the supervisors (*mubāshir*) of the *kharāj* in Syria, it begins by making the *raises* of the country classify and sum up what is sown (*zurāʿa*) and what is fallow (*kerāb*). The terminology they use in this connection is: 'red' (*aḥmar*) and 'green' (*akhḍar*), the 'red' meaning fallow, the 'green' meaning sown, either in winter or in summer. 'Winter' (*shatawi*) indicates wheat, barley, spelt, beans, chick-peas, lentils, vetches, (*al-julubbān*), peas (*bistilya*), which are called in Egypt *al-bisilla*, and on the coast of Tripoli *al-ḥālibah* (Star of Bethlehem?). 'Summer' (*ṣayfī*) denotes: sorghum (*dhura*), millet (*dukhn*), sesame, rice, 'black grain' (*al-ḥabba al-Saudā*', perhaps fennel), coriander (*kuṣbara*), cucumber, indigo (*wasma*), saffron (*qirtim*), cotton and hemp . . . As to carobs, olives, cotton, sumac, pistachio, nuts, almonds, rice, the supervisors control them until they come to the threshing floor and they are divided according to the customary tax. This is divided according to the tax and is received(?) and inscribed on the register of revenue (*mutaḥaṣṣal*).

Sowing and Harvesting

The quantity of grain sown in a *carruca* is, according to the Venetian inventory, the same everywhere: 9 *modii* to a *carruca*. There were two *modii* that could have been used in this calculation: the *modius* of Venice and the *modius* of Acre, but as our text explicitly says *modium regale*,[123] it clearly points to the royal measure of Acre, which appears in another document as *modius domini Accon*.[124]

This *modius* equals 176 litres[125] and 9 *modii* equal 1,584 litres. This quantity was consequently sown in *c.* 35 ha of land or counting 0·74 kg of wheat grain to 1 litre—33·5 kg per hectar. For barley, the quantity is smaller—0·58 kg to the litre or 26 kg sown per hectar.

This is obviously a theoretical evaluation and has to be considered in terms of agricultural practice. When the Venetian official stated the quantity of grain to be sown in a *carruca*, he could hardly have referred to the *carruca* as a whole, but rather to that part of the *carruca* that was actually sown with winter or summer crops. Unfortunately, as we have already pointed out, the respective proportion of fallow and cultivated land is unknown. Assuming that the arable was divided into halves (and

[123] Tafel–Thomas ii. 369.
[124] F. B. Pegolotti, *La pratica della mercatura,* ed. A. Evans (Cambridge, Mass., 1936), p. 64: 'Grano e orzo e tutti biadi, e noce e castagne e nocelle, si vendono in *Acri a moggio*, ed è il *moggio del signore* e della ruga di Pisa e della ruga di Vinegia tutto uno con quello delle magione dello Spedale del Tempio, ed è modelli 24, e quelle della fonda, cioè la piazza ove si vende, si è altressi mondelli 24.'
[125] A Schaube, *Handelsgesch. der roman. Völker* (Munich and Berlin, 1906), p. 814. The Venetian *modius* had 10 hl, almost five times the *modius* of Acre.

this seems to be implied by Nuwayri) we shall count 1,584 litres of wheat per 17½ ha, that is to say 66·8 kg and 52 kg of barley actually sown per ha.

As to leguminous plants, it was 1 *modius* per *carruca*, that is theoretically 176 litres per 35 ha. Here it is more difficult to evaluate the quantities as the different species have different weights. If we take peas for example, where 1 litre corresponds to 0·45 kg, we find 2·3 kg sown per 1 ha. But we cannot reach any conclusion as we do not know the area sown.[126] Assuming hypothetically that it is half of the *garet*, or a quarter of the *carruca*, we shall evaluate the quantity at 9·1 kg.

Comparing the above date with the modern Arabic 'dry farming' we find that in the latter 120 kg are sown per 1 ha, that is twice as much as in the Crusader period, whereas the leguminous plants are sown 4 to 15 kg according to the species. That is roughly as much as in the medieval period.[127]

Information on the harvest comes from one village only, Bethoron; in fact, this seems to comprise the only data for the Crusader period.[128] Seeing, however, the uniformity in the quantity of sown grain in the different villages, we can assume that the harvest differences were rather small.

The Venetian part of Bethoron[129] had 5 *carrucae*. This area received 12 *modii* of winter crops and 3 *modii* of leguminous plants in the *garet*. The harvest brought the Venetians, according to Marsiglio Zorzi's evaluation, 20 *modii* of cereals and 10 *modii* of leguminous plants. These numbers represent a quarter or a third of the total production (three-quarters or two-thirds remained with the peasant) and not the whole harvest. Thus to evaluate the whole harvest we have to multiply the Venetian revenue by 3 or 4. Consequently, the harvest for 12 *modii* of sown cereals was 60 or 80 *modii* and for the 3 *modii* of leguminous plants, 30 or 40 *modii*. That is to say, there was a varying relation of 1 : 5 or 1 : 7 for cereals and 1 : 10 to 1 : 13 for the leguminous plants. In absolute numbers, the peasant harvested

[126] Arab folklore has it that peas are 'calling out' to each other, whereas beans 'whisper' to each other (Dalman, op. cit. iv. 183).

[127] Similar quantities were noted by A. Rupin in 1917, op. cit., p. 90, and cf. Eleazari-Volcani, op. cit., p. 31. L. Anderlind, 'Ackerbau und Thierzucht in Syrien', *ZDPV* 9 (1886), 49, noted at his time in the Palestinian plain: 60 l. to 1 acre, or 150 l. to 1 ha, or 67·5 kg to 1 ha. Our estimates obviously depend on the proportions of fallow and worked land.

[128] Some indications on the harvest can be gathered from chronicles and itineraries, but they are too often influenced by biblical praises of the 'land of milk and honey' to reflect reality.

[129] Tafel–Thomas ii. 383–4.

in 1 ha of land around 233 kg (or 167 kg) of wheat, 183 kg (or 131 kg) of barley and 30 kg (or 23 kg) of peas per ha.

In the traditional agriculture the fellah harvested around 500–600 kg of wheat in 1 ha and 200–600 kg of leguminous plants to 1 ha,[130] and the relation varies between 1:4 and 1:8 for cereals and from 1:4 to 1:5 for leguminous plants. Note also that the average harvest in antiquity in the same country was 1:5 between the amount of grain sown and harvested, precisely as in the Arab farm of the thirteenth century under Crusader rule.[131]

The constancy of these proportions between the thirteenth century and our own days, although the quantity sown almost doubles or triples, shows the constant fertility of the soil during the ages on this coastal plain of Syria. These results can serve as a basis for general evaluation, but we have to remember that they are based on one village only and reflect, even in the best of cases, particular conditions. Finally, we have to remember that we are using fiscal evaluations which here, as everywhere else, are certainly underestimating the real quantities of production. However, in the state of our documentation, an evaluation, even limited in scope,

---

[130] Cf. the statistical tables of Eleazari-Volcani, op. cit., pp. 41 and 49. Z. Abramowtiz and J. Gelfat, op. cit., p. 31, evaluated the harvest of 1935 at 460 kg of wheat per ha, 260 kg of barley. In 1938 the corresponding quantities were: 210 kg for wheat but 330 kg for barley. The evaluations for Lebanon and Syria were higher: 800–1,000 kg of wheat, 1,000–1,100 for barley (ibid., p. 148).

[131] F. M. Heichelheim, 'Roman Syria', *An Economic Survey of Ancient Rome*, ed. T. Frank (Baltimore, 1931), p. 129. It is worth noting that in twelfth- and thirteenth-century England the relation was 1:5. A. L. Poole, *From Domesday Book to Magna Carta*, p. 49. A. Rupin noted for 1917 (op. cit., p. 90): wheat 1:8 to 1:10; barley 1:10 to 1:15; beans and other leguminous plants 1:10 to 1:15. Summer grains produced 1:40 to 1:50. The *Handbook of Syria prepared by the Geographical Society of the Naval Intelligence Division* (Admiralty, London, n.d.), p. 257, noted 1:12, the relation between sowing and harvesting, as 'good' for Palestine. There are real difficulties in obtaining reliable data on traditional agriculture, as these obviously vary with soil conditions and changes in climate which affect this type of agriculture more than the modernized kind, and finally, as far as official statistics are concerned, with the reticence of the peasants (because of taxes). For the vicinity of Tyre we find a statistic dating from before the First World War (which partially eliminates modernizing influences): F. Grobler, *Die Getreidewirtschaft Syriens und Palästinas seit Beginn des Weltkriegs* (Hanover, 1923), table 2, p. 140, and table 7, p. 145. For the years of 'good harvest', 1912–13 (cf. above *Handbook*, p. 257), it furnishes the following data for the district of Sour (Tyr):

Plants	Area sown	Harvest
Wheat	50,000 *dönüm*	577 t.
Barley	30,000 *dönüm*	4,200 t.
Leguminous plants	25,500 *dönüm*	2,436 t.

Counting 912 sq m to the *dönüm* we evaluate the harvest as 130 kg of wheat, 1,500 kg of barley, and 1,100 kg of leguminous plants to the ha.

should not be neglected if we want to envisage agricultural life under the Crusaders. We do not intend to extend our study to the whole territory under Crusader domination. However, a comparison with some data coming from other regions of Crusader establishments will allow us to size up better the character of agriculture in our lordship.

To begin with southern Palestine: in a deed of 1257—almost contemporary with Marsiglio Zorzi's memorandum, John of Ibelin, count of Jaffa and of Ascalon, promised to give to the Hospitallers 650 *charruées*[132] of land in his lordship of Ascalon if it ever came back into Christian hands. The definition of the *charruées* is as follows: 'C'est assaveir à chascune charruée terre à quatre guarelles de semaille et à autre quatre de guaret.' And in a confirmation: 'C'est assaveir a chascune charruée terre à quatre gareles de blé de semaille, et à autres quatre de gareit.'[133]

As we have seen, the system of cultivation in this southern part of the country was different from that used in Tyre. In fact, in the vicinity of Ascalon, 1 *carruca* of land received the same quantity of grain as the leguminous plants whereas in the lordship of Tyre the quantity of leguminous plants was hardly one-ninth of the quantity of the cereals. The unit of measure here was the *guarelle* or *garele*. This measure of capacity was mentioned by Marsiglio Zorzi who gave it the value of 3 *modii*.[134] Consequently, in the vicinity of Ascalon the sowing was of 12 *modii* of grain to one *carruca* or a quarter more than in the lordship of Tyre.[135] In absolute numbers it means 2,100 litres of grain as compared with 1,500 sown in Tyre.

In the vicinity of Beirut, Claude Cahen found that 4 *ghiraras* were sown

---

[132] Delaville, no. 2845 (ii. 833). There is a mistake in the printed title: '150 charrué de terre'. The text says: 'sis cenz cinquante'.

[133] Delaville, no. 2853 (ii. 838). This amount of land was given in fourteen villages. This means that a village had on the average 46 *charrués*, i.e. slightly more than 1,600 ha. These were obviously important villages. But we have little confidence in a passage of Marsiglio Zorzi relating to the vicinity of Ascalon. He mentions seventy-two villages in the area: 'eciam id, quod minus inter dicta habetur, ducente familie reperiuntur, exceptis minoribus casalibus, que sunt circha XX vel plus vel minus' (Tafel–Thomas, ii. 398). These are Levantine exaggerations. On the other hand villages with twenty families, each in possession of two *carrucae* (as in Beit-Jibrin in the same vicinity, see Ch. 5 above, p. 121), corresponds quite well with the 46 *carrucae* per village. The expression 'guaret' and 'gareit' mean the same; Quatremère mistakenly explained it as *ghirara* (Maqrizi, *Histoire des sultans mamelouks*, ed. F. Quatremère, ii. 85 n. 102). On the *ghirara, ardeb*, and royal *modius*, see J. Prawer, 'Le muid royal de St. Jean d'Acre et les mesures arabes contemporaines', *Byzantion* 22 (1952), 58–61.

[134] Tafel–Thomas ii. 377: 'que terra [sc. Belemed] seminatur iusta modiis XXX vel garellis X.'

[135] Assuming that we are dealing with the same *carruca*.

to 1 carruca.[136] The measure is of Arab origin and means a sack. Pegolotti mentioned two different measures which have, it seems, the same name: the *carra* of Ramleh and the *carrara* of Beirut. The first one was evaluated at 26 Cypriot *moggia* and was twice as big as that of Beirut which contained only 13.[137] If we evaluate the *modius* of Cyprus at 35 litres[138] we shall conclude that in the vicinity of Beirut they sowed either 3,600 or 1,800 litres per *carruca*. We prefer, rather, to accept the smaller number. Summing up, we arrive at the following quantities of grain sown in 1 *carruca*: Tyre—1,500 litres; Beirut—1,800 litres; Ascalon—2,100 litres.

Our knowledge of other cultivated crops in the region of Tyre is minimal. It is more in the description of medieval travellers than in documents that we find the mention of orchards and gardens which surrounded the city. Comparing the descriptions of *itineraria* with the documents at our disposal, we see that the gardens were concentrated on the coast up to the hilly and mountainous region which limited them on the east. As we have already indicated, the number of villages on this plain was very small, and the area of villages began with the hills. This situation had not changed 200 years later when, in 1432, Bertrand de la Brocquière visited the city of Tyre.[139]

Among the fruit-bearing trees[140] a privileged place is taken by the olives. They formed real plantations, as in Bethoron where 2,040 trees were counted in the domain of the Archbishop of Tyre along with smaller groups composed of fourteen, twenty-five, and forty trees.[141] As has been shown, these trees were not included in the area measured in *carrucae*. They were maintained by families of peasants, especially designed for that

[136] 'Le régime rural', p. 295 n. 5.

[137] Pegolotti, op. cit., p. 101.

[138] Pegolotti, op. cit., p. 94 indicates 100 Sicilian *salmae* as equivalent to 825–30 Cypriot *modii*. As 1 *salma* (Messina) was equivalent to 315·5 litres (Schaube, op. cit., index), 1 Cypriot *modius* was equivalent to 38 litres. On the other hand following Pegolotti, 1 *salma* (Apulian) = 239 litres, then 1 Cypriot *modius* = 31 litres. We are using the average of 35 litres. Cf. J. Richard, *Documents chypriotes des archives du Vatican* (Paris, 1962), pp. 19–20 and notes, who arrived at similar measures from different data. The *ghirara* of Ramle was then equivalent to 900 litres and that of Beirut 450 litres. The permanancy of this measure is astonishing. G. Dalman, 'Getreidemass und Feldmass', *ZDPV* 28 (1905), 36, found the *ghirara* of 432 litres as a measure in Beirut.

[139] Engl. transl. by T. Wright, *Early Travels in Palestine* (London, 1848), p. 298: 'The mountain near Sur forms a crescent, the two horns advancing as far as the sea: the void between them is not filled with villages, though there are many on the sides of the mountain.'

[140] Fig trees and carobs are mentioned by Marsiglio Zorzi (Tafel–Thomas ii. 383 and 380).

[141] Ibid. ii. 383. Counting 100 olive trees to 1 ha, the archbishop's plantation covered 20 ha.

purpose. Their work was remunerated, if at all, in a way we do not know, perhaps by crop-sharing.[142] We know the revenue from these olive trees. Forty trees brought in 5 besants annually; another group of forty trees brought in 6 besants; the group of twenty-five trees—4 besants only. The average, consequently, was 1 besant of income from seven to eight trees. The total number of the three groups, 105 trees, which covered, if our evaluation of the local *faddān* is correct, around 2 ha, brought in 15 besants in all. We may recall that in the same country under Diocletian, a group of 450 olive trees was counted by the Roman treasury as 1 *iugum*, this is an area sufficient for the maintenance of a peasant family.[143] Supposing that 15 besants represent only the Venetian revenue of one-third, we could evaluate the total income from the harvest of these 100 trees at 45 besants.[144] It is not impossible that the income was really higher if we admit that the peasants also tilled the land on which the olive trees were planted, a procedure which is quite well known from antiquity and still practised in the country as well as in the south of France.[145] However, this seems improbable because of the abundance of land. Perhaps the small revenue (and it seems to us to be quite small), can be partially explained by the bad quality of the olives of Tyre. In any case, in our own days, the olive called *Suri*, from Tyre, is not edible and is used for the fabrication of soap and other products based on oil.[146] In addition, the peasants were not so much interested in the pecuniary or commercial aspect of their olives. This was something that was more regarded by their overlords. For them, the olives and oil were products of primary importance in the economy of the farm and a vital part of their nourishment.

Grapes were also among the privileged plants. The area of the vineyards, just like that of olive groves, was not evaluated in *carrucae*. In one case, near the famous Ras al-ʿAin aqueduct, the vineyard was planted and cultivated

[142] A famous passage of Ibn Jubayr, *RHC HOr.* iii. 448, mentions only a 'light tax on trees'.

[143] W. Ensslin, 'The Reforms of Diocletian', *Cambridge Ancient History* xii, ch. ii, based on Bruns–Sachau, *Syrisch-römisches Rechtsbuch* (1880), § 121. In the maritime plain 225 olive trees were counted as a *iugum*.

[144] An olive tree ordinarily yields 13 to 23 kg of olives and a little less every second year: cf. A. Rupin, op. cit., p. 45. A hundred trees will thus produce at least 1·300 kg of olives, worth 45 besants, or 28 kg for a besant.

[145] C. G. Stevens, 'Agricultural and Rural life in the Later Roman Empire', *Cambridge Economic History* i. 96–7. Cf. R. Grand and R. Delatouche, op. cit., p. 361. In southern France the olive trees are planted in the midst of vineyards. Attention should be paid to Marsiglio's expressions: 'Redditus terre cum oliuis sunt' etc., 'Redditus terre cum arboribus' (Tafel–Thomas ii. 380–1).

[146] Cf. *Handbook of Syria*, p. 262.

on the basis of a *complant*-contract: the Oriental Christian peasants received three-quarters of the yield, whereas the landlord, in this case the abbot of Notre-Dame of Josaphat, received the remaining quarter. After three years the peasants were allowed to sell their holdings, preserving the rights of the abbot.[147] The normal style of cultivation seems to have been the *champart* with the ensuing division of the yield in a ration of two-thirds to the tenant and one-third to the proprietor.

We have no information as to the size of the vineyards, but we have some data as to their revenue. At Bethoron 'pro tertia parte' the landlord received 2, 3, 4, 6, and 10 besants respectively.[148] Elsewhere, three vineyards brought the proprietor: 'tres salmas vini de camello, qui equiparantur esse VI biguncios vini de Venecia'.[149] Four *bigonciae* of Venice equalled 6 hl[150] (a camel-load was thus evaluated at 3 hl) and consequently, the revenue of the proprietor was 9 hl of wine. Unfortunately, we do not know what price wine fetched in the market of Tyre.

On agricultural livestock the documentation is extremely poor.[151] Here we encounter oxen and, in some instances, camels also,[152] both a source of meat and beasts of burden; then cows, goats, from whose milk cheese was made. Chickens were part of the *xenia* payments to the proprietors—in this case, the Venetians.[153] We also find beehives, the honey of which was sold in the markets of Tyre.[154]

2. General Evolutionary Trends

The Pattern of Settlement

The area of the lordship was small but thickly covered by numerous villages: on average, one village or agglomeration every 2 km.[155] The

---

[147] Kohler, no. 30, pp. 33–4. This mid-twelfth century document has not been published *in extenso*. Cf. (of a vineyard in Bethoron): 'vinea Archiepiscopi, quam tenet noster rusticus Maummet; et tradit Archiepiscopo suam partem' (Tafel–Thomas ii. 383).

[148] Tafel–Thomas ii. 370 and 381.

[149] Ibid. ii. 383.

[150] Schaube, op. cit., p. 816.

[151] For more details see below, p. 185.

[152] Tafel–Thomas ii. 383.

[153] Ibid. ii. 371: 'una galina, X ova et media rotula casei recentis.'

[154] Measures used for honey in the market (ibid. ii. 385).

[155] In the lordship of Caesarea we find a maximum of 100 villages in an area of 1,200 sq. km, viz. one village to 12 sq. km. In the lordship of Nablus a maximum of 300 villages in 2,000 sq. km, theoretically one village to 7 sq. km. The numbers of villages and areas of the lordship are calculated on the basis of G. Beyer, *ZDPV* 63 and 64 (above, p. 152 n. 30).

density of population however, was low, the village population being very small. Some of the agglomerations were no more than hamlets inhabited by some three families. How should we interpret this pattern of settlement? There was clearly no scarcity of land. If anything, the contrary is true, witness the fact that a peasant's tenure occupied 35–70 ha—rather nearer the larger figure. The climate and quality of soil doubtless played a major role in creating this pattern of settlement,[156] but these two factors were permanent features, and consequently we should expect to find a similar pattern in more recent times. The picture however, is entirely different.

In 1918 the district of Tyre counted a population of 17,000 in '133 cities, villages and hamlets', 6,000 of which (slightly more than a third) lived in the city.[157] This leaves us with 11,000 inhabitants in about 130 agglomerations, an average of 83 inhabitants, or 10 to 15 families, per agglomeration. If we take into consideration that in three centres, Tibnin, Qana, and Mearka (capitals of *nahiés*), there was a far larger than average population, we can safely evaluate 10 families per agglomeration. In 1918 (or rather 1914) the agricultural countryside of the district of Tyre greatly resembled its medieval ancestor. The picture becomes entirely different, however, if we compare the component parts of the Crusader lordship of Tyre, both city and countryside, with the same district in the nineteenth century, when there were some 11,000 peasants, or, excluding the three larger agglomerations, *c.* 9,000 villagers[158] living in the countryside, as against *c.* 6,000 inhabitants in the city. The medieval picture is entirely different. We have stressed the preponderance of the medieval city over the rural district, a situation which found expression, for example, in the list of military services. We arrive at similar conclusions starting from

[156] In the classic work of R. Thoumin, *Géographie humaine de la Syrie centrale* (Tours, 1936), p. 284: 'les villages (actuels) de la région beyroutine situés entre les premières crêtes' are qualified as 'villages de croupe', which 'sont remarquablement agglomérés. Les habitants s'isolent les uns des autres, ou se groupent par trois ou quatre au milieu de cultures et sur les pentes relativement douces.' It is impossible to determine to what extent this description corresponds to the neighbouring district of Tyre.

[157] G. Samné, *La Syrie* (Paris, 1920), pp. 259 and 279–80. These data are based on statistics prior to 1914. They must, however, be compared with the results of a German study, of 1918, which fixed the number of the inhabitants of the district of Sur at 41,200. (F. Grobler, *Die Getreidewirtschaft Syriens und Palästinas seit Beginn des Weltkrieges* (Hanover, 1923), table XIX, p. 157).

[158] In 1907 Qana had *c.* 1,000 habitants (B. Meistermann, *Nouveau Guide de Terre Sainte* (Paris, 1907), p. 530). In 1880 Tibnin had a population of 800 (V. Guérin, *Description . . . de la Palestine*, 3rd pt.: *Galilée* ii (Paris, 1880), 377). But the rural population was more important, according to the figures provided by Grobler's study.

demographic premisses. If the data for Crusader Jerusalem and Acre, which are more or less reliable, are any indication, the population of medieval Tyre should have reached *c.* 25,000–30,000 inhabitants.[159]

Bertou evaluated the population of Tyre in antiquity at 25,000 souls, Renan, starting out from the built-up area, came up with 50,000. If we remember that in the eleventh century, on the eve of the Crusades, the Persian traveller Nasir-I-Khusrau[160] described the caravansereis of the city as having five and even six storeys (Strabo remarked that the houses in Tyre in his time were as high as those of the capital of the Empire), we shall reach the conclusion that almost the whole city area was built up (excluding the ruins and empty spaces found everywhere in the Near East) and that the population of Crusader Tyre, in its heyday, was no smaller than in antiquity.

Thus, we have to envisage an entirely different population pattern for the Crusader lordship: something like 30,000 city inhabitants as against 9,000 peasants. Inside its walls the city housed almost 75 per cent of the lordship's population. This is the most salient feature of a remarkable change which took place between the time of the Crusades and modern times. In the Crusader period, a quarter of the population lived in the rural district and three-quarters in the city, as compared with two-thirds or so in the rural district and one-third in the city at the end of the Ottoman period.

We may rightly ask if the data on the rural and urban population at the end of the Turkish domination are also valid for the intervening five centuries between the Mameluke conquest and the end of the nineteenth century. Some random indications (the framework of this study renders it impossible to collect all available data on the continuity of city life in Tyre) seem rather to point to the fact that the contrast between city and rural population in the nineteenth century was even stronger than in the previous centuries.[161] Beginning with the Muslim chronicler Abu-l-Fida and the traveller Ogier d'Anglure in the fourteenth century, then Khalil

[159] M. F. Lot, *L'Art militaire et les armées au moyen âge*, i. 199, doubtless underestimated the population of Acre as that of 20,000 habitants. 40,000 is probably closer to reality.

[160] Nasir-I-Khusrau, *Diary of a Journey through Syria and Palestine*, ed. Le Strange, *PPTS* 4, pp. 11–12.

[161] The need for a study of the continuity of life in the Levant is too obvious to need any explanation. A work such as that of H. A. R. Gibb and H. Bowen, *Islamic Society in the West* i: *Islamic Society in the Eighteenth Century* (Oxford, 1950), has very little on these questions. A large number of Arab sources was collected by A. N. Poliak in *Feudalism in Egypt, Syria, Palestine and Lebanon, 1250–1900* (London, 1939) and in his many other articles. Cf. J. Sauvaget, *Introduction a l'histoire de l'orient musulman* (Paris, 1964), pp. 90 and 157.

al-Zahiri (fifteenth century), Goujon, Cotovicus (1596), Sandys (1610), Quaresmius (1618), Nau (1666), Laffi (1679), Maundrell (1697), C. Le Bruyn (1698), Morison (1705), up to Pococke in 1739, we find, time and again, a ruined city hardly inhabited. At the turn of the seventeenth century the city was described as 'a mere Babel of broken walls, pillars, vaults, etc ... there being not so much as one entire house left.' Its population is composed of two or three Christian families, 'besides these, there are few other inhabitants, except some yanizaries, who live in a near castle'. A. Morison has this remarkable description: 'un état qu'on peut dire d'un anéantissement total, puisque les ruines même sont, pour ainsi dire, ruinées.' It was not until the middle of the eighteenth century, in 1766, that the Mutawalis came down from the mountains and revived the city by settling in the midst of its ancient walls and ruins. Volney (1785–93) was the first to indicate the revival of city life. Buckingham (1816) and T. R. Joliffe (1817) counted 5,000 to 8,000 inhabitants in the city by that time.[162]

This gloomy picture, which reads almost like a fulfilment of the ancient prophecies of Israel (Ezekiel 26:1 ff.) refers to the city only. The district of Sour—that is its agricultural plain—is painted in contrastingly glowing colours. The area is praised for its extraordinary fertility. In the sixteenth century we hear from Goujon that the coastland between Sidon, Sarepta, Tyre, and Acre 'is beautiful and the most pleasant to be found on the shores of the Mediterranean'. In the first half of the eighteenth century when the city lies in ruins, we learn that a great quantity of wheat was exported

[162] The material was partly collected by E. Robinson, *Palästina und die südlich angrenzenden Länder*, iii (Halle, 1842), 675 and 682–3, as well as by V. Guérin, *Description ... de la Palestine*, 3rd pt.: *Galilée*, ii (Paris, 1880), 231. The quotations in the text were taken from H. Maundrell, *A Journey from Aleppo to Jerusalem*, in T. Wright, *Early Travels in Palestine* (London, 1848), p. 423, R. Pococke, *A Description of the East and some other Countries*, vol. 2, pt. 1 (London, 1745), p. 82, and A. Morison, *Relation historique d'un voyage nouvellement fait au Mont de Sinai et à Jérusalem* (Paris, 1705), p. 580. Other sources mentioned are Abu-l-Fidā, quoted by Guérin, op. cit., p. 231, and by Robinson, op. cit., p. 682. Seigneur d'Anglure, *Le Saint Voyage de Jhérusalem* (Paris, 1878), p. 11. Khalil az-Zahiri, ed. Ravaisse, p. 44. J. Goujon, *Histoire et voyage de la Terre Sainte* (Lyons, 1571), p. 571. J. Cotovicus, *Itinerarium Hierosolymitanum et Syriacum* (Antwerp, 1619), p. 120. G. Sandys, *A Relation of a Journey begun in 1610* (London, 1615), pp. 216–17. G. Quaresmius, *Historica, theologica et moralis Terrae Sanctae Elucidatio* (Venice, 1881), ii. 906. M. Nau, *Voyage nouveau de la Terre Sainte* (Paris, 1659), pp. 663–7. D. Laffi, *Viaggio in Levante al Santo Sepolchro* (1679), p. 112. C. Le Bruyn, *Voyage en Levant* (Rouen, 1725) i. 535; ii. 339, 341, 345. Volney, *Voyage en Égypte et en Syrie pendant les années 1783–1785* ii. 69. J. S. Buckingham, *Travels in Palestine* i. (1822), 71–6. T. R. Joliffe, *Reise in Palästina, Syrien und Aegypten im Jahre 1817* (Leipzig, 1821), p. 12.

from the countryside—even provisioning the island of Malta.[163] Volney, always a shrewd observer, wrote: 'The plains of Acre, Esdrelon, Sour, Hule and ... Baqa are praised, and rightly so, for their fertility. Wheat, barley, maize, cotton and sesame yield 1:20 or 1:25, despite the backwardness of the cultivation.' A characteristic description is that of D. Laffi at the end of the eighteenth century: 'Per quanto si entendeua il giro della Città con suoi Borghi é tutto sterile, e coperto d'arena ... ma il Territorio fuori di detto circuito e molto fertile, bello e d'aria allegra, e salubre. Qui appresso terminano li Monti fertillisimi dell' Antilibano.' It was the medieval city and its population that disappeared. The countryside, if it suffered at all, certainly suffered considerably less. The responsibility clearly lies here with the Mamelukes, who destroyed the coastal cities of Palestine and Syria to prevent any possible new European invasions.

Our conclusions for Tyre can also be generally regarded as valid for the whole maritime plain: a hiatus in city life, a humanly induced cataclysm, interrupted and turned back the millenary urban tradition of this area. And yet the whole urban tradition was not reversed. There was, rather, a shifting of centres of gravitation. The great urban centres moved from the littoral into the interior. In the Mameluke and Ottoman periods and up to the end of the eighteenth century, the great city centres of the country were in Safed, Tiberias, and Ramle. It was only at the turn of the eighteenth century, and during the nineteenth, that the urban centres on the littoral slowly began to develop, though the real renaissance did not take place until the end of that century, when European influence, Christian and Jewish, revived the ancient coasts of Phoenicia and Palestine. After the middle of the nineteenth century, though for different reasons, Jerusalem also was to reawaken.

Agriculture

At the beginning of this study, we did not expect to find anything exceptional or new in the realm of agriculture. We started out from the common premiss in biblical studies, that the Arab farm at the beginning of our century represents the ancient and traditional farm *par excellence*. In face of the documentary evidence this premiss can no longer be maintained.

---

[163] J. Goujon, op. cit., p. 54; R. Pococke, op. cit., p. 82: 'I went to the house of a Maronite [in Tyre], who was agent of the French here, it being a place where they export great quantities of corn, and even Malta itself is supplied from this place.' It is not necessary to suppose that this refers only to the use of the port. The great port at that period was actually a French commercial centre in neighbouring Sidon.

Certainly the farming of the Crusader period and traditional Arab farming are directly related. They have much in common in agricultural technique, but here the similarity ceases. Palestino-Syrian agriculture, at the time of the Crusades, was far more extensive than the retarded agriculture of that area at the beginning of our century. The intensity of agriculture had almost doubled. There is little doubt that after the Middle Ages agriculture underwent a drastic change, if not a revolution. The extensive farming under Crusader rule was conditioned by two factors: abundance of land and scarcity of manpower. Its main features were the immutability of crop rotation, concentration on winter crops to satisfy the needs of man and beast, inadequate and often only sporadic summer crops, long periods of total or almost total fallow.

This situation could hardly have changed in view of the obvious limitations. The first was manpower. More sowing meant either cultivating larger areas or ameliorating the labour by more intensive cultivation or different crop rotation. Both alternatives depended on the existence of a population surplus, which was obviously not the case in the thirteenth-century lordship of Tyre. In fact, it probably never existed in this area from that period up to the nineteenth century.

Another possibility was that of augmenting the yield of harvests by better fertilization. Unfortunately, the only system of fertilization in the thirteenth, as well as in the following centuries, was the use of manure, the supply of which depended upon the availability of livestock. In our texts we sometimes come across oxen, horses, goats, sheep, and chicken. But here, the texts strike a very minor note. This we can assert to be common to the whole area of the Latin Kingdom. Only small quantities of cheese, eggs, and chicken appear among the payments owed by peasants to the lord of the land. This would have been different if the available livestock had been more plentiful. A comparison with contemporary Europe, with e.g. its *Besthaupt* payments, bring this point into relief. However, in Syria and Palestine scarcity of livestock has a very ancient history. One remembers that the Emperor Valens (363–78) prohibited the slaughtering of beasts in the eastern part of the Empire to save agriculture.[164]

This shortage of livestock seems to explain curious customs in some villages of the lordship. The entire *palea* after the harvest, we are told, was

[164] C. E. Stevenson, 'Agricultural and Rural Life in the Later Roman Empire', *Cambridge Economic History* i. 92. We find only one tax on oxen: 'de bubus Surianorum', in the vicinity of Tripoli (Delaville no. 79 (i. 74–5)).

brought to the landlord. The limited amount of livestock made the *palea* in some measure superfluous.[165] It is also a remarkable fact that the only tax on livestock in the markets of Tyre was imposed on pigs, animals not commonly raised by either Muslims or Oriental Christians.[166] The same can be deduced from the very detailed list of taxes in the markets of Acre. Meat was not listed among the taxable agricultural products.[167] Meat consumed was probably from sheep, which are a poor source of manure. This shortage of livestock resulted in inadequate manure with little possibility of augmenting the yields of harvest—the old tragedy of the Near East until the introduction of better crop rotations and chemical fertilizers.

The third factor was the available quantity of grain for sowing. To augment crops it was necessary to sow more, to invest more working capital in agriculture. Here we encounter the vicious circle which gripped the Near East for centuries. The harvests were so poor that what remained, once the landlord got his share, was hardly, or only just, sufficient, for the needs of the peasant family. If the area was hit by a drought, the situation of the peasants became unbearable. If they did not die of starvation, they certainly did not have enough for the next year's sowing. In such cases they remained at the mercy of the capitalists or landlords living in the city.

We are not projecting modern notions into the Crusader period. The scarcity of grain was a permanent and sad phenomenon of agriculture. The situation was stated explicitly by Marsiglio Zorzi: 'Est consuetudo quod mutatur frumentum rusticis, qui manent in casalibus communis ad hoc ut melius terra seminetur. Et ipsi, cum accipiunt, quantum sit eis necesse, tribuunt (h)ob honorem curie pro qualibet caruca unum pullum paruum.'[168]

The scarcity of seed grain and the consequent poor harvests virtually precluded the possibility of augmenting the next year's harvest. And one wonders how the borrowing of grain over long periods of time in a land often ravaged by recurrent droughts influenced the standing of the peasantry. Three generations or so later the Arab chronicler Nuwayri,

[165] On Batiole we read: 'Tota palea (que) pervenit in parte communis; et est consuetudo, quod sit Baiuli cum dictis galinis, ovis, caseo et lingnis [*sic*]' (Tafel–Thomas, ii. 371). Cf. the description by Nuwayri, below, p. 193.

[166] A tax imposed by the Venetians called *tuazzo* (Tafel–Thomas, ii. 360). We do not believe that the breeding of pigs can be attributed to the 'Suriani'. The aversion of Oriental Christians to pork is well known.

[167] Cf. J. Prawer, 'L'établissement des Coutumes du marché à Saint-Jean d'Acre et la date de composition du Livre des Assises des Bourgeois', *RHDFE* 29 (1951), 329–51.

[168] Tafel–Thomas, ii. 374–5.

describing the conditions of Syria and Palestine, regards it as normal, that the fellah on the Sultan's properties should receive yearly provision for next year's sowing (*taqāwī*), which he had to pay back next year as part of the system. In addition, grain was also advanced (*qukūḍ*) to him by the Sultan's authorities. Until very recent times this brought about the peasant's social and economic enslavement. In the Middle Ages, as quasi-serfdom was the normal status of peasantry, the situation was perhaps less acute. The landlord's interest in preserving his manpower, precious because scanty, probably saved the peasant from total catastrophy. Still, there was truth in the Arab proverb: 'Borrowed grain destroys the land.'

The question to be posed, even if we cannot answer it satisfactorily, is: how and when did a change in Syro-Palestinian agriculture take place? C. Cahen, in a review of an earlier form of this study, suggested that it was the result of the abandonment of poor lands and a concentration of richer soils. This seems plausible, but we would also suggest another factor which complements the former argument—the renaissance of urban life on the Syro-Palestinian coast, to which we have already alluded. The revival of cities, the need to feed growing numbers of townspeople, the pressure of urban capitalism—all led the villages and their peasantry to intensify their agriculture. Naturally this was not an unmixed blessing, as it brought in its wake a growing dependence, or quasi-serfdom, of the peasantry upon city wealth.

Collective Property or Private Ownership

The charrué. It is a well-known fact that there is no contemporary description of a medieval village for Egypt, Syria, or Palestine. The earliest that have come down to us date from the Mameluke period and even then leave much to be desired. As once suggested by Cahen, it is the Crusader documentation, that, barring unexpected discoveries, will probably remain the only documentation permitting us to envisage a medieval village in this area before the fourteenth century.

Palestinian villages preserved institutions allegedly 'immemorial' deep into the twentieth century. One of them was the famous *mushā'a*—that is, collective property with a periodical redistribution of the arable in the village territory between the peasant households. This was accomplished on the basis of a traditional number of *faddāns* (or parts of it: *quirāt* = one-twenty-fourth of a *faddān*), to which a family had a rightful claim.

How 'immemorial' is this institution? We were taught by Marc Bloch that three generations were counted as 'immemorial' in the Middle Ages.

Does Crusader documentation furnish any indication as to the existence of collective property and periodical land distribution in the twelfth and thirteenth centuries?

At the end of the nineteenth century it was *à la mode* to regard the still-existing collective property as going back to antiquity, a survival from biblical times.[169] F. Seebohm used this notion to corroborate his theory that collective property was common to all human societies at a given level of evolution. Since then many of these collectives, 'Village Communities in the East and West', to use the name of H. S. Maine's famous study (1872), have received a different explanation. Like the Russian *mir*, they have found a less venerable and more recent parenthood.

In our case, the accepted view is overshadowed by such notions, but as far as we know, no attempt has ever been made to find any affiliation or continuity between biblical times and the recent past. A. N. Poliak, who once advocated biblical origins, later claimed that whatever the origins, it antedates the Mameluke period.[170] H. A. R. Gibb and H. Bowen accepted Poliak's thesis, whereas A. Bonne suggested an affiliation with the *epibolé* of the late Roman Empire. The studies of Weulersse did not touch upon the problem.[171] Only Cahen has actually tried to find some indication that perhaps the institution existed under the Crusaders.

Before studying the *mushā'a* land, as this type of property is termed in Arabic, we have to keep in mind that common and fixed crops rotation, the *Flurzwang* as it is called in German, is as compatible with collective property as it is with private ownership.[172] The common use of harvested fields for pasture was in itself sufficient to determine a uniform cultivation.[173]

---

[169] e.g. J. Neil, *Palestine Life, its Light on the Letter of Holy Scripture* (London, n.d.) especially chs. XIV–XV and appendix b: 'Discussion of Paper on Land Tenure in Ancient Times as Preserved by the Present Village Communities in Palestine', pp. 365–84.

[170] A. N. Poliak, 'Some notes on the Feudal system of the Mameluks', *Journal of the Royal Asiatic Society*, 1937, p. 105.

[171] J. Weulersse, *Paysans de Syrie et du Proche-Orient* (Paris, 1946), p. 106: 'Quelle origine attribuer à un system agraire aussi original et complexe? Il faut avouer que le problème demeure actuellement sans réponse. D'abord faute de précision d'ordre historique; nous ne possédons jusqu'à présent aucun document qui nous permette d'éclaircir le passé du mouchā'a' (H. A. R. Gibb and H. Bowen, op. cit., p. 259; A. Bonne, *State and Economics in the Middle East* (London, 1955), pp. 117–18).

[172] We use the word 'property' in the meaning of hereditary possession of the tenant.

[173] This is what made Poliak (cit. p. 173 n. 122) read a triennial rotation into Nuwayri. He also argues that this is the earliest source dealing with rotation. But we are dealing with biennial rotation, for which the earliest *medieval* description is that of Marsiglio Zorzi.

The only indication[174] from which the existence of *mushā'a* property could possibly be inferred was pointed out by Cahen—namely, the fact that *carrucae* given in fief or in *frankalmoign* are not topographically defined or described. This, he argues, 'suggests the possibility, at least in certain cases, of investiture not with particular parcels of land but with non-specified quotas of land periodically distributed'.[175]

If we are prudent, like Cahen, we shall not generalize. Such donations as, for example, that of William of Bures who gave to the abbey of Notre-Dame of Josaphat (1121) 'in territorio Tyberiadis, prope civitatem *quandam* carrucatam terra et unum Sirium cum sua sequentia ad eandem terram operandam',[176] or that of Hugh of Giblet, alienating a *casale* near Tripoli (1284) to the Order of St. John: 'sauf une charruée de terre avoec ses vileins' can prima facie be interpreted as portions of land not individually attributed. What was actually given or sold, it can be argued, was the villein with his rights to a certain quota of arables in the village. However, the expression runs: '*carruca with* its villeins', [177] which can more plausibly be interpreted as a well-defined area. Otherwise the expression would rather have read: 'the villeins with their *carruca*', and even then the meaning would have been at least doubtful.

But let us analyse a different case, that of the village of Bethoron, where each of the fifteen families held 1 *carruca* of land. Only the steward of the Archbishop of Tyre had 2 *carrucae*. There is no description of the boundaries of the *carrucae*. This can be construed, then, as indicating collective property. But in the same document we hear of the *praepositus' carruca*: 'Que carruca valet bene tres de alijs, in qua terra dicte carruce seminant IV modijs frumenti et plus et in terra de gareto, quam frangunt, XX modia leguminum cum ordeo et blado.'[178] There is not the slightest doubt that we are dealing with a well-delimited *carruca*, an area with particular properties. Another example is even more illuminating. About the year 1130 King Baldwin II gave the village of Sardanas, in the lordship

[174] The hypothesis of community of property in the Byzantine villages, which could lead to the possibility of the continuity of the system through the Arab period and Crusader period, has no followers. G. Ostrogorsky, 'Agrarian Conditions in the Byzantine Empire in the Middle Ages', *Cambridge Economic History* i. 199; cf. P. Charanis, 'Social Structure of the Later Roman Empire', *Byzantion*, 17 (1944/5), 28 and 44, n. 21. In a review of my *Latin Kingdom* in the *Journal of Economic and Social History of the Orient* 19 (1976), 106–8) C. Cahen suggested that a system similar to *mushā'a* already existed. In a private communication to me it was made clear that proof exists for the planes of Syria and Iraq, but not for the maritime area with which we are concerned.

[175] C. Cahen, p. 295.   [176] Delaborde, no. 10, p. 36.
[177] Kohler, no. 71, p. 73.   [178] Tafel–Thomas ii. 384.

of Tyre, to the abbey of Notre-Dame of Josaphat. The act of donation had a reservation clause for the benefit of the church of Mt. Zion: 'in casali Sardanas. . . duas carrucatas terrae libere et quiete. . . habendas et possidendas jure perpetuo.'[179] The text can apparently be interpreted as indicating not individualized but collective property. Fortunately for the historian, a quarrel broke out in 1243 between the canons of Mt. Zion and the monks of Notre-Dame of Josaphat: 'super finibus duarum carrucatarum terrae. . . in casali de Sardanas'.[180] Without doubt, though not spelled out in the original donation, the grant did actually refer to well-delimited *carrucae*. The conclusion that can be drawn from the above example is that though a grant may not mention boundaries of *carrucae*, it does not mean that rights of usage and not specific areas were intended. To put it differently, the wording of the donations is no proof of the existence of collective property, the famous *musha'a*, at the time of Crusader domination. The document that relates the quarrel of 1243 is even more explicit. The case finally had to be decided by arbitration, the terms of which prove beyond any doubt that we are dealing with well-defined private ownership. The document in case proposes several solutions, but if the judges could not agree, then:

per tenorem dictorum privilegiorum. . . ipsi debent habere recursum ad Secretam Tyri, et, si per Secretam Tyri certi esse non possunt, debent secundum usus et consuetudines civitatis Tyrensis procedere et arbitrari. Et si forte de antiqua consuetudine constare non posset de dictis finibus, predicti arbitri tenebuntur habere recursum ad Secretam Acconensem, et secundum quod ibidem invenerint, fines dictarum carrucatarum tenebuntur dividere et mensurare, et partibus adjudicare.

We have, then, four possible sources: a description of boundaries in the privileges of Notre-Dame of Josaphat and Mt. Zion; the information in the royal *Secrète* of Tyre (possibly a registration act, proof of taxation or proof of actual *saisine*); the customs of Tyre; and finally the archives from Acre. Each of these sources must lead to the fixing of the boundaries of the controversial *carrucae* and their assignment to the respective parties. Clearly, it is accepted as normal that the *carrucae* are individualized, have proper boundaries, and belong to individual households.

As the fixing of boundaries is of special interest in our context, it is worth while seeing it in action. An excellent description of such a procedure, almost contemporary with our document, is preserved in the two famous treatises of Crusader jurisprudence, those of Philip of Novara

---

[179] Kohler, no. 18, p. 21.   [180] Kohler, no. 71, p. 73.

and of John of Ibelin. If a contention arose regarding boundaries of property, the lord had to appoint an inquiry commission. The commission proceeded to the place and fixed the boundaries by interrogation of the local peasants:

Les devisors deivent venir en la marche de la devize, et là deivent assembler les plus ansiens de la contrée et toutes manières de gens par qui il cuideront estre assenés; et lor deivent faire jurer que il diront et moustreront verité et se contendront bien et loiaument au fait de cele devise, se il rien en seivent. Quant il auront ce juré, les devisors doivent chascun apeler à une part et deivent oir son dit, se il rien en seit, et faire le dit escrire, et enquere le estroitement coment il seit ce que il dit.[181]

The procedure seems to derive from the Carolingian *inquisitio per testes*,[182] the *antiqua consuetudo*, which could have varied from lordship to lordship.[183] The recourse to the *Secrète* of Acre can perhaps be explained by the fact that in the middle of the thirteenth century the city was the capital of the kingdom and in a sense could have been regarded as the repository of 'authentic' customs.

May we then definitely dismiss the existence of a *mushā'a* tenure under Crusader rule? We must remember that out of hundreds of donations we hear of boundaries in only a few. It is a tantalizing problem and of the utmost importance in the analysis of the rural regime in Syria and Palestine. It is our view that the rare mention of boundaries in our documents, which seems to point to collective property, depends on how the Crusaders envisaged the *carruca*, and this in turn was linked with their system of taxation. Theoretically, the *carruca* was a rectangle 2 × 3 (16 × 24 *cordes*). Nothing was more abstract than these proportions. No cultivated land ever had such proportions—they were the creation of the human mind. And yet, it was not just an abstraction. The concept had

---

[181] Philip of Novara, ch. 62 (*Lois* i. 533) and John of Ibelin, ch. 247 (ibid. 395).

[182] Cf. H. Brunner, *Die Entstehung der Schwurgerichte* (Berlin, 1872), p. 85. Should we think of Norman influence in the case of this *leal enquête*? Note that it appears not only in the case of a *nouvelle dissaisine*, as suggested by Brunner.

[183] Some examples of this procedure are on record: e.g. in the donation of *Acheldemach* by William, Patriarch of Jerusalem (1143) to the Knights of St. John, we read: 'ecclesia . . . cum tota ejusdem agri terra, *ab antiquis Surianis*, nobis praesentibus, *divisa* [erat]' (Delaville i, no. 150, p. 122). A detailed description of a division of possessions between the prior of the Holy Sepulchre, Arnald, and one Robert de Retest is preserved for Mahumeria: 'egressi sunt ut viderent et peragrarent terrarum fines et metas. Elegerunt autem quendam Sarracenum antiquum, Pedem Tortum nomine, qui preiret; ipse enim sciebat terrarum divisiones et terminos. Precepit autem ei dominus Robertus, cuius homo rusticus ille erat, ut veritatem diceret . . . minando ei pedem bonum facere incidi, si mentiretur, et si aliquando a via recta deviaret' (Rozière, no. 129, p. 241).

roots in agricultural reality. The surface corresponded to an area of arable land sufficient to nourish a household at a given moment. But in this case we would expect *carrucae* of different sizes, according to the quality of climate and soil. But Crusader documentation has a uniform *carruca*. The reason is obvious. We are dealing with a fiscal measure, which also explains the fact that its component units (*corde*, *toise*) were established by legislation and preserved in the royal *Secrète*. As such, its use was first and foremost fiscal, namely that of an entity of taxation, a fiscal notion of a household tenure unit. For the administration, the whole kingdom, so to speak, was composed of regular rectangles, a kind of chessboard with regular squares.

In everyday life the difference between the fiscal and the real *carruca* did not pose any great problems. Each village was evaluated at a given number of *carrucae*, which roughly corresponded to the totality of its arable. When a village was alienated in its entirety, the beneficiary received a quarter or a third of the harvest from its arable. Nor did the donation of part of a village, or of a number of *carrucae* therein, pose difficult problems. We have seen this in the lordship of Tyre, where villages were divided between the Crown and the Venetians. The two parties divided the whole harvest in proportion to their respective rights, without any preliminary interference with the cultivation.[184]

Theoretically a difficulty may arise. If, for example, one-third of a village was given as a fief, then it might happen that the corresponding one-third of the harvest would not have been taken from a round number of peasant tenures but also from a fraction of a tenure. Similarly, this may occur if the donation was expressed in *carrucae*, because there was no exact correspondence between the peasant family and the basic unit of tenure. We have seen that a family normally held more than 1 *carruca*, let us say $1\frac{1}{2}$ *carrucae*. Consequently, a tax on 2 *carrucae* would be imposed on one household and the totality of its tenure and a fraction of another household's tenure. This would actually have been the case if the Crusader landlords had collected their taxes directly from the tenures of their tenants. But this was not the regular practice. As a rule, the Franks did not divide the arable and did not collect taxes from specific tenures. It was after the reaping and gathering that the totality of the harvest was divided

---

[184] Tafel–Thomas ii. 373: 'Ita quod omne, quod reddit dictum casale, integre habemus nostram partem terciam tam de arboribus quam de blado', and ibid., 'Et quicquid reddunt *acumulatur et postea diuiditur* ita quod terciam integram habemus.'

according to respective quota rights.[185] If a village was evaluated at 10 *carrucae*, and a given Frankish lord had 6 and another 4 *carrucae*, then the one-third of the harvest (two-thirds remained with the peasant) was proportionally divided: 6 parts to one and 4 parts to the other, and nobody worried which *carrucae* 'belonged' to one Frankish lord or another. If there were controversies, they were not between peasants and landlords but between Frankish landlords among themselves.[186] The same system is picturesquely described by the fourteenth-century Mameluke chronicler Nuwayri:

Then the order is given to guard what is on the threshing-floor and they begin the threshing of the grain. Once this is done and the threshing-floors clean, so that there is nothing more to be done but to winnow, they bring a winnower (*mudharri*) and his task is to free the harvest from straw and impurities and clean it. And when this is done and the threshing-floor is clean and the harvest is cleaned from straw and impurities, the governor of the province, with his supervisors, comes to that area and orders the divisions to be made, according to the tax imposed on the village and its customary proportions: one half in irrigated lands; from one-third to one quarter in the greater part of the country; then, one-fifth to one-sixth in cultivated lands and districts devoid of inhabitants, which are laboured by tenants; one-seventh and one-eighth in areas near the sea coast bordering on enemy territory. After the division is made, the supervisors take what belongs to the *diwān*, then it is estimated what is still on the threshing-floor—chaff, bits of straw, and particles, and this is again divided so as to take what belongs to the *diwān* and give the fellah his part according to the tax of the district (*nahiya*).[187]

Although non-division of property and only division of harvest and revenue was the rule, we sometimes witness, though rarely, an actual division of property between Frankish landlords, as in the cases of Sardanas, Sedim, or in the case discussed by Crusader jurists. This was somewhat exceptional and probably only took place when a particular type of crop was concerned or in cases of very fertile land or of particular soil qualities. In such cases the Frankish landlord had an obvious interest to attach his rights to given parcels of land. In addition, whenever a landlord was willing to administer and manage his property directly—a procedure more common, possibly even exclusive, to ecclesiastics and

[185] This explains why a jury sent to fix boundaries between two Frankish lords found itself facing a strange situation: 'Se il ne treuvent *que devise ait esté faite*, les devisours le deivent faire à bone fei, selon lor consience, toute novele' (Philip of Novara, ch. 62, *Lois* i. 533).

[186] Here is a tragic example: 'Dimisit [casale Sedim], quod tenebat, propter occasionem divisionis, quam volebat fieri cum rege dominus Pantaleo Barbo, qui rex noluit facere divisionem' (Tafel–Thomas ii. 389).

[187] See above, p. 173 n. 122.

Military Orders—such attachment of rights to given portions of the arable would occur. The frequent disputes between ecclesiastical establishments regarding tithes may also have played a role in such cases.[188] By law, every Frankish landlord was obliged to pay the tithe. If in his village, as often happened, some tenures belonged to an ecclesiastical establishment, the latter might have been interested in defining the boundaries of the property in question.

How were these boundaries fixed? There was the obvious difficulty that peasant plots were scattered in the different fields of the village's arable. Moreover, the donor transferring a number of *carrucae* was naturally concerned with the *carrucae* and the tillers. But this, as we have seen, was not always practical, as it assumed a correspondence between an abstract fiscal unit and the social entity of a family. To avoid such difficulties the Franks had recourse to a special formula of donation. Thus in a donation to the Order of St. John we read: 'unum hominem cum muliere et infantibus suis *et mansum* quem possidet'.[189] Another way to circumvent the difficulty is exemplified by Gautier Granier's donation to the Order of St. John near his city of Caesarea: 'duas carrugas terre in Cafarsalem . . . praeterea iuxta istam terram concedo iis ex parte mea duas carrugas terre [with boundary description] . . . *si vero hac terra defecerit* eis, accipiant tantum de meliori terra quam invenerint in Sabulone, *quod satis habeant ad opus quatuor carrugarum*.'[190] Thus the chancery of the lord of Caesarea started out from the abstract fiscal notion of *carruca*, but knowing that it would have to tackle reality, provided a way to accommodate theory and reality.

However, it may be legitimate to ask if the procedure of dividing the entire harvest of the village *pro rata* instead of fixing boundaries in the arable implies collective property, at least indirectly. It seems to us that the answer is definitely negative.

In the *mushā'a* system there was collective property and periodical redistribution of the arable between the peasant households, but it did not imply collective tillage or harvest (besides the mutual help of neighbours) and in no case did it mean that there was a collective sharing of the harvest. The parcels once allocated to the families for a fixed span of time were individually worked and harvested. *Collective responsibility* of the village for its taxes was only one of the characteristic features of the *mushā'a* system. This could have existed, although there is no direct proof for it, *de*

---

[188] Riley-Smith, *Knights of St. John*, index, s.v. 'privileges: tithe privileges'.
[189] Delaville i, no. 7, p. 12.   [190] Ibid. i, no. 94, p. 84.

facto in Crusader times, as seems to be implied, though not explicitly, by two passages of Nuwayri. In the first, he states the obligation of the fellahs to labour the land 'forbidding them to leave any land fallow. Who leaves it fallow is responsible to put the [tax] on the cultivated land equivalent to that of non-cultivated.' Basically, he was describing a system of forced labour imposed on the village to ensure the taxation. Another passage is perhaps more explicit. 'As to villages, which were *iqṭāʿs*, and properties from which the tithe belonged to the *Dīwān*, there were some which had a fixed tax every year, whether the harvest was good or bad' and others where there was an annual evaluation of the harvest. The first case (without regard to the harvest) comes very near another type of property mentioned by Nuwayri:

In some districts of Syria there are villages *mafṣūl*, farmed out to proprietors for a fixed sum, which is taken from them at the time of the harvest without measuring or dividing, similar to what is done in farmed-out land in Egypt. The word *faṣal* [= vassal?] is throughout Syria a Frankish word according to their custom, which was preserved in all lands captured from them.[191]

This curious passage (whatever the veracity of the etymology of *mafṣūl*), as well as the preceeding one, can be regarded as possibly pointing to the village community's collective responsibility for taxes. This is not the *mushaʿa* system, but possibly the root from which it grew up.

The Continuity of the Rural Regime

One of the striking features of Syro-Palestinian agriculture under the Crusaders was the average peasant tenure, which exceeded the *mansus* or *carruca*. This was a remarkable fact and is put into relief if compared with the situation in Europe, where in the beginning of the eleventh century we witness a quite opposite phenomenon, namely the splitting up of the one family *mansus* between a large number (often four to eight) of peasant households.

Whence the difference between the peasants in Western Europe as compared with the Near East? Since the *carruca* was of local origin, as it must necessarily have been, and since the Crusaders did not embark upon a redistribution of land among the native peasantry, we must conclude that this situation antedated the Crusaders and already existed in the previous Arab, or even Byzantine, period.

The problem is of major importance in the history of Syro-Palestinian

---

[191] See above, p. 173, n. 122.

agriculture: it is the question of continuity or disruption of property relations and rural institutions. Although we cannot suggest a definite date for the emergence of this disparity, we can try to explain its meaning and perhaps even get a glimpse of the Frankish impact on the situation.

If we were dealing with a European village, our first concern would be the basic division of the village arable between the *dominicatus* of the lord of the *tenurae* of his peasants. These two poles of proprietary rights and obligations determined the life of the peasant. It is here that we find the decisive difference between the European and the Crusader rural regime. With rare exceptions, there was no *terra dominicata*, no lordly demesne in the Crusader Kingdom. There is no reason to accuse our documentation. Dozens of villages are minutely described, but the demesne is conspicuous by its absence. The Muslim traveller Ibn Jubair, in a famous passage referring to the obligations of the peasants to their Frankish lords at Tibnin, the closest eastern neighbour of our lordship of Tyre, minutely described payments due from the peasants, but no *corvées*[192] are mentioned; it is futile to speculate that such a striking aspect of serfdom escaped the attention of that shrewd traveller—obviously there were no *corvées* because there was no demesne land.

It is only in one passage of Marsiglio Zorzi's comprehensive inventory that we come across the mention of *corvées*: 'Sciendum est quod rustici pro angaria exibent pro qualibet carruca in terra communis una die, sicut rustici Regis consueti sunt facere.'[193] One day of *corvées*, but where, and was it weekly or monthly? Even supposing a day weekly, that is four to six days monthly (counting more than 1 *carruca* per household), this amount of work was hardly sufficient to work any meaningful demesne land (no additional boon-work is ever mentioned). As such demesne was non-existent, we suppose that the sensible way to use labour services was by concentrating them in the only area the Venetians cultivated directly for their own profit—the sugar plantations along the coast. In describing these sugar plantations the Venetian inventory does not mention any specific household connected with its cultivation. Although we can assume that some labour, working for wages, could have come from the city, it would have been rational to use the servile labour services due from the

---

[192] 'Extrait du voyage d'Ibn Djobeir', *RHC HOr*. iii. 448. We should, however, restrict the description of Ibn Jubayr to the vicinity he describes. Generalizations made on the basis of this description are doubtless faulty. Cf. Ch. 5, p. 134. Cahen views this passage in the same manner. Cf. H. E. Mayer, 'Latins, Muslims and Greeks in Latin Kingdom of Jerusalem.' *History* 63 (1978), 175–92.

[193] Tafel–Thomas ii. 375.

different villages by concentrating them in this area.[194] Such use of servile labour was probably sufficient to cultivate the precious sugar-cane. Other uses of the *corvées* were required for the transportation of the agricultural rents from the villages to the granaries of the commune in the capital and the maintenance of the irrigation system connected with the famous water-spring at Ras al-ʿAin, and perhaps also the maintenance of some houses which belonged to the commune in the city.

If our interpretation is correct, we can draw an interesting parallel to the Mameluke Empire, which succeeded the Crusader Kingdom. It was precisely in the sugar plantations that the Mamelukes made use of the servile services of their peasants.[195] It seems very plausible that this represented a Crusaders legacy to their Mameluke successors.[196]

At the time that the first essay of this study was published and the conspicuous absence of demesne land noted,[197] C. Cahen, who reached the same conclusion, explained the phenomenon by approaching it from a different angle. His point of departure was the existence of large landed properties in the Byzantine, as well as in the Muslim Empire. There were two types of property: private property which payed its taxes to the state, and the *iqṭāʿ*, which conferred this enjoyment of administrative and fiscal rights upon its holder. From the peasant's point of view, there was little difference whether he paid a part of his produce as *kharaj* to the holder of the *iqṭāʿ*, or the equivalent *muzaraʿ* (the rent for his possession) to the state. Some beginnings of serfdom already existed in the great private landed properties and in the *iqṭāʿs* before the Crusader conquest and it was simply taken over by the Crusaders. But neither in Byzantium nor in Islam do we encounter a *terra indominicata*. If the Crusaders had introduced it, it would have been tantamount to a revolution.[198]

[194] What has been said about *corvées* owed to Venice obviously also applied to the king's peasantry.

[195] A. N. Poliak, 'La féodalité islamique', *Revue des études islamiques* 10 (1936), 262.

[196] We do not see any reason to suppose that a *dominicatus* existed in the twelfth century and disappeared in the thirteenth. The evolution in Crusader Syria has at this point nothing in common with European evolution.

[197] The *dominicatus*, however existed in some parts of the Crusader states. But it can be stated that its diffusion was very restrained, nothing to compare with Europe.

[198] Cahen, 'Le régime rural', pp. 287–8 and 297. A new approach to the *iqṭāʿ*, which partially vindicates the studies of A. N. Poliak against their criticism by Cahen, is that of R. Irwin, 'Iqṭāʿ' and the end of the Crusader States,' in *The Eastern Mediterranean Lands in the period of the Crusaders*, ed. P. M. Holt (1977), pp. 62–78. The present study, which is quite relevant to the problem, has escaped the author's attention. The continuity of village life and institutions has been studied by N. Iorga, 'Le village byzantin', *Études byzantines* 2 (Bucharest, 1940), 375–412. His conclusions regarding the villages of Syria (pp. 394–5) seem somewhat hazardous. Cf. P. Lemerle, 'Esquisse pour une histoire agraire à Byzance', *Rev. hist.* 219–20 (1958).

In this general picture of evolution in the Near East there is one exception: the *paroikoi* of Cyprus. In the fourteenth and fifteenth centuries the Cypriot peasants were obliged to three days of *corvées* weekly.[199] 'Is this', Cahen asks, 'a later evolution, created under the influence of Western immigrants (but in the West at that time the demesne disintegrated), or is it a survival of a particular situation in byzantine Cyprus, where the position of the *paroikoi* worsened in a more radical way than in northern Syria before the coming of the Crusaders?'

Without prejudicing the exactness of the whole picture drawn by Cahen,[200] we would prefer to explain the absence of Crusader demesne in a different way. It seems that the key to the problem has to be sought in the disparity between the household and the *carruca*. In the second half of the eleventh century Syria and Palestine were afflicted by waves of calamities. The annals of that period are filled with droughts, famines, earthquakes, and bloody incursions of Bedouin, Arabs, and Turks which culminated in the Seljuq conquest of *c.* 1070. There is little doubt that the native population suffered. Then came a new terror: the Crusaders. The major battles were fought in and around cities, but as always, it was the countryside that had to supply the provisions of the combatants. Oriental and Western sources alike prove the desolation of the country. We also know of flights and refugees from the ravaged regions.[201] For one or two generations the population was decimated. It was this marked decline in population that characterized Syria and Palestine in the eleventh century and we would suggest that it was at the root of the double phenomenon: (a) the absence of demesne land and (b) the family tenure larger than the *carruca*. Thus we witness here a process of evolution tending in the opposite direction to that of early medieval Europe, when a demographic increase split up the household tenure, the *mansus*, into smaller and even tiny tenant units.[202] In Syria the demographic decline of the eleventh and the beginning of the twelfth centuries created an opposite disparity: an abundance of land compared with a thin and thinning population. If this

---

[199] The word *paroikoi* is explained by F. Bustron as 'huomo obligato star appresso la casa, che non si puo partir da quella casa, overo casale, senza licenzia del patron di quel casale', quoted by G. Hill, *History of Cyprus*, ii (1948), 8 n. 5. The word for *corvées* is *angaria*. The existence of *corvées* obviously proves the existence of the *dominicatus*.

[200] Cf. C. Cahen 'L'évolution de l'Iqṭāʿ du IXᵉ an XIIIᵉ siècle', *Annales* (1953), pp. 25–52.

[201] Cf. E. Sivan, 'Refugiés Syro-Palestiniens au temps des Croisades', *Revue des études islamiques* (1967), pp. 135–47.

[202] Cf. the classic work of C. E. Perrin, *Recherches sur la seigneurie rurale en Lorraine d'après les plus anciens censiers, IXᵉ–XIIᵉ siècles* (Strasburg, 1935), pp. 634 ff.

happened in such a fertile area as the plain of Tyre, we can assume that it was even more pronounced in less productive areas. Everywhere there was more land than manpower to till it.

This was the situation the Crusaders had to face. Hence there were two possibilities: one-third of the harvest from smaller peasant tenures and crops from a demesne worked by an inefficient and certainly reluctant peasantry, or one-third of crops from larger tenures cultivated by a family which worked for its own subsistence. The Crusaders chose the second alternative. If a *dominicatus* ever existed before, as in Cyprus,[203] it disappeared and was split up between the peasant households against customary payments. If there were any *corvées*, they also disappeared, as there was no need for them in the absence of the demesne. No new *corvées* were introduced; at most, perhaps a fraction would have been preserved, to be used in the most lucrative parts of the land, in the sugar-cane plantations.

The difference is clearly apparent if we compare the situation with the neighbouring island. In Cyprus the Crusaders entered into the legacy of Byzantium. The conquest was short and not destructive. The revolts, though sometimes bloody, were short-lived. The native population was spared; the geographical position virtually prevented any mass flight or emigration. No demographic change similar to that which we envisage for Syria accompanied the conquest of the island. The former rural system could have persisted or a new one, familiar to the conquerors, could have been introduced, a system based on the *dominicatus* and the *corvées*.

The following remark was added by Henri Grégoire: 'One can no longer doubt that the condition of the Cypriot *paroikoi* in the fourteenth and fifteenth century only perpetuated an existing situation, which goes back to the period of Byzantine domination of the island.' Thanks to the monumental work of M. G. Ostrogorsky on the *Pronoia*,[204], we know

---

[203] G. Hill, op. cit., p. 8, rightly suggests, it seems to us, the existence of the *dominicatus* and of *corvées* in the Byzantine period, which preceded the Crusader conquest, although the fact is not evident. There certainly were Cypriot *corvées* in the fourteenth century. Philip de Mézières indicates three days, Francesco Attar two days a week. There can be little doubt of the existence of *corvées* in the thirteenth century if they are found in 1317–18, and at the same time a *dominicatus*, which comprised approximately one-seventh of all arables. Cf. J. Richard, 'Le casal de Psimolofo et la vie rurale en Chypre au XIVᵉ siècle', *Mélanges d'archéologie et d'histoire*, 59 (1947), 130 and 135. We also think that a document dated 1330 from Limassol, mentioning a 'vilain fasant le service à coutume del vilenage', indicates *corvées* (Delaville iii, no. 4515, p. 811). E. Lusignan, *Description de toute l'île de Chypre* (Paris, 1580), p. 68, indicates two days a week as a *corvée* and assigns the creation of the *paroikoi* to very ancient times.

[204] Cf. *Byzantion* 22 (1952), 437–518.

how this institution, a true equivalent to the western 'fief', was diffused throughout the Byzantine Empire, beginning with the eleventh century. According to this system, the *paroikoi*, or serfs, were obliged not only to pay to the *pronoiaire* the taxes they had paid previously to the state, but also to serve 'as slaves'—that is to say, to perform the *corvées* .[205] If we do not find any traces of a *dominicatus* in Crusader Syria, this was probably due to the fact that this region had for a long time ceased to be a part of the Greek Empire, and consequently the institution of *pronoia* had no opportunity to develop.[206]

---

[205] Ibid., p. 464.

[206] Two studies, which appeared after the first publication of this essay are to be noted: W. Hütteroth, 'The Pattern of Settlement in Palestine in the sixteenth century', *Studies on Palestine during the Ottoman Period*, ed. M. Ma'oz (Jerusalem, 1975), pp. 3–11. Idem and Kamal Abdulfattah, *Historical Geography of Palestine, Transjordan and Southern Syria in the late XVIth century* (Erlangen, 1977). These authors do not use Crusader documentation. On the Crusader lordship of Tyre see the important study of M. H. Chehab, *Tyr à l'époque des Croisades* (Paris, 1975).

7 Serfs, Slaves, and Bedouin

One of the more remarkable aspects of the Crusader Kingdom was the legal status of the conquered population. As the Crusaders did not replace the population of Syria and Palestine, they were faced with the problem of defining its social and legal position.

The complexity of the problem was as much the result of the ethno-religious as of the demographic and social structure of the conquered land. On a situation created by centuries of history, the Crusaders imposed, or presumably wanted to impose, their own notions of society. Yet Syro-Palestinian reality did not lend itself easily to contemporary notions of a European society. On the one hand there was the decisive factor of the Levantine cities and their inhabitants. On the other there was the countryside and its peasantry, slightly less heterogeneous in its ethno-religious composition than the urban agglomerations. The countryside was settled in an overwhelming majority by Muslims, but with a fair sprinkling of Oriental Christians of different denominations, whereas in Galilee there were additional Jewish agglomerations and in Samaria autochthonous Samaritan villages.

Whatever the early sentiments of the Crusader conquerors towards Oriental Christians,[1] once the conquest was over, the Crusaders established a uniform policy towards the *whole* conquered population without regard to their religious affiliations. The native population was classified as non-Franks and as such lower-grade subjects of the conquerors. In everyday life Crusader attitudes might have been different, but this was seldom, if ever, expressed in terms of a different legal status accorded to Christian 'minorities'.

There is no doubt that all the conquered populations entered into the legal status of the *dhimmis* of the previous Muslim state. Payments of *jizya*, i.e. *capitatio*, seem to have been the outward sign of their legal status, paid by all non-Franks regardless of their religious affiliation. The situation was not new either to the Oriental Christians or to the Jews who were in the

---

[1] See Prawer, *Latin Kingdom*, pp. 214 ff.

same position under the previous rule of Islam. The change mainly affected the Muslim population, which from the status of rulers became that of ruled and dependent, the protected clients of the Christian state.[2]

Yet the wholesale classification of all non-Franks as second-rate subjects of the Crusader Kingdom did not solve all the problems connected with the control of the native population. There was the major question of the peasant population on whom the Crusaders depended for their livelihood and the question of the non-Franks inhabiting Crusader cities. For the peasants the Crusader had the ready-made formula of serfdom; and there were European notions of a special class of society inhabiting the cities.

At the turn of the eleventh century even the small European urban agglomerations had a class of inhabitants neither noble nor serf, the free burgesses. But what was still a peripheral occurrence in Europe was a major phenomenon in the Levant with its uninterrupted millenary urban traditions. During the time of conquest and the first ten years of Crusader rule, it looked as if the problem would be solved by the sword, since in all captured cities there was a wholesale massacre of the native city population. This changed in the second decade of Crusader rule when the local population was spared and at the same time the survivors of massacres, as well as new immigrants, Muslims, Oriental Christians, and Jews, flocked back and settled in the cities. Towards this non-Frankish city population the Crusaders had to adopt a legal policy.

The Crusaders, then, had to solve the problem of the legal standing of the non-Frankish population on two levels: on the one hand city inhabitants from among the 'minorities' (which in some places were the numerical majority of city inhabitants)[3] and on the other hand the non-Franks in the countryside. Religious affiliation had very little to do with economic occupations. A Melkite or Jacobite, to mention the largest group of Christian non-Franks, a Muslim or a Jew, was almost a free man or at least enjoyed several privileges characteristic of freedom when he lived in a city, but lost them if he lived in the villages or farms of the countryside. Basically, although it may have been different in the early period, there were no serfs in the cities.

---

[2] Ibid., pp. 504 ff. Idem, 'Minorities in the Crusader East', *History of the Crusades* v, ed. K. M. Setton. Cf. H. E. Mayer, cit. above, p. 196 n. 192.

[3] This was certainly the situation in the maritime coast north of Beirut in Lebanon and Antioch. James of Vitry needed an Arab interpreter when he attempted to preach in this area (*Lettres de Jacques de Vitry*, ed. R. B. C. Huygens (Leiden, 1960), p. 93 and below, p. 211 n. 50).

The expression *servus* in the usually accepted sense of *serf* is hardly ever found in Crusader documents; it does appear, but often, as we shall try to prove, with another meaning, in the writings of Crusader jurists. In Crusader acts all non-Frank peasants are *villani* or *rustici*.[4] Even as a linguistic phenomenon this is not easy to explain. It is certainly more difficult as a legal definition. The feudal vocabulary of the Crusaders is explicitly that of northern France (with some exceptions in Antioch and Tripoli) and one wonders if the Crusader use of *villanus* rather than *servus* corresponds to the European legal distinction, obscure as it often was, between the two. Yet the *villanus* of the Crusaders was to all practical purposes a serf and did not enjoy any benefits from his more liberal designation. It could perhaps be envisaged that the Latin appellation was influenced by the Arabic *fellaḥ* which is precisely *rusticus*, because there was no Arabic equivalent of *serf*. This is possible but not very plausible. In some cases peasant families, or rather their heads, are called *homliges*. And again despite the more noble origin of their designation, they do not seem to differ from other villeins and the noun does not seem to mean more than 'subjects', people dependent on an overlord.[5]

If we had to describe the position of the Crusader *villani*—Oriental Christians, Muslims, and Jews—according to the legal treatises only, the picture would perhaps be clear, but extremely scanty. Only John of Ibelin pays attention to the problem, whereas the other treatises of Crusader jurisprudence, which have a lot to say about witnesses and pledges, have very little or nothing on the overwhelming majority of the inhabitants of the kingdom.

In five concise chapters John of Ibelin describes the major legal features of Crusader serfdom, but we have to rely on Crusader documents to reconstruct their economic obligations and to complement his sparse data. The most interesting aspect of John of Ibelin's description is the existence of a special court and special legislation, which have attracted very little

---

[4] For some reason the noun *rusticus* is more frequent in the colonial Venetian than in the Crusader documents. Cf. e.g. Tafel–Thomas ii. 371.

[5] We do not see any reason, though there are opinions to the contrary, to regard these *homliges*, found in a Venetian inventory of the middle of the thirteenth century, as anything but serfs. In the village of Theiretenne in the lordship of Tyre the *homliges* represent the whole peasant population which belonged to the Venetians: 'sunt in dicto casali XII homliges' (Tafel–Thomas, ii. 374). A clear proof is furnished by the village of Homeire in the same lordship: 'Habemus in dicto casali nostro tres *homliges*. Nomina *rusticorum* sunt hec: Raysinegid, Couaha, Habdeluaif' (ibid. ii. 374).

attention from modern historians.[6] A special *assise*, he tells us, was promulgated to deal with some aspects of serfdom, but the date of its promulgation, though probably the first half of the twelfth century, is not stated. This act of Crusader legislation is called *L'Assise et l'etablissement des vilains et des vilaines*. The same *assise* is called by Philip of Novara *L'Assise dou remuement des villains* and by Geoffroy le Tort *Assise ou usage des vilainz*.[7] In the two last treatises the problem of villeins is only accidentally mentioned in connection with a contested claim as to the possession of a fief. So far we do not know if there was any difference between *assise*, *établissement*, or *usage*, though theoretically it can be assumed that *usage* was not an official enactment, whereas *assise* and *établissement* suggest official legislation. *Remuement* used by Philip of Novara and Geoffroy le Tort probably means dependence or belonging, like the feudal expression *mouvance*. The aim of the *assise* was to safeguard the rights of the feudal landlords over their villeins. At the same time it also ordered the establishment of special courts to deal with fugitive villeins. The members of this special court are called indifferently: *juges, enquereors*, or *ciaus qui tienent l'assise*. The appointment of these judges was the obligation of the overlord (it is not clear if it is the king or the lord of the lordship). They have to be 'three liegemen to hold the assize' and they are to be established 'par les contrées et par les seignories'. If one of them fails to act or changes his place of residence, he has to be replaced by the overlord.[8]

The competence of the court was to decide questions of lordship over villeins, to raise the hue and cry for the pursuit of fugitives and the restoring of the captured serfs to their legal owners. In disputed cases the ownership of the villein can be decided by an *enqueste* using the testimony of other villeins. The procedure of the court is very reminiscent of the Carolingian *inquisitio* or the Anglo-Norman inquest. A fugitive villein had to be returned to his legal lord, otherwise his former lord could bring him back by force.

Thus the peasants were *ad glebam adscripti*. They were not allowed to leave their villages without permission of their lords. *Formariage* was

---

[6] The *assise* is mentioned by M. Grandclaude, 'Liste d'assises remontant au premier royaume de Jérusalem (1098–1187)', *Mélanges P. Fournier* (Paris, 1929), p. 334 n. 77. H. Prutz, *Kulturgeschichte der Kreuzzüge* (Berlin, 1883), pp. 326 f., confused serfs and slaves and follows Beugnot, 'Mém. sur le régime des terres dans les principautés fondées en Syrie et en Palestine par les Francs', *Bibl. de l'École des Chartes*, 3rd ser. iv. 529 ff. and v. 31 ff.

[7] John of Ibelin, chs. 251–5, Philip of Novara, ch. 65, p. 535, ch. 66, p. 536, Geoffroy le Tort, ch. 8 (*Lois* i. 437).

[8] John of Ibelin, ch. 253.

forbidden, but if it took place with the connivance of another lord, he had to replace the loss of the female serf by another woman of the same age and condition.

All this sounds very much like European feudal legislation. Although links of dependence, even strict dependence, existed in the previous period, Islamic law, which sanctioned slavery, did not recognize the status of serfs. Muslim legislation made a distinction between Muslims and the non-Muslim clients of the Muslim state (*dhimmi*), but this reflected their position as subjects of the state, not their personal servitude.

And yet the Crusader conquest did not perceptibly change the position of Syrian and Palestinian peasantry. By the eleventh century free and independent peasants had become rare in the Muslim Near East. There was a proliferation of large domains belonging to charitable or pious institutions (*wāqf*), a process probably accentuated by the Seljuq neophytes. In addition the spread of the *iqṭāʿ*, a benefice or fief grant (in the beginning its income only, but later regarded as a kind of property), made the peasant dependent on an overlord. Finally the payments to state authority which became private by usurpation tended in the same direction, towards the disappearance of small independent properties.[9] The Frankish lords were thus easily able to move into the existing system of servitudes. If there was a Crusader impact on the prevailing situation it should be described as the generalization of serfdom.

The legal situation of the villeins, as described by Crusader jurists, finds full confirmation in the legal acts of the period. Land transactions state explicitly or imply clearly that the alienation of land means 'cum omnibus terris, villanis et pertinentiis suis'; or that the land goes and so do the 'praedicti villani cum eorum posteritatibus';[10] or 'cum omnibus villanis Surianis vel Sarracenis ubicumque sint';[11] or 'cum vineis et olivetis et iardinis, cum omnibus terris cultis et incultis, cum omnibus villanis terre et cum omnibus pertinenciis et divisionibus suis'.[12]

Serfdom, being a personal condition, is carried by the villein wherever he may be. Thus land is alienated 'cum rusticis quoque, qui de eisdem casalibus nati sunt, ubicumque sint',[13] or 'simul cum rusticis omnibus qui in praedicto casali habitant presentialiter et quicumque convinci potuerint

[9] C. Cahen, 'Le régime rural au temps de la domination franque', *Bulletin de la Faculté des Lettres de Strasbourg* (April 1951).

[10] Rozière, no. 44, p. 81, no. 48, p. 88.

[11] Strehlke, no. 3, pp. 3–4.

[12] Ibid. p. 14.

[13] Ibid. p. 15.

inveniri fore de predicto casali'.[14] This may possibly have applied to fugitive villeins pursued by their lords, for whom, as we saw, a special type of jurisdiction was established. In some cases Frankish lords even entered into special agreements with their neighbours to prevent their villeins from running away and settling in other villages. Thus in 1186 Bohemond of Antioch, when selling Margat to the Hospitallers, specifies that

[if] my or my men's villeins who are Saracens, if by any chance they come into the territory of Valania or Margat, the Brothers of the Hospital will return them to us according to the *assise* and to the customs of the land. But should they be Christians, the Hospitallers will recompense us (*pacificabunt*) within fifteen days or will license them from their land. But if they are their villeins and by chance come into my land or the land of my men, we shall likewise give them back to the Brothers of the Hospital.[15]

A curious agreement from the neighbourhood of Beirut stipulates that the Boḥtar emirs of al-Gharb will hand over all fugitive villeins from Beirut to the Frankish lord of the city (1280) within eight days.[16] Naturally one may doubt the *bona fides* of the contracting party.

Flight of villeins is also known from the early years of the existence of the kingdom, as a result of political circumstances.[17] Later on, in the middle of the twelfth century, in a specific case, Muslim peasants, because of maltreatment by a Frankish lord in the vicinity of Nablus, set up a clandestine organization to enable them to escape from Frankish lands to their Muslim co-religionists in Damascus.[18]

All this reminds us of European serfdom. But there are some peculiarities which need explaining. Many documents mention the alienation, through sale or grant, of single villein families. Thus in a generous grant of villages to the Hospitallers, Pons of Tripoli adds: 'And I allow all my men who hold land from me, that if they wish, they may give *one villein* to the Hospital . . . every one in his fief. And if more, then I will allow it with my consent.'[19] A confirmation of the Hospital's privileges in 1154 reads like an inventory of donations of single villeins: 'one rich villein who lives

---

[14] Delaville ii. 135.

[15] Delaville i, 163.

[16] Clermont–Ganneau, 'Deux chartes des Croisés dans les archives arabes'. *Rec. d'archéol. Orientale* 4 (1905), 5–31.

[17] Cf. Prawer, *Histoire* i. 289.

[18] E. Sivan, 'Les réfugiés Syro-palestiniens à l'époque des Croisades', *Rev. des études islamiques*, 25 (1967), 135–147.

[19] Delaville, no. 82,

in Nablus . . . three villeins given by the bishop of Nazareth, one given by William de Tenchis, another by Pagan Vacca, another given by Drogo' etc.[20] There are many similar donations to prove that this procedure was customary in the Latin East. The frequency of this type of donation, though not unknown in the West, seems to be the result of the Frankish agricultural regime.

In theory, the selling or the donation (which was more common) of a villein, meant the transfer of the man, his family, and his descendants into someone else's power. It also meant the transfer of his tenure and of the dues and services to the new lord. Our documentation however points apparently to the transfer of economic rights only, whereas the jurisdiction remained with the former lord, unless a whole village or a larger territory was transferred. This can be understood if we remember that the Crusaders hardly created a manorial system and had little or no demesne land. Consequently payments in share of crops, or cash in particular cases, and in product dues on special occasions were the main individual villein obligations. However, the bulk of dues, except the *xenia*, was paid by the village as a whole.[21] *Corvées* were almost non-existent or very limited, and concentrated on special crops (such as olive groves, vineyards) or occupations, such as fishing.[22] As the Frankish overlord was thus more of a *rentier* than a squire with land in the village, the easiest way of making a donation was to mention the villein and his family rather than to describe the villein's property.

Economically and socially a number of villein families enjoyed a more prestigious position. Such were the families of the *raïs*.[23] To this group there also belonged a number of rich villeins who were village notables, perhaps a class similar to the European *villici*—for example a villein given by Pagan, lord of Haifa, to the Hospitallers, 'with lands and houses in Haifa and Capharnaum';[24] he was obviously a man of some standing, as was his counterpart, a *divis villanus* in Nablus.[25] In some cases villeins came into more property or income by performing special duties. In such cases they

[20] Delaville, no. 225 (i. 172).

[21] e.g. 'quicquid reddunt accumulatur et postea dividitur ita quod terciam integram habemus', from the inventory of Venetians possessions in Tyre. The same arrangement held for fines (Tafel–Thomas ii. 373).

[22] Rozière, no. 74, p. 149: 'angaria et auxilium piscatorum' in the Sea of Galilee.

[23] J. Riley-Smith, 'Some lesser officials in Latin Syria', *EHR*, 77 (1972), 1–26.

[24] Delaville, no. 225 (i. 172). This 'Capharnaum' is not the biblical site on the coast of the Sea of Galilee, but Shiqmōna near Haifa. This strange identification was common to Jews and Crusaders.

[25] Delaville, no. 225 (i. 172).

held service tenures, such as the Oriental Christian 'Abd al-Massīḥ (Abdelmessie), the *raīs* of Margat, who possessed three-quarters of a village,[26] or Guido Raicius who seems to have held a large tract of land near Nablus.[27] In Antioch a mill belonging to the Holy Sepulchre was in the care of three Syrians, Nicephor, Michael, and Nicholas; their office is hereditary and described as *feodum villanie* and *villania*.[28] Others received real fiefs—for example, an Arab knight or warrior (*Arabicus miles*) who possessed two villages, Odabeb and Damersor,[29] the *Turcople* who held land near Nablus,[30] or Barda Armenus, who gave a whole village near Acre to the Order of St. John.[31] These were, however, exceptional and we do not feel that one can draw conclusions from such cases of Muslims serving the Franks in a military capacity.

In addition to the villeins, the treatises of jurisprudence also mention serfs. John of Ibelin is very careful to distinguish between serf and slave. The former is called *villein* and the latter *esclaf*.[32] But confusion rules in another work of Crusader jurisprudence, the *Livre des Assises des Bourgeois*. Here the expression *serf* is often used indiscriminately for villein and slave.[33]

The appearance of the noun *serf* is so rare that we feel we are dealing not really with serfs but with slaves. It was a Crusader rule that no Latin Christian could be or become a slave. Slaves were Muslims, Oriental Christians, or Jews, usually captured in conquered cities, or men bought in the market.[34] The ransoming of captives from the hands of Franks is attested for Jews and Muslims just like the ransoming of Oriental Christians and Franks from the Muslims.[35] If a slave ran away, the *ban* was

[26] Ibid., no. 457 (i. 314).

[27] Delaborde, p. 91.

[28] Delaville, no. 90 (i. 179).

[29] Rozière, no. 56, pp. 110, 120, 128.

[30] Delaborde, nos. 34–5, pp. 80–1.

[31] Delaville, i. 172.

[32] John of Ibelin, ch. 80, p. 129; ch. 132, p. 207. In both cases he is dealing with *esclaf mesel*.

[33] Thus *LdAdB*, ch. 208, has in the title *serf* and in the text *esclaf* and see below, p. 209 n. 40.

[34] In Acre the selling of a slave was burdened with the payment of 1 besant (Tafel–Thomas ii. 398).

[35] The ransoming of Jews captured by Franks by Jewish communities in Apulia and the different communities of Syria, Palestine, and Egypt is well known from the Geniza documents. Cf. B. Kedar, 'Notes on the history of the Jews in Palestine in the Middle Ages', *Tarbiz*, 42 (1973), 405 ff. Oriental Christians were ransomed e.g. after the capture of Edessa by the Muslims (Matthieu d'Edessa, *RHC HArm*. i. 329 ff.). Ransoming of noble Franks by their vassals was a feudal obligation. The aim of the Order of the Holy Spirit was the ransoming of Christian prisoners from Muslim captivity. Cf. Riley-Smith, 'Note on Confraternities', above, p. 46 n. 1.

called by the town crier throughout the city and the hiding of a fugitive slave was a criminal offence punished by hanging.[36]

Wherever there are villeins and slaves, there is also manumission. The Crusader feudal jurists have nothing to say about it and it is only the mid-thirteenth-century *Livre des Assises des Bourgeois* that furnishes details. However, this is not the most reliable source, as the chapters dealing with manumission can be traced back to the Provençal *Lo Codi*, and indirectly to Roman law.[37] And yet some of the customs were certainly part of Crusader law.

The manumission of a slave (*serf*) can be performed in three ways: before three witnesses, by charter, or by valid testament.[38] The bequeathing of his heritage to a slave (*serf*) automatically sets the slave free, to become *libertin*.[39] But there is another way of being liberated from slavery—by conversion. So at least runs the legal theory: 'Because the Christian land and the people are called "the land of Franks" they [the baptized] should be entirely free.'[40] Thus if a fugitive slave returns from the Muslims, and is converted, his former lord has no power over him. Strangely enough, if the slave is a Christian and runs away into Christian territory, once he comes back he is not free because he acted through *male fei*. His former lord can even sell him, but only to a Christian.[41]

The relations of the *libertin* to his benefactor are strictly prescribed and they follow the rules of Roman law.[42] He cannot plead against his former lord or he will be fined or even run the risk of mutilation. If the slave freed by conversion dies without testament, his property goes to his benefactor or to the benefactor's children. In the absence of these, it goes to the lord of the land.[43] If he offends his former lord he can be returned to slavery (in the text: *serf*), but cannot be sold, and his children are free.[44] Though some of the chapters of the *Assises des Bourgeois* mention *serf*, *serve*, and *servage*, there is no doubt that they refer to slaves and slavery and *serf* is a

[36] *LdAdB*, ch. 207.
[37] Cf. Ch 15 below, pp. 358 ff. And see C. Verlinden, *L'Esclavage dans l'Europe médiévale* ii (Ghent, 1977), 964 ff.
[38] *LdAdB*, ch. 204 = *Lo Codi* vii. 1, 1–2. *Lo Codi* following Roman law demands five witnesses and also adds the manumission in a church.
[39] *LdAdB*, ch. 203; cf. ch. 16 = *Lo Codi* ii. 2, 3–4.
[40] *LdAdB*, ch. 249. Although the title has *serf* the text has *esclaf*. There is no doubt that he is dealing with slaves.
[41] Ibid., ch. 249.
[42] Ibid., ch. 16 = *Lo Codi* ii. 2, 3–4. The penalty imposed on the freedman by the *LdAdB* is 50 besants. *Lo Codi* has: 'pena L aureorum, id est de L bisantis'.
[43] Ibid., ch. 201 = *Lo Codi* vi. 20, 1.
[44] Ibid., ch. 202 = *Lo Codi* vi. 24, 1–3.

slip of the pen during the translation from *Lo Codi*, where, naturally, the Roman legal expression *servus* meant 'slave'.

Conversion and manumission of a villein are incidentally dealt with in one of Philip of Novara's typically hair-splitting chapters. Among those excluded from sitting in a seignorial court because of religion or former trespasses he notes the case of a villein (*serf*) to whom the lord had given a fief.[45] The defendant can claim that the freed serf should not sit in court, by addressing his lord: 'he is your man, you keep faith with him . . . but you cannot make him our peer'.[46]

The problem of conversion was a complex and somewhat thorny problem. Whatever the ideology of the First Crusade, the Crusaders in the East never became a missionary establishment, if 'missionary' is taken in the sense of the conversion of individuals, whether Oriental Christians, Muslims, or Jews, as opposed to efforts to bring about a wholesale unification with Rome (this naturally applied to the Oriental Christians only). Far from engaging in missionary activities, the Crusaders were in the best of cases indifferent to conversion and in many instances actually opposed it. Nothing is more significant than the complaints of the virulent bishop of Acre, James of Vitry. Discounting his claim to the efficiency of his preaching to Oriental Christians and Muslims, we have his formal statement that Franks and even the Order of St. John were opposed to preaching and conversion.[47] Frankish opposition to conversion must have been strong enough if even the Papacy had to intervene, though in a rather soft-spoken way, which makes us suppose that the Curia knew the Crusaders' attitude to the problem. Thus in 1237, in a letter to the Patriarch of Jerusalem, Gregory IX mentions the fact that Muslim slaves (*sclavi*) are being refused baptism, as this might bring about their manumission. The Pope orders that they should be baptized if they

---

[45] Philip of Novara, ch. 28 (*Lois* i. 502): 'Se le seignor a doné feme au serf'. No doubt the correct reading is of MS. B: 'a doné fié'.

[46] Ibid.: 'Sire, vous en dret le poés franchir, puisqu'il vos plot; et s'il est vostre home, vos garderés bien vostre fei vers lui si come vous devriés... Sauve seit vostre henor, ne le poés vous ne devés franchir le, ne nostre per faire.' This is a reminder of the argument of Ralph Glanville, that a peasant emancipated and knighted was free only in relation to his master and other peasants and not in relation to a man of any other order. Cf. J. G. Mundy, *Europe in the High Middle Ages* (London, 1973), p. 259.

[47] *Lettres de Jacques de Vitry*, ed. Huygens, ii. 206–10: 'Christiani servis suis Sarracenis baptismum negabant, licet ipsi Sarraceni instanter et cum lacrimis posturalent. Dicebant enim domini eorum: "si isti Christiani fuerint, non ita pro voluntate nostra eos angariare poterimus".' Cf. Prawer, *Latin Kingdom*, p. 507 ff.

promise 'to remain in the state of their former serfdom.'[48] Some efforts
were made in this direction and the Latin clergy tried to convert non-
Latins from among the poorest by establishing a house of converts,
offering them food, shelter, and baptism.[49]

Thus the status of the great majority of population was compounded by
their legal status as second-rate subjects, the former *dhimmis*, and that of
their personal status as serfs. If this was not entirely an innovation, it was
still a meaningful change, because under Crusader domination it became
the general and legally fixed condition of the peasant population.

Moving from the countryside to the cities, the picture changes entirely.
Once the period of conquest was over, the native population, not only
Oriental Christians, but also Muslims and Jews, who had left the cities
before the siege or escaped the massacres that accompanied the conquest,
returned and settled in them again. This happened, for example, in the case
of the Oriental Christians who were expelled by their Muslim co-citizens
from Jerusalem on the eve of the Conquest or in that of their co-religionists
who fled from Ramleh, afraid of the turmoils of war, but later settled
again in the same places. The only exception was Jerusalem, where a law,
promulgated almost immediately after the Conquest, barred Muslims and
Jews from settling in the Holy City.

In almost all Crusader cities there were many Oriental Christians,
especially in places such as Jerusalem, Nazareth, Bethlehem, and in the
ports of Jaffa, Acre, Tyre, Sidon, Beirut, Antioch, and Tripoli. The
Muslims were probably more numerous in mountainous parts than in the
coastal plain of Palestine. It was different in the north where a considerable
Muslim population existed on the coast on the confines of the kingdom
and of Tripoli. According to a Muslim source, in some of these cities they
were the majority of inhabitants even under Crusader rule.[50]

The non-Frankish population of the cities was not regarded—certainly
not in a later period—as villeins. They certainly were not bound to city
soil and there was no personal servitude. Their movables were their own
and they were also proprietors of city land and houses. They paid rent and
probably a recognition tax, *cens* (distinct from rent), and were bound to

---

[48] A baptized Muslim is automatically set free according to *LdAdB*, chs. 204–12. The
quotation from the papal letter: 'in servitute pristina permaneri', *Acta Honorii III et Gregorii
IX, 1227–1241*, ed. A. T. Tautu (Vatican, 1950), no. 228, pp. 307–8.

[49] See the letter of Urban IV to the Patriarch of Jerusalem (1264), published by B. Kedar
in *Tarbiz* 42 (1973), 416: 'Sarraceni pauperes et Judei, converti ad unitatem ecclesie cupientes
ad civitatem Acconensem accedunt et postulant baptizari.'

[50] 'Imad al-Din, *RHC HOr*. iv. 309, 353, 356, 358, 362.

some more specific payments obligatory on non-Latins only. Such a payment was the *capitatio*, doubtless a descendant of the Muslim *jizya*, paid by every male over fifteen. This payment, derived from a former state tax, was due to the *seigneur justicier* and not to the landowner. So, for example, the Venetians in Tyre collected a poll-tax from Jews and Syrians,[51] a privilege every *seigneur justicier* enjoyed over his villeins in his landed estate.

It was again in connection with taxation that the non-Latins were discriminated against. In Acre after the Third Crusade the non-Latins were barred from living in the older part of the city and relegated to the new suburb, Mont Musard, not yet fortified. Moreover it is almost certain that they were compelled to use a special market, which belonged to the king; they were taxed differently from those using the markets that did not belong to the king.[52]

Yet royal legislation could not always refer to all the non-Franks in a city. The autonomous city quarters of the communes (perhaps also of the Military Orders) carefully guarded their 'own' non-Franks, whose taxation was a major source of income. In a city such as Tyre the king used what today would be called dishonest practices by enticing the Syrians of the Venetian quarter to settle in his own quarter.[53] Again in Acre the *Maggior Consiglio* of Venice decreed in 1271 that its 'own' Jews were not allowed to live in the city but only in the Venetian quarter.[54]

Though we do not know of any special taxation in Jerusalem, the fact that the non-Latins lived, but were not compelled to live, in a special quarter and had their own exchange benches and stalls in distinct parts of the bazaars of Jerusalem, could have facilitated special taxation.[55]

Members of a minority group who lived in a city were personally free and as a rule could move from place to place, acquire possessions (theoretically burgage-tenures), or rent property.[56] Yet a number of

[51] Tafel–Thomas ii. 359.

[52] J. Prawer, 'L'établissement des coutumes du marché à Saint-Jean d'Acre', *RHDFE* 1951, pp. 329–51. Not convincingly opposed by C. Cahen, 'A propos des coutumes du marché d'Acre', ibid. 1963, pp. 287–90, who agrees on the space limitations, but argues against the term 'ghetto'. The difference of taxation in different markets was proposed by J. Richard, 'Colonies marchandes privilegiées et marché seigneurial', *Moyen-Âge*, 1953, pp. 325–39. Cf. Prawer, *Latin Kingdom*, pp. 412 ff.

[53] Tafel–Thomas, ii. 384: 'Rex Johannes liberauit omnes Surianos ad dationem cathene, qui essent de suis partibus.'

[54] *Deliberazioni del Maggior Consiglio di Venezia*, ii, ed. R. Cessi (Bologna, 1931), *Septima rubrica*, i. 15–16.   [55] Prawer, *Latin Kingdom*, p. 410.

[56] Yet in some cases they were explicitly excluded from buying burgage tenures, see below, Ch. 12, p. 324 n. 38.

Crusader documents point to the existence of another class among the minority of city inhabitants. For some reason they seem to have been confined to the northern principalities and we did not find them in the Latin Kingdom proper. These were individuals who lived in cities and were alienated by the lord of the place. So a Syrian, Ben Mossor, is given by Bohemond III to the Hospitallers (1175) in Jubail together 'with his children and all their rights and possessions' ('cum omni eorum jure et rebus'), and in Laodicea a Jew, called Garinus, is alienated in the same way.[57] Again, in 1183 Bohemond III in Laodicea gives to the Order of St. John a large number of Greeks (six), Armenians (five), and Jews (seven). The text of the donation ends as follows:

> And those men mentioned above, Latins as well as Greeks, and Armenians and Jews, will belong to the House of the Hospitallers who will hold them and possess them in perpetuity, in peace, and without appeal, free and liberated from any *tallea*. And these are all that belong to the Hospital in Laodicea and no others unless I give to them.[58]

There are only few donations of this type and they are in the northern principalities.[59]

The interpretation of these texts is not easy. The donation clearly meant that these city inhabitants would now be bound to make payments to their new lord. It is not impossible that these were former serfs who had lived in the countryside and although they had moved into the city, their former legal status (as was the case sometimes in Europe) was preserved. In a donation of Bohemond III to the Hospital of 1194 one such man, George the notary, son of Vassilius, son of Uardus, is described as *homo peculiaris*. His property (*hereditas*) at the time of alienation will remain with Bohemond III, but new acquisitions after this date will belong to the Hospital.[60] The adjective *peculiaris* possibly points to the noun *peculium* or *peculiaris*, usually *peculiare*—the property of a serf. Thus George the notary, despite his social standing, inherited the legal position of his ancestors and did not get rid of it, even in an elevated position in the city.[61]

Whatever the case, we have very few such examples which would

[57] Delaville, no. 472 (i. 324).

[58] Ibid. i. 436–7.

[59] A similar case for Tibnin (1183), but this may perhaps be regarded as not dealing with a city (E. Strehlke, p. 10).

[60] Delaville, no. 966 (i. 613).

[61] The presence of Latins in the donation of Bohemond III is puzzling and we would regard it as a slip of the scribe. As a matter of fact in the detailed name enumeration no Latin is mentioned.

point to serfdom in the cities and we are inclined to regard them as the result of particular circumstances.

A few words should be said about the legal status of the Bedouin.[62] Several documents which enumerate Bedouin inside the borders of the kingdom, though they do not enable us to link them with a specific tribe,[63] point to the fact that the Crusaders found a legal formula for these nomads. By definition neither city inhabitants nor *ad glebam adscripti* serfs, they had a special legal status, by being the king's property. This meant that they paid for pasture rights probably in horses, camels, or sheep and were under royal and not a particular lordship's jurisdiction. This rule was well adapted to the mode of their existence as they moved from place to place: the Crown, theoretically at least, was the only factor that could assure them protection in every place in the kingdom. It needed a special royal grant to alienate a tribe or its branch to a lordship.[64] However, we do find Bedouin tribes in the possession of the Templars[65] and in a special grant the king permits the Order of St. John to allocate areas in Galilee to 100 Bedouin tents with the condition that they come from outside the frontiers of the kingdom and were never before under the king's or any other lord's domination.[66]

[62] See a list of Bedouin tribes in the kingdom in Prawer, *Latin Kingdom*, pp. 49–50.

[63] A detailed description of a Bedouin tribe and its branches or families is furnished by a charter of Baldwin IV to the Hospitallers in 1178. The tribe was once given by Queen Melissenda to Baldwin and his son Amalric, viscount of Nablus. They were sold to Baldwin of Ibelin, lord of Nablus, for the substantial sum of 5,500 besants. All in all there were 103 tents (families). It seems that the tribe is called Beni Karkas or Beni Karguas (Delaville, i. 132–4). The Beni Karkas and Solta (from al-Salt?) are called *gens*; then three units (Hassan, Beniflel, Serif) are called *radix*; these seem to be divided into families (in all ten such units), each composed from seven to twenty-one *tentoria* (on the average ten) (ibid. i. 372–3).

[64] When Baldwin III invested Philip of Nablus in 1161 with Transjordan he adds: 'salvis eciam Beduinis meis omnibus, qui de terra Montis Regalis nati non sunt' (Strehlke, no. 3, pp. 3–4).

[65] In 1179 in a peace agreement between Templars and Hospitallers the document mentions a settlement: 'de quaedam praedatione Beduinorum Templi facta a Turcopolis Gibelini' (Delaville, i. 378–9).

[66] Baldwin IV's privilege for the Hospitallers in Belvoir of 1180. They will have income: 'illorum videlicet Beduinorum quos ab alienis partibus convocare poteritis et qui in regno meo sub meo vel hominum meorum potestate nunquam fuerint' (ibid. i. 147).

Social History

8 The Italians in the Latin Kingdom[1]

Italian expansion in the Mediterranean since the eleventh century is a well-studied subject. Since the monumental works of W. Heyd (1885) and A. Schaube (1906), a large amount of new material has been published, enriching our knowledge of a famous chapter in maritime adventure and commerce. One has only to read the excellent chapter by R. S. Lopez in the *Cambridge Economic History* to realize the progress in this field of study.[2] The perspective adopted by these writers is that of the Rialto and the Porte Vecchio,[3] whereas relatively little presents the view from the Levant. It goes without saying that in the history of Italian expansion the Crusades are a favourite topic. Yet even in this domain, current studies deal mainly with the privileges of the communes, the political history of their expansion, and the volume and variety of their commerce. Very little is devoted to the colonists themselves.[4]

The aim in this chapter is to deal with the colonists and their environment in the special case of the Venetians. We shall attempt to describe the Venetian colonists and their communal quarters in the ports

---

[1] This chapter is an enlarged version of a study published as 'I Veneziani e le colonie Veneziane nel Regno Latino di Gerusalemme', *Venezia e il Levante fino al secolo XV* (Florence, 1973), pp. 625–56.

[2] W. Heyd, *Histoire du commerce du Levant au moyen-âge* i–ii (Leipzig, 1885); A. Schaube, *Handelsgeschichte der romanischen Völker des Mittelmeergebiets bis zum Ende der Kreuzzüge* (Munich, 1906); R. S. Lopez, 'Trade of Medieval Europe: the South', *Cambridge Economic History* ii (Cambridge, 1952), ch. V.

[3] For a different perspective see C. Cahen, 'Orient latin et commerce du Levant', *Bulletin de la Faculté des Lettres de Strasbourg* 29 (1951), 328-46, and Prawer, *Latin Kingdom*, pp. 352 ff.

[4] A. Sapori, 'Il commercio internazionale nel medioevo', *Studi di storia economica, sec. XIII–XIV* i (Florence, 1955, orig. 1938); G. Luzzatto, *Storia economica di Venezia dall' XI al XVI secolo* (Venice, 1961, with bibl.); G. Cracco, *Società e stato nel medioevo veneziano, sec. XII–XIV* (Florence, 1960). See also the collective volumes published by the Centro di Cultura e Civiltà della Fondazione Giorgio Cini: *Venezia della prima crociata alla conquista di Constantinopoli del 1204* (Florence, 1965); *La civiltà veneziana del secolo di Marco Polo* (Florence, 1955); *La civiltà veneziana del Trecento* (Florence, 1956); C. Errera, 'I crociati veneziani in Terra Santa dal concilio di Clermont alla morte di Ordelafo Falier', *Archivio Veneto* 38 (1890), 238–77; C. Manfroni, *Storia della marina italiana, 400–1261* (Livorno, 1899); R. Cessi, *Storia della Repubblica di Venezia* i–ii (Milan, 1944–6); R. Cessi, *Le colonie medievali italiane in Oriente* i (Bologna, 1942): *La conquista*.

of the Latin Levant and thus to arrive at some conclusion as to their way of life in the physical framework of the East. A comparison with data on similar Genoese communal quarters should contribute to a better understanding of some aspects of Crusader cities and their Italian inhabitants.

The earliest period

In the great movement of the First Crusade and the foundation of the Latin establishments in the East, Venice played a particular role. Three episodes mark her participation in the First Crusade and in the early history of the kingdom. The earliest, described by an anonymous monk from Lido some twenty years after the event, should be considered with some reservations as to the exactness of detail. He describes an expedition of 200 ships commanded by Henry, bishop of Castello, and by John, son of the Doge Michiel, which reached Jaffa in June 1100.[5] This expedition, aimed at the capture of the great port of Acre, ended up in the siege of the less important Haifa (August 1100). This brought the Venetians their first privileges in the Latin Kingdom. It was only ten years later that they reappeared to participate, together with the Palestinian Crusaders and a Norwegian fleet commanded by Sigurd I, in the capture of Sidon (December 1110). Again more than a decade passed until their appearance at the siege of the great city of Tyre with a fleet of 120 ships, commanded by the Doge Ordelafo Falier (1123).

Strangely enough, despite this sporadic and hesitant participation, the Venetians acquired more privileges in the Latin Kingdom than their Italian rivals did. By 1123 Genoa and Pisa had already received large, and one may add, almost ruinous privileges in the kingdom. And yet Venice received more, not so much in quantity as in the peculiarity and quality of her privileges.

If we were to judge by the contents of the privileges, we might be tempted to conclude that among the 'Big Three', Venice had grander political views. It is tempting to say that Venice had a sense of vision and was more conscious of her aims than her rivals were. It is of course debatable whether this was due to her earlier experience, which certainly was rather limited, or to the quality of her leadership. Venice alone seems to have thought along political lines and not only in terms of trading concessions.

The first privileges granted to the Italian communes are not always

[5] Monachus Littorensis, *RHC HOcc.* v. 253.

explicit or conclusive enough as to the kind of enterprise or settlement envisaged by their leaders and commanders. It seems that at this early stage the Italians did not think in terms of migration and settlement, but rather of domination over the lines of communication and commerce between Europe and the eastern shores of the Mediterranean. Warehouses for merchandise to be transported to the West, lodgings for travelling merchants, a number of people on the spot to guard property, guardians of privileges against encroachments, and arbiters in quarrels between merchants and sea captains, these were probably the immediate aims of the enterprising merchant adventurers at the opening of the twelfth century. 'Pro hospitatione Venetorum quando illuc irent', wrote the Doge Vitale Michiel, referring to Tyre. It is true that the privileges granted far more and referred to a third of a city, sometimes to quarters in cities to be conquered, or even in all the cities of the kingdom.[6] These privileges, if realized according to the letter, would hardly have left any city in the kingdom to the king or his vassals.

The lavishness of grants and privileges certainly reflects the urgent needs of the kingdom, but it also depicts a mutual state of ignorance as to real needs and possibilities on the part of the contracting parties. Rulers might have hoped to have Italian merchants in all their cities. The Italians, with the bargaining power on their side, demanded as much as possible. But experience soon proved that a quarter in the capital, Jerusalem, was of no practical use to merchants. Their main interest was in the *catena*, in the jetties and custom-offices of the port, where ships anchored and cargoes were exported to Europe, and not in an inland city without commercial outlets, even if it were the capital of the kingdom.

The communes never took root outside coastal cities and were concentrated in a few ports only. Although some communes had privileges in cities such as Caesarea, Ascalon, and Jaffa they never founded their colonies there. Antioch, Tripoli, Tyre, and Acre dominated commerce and in turn, were dominated in their economy by the communes. Consequently, the purely commercial clauses of the privileges and the grants of space needed for lodgings, warehouses, and bazaars, were at that stage far more important than the rights of autonomy.

If our interpretation is correct, the earliest population of these colonies was essentially and predominantly a shifting population. They were not settlers and colonizers, they were merchants on the move, in need of a

[6] A short, convenient list of privileges granted to the communes may be found in La Monte, *Feudal Monarchy*, Appendix D.

foothold in the port and custom franchises in commerce. Their families and properties stayed on in Genoa, Pisa, and Venice. The ports of the kingdom, as well as of the Muslim Levant were only so many halting places on their voyages. Of course the exigencies of commerce made their halts somewhat prolonged. Genoese or Venetians, embarking for a Crusaders' port in the last days of September to be on the spot just before Christmas, usually remained there for several months until Easter, although the bulk of their business seems to have been transacted during the first fifteen or thirty days after their arrival.

During his months of stay in the East, the Italian merchant found his compatriots in the communal lodgings, the chambers (*camerae*) above the shops and stores of the huge warehouse in his national quarter. The 'commune' in the East supplied the social frame of cohesion, a substitute for family and neighbours in far-away Italy. Its members spoke their local dialect of Italian among themselves; their agreements were written in a barbarous Latin stuffed with Italian commercial expressions. When it came to writing down a phrase not dealing with the usual objects of commerce, the notary, although an ecclesiastic, phrased it in a disastrous Latin.[7] Their own bakery and their own bath (later indicted by the virulent bishop of Acre, James of Vitry) catered for their customary tastes and habits. The church in their quarter, subordinated to the cathedral in the metropolis, with a familiar ecclesiastic, took care of their souls and, at death, of their testaments and bodies. Anyone who has tasted the griefs of exile or the anxieties of emigration can appreciate the importance of a substitute for familiar surroundings when transplanted into a foreign country.

These 'hibernating' early colonies—and we may rightly use this expression, seeing that the merchants remained in the East from December to April—were predominantly a society of sea captains, sailors, and merchants. Combining sea-going and commerce, money changing with import, export, and pirating when the conditions were propitious, they moved back and forth from Venice or Genoa to Alexandria, Acre, or Constantinople, sometimes to Cyprus, Crete, and Croton. Once a year, or once in two years, they made a longer halt, staying on in the East for four or five months. These people had no real homes except in Italy. A typical

---

[7] Cf. a deed of November 1192 written in Tyre: 'Istum sclavus fuit de imprestito marchionis bonae memoriae quod nobis dedit domino comes Enricus, quod vocatum est nomine eius Cotoble'! R. Morozzo della Rocca and A. Lombardo, *Documenti del commercio veneziano nei secoli XI–XIII* (Turin, 1940), nos. 411, 412.

representative of this type of man was, for example, the Venetian Romano Mairano.[8]

This early phase of existence roughly covers the first decade of the history of the kingdom, the period of conquest. It was probably only during the second decade, when all the coastal cities from Antioch southwards had been captured (with the exception of Tyre and Ascalon, captured in 1124 and 1153 respectively), that commerce took on a more regular rhythm. The Muslim danger on the seas was diminishing, emigration from Europe was growing and turning the exceedingly small Crusader settlements into sizeable colonies. These more normal conditions favoured the extension of commerce and the growth of the merchant colonies. It is not inappropriate to compare the next stage in the existence of the communes in the East with the process of transition from a sporadic or seasonal fair or market with wandering merchants to a fixed market favouring the emergence of a permanent merchant class in an urban settlement. It was a slow process whose main feature was the transition from prolonged stays in the East to permanent settling in the place.

The Pactum Warmundi: *The Venetians*

It is difficult to fix the exact date of this transformation, but we would suggest that it happened in the second quarter of the twelfth century, a generation after the Conquest. The famous *Pactum Warmundi*, signed by Warmund, Patriarch of Jerusalem in 1123, in the absence of Baldwin II, taken prisoner by the Muslims in April of that year, to assure Venetian help in capturing the opulent and still Muslim Tyre, may indicate a new phase in the life of the communes beyond the sea.

To evaluate the change, and the importance of the *Pactum Warmundi*, which we regard as a milestone in the evolution of the political thinking of Venice, it is worth while reviewing the earlier agreements and privileges granted to the Queen of the Adria. The earliest one is not preserved but its existence is known from the anonymous Monk of Lido.[9] According to his narrative, Godfrey of Bouillon granted (June 1100) to the Venetians a privilege in payment for their services during the summer of that year. This included the grant of a church and market-place, and an exemption from customs; it also stipulated a division of spoils in cities captured in a proportion of two-thirds to the king and one-third to the Venetians ('because the kingdom was poor', adds our chronicler). In

[8] R. Heynen, *Zur Entstehung des Kapitalismus in Venedig* (Stuttgart, 1905). Ridiculed by M. Weber, it is revindicated by G. Luzzato (Padovano), see below, p. 228 n. 27.

[9] Monachus Littorensis: see above, p. 218 n. 5. The agreement is not mentioned by Tafel–Thomas i. 64, who quote a vague note of Andreas Dandolo.

addition, if Tripoli (claimed by Raymond of St. Gilles) should be captured, the spoils would be divided on an equal basis. What really seems to have mattered at the moment was the division of spoils in cities conquered with Venetian help.[10]

At the end of 1110 another agreement was signed with the Venetians. This is known from the *Pactum Warmundi* and from a confirmation of Baldwin II in a privilege of 1125.[11] The privilege was granted by Baldwin I at the time of the capture of Sidon (December 1110). It gave the Venetians a piazza in a street in Acre (*rugae platea*), which is henceforth called *vicus Venetorum*. It seems that the king did not resign his *ban*-rights inside the *vicus*, such as the bakery, mill, bath, weights and measures, because a special grant was needed in 1123 to make them Venetian, although without *ban*-rights, that is, without the rights of monopoly on these installations. The inhabitants were able, but not forced, to use these Venetian *banalités*.[12]

The turning-point came thirteen years later with the *Pactum Warmundi*. This agreement assured the Venetians not only commercial privileges and a third of Tyre, but a kind of autonomy, which we might regard, in accordance with the later Venetian interpretation, as a creation of a state within the kingdom. It was only the belated intervention of Baldwin II that ensured some semblance of reciprocal obligations between the commune and the kingdom in the form of the service of three knights owed by the Venetians to the Crown.[13] The Venetians now claimed not only full jurisdiction (the limitation to civil cases was probably a later royal interpolation or interpretation, because there is nothing about it in the *Pactum*) over their nationals and in mixed cases, but also complete sovereign power over all inhabitants of the Venetian quarter in Tyre. The formula used to describe the new situation is significant and explicit: 'Besides, the Venetians will have the same rights of jurisdiction and

[10] Still, in 1098 Genoa received an area with thirty houses in Antioch (*Regesta*, no. 12).

[11] Tafel–Thomas i. 86 and 91: 'Praeterea illam eiusdem ruge Achon platee partem...quam rex Balduinus Jerusalem primus beato Marco dominoque Duci Ordelafo suisque successoribus in Sidonis acquisitione dedit.'

[12] *Pactum Warmundi*, Tafel–Thomas i. 85: 'Quodsi apud Achon furnum, molendinum, balneum, stateram, modios et buzas, ad uinum, oleum vel mel mensurandum, in uico suo Venetici facere voluerint, omnibus inibi habitantibus absque contradictione, quicumque uoluerit, coquere, molere, balneare, sicut ad regis propia, libere liceat.' Repeated verbatim in Baldwin II's confirmation, ibid. 91. The last phrase reads: 'absque omni contradictione, pretio suo, quoquere, mollere, balneare et mensurare.'

[13] Tafel–Thomas i. 93. The number of knights is not mentioned in the original grant where only the participation of the Venetians in the defence is announced. In the middle of the twelfth century it was reckoned as the service of three knights.

taxation over *burgesses of whatever origin,* living in the quarter and the
houses of the Venetians, *as the king has over his own.*'[14] This is a new
attitude, an almost revolutionary change, and the Venetians, like one
toying with a new idea, came back to it when they summed up the treaty:
'They will hold their third of Tyre and Ascalon, *libere et regaliter, sicut rex
alias duas [partes].*'[15]

This new definition, created in 1123, was vindicated by the Venetians
as long as the kingdom existed. The kings of Jerusalem, on the other hand,
tried to narrow down and disregard the relative clauses of the agreement,
but the Venetians came back to it again and again. In 1243 the famous
Venetian *bailli,* Marsiglio Zorzi, who was instrumental in overthrowing
the Hohenstaufen rule, indicated in his report to Venice: 'We have in the
city of Tyre one third . . . and we have our court perfect, as has the king
his own.'[16] This concept of sovereignty came to its fullest expression in
1277 when John of Montfort, lord of Tyre and Toron, tried to renew his
relations with the Commune of Venice. The agreement written by the
Patriarch's notary, Bartholemew de Firmo, for John of Montfort and the
Venetians, the *bailli* Albert Maurocenus and his counsellors Marco
Foscareni and Philip Cornaro, contains the following: 'Whereas the Doge
and the commune of the Venetians have by their privileges one-third of
the city of Tyre and its appurtenances . . . freely and royally, as *consorts and
true lords* of that third part, therefore they can exercise justice, criminal and
civil, over all men who belong to their jurisdiction.'[17] There is more to

[14] Tafel–Thomas i. 88: 'Praeterea super cuiusque gentis burgenses habitantes in uico et
domibus Venetorum eandem iusticiam et consuetudines, quas rex super suos, Venetici
habeant.' It may be argued that this contradicts other regulations of justice in the same
privilege (ibid. 87 and 93), which state that if the defendant is not a Venetian the case will
come before the royal court. The contradiction is apparent only, as this probably refers to the
inhabitants of Tyre who did not live in the Venetian quarter.

[15] Tafel–Thomas i. 88 and 93. Here we also find a general declaration (i. 85) of policy,
especially for Jerusalem: 'In omnibus . . . ciuitatibus Venetici ecclesiam et integram rugam
unamque plateam siue balneum, nec non et furnum habeant, jure hereditario imperpetuum
ab omni exactioni libera, sicut sunt regis propria. Verum in plathea Jerusalem tantum ad
proprium habeant, quantum rex habere solitus est.' Cf. i. 90. This refers to property only but
not to lordship rights over the territory.

[16] Tafel–Thomas ii. 358: '. . . habemus in ciuitate Tyri terciam partem, que bene diuisa est
a partibus regni . . . Nam habemus nostram curiam integram, secundum quod rex habet.'
Again in the same report: 'Et banna in nostro tercierio imponimus et exigimus libere, ut rex
in suis duabus partibus imponit et exigit' (ibid. ii. 359).

[17] Tafel–Thomas iii. 152: 'Quod, cum dominus dux et commune Venetiarum per
privilegium eorum habeant tertiam partem civitatis Tyrensis et suarum pertinentiarum,
secundum terminos definitos ab antiquo *libere et regaliter, sicut consortes et veri domini ipsius
tertiae partis,* quod ipsi possint exercere justitiam tam civilem quam criminalem super omnes
homines, qui pertinent ad jurisdictionem suam, sive Venetos, sive alios habitantes et manentes

(continued)

come. A curious paragraph, which seems somewhat brazen and expresses contemporary Venetian bargaining power, reads:

> And although in the above agreement, the Lord John of Montfort is in many places called 'lord of Tyre', according to the custom which is generally followed in these regions, still it is hereby declared by the above-mentioned arbiters, that this title or name should not and will not prejudice any of the contracting parties, in no way and in no manner, not here and not elsewhere, neither will it add or diminish their rights.[18]

This use of the term *regaliter* to qualify possession and the noun *consortes* to describe the legal standing of the Venetians *vis-à-vis* the king or the state point to the emergence of a new concept and a departure from the existing relations between commune and state. If we remember that at the time of the signature of the *Pactum Warmundi*, the city of Tyre was a royal city, then the claim of the Venetians is not to the status of a vassal, not even to that of a tenant-in-chief of the Crown, but to that of an independent sovereign limited by an obscure notion of the general framework of the state. Patriarch and barons who signed this agreement were certainly conscious of the meaning of the *Pactum*. This explains the strong sanction clause of the agreement:

> We Warmund, the Patriarch of Jerusalem, will, with the help of God, bring the king, if he is ever released from his captivity, to confirm the above agreement taking oath on the Gospels; and if it happens that someone else becomes king in the Kingdom of the Jerusalemites, then, either he will be made to confirm the above-mentioned promises before he is appointed or otherwise we shall not agree in any way that he should be elevated to kingship. In the same way the successors of the barons and new barons will make the confirmations.[19]

In the whole constitutional history of the kingdom there is only one unique parallel to that type of sanction and that is the coronation oath of the kings of Jerusalem to observe the laws and the customs—that is, the whole legal foundation of the kingdom!

Thus the *Pactum Warmundi* is more than the result of haggling over

in tertiaria sua, exceptis hominibus ligiis domini Tyri et burgensibus suis, quos habitare contingeret in tertiaria praedictorum Venetorum.' The lord of Tyre has the same rights over all the inhabitants of the remaining two parts of the city, except Venetians who happen to live in his area.

[18] Tafel–Thomas iii. 157–8: 'Licet autem in supradicta compositione in pluribus locis supradictus Dominus Joannes de Monteforti appellatur Dominus Tyri, secundum modum in partibus istis generaliter observatum, tamen per praedictos arbitros extitit declaratum, quod praedicta nominatio sive appellatio neutri partium possit vel debeat aliquo modo vel ingenio, vel hic, vel alibi, aliquod praejudicium generare, nec jus addat, vel minuat inter partes.'

[19] Tafel–Thomas i. 88. This clause is left out of the royal confirmation of Baldwin II.

exempted quarters or economic privileges; it is an attempt to create a semi-independent state in the framework of the kingdom. Nothing similar happened again until 200 years later when the Genoese Benedetto Zaccaria attempted to create a Genoese state in the kingdom.[20]

In the light of this we would suggest that the later title of the Doge of Venice, *Quartae partis et dimidiae totius Romani Imperii dominator*, was conceived in the Lebanese city of Tyre, three generations before the capture of Constantinople.

The *Pactum Warmundi*, which marks a new departure in political thinking, played a similar role in shaping the character of the Venetian establishment in the East. The point of departure was the clause that granted the Venetians a third of all land belonging to the city. Earlier treaties sometimes accorded the communes land adjoining the city, 'one mile' around it. This might have been a deliberately vague phrase or a conscious precaution to assure food and provision to a commune. In Tyre we meet with a different approach. A whole third of a rich lordship, which, despite its narrow frontiers, counted some 120 villages, would henceforth belong to the commune.[21] Having gone so far as to create an independent lordship in the city, they demanded, and were granted, a seignory of the normal Palestinian type, that is, a city as capital and the surrounding rural area with its villages and peasants as its domain. But we suppose that beside this reasoning, there was another factor that influenced the Venetian demand. The last generation, between 1100 and 1123, although mainly non-Venetian, had witnessed the crystallization of a local Italian population. It is hard to believe that the Venetians claimed jurisdiction over all the inhabitants in their quarter and over a very rich rural area, which needed their constant vigilance and the establishment of an administration, solely for the benefit of the shifting population of sailors and merchants in the maritime city. Certainly, any income accruing from these possessions would profit the metropolis, but it seems more plausible to suggest that the Venetians began to think in terms of colonization and settlement. It is true that the main occupation of their settlers was and remained commerce, but at the same time, the enfeoffment of a part of their property to their nationals, the establishment of a local administration to supervise the rural area and exploit it, to collect dues and customs from the inhabitants of the quarter—in brief the establishment of

[20] See R. Lopez, *Genova marinara nel ducento* (Messina–Milan, 1932) pp. 137 ff., and cf. Prawer, *Histoire* ii. 533–6.
[21] See above, Ch. 6, pp. 145–8.

an organization to run a lordship—seems to indicate a major change in the social and demographic composition of the commune in the East. And although it might be argued either that this change had already taken place before the signing of the *Pactum Warmundi*, or that it was the *Pactum* that created the necessary conditions for such a change, it seems to fit in with the whole situation of the Latin Kingdom that the second quarter of the twelfth century witnessed the crystallization of an Italian settlement, real colonies in the ports of the kingdom.

From merchant to colonist

The nucleus of the more sedentary population was linked with the possession of landed property in city and countryside. Someone had to administer this and keep an open eye on the rulers who blissfully tended to forget the privileges granted. At the same time commerce was getting more voluminous, more people were coming with the *stolae*, and more would stay on in the East. There were evident advantages in establishing business headquarters in a communal quarter in Antioch, Acre, or Tyre, although big transactions were rather concluded for Muslim or Byzantine ports. Until the thirteenth century no riots or pogroms against the communes, like those in Constantinople, no sequestrations of property, were ever witnessed in the Crusaders' establishments in the East. The officials of the commune and the mercantile population were taking root in the ports of the Levant.

Merchants concluding agreements for the East knew beforehand that they would stay there for three or five years. Some even brought over their wives and children. Genoese contracts show names with Crusaders patronymics, such as Bertrand from Syria, John Andrew of Tripoli, John of Acre, Bonvassal of Antioch. Some introduce clauses into their contracts, such as: 'if I stay overseas', 'if I do not come back from Syria'. This is not limited to the Genoese only. Earlier Venetian contracts already mention Venetian merchants who add to their signatures: 'inhabitant of Acre', 'inhabitant of Tyre'—we even find a Venetian 'inhabitant of [Genoese] Gibelet'. These examples illustrate the fact that in the middle of the twelfth century we reach a new phase in the existence of the communes. These merchants are no longer occasional residents for the duration of a business voyage, a winter, or even a year, but genuine colonists, subjects of their mother-cities who are already moving to settle in the Crusaders' Levant. No wonder then, that at the end of the First Kingdom we find Italian families which had lived in the East for three consecutive generations. An example, happily preserved in a Venetian contract, shows a Peter

Morosini, an inhabitant of Acre in the second half of the twelfth century; his son James established himself in Tripoli and his grandson Nicolino lived again in Acre when he signed an agreement with one of the merchant captains. The first Morosini, Peter, still possessed property in Venice, although he is already described as 'Petrus Maurocenus de Acris'.[22] As to his descendants, they probably sold out their property in Venice before definitely settling in the East.

The sources, so rich in relation to commerce, fail us bitterly when it comes to describe the Italian colonists established in the East. Still we have some indications which may help to draw at least an outline of the human element living in these colonies.

Whereas in a city like Genoa the wealthy nobility controlled the Eastern trade, but, as far as we can ascertain, did not settle in the East, the Venetians had a different capital structure at home and a different type of colonist in the East. Among the Venetians we discern a higher class of society established in *Outremer*, such as one Rolandus Contarenus, who was richly enfeoffed in Tyre and whose family can be traced for three generations in that city.[23] A Guillaume Jourdain might be a Venetian or a Provençal knight married to a Pantaleone and holding rich property in the place.[24] The existence of this element in the Venetian colony should be sought in the fact that the Venetians, masters of a third of the lordship of Tyre, organized their administration by enfeoffing a part of their land and income to Venetians of knightly origin against rents and military services. But whereas a similar procedure by the Genoese in Gibelet ended with the full independence of the Embriacci, the Venetians, far better organized, did keep an eye on their nationals, although some losses were inevitable.[25]

Another reason for having settlers of a higher social class is probably connected with the fact that some of the Venetian representatives in the East, of knightly origin, stayed on there. Some had commercial connections before being appointed and then remained in the place. As an example, we might cite Domenico Acontano, who in 1184 administered the possessions of San Marco in Tyre. The same man served later as *bailli* of Venice although not a very successful one. Members of the same family, the

---

[22] R. Morozzo della Rocca and A. Lombardo, *Documenti*, no. 463 (A.D. 1203): 'Nicolinus Maurocenus filius quondam Iacobi Mauroceni habitator [*sic!*] Tripoli, quod Iacobus filius fuit quondam Petri Mauroceni habitatoris Acconis.' Ibid. no. 171 (A.D. 1166): 'Petrus Maurocenus habitator in predicta Acres' (an agreement with Romano Mairano).

[23] On the Contareni in Tyre, see above, p. 149 n. 14.

[24] Above, p. 149.

[25] See Prawer, *Latin Kingdom*, pp. 495 ff.

Guido, witnessed an act of Philip Cornaro, *bailli* of Venice in 1222 in
Acre, and another Acontano, John, served in the same year as ambassador
of the Venetian *bailli* in Acre to the consul of Pisa in the same city.[26] The
commercial contracts of the Venetians show a fair number of noble
families not only investing in trade with Acre and Tyre, but actually
staying on and doing business in the Latin Orient.[27] We see, for example,
James (Jacopo) Dandolo doing business in Acre in 1186; his son Giovanni
acts as *vicecomes* of Venice in Tyre and Acre. As he guaranteed the loans of
his brother Marco, he found himself in an embarrassing position, when,
as viscount, he had to announce his insolvency in the court over which he
was presiding. Another family are the Dulce (written also Dulcis, Dous).
Manasse Dulce was viscount of Venice in Tyre, a Thomas Dulce had
property in the city and was administrator of the property of San Marco,
a Petrus Dulce is known in Acre after 1209, Domenico Dulsi in Tyre in
1211. Another case is that of the noble family of Falieri. They appear as
early as 1129 and 1130 transacting business in Acre, although we do not
know if Otto Falieri, mentioned in these early documents, had any fief in
Tyre. Members of the Falieri family, still living partly in Venice and
partly in Syria, appear again in 1206, when at the death of Leo Falier, his
brother Vitale, still living in Venice, was enfeoffed by the Doge of Venice
with his late brother's property.[28]

   The settling of knightly or patrician families in the East seems to have
been a particular feature of the Venetian colony. Despite the far richer

---

[26] Domenico Acontano, *Regesta*, no. 639 (A.D. 1184); *Reg.* no. 1114; ibid., pp. 292, 297.
Philip—*Reg.*, no. 956; John—*Reg.*, no. 961.
   [27] The following names are from R. Morozzo della Rocca—A. Lombardo, *Doc. del
commercio veneziano* (see above, p. 220 n. 7). Domenico Michiel (1104) possibly in Antioch—
no. 31; Marino Michiel and Otto Falier in Acre (1129)—no. 53; Otto Falier in Syria
(1130)—no. 56; Marino Michiel in Tyre (1132)—no. 62; Enrico Contarini in Acre—no.
71; Marino Michiel in Acre (1147)—no. 90; Giovanni Dandolo in Acre (1161)—no. 155;
the three generations of the Morosini—see above, p. 227 n. 22; Pietro Ziani in Acre
(1178)—nos. 289, 292; Iacobus Dandolo in Acre (1186)—no. 376; Marco Contarini in Tyre
(1190)—no. 385; Domenico Contarini in Tyre (1192)—nos. 411–12; Iacobus Dandolo in
Acre (1192)—no. 463; Giovanni and Marco Dandolo in Acre (1209)—no. 509; Marco
Giustiniani in Tyre and Acre (1209)—nos. 510, 514, 521; Giovanni and Marco Dandolo in
Tyre (1211)—no. 529; Viviano da Molin in Acre—no. 59; Leonardo Querini (1209) in
Acre—no. 514; one of the Nenni is presbyter in Acre (1209)—no. 514. These examples may
contribute to the clarification of Sayous's controversial theory regarding capital and capitalist
factors in Venice, Cf. G. Luzzato, 'Capitale e i lavoro nel commercio veneziano dei sec. XI e
XII'. *Studi di storia economica veneziana* (Padua, 1954), pp. 117–23.
   [28] On the Dandolo see in the previous note. On the Dulce, see *Regesta*, nos. 114, 1332. On
the Falieri, Tafel–Thomas ii. 11–13. On Venetian families which settled in the East see
also D. Jacoby, cit. p. 249 n. 99.

Genoese documentation, we can scarcely discern such cases in their Levantine colonies.

The Venetian quarter in Acre

Our description of the human element that settled in the East may be complemented by one of the Venetian quarter in Acre. Two detailed inventories of the quarters in Tyre and in Acre, drawn up in 1243 and 1244 by the *bailli* Marsiglio Zorzi and the newly executed archaeological survey of Acre in addition to the fortunate survival of original maps of the city drawn up at the end of the thirteenth century, make this reconstruction possible. Naturally, much will be hypothetical, but for an age in which topographical and quantitative evaluations are hard to come by, such a reconstruction is worth attempting.

Our best guide for a physical description of the Venetian quarter in Acre are the maps probably drawn by Pietro Vesconte for Marino Sanudo (British Library, Add. 27.376 and Oxford, Tanner 190, fo. 207).[29] The archeological survey of Acre undertaken in 1962 by the architect A. Kesten[30] on behalf of the National Parks Authority facilitates topographical identification.[31]

The nucleus of the Venetian property in Acre was acquired during the siege of Sidon in 1110. Its central part was the *ruga*, a street or thoroughfare, perhaps with a larger square (*platea*), which began at the house of one Pietro Zanni,[32] and had inside its boundaries a former mosque (*machomaria*) and some stone houses. Its location can be ascertained by the fact that the *ruga* ended in the monastery of St. Demetrius.[33] This monastery or church[34] must have been located at the north-eastern corner of the

[29] The maps were published by J. Prawer, 'Historical maps of Acre' (Heb.), *Eretz Israel* 2 (1952), 175–84. Cf. B. Dichter, *The Maps of Acre. A Historical Cartography* (Acre, 1973). The problem of Marino Sanudo's maps and their relation to the work of Pietro Vesconte, and the maps commissioned by Paolino of Pozzuoli is rather complicated. We also have an earlier map of Acre in the manuscript of Matthew Paris. Cf. J. Prawer in the Introduction to the reprint of Marino Sanudo, *Liber Secretorum Fidelium Crucis* (Toronto Univ. Press, 1972), pp. xviii–xix.

[30] A. Kesten, *Acre. The Old City, Survey and Planning* (Jerusalem, 1962).

[31] A. Kesten's survey almost entirely changes the conclusions of earlier studies of Acre by E. Rey, 'Étude sur la topographie de la ville d'Acre au XIIe siècle', *Mém. de la soc. nat. des Antiquaires de France*, 39 (1878), 115–45; idem., 'Supplément à l'étude sur la topographie de la ville d'Acre', ibid. 49 (1888), 1–18, and even the still-indispensable N. Makhouli and C. N. Johns, *Guide to Acre* (Jerusalem, 1945). Cf. Benvenisti, *Crusaders*, pp. 78–114. A topographical study of Crusader Acre remains a *desideratum*.

[32] A Theophile Zeno is mentioned in 1117 as the earliest representative of Venice in the Latin East (Tafel–Thomas i. 77).

[33] Tafel–Thomas i. 86

[34] The origins of this church are unknown. St. Demetrius, the Megalomartyr of Sirmium

(continued)

Venetian quarter, hard on the seaboard since it was swallowed up (*c.* 1290) by the sea.[35] This major thoroughfare was the pivot line, running from north-east to south-west of the Venetian quarter. Using thirteenth-century data and the existent maps, the following picture might be drawn of the quarter as a whole.

Its shape was that of a swollen cresent. Its southern side clung to the seaboard, taking up almost half of it. In the north-east, the quarter was limited by the royal *arsenal* (from Arabic: *dar al-ṣan'a*—repair place of ships), and in the north-west it was limited by the quarter of the Order of St. John; along its western front the Venetians confronted the Genoese, and on the borderline was the famous monastery of St. Sabba which gave its name to one of the bloodiest fratricidal wars in the Latin East.[36] In the south-west the Venetian, as well as the Genoese (who had no direct outlet to the sea) and Pisan quarters converged on the port area near the Iron Gate (*Porta Ferrea*).

By the middle of the thirteenth century the quarter was enclosed on all sides by newly built walls.[37] Here we may follow a description dating from 1260 which perfectly tallies with the extant maps of the period. The description is part of an agreement by which the church of St. Demetrius is recognized as dependent on the parish church of St. Mark. The presbyter of St. Demetrius will henceforth be appointed by the parish priest of St. Mark but with the consent of the bishop of Acre. The parish priest of St. Mark will recognize his dependence on the bishop by assisting ceremonies at the cathedral church of *Sta Crux* and by receiving the consecrated oil for his church from him.

The new fortifications began at the south-western corner of the quarter, the meeting-point of the royal, Pisan, and Genoese possessions.[38] From

---

(Mitrovic) was primarily an Oriental saint. He was 'adopted' by the Crusaders as a warrior-saint and appears in 1098, together with St. Mercurius, at the battle of Antioch. The church of St. Demetrius in Acre was possibly a Greek church usurped by the Latins, though St. Demetrius had his earliest chapel in the West, in Ravenna, and it is not impossible that his cult was a Venetian import.

[35] *Registre de Nicolas IV*, ed. V. Langlois, no. 2919. The topographical position of this church can additionally be ascertained in relation to the church of St. Mark in its immediate neighbourhood (Tafel–Thomas iii. 32), and its proximity to the Great Palace of the Fondaco (ibid. ii. 394). See below, p. 233.

[36] Prawer, *Histoire* ii. 359–75.

[37] The newly built walls against the neighbouring quarters of St. John, the Genoese, and the Provençals are indicated in the agreement (A.D. 1260) between Florence, bishop of Acre, and the Venetian *bailli* in Acre, John Dandolo (Tafel–Thomas iii. 32).

[38] The Genoese, Pisan, and Hospitaller quarters are clearly indicated on all Crusader maps of Acre.

ITALIAN QUARTERS
IN MEDIEVAL ACRE

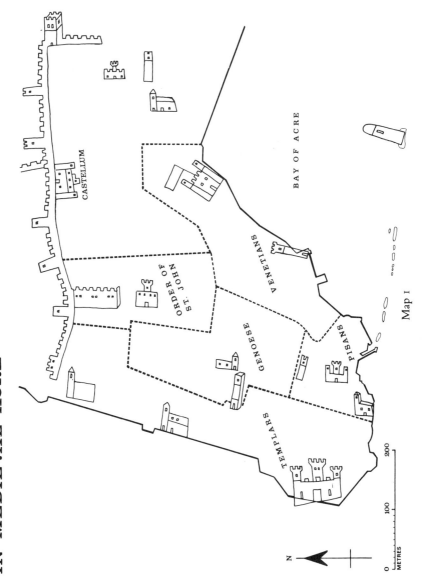

CASTELLUM

ORDER OF
ST. JOHN

GENOESE

VENETIANS

PISANS

TEMPLARS

BAY OF ACRE

Map I

N

METRES

0   100   200

here the wall proceeded to the north, dividing the Pisans in the south and the Genoese in the west from the Venetians. There was a *ruga Paleacia* or *Palearea* in this neighbourhood and a church of the Amalfitans close by. Reaching the north-western corner of the quarter, the walls divided the Venetians from their mighty neighbours, the Order of St. John. Up to here there was no gate in the walls. It was only on turning to the east that a fortified gate was opened connecting the Venetian with the neighbouring Provençal quarter. At this point, inside the quarter, was the 'Great Palace of the Bailli'; on the other side the church of St. Mary of the Provençals, which belonged to the Commune of Marseilles.[39]

The new Venetian walls against the Quarter of St. John were built in this area on an earlier 'Onion Market'. Near the Provençal quarter, turning now from north to south, a Lombard community once settled. Later this area was integrated into the Venetian quarter. From here the walls continued to the south, dividing the quarter from that of the Patriarch and the Arsenal. If our identifications are correct, the Venetian seaboard measured some 300 m and the parallel north-western perimeter some 463 m, whereas its southern and northern sides were very narrow indeed. The whole area comprised approximately 3·16 ha.[40]

The Venetian quarter was divided into four subdivisions, three of which we can place and identify. The one we find difficult to identify is along a *ruga Firmi*, a small quarter, where the commune had a bakery (*furnus*) and three houses, two of them built in two storeys. One of the houses had two shops on its ground floor.[41]

The central part of the quarter was taken up by the Fondaco (*funticus*), which, at least as used by Marsiglio Zorzi, denotes not only the 'warehouse'

[39] The *ruga Paleacia* is mentioned (Tafel–Thomas iii. 32) near a royal bakery. The *ruga Palearea* and the property of the Amalfitan church are known from a deed of 1267, *Regesta*, no. 1346. The new fortified gate connecting with the Order of St. John is noted in Tafel–Thomas iii. 32. The vicinity of the Provençal complex is described in a confirmation of John of Brienne to Marseilles, *Regesta*, 855, and in a grant to the Order of St. John by Henry I of Cyprus and Jerusalem (A.D. 1252) to build two new gates in their quarter connecting with the Genoese and Provençal quarters, *Regesta*, no. 1200.

[40] The 'Onion market' ('platea ubi vendebantur cepae') and a new gate, 'the small gate of St. Mark' are mentioned in 1259. *Regesta, Add.* 1273a. The Patriarch's quarter and the Arsenal are indicated on all contemporary maps of the city. M. Benvenisti has kindly supplied an evaluation of the surface of the communal quarters in Acre: Venice, 4·5 ha; Genoa, 6·5 ha; Pisa, 3 ha. This includes non-built-up areas such as streets and piazzas (probably over 25 per cent of the surface).

[41] The *ruga Firmi* is mentioned only once in our documentation (Tafel–Thomas ii. 390). *Domus* means here, as in some other places, 'apartment' or 'room'. *Domus in solario* is a second-floor apartment. See below, p. 234 n. 50.

but the whole complex of buildings, magazines, and lodgings.[42] Three landmarks characterized the area: the palace of the *bailli*, the Great Palace of the Fondaco, and the tower near the sea. The northernmost of these buildings was the palace of the *bailli* which faced, across the small Provençal quarter, the cantons of the Genoese and of the Order of St. John.[43]

The palace of the *bailli* was a two- or three-storey building.[44] Its ground floor was taken up by six large shops. It was the size of the shops, or possibly their location, that brought the commune a more than handsome income; their lessees paid 153 and 160 besants in rent, and the remaining three shops 180 besants yearly.[45] Here, in addition, there were six apartments on the second floor paying 16, 17½, and 18 besants in annual rent. Outside the house was a portico or loggia which almost connected the palace with the church of St. Mark.[46] Around it were eight benches or tables (*tabule siue banche*) for displaying merchandise. The rent here was quite high, from 12 besants paid for a small bench, to one which paid 25¾ besants.

Near by, between the palace of the *bailli* and the church of St. Mark, were four more shops and a house which could be reached by crossing the courtyard of the palace.

The next building was the major Venetian establishment in Acre. This was the Great Palace of the Fondaco, no doubt the large building facing the sea, marked on contemporary maps of the city as flying a huge banner. The whole ground floor and its basement were taken up by shops and apartments. Sixteen shops on the ground floor (one called *de la cocorda*), paid from 34 to 61 besants rental; the rest were small rooms,[47] twelve in

---

[42] There is some confusion as to this expression. See W. Heyd in *Sitzungsber. der Münchener Akad. Hist. Classe* 5 (1880), 617–27; idem, op. cit. ii. 430; A. Schaube, op. cit., p. 123 and n. 3. Normally it should denote a warehouse, often a warehouse and tavern (so in Aramaic and Hebrew, differently in Greek). In this the *fonticum, funticus*, etc., or *Fondaco* differs from *funda*—'land', 'market', 'market-place'. But Marsiglio Zorzi has 'sub magno palatio fontici super viam et campum' (Tafel–Thomas ii. 391).

[43] Tafel–Thomas iii. 32.

[44] Tafel–Thomas ii. 390: 'sub palatio ubi habitat Baiulus' and ii. 391: 'juxta portam ecclesie versus domum ubi habitat Baiulus'; ii. 390: *in solario medio*, which can only mean that there was one floor above the middle one.

[45] The list of *stationes* and their rents (Tafel–Thomas ii. 390).

[46] Ibid. ii. 391: 'Tabule siue banche circa logiam existentes'; 'item quatuor stationes, inter dictum palatium et ecclesiam Sancti Marci existentes'.

[47] Ibid.: 'Stationes sub *magno palacio fontici* super viam et campum existentes'. Possibly ground floor and basement, ibid. ii. 392: 'Camere in magno palatio fontici *intra et inferius* existentes'.

all, paying 3 besants monthly rental during the season. One of the rooms was kept by the *bailli* as a store-house for property recommended to him by merchants, perhaps also for property of deceased merchants to which their relatives had a legitimate claim. In another room lived the parish priest of St. Mark and, in a room beneath him, the *placearius*, that is subaltern officer, crier, and assistant to the court.[48]

Prices were higher on the second floor of the Great Palace of the Fondaco:[49] here we count eleven rooms paying from 6 to 15 besants per apartment during the arrival of the *carauana*.[50] The upper third floor of the Great Palace of the Fondaco had four small rooms facing St. Demetrius, which paid 4 to 5 besants monthly during the season. Here, in addition, were two large rooms, paying 5 besants monthly and 4 smaller ones, perhaps without windows, leased for 2 besants per month.[51] The smaller number of rooms in the upper floor can be explained by the defence towers of the building, which already appear on the second floor.[52]

The great Fondaco was near the church of St. Demetrius and a narrow courtyard connected the two.[53] Here there was a cistern, so important in the Near East, and even more so during the War of St. Sabbas when the quarter was in a state of siege. A two-storey house, a four-storey house, and its ground floor which was used as a stable, were rented yearly for moderate sums of 8, 16, and 30 besants respectively.[54]

There were some buildings inside the Fondaco. It is interesting to note that one of the houses was not rented by the commune, but paid a recognizance *cens* only. It was a two-storey building with eleven rooms.[55]

---

[48] Ibid. ii. 392.

[49] The Great Palace of the Fondaco should probably be identified with Khan al-Shawarda, whose Burj al-Sultan is certainly of Crusader origin.

[50] The usual vocabulary of the inventory makes analysis difficult. For 'apartment' or 'room', it has not *camera* or *habitatio*, but *domus*. So the heading has the curious note: 'Domus in palatio magno fontici in *solario de medio* (upper floor) existentes' (ii. 393). That in reality apartments were meant, is proved by a comparison with the items: 'Est *tertia domus*, ubi habitat plebanus, que est super illa, ubi habitat Johannes Gastaldo' (ibid.) and the description of the ground floor: 'Est *camera* una parua in qua habitat Johannes Gastaldio, plazarius communis, que camera est subtus cameram ubi habitat plebanus' (ibid. ii. 392). For other *termini* see below, p. 235 n. 56.

[51] Ibid. ii. 394: 'Alie quatuor qui sunt intus a predictis, et sunt parue.'

[52] Ibid. ii. 393: 'Est quarta domus [in solario de medio], ubi est turris.'

[53] Cf. ibid. ii. 394: 'In capite fontici iuxta sanctum Dimitrium sunt V habitationes' and ii. 395: 'curia que est iusta ecclesiam.'

[54] Ibid. ii. 394.

[55] Ibid. ii. 394. It was held by one 'domina Pauia'. She paid 7 besants to the church of St. Mark. The Venetian *bailli* notes that '. . . est iam longum tempus quod antecessores sui et ipsa habuit a commune Venecie'. This might point to an old-established family.

As in many medieval cities, and even more so in the Near East, houses were built one leaning against one another. Even the Great Palace of the Fondaco did not escape this pattern. Near the outside staircase which led to the upper floor of the Palace was a huge building, some four storeys high, with ten rooms or apartments, which used the palace staircase.[56] Part of this building was employed for communal purposes: two storage rooms for keeping stones, chalk, and timber and another kept by a second *placearius* of the commune.[57]

The next group of buildings in the Venetian quarter was in the southern part of the area, directly on the seaside. Its two major buildings were a church and a tower. This tower figures on the contemporary maps of the city just outside the inner port of the city.[58] It was three floors high: its room on the highest floor was rented for 14 besants per month during the caravan season; one room on the second floor for 7 besants per month. A vaulted room beneath the tower served as a prison.[59]

To the west of the Fondaco was a group of buildings which seem to have belonged to the church of St. Mark.[60] Near by was a two-storey house with three apartments on the lower floor and one above them. This was held half and half by the commune and one Pandulf.

Near the tower was the inner port of the city and on its western side, the Iron Gate (*Porta Ferrea*). From here an iron chain was strung across the sea-entrance to the lighthouse tower in the middle of the bay.[61] From the

[56] Ibid. ii. 394. Inside a 'domus communis . . . est secunda habitatio, que est iusta scalas magni palacij.' The building had four storeys, and rooms are indicated as 'inferius', 'solarium medium', 'solarium', and 'superior pars'. The entrance to the last was 'per scalas magni palacij' (ii. 395).

[57] Ibid. ii. 395: '. . . due camera . . . quas commune tenet pro imittendo lignamina, calcinam, lapides'; another room 'ubi habitat Buraffus Plazarius'.

[58] Marked on the Vatican and Oxford maps of Acre. The inner port is marked on all medieval maps of the city. It can also be clearly seen on the French map of Jacotin drawn up during the Napoleonic expedition. It seems to have been in the place which later served as a stable for the Turkish garrison. Today it is partly in the area of a restaurant.

[59] ii. 395: 'Habemus unam turrim iusta ecclesiam super mare'. Besides the churches of St. Demetrius and St. Mark, there was also a church of St. Matthew in the quarter. The latter was probably near the palace of the *bailli*, as it is described 'sub logia Venetorum que est iuxta ecclesiam Sancti Mathei', if it is not a mistake for 'Sti Marci'. See G. Bigoni, 'Quattro documenti genovesi sulle contese d'Oltramare nel secolo XIII', *Arch. stor. italiano* 24 (1899), 65. On the loggia see above, p. 233 n. 46. Cf. Tafel–Thomas ii. 397: a house bought 'ex opposito logie nostre Sti Marci'.

[60] Marsiglio Zorzi's inventory does not detail this property, possibly because its income did not belong to the commune; he says: 'Firmatur versus occidentem in domibus de *helemosina* existentibus' (Tafel–Thomas ii. 395), which may refer to St. Mark. See further below, Ch. 12.

[61] The name *Porta Ferrea* is indicated on all maps. The position of the Iron Gate, the chain, and the lighthouse is remarkably well marked in MSS. Vatican and Oxford–Tanner.

economic as well as from the military point of view, especially in the fabric of inter-commune relations, this was a most important area. Though we do not know the details, it may be assumed that the different powers which had access to the port area split it up between them, either by simple division or by building short jetties as landing points for their ships.[62] The most ancient part of the commune's property was around the mosque, mentioned as early as 1110, which became a two-storey lodging house, but was still called *Machomaria*.[63] Two houses, both three storeys high, stood near by; one with two shops on the ground floor, two rooms on the first and one on the second floor, and the other with one shop and two rooms on the ground floor and one each on the second and third floor. The strategic and economic position of this area explains the extremely high property prices. For a house which had a large magazine or shop (*statio*) and two apartments one above the other, Marsiglio Zorzi paid 1,200 besants; half the annual income was 82 besants and an additional 16 besants for the benches outside the house.[64]

We have tried to describe the Venetian quarter of Acre, but we have to be careful not to draw more conclusions from it than our sources warrant. Whereas a contemporary Genoese inventory listed *all* houses in its quarter, Marsiglio Zorzi's report lists (with one exception) *communal property* only. Thus we do not know the actual number of houses in the Venetian quarter. Even so, the description with its topographical and architectural details is of interest and importance.

Summing up, we arrive at the following results: the commune possessed only fourteen houses in its own quarter. Half of them were two-storey buildings, two were four-storey buildings, one house had only one floor, and the two major buildings, the palace of the *bailli* and the Great Palace of the Fondaco had three storeys. Almost all these houses had shops and magazines of different sizes. Their total number was thirty-one. The number of rooms or apartments, whether leased on an annual basis or

[62] M. Benvenisti as well as J. Riley-Smith and D. Jacoby argue that the seaboard, the *catena*, was undivided and remained royal property. The *catena* should be carefully distinguished from the *funda*. I previously misread the phrase: 'Hec sunt domus comunis Venecie, que sunt supra capum nostrum' (Tafel–Thomas ii. 396) as meaning 'Supra caput nostrum'. Jacoby rightly reads 'supra campum nostrum' and his reading is confirmed by the MS. Querini. Yet cf. above, p. 235 n. 59 which mentions a Venetian tower 'super mare'.

[63] Ibid.: 'Habet . . . domum cum solario, que vocatur Machomaria.' The earliest grant to Venice must have concerned an area near the seaboard.

[64] Ibid. ii. 397. It is not clear if the 1,200 besants represent half or the whole price. The 82 besants certainly represented half the rent. If 180 besants (164 + 16) was the annual rent, then they represented less than 7 per cent of the value of the property.

rented with the arrival of the fleets, was seventy-four. The number of houses is very small indeed, but they only represent houses that belonged to the Commune of Venice and not the total number of buildings in the quarter. To visualize a communal quarter as a whole, the Venetian inventory is not sufficient, but we may have recourse to another inventory—that of the Genoese in Acre. Contemporary with the description of Marsiglio Zorzi, the inventory drawn up in 1249 by the Genoese authorities, Guillielmo di Bulgaro and Simone Malocello, furnishes data of the greatest importance.[65]

The Genoese quarter in Acre

The study of this inventory has caused some confusion and even the critical edition of C. Desimoni has not been correctly interpreted. The inventory has five main divisions, often summarized as allegedly representing the total annual income of the commune. This was straightened out by W. Heyd and followed by Desimoni, who pointed out that there are basically two divisions, each composed of two parts, the second division being no more than a repetition of the first for another (the next) year.[66] This is essentially correct, but what escaped Desimoni's attention is a fifth division of the inventory, which complements data not found elsewhere.

In drawing up its inventory, the Genoese administration proceeded according to the following divisions: '(a) the possessions of the commune, which were rented for the *passagium*; (b) how and for how much they were rented at the time of their office of the [foregoing] consuls; (c) inspections of the possessions of the commune which were rented yearly during the [present] consulate; (d) how the possessions of the commune were usually rented for the *passagium* as well as yearly at the time of the [consulate of] Simone Malocello and Ogerio Ricci, including also the possessions of the commune outside Acre; (e) and finally, what was paid to the commune annually.'[67]

(a) The list of houses rented *ad passagium*, shows four houses and six palaces. We also learn of the church of St. Lawrence, the major church of the quarter, leaning on the 'commune's Old Tower' and a 'New Tower'. In the Old Palace the ground floor was used for the *curia* of the commune. Two of the palaces were in the 'Covered street', which probably refers to

---

[65] C. Desimoni, 'Quatre titres des propriétés des Génois à Acre et à Tyr', *AOL* ii. 215 ff.
[66] Ibid. 213.
[67] The rubrics are as follows: 'apautus ad passagium'; 'apautus ad annum'—both listed for two consecutive years. For the next rubric see below, p. 239 and n. 72.

a covered bazaar similar to that in Jerusalem. Soap-makers lived in one of them.[68] Another palace was distinguished as being in the loggia. The last palace to be mentioned must have been in the north-western part of the quarter. Its location is 'deversus ordamer', which corresponds to the 'lordamer iuxta murum hospitalis'.[69] According to the maps appended to the work of Marino Sanudo, the Hospitaller quarter did not reach the port area. Yet on the western border of their quarter there was an area called *Boverel*, cattle-pen or cattle market (the Templars had a *Boveria Templi* in the northern suburb of Mt. Musard). This area, at least in the maps of the city of Paolino of Puzzeoli (Venice, St. Mark, Cod. Lat. 394 and Paris, B. N. Lat. 4939, fo. 113),[70] is actually on the western beach of the city. We know that the Hospitallers built a repair-dock for ships and this seems to have been the most convenient area for such construction.[71]

(b) In the list of property rented for the whole year, we count six houses; one near the *platea* of the commune and again another near the *darsana* (of the Hospitallers) adjoining the pig-sties (*bacconeria*) and a house in the south-eastern part of the quarter near the Pisan quarter. Another house was in a street with the picturesque name of the Three Magi.

All in all, the buildings leased for the 'passagium' and for a whole year were six palaces and ten houses. The next year's data roughly correspond to the former list. Amongst the houses leased for the 'passagium', one house is missing. As to buildings leased for a whole year, the differences are greater. Instead of the five houses listed for the previous year, ten houses are listed, but one is the missing house of the former list. It was now leased for a whole year instead of the 'passagium' period only.

The marked difference between the Genoese and Venetian inventories lies in the fact that the former never indicated rooms or apartments, but entire houses, even 'palaces'. Does this indicate a different way of renting? Not necessarily. It is quite possible that the inventory that we have is already based on a more detailed list of which it is a summary.

All in all, the direct property of the Genoese is slightly superior to that of the Venetians: fourteen houses of Venice as against ten houses (or

[68] *AOL* ii. 217: 'Palacium tercium Ruae Coopertae iuxta domus Thomae et Iacobi quondam Saboneriorum.'
[69] Ibid. 216. On the *ordamer* or *lordamer* see Prawer, *Histoire* ii. 531; idem, *RHDFE* 29 (1951), 335 ff.; Benvenisti, *Crusaders*, p. 98.
[70] The St. Mark MS. published in *De passagiis in Terram Sanctam*, ed. G. Thomas (Venice, 1879). The B. N. MS. published by J. Prawer, above, p. 229 n. 29.
[71] *AOL* ii. B. 244: 'ab uno latere deversus mare, retro murum darsana facta per hospitale Sti Johannis.'

fourteen houses) of Genoa. The Genoese, however, have a larger number of 'palaces'. One just wonders if a three- or four-storey house would not merit such a name in the Genoese administration.

But, in addition to these houses and 'palaces', our inventory has another list of the greatest importance:

Here is the list of the *census* which was returned and paid to the commune on the Purification of the Virgin Mary [2 Feb.] from houses and buildings placed and built *super burgensiam* and in the *ruga* of the commune; also recognizance payments (*recognoscimenta*), which were returned to the commune from houses, which are enumerated in what follows.[72]

The distinction is important. The first lists dealt with property directly managed or administered by the Genoese; the following list enumerated *all* the buildings to be found in the quarter paying *cens* to the commune. The land on which they were built belongs to the commune—this was the *burgensia* or *ruga* of the commune.[73]

An arbitration decision of 1212 may well be adduced to illustrate problems connected with such tenures. A lady by the name of Agnes Gastaldi, together with her relatives, had a house in the Genoese quarter of Acre in the *ruga Sti Laurentii*. The Lady Agnes sold part of the house to another lady, Lucensis, widow of one Bartholomeo de Dominis. Summoned to appear before the viscount and *curia* of the commune of Genoa, which claimed jurisdiction 'ratione domi, quam in ruga Sti Laurentii tenebat ad censum a dicto communi', Lady Agnes refused. For reasons unknown, she found a defender in the Commune of Pisa. One possibility would be to assume that Agnes was a Pisan national, although she had property in the Genoese quarter. The Pisans argued that the Genoese had no other rights 'praeter solum censum, quem in ipsa domu habebant'.[74] The communes and the defendant agreed on arbitration by the Patriarch Albert, by Walter, bishop of Acre, and Andreas, viscount of Venice. The Pisans had stressed in the proceedings: 'the Commune of Genoa cannot demand from the above-mentioned Agnes anything but the *cens* only'. The outcome of the arbitration was to restore Agnes to the good graces of the Genoese; the illegal transaction was sanctioned and the Lady Lucensis would have to pay half a besant annually; Lady Agnes would pay the annual *cens* of 10 besants (which would include the half-besant, that is, she herself would pay $9\frac{1}{2}$ besants). Finally: 'Agnes and

---

[72] Ibid. ii. 219.   [73] See below, Ch. 12, pp. 318 f.
[74] Müller, pp. 439–40, no. 63.

Lucensis would be responsible for the above-mentioned houses of the *burgesia* to the viscount [of Genoa] and his *curia*, like other *burgenses*.'[75]

The last part of the Genoese inventory dealt precisely with this type of real property in their quarter. The houses were held by burgage-tenure and the hereditary *cens* was paid to the Commune of Genoa. Their total number of houses was fifty-one.

As the *cens* certainly reflected in some measure the size of house, it is worth tabulating the respective *cens*;

Houses	Besants	Houses	Besants	Houses	Besants
2	30	1	12	1	$3\frac{1}{2}$
1	29	1	11	5	3
1	25	1	10	1	$2\frac{1}{2}$
1	22	1	9	4	2
1	18	2	8	4	1
2	17	1	7	2	$\frac{3}{4}$
2	$13\frac{1}{2}$	3	4	2	$\frac{1}{2}$

Six houses did not pay *cens*, as they now were directly administered by the commune, and four houses did not pay *cens* for unstated reasons. This gives a total of forty-five or fifty-one houses (if the last six were counted among the ten or fourteen directly administered by the commune). Together then with the houses directly held by the commune, the total number of houses was sixty-four. As the area of the Genoese quarter can be evaluated at *c*. 6·5 ha, it was quite crowded.

Our list mentions two items of some interest. Two houses did not pay *cens* but 'pro recognoscimento annuatim'—7 and 4 besants respectively; in addition four houses, as the Genoese authorities noted with some dismay, 'quamvis sint in burgensia et ruga Ianuensi, liberae sunt et nihil dant nec sunt de communi'. Such occurrences are also known from Europe, where the laxity of medieval administration created a *de facto* state of non-payment. But it is not impossible here that we are dealing with allodial property which came into burgesses' hands by marriage or acquisition.[76]

It is interesting to compare the annual incomes of the commune. In 1249 the rents 'ad passagium' totalled $750\frac{1}{2}$ besants; the rents 'ad annum' 297 besants. The same property a fiscal year later totalled 839 besants and 521 besants respectively (the inventory totalled $1,003\frac{2}{3}$ besants but included 482 besants for a bakery and garden not counted before), that is

[75] Ibid., p. 440.   [76] See Ch. 14 below, pp. 350 f.

1,047 besants and 1,360 besants respectively for two consecutive years. On the other hand, the *cens* from tenancy totalled only 358½ besants per annum.

The Venetian quarter, like that of Genoese, with some sixty houses in a restricted area of their *rugae* in Acre, may be described as extremely crowded. This can also be gathered from other indications, such as the privilege of Baldwin IV in 1182 to the Pisans in Acre. Their quarter seems to have been the smallest of the communal quarters. Trying to reach the commercial heart of the city, the port area, the Pisans received 'a given *platea* at the port of Acre . . . but on condition that they will be allowed to build vaults or arches (*voltae*) above this *platea*, and above the vaults they can erect any type of building, but the *platea* beneath the vaults will remain empty and free for the service of the Commune of Pisa and of the city.'[77]

In these very crowded areas of Acre, the communes administered only ten to fourteen houses directly, some used for the needs of administration and its officials; others were a source of income far more important than the income from the *cens* of the burgage-tenures in the quarter. Remarkably enough, the same picture seems to be true for Tyre also. One would expect that the Venetians, the 'consorts of the king' and lords of one-third of the city, would have a stronger grip on their property there. Yet an inventory of Venetian property in Tyre, drawn up at the same time as that for Acre, comes up with a similar number of houses. If our calculations are correct, the commune had eight houses there in direct property (three lost by usurpation) and five houses belonging to the Venetian parish church of St. Mark. Altogether there were only ten houses, to which we should add an unspecified number of houses destroyed in an earthquake.[78]

The nationals of the communes and the Frankish burgesses

By the middle of the thirteenth century the population of the communal quarter differed very much from that of the previous century. One has the impression that although many buildings or rooms were reserved for the *caravanae*, there was a large, settled local population, the same that took up arms during the infamous War of St. Sabbas.

The interests of these two categories of Italians, the occasional visitors and the permanent settlers, were not identical. Whereas the purely ever shifting, mercantile element was first and foremost interested in *commercial*

[77] Müller, p. 23.   [78] Tafel–Thomas ii. 362–8.

privileges, the local Italians—the real colonists we may call them—were no less interested in their possessions and their general standing in the kingdom. With the settling of the nationals of the communes, their taking possession of vineyards and courtyards, homes and magazines, they became citizens of the city, and indeed of the kingdom, enjoying incredibly large privileges in commerce in comparison with their Frankish co-citizens. The latter, who paid customs and taxes in the port and market-place, in addition to occasional *tallia* and eventual military service, were at a great disadvantage. It does not need much imagination to realize how the Italians' exorbitant privileges offended the local Frankish middle class. Their special position prevented the rise of an opulent Frankish mercantile class engaged in maritime commerce. In the best of cases the local Franks could function as mediators only, between the Italians and the local market and eventually between the Italians and the Islamic hinterland. But even here the Italians preferred to establish their own direct contacts with paynim; in any case, in the import and export from this hinterland, they enjoyed privileges not accessible to the local population.

It is a remarkable fact that Crusader authorities, whether Crown or lordship, never followed the European municipal examples which safeguarded the local commercial class by barring the great merchants from the retail commerce and left them the role of wholesalers only. The sentiments of the local population had their counterpart in the attitude of the royal, and in the thirteenth century, of the lordships' administration. Since fifty years after the conquest was a period long enough to forget the services of the Italians during the first decade of the kingdom's existence, it was not surprising that attempts were made to abrogate their privileges. But this was not easy to do: even the Holy See intervened on their behalf. If Italians bringing in ships and merchandise could claim some service to the kingdom, this was not so for the permanent settlers. They had land in and around the great cities and if they paid any taxes, it was only to their own *curia*.

The problem had two distinct aspects, both originating in the same source. There was the purely economic side, which from the point of view of the state meant exemption or near-exemption from custom duties and consequently a serious diminution in the potential revenue of the royal, or the lordship's, treasury. But there was also the all-important aspect of jurisdiction, which in the framework of the feudal state meant not only immunity from royal, or from a lordship's, jurisdiction, but actually the creation of a particular estate of subjects—those of the commune, beyond the reach of the Crown or of the territorial ruler of the Crusader Kingdom. Although some particular aspects of the problem have been considered, such as the attempts of Crown and lordships to safeguard their rights against the Italian claim to enjoy autonomous criminal and civil jurisdiction, these national subjects deserve more attention.

As is well known, the Frankish population was composed of nobles and non-nobles or *burgenses*, burgesses. Perhaps the nearest we can come to defining their status by a positive expression would be to use the French term *roturier* or the English *commoner*. The suggestion of such a definition was made a hundred years ago but was somehow not noticed or did not become popular with the historians.[79] But the term *burgenses* or *borjois* was not only a definition of a social class, it also denoted belonging to a definite jurisdiction. A *burgensis regis* was the Frankish subject of the king in a royal city or in the royal domain, and a *burgensis Acconensis* was a Frankish subject of the *seigneur justicier* of Acre (in this case the king).[80]

The creation of the autonomous Italian quarters created a plethora of legal problems which made the day of the Crusader law practitioners. To visualize the problem we may try to reduce it to its most simple aspects. According to the Venetians' *Pactum Warmundi*, and similar privileges of the Genoese, everyone living in their quarter was under the jurisdiction of the commune.[81] The most obvious exception was that of a Frankish noble who lived in the Venetian quarter, but was a vassal of the Crown or of the lord of the city. He obviously could not be judged *ratione personae* by the Venetians, but by the feudal court of his lord or king; and he was judged by the Court of Burgesses for his burgage holdings. Theoretically if the burgage-tenure was in a communal quarter he should have been judged by the communal court. However, there were certainly frequent cases of people belonging to the same strata of society—for example royal burgesses who had property in a communal quarter and conversely nationals of the communes who had property in the royal quarter. A parallel case was that of nationals of different communes who had property not in their own quarters. The variations on the theme were numerous and the situation inevitably invited bickering and litigation.

[79] Cf. T. Smith, *The Assize of Jerusalem* (Leicester, 1842).

[80] See below, Ch. 13.

[81] See above, p. 223 n. 14. The Genoese right of jurisdiction, e.g. in the privilege of Henry of Champagne of 1195: 'non debeam nec possim aliquem uirum cum femina capere ex quocumque genere sit (in ruga beati Laurentii) ... et quod non possim nec debeam habitantem in predicta ruga in alia curia compelli nec uocari pro aliquo melefitio seu placito' (*Liber iurium* i. 412, no. 310).

It was in these circumstances that a new legal notion arose regarding the Italians. It might be termed a medieval notion of 'nationals'. The more vigorous kings and lords of the Latin Kingdom would try to differentiate between Italians—Venetians, Genoese, Pisans, etc.—who came to the kingdom on business, and those who settled in the kingdom and acquired property in it. Some legislation would attempt (without success) to confine the commercial privileges to the former only, other legislation, more important in our context, would attempt to regain jurisdiction over the latter.

Perhaps the Crusader Kingdom might have learned not only from its experience, but from that of its ally, the Byzantine Empire, although it might have happened the other way round. It was Manuel Comnenus who introduced the distinction between the travelling Venetian merchants and those permanently established in the Empire. The latter were to lose their privileges and become, as our source puts it, *bourgesioi* of the *basileus*.[82]

A few years earlier, in 1168, King Amalric of Jerusalem wrote in a privilege to the Pisans: 'I concede . . . a court against all people, excepting myself, to judge there all Pisans, *praeter illos qui homines mei sunt et mansiones seu redditus et possessiones stabiles in regno meo habent*, who will be judged by me and my judges.'[83] The distinction is clear: a Pisan had the right to be judged in his communal court as long as he had no real property (*mansio*) or fixed income, which could only mean, in this case, income from real property in the kingdom; to put it another way, if he was not a permanent inhabitant of the kingdom. In the latter case he became, as King Amalric put it, *homo meus*, the king's subject. The motives behind such a decision are clear. Amalric was trying to abolish the exterritorial status of a Pisan, who claimed it by right of Pisan nationality, enjoying all its privileges, without benefiting the king and in fact encroaching on his rights of sovereignty.

This became even more explicit under Henry of Champagne who tried to curb the exorbitant privileges conferred in times of need by Conrad of

---

[82] J. Kinnamos, *Epitome rerum ab . . . Ioanne et Alexio* [sic] *Comnenis gestarum* (Bonn, 1836), p. 282. Cf. W. Heyd, *Histoire du commerce du Levant au moyen-âge* (Leipzig, 1885), i. 200. Cf. *Deeds of John and Manuel Comnenus by John Kinnamos*, transl. C. M. Brand (New York, 1976), pp. 210–11. The date seems to be slightly prior to 1170. I would like to thank Professor D. Jacoby who drew my attention to the dating.

[83] Müller, p. 14. Cf. *mansiones seu redditus stabiles* in this privilege with their privilege in Tyre of 1156, where they receive land: 'ita quoque ne aliquis ibidem aliquem mansionis stabilitatem facere presumat.'

Montferrat and Guy of Lusignan. In a privilege of 1193 he stated forcefully: 'If any Pisan holds from me a *burgesia*, either he leaves the *burgesia* to me and then will be free like other Pisans, or if he wants to hold my *burgesia*, he should be obliged to me like my other *burgenses*.'[84]

The underlying legal notion of this conflict was the royal claim that a national of a commune who acquired land in the kingdom became *eo ipso* a *burgensis regis*. A generation later Bohemond of Antioch would go one step further. In a privilege to the Genoese in 1199 he promised them 'a court in Antioch, a court in Laodicea and privileges', excepting for criminal jurisdiction, and 'with the exception of *meis burgensibus Ianuensibus* of Antioch, Laodicea, and Jubail, whom I do not allow to accept into their commune'.[85] Here the new legal notion of 'my Genoese burgesses' is explicitly stated. More than that, the prince of Antioch formally decreed that such 'burgesses', although Genoese, should not be allowed to enter the privileged Commune of Genoa. A few years later, in 1205, Bohemond, his son, confirmed privileges 'to the city of Genoa, to all Genoese and sons [descendants] of the Genoese, except the burgesses of the kingdom of Jesusalem, or of the County of Tripoli or of Cyprus or of the principality of Antioch'.[86]

Opposite demands were obviously put by the communes, who pointed to their original privileges, given to them *iure hereditario*.[87] Even long before the Venetian Marsiglio Zorzi had vehemently defended the rights of his commune, the Pisans did the same, wresting them from Conrad of Montferrat and the competing Guy of Lusignan. The former agreed to full Pisan jurisdiction in Tyre and even in the whole kingdom (which did not belong to him). The privilege was given 'to all Pisans and those who are regarded as Pisans, sailors as well as burgesses and also knights and nobles and laymen of whatever status, who will be judged in the Court of the Pisans' except 'what applies to fiefs and *assises*, in which case it will be judged in the court of the lords. But in no other case will a Pisan be judged in the royal court of Tyre and its district, or in the whole territory of the

---

[84] Müller, p. 60: 'Si Pisanus aliquis teneat a me burgesiam aud [*sic!*] burgesiam quam de me tenet mihi relinquat et sit tunc liber ut alii Pisani, aud si vult tenere meam burgesiam, sicut alii burgenses mei mihi teneatur.' *Liber* may mean here 'enjoying the *libertates* of the Pisans'.

[85] *Liber iurium*, p. 432, no. 424: 'In Antiochia curiam et apud Laoditiam curiam et libertatem exceptis tantum de proditione etc. et exceptis meis burgensibus Januensibus de Antiochia et Laoditia et Gabulo, quos in eorum communione recipi non permitto.'

[86] Ibid., p. 522, no. 477: 'ciuitati Ianue et omnibus Ianuensibus et Ianuensium filiis exceptis burgensibus regni Ierusalem uel comitatus Tripolis siue Cypri uel principatus Antiochie'.

[87] Baldwin IV's privilege of 1156 to Pisa (Müller, p. 7).

kingdom.'[88] At least Conrad succeeded in safeguarding some privileges in the royal city of Tyre. The royal writ did not run in the Pisan quarter of Tyre; and Pisans living outside their autonomous quarter (significantly described as *honor*, which would normally be understood as a noble fief), could not be judged by the lord of the city. But if the lord imposed an extraordinary tax on the city, then 'from the houses of Pisan *burgenses* outside the *honor* of the Commune of the Pisans, the king will be allowed to receive the *talia*, if he receives it for the commune of the city of Tyre.'[89] This was twisted or interpolated by the Pisans when, two years later (1189) they demanded a confirmation of their privilege from Guy of Lusignan. Here we read (although the interpolation sits badly in the phrase): 'the king cannot receive the *talia* from them [the Pisans].'[90] Moreover they introduced a new clause: 'But from the houses of Pisan burgesses outside the *honor* of the Commune of Pisa, the Pisans will be allowed to receive the *talia*, if they receive it for the commune [of the Pisans in Tyre].'[91] The Pisan therefore carried his status outside the quarter of his commune.

The expression *burgensis* in all these documents now has an entirely different meaning from that usually accepted for the kingdom. The *burgensis* was not only a 'commoner', he was also a subject and national of

[88] Ibid., p. 27: 'ut omnes Pisani et qui Pisanorum nomine censentur, tam scapuli quam burgenses seu etiam milites et comites seu cuiuscumque conditionis laici in Pisanorum curia iudicentur ... preterquam ... que ad feoda et assisias pertinent, de quibus omnibus in dominorum curia iudicentur. De nulla autem alia re Pisanus iudicetur in regali curia in Tyro et eius partibus, nec etiam in toto regno.' The noun *scapuli*, as far as we know was never explained. Obviously it cannot mean 'clergymen' (*scapulati*), as the text indicates that they are laymen. But in a sixteenth-century Venetian description we have found *gondoliers* designated *scapoli*. We suggest that *scapuli* derives from the Germanic *scip*, ship. It is found in Ammianus Marcellinus and reappears in *scapwardus* in the early Middle Ages in Lombardy and Gaul. See J. F. Niermeyer, s.v. *scapoardus*. The 'comites', translated as 'nobles', and 'curia dominorum' for the 'curia regis' are non-Crusader expressions. They must have been introduced by the Italian Bandini, Conrad of Montferrat's *scriba*. This privilege also proves that the Italians acquired fiefs in the kingdom and in this case *ratione materiae* were judged in the 'curia regis'. The 'assisiae' mentioned here are money assignments, very often money-fiefs, to be paid from the royal treasury or monopoly, like the income from market duties or port customs. Cf. Müller, p. 33: 'ad fundam et catenam Acconis singulis annis percipiendorum per terminos statutos de assisiis'.

[89] Müller, p. 27: 'De domibus autem burgensium Pisanorum extra honorem Pisani communis positis, rex taliam possit percipere, si pro communi civitatis Tyri taliam receperit'. On the Commune of Tyre, see H. E. Mayer, 'On the Beginnings of the Communal Movement in the Holy Land: The Commune of Tyre', *Traditio* 24 (1968), 443–57.

[90] Müller, p. 38: 'et rex non possit de eis taliam recipere.'

[91] Müller, p. 38: 'De domibus autem burgensium Pisanorum extra honorem Pisani communis positis, consules Pisani possint de eis taliam recipere, quando eam pro communi recipere voluerint.'

a given state or communal authority. When a coalition of native nobles and Venetians took Tyre from the hands of Frederick II's 'Lombards', the Venetian *bailli* wrote that the city was captured in three days: 'et hoc occasione nostrorum Venetorum qui ibi sunt burgenses'.[92] Thus the Venetians too had jurisdiction in Tyre over all the inhabitants of their quarter, except the vassals of the lord of Tyre, 'et burgensibus suis [of the lord] quos habitare contingeret in tertiaria praedictorum Venetorum'.[93] Commercial contracts signed in Acre in 1284 between Pisans made the clear distinction between a Henricus Nai 'burgensis Pisanus de Accon' and a Raynerius de Gaytanis de Malpilio 'Pisanus civis', the latter being a permanent inhabitant of Pisa in Italy.[94]

The repetition of the limitation clauses in the privileges is in itself proof enough that it was the Italian colonies that triumphed and not the Frankish rulers who undertook legislation too late. We have to wait for the Kingdom of Cyprus, seven years after the fall of the Latin Kingdom, to find a general legislation regarding *borgesies*' property in the hands of the Italian settlers. By an ordinance proclaimed in 1298, Henry II ordered the nationals of the communes, and also the clergy, to get rid of their *borgesies* during the half-year following the proclamation, under threat of confiscation. Only with the king's assent were they allowed to hold *borgesies* in the Kingdom of the Lusignans.[95]

The relative importance of the communes grew steadily from the time of the Third Crusade. Diminishing immigration from Europe, internal political strife, and the financial situation brought into prominence those groups of society, which, with their foreign affiliations, escaped in some sense the realities of the kingdom. Such was the case of the Military Orders and communes, which became controlling powers in the state. The physical bases of their strength were the inhabitants of their quarters in the maritime cities and their navies controlling the seas and fighting to maintain that hegemony.

With the end of the Crusade of Frederick II we enter the gravest period in the history of the kingdom. The state seems to have disappeared as a political entity. Society was in chronic ferment. In a sense, the whole frame of state and society was disintegrating.[96] The rival factions of

---

[92] Tafel–Thomas ii. 356.

[93] Ibid. iii. 152, in John of Montfort's privilege (1277) to the Venetians in Tyre.

[94] Müller, no. 71, p. 103.

[95] 'Bans et Ordonnances des rois de Chypre', *Lois* ii. 361.

[96] See above, Ch. 3, pp. 79–82.

nobility, the rivalries of the Military Orders, the wars of the communes, made the kingdom the most unedifying spectacle in Christendom in the middle of the thirteenth century. In these conditions, any organized group became a power courted by the different factions. One has only to read the report of the Venetian *bailli* Marsiglio Zorzi in 1243, offering his commune's help to give the throne to the Princess Alice against the claims of the Hohenstaufen, to realize that state and society were entirely atomized; there was no moral backbone left. No state interest could call for unity and prevent decadence and utter failure.

We would like to know more about the Italian colonies in the period following the murderous War of St. Sabbas in the middle of the thirteenth century but our documentation is somewhat scanty. One feature, however, seems to be clear—the growing number of Italians permanently settled in the kingdom. This can be learned from the registers of the notaries of Genoa and deduced from the history of the kingdom itself. Another aspect of the growing number of colonists in the Latin East is the emergence of institutions which enabled the colonists to express their wishes and to impose, in some measure, a kind of control over officials sent from the European metropolis. The *consules* and *vicecomites* were usually appointed in the mother cities in Europe, from men who had experience in the East. But they were appointed for a short term, usually not more than a year. Consequently an institution grew up which guaranteed that the management of local affairs should be based on knowledge of local conditions and would assure the continuity of local policies. This institution was the *consilium*, mentioned several times after the middle of the thirteenth century, but certainly existing earlier, perhaps from the beginning of the century.[97] The nature of this body is not very clear. It may have been a general assembly of the settlers, a kind of *magnum consilium*, but in all probability it was a select body of the outstanding members of the colony, more or less formally elected by the settlers. The scarcity of published documents does not allow more to be said about these *consiliarii* for the time being.

Another aspect of the greater cohesion of the colony is indicated by the use of oaths, which in medieval usage gave the feeling of corporation to the colony. We hear (1243) that the inhabitants of the Venetian quarter of Tyre were obliged to give an oath of allegiance to Venice and this was also imposed on non-Venetians buying houses in the Venetian quarter.[98]

[97] Tafel–Thomas ii. 151 and the oath of the 'iurati' (ibid. ii. 360).

[98] Ibid. ii. 360–1. This oath even forgoes the traditional exception clause, *salvo iure regis*, or any similar formula for the lords of the city.

The fall of the Crusader Kingdom in the Holy Land and the principalities in the north ends this first chapter in the history of European expansion and colonization. But a hundred years earlier a new European kingdom had been created in Cyprus and a new pattern of colonization had come into being. And a few years later the maritime empire of Venice, from the Aegean to the Bosphorus, came in the wake of the Fourth Crusade. A more solid basis for a successful enterprise was created.[99]

[99] The following studies should also be consulted: D. Jacoby, 'L'expansion occidentale dans le Levant: les Vénitiens à Acre dans la seconde moitié du treizième siècle', *Journal of Medieval History* 3 (1977), 225–67; H. E. Mayer, *Marseilles Levantehandel und ein Akkonensisches Fälscheratelier des 13. Jahrhunderts* (Tübingen, 1972).

9 Burgage-tenure

When a former juror of the Court of Burgesses of Nicosia in Cyprus decided at the age of seventy to write a manual on pleading in his court, he prefaced it with a singular remark: 'And in this matter one has many misgivings to dare such an enterprise; and it has often been said on this subject: pleading in *bourgezies* is like a sea, it has no bottom.'[1] His learned editor Beugnot remarked that is was surprising to see questions dealt with daily in the courts, problems exposed by so many jurists, compared, at the beginning of the fourteenth century, to a bottomless sea. It is a matter of opinion whether the juror's statement or his editor's criticism was more justified, but it is still a fact that until now, except for Beugnot's introduction, there is no single study of the problem.[2]

And yet the *borgesie* not only was of the utmost importance in everyday life of the Crusader Kingdom, but it presents problems of origin, function, and position in the social and economic web of Crusader life which by far transcend its legal aspects. To stress the importance of the subject it will be enough to remember the place of cities in the structure of Crusader society.[3] This quite recent acquisition of modern scholarship explains perhaps in some measure why the subject has been overlooked and neglected until now.

We shall look in vain in the Crusader treatises of jurisprudence for any legal definition of the *borgesie*, despite the fact that the *Livre des Assises des Bourgeois* of the Latin Kingdom and its Cypriot counterpart, the *Livres du plédéant et du plaidoyer*, whenever they deal with real property, deal almost exclusively with *borgesies*. Moreover, the *Livre au Roi*, Philip of Novara, and John of Ibelin often refer to them, whether in connection with the High Court or with the non-feudal property of knights and nobility. However, medieval jurists did not always feel the need for such definitions, until the revival of Roman law created a different mentality and a different type of legal thinking.

[1] *Livre du plaidoyer*, ch. 1, *Lois* ii. 293.

[2] The only exception is the judicious pages of Riley-Smith, *Feudal Nobility*, pp. 82–3.

[3] J. Prawer, 'Crusader Cities', in *The Medieval City. Studies presented to R. S. Lopez*, ed. H. A. Miskimin, *et al.* (Yale, 1977), pp. 179 ff.

By bringing together the large number of references to the *borgesies*, we can put forward the following definition. The *borgesie* is a type of tenure, different from fief and servile tenure, typical, though not a monopoly, of the commoners—that is, of non-noble Franks. In addition, a *borgesie*, which we shall call burgage-tenure, because that is what it really was, is predominantly a tenure of land or property inside, or in the neighbourhood of, the city walls. As such it is almost always described as houses, vineyards, land plots, and sometimes fields. Frequently *borgesie* is also described as heritage,[4] but neither its economic function nor its location suffices to define its legal status, not even the legal standing of its possessor. In fact knights and nobles possessed burgage-tenures (though city properties in the hands of the nobility were frequently not burgage-tenures, but parts of fiefs),[5] whereas burgesses were by law barred from holding fiefs. Sometimes attempts were made to prevent non-burgesses from holding burgage-tenure.[6] The latter were also jealously guarded against acquisition by ecclesiastical and monastic establishments, as well as against Military Orders.[7] The difficulties of keeping burgage-tenures for burgesses only was heightened by the fact that noble and non-noble Franks lived side by side in the same cities and intermarried, bringing burgage fortunes into knightly families.[8] The proof of the legal status of property (fief, *eleemosyna*, *allodium*, *borgesie*, free *borgesie*[9]) must have been in the last resort, in the early period of the kingdom, the services or payments due to, or claimed by, the lord of the city or the *seigneur justicier* of the place (if

---

[4] *Livre au Roi*, ch. 20: 'chans ou vignes ou maison'; ibid., ch. 37: 'toutes ycelles borgesies qui au fié n'apartienent, si come sont maisons et terres et jardins et vignes', cf. ch. 44. *Livre du plédéant*, ch. 21: 'borgezies qui sont dedens la ville, si come sont heritages de maizons, et jardins et chans et autre chozes semblables', ibid., ch. 40, p. 224: 'bourgesies... qui s'apellent heritages pour ce que il sont dedens ville.' Cf. *LdAdB*, chs. 30, 31, 144, etc. The sixteenth-century Italian translation has systematically for *borgesies* 'stabili' or 'heredità'.

[5] e.g. Strehlke, no. 22: 'domus in Accon, qua ad feudum Chabor pertinet'. Cf. *Livre du plédéant*, ch. 13: 'maison et jardins et chans qui sont joins as fiés, lesquels borgesies sont et franches, ou en aucune redevance au chief seignor.'

[6] There are some examples from the kingdom in deeds of sale or rent to prevent knights from acquiring burgage-tenures: see e.g. 'Partriach's lordship', p. 310 n. 88. This became a rule in Cyprus, where non-Latins, knights, clergymen, nationals of communes, and Military Orders were excluded from holding burgage tenures (*Livre du plédéant*, chs. 17 and 25). But cf. 'Patriarch's lordship', no. 89.

[7] *Livre au Roi*, ch. 43: 'nules borgesies... qui soyent es devises dou roy, ce est en ca terre, ne en la terre de ces homes, ne peut etre doné a yglise ne a religion.' Many actual examples are to be found in deeds of sale or of rent. See below p. 324 n. 38.

[8] A noble may receive as dowry from his burgess wife's property a burgage-tenure (*Livre au Roi*, chs. 20, 37, 43).

[9] On 'free *borgesies*', see above n. 5, p. 258 n. 26, and Ch. 14, p. 351.

there were independent jurisdictions in the city) from the tenure. In addition there was the legal rule that all transactions in fiefs could only be performed legally in the High Court or in the baronial court of the lordship, which drew a sharp line between fief and burgage-tenure.[10]

The importance of burgage-tenure in the life of the kingdom cannot be overestimated. Wherever in Europe—in Normandy, Norman England, or even in Flanders, the most urbanized part of northern Europe—burgage-tenures did exist, they were confined to the nascent cities which were exceptions, enclaves in the lands of fiefs and manors. The picture was different in the Latin Kingdom. Here the Crusader population, Franks of all strata of society, lived in cities, and burgage-tenures were consequently of paramount importance in their lives and occupations.

How did burgage-tenures come into existence? In Europe they were the result of an organic growth, part of the process of urban evolution. In a somewhat later stage, when such tenures became more clearly defined in the nascent cities, they often became part of the privileges bestowed on places which were expected to develop into cities—part of the process of the urban foundation that dominated the twelfth and thirteenth centuries. Both lines of development hardly fit the Latin establishments in the East. Physically cities preceded the Crusader conquest; it was only their population that was almost entirely new. Burgage-tenure was thus a European institution imported wholesale. Moreover, we find burgage-tenures overlaid by so many notions of feudal customs and procedure that although one could look to southern Europe for elements of city life which could have been brought to the East, it is more probable that the tenure did not originate in the south. The vocabulary is that of the north and so is the procedure followed in the legal acts connected with this tenure.

Before suggesting a working hypothesis as to the origins of the Crusader burgage-tenures, we have to explain some characteristics of our documentation. As far as legal practice is concerned, our documentation goes back to the beginnings of the kingdom; on the other hand we shall have to rely on treatises of jurisprudence of a more recent date. The *Livres du plédéant et du plaidoyer* is very late indeed, as it dates from the second

---

[10] This important rule could have been, and actually often was, circumvented. Ultimately it depended, as rightly seen by John of Ibelin, on the good faith of the parties concerned. John (ch. 38) discussed the case of a buyer who did not know the legal status of the property he was acquiring: 'Et se ciaux a qui l'on vent ou done ou aliene heritage dedenz ville, ne puent pas saveir se il est de fié ou non; cil qui le vent ou aliene s'en deit garder par la fei qu'il deit au seigneur.'

decade of the fourteenth century and was written in Cyprus. The justification for using so recent a source is that the Lusignans of the island continued the traditions of the mainland. The Cypriot customs, as we shall see, are so traditional, that they may rightly be called archaic, and by no stretch of imagination can it be assumed that they were created on the island. They were transferred from the mainland where there are ample proofs of their uninterrupted continuity from the beginning of the twelfth century.

How did the Crusader burgage-tenures originate? There is no trace of their creation either in chronicles or in legal documents of the period. Yet we can assume with certainty that burgage-tenures, although perhaps not immediately so called, were created during, or immediately following, the period of Crusader conquest, that is to say in the first or second decade of the kingdom's existence. We would like to postulate that their creation was the result of the social composition of the armies of the First Crusade and of the waves of immigration that reached the shores of the kingdom in its wake. *Milites* and *pedites* were the basic divisions in the armies, the former furnishing the nucleus of the knightly class, the latter that of the non-noble Franks, the burgesses. Many a *pedes*, serf or villein, probably slipped into the higher class by the fortunes of spoil and fighting. As these basic divisions in the armies of the First Crusade were a legacy to the social classes of the kingdom, so were their conquests to the economic basis of its existence. We shall deal with the creation of fiefs and allods in Chapter 14 below, and concentrate here on the type of property acquired by the *pedites*, the non-noble conquerors and colonizers of the kingdom.

The earliest property of the burgesses, excluding movable spoils, were houses in conquered Jerusalem, Ramle, Jaffa, and later in other conquered cities. The 'Law of Conquest' ruled that if a man put a lance, a shield, or any other sign on a house in a captured city, he thereby assured to himself its possession.[11] We can assume with certainty that lordly houses of the

---

[11] Fulk of Chartres i. c. 29: 'Et post stragem tantam ingressi sunt domos civium, rapientes quaecumque in eis reppererunt: ita sane, ut quicumque primus domum introisset, sive dives sive pauper esset, nullatenus ab aliquo fieret injuria, quin domum ipsam aut palatium, et quodcumque in ea repperisset, ac si omnino propria, sibi assumeret, haberet et possideret. Hoc itaque jus invicem tenendum stabilierant. Unde multi inopes effecti sunt locupletes.' This is also stated by Albert of Aachen vi. 23: 'Quicunque vero domum aut palatium prior invadebat, cum omni suppellectili, frumento, ordeo, oleo, et vino, pecunia aut veste, vel qualibet re pacifice obtinebat. Et sic possessores totius civitatis facti sunt.' William of Tyre's description is detailed (viii. 20): 'Quam vero quisque domum effregerat, eam sibi cum universa ejus substantia jure perpetuo vendicabat: id enim prius ante urbem captam inter eos convenerat, ut, urbe violenter impugnata, quod quisque sibi acquireret, id jure proprietatis
(continued)

previous Muslim period became the property of the noble or knightly Franks. But this did not disinherit the *pedites*. Nowhere was the Crusader population able to fill the inhabited area of the former cities. There was more property than potential possessors. The acquisition of houses and other property in the cities by both knight and burgess created the problem of differentiation in the legal status of their possessions. One feature was obvious, namely the military obligations demanded from royal vassals, and later on—when cities were actually handed over by the Crown to vassals[12]—military services due from vassals to their respective lords. The bases of these obligations were the fiefs, but taking into account that the Crusader nobility rarely lived in manor houses, and certainly not at that early period, the question arose as to the legal status of their places of habitat, the houses in the city. Thus a particular feature of the Crusader fief was created—that, in addition to land or rent fiefs, it comprised a house and its appurtenances inside the walls of the city. In the more than half-empty cities, it was not a question of lodgings but of houses inhabited by royal vassals, if they did not chance to be part of the royal household. City properties forming part of the fiefs are well attested by Crusader sources.[13] There was no doubt that since they were part of the fiefs, all litigations or transactions regarding such properties were ruled by the customs of the fiefs. No alienation was possible without the seignor's agreement, no alienation valid unless done in the High Court in royal cities or the baronial court in the lordships. There were feudal rules of succession, of investiture, and of relief. Thus a part of the city's acreage

---

sine molestia possideret in perpetuum. Unde urbem perlustrantes diligentius . . . secretiora civium effringebant penetralia, clypeos vel quodlibet armorum genus in introitu defigentes, ut esset signum accendentibus ne gressum ibi figerent, sed loca praeterirent, quasi jam ab aliis occupata.' The French translation has more details: 'il avenoit que li baron metoient seur les mesons qu'il avoient conquises leur banieres, li meneurs chevaliers i pendoient leur escuz, la gent à pié i metoient leur chapiaux et leur espées, por monstrer leur enseignes que la meson estoit jà prise, si que li autre n'i venissent mie.' Raymond of Aguillers, *RHC HOcc.* iii. 275, c. 7, says more about capturing cities and castles than about property inside cities: 'etenim mos erat in exercitu ut, si signum alicujus Franci in civitate aut castello reperiretur, a nullo postea expugnabatur'; cf. ibid., p. 292e. This 'Law of Conquest' is still mentioned in the second half of the twelfth century by Usamah ibn Munqidh (transl. by P. K. Hitti, p. 178), during the capture of Apamea: 'They [the Franks] took possession of the houses, and each one of them put the sign of the crucifix over one house and planted over it his flag.' Cf. Prawer, *Latin Kingdom*, pp. 63–4, 80, 473.

[12] See above, Ch. 1, p. 14 and Ch. 2, pp. 21–2.

[13] *Livre au Roi*, ch. 43, where a heritage composed of a fief and a burgage tenure escheated to/a nun. For the former she will plead in the High Court, for the latter in the Court of Burgesses. *Livre du plédéant*, ch. 13: 'bourgesies... qui sont joins as fies'. Cf. John of Ibelin, ch. 38, and cf. above, p. 251 n. 5.

entered the mesh of feudal relations. There were however some exceptions, possessions which somehow escaped the web of feudal relations and kept the status of allods. This situation changed later when the cities were more densely populated and knights, probably smaller fry, rented lodgings. These lodgings were consequently not part of the fiefs.

The *pedites* settled alongside the knights and nobles. By joining the Crusade or by migrating to the Holy Land, whatever their original legal status, they became personally free, forming a class of commoners, *roturiers*, with no links of dependence on any overlord, unless in a contractual service relation, as servants, soldiers, officials, etc. From the beginning, according to Crusader tradition even under Godfrey of Bouillon, two different codes of law and two different courts ruled the two classes of the earliest Crusader settlers. The first part of this tradition seems partly plausible. The knights, by the nature of their vassalic nexus and their feudal obligations, were obviously ruled by their own traditional or customary law. But what about the burgesses? We doubt if Godfrey of Bouillon had the time or leisure to create specific courts. What seems more likely is that in the earliest period the ruler's lieutenant in the city, probably the *castellanus* and then the *vicecomes* had a kind of summary jurisdiction over the non-noble Frank inhabitants of the city. Such summary jurisdiction over burgesses was still exercised even in the thirteenth century in Crusader armies by the constable of the kingdom.[14] This jurisdiction *ratione personae* must have been extended to jurisdiction over their property.

With the evolution of the kingdom, with more stability, we enter into a period of the crystallization of its institutions, accompanied by some legal or constitutional notions of organization. The most obvious, deriving from European traditions, was that the lord of the city, whether king or *seigneur*, was the man from whom all land was ultimately held,[15] but this implied a differentiation and definition of the legal status of possessions. Their distinctiveness was self-evident. The commoners did not owe any military or servile services for their property, whether fief or servile tenure. True, they were mobilized for the defence of the city, possibly for military expeditions, an almost permanent feature the first two decades after the conquest. This was a measure of self-preservation not linked to possessions. It was not only convenient but a real necessity for any attempt

---

[14] *Livre au Roi*, ch. 14.

[15] Places of general utility such as streets and markets are called by Philip of Novara, ch. 77: 'ces leus sont *chambre dou seigneur.*'

at administration to classify the possessions of burgesses under a distinct type of tenure and a distinct name. Hence the emergence of the name *borgesie* or burgage-tenure.

There is no lead as to the origin of the name. On the one hand there was a native word, in Arabic *burj*, with more ancient antecedents in Hebrew and in Aramaic: *bûrgîn*, and their inhabitants *bûrganîn*.[16] It would be tempting to connect it with *borgesie*, but this is not plausible. The Hebrew and Aramaic expressions denote 'caravanserais', towers or fortified places on the royal roads and their inhabitants. In Arabic *burj* means the same: a fortified place, or tower, and the Semitic expressions are thus linked to the Greek *pyrgos*. This could have hardly served as a point of departure for burgage-tenures. We believe that the expression used by the Crusaders came from Europe, and more specifically from Normandy, the only place in which not only the institution, which can also be found in other areas of urban growth, but also the particular name *borgesie* appears.[17]

Another indication can perhaps in some measure corroborate our hypothesis. Crusader city administration was directly linked to the *vicecomes*, the viscount, not a noble *seigneur justicier*, but simply a royal officer who served a limited term and was recallable. This is a reminder of the Norman viscount, whereas his namesake in France was already by the end of the eleventh century an independent *seigneur*. It is not impossible that before the viscount it was the Crusader *castellanus*,[18] the commander of the citadel, who also fulfilled civil tasks later transferred to the *vicecomes*; in fact even in a later period the tasks of castellan and viscount were sometimes performed by the same person.[19] The former with military

---

[16] M. Jastrow, *Dict. of the Targumim, Talmud Babli etc.* (Philadelphia, 1903), s.v. *burgîn*, p. 149.

[17] The name *bourgage* is typical for Normandy. The same tenure is called *échevinage* in Artois, Hainaut, and Flanders; *albergement* in Savoy, Dauphiné, Provence, and Languedoc, etc. See E. Chénon, *Histoire du droit français* ii. (Paris, 1929), 198–201. For France, Flanders, and Germany see also R. Genestal (below, p. 257 n. 23), pp. 175–8. The term is found wherever we find Normans. Burgage-tenure is found in England and in Sicily. Glasson, op. cit., thought it came to Normandy from Anglo-Saxon England, but the term was not used in Domesday Book. Cf. Morley de Wolf Hemmeon, *Burgage tenure in mediaeval England* (Cambridge, Mass., 1914), p. 162. For Sicily the most important is H. Niese, *Die Gesetzgebung der normannischen Dynastie im Regnum Siciliae* (Halle, 1910), pp. 102 ff. Cf. E. Loncao, *Considerazioni sulla genesi della borghesia in Sicilia* (Palermo, 1899). E. Mayer, *Italienische Verfassungsgeschichte*, i (Leipzig, 1909), 321 ff. F. Ciccaglione, 'La vita economica siciliana nel periodo normanno-suevo', *Archivio storico per la Sicilia orientale* 9 (1912), 331.

[18] In 1110 one Anselmus had the title 'turris David custos' (*Regesta*, no. 59). He also signs as 'Anselmus de Turre David' (ibid., no. 57).

[19] See below, Ch. 10, pp. 264 n. 7; 271 n. 29; 274; 279.

and civil competences may have originated in Flanders, near the Bouillon patrimony, but by the end of the eleventh century the Crusader viscount did not correspond to Flemish traditions.[20] Without being sure, we are very much inclined to postulate a Norman origin for the burgage-tenure. Its emergence was part of the legacy of the ruling class and not the contribution of the ruled.[21]

This hypothesis faces an apparent chronological difficulty. Contemporary Normandy and the Domesday Book do not know the term *burgagium*. Whereas the term *burgus* is attested for Normandy at the end of the tenth century, this is not the case for the particular term *burgagium*, though certainly conditions were ripe for such development,[22] as by the end of the eleventh century—that is, almost contemporary with the First Crusade—we find in Normandy a *consuetudo burgi* and a payment from city land is called *burgagium*.[23] Chronologically then the affinity is clear, but it remains a fact that the particular term appears somewhat late in the course of the twelfth century only.

We do not know how these Crusader non-noble possessions were administered, if they were at all, in the first decade of the Latin Kingdom. Yet one thing is clear: the order of the day, the great effort of the rulers, was to colonize and settle the captured and empty cities. Such a conscious project as settling Christian Syrians from Transjordan in a special quarter of Jerusalem must have been accompanied by some kind of agreement

[20] In Flanders during the twelfth century the castellans became hereditary and were replaced in the cities by *baillis*. J. Duesberg, *Les Jurisdictions scabinales en Flandre et en Lotharingie au moyen-âge* (Louvain, 1932), pp. 24 ff. F. L. Ganshof, 'Les transformations de l'organisation judiciaire dans le comté de Flandre jusqu'à l'avènement de la maison de Bourgogne', *Revue belge de philologie et d'histoire* 18 (1939), 46 ff. R. Monier, *Les Institutions judiciaires des villes de Flandre* (Lille, 1924), esp. pp. 135 ff. F. L. Ganshof, 'L'origine des constitutions urbaines en Flandre', *Moyen-Âge* 1926, pp. 349 ff. R. Monier, *Les Institutions centrales du Comté de Flandre de la fin du XIe siècle à 1384* (Paris, 1943), esp. pp. 22 and 61. On the Norman viscount see C. H. Haskins, *Norman Institutions* (New York, 1918), pp. 45–7. L. A. and T. A. Warnkönig, L. Stein, *Französische Staats- und Rechtsgeschichte* i (Basel, 1846), 242, cf. 357–8. H. M. Cam, *Liberties and Communities in Medieval England* (Cambridge, 1944), pp. 51–4.

[21] This would be corroborated by a study of the laws of succession in burgage-tenures which follow common European customs. Cf. below, Ch. 10, p. 279.

[22] H. Lagouëlle, *Essai sur la conception féodale de la propriété foncière dans le très ancien droit normand* (Paris, 1902), p. 135.

[23] Ibid., p. 140. The English customs derived from Breteuil have *burgagium* to denote property or the quit-rent due from it. Cf. M. Bateson, 'The laws of Breteuil', *EHR* 15 (1900), 304, 313, 496, 599, etc. For Normandy see R. Genestal, *La Tenure en bourgage dans les pays régis par la Coutume de Normandie* (Paris, 1900), pp. 164 ff. The expression *bourgage* does not appear before 1180 (ibid., pp. 207–19). The noun *burgenses* appears for the first time in Crusader sources in 1110 (W.T. xi. 12).

between Baldwin I and the 'Syrians' as to their future possessions.[24] Such a single event and also the everyday settling of Frankish colonists in the cities must have brought about a tighter administration of city property.

In the second and third decades the basic concept of burgage-tenure had already crystallized, to leave an indelible mark on the legal system of the Latins in the east for more than 400 years. Burgage-tenure was a perpetual and hereditary tenure, which paid to the lord of the city a *cens*—a nominal quit-rent—a small payment, to mark its dependence as a tenure held from the lord of the city. We may even note a degree of strictness in the royal administration. Even in property which could hardly ever have reverted to the Crown, such as in ecclesiastical *frankalmoigns* (*eleemosinae*), the lord insisted on safeguarding his rights.[25] *A fortiori* this was the case in the lay properties of burgesses. It is therefore remarkable that alongside the normal burgage-tenure we also find a *franche borgesie*, or burgage-tenure which did not pay any *cens*.[26] The insufficiency of Crusader administration can be blamed for it, but we have also to take into account a special type of royal or lordly grant. It was a part of the prerogative to bestow on a knight city land which would not be part of a fief but explicitly burgage-tenure, that is, properties held without any feudal obligations. Thus a deserving noble who received such property received it with a remittance of *cens*. As burgage-tenures were easily alienable, such property, once declared free, kept its legal standing, even if transferred to a third party.

We do not know the quantitative relation of burgage-tenures to free burgage-tenures. Obviously the former were the rule. But this distinction supplies important information, which will corroborate some of our earlier assumptions. The emergence of a full-fledged concept of burgage-tenure with its various legal rules must be linked with the development of the Court of Burgesses. It probably started out, as assumed, from the summary jurisdiction over non-nobles by the castellan or viscount. Disturbances of the peace by burgesses, and, even more, property claims of non-nobles, could hardly have been judged by feudal courts composed of knightly vassals. Not only was this an offence against legal tradition, but such a procedure would certainly have been inadequate to deal with

---

[24] See above, Ch. 4, pp. 92–3.

[25] See a privilege of King Fulk to the Holy Sepulchre. The property is given: 'ab omni consuetudine solutas, salva iustitia regali, quam rex debet habere in helemosina' (Rozière, no. 32. *Regesta*, no. 181, cf. no. 309).

[26] Philip of Novara, ch. 78: 'bourgesie franches et quites' and see above, p. 251 n. 5, and below, n. 28.

questions connected with city life and economy. A distinct judicial instance was imperative. This was the future Court of Burgesses.[27]

With the emergence of the Court of Burgesses some legal notions connected with burgage-tenures were put into practice. Though no formulated legal theory is extant, court procedure points to its existence. Its clearest expression is in the elaborate form of transactions before the Court of Burgesses. Traditional, it preserved, even for centuries to come, ancient notions and concepts in the formalistic rituals of its procedure.

The *Livre des Assises des Bourgeois* gives the following instructions:

> Who so sells his heritage, if it is in the land of the king and pays a quit-rent (*cens*), he is due to pay for that sale (*por cele vente*) 1 mark of silver and the man who buys the land or the house has to give 3 besants. But if the land or house are *franc*, that is they do not pay any *cens* to the king, nor to anybody else, the law commands that he is not obliged to pay anything for the sale of the house, except that the buyer will pay to the court 3 besants only, and thereby will be free, by law and *assise*.[28]

The difference between burgage-tenure and the free burgage-tenure resides in the seller's payment of 1 mark of silver to the lord, a payment absent in the case of a free burgage-tenure. In both cases, however, there is the payment of 3 besants to the court. It is not difficult to see in the seller's due of 1 mark of silver the European equivalent of the *laudemium* or *lods et ventes*, universal in alienations of burgage-tenures. As it existed in the Latin Kingdom, the payment was not the *treisième*, the thirteenth of the value, but a uniform payment of 1 mark of silver, independent of the real value of the property. The amount was not expressed in current coinage but in *monnaie de compte*, which in practice must have been evaluated in besants or deniers.[29] European usage varied in the amount and in the way it was paid by seller and buyer,[30] but the idea behind the payment was the same everywhere: this was the *laudemium*, the payment for the lord's permission for the transaction in property, which was a tenure held from him. The origin of the payment goes back to a time when such permission was legally needed. It proclaimed the lord's original right to a plot of land, which he or his predecessors bestowed on any individual tenant, or on a collectivity in the *villae novae*. As a rule, a

---

[27] See below, Ch. 10.

[28] *LdAdB*, ch. 31.

[29] See below, p. 262 and Ch. 16, p. 428 n. 66.

[30] H. Legras, *Le Bourgage de Caen. Tenure à cens et tenure à rente, XIe–XVe siècles* (Paris, 1911), pp. 61 f. and 109 f.; Glasson, op. cit. iv. 401–2.

uniform payment points to a process of urban colonization, when settlers received land on which to build their houses, or to a later development when a whole township received the privilege of a uniform payment, independent of the actual and real value of their property.

As to the Crusader Kingdom, it is impossible to suggest that its burgess settlers went through the whole historical process. The conquest and forceful appropriation, the availability of land and scarcity of settlers in the empty cities, all point to a different evolution. We are inclined to believe that it was during the process of consolidation of city administration that a theory came into being of an original distribution of city land by the lord of the city. The *laudemium* was a reminder of such an alleged act and the payment in a sense legitimized a legal theory. Actually things were different. The emergence of administration brought with it the classification of landed property. The legal notions of the ruling administration were brought over *in toto* from Europe and among them the burgage-tenure with all its freedoms but also with its archaic customs. Hence the *lods et ventes* in the Court of Burgesses.

Burgage-tenures survived the Latin Kingdom and we find them in full bloom at the beginning of the fourteenth century in the Court of Burgesses in Cyprus. Moreover, Cypriot practices, without a shadow of doubt brought over from the mainland, complete and corroborate our reconstruction of the developments in the Latin Kingdom.

The Cypriot procedure seems to have preserved the customs of Jerusalem slightly changed and adapted to newer circumstances. The simplest case was that of sale of a burgage-tenure.[31] The sale took place before the Court of Burgesses, a procedure which was optional, it seems, but not obligatory in Jerusalem.[32] The transaction was made in three phases: The seller announced the sale, naming object and price. Then followed the act of *dessaisine et saisine*, as it was called by the Crusaders. The seller handed over a stick (*verge*) to the vicomte, who in his turn passed it to the buyer, announcing that the seisin was delivered to him. The payment was the traditional 3 besants to the court and 2s. to be split between the clerk and the sergeants.

These formal, symbolic actions preserve the memory of a fictitious bestowal of the tenure by the lord of the city, now represented by the viscount, upon an original possessor of the tenure. For a moment the

---

[31] *Livre du plédéant*, ch. 15.

[32] But even in Cyprus *louages* could have been enacted before the Court, or with pledges without a court, or even with simple witnesses (*Livre du plédéant*, ch. 41, pp. 224 ff.).

viscount symbolically holds the tenure in his hand and repeats the action of the original bestowment.[33] The remarkable feature of this transaction is the disappearance of the payment of 1 mark of silver we met with in the Latin Kingdom, and there is no indication that we are dealing with a *borgesie franche*. We conclude rather that this payment to the lord of the city fell into abeyance.

Yet the payment of the traditional mark of silver did not disappear entirely.[34] It reappears in connection with burgage-tenure, but in a different context. The Cypriot treatise on jurisprudence deals in some chapters with a more complex problem than just the sale of a burgage-tenure. This tenure, 'far freer than any other',[35] became with time, as it happened in Europe, not only marketable real property, but also an object of investment. Renting or mortgaging real property, houses, gardens, and their like was a profitable enterprise. Real property was rented for a fixed or unlimited period by a contract, called in Europe *bail à rente*, and assured the renter a fixed annual income. The renter was the lord of the *encensive* and the payment was called *cens* causing us some difficulties, as it was the same term which was once applied to the quit-rent due to the *seigneur justicier*.[36]

New types of transaction and new legal rules came into being, and are recorded by the Cypriot jurists. As in former times, when the possessor of a burgage-tenure wants to sell it, he has full freedom to alienate,

---

[33] Actually the payment of the *lods et ventes* would have been sufficient to establish the title of the new buyer. This was the common European usage, but in some places, as in our case, there was also the act of *ensaisinement*. Cf. Glasson, op. cit. iv. 404.

[34] See below, Ch. 10, p. 294 n. 136 and p. 281 n. 67.

[35] *Livre du plédéant*, ch. 32: 'la franchise de la bourgezie qui est une chose mout franche'.

[36] In Europe *cens* was generally understood as the recognition payment, or quit-rent to the feudal lord and later to the communal authority. The *censitaire* could not create a new *cens* and thus become a *seigneur justicier*. This was expressed by the legal maxim: 'Cens sur cens n'a point de lieu' (A. Loysel, *Institutes coutumières*, ed. E. de Laurière (Paris, 1846) l. iv. tit. 2, 4, § 523). The real rent was established by a *bail à rente* and the rent called *croi de cens* or *cens costier* (Glasson, op. cit. iv. 399). Crusader vocabulary is less clear. The LdAdB, ch. 254, describes what seems to be a *bail à rent*, but says: 'Ce aucuns hons ou feme apaute aucune mee terre... por douner me chascun an I cert pris noumé, et il avient puis que celuy ne me paie pas mon *cens*, si come il deit.' The original *censitaire* is called in the same chapter *seigneur de la terre*. The *Livre du plédéant*, ch. 13, lists among the competences of the Court of Burgesses: 'borgezies qui sont dedens la ville... et de rentes et encensive desdites *borgesies*', which are in the competence of the High Court because they are part of the fiefs. Thus *encensive* corresponds here apparently to the *croi de cens*. This is corroborated by the same chapter, which lists transactions to be pleaded before the Court of Burgesses and among them: 'et en douner les (héritages) à encensive, à terme et sans terme'. Finally, ibid., ch. 21 seems to be conclusive: 'Pour ce que l'om doit savoir le fait des encensives, encores si a ventes que l'om fait d'aucuns héritages qui doivent encensive.' *Encensive* is translated into Italian as 'liuello'.

safeguarding the rights of the lord of the 'encensive'. The latter will in such a case receive the payment of 1 mark of silver, evaluated at 25 Cypriot besants. Moreover he has a pre-emption right over any prospective buyer and if he decides to buy, he will pay 1 mark of silver less than the agreed price. From the seller's point of view there is no difference, as in both cases he will pay the mark of silver to the lord of the *cens*.[37] The survival of the mark of silver payment, the traditional amount we encountered in the Latin Kingdom, proves the transmission of the institution to Cyprus. But the tenure became freer than before and the *seigneur justicier* lost his rights. What remained was the payment for the seizin. This we find again when a tenure is sold by an order of the court to the highest bidder[38] and in many other cases.[39] It was now in the spirit of this greater freedom that not only the tenure was free on the market. The *encensive* itself, that is the *bail à rente* became a commercial commodity, and *encensives* were sold before the Court of Burgesses. This commodity was now bought by everybody not legally excluded from possession[40] and even the king himself invested or transacted in *encensive*. The only payment that remained was that of *dessaisine–saisine*.[41]

[37] *Livre du plédéant*, ch. 21.   [38] Ibid., ch. 23.   [39] Ibid., ch. 21.
[40] See above, p. 251 n. 6.   [41] *Livre du plédéant*, ch. 17 *in fine*.

10 The Origin of the Court of Burgesses

In the middle of the thirteenth century John of Ibelin, meditating on the institutions of his country, told the story of how Godfrey of Bouillon established two courts in the kingdom, the High Court to judge knights and nobles and the Court of Burgesses to judge the Frankish non-nobles, called *burgenses*. In all probability it was not John of Ibelin who invented the story, but he put into writing what was a current tale. Henceforth the story was repeated in different treatises of law of the kingdom, transmitted to the Latins of Constantinople, to the Franks in Cyprus, and to the French in Morea, and finally handed down to modern historiography.[1] The problem has been debated to some extent, but whatever the conclusions, they are ultimately based on the treatises of jurisprudence. But these treatises represent only one type of source; the others are the legal documents, which have seldom, if ever, been used to elucidate the origins and competences of the Court of Burgesses.

The Court of Burgesses was often called the Court of the Viscount from the title of the officer who presided over it. It was also called the Lower Court *(Court basse)*, which points to its original birth-place in Jerusalem, where it was distinguished from the royal High Court. It was even called *Court petite*, the 'Small Court'. What is remarkable is the name *Cour de borgesie*, a name found not only in legal treatises but in actual charters.[2] Obviously, the *borgesies* were its main concern, and a Cypriot jurist even thought of deriving its name from these burgage-tenures.[3]

The number of documents that can be assigned directly to the Court of Burgesses, in view of the abundant documentation at our disposal, is disappointingly small. For the twelfth century we find twenty-five only, the majority from the capital of the kingdom, Jerusalem, a single one from Caesarea, and two from Tyre and Acre.[4] All, except that from Caesarea,

---

[1] On the vicissitudes of this story, see below, Ch. 14.
[2] Cf. below, p. 293; 'in presentia curie burgesie'.
[3] *Livre du plédéant*, ch. 13, p. 68.
[4] John of Ibelin, ch. 270, listed thirty-six Courts of Burgesses. Richard, *Royaume latin*, p. 119, counted four additional viscounts which makes a total of forty.

come from royal cities. In the thirteenth century the main bulk of documents originated, as we might assume, in Acre. It is also a matter of interest that only two surviving deeds emanate directly from the Court of Burgesses, sealed by its official seal. Both belong to the second half of the thirteenth century and are related to a reform in court procedure.

The legal procedure described by the treatises of law does not always correspond to the actual deeds. Moreover there is a large number of deeds in which one would expect the intervention of the court, but in which the latter is conspicuously absent. Conversely, there are also cases which were passed before the Court of Burgesses, but the name of the institution is not mentioned. In both cases we are dealing with peculiarities of Crusader law and procedure.

The name *burgenses* was not used by any chronicler of the first Crusade; it appeared for the first time in 1110 in a privilege of Baldwin I. The privilege empowered the members of the three orders *optimates, milites,* and *burgenses,* to endow the newly created bishopric of Bethlehem.[5]

For the earliest appearance of the name *curia* for the Court of Burgesses we shall have to wait until 1149, when a charter mentions the *curia regalis,* definitely the Court of Burgesses in Jerusalem.[6] The very late appearance of the name *curia regalis* to describe the Court of Burgesses does not mean that the court did not exist earlier. It points rather to the fact that the Court of Burgesses did not come into existence in one piece and that there was a period of incubation and growth which culminated in the middle of the twelfth century.

How and when did this institution develop? To follow its evolution for almost two generations after the conquest, we shall rely on three factors: the Court of Burgesses was presided over by a viscount, or sometimes, as we shall see, by the castellan;[7] the names of people who witnessed charters often appear with the adjective *burgenses* or *iurati*; the competences of the court and consequently the type of transactions to be carried out before it, are known to us from the treatises of law. Consequently, a large number of transactions can be assigned or linked to the Court of Burgesses.

As court registers were not kept until the middle of the thirteenth century, and even these did not survive, we shall have to rely on another

---

[5] The privilege was copied by W.T. xi. 12.

[6] Rozière, no. 112: 'Hoc totum factum est in presenti regali curia' (*Regesta,* no. 225). The list of witnesses begins with the Viscount Roart, followed by the names of nine well-known burgesses of the city. The same people appear in other documents as *iurati*.

[7] e.g. Delaville, no. 312; *Regesta,* no. 391, and more examples below. It is remarkable that the *LdAdB* never mentioned such a possibility.

type of documents, those belonging to establishments which, when buying or receiving property, drew up charters and often asked for all earlier deeds relating to the acquired property. This was done to prove legitimate rights in a case of claim (*calumnia, chalonge*).

The earliest document that has a bearing on our matter was written in 1125—a generation after the establishment of the kingdom. The document is called *carta*, and seems to be a summary of proceedings which was inserted into the Cartulary of the Holy Sepulchre.[8] It recorded the essentials of the sale of a house by one George Rais and his partner Bursard to Bernard of Castellum Radulfi and his wife Havidis. The house itself once belonged to a Breton Peter and his partner Geifrid. The price of the first sale was 80 besants 'inter omnes consuetudines' (the price of the present actual sale is not mentioned), and it was done 'coram Anschetino vicecomite, qui rectitudinem inde accepit', in the presence of twenty-one witnesses, including the viscount's son Albert, the 'placearius' (the subaltern official of the court, a kind of beadle), William Grossus, and Robert, 'janitor portae David'. The overwhelming majority of the witnesses were of non-knightly origin.[9] The *carta* was written by Oger, 'clericus in turre David'. The house is sold 'sine aliqua calumpnia ad vendendum et ad dandum ad suam voluntatem fatiendam'. The witness to the charter (as distinct from the witnesses of the sale) was Marages, son of the seller Bursard, 'qui fuit ad potationem huius rei'. The transaction was thus clinched by the popular custom of having a drink together.[10]

The charter was not an instrument of transaction, it was in the best of cases a *recordatio*. According to Crusader law it was no proof in itself, and its importance was in the list of twenty-one witnesses, the potential warrantors (*garens*) to the act. The actual sale was performed before the Viscount Anschetinus. His presence signified public recognition of the transaction, but it was also determined by the legal nature of the property involved, as the house was doubtless a *borgesie*. As burgage-tenure it was held from the lord of the city and theoretically needed his consent to any alienation. This right, now vested in his representative, the viscount, was expressed by the payment of a *rectitudo*, which the buyer included ('inter omnes consuetudines') in the price of the property.

---

[8] Rozière, no. 103; *Regesta*, no. 110.

[9] Cf. names such as Stephanus Stultus, Radulfus Faber, Brunet Cambiator, Petrus Faber.

[10] This popular custom of *vin du marché, Friede Wein, Weinkauf*, is well known in France, Germany (A. Esmein, *Étude sur les contrats dans le très-ancien droit français* (Paris, 1883), pp. 24–5), and England (M. Bateson, *Borough Customs* ii (London, 1906), 116–17).

What we miss in the whole procedure is the Court of Burgesses in which such a transaction would or should have taken place. Does that mean that it did not exist? This depends on the interpretation of the list of the twenty-one witnesses. They sign as *testes*, and apparently there is no warrant to see in them the Court of Burgesses of Jerusalem. The writer of the charter is the 'clericus in turre David', who in all probability kept the accounts of customs paid at the entrance into the city,[11] and as such was connected with the viscount, the man responsible for the king's revenue in the city. Two other people signing the document are also connected with the viscount: the 'placearius' and the 'janitor portae David', though the latter might rather have been connected with the castellan, but often both tasks were discharged by one and the same person. Among other signatories there was Albert, the viscount's son. These three people were scarcely official members of any hypothetical Court of Burgesses. The other witnesses were no doubt burgesses; they made the transaction public, and signed because they knew the parties concerned; they may have been even their *vicini* in the city. Nothing indicates that they were jurors of the court. And yet such a possibility, far from being excluded, is very plausible.

What we are witnessing here and in the following documents is a process whereby some of the witnesses to transactions became in time some sort of 'official witnesses', the nucleus of the *iurati* of the Court of Burgesses, headed by the viscount of the city. This process is well illustrated by the transition from the fluid vocabulary of our documents which prevailed for almost two generations to a more precise one, and finally to the appearance of a full-fledged Court of Burgesses. This corresponds closely to the contemporary evolution of European urban institutions. It can best be described as a process which begins with the emergence of an officer or official representing the feudal lord specifically in city affairs and a group of people witnessing urban transactions and ending with the creation of a communal or urban court with well-defined competences. From the beginning the witnesses were not just people chosen at random. Some might have been *vicini*, the neighbours of the parties or properties concerned, who still exercised in some places the *retrait des voisins*, a pre-emption right in properties in their neighbourhood. More important for future development was the fact that to assure legality to the transaction and to make a private act into a public and unimpeachably valid one, the witnesses were chosen from among the

---

[11] Some were abolished in 1120 (Rozière, no. 45; *Regesta* no. 91).

better-known burgesses, or from burgesses of standing in the city or township.[12] They were the nucleus of the future *iurati* of the court. The title *iurati* will obviously not appear until they take a specific oath. In our context it is of no consequence that in Europe this institution became an urban institution when the lord of the city abandoned his rights and delegated them to the city commune. The institution remained basically the same even if the fines were poured into the community chest and not paid to the lord's treasury. This later evolution did not take place in the kingdom, because urban communes never came into being. Conversely, the beginnings of the urban jurisdiction vested in a particular Court of Burgesses was common to Europe and to Outremer.

By the second quarter of the century a process of crystallization, which probably started earlier, is apparent. The same witnesses appear time and again in transactions passed in the presence of the viscount. Moreover, their number becomes smaller, an unmistakable sign of the development of a more precise and better-defined institution, which we find in the forties of the twelfth century. This process of crystallization of the institution can be followed in the surviving deeds of the period.

A grant made *c.* 1125 by one Radulf de Fontanellis to a well-known burgess in Jerusalem, Gaufridus Acu, is witnessed by the Viscount Anschetinus and seven burgesses: 'Rainaldus de Ponto, Bonet de Tolosa, Porcellus, Gerardus Bocherius, Soherius de Baruth, Petrus Provintialis, Bachelerius'.[13] The property was a vineyard, perhaps a *franc-borgesie*, since the grant says explicitly that no service or payment will be due from it. In this case the viscount exercised a *juridiction gracieuse*, a non-litigating function, and though there is no indication that the witnesses comprise a court, they are already a more coherent body. When four years later Baldwin II confirmed possessions given to the Hospitallers during his reign,[14] he mentioned, among others, three properties given in Jerusalem[15] between 1118 and 1129. The witnesses to these donations were, in the first

---

[12] Parallel developments can be found in Flanders and north Germany (G. Des Marez, *Étude sur la propriété foncière des villes du moyen-âge et spécialement en Flandre* (Paris, 1898), p. 241). In Norman Sicily and Italy the same position is taken by the *boni homines*. V. Giuffrida, 'Sulla formazione delle consuetudini giuridiche delle città di Sicilia', *Archivio storico per la Sicilia orientale* 5 (1908), 195–6; L. V. Heinemann, *Zur Entstehung der Stadtverfassung in Italien* (Leipzig, 1896), pp. 15 and 19.

[13] Rozière, no. 121; *Regesta*, no. 111.

[14] Delaville, no. 84 (i. 78–9); *Regesta*, no. 130.

[15] A house near the Temple area given by Adam de Ramis; Alfanus, who gives his property in the Changers' Street to the Order; a house given in Jerusalem by Alanus Boccerius.

case, the Viscount Anschetinus, Hugo de Ramis, Goffridus Acula, Alfanus, Siherius de Beritto, Porcellus, Rainaldus de Ponzo;[16] in the second, again the viscount and all the previous witnesses in addition to Hugo de Ramis (probably Ramle),[17] and Alfanus who made the donation. The same witnesses with three additional names had figured before in the donation of Radulf de Fontanellis. The last donation, that of Alanus Boccerius has, besides the viscount, only two witnesses, Guerricus and Henricus the Burgundian, not found in other documents. Thus we see by about 1129 a nucleus of burgesses who clustered around the viscount. Still, not all the witnesses were burgesses. A knight such as Hugo of Ramle, for example, signed a deed after the viscount and before the burgesses. But the non-noble witnesses became, so to speak, 'professional witnesses', a good nucleus for the future Court of Burgesses.

The organization of the court, even when it was already becoming a more defined body did not proceed without difficulties, and it could not have been otherwise. The unruly participants of the First Crusade and the heterogeneous population that settled in the kingdom afterwards were certainly not the most law-abiding elements. Once outside their native places, with no tradition or established order to impose rules of conduct, these newcomers who settled in the almost empty cities and fought daily for their existence, were not easily mastered. There were also the social differences which made knight and noble look down at the Frankish commoners and even more on city institutions unknown in their native lands and now, in a sense, imposed on them by the fact of their city habitat. Because of their city possessions, if they were not part of a fief or an allod, the knight and noble were under the jurisdiction of the local Court of Burgesses, a rule which could scarcely have been popular with the nobility of the kingdom. The royal court in Jerusalem and royal courts in other crown cities, a baronial court outside the royal domain, were the competent authorities for burgage-tenures even for the nobles of the kingdom.

Once the Court of Burgesses came into being, it was in the logic of things to define its competence. The area of its jurisdiction was defined (perhaps identical with that of the *chambre du seigneur*)[18] as the lordship. This was an important feature of the new organization, which could not

---

[16] Donation of Adam de Ramis.

[17] The chancellor and two knights sign before the viscount. Hugo de Ramis gave Bethiben and Gendas near Lydda to the Hospitallers with the consent of his overlord Hugh of Jaffa.

[18] See above, ch. 9, p. 255 n. 15.

look back to the *comitatus* or *castellaniae* of a previous Carolingian period. The notion was pushed to the extreme. If two lordships found themselves united, neither lost its former identity, and it goes without saying that each jurisdiction was absolutely autonomous. This was strengthened by the parallel feudal structure, as the body of vassals was that of knights holding fiefs in the lordship. A curious aspect of the system was a kind of non-recognition of acts performed before a Court of Burgesses by another court in a different lordship. Any claim in burgage-tenure had to come before the court in whose jurisdiction district the property was situated. A burgess of Acre or Bethlehem could not claim property in Jerusalem except in the Court of Jerusalem.[19] Finally, any litigation concerning burgage-tenures had to be judged exclusively by the Court of Burgesses. This was so strictly observed that Frankish nobles, including royal vassals, had to plead for their non-feudal properties in the Court of Burgesses.[20] Thus the Courts of Burgesses brought under their competence the burgesses and their properties *ratione personae* and even knights and nobles *ratione materiae*.

Such developments encountered difficulties and even violent opposition. Philip of Novara preserves a record of the early process of this emergence of the Court of Burgesses. He mentions the promulgation of an old *assise* of an uncertain date: ' a long time after the other *assises*'.[21] Obviously, in the middle of the thirteenth century there was no detailed knowledge of the chronology of the *assises*. What he has to say can be summarized as follows: outrages and insults were heaped on the jurors of the Court of Burgesses. This created a situation in which 'the seignor could hardly find a man who was willing to be a juror of the Court of the Viscount and that of the Burgesses.' To remedy this situation a special *assise* had to be promulgated, that no judicial combat (*bataille*) would be allowed against members of the court if they were accused of false judgment or of being corrupt ('que la court est fausse ou que elle a fait faus jugements'). The punishment for such accusation would be loss of life and this would happen even 'to the greatest man of the country'; at the utmost, if the king should show mercy, the tongue of the accuser would be cut out. Moreover

---

[19] *LdAdB*, ch. 221.

[20] John of Ibelin, ch. 24: 'De borgesie, de quoi l'on ne deit plaideer que en la Court de Borgesie. Car ceste franchise ont anciennement les seignors dou reiaume de Jerusalem doné as borgeis, par la volenté et l'otroi de leur homes.' Cf. ibid., ch. 38; *Livre au Roi*, ch. 340; *Livre du plédéant*, ch. 13.

[21] Philip of Novara, ch. 87, p. 561.

the testimony of jurors would be sufficient and final and they would not need either pledges or proof.[22]

And because of the security of this *assise* [says Philip of Novara], do burgesses dare to be *jurés* of the Court of the lord, and pronounce and judge in security. Because the Court of the Viscount and of the Burgesses is well that of the lord, because he would have made the judgments if he were present.'

Philip of Novara did not explicitly state what kind of litigation caused outbursts of violence against the jurors of the Court of Burgesses. And though there is no reason to think that the burgesses of the kingdom were more law-abiding than its nobles, he seems to indicate clearly that it was the nobles litigating for their tenures (otherwise they would not come before the Court of Burgesses), whose behaviour not only constituted a contempt of court, but physically threatened the jurors. Without being sure, we may assign this *assise* to the first half of the twelfth century.

It is around the middle of that century, *c.* 1146–9, that the contours of a better-defined institution can be seen emerging from our evidence. The documents in question do not come from Jerusalem but from Tyre. Both are acts of sale of city land to the Hospitallers. In the first (1146), Gilbert, the Master of the Knights of St. John, buys land from a 'domina Beliorna' widow of Robert of Scandalion.[23] The document ends with a list of witnesses, introduced by: 'tali vero testimonio, quod istius emptionis pro hac terra testis veraciter est Willelmus de Japha', followed by a Hospitaller and some burgesses, a 'cementarius', two 'corviserii', and one tanner, and this is followed by: 'et alii quam plures *boni homines et legalitatis et justitie exsecutores*'. In the second charter (1149–50) of the same Gilbert,[24] the eschatocol states: 'tali modo, quod Giraldus Passerel fuit inde *auctorixator* et testis, Willelmus de Japha testis', followed by the signatures of one Hospitaller and three other people who were burgesses (Petrus Cementarius, Guillelmus Anglicus, Petrus Rex). In both cases we are dealing with more than a list of witnesses. The 'boni homines et legalitatis *et justitie* exsecutores' cannot be thought of as only qualified witnesses.[25] They have a far more important standing in the transaction. They seem to be actually members of the Court of Burgesses although not described as such. They assist the transaction,[26] authorize it by their presence, and make it legal

---

[22] Ibid., ch. 87.   [23] Delaville, no. 184 (i. 145); *Regesta*, no. 254.

[24] Delaville, no. 166 (i. 132); *Regesta*, no. 242.

[25] It is not clear what *auctorixator* means. It is certainly not the man from whom the land is bought. It may mean the man who warrants the legality of transaction.

[26] The viscount is not mentioned, unless Willelmus de Japha was the viscount.

and binding. In this sense they are *justitie exsecutores*, but they are not yet clearly separated from other witnesses. Giraldus Passerel, described as 'auctorixator et testis', exemplifies well the fluidity of the vocabulary.[27]

A charter from Jerusalem, of 1149, proves that the Court of Burgesses had already reached its definite form—probably a decade or so earlier. Anfred, castellan of Hebron, bestowed on Martin and his wife a courtyard in perpetuity for an annual *cens* of 2 besants. The place of transaction is explicitly stated: 'Hoc totum factum est in *presenti regali curia*, testibus: Domno Roart Benscelino vicecomite', followed by the names of nine well-known burgesses.[28] Following that we read: 'Fulcherio existente patriarcha, regnante Baldoino rege, testibus: Domno Philippo, Johanne de Valentina, Gervasio, Petro Burdillo.' It is the first time that the *curia*, presided over by the viscount, is officially and explicitly mentioned.[29] No doubt the other signatories are members of the court. Their standing, not as simple witnesses, is proved by the fact that after an intervening line, the charter mentions another set of four witnesses who did not belong to the court—in all probability not even burgesses—in the retinue of the castellan of Hebron, witnessing on behalf of the original landlord. Despite this distinction and a better perception of the respective standing of people present in court, the difference between court members and witnesses is still blurred. The addition of 'multi alii' at the end of the list of witnesses may have been due to a scribe's flourish, but possibly also reflects a current usage of making the transaction public.[30]

The stage of development which our court had reached *c.* 1149 is well illustrated in Acre by a charter of Queen Melissenda to the Knights of St.

---

[27] The man seems to have been a knight attached to the royal households of Fulk of Anjou, Baldwin III, Melissenda, and Theodora. If he was viscount of Tyre, the title *auctorixator* would be even more meaningful.

[28] Rozière, no. 112; *Regesta*, no. 255.

[29] *Regesta*, index, s.v. identified Roart Benscellinus with a viscount of Hebron. This is inadmissible, as all the signatures are of well-known burgesses of Jerusalem. We should possibly read: 'Domino Roart vicecomite, Benscellino'. Roart was actually castellan and viscount of Jerusalem (*Regesta*, s.v.), whereas Bencelinus (Bentulinus etc.) was a burgess of Jerusalem. The other signatories were Brictius, Rainaldus, Sicherius Petraguoricensis, Petrus Salomonis, Ymbertus de Baro, Symon, Hugo de Tolosa, Arbertus de Arcu, Iudas, 'et alii multi'.

[30] Another deed concerning the same Martina and another castellan of Hebron, Hugh of St. Abraham, deals with a courtyard bestowed on her in perpetuity for a quit-rent of 2 besants (Rozière, no. 113). *Regesta*, no. 169, assigns it to 1136, but it could be argued for *c.* 1149 as a confirmation of the charter analysed above. In any case this grant does not mention any *curia*. Of its witnesses (all, it seems, from Hebron) it is said: 'omnes isti testes suprascripti audierunt et viderunt.'

John.[31] It refers to three transactions, each performed before a different forum. In the first Melissenda received from the Hospitallers baths in St. Leonard's quarter in Acre and gave them a loggia, some houses, till then kept by Franco, the former castellan of the city, and some land outside the city. This part of the charter concludes: 'Testes vero sunt cambitionis . . . hii quorum subter adnotata sunt nomina: Geraldus de Valentia, per manum cujus facta est cambitio diebus vicecomitatus sui, Menardus de Portu et Deauratus et alii plures.' The next part is a confirmation by Melissenda and King Baldwin III of a formal transaction of the Hospitallers, described by the queen: 'vendicio legitime facta est . . . per manum Clarembaldi, itidem vicecomitis Acconensis.' In both cases the land is a burgage-tenure and the sale is performed through the intermediary of the viscount. The 'cambitio . . . per manum' denotes more than a simple presence. The viscount, as we saw, was instrumental in the seisin and investiture of property and his symbolic action was paid by the parties concerned. The two burgesses mentioned in the first charter are doubtless members of the Viscount's Court. In the original sale they were probably distinctly marked out from other burgesses, but Melissenda's charter mentions their names only, as this is sufficient to prove the validity of the transaction. These documents, written in 1149, show the Court of Burgesses already fully composed and functioning.

After the middle of the century the number of documents connected with the court grows constantly and permits a more detailed picture of its proceedings. The series begins with a donation—actually in the creation of an *encensive*—by a knight, Gibelin son of Anchetinus, for the canons of the Holy Sepulchre (*c.* 1151).[32] This is the first time that the name *iurati* appears, though, as we saw, the court had probably existed for more than a generation, and two years earlier was explicitly mentioned in a charter. The property in question was a *casale Sapharoria*, and therefore somewhat exceptional, as it does not refer to city property. But as we shall see, some *casalia*, villages, were not fiefs, but were held by burgage-tenure. The *casale* Sapharoria seems to have been one of them. How it came into the hands of Gibelin is not known, but in all probability through marriage, as his wife Agnes and his son Anselinus take part in the concession, and their consent is not simply mentioned, as was usual, but is far more formal and added in a separate clause with a special set of witnesses. There is no mention of the Court of Burgesses, the signatures being introduced as

[31] Delaville, no. 180, pp. 140–1; *Regesta*, no. 256.
[32] Rozière, no. 133; *Regesta*, no. 273.

'huius itaque venditionis testes sunt', but in the second set of witnesses, introduced by 'concessionis vero Agnetis, uxoris Gibelini, et filii eorum Anselmi testes sunt', we find signatures introduced by 'et de *iuratis* Jerusalem'. The first set of witnesses is composed of people who are often in the Court of the Holy Sepulchre, except for the first signatory, John 'dapifer regis', the king's seneschal. His legal position is not very clear. He might have been a simple witness, but it seems rather that Gibelin's knightly origin explains his signature in the deed. Whereas Gibelin's list of witnesses includes nine signatures, the consent of Agnes and of her son include only three, two of whom witnessed Gibelin's concession. Finally, from among the five witnesses signing with the additional adjective of *iurati*, one, Symon Rufus, had already signed Gibelin's concession as a witness (without the title *iuratus*). We can reconstruct the whole procedure as follows. The burgage-tenure was given in perpetuity to the canons, who paid for it 180 besants and furs. The tenure is entirely free and at their will, but an *encensive* is created and settled on Gibelin's son Anselin. The *encensive* is an annual payment of 5 besants and a sword. Such a transaction to assure its validity is performed with *fideiussores*, who correspond to the *garens*[33] of the Crusader treatise of law. The *garens* not only take upon themselves to defend the legality of the transaction, but even oblige their descendants to the third generation.[34] The sale by Gibelin was witnessed by a number of people connected with the Court of the Patriarch and by some prominent burgesses; the consent of his wife and their son was given at the same time and witnessed by burgesses, some of whom were *iurati*. This double agreement was then drawn up in a record, probably by a clerk of the canons of the Holy Sepulchre.

But one point remains unclear, the absence of the viscount. The explanation is to be found in the character of our document. The transaction must have been performed in a Court of Burgesses, but our document is a private record of it. The validity of the transaction depended on the *fideiussores*, who will prevent any claim (especially from the family involved) and on the witnesses. The *iurati* who appear here were present at the official transaction before the Court of Burgesses. Their testimony has a special value in litigation as is clearly expressed in the *Livre des Assises des Bourgeois*.[35]

[33] They are Gibelin's son-in-law Hugh and one William the Norman. The presence of Hugh as a potential claimant to his father-in-law's possession was obviously important.

[34] Cf. *Livre du plédéant*, ch. 15 *in fine*.

[35] *LdAdB*, ch. 138: 'Mais bien saches que II iures pueent bien porter garantie de toutes choses qui sont faites ou dites devant yaus en la cort sans nulle bataille que estre y puisse.' Ibid.,

(continued)

A similar case was that of a transaction in city property preserved in a document of 1163. The families of one Eustace and Adam le Noir sold land to the Hospitallers.[36] The land was at St. Stephen's Gate near other property of the Hospitallers. The transaction (500 besants) was made before four different groups of people, all described as *testes idonei*. The first comprised members of the Order of St. John; the second, that of *milites*, headed by Rohard the castellan and at the same time viscount of Jerusalem; the third was that of *de juratis Jherusalem*, and, finally, we find the names of nine well-known burgesses of Jerusalem introduced by 'interfuit etiam . . .'. The wives of the sellers, Agnes and Osmonde, were sisters, daughters of Bertrand Pons, and possessed in common some other land in the vicinity, which they also sold (in 1163) to the Hospitallers.[37] The land was probably part of the succession of their father and entered into the property of their respective marriages. Bertrand Pons is unknown, but seeing the location of the property and the type of witnesses we assume a knight–burgess marriage, through which a burgage-tenure came into knightly possession. Here again the Court of Burgesses is not expressly mentioned, but as we have seen already, there is no direct or formal relation between the dealings of the court and the documents describing the transaction. In our document we have at least all the component parts of the court: the castellan Rohard, who is also the viscount, and the *iurati*. The presence of Hospitallers and other knights is explained by the fact that the first are the interested party and the others belong to the social class of the alientators. The distinction between the *iurati* and other burgess witnesses is the same as in the previous document. Yet this transaction has some peculiarities. The transfer of the seisin of the property is made by the seller who says: 'fratribus ejusdem et successoribus eorum in helemosinam contradidimus et per impositionem manuum nostrarum super altare sancti Johannis investituram eisdem bono animo parique voto fecimus.' The land, whatever its former legal status, will henceforth be a *frankalmoign*. The seisin is directly transferred by the seller without the viscount's intervention, by putting his hands on the altar, thus, so to speak, investing St. John with the property. This seems to exclude the intervention of the Court of Burgesses. It is possible to argue that the former status of the property was that of an allod, or *franc borgesie* and there was no need for

---

ch. 137: jurors, although Franks, are legitimate warrants even against a non-Frank, a rule not admitted for anybody else.

[36] Delaville, no. 312 (i. 225–6); *Regesta*, no. 391.

[37] Delaville, no. 314 (i. 227); *Regesta*, no. 391a.

the lord's, or his representative's authorization. What was needed was simply the signatures of witnesses who would keep the 'record', as the Crusaders called it, of the transaction. The direct seisin would point more in this direction.

The evolution of the Court of Burgesses in royal cities such as Jerusalem, Tyre, and Acre, was paralleled in the baronial cities of the kingdom. A good example of the working of the Court of Burgesses in a non-royal city comes in 1167 from Caesarea.[38] It is a deed recording the sale of a house for 30 besants and 12 *nummi* (probably *deniers*) in full hereditary possession by one Isabella, 'civitatis Cesaree Palestine colona', to one Alberic. The seller states: 'verum ut hac mea legitima venditio firma et inconcussa perpetuo permaneat, *in curia coram juratis civitatis* Cesaree Palestine concessi.' The same is guaranteed by her daughter in her own name and that of her successors. The terms of sale stipulate complete freedom of alienation and the property is not burdened by any *cens*.[39] The house was certainly a burgage-tenure and possibly *franc borgesie*. The witnesses are unknown from other sources, but they are no doubt burgesses, as proved by their occupations, such as *cambiator* and *cordonarius*. They were probably members of the court and headed by a Hugo 'senescalus domini'. As the seneschal was one of the highest officers who represented the king or the lord, it is plausible to suggest that in a small lordship like Caesarea he sometimes fulfilled the task of the viscount.

A particular example of the working of the Court of Burgesses and its relation to witnesses signing the deeds is furnished by a charter of *c.* 1169 from Jerusalem.[40] It is an act creating a perpetual rent (27 besants a year) from houses in Jerusalem for one Bonjean 'linarius'.[41] Ancelin, son of Lady Gille, who was the original landlord, retained a pre-emption right, and in case of alienation the eventual payment of 2 marks of silver less than other bidders.[42] The description of the conditions of the transaction is followed by a list of twelve witnesses, headed by Guido de Beteras 'miles', Goncelinus, and Gaufredus, 'senecalcus patriarchae'. All the other witnesses are well-known burgesses of Jerusalem, some of them known as *iurati* of

[38] Delaville, *Archives*, no. 27, pp. 110–11; *Regesta*, no. 432.

[39] Ibid.: 'absque omni contrarietate vendendi, alienandi vel cui libuerit religioni donandi potestatem habeant.'

[40] *ROL* xi (1905–8), 185–7.

[41] The legal status is defined by the expression: 'et habeant postestatem dare, vendere, impignorare, et quicquid illis facere placuerit sicut de propria hereditate sua.'

[42] The usual payment is 1 mark of silver, but we have here at least two houses ('que . . . domus sunt') and possibly the payment indicated is 1 mark less for each house.

the court.[43] The most illuminating is the phrase at the end of the charter: 'Facta sunt hec in *curia Jerosolimitana*.' The transaction was thus made in the court of Jerusalem, but the charter was not written by the court and was technically a private one. The most important personality among the witnesses is Goncelinus who appears here without any title, but we know him from other deeds a few years later as a member of the Court of Burgesses and in the entourage of King Amalric.[44] In all probability he was connected with the viscount or castellan of the city. Another interesting personality is Godfrey, the Patriarch's seneschal, known between 1153 and 1186, whom we shall discuss in connection with the Patriarch's lordship in Jerusalem.

An exchange transaction in an important complex of burgage-tenures in Jerusalem[45] is represented by a deed of 1171. Some features of this transaction are particularly important as they deviate from the rules of the legal treatises. The abbot of the church of Ascension on the Mount of Olives exchanged the village of Cafran for houses belonging to the Order of St. John of Jerusalem. The number of houses is not specified but there were twelve tenants,[46] and the total annual rent was 130 besants. 'Istud prefatum concambium', we read, 'factum fuit in civitate Acconensium, in presentia domini Amalrici, patriarche Jherosolimitani et concilio et laudamento Amalrici ... regis.' The signatories are grouped into churchmen, then *de baronibus* and among them Rohard, castellan of Jerusalem, and finally *de juratis*, a dozen well-known burgesses of Jerusalem, including Adalbert, the patriarch's butler. The peculiarity of this deed is to remind us that the Court of Burgesses of Jerusalem was a royal court and could function as an entity, but also as a part of the *curia regis* in the larger sense of the word. In our deed the transaction is performed with the consent of the *curia regis* at large, the king, his barons, and his burgesses, who were jurors of the Court of Burgesses. The presence of the Patriarch was probably a legal necessity as the abbot of the church of the Ascension was his suffragan.[47] More intriguing is the fact that the transaction did not follow the strict rule that a burgage-tenure could be alienated only in the court to whose jurisdiction it belonged.[48] These

[43] See the identifications of Delaville, *Archives*, pp. 186–7.

[44] *Regesta*, nos. 501, 504, 516. He signs as 'magister' Guncelinus and Guncelinus Castelli between 1173 and 1174.

[45] Delaville, no. 422 (i. 291–2); *Regesta*; no. 492.

[46] The number of houses is unknown as some tenants pay 'de domibus'.

[47] Prawer, *Latin Kingdom*, p. 166.

[48] See above, pp. 268–9.

burgage-tenures, though located in Jerusalem, were actually alienated in Acre. This is not a glaring contradiction of the rule; it rather points to the fact that the court does not necessarily sit in Jerusalem. When it moves with the whole *curia regis* to Acre, it is still the Court of Burgesses of Jerusalem and as such preserves its jurisdiction over burgage-tenures in that city.

All the component parts of the Court of Burgesses and its working routine are finally illustrated in a deed of 1173, of the sale of a courtyard to the Hospitallers near the 'lacus Germani'—that is, near Mt. Zion in Jerusalem.[49] The sale was performed by one Hodeardis, widow of Otto of Verdun of a burgess family, which had for a long time played a part in the administrative life of the city.[50] The transaction, we read, 'factum est autem hoc in curia domini regis Amalrici in Jerusalem, qui hoc donum laudavit, consensit, et pro salute anime sua et totius generis sui confirmavit.' The *curia* in this case was obviously not the High Court, but the Court of Burgesses. This is clearly indicated: 'huius rei testes sunt: Hernulfus de Blanca Guarda, tunc vicecomes, qui venditiones inde accepit jure regio.' There follow twelve signatures, including that of *magister* Gonscelinus,[51] and two with the adjective *iuratus*.[52] Here we are in the presence of a full-fledged Court of Burgesses headed by the *vicecomes*. The transaction was made in the presence of the king, but it was the viscount who received the payment called *venditiones*. The transaction, though it appears as a simple sale, was actually that of creating a *frankalmoign*. The sum of 760 besants paid by the Hospitallers is described as: 'pro recognitione et eiusdem doni confirmatione', a rather strange definition.[53] Whatever this meant, the land clearly changed its status from a burgage-tenure into a tenure-in-

---

[49] Delaville, no. 444, i. 308–9; *Regesta*, no. 504.

[50] Otto of Verdun appears in 1154 in the Patriarch's court (*Regesta*, no. 295). His daughter, Isabella, was wife of Johannes Aschetinus, whom Delaville identified, probably rightly, as the son of Anschetinus, former viscount of Jerusalem; another daughter was wife to Godfrey, son of Simon Judex, a well-known Jerusalem personality attested by numerous documents between 1149 and 1178. He seems to be identical with Simon Rufus, who often appears among the burgess signatories. See below, p. 278 n. 56.

[51] The title *magister* was probably that of the former *clericus* of the Tower of David. See above, p. 265 n. 8. Another *magister*, this time explicitly 'magister castelli' appears in 1175. See below p. 279 n. 60.

[52] There were possibly more titled signatories but there are lacunae after their names in the text.

[53] The families concerned were Hodeardis, widow of Otto of Verdun, her three daughters Isabella, Benedicta, and Jasze married respectively to John son of Aschetin, Geoffrey son of Simon Judex, and Henry Balistarius; her two sons, Henry and Guido, were received into the *confraternitas* of the Order of St. John.

alms. The charter recorded proceedings before the court and perhaps the *magister* was an official of the court. Here we have a clear case in which the viscount receives as payment the *venditiones*, that is, the *lods et ventes* for the king's *laudemium*.

The way in which the burgesses appear in our document is striking. Officially they are *testes*, including those who sign as *iurati*. As we saw in earlier documents, the distinction between the two is blurred. We would not, however, hazard conclusions. Some of the *testes* appear in different documents two years earlier as *iurati*, and perhaps we should assign to the clerk's whim the fact that he did not specify their standing here.[54] The charter is not the court's charter and in the eyes of the clerk, having once mentioned the authorization to the deal given by king and viscount, the presence of the *iurati* is as that of *testes* to his charter. It is interesting to note that the same transaction was confirmed a year later in a special charter by King Amalric.[55] Such a confirmation seems superfluous, since the original deed recorded an act passed in his court. There is no explanation for it but the medieval concern for lost documents, which prompted people to receive new confirmations.

A comparison of a group of three deeds from 1171, 1173, and 1174 respectively is rewarding. It proves that whether or not the name *curia* is explicitly mentioned, the transactions were performed in the Court of Burgesses and that we are dealing with the same group of people, members of the court. Only in the deed of 1171 are they specifically distinguished under the heading *de juratis*; in 1173 they are simply *testes*, though some of them bear the title *juratus*, whereas in 1174 they are grouped under the heading: *de viris Jherusalem*.[56]

---

[54] Some of them appear at different dates as *iurati*: e.g. Gilbertus de Pinkeni in 1171 (*Regesta*, no. 492); Lambertus Patriarcha in 1175 (ibid., no. 534); Guillelmus de Ponz in 1171 (ibid., no. 492); etc.

[55] The document is lost but registered in the Hospitallers' *Inventaire* (Delaville, no. 455; *Regesta*, no. 517[b]).

[56] In 1171: 'De juratis: dominus Symon, Gaufridus Turonensis, Gillebertus de Pinguigni, Robertus de Balgenci [*lacuna*], Pesellus Rex, Johannes Bricius, Willelmus Beraldi; Gullielmus Patron, Guillelmus de Pons, Bartholomeus Luscus, Balduinus [*lacuna*], Petrus de S. Jacobo, Petrus de S. Lazaro, Adelbertus, pincerna patriarche.' In 1173: 'Huius rei testes sunt: Hernulfus vicecomes . . . magister Gonscelinus, Symon juratus, Joffrid [*lacuna*] Gillebertus de Pinkeni, Lambertus patriarcha, W. de Ponz, Johannes Briceii, Bartholomeus juratus [*lacuna*], Gaufridus Tortus, Petrus de S. Lazaro, Jacobus, gener Gilleberti de Pinkeni, Rice [*lacuna*].' In 1174 (*Regesta*, no. 516) a donation by King Amalric to the Order of St. John and the nuns of Sta Maria Major, is signed by Hospitallers, nuns, and 'de viris Jherusalem: Harnulfus vicecomes, Robertus de Pinquineo, Goffridus de Turonis, Lambertus Patriarche, Albertus Lonbardus, Johannes Bricius, Willelmus de Punz, Thomas Patriz, Rainaldus de Belgrant,

A typical document relating to the functioning of the Court of Burgesses comes again from the Hospitallers in 1175 and it represents the most formal deed of its kind in the twelfth century.[57] Peter, son of Peter of Cahors, sold to his brother Clarembald his share in their father's heritage in Jerusalem, a house and an empty plot of land on Mt. Zion.[58] The seller promised to defend the buyer against any claim 'according to the usages and customs of the city of Jerusalem'. His brother will henceforth have the right to sell, give, and pledge the property to whomsoever he wants, again 'iuxta usus et consuetudines civitatis Jerusalem'. This sale, the document goes on to say, was confirmed 'in plena curia in presentia domini Rohardi, tunc temporis Jerusalem castellani, assistentibus ibidem Bernardo Broet, tunc castelli magistro, et juratis civitatis ejusdem'. The names of the *iurati* are not listed here, but at the end of the document where they are introduced: 'verum sunt testes' followed by fourteen names, none of which is accompanied by the title *iuratus*.

The Court of Burgesses intervened in the last transaction at two points for two different reasons. The land was without doubt a burgage-tenure held by a burgess family from Cahors. Following the common rules of succession in burgage-tenures, there was a division of the heritage between the brothers,[59] one of whom was now selling out his part to his coheir. The sale was finalized by being transacted in the Court of Burgesses before the lord's delegate, in our case the castellan, who, as we have seen already, often united the functions of viscount and castellan. The *magister castelli* had little to do with military affairs. The civil and non-military character of his functions is corroborated by the fact, that the *magister castelli* was Bernard Broet or Proet, a well-known burgess and a juror of the Court of Burgesses of Jerusalem.[60] The transaction performed in court included a payment: 'rex inde habuit de jure suo II bisancios et II solidos.'[61]

This payment of 2 besants and 2s., which we often find in other transactions, is not easy to interpret. We know from the *Livre des Assises*

Petrus de S. Lazaro, Constantius, magister Guncelinus, et alii plures'. Again some of these names appear in 1175 (*Regesta*, no. 534).

[57] Delaville, *Archives*, no. 34, pp. 119–20; *Regesta*, no. 534.

[58] Mt. Zion inside the walls. As the parcel of land had 'viam arcus Jude in medio', it means in the actual Jewish quarter of Jerusalem.

[59] e.g. *Livre au Roi*, ch. 47.

[60] He signs as 'de burgensibus Jherusalem' in the same year 1175 (*Regesta*, no. 531); 'de curia Jerusalem' in 1178 (*Regesta*, no. 558); as 'iuratus' in 1178 (*Regesta*, no. 559).

[61] In 1178 the Hospitallers authorized a sale of houses near Mt. Zion Gate in Jerusalem, from which they had a *cens seigneurial* of 1 besant a year. They add: 'de hoc autem vendicione recepimus bisancios II et solidos II' (Delaville, *Archives*, no. 47, p. 137; *Regesta*, no. 558).

des Bourgeois that the lord received 'por la vente', that is for the *venditio* or *lods et vente*, basically for his consent or *laudemium* 1 mark of silver from the seller and the payment of 3 besants from the buyer.[62] A similar situation seems to have existed in the beginning of the fourteenth century in Cyprus, where the *Livre du plédéant*[63] mentions a payment due from the buyer 'pour la saizine basanz III et II sos, lesquels III besanz sont dou seignor et les II sos, l'un à l'escrivain et l'autre as sergens'. For reasons we are unable to explain, unless we are dealing with a 'free burgage', the mark of silver was not paid, and in any case is not mentioned in our text. Nor do we encounter here the payment of 3 besants paid by the buyer, but a payment of 2 besants and 2s. The latter must be related to a payment mentioned in the *LdAdB*, namely: 'Sil avient que aucuns home ou aucune feme vende sa maison, celuy qui l'achete, qui que il soit, det douner a la cort I besant et I rabouin por la vente.'[64] The Italian version proves that 1 besant was traditionally counted as 4 *solidi* ('deue pagar ... bisanti tre et mezo'), that is the *solidus* was counted as a quarter of the besant. This fits well with the *rabouin* of the *LdAdB*, which was one-fourth (from Arabic *ruba'*) of the besant. If both buyer and seller paid 1¼ besants each then the total payment was that of 2 besants and 2s., as indicated in our document. Still, this is a hypothetical explanation, because the *LdAdB* mentions a payment by the buyer only.[65] Moreover the payment of 1 mark of silver was still actually paid in the middle of the thirteenth century in Acre and later in Cyprus, though in some cases it was stipulated as payment of 1 besant only,[66] and we have it on record that the payment of 3 besants was

[62] *LdAdB*, ch. 31.   [63] *Livre du plédéant*, chs. 15, 18, 19, 20.

[64] *LdAdB*, ch. 295. For the same payments in the communal court of Venice, see below, p. 319.

[65] The payment of *lods et ventes* in Europe often poses the same question. In some places it is paid by seller and buyer, so, e.g. Pontefract and Northampton in England, sometimes by buyer only, e.g. Egremont (M. Bateson, *Borough Customs* ii (London, 1906), 82). The same in France, where *ventes* is explained as payment by the seller and *lods* by buyer, but quite often it is the buyer only who pays (J. Brissaud, *Cours d'histoire générale du droit français public et privé* i (Paris, 1904), 730).

[66] The payment of 1 mark of silver has been explained above, p. 259, and its value is explained below, p. 428 n. 66. A Hospitaller deed of 1184 records such payment linked to a pre-emption right: 'si capitulum Hospitalis illas [domos] emere voluerit, *unam argenti marcham minus*, quam aliis emptoribus capitulo remittis' (Delaville, *Archives*, no. 62, p. 155; *Regesta*, no. 640). In other cases the payment is smaller. In a deed of 1173 the Hospital stipulates for the Order: 'vendent minus uno bisantio quam alteri' (ibid., no. 30, p. 114; *Regesta*, no. 504). Again (May 1178) the Hospital authorizes the sale of a burgage-tenure: 'si vendere vel invadiare voluerint, nobis vendent uno bisancio minus quam alteri' (ibid., no. 47, p. 136: *Regesta*, no. 558). Similarly, in a deed of 1186 (ibid., no. 63, p. 156–7; *Regesta*, no. 651).

actually paid in Acre in 1269.[67] We may perhaps suggest that we are dealing with different payments. One was that of *lods et ventes* of 1 mark of silver, which became directly linked with a pre-emption right, the others were for the seisin and varied according to different types of transaction. This seems to be indicated by the *Livre du plédéant* (ch. 31), which describes two types of transactions involving an exchange of properties. If the parties simply exchanged them, each party went through the formality of *devest–vest*: 'et le Visconte les doit saizir chascun d'eaus de celui héritage . . . et il doivent paier à la court les saizines chascun V sos, de quei les IV sos sont dou Visconte et l'autre à l'escrivain et as sergens.' This means that each party will pay 1 besant to the viscount and a quarter to the scribe and sergeant, the total payment being 2 besants and 2s. But if the exchange involves an additional payment, the transaction becomes a sale (*vente*). The buyer (who adds money) pays in this case 'pour la saizine que il a heu par l'achet que il a fait III bezans et II sos, et l'autre qui a vendu payera les V sos.' The buyer pays then the traditional 3 besants and 2s., whereas the seller pays 1¼ besants only.

Returning to our document we see that the payments to the court assured the seisin; whereas the witnesses gave some kind of guarantee against possible claims. There is no distinction between the members of *plena curia*, the *iurati*, and the witnesses in the eschatocol of the deed. Here we find fourteen signatures, whereas according to the legal treatises the number of *iurati* was twelve. This probably means that there was a panel of *iurati*, but twelve sufficed for a *plena curia*.[68] Moreover we know that the viscount and two *iurati* were in some cases sufficient to function as a court.[69]

An analysis of two more deeds relating to the same property and the same transaction, both of 1178, adds some information on the Court of Burgesses and the procedure followed therein. Both deal with the alienation of a house in Jerusalem[70] in the Mt. Zion quarter ('ad Portam Novam que vocatur Belcayra'). They were burgage-tenures which owed a *cens* of 1 besant annually to the Knights of St. John. Their present tenant, one John Fulco, sold them to a William Baptizatus of Blanchegarde. The alienation is recorded in two parallel documents: one containing the act

---

[67] See below, p. 294 n. 135, and for Cyprus the *Livre du plédéant*, ch. 31, quoted in the text.

[68] This is also proved by a full list of fourteen jurors in Acre in 1250 (*Livre du plédéant*, ch. 12).

[69] *LdAdB*, ch. 311; *Livre du plédéant*, ch, I. p. 18.

[70] Delaville, *Archives*, nos. 46–7, pp. 135–7; *Regesta*, nos. 558–9.

of alienation before the Court of Burgesses of Jerusalem; the second the Hospitallers' consent to the alienation. The former was written in the first person by the seller. After relating the sale for 97 besants it ends: 'Hujus rei sunt testes: Balianus, castellanus Jherusalem' followed by nine names, and then: 'factum est autem hoc scriptum precepto Baliani, castellani Jerusalem et juratorum ad confirmationem hujus venditionis.' We do not know if the deed was sealed but it was certainly not the seal of the court, which did not yet have a seal of its own. It may have been the seal of the castellan, who also ordered the writing of the document. The deed was a proof of sale transacted in public before the court presided over by the castellan. No payment to the court is mentioned, but there is no reason to suppose it was not paid.

This transaction offers some peculiarities, since so far we have dealt with transactions that were almost all burgage-tenures held from the king, who, consequently, besides being the *seigneur justicier* was also the *seigneur foncier*. In the present case the land is a burgage-tenure held from the Hospitallers, whose *cens* is being reserved in the charter. Has the king then any rights of intervention? It is difficult to answer this question. What seems plausible is that the Court of Burgesses functioned as dispensing a *juridiction gracieuse*, a non-litigating but recording function.[71] Whereas royal authorization of the sale was perhaps superfluous, the transaction had to be made with the authorization of the Hospitallers from whom the land was held. They authorized it and record: 'concessimus et tradidimus', and 'de hac autem vendicione recepimus bisancios II et solidos II', the customary amount paid in other cases to the royal court. The second charter was written by a brother of the Hospital on behalf of Roger, Master of the Order. It must have been written simultaneously with the deed of sale, and after the signatures of some Hospitaller witnesses we read: 'de curia Jerusalem: Balianus regius castellanus' followed by eight witnesses, seven of whom did sign the former charter ordered by the castellan.

An interesting document relating to the Court of Burgesses comes again from the archives of the Hospitallers in 1179.[72] It deals with a burgage-tenure paying an annual quit-rent to the Order. Unfortunately, the phrasing is somewhat confused and we are not sure as to the details. We can try to reconstruct the property situation as follows. The tenure belonged to one Nicolas Manzur (possibly an Oriental Christian: Mansur). He sold it, as well as a vineyard on the road to Bethlehem, to the

---

[71] See below, Ch. 12.
[72] Delaville, no. 554 (i. 376); *Regesta*, no. 580.

Hospitallers, but created a *bail à rente* of 10 besants a year for the house and 20 besants for the vineyard. The *bail à rente*[73] of 30 besants is now sold to the Order for 300 besants.[74] The tenure was on royal land and the alienation transacted in the royal court, in fact in the presence of the king: 'in curia coram domino rege'. The charter goes on to say that the king approved the sale and called upon Rohard, the castellan, to ratify it. It is Robert of Pinqueni (Pincheni), a well-known burgess and *iuratus*, who 'pro jure regio venditiones inde (lacuna) castellani Ro(ardi) II bisancios et II solidos'. We suggest the reading: 'venditiones inde accepit nomine castellani'. The names following ('hujus rei testes sunt') begin with Robert of Pinqueni and Rohard the castellan followed by the names of six well-known burgesses 'et plures alii'.[75] It is worth noting that the man who received the payment, or one of the payments, Robert of Pinqueni, may have functioned as a 'magister castelli', as no viscount is mentioned.

If our twelfth-century documentation came mainly from Jerusalem, that of the thirteenth, as might be expected, comes from Acre, the new capital of the kingdom. But even here, despite the great concentration of population, the number of documents dealing with the viscount's court is relatively small. Amongst the hundreds of documents that emanated from the city, fewer than a dozen related to the working of the Court of Burgesses. Nevertheless they suffice to reconstruct its competence and functioning in the thirteenth century.

The earliest document connected with the Court of Burgesses comes from Acre in 1200.[76] It is a transaction performed in the court of King Aimery. A five-year-old litigation about property bestowed (1195) by Henry of Champagne, former ruler of the kingdom, on the Teutonic Order included a house in Tyre of one Theodor of Sarepta. His sons, Paul and Theodor, challenged the donation, but settled now with the Order against a payment of 200 besants. The king authorized and guaranteed the transaction, ordering that no future claim would ever be heard. This transaction was performed in Acre: 'in presencia nostra et in curia nostra et eciam *curia iuratorum nostrorum*'. The particular feature of this privilege

---

[73] The document says 'illos X bisancios . . . censuales supra domum', and 'vinea . . . quam dederat *ad censum*'.

[74] This badly phrased document was differently understood by R. Röhricht, *Regesta*, no. 590.

[75] Perhaps more names, as there is a lacuna in the text. The names preserved are: 'Willelmus Beraldi, Willelmus Patrun, Lambertus Cambitor, Joffridus d'Issoudun, Johannes Bricii, Petrus de Sancto Lazaro et plures alii'.

[76] Strehlke, no. 36, pp. 29–30; *Regesta*, no. 774.

is the meeting of the royal court and that of the burgesses, a procedure which was not very common. Stranger still, the transaction was made in Acre, and consequently with the Court of Burgesses of that city, whereas the property was in Tyre. According to our legal treatises, this was inadmissible,[77] but we have already seen exceptions to the rule in the twelfth century. Technically the charter was a royal privilege whereby the king constituted himself as warrant against any future claim, a rather extraordinary task for a king. Being a royal charter, it is witnessed by the king's entourage, in which we fail to detect a burgess witness. The procedure does not follow the accepted rules, but it clearly characterizes the type of document: not a charter of the court, not even a 'record' of its proceedings, but a royal privilege which mentions that the problem was transacted in the Court of Burgesses.

Even small places with a Frankish population had their own Courts of Burgesses. In the twelfth century we encounter one in session in Caesarea; in the thirteenth there is one from the small lordship of Haifa.[78] As it is a somewhat exceptional case we mention it here, although it had nothing to do with burgage-tenure, but with the sale of a fief by Christin, daughter of Roger of Haifa to the Order of St. John. This was transacted in 1232 with the permission of the lord of Haifa, Rohard. Among the witnesses we find after the Hospitallers and the *milites* of the lordship and a list of *jurati de Cayphas*, nine signatories, including the well-known Hugh Pellevillanus, viscount of Acre. The transaction must therefore have been done in the full *curia* of the lordship.

A similar procedure was probably followed in another small town—in Jaffa in 1238, where John Poilvilain, the viscount presided over a court in which some property in Jaffa and Ascalon was transferred to the Order of St. John.[79] Unfortunately the details are meagre and known to us from an inventory of the Order only.

The type of transactions carried out in the Court of Burgesses is illustrated by a number of documents from Acre. They concern a complex of properties in the city and their special interest lies in the fact that they deal with the highest nobility of the kingdom, the Ibelins. Part of their city property was sold to the Order of St. John. It is recorded in the earliest charter (April 1232), that John of Ibelin, son of Philip, sold some houses to the Hospitallers 'in curia Acconensi'. The transaction was opposed by

[77] See above, p. 269.
[78] Delaville, no. 1146 (ii. 8–9); *Regesta*, no. 784.
[79] Delaville, no. 2212 (ii. 536); *Regesta*, no. 1084a.

Alice, the sister of the deceased John, and her daughter Maria. Our charter is a promise given by John of Ibelin, lord of Beirut, and by John, lord of Caesarea, to defend the legality of the transaction against the claims of a third party. The charter is corroborated by the seals of the two pledges, and by 'subscriptorum virorum testimonio'. The witnesses were headed by Étienne Boutier, viscount of Acre, and seven burgesses described as 'jurati curie Acconensis'.[80]

The transaction and the charter are extremely curious. Our deed records not the alienation which took place before the court earlier, but the fact that John of Beirut and John of Caesarea constituted themselves directly responsible, with their property, to a potential victorious claimant.[81] The people concerned belonged to the leading aristocracy of the country and we hardly expect them to appear before the Court of Burgesses. Yet the whole procedure was well embedded in current Crusader law. The house, though belonging to a noble, was a burgage-tenure, not a fief, and consequently was sold in the Court of Burgesses. Linked to this charter is another,[82] written six months later by the potential claimant, the aforesaid Lady Alice. We are obviously dealing with the same complex of property. Possibly one of the houses of John of Ibelin remained with his sister Alice, and the Hospitallers, instead of going into court, preferred to come to an agreement with her. The house remained with her for her lifetime on condition that it would return to them upon her death. Lady Alice promised the property to the Knights of St. John with the exclusion of all possible bidders. This was done in the presence of Eude, constable of the kingdom, Philip of Troies, the viscount of Acre, 'ac juratorum subscriptorum'. The promissory charter was sealed with her own seal and 'testimonio juratorum curie regie robaratum', followed by the signatures of seven people. Here then the *iurati* are clearly the legal witnesses to a promise made in their court.

Some of the surviving charters connected with the Court of Burgesses permit us, incidentally, to trace the story of a property and its possessors. In many cases we find burgage-tenures which entered knightly families through marriage. A charter of this type records an exchange of property between a Nicholas Antelini[83] and the Hospitallers (Acre, November

---

[80] Delaville, no. 2015 (ii. 434–5); *Regesta*, no. 1036.

[81] Ibid.: 'facimus nos plegios et principales debitores ac defensores'. The guarantee is given for a year and a day 'secundum usus et consuetudines civitatis Acconensis'.

[82] Delaville, no. 2033 (ii. 442); *Regesta*, no. 1038a.

[83] A knight known between 1226 and 1249, *Regesta*, nos. 974, 1027, 1073, and 1181. Cf. Delaville, *Archives*, p. 173 n. 1.

1235).[84] In October 1198 King Aimery gave to one William of Petra, a prison tower ('turris carceris') and a house to the east of it, as well as 'censum domus inter murum et barbacana sitae'.[85] We can roughly ascertain the position of this property, which was near the 'Bovaria Templi', marked on Marino Sanudo's map as in the suburb of Mont Musard. At William's death his property came to Isabella of Petra, probably his widow, who sold it to the Hospital. The Order now exchanged this house for that of Nicholas in the same neighbourhood. This exchange was performed 'in presencia curie et juratorum Acconensium'. No special document was drawn up; as to the part played by the court, its members were not even called upon to sign the document. It is a private charter signed by the Order and sealed by Guerin, the Master of the Hospitallers. The members of the court do not appear as witnesses to the deed. Why then the intervention of the court at all, as both parties were 'non-burgesses'? The reason was doubtless the legal status of property. As the deed of sale of Isabella of Petra to Nicolaus Antelini did not survive, it is impossible to be more precise, but we suppose that the house of Nicolaus Antelini was a burgage-tenure which paid *cens* to the king. In fact the neighbouring houses are described as 'domus *sub censu regio* constituae'.

From the same year, 1235, we have an act connected with the Court of Burgesses from a most unexpected quarter, Jerusalem.[86] The city was in the precarious hold of the Crusaders by virtue of the treaty of 1229 made between Frederick II and the Sultan of Egypt, al-Malik al-Kamil. It was only partly fortified and its population was under the permanent threat of attack and siege. But the Franks, as we know, tried to resettle the city, until then inhabited only by a small Muslim and Oriental Christian population. Thus it is curious to see that the new, small Frankish population immediately revived its institutions, which had disappeared some forty-five years earlier with Saladin's conquest in 1187. Stephania, we learn from the deed, daughter of Bonus Johannes, donated her paternal home to the Hospitallers 'in puram elemosinam'. This donation, she says, 'ut ... firma sit et stabilis in perpetuum, facta fuit in curia Jerusalem', in the presence of Baldwin of Pinquigny the castellan, Girard of Saises, the viscount, 'et quoram judicibus'. This is followed by four signatures. The charter is witnessed by the military and civil governors of the city, in all

[84] Delaville, no. 2126 (ii. 493–4; *Regesta*, no. 1063).
[85] *Regesta*, no. 746.
[86] Delaville, no. 2127 (ii. 494); *Regesta*, no. 1065.

probability in the name of the absentee lord, the Emperor Frederick II. The fact that the transaction was performed in the Court of Burgesses, whose *iurati* are here called *judices*, proves that the prohibition of selling burgage-tenures to Military Orders was still enforced and that special permission was still needed to alienate such property, which, it seems, became automatically an *eleemosina*.

Acre in the thirteenth century, like Jerusalem a century earlier, had its own quota of burgesses of standing. It seems, however, that these burgesses had a different position from that of their predecessors in Jerusalem. We have the impression that they belonged to a city patriciate, people of means and influence, who did not rise to their position by being in attendance on the viscount or the Court of the Patriarch. In all probability it was the other way around: they entered royal service in the new capital because of their position in the city. Such an expression as 'granborjois'[87] given to some of them in a Crusader chronicle, as well as their participation in the political struggles in Acre,[88] would rather point in this direction. This was probably the outcome of two concurring factors. On the one hand the objective, physical conditions—Acre was not only the capital, sometimes it was the state. Nothing important was decided outside Acre, and this gave to its inhabitants a new standing in state affairs. On the other hand, whereas Jerusalem was never a rich city, not even at the peak of its power in the second half of the twelfth century, Acre, with a larger population, was also much richer. Both factors prompted the rise of a local patriciate, the 'grands bourgeois' as they were called by Philip of Novara.

It was in the logic of things that some of these burgesses, barred from ruling their city, as urban autonomy never existed, found an outlet for their energies in royal service and in the administration of justice. In fact they followed a pattern well established by the nobility. Some of the most famous names in Crusader history were those of nobles who at the same time were great jurists.[89] This attracted the burgesses and we can actually follow burgess 'dynasties' concerned with customary law or with the service in the court. Their prominence was such that they were even consulted by the High Court of the kingdom. Not everybody accepted this rise to prominence with magnanimity. Raoul of Tiberias, whom

---

[87] *Gestes des Chiprois*, ed. G. Raynaud (Geneva, 1887), § 221: 'Il gransborjois d'Accre quy mout avoyent grant pooir sur le peuple de la ville.'

[88] See above, ch. 3, pp. 54 ff.

[89] The knowledge of the customary law was of paramount importance in the constitutional struggles of the thirteenth century. Cf. Prawer, *Histoire* ii. 215 ff.

King Aimery asked to reconstitute the *assises* of the kingdom lost with the fall of Jerusalem, gave the famous haughty answer that he would not co-operate with Antiaume, a man of low extraction.[90] One wonders how he would have reacted two generations later when political factions tried to woo the burgesses of the city.

One such prominent burgess family was the Briccii. If we are actually dealing with the same family, we can trace their history for almost 150 years. They appear in Jerusalem in the middle of the twelfth century. We see them, between 1148 and 1186, moving in the royal entourage of Queen Melissenda, King Amalric, and King Baldwin IV, and at the same time, we find their signatures in the Court of the Patriarchs of Jerusalem and the Court of Burgesses of the city. A burgess by the name of Bricius signs charters between 1148 and 1161. In 1148, 'Brictius' (spellings vary) signs a charter as *burgensis* and a year later he signs in *curia regis*. This type of signature, among the *burgenses regis* continues until 1161.[91] Ten years later we encounter 'Johannes Briccius', in all probability the son of the former. The father's connections stood his son in good stead, as we find him associated with the same royal and ecclesiastical institutions.

In 1171 'Johannes Briccius' or 'Bricii' is a *iuratus* of the Court of Burgesses in Jerusalem, and his signatures in the *curia regis* continue until his last, again as *iuratus*, in 1186, a year before the fall of the city.[92] We do not know what happened to him and his family after Hittin and the fall of Jerusalem, but by 1187 a 'Peter Brice', a man of prominence, lived in Acre and achieved a sad distinction when he was chosen to hand over the keys of the capitulating city to the victorious Muslim army commanded by Taki al-Din.[93] A generation later, in 1225, a 'Peter Briccius' reappears, but we doubt if it was the same man; we would rather think it was his son.[94] After 1249 we see a 'Peter Bricius' connected with the Venetians in Acre. He served as counsellor to Marco Giustiniani the Venetian *baiulo* in Syria in 1259 and signed an agreement between the church of St. Mark with Florentius, bishop of Acre.[95]

Another prominent burgess family of Acre was the Conches. Seven people bore the name 'de Conchis' and there is every reason to suppose that

[90] Philip of Novara, ch. 47, p. 523: 'Remont Anciaume ne autre soutil borgeis ou bas home letré.'

[91] *Regesta*, nos. 251, 255, 259, 273, 280, 299, 300, 301, 333, 369.

[92] Ibid., nos. 492, 504, 516, 535, 556, 558, 590, 651.

[93] *Eracles*, xxiii. 46, *RHC HOcc.* ii. 70, var. b.

[94] *Regesta*, no. 973.

[95] *Templier de Tyr*, § 268, p. 149; *Regesta*, nos. 1273a, 1285.

they belonged to the same family. Together they span a period of almost 100 years. The first known was an 'Odo de Conchis', who in 1183 appears in Acre and a year later signs as *iuratus curie regis*.[96] 'Heude de Conches' who, in 1251, took part in the meeting of the courts on the reform of registers,[97] was probably a son or grandson of Odo. A contemporary of the first Odo (Heude) was Nicholas, who in 1193 signed a charter connected with another famous burgess family of the city, the Antelmi.[98] Two contemporaries of the Conches family lived in Acre *c.* 1232–9, Raymond and Bernard. Raymond, who signed charters in 1232 as *iuratus* of the Court of Burgesses,[99] became famous as one of the great experts in the customary law of the kingdom. No greater compliment could have been bestowed upon him than the eulogy of no less a specialist than Philip of Novara: 'Sire Raymon de Conches qui estoient [with Philip le Beau, perhaps de Bauduyn][100] moult sages borgeis et qui veneit et plaidoit moult souvent en la Haute Cour.'[101] In 1236 we find him with Geraut Olivier, consul of Marseilles, receiving privileges for that city in Cyprus.[102] Bernard was a *iuratus* of the Acre Court of Burgesses in 1232.[103] A generation later we find three other representatives of the same family. Heude de Conchis, whom we have already mentioned as present at the reform meeting in Acre, was there in the company of 'Henry de Conches', who in 1260 and 1269 served as *iuratus* of the Court of Burgesses.[104] His companion at the court session of 1269 was 'Giles de Conches', who still exercised the same function in 1274.[105]

The best-known of the burgess families in Acre was probably that of the Antiaumes. Two members of the family, Raymond and Guido, were in the entourage of the ruler of the kingdom, Henry of Champagne, in 1193,[106] the former making a name for himself as expert in the customary law of the kingdom and incurring the scorn of Raoul of Tiberias. We know nothing of their family connections, but as in the case of the Conches, service in the royal court ran in the family. Guido is still attested a generation later, in 1232, as a *iuratus* of the court of Acre.[107] Raymond's son Nicholas, a generation later, kept the family tradition and even enhanced it. Philip of Novara praised his knowledge; he used to appear in

---

[96] *Regesta*, nos. 624, 640.   [97] *Livre du plédéant*, ch. 14.   [98] *Regesta*, no. 716.
[99] *Regesta*, nos. 1036, 1038.   [100] *Les Gestes des Chiprois*, § 225, p. 129.
[101] Philip of Novara, ch. 38.   [102] *Regesta*, no. 1071.
[103] *Regesta*, no. 1036. Another contemporary was John de Conchis who had a vineyard near Acre, ibid., no. 1093 (A.D. 1239).
[104] Ibid., nos. 1291 and 1364.   [105] Ibid., nos. 1364 and 1400.
[106] Ibid., nos. 710 and 716.   [107] Ibid., nos. 1036 and 1038.

the High Court[108] and reached fame by finding a loop-hole in the legal procedure regarding murder.[109] He was even consulted by John of Ibelin at the request of Constance, *bail* of Armenia.[110] Nicholas Antiaume, though burgess by origin, was socially accepted by the nobility, as is clear from Philip of Novara's eulogy. Moreover we find him in the entourage of the rulers of the kingdom. In 1226 he signs a privilege of Frederick II to the Teutonic Order [111] and even ten years later in 1236 he signs, among the *homines imperatoris*, a sale of a fief in the lordship of Toron to the same Order.[112] He was in the entourage of Balian of Sidon, *bailli* of the kingdom in 1231.[113] His hostel in Acre, near the property of the Hospital, was an object of exchange with the Order[114] and later came into the hands of the Genoese.[115] He reached the peak of his career when, during the minority of 1240, he became, together with the lord of Toron, the guardian of the citadel of Acre.[116] He died some time between 1240 and 1249. Nicholas's fame paved the way for his son Balian,[117] but the latter seems to have had little to do with the burgesses. Possibly his father had already been made a knight, as witnessed by his standing as *home liege* of the kingdom. Balian was certainly no more a burgess. We find him signing a privilege of Garcia Alvarez, lord of Haifa, in 1250,[118] and he is officially a vassal of John of Ibelin, lord of Arsuf in 1257,[119] and finally marries into the family of the lords of Gibelet.[120] We find him for the last time in 1277 in the council of the *bailli* Balian of Ibelin, lord of Arsuf.[121]

It is this type of burgess that we find represented at an important moment in the history of the Court of Burgesses in the middle of the thirteenth century.

In March 1251 the Court of Burgesses, which had already existed for almost 150 years, underwent a major reform which was to be transmitted to Cyprus. Some three generations later, the author of the Cypriot *Livre du plédéant* tells its story.[122] In a meeting of the High Court in which twenty-nine nobles participated and which was attended by the jurors of

---

[108] Philip of Novara, ch. 49, p. 525.

[109] *Livre du plédéant*, ch. 28 (ed. Beugnot), p. 339.

[110] John of Ibelin, ch. 145, p. 220.   [111] *Regesta*, no. 974.   [112] Ibid., no. 1073.

[113] Ibid., no. 1027.   [114] Ibid., no. 1063.   [115] Ibid., no. 1181.

[116] 'Doc. relatifs à la successibilité au trône et à la régence', *Lois* ii. 401: 'por ce que les homes liges deivent garder les forteresces dou reiaume' during the time of minority.

[117] *Livre du plédéant*, ch. 28 (ed. Beugnot, p. 339).   [118] *Regesta*, no. 1189.

[119] Ibid., no. 1259.   [120] 'Lignages d'Outremer', *Lois* ii 466.

[121] F. Amadi, *Chroniques de Chypre*, ed. L. de Mas Latrie (Paris, 1891), p. 214.

[122] *Livre du plédéant*, ch. 12, pp. 48–66.

the Court of Burgesses (their number was fourteen), the lord of Arsuf proposed the establishment of French registers of proceedings for both courts and the appointment of a clerk to keep them. The Court of Burgesses, we are told, 'par générau conseill, et le assent et l'avisment des sages' then ordered 'escrivain et livres en la basse court'. The proposals of the lord of Arsuf were certainly salutary and conformed to European developments, attested to as early as the second quarter of the twelfth century for Cologne (the famous *Schreinskarten*), which spread to Metz (1197), north-west Germany, and Flanders.[123] As the Crusaders never had anything like a city-hall, the registers were kept in a *huche* in a house of one of the *jurés* of the court.[124]

The establishment of an official register, which would facilitate the memory, the 'record' of the court, and which to all practical purposes would have the power of a written proof, was a revolutionary change in the Latin Orient. Anachronistic principles, which admitted oral proof only according to the old traditions of Germanic law, were to be transformed. Yet despite the obvious advantages, the deeply engrained principles died hard. In fact the lord of Tyre and Tibnin, who participated in the debate, accepted the proposal in lukewarm terms. He praised it, says our source, and added: 'that all that was remembered by part of the court should be done accordingly; but if something else was found, that the thing should be done according to the sayings and the "record" rather than the writing.'[125] This sentiment was shared, it seems, even seventy-five years later by the author of the *Livre du plédéant*. Commenting on the events, he says: 'And as in the introduction it was said that the "record" of the court has to have more value than the writing, there is a reason for it, that is to say, in its proper place and for just causes'.[126] Thus, it seems that

---

[123] A. de Boüard, *Manuel de diplomatique française et pontificale*, ii (Paris, 1948), 238–40. Beugnot remarks that the French *Olim* began in 1254.

[124] A transitional period of this kind was also current in Europe. Cf. A. de Boüard, loc. cit. It still existed in Nicosia in Cyprus as late as 1325, when Hugh IV ordered a 'maison à vote dedens le porpris de la court de la visconté' to be built where the boxes with registers were kept (*Livre du plédéant*, ch. 12, p. 66).

[125] The phrase, though not difficult to understand, is awkward: 'il looit que tout ce de coy partie de la court fusse membrant fust enci; et se autre maniere se trovast, que la choze fusse celonc le dit et le recort de la court et plus tost que l'escrit.' The Italian translators ran into difficulty and translated verbatim: 'che di quello che parte de la corte fusse memorato, si faccia così; et se in altro modo se trovasse, che la cosa sia secondo el ditto et el recordo de la corte, più tosto ch'el scritto.' Actually this means that the decision to keep books or registers, though not opposed, will be 'neutralized' in its legal effects.

[126] *Livre du plédéant*, ch. 12, p. 62: 'Et pour ce que au premier prologue fu fait mencion que le recort de la court doit veloir plus que l'assent [=l'escrit], raison le viaut, c'est assavoir en

(continued)

the old principle remained intact and yet the usefulness of the new practice was too evident to be disregarded. The High Court did not install registers, but this was done in the Court of Burgesses.

It seems plausible to assume that it was at that time, and connected with this reform, that the Court of Burgesses began delivering to interested parties charters corroborated by its own seal, one example of which is known to us.[127] And yet, despite some examples of such procedure, it did not become general. This meant far more than a simple new procedure of dispatching business, it meant also the creation of a system of verification not only of the legality of claims but also, when needed, to ascertain the legal status of the property.

To judge by our documents, the results of this reform were not as far-reaching as one would expect. The clinging to the old tradition is illustrated by a number of charters. Just two years later (1253), one 'Nicola de Arcu', who declared himself to be a Genoese, gave his home as a *donatio inter vivos* to the Hospitallers. The transaction was performed 'coram curia burgesie Acconensis, videlicet domino Joanne Griffo, vicecomite', three *jurati curie*, and a number of witnesses. The house was then let for a lifetime to Nicola, who paid henceforth 1 denier as *cens*.[128] We would have expected that this transaction which took place before the *Curia burgesie* (this is the first time that this form appears) would have resulted in a charter of the *escrivain* of the court sealed with the court's seal. But this was not so. The charter is the traditional private charter, whose claim to being official and public is based on its being written by one Aliottus Uguicionis, 'imperiali auctoritate iudex et notarius publicus', the new kind of clerk, who appears after *c.* 1230 in the Holy Land, drawing up *notitiae* and *cartae*, full of new Roman legal learning.[129] Supposing that the document tells us all that is to be told about the transaction, we fail to see in the court's intervention any other purpose than the simple wish to make

---

propre leuc et pour juste achaizon.' *Lois* ii. 249, note b, understands 'prologue' as the speech of the lord of Tyre. The Italian translation reads: 'et per che el principio del prologo fu fatto mention, chel recordo de la corte deue valer più che la scrittura, la rason el vole, cioè in proprio loco, et per iusta causa.'

[127] Two charters corroborated by the seal of the court are preserved. See below, p. 294 n. 135, and p. 295 n. 138.

[128] Delaville, no. 2662 (ii. 750–1); *Regesta*, no. 1209.

[129] The earliest trace of such influence seems to be an agreement of 1211 between a Genoese and the Teutonic Order where we read that the parties agreed: 'abrenunciare excepcioni non numerate pecunie vel non ponderati auri vel non accepte rei'. This was written by Stephanus de Valencia, *Ianuensis notarius* in Syria (Strehlke, no. 45).

the deal public. However, it is possible that the bringing of the transaction before the court was meant to give legality to the transformation of a *borgesie* into an *eleemosina*.

It was the same notary Aliottus that drew up a similar document two years later, in 1255, when a knight Johannes Marraim gave the Hospitallers land outside the walls of Acre as a 'donatio inter vivos . . . in perpetuam elemosinam'.[130] The transaction was made in the presence of the vicar of the bishop of Acre, Hugh Pellavillanus, the viscount of the city, and three 'jurati curie burgesie Acconensis'. The investiture was performed in court, but the physical handing over was done on the land without the presence of the members of the court. It was Aliottus who on the demand of the two parties redacted the deed 'in publicam formam'. The handing over was done 'de manu in manum' without the seisin of the viscount. Obviously, the intervention of the court was conditioned by the fact that the parcel of land near the city was a burgage-tenure. The transaction did not apparently need any approval of the lord of the city. The court recorded the transaction, the notary wrote the charter, and the clerk probably registered it in the new *livre* of the court.

The same pattern was followed in 1260, when a knight, Johannes Grifus,[131] gave his houses on Mt. Musard *in elemosinam* to the Knights of St. John. One of the houses was clearly held by John Grifus as a burgage-tenure which paid a quit-rent to the Hospitallers and now reverted to them.[132] The concession was made 'in presentia curie burgesie Accon', headed by a lieutenant of the viscount, *magister* Arnulf of Perona, and five *jurati* of the court. The handing over was accomplished 'par quemdam baculum, quem in manu tenebat'. The protocol was written by the notary Aliottus. It says: 'hec acta sunt apud Acon, coram dictis curia et juratis'; and eight people described as *testes rogati* are signing this *notitia*. The court's clerk is not mentioned, nor any action of court except its presence. It is difficult to assume that its role was more important and not noted by the notary. It may well be that the status of 'free *borgesie*' or its new status of *elemosina* did not require any additional intervention. One is almost tempted to ask if this 'donatio in puram elemosinam' was not a fraudulent transfer to escape payments or to escape the limitations of selling property to Military Orders.

It is not out of place in this connection to recall an event which shook

---

[130] Delaville, no. 2714 (ii. 772–4); *Regesta*, no. 1212.
[131] In December 1253 he was viscount of Acre (*Regesta*, no. 1209).
[132] Delaville, no 2949 (ii. 886–8); *Regesta*, no. 1291.

Acre in 1276 and caused King Hugh Lusignan to abandon the city and leave it without any government, lieutenant, or viscount. The event which so upset the king was caused by the Templars, who bought a village, called Fauconerie, from a knight, one Thomas of Saint Bertin. One can imagine the king's wrath when the Order flouted the king's authority, because no fief could have been sold without its overlord's permission. This is what we learn from Marino Sanudo,[133] who states 'qui illud [casale] sub homagio a Rege tenebat'. Things look different in the French continuation of William of Tyre, which states that the knight 'tenoit le dit casal de *borjoysie*, dont il ne devoit homage ne servise.'[134]

It is not until April 1269 that we see the Court of Burgesses exercising more than a recording part in transactions in city property. Here finally we come across a title written by the court in its own name and sealed with its own seal. This is one of the two surviving documents of the Court of Burgesses in the Latin Kingdom. The document is a French written charter of Hue of Hadestel, viscount of Acre, and of the 'jurés de la cort de borgeis d'Acre', drawn up by one Renier. The procedure followed can be reconstructed, and the practice and the type of deeds which emanated at that time from the Court of Burgesses established. Though only a single example,[135] it is certainly typical of hundreds which must have been expedited by the court but have not reached us.

A burgess of Acre, actually one of the *jurés* of the court, Pèlerin Coquerel, sold his property in the Street of the Provençals to the Hospitallers for 1,700 besants. The house was no doubt a burgage-tenure and Godfrey of Sargines, the *bailli* of the kingdom, authorized the sale. The seller then, according to Crusader custom described in detail in the *Livre du plédéant*,[136] put the viscount 'in seisin of the heritage'; the latter then put the treasurer of the Hospitallers in seisin of the property. The price of the sale was handed over by the buyer to the viscount and from viscount to seller. The court received 'iij bezans por la raison doudit achat'.

The reform of 1251 put new proofs of legality at the disposal of the contracting parties. The representative of the Hospitallers appeared before

[133] Marino Sanudo, *Liber Secretorum Fidelium Crucis*, p. 226.

[134] *Eracles*, ch. 28, *RHC HOcc.* ii. 474.

[135] Delaville, no. 3334 (iii. 195–6); *Regesta*, no. 1364. The seal mentioned disappeared but it was copied by Amico in the seventeenth century and reproduced by Paoli. It represents a session of the court, the presiding viscount holding a *verge* in his hand. The inscription reads: LE SEEL DE LA COR DE (B)ORGEIS DACCRE (A. Blanchet, *Sigillographie de l'Orient latin* (Paris, 1943), p. 69).

[136] Ch. 15; see above p. 260.

the court: 'et nos requist recort del fait'. The viscount asked the jurors to do it and they actually found it 'en nostre record', which we think means in the register of proceedings (and not the 'memory of the court'), in the *livre*. This stated, the viscount declared: 'Et por ce que nos volons que chascun sache que nos ladite cort feimes et deimes ce devantdit recort en la maniere dessus dite, avons nos fait faire ceste presente chartre, seelée de nostre seel de cyre pendant, escrite par la main de Renier, nostre escrivain.' Therefore, though no charters of transaction were given by the court, a new way was found to make transactions assured of legal proof by way of demanding an official charter of the court, based on its collective memory ('record') and its register. It is relevant to remember that this procedure was used in northern France in several localities, picturesquely described by M. de Boüard as 'preuve écrite grefée sur le record'.[137] The European development will soon go beyond this intermediate stage and finally succumb to the utility of the written proof. This never happened in the Latin Kingdom. Our last document, from 1274, shows us one stage of later development than that reached five years earlier, though we might justly suppose that it actually goes back to the reform of 1251. The document[138] is not a notice of *res gestae*, nor is it exactly a charter legalizing a transaction. The transaction could have taken place without the charter and be for all that entirely legal. The document is an *instrumentum* written by Bienvenue the *escrivain* of the court, and sealed with the seal of the Court of Burgesses. It is written immediately after clinching the deal: 'et por ce que nos volons que chascun sache que la dite comande en la maniere come ele est dessus devisée fu faite en nostre presence, avons nos fait faire ceste presente chartre seeler de nostre seel de cire pendant.' The gist of the transaction was a repayment of debts to the Teutonic Order by leaving them rents of houses in Acre, with the exception of some 60 besants annually reserved for the debtor. The *devest-vest* procedure was performed without the mediation of the viscount, as the property of the houses itself did not change hands. We are not sure that the same procedure would have been used if there was a real case of property alienation. They would possibly have used the earlier procedure of the 'recorded [written] record', but developments were clearly moving in the direction of simplification. This was never attained, as several years later the kingdom was lost.

---

[137] M. de Boüard, *Manuel de diplomatique française et pontificale*, ii (Paris, 1948), 236.
[138] Mas Latrie, *Histoire de l'île de Chypre*, iii (Paris, 1861), 677, no. 2.

11 The Patriarch's Lordship in Jerusalem

One of the best-known incidents in the early history of the Latin Kingdom is the famous clash between ecclesiastical and lay interests which accompanied the election of the future ruler of the kingdom. The ecclesiastical party demanded the election of a Patriarch before that of the lay ruler, either intending to create an ecclesiastical patrimony, headed by a churchman, or by this order of election to ensure for the Patriarch a decisive vote in the choice of ruler. It was the lay faction that won the day, but time and again the claims of the Patriarchs of Jerusalem were voiced and the early history of the kingdom was accompanied by tension between the two heads of the newly created Christian Kingdom in the East. However, the importance of this tension should not be exaggerated, as it did not survive the third decade of the kingdom. If later on there are signs of friction, such as that between the Patriarch Gerold and Frederick II, they were motivated by a different set of circumstances.[1] It should only be noticed that the Church's claim to supremacy was never wholly abandoned, and when circumstances permitted, it was renewed. It was expressed in the clearest way by Pelagius in Damiette when opposing John de Brienne:

Devant I contens estoit sors entre le legat et le roi Johan, car li rois avoit eu la seignorie de l'ost et de la conqueste, ensi come vos aves oi; et li legaz la voloit avoir. Car il diseit que les movement et le fait avoit esté fait par l'Iglise et par la croisée; et si metoit quan que il poeit et useit en plusors choses. Li rois n'en faisoit semblant, ains usoit come seignor.[2]

The clash between *regnum* and *sacerdotium* in the beginnings of the kingdom was of no consequence in its later history. Its interest lies in its reflection of a current Hildebrandian notion of theocracy and the testimony to an undercurrent of popular sentiment that somehow Jerusalem belonged to God and his representatives upon earth.

But the quarrel left traces where we would hardly look for them—in the administration of the city of Jerusalem. The Patriarch's claim to an

[1] La Monte, *Feudal Monarchy* pp. 203–16; Prawer, *Histoire* ii. 160 ff.
[2] *Eracles*, i. 32, ch. 12; *RHC HOcc.* ii. 343–4.

overlordship over the kingdom and its northern principalities found some satisfaction in the acts of homage of Godfrey of Bouillon and of Bohemond.[3] But the ambitious Daimbert, sure of his Pisan fleet in Jaffa, was not content with this external recognition of his suzerainty. He demanded more tangible results. On 2 February 1100, either from conviction or necessity, Godfrey granted the Patriarch the fourth part of Jaffa; two months later during Easter, on 1 April, he resigned to him the city of Jerusalem with its citadel.[4] The execution of this grant was suspended until Godfrey succeeded in conquering two more cities in the Holy Land. But should he die without heirs the grant would immediately go into execution.[5] According to another version the handing over of Jerusalem was conditional upon the conquest of Ascalon.[6]

This story told by William of Tyre is partly based on Daimbert's letter to Bohemond (at the end of July 1100), which he inserted into his great chronicle. But whatever the claims of Daimbert, William of Tyre himself tries to explain the origins of the claim. Daimbert's explanation has little to do with that of William of Tyre. For Daimbert the claim is based on Godfrey's oath of homage. 'He became the man of the Holy Sepulchre', in the words of the Patriarch, and there is only a secondary reference to the Patriarch's possessions at the time of the Turks.[7] William of Tyre, surprised at the Patriarch's claim, as he himself states, because Godfrey was elected to rule the country without being subject to anybody, made a special study of the problem.

According to William of Tyre, the origin of the Patriarch's claim to a quarter of the city of Jerusalem, goes back to the middle of the eleventh

---

[3] W.T. ix. 15. See now H. E. Mayer, *Bistümer, Klöster und Stifte im Königreich Jerusalem* (Stuttgart, 1977), pp. 9 ff.

[4] William of Tyre, explaining the oath of Godfrey of Bouillon and Bohemond to Patriarch Daimbert, says: 'ab eo susceperunt investituram, ei arbitrantes se honorem impendere, cujus tanquam minister ille in terris vicem gerere credebatur' (ix. 15). In another chapter (ix. 16) William says that Daimbert demanded: 'civitatem sanctam Deo ascriptam'.

[5] W.T. ix. 16: 'Dux ... [2 Feb. 1100] quartam partem Joppe resignavit. Postea [1 Apr. 1100] urbem Hierosolymam cum turri David et universis ejus pertinentiis, in manu domini patriarchae resignavit.'

[6] See the sources *Regesta*, no. 34, and cf. H. Hagenmeyer, 'Chronologie de la première Croisade', *ROL* 8 (1900–1), nos. 447 and 455. In a later version, in the letter of Daimbert (see next note), he speaks of the conquest of Cairo.

[7] In the famous, though suspect, letter of Daimbert to Bohemond, quoted by W.T. x. 4: 'Vix enim Dux Godefridus ... ea reliquit ecclesiae tenenda, quae Turcorum temporibus, qui tunc fuerat patriarcha tenuerat ... de Joppe quartam partem ecclesiae Sancti Sepulchri dedit; et post ... cuncta quae juris erant Ecclesiae libera reddidit ... Reddidit itaque nostrae potestatis turrim David cum tota Hierosolymitana urbe, ejusque pertinentiis, et quod in Joppe ipse tenebat.'

century when an agreement reached between the Caliph of Egypt and Constantin X of Byzantium stipulated the latter's financing the fortification of part of Jerusalem, if its Christian inhabitants were the sole inhabitants of their quarter.[8] The fortifications ended in 1063, the Muslim inhabitants left the quarter, and in the words of William of Tyre:

> If [the Christian inhabitants] had any litigation, they referred it to the Church, and by the intervention of the then ruling Patriarch and his arbitration, they decided about their controversies. From that day on, this part of the city did not have any other judge or lord but the Patriarch and the Church claimed it as it were its own in perpetuity.[9]

The disparity between Daimbert's claim to the whole of Jerusalem and a fourth of Jaffa and the former Christian quarter in Jerusalem is so striking that one wonders how a great historian like William of Tyre should have passed it over in silence. It is inconceivable that he was unaware of not proving what he intended to. Moreover, as late as 1128 a newly elected Patriarch, Stephen of Chartres, voiced again the whole of Daimbert's claim, demanding from Baldwin II a fourth of Jaffa and the whole of Jerusalem.[10]

William of Tyre's story, consequently, hardly explains Daimbert's claim, but it does explain a situation which existed when William wrote his History in the eighties of the twelfth century. What he was actually explaining was the existence of an ecclesiastical lordship in the royal city of Jerusalem. Let us not forget that at the time he wrote his chronicle, he was a candidate to the Patriarchate, and may have had more than a purely academic interest in its possessions and privileges.

The treatises of Crusader law are somewhat reticent on ecclesiastical jurisdiction. Generally speaking the Church had jurisdiction *ratione materiae* in cases of heresy, adultery, and cases devolving from family relations. The Church also had jurisdiction over its own members and property. But in no case could it judge murder and treason.[11] An interesting phrase of Philip of Novara indicates that the Church was not

---

[8] W.T. ix. 17–18.

[9] W.T. ix. 18: 'Sic ergo ab ea die et ea ratione . . . praedicta pars civitatis quarta, alium non habuit judicem vel dominum nisi patriarcham, et eam quasi propriam Ecclesia sibi perpetuo vendicavit.'

[10] W.T. xiii. 25.

[11] *LdAdB*, chs. 14, 18, 131, 134, 186. *Clef des assises*, ch. 9 (*Lois* i. 579), counts testaments as belonging to church jurisdiction. There are cases in which members of Military Orders had to appear before the court of the viscount, *LdAdB*, ch. 129. Cf. La Monte, *Feudal Monarchy*, p. 215.

even opposed to judging according to the customs of the kingdom or to invoking canon law.[12]

The problem which interests us here is that of church jurisdiction over its members and property. The definition 'et ce a iaus aucun plait apartient, si se deit desfenir devant les prelas de sainte yglise' is certainly vague. How should this be understood: is all church property under its own jurisdiction?

A clue to an explanation is to be found in a privilege of Fulk of Anjou (A.D. 1138) granting houses in Jerusalem to the canons of the Holy Sepulchre. He states: 'has itaque domos liberas et quietas ego rex Fulco concedo et confirmo habendas... iure perpetuo... ab omni cousuetudine solutas, *salva iustitia regali*, quam rex debet habere in helemosina, quam ipse dat sanctae ecclesiae.'[13] The same is repeated seventeen years later by Baldwin III: 'quas [domos] omnes pater meus ... ab omni exactione liberas et quietas, *salvo tamen regio iure*, quod in helemosine, quam rex ecclesie facit, debet habere, canonicis Sancti Sepulcri concessit.'[14]

The property described in these documents is classified as *elemosina*, but the king reserves to himself a *iustitia regalis* or *regis ius*. One interpretation of the meaning of the *ius* is the legal status of the property. Fulk's privilege says: 'concedo et confirmo habendas', which is not sufficiently clear since both verbs were used indifferently for concession and simple confirmation.

Fortunately we can check the origin of the properties concerned, because the Cartulary of the Holy Sepulchre preserved deeds dealing with them before they came into the hands of the canons. Out of the houses mentioned,[15] three are described as follows: 'domus Petri Bernardi canonici, item domus alterius Eurardi canonici'. The 'domus Mabile' is the house sold by Mabilia to the canons in 1132,[16] the 'domus Rogerii fratris eorum canonicorum' is the house given by Roger of St. Lazarus to the canons on entering their fraternity, [17] the house of Martinus Caraona is known to have been given by him to the canons.[18] The 'domus Bernardi Bursarii' can be identified with a house that once belonged to Bernard

---

[12] Philip of Novara, ch. 47, *Lois* i. 522: 'Il y aveit plusors cas qui touchoient à la juridiction de l'Iglize, dont l'Iglize de Jerusalem avoit fait otroi que se teil cas venoit devant eaus que il n'i alegeroient decrès ne decretale ne lei, ains jugeroient selon l'usage et l'assise de la terre.'

[13] Rozière, no. 32; *Regesta*, no. 181.

[14] Rozière, no. 53 (A.D. 1155); *Regesta*, no. 309.

[15] Rozière, no. 32. All the following quotations are from the same document, *Regesta*, no. 181.

[16] Rozière, no. 106. Regesta, no. 141.   [17] Rozière, no. 111; *Regesta*, no. 156.

[18] Rozière, no. 114; *Regesta*, no. 280.

Bursarius and was leased by the canons in 1160 to one Richard Jaferinus.[19] In all probability the house was given or sold by Bernard Bursarius to the canons. We can clearly establish, then, that six of the ten houses were not a royal gift to the canons, but a confirmation of their acquisition. The property clearly consisted of burgage-tenures, and when they became a *helemosina* the king, who in this case was also the lord of the city, safeguarded his rights in the tenures.

The royal confirmation of ten houses only would have been arbitrary, unless we suppose that only these houses came into their hands during Fulk's time, or that there was another reason for this particular confirmation. We think that it is their location in the city area that explains Fulk's charter. The 'domus Garsie' mentioned in Fulk's confirmation of 1141 was described in 1136 as being in *parte regis* of the city.[20] As to the house of 'frater Roger', he received a 'fief' from the canons in 1135 on condition that he sold his property in the city and settled 'cum consilio canonicorum *super terram Sancti Sepulchri* vel ad Sanctum Lazarum vel in Jerusalem'.[21] Consequently his house, like that of Garsia, was at that time not 'in parte Sancti Sepulcri' but in 'parte regis'. Bernardus Bursarius' house was possibly a house built on a plot of land given to him by the canons under the obligation 'aedificare domum de proprio *super terram Sancti Sepulcri, que est in* Jherusalem in parte regis'.[22] Another house, that of Martin Caraon, was in 'vicus de Repoes' near the Temple area.[23]

The location of the different houses points clearly to the conclusion that Jerusalem was divided between a *pars regis* and a *pars Sancti Sepulchri*. This division has nothing to do with property rights. The Holy Sepulchre's properties were in both parts of the city. In the royal part the Holy Sepulchre possessed *elemosinae*, which were legally tenures: in the *pars Sancti Sepulchri* the Patriarch was *dominus terrae*, the lord of the lordship. This difference obviously had legal consequences. The *elemosina* held in the *dominium regis* and the confirmation prove that they needed the king's consent to alienation, as was the case with fiefs and other burgage-tenures. Moreover, should the Church alienate this property to a layman, the property would lose its status of *elemosina*, of an absolutely service-free tenure, and return to its former status. This explains the *ius regis*, or

[19] Rozière, no. 105; *Regesta*, no. 343.   [20] Rozière, no. 107; *Regesta*, no. 166.
[21] Rozière, no. 111: *Regesta*, no. 156.   [22] Rozière, no. 107; *Regesta*, no. 166.
[23] Rozière, no. 185; *Regesta*, no. 421.

servicium, which the king has in the *elemosinae*.[24] Naturally, he would not have any such rights in property in the city *dominium* of the Church.

The point is well illustrated in Alexander III's confirmation of the privileges of the church of the Holy Sepulchre of 1170. The Pope confirmed all their possessions to the canons: 'domos insuper, stationes, terras et quicquid *in quarterio ecclesie et patriarche* habetis, et de cetero iuste acquirere poteritis, et omnes alias domos, stationes, et terras, quas infra Jerusalem vel extra possidetis.'[25]

The *quarterium ecclesie et patriarche* is that minutely described by William of Tyre in the north-western part of the city. It formed a quadrangle, two of its sides being the western and northern walls of the city, stretching from the city citadel and David's Gate (Jaffa Gate), passing through the north-western angle of Tancred's tower to St. Stephen's Gate (Damascus Gate) in the centre of the northern wall of the city. The two other sides were part of David's Street, from Jaffa Gate to the Temple Mount, and the street which led from St. Stephen's Gate to Mt. Zion. The streets intersected at the triple bazaar of the city, near the benches of the Latin money-changers. The centre of the quarter was the Church of the Holy Sepulchre and the Patriarch's palace, from which the quarter took its name as 'quarterium Patriarchae'.[26]

The existence of an ecclesiastical lordship in the capital created a special relationship between the lord and the inhabitants of this lordship. One of its results was the creation of special institutions to rule the lordship. The administration of the *quarterium ecclesie et patriarche* was in practice exercised by the prior, who on the death of the Patriarch also administered all his possessions.[27] We have not succeeded in drawing a line between the Patriarch's and the prior's prerogatives in the quarter, but we do not

[24] A similar case referring to a house in Acre is furnished by a confirmation (1155) of Baldwin III to the canons of the Holy Sepulchre. The king, following an earlier privilege of King Fulk, laid down the following conditions: 'ne venditione vel commutatione sive quolibet alio modo a se eicere liceat, et, si fecerint, regia maiestas ex ea servicium habeat' (Rozière, no. 54, p. 104; *Regesta*, no. 354).

[25] Rozière, nos. 166–7. This is based on a confirmation of privileges of the canons by Patriarch Amalric of 1169: 'domos, stationes, terras et quicquid in quarterio ecclesiae et nostro habeatis' (*Regesta*, nos. 474, 469). In Patriarch Arnulf's privilege of 1114 this phrase does not appear (Rozière, no. 25).

[26] W.T. ix. 18. It also included the compound of the Hospitallers, which created a problem. The canons had 'plateam vero, quod est inter portam ecclesie et columpnas et Hospitale Sti Johannis, sicut in longum et latum protenditur' (Rozière, no. 167, p. 302).

[27] Rozière, no. 167: 'Obeunte vero vel transfretante Patriarcha ... prior et canonici ... domum ut iustum est, et familiam patriarche, et omnia que ad ius eius spectant, intus et extra fideliter custodient et regent' (*Regesta*, no. 469).

THE PATRIARCH'S LORDSHIP
IN JERUSALEM

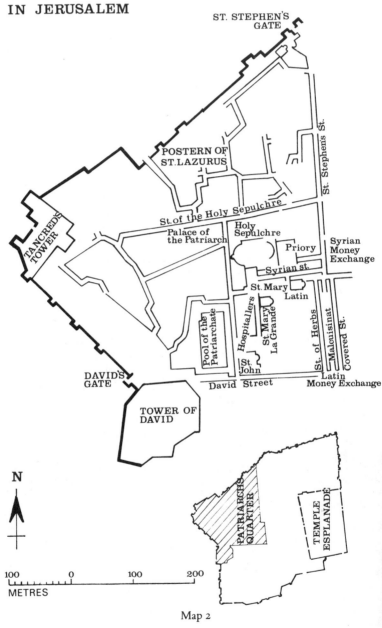

Map 2

envisage a geographical division of the lordship between the Patriarch and the canons,[28] though there were particular properties that belonged to the canons. In the overwhelming majority of recorded cases, property acquisitions were made by the prior with the consent of, or in the presence of, the Patriarch and usually in the name of the chapter.[29] But there are some deeds in which the Patriarch does not appear.[30] The ecclesiastical lordship had a population of several thousand souls and included market places, piazzas, houses, shops, and workshops. This was actually the first quarter to be settled by the Latins.[31] In time it developed special administrative institutions.

The central instrument of administration was the *curia Patriarchae*, distinct, when dealing with its city lordship,[32] from the one that dealt with strictly ecclesiastical matters. The *curia Patriarchae* of the lordship was a mixed ecclesiastical and lay body. It was composed, as far as we can ascertain, of a number of clergymen from the Patriarch's household and some canons, whereas its lay members were *burgenses* of Jerusalem.

We know a good many of these burgesses whose signatures accompany deeds that recorded transactions passed before the Patriarch's court. They are usually introduced by their social rank or their lay status. Thus in a donation of Patriarch Amalric of Nesle in August 1175, their signatures follow that of a presbyter, a dean, and a subdeacon, and are introduced by: 'De hominibus nostris laicis'.[33] In a charter of June 1177 the same Amalric of Nesle[34] calls them 'de familia mea' and their signatures mingle with those of the clergymen of the household, the Patriarch's seneschal (*dapifer*)

---

[28] A distinction should be made between rights of lordship and simple rights of property. The canons had particular property in the ecclesiastical lordship, as is clear from the privilege quoted above, p. 301 n. 25. The problem needs a more detailed study.

[29] Rozière, no. 82; *Regesta*, no. 154: 'annuente Patriarcha'; no. 101; *Regesta*, no. 183: 'testes sunt: domnus Patriarcha etc'. no. 109; *Regesta*, no. 158: 'iubente Patriarcha'; cf. nos. 110, 77; *Regesta*, no. 295. The canons also appear in Rozière, nos. 107, 80, 81, 78; *Regesta*, nos. 166, 223, 267, 129. Three different seals were used: the Patriarch's, the prior's, and the chapter's. Cf. Schlumberger, Chalandon, Blanchet, *Sigillographie de l'Orient latin* (Paris, 1943), nos. 162–6. Cf. the previous note.

[30] Rozière, nos. 102, 104, 105, 106, 108; *Regesta*, nos. 160, 146, 343, 141, 310.

[31] Cf. above, Ch. 4, pp. 94 f.

[32] In thirteenth-century Acre the Patriarch of Jerusalem used a special seal when dealing with non-ecclesiastical matters. The Archdeacon William who served as *officialis* of the Patriarch in 1286 and judged 'in domo episcopali, in loco scilicet ubi iura redduntur' says: 'sigillum predicte curie quod *ad causas* utitur, appendi feci' (H. Prutz in *Altpreussische Monatsschrift*, 20, no. 10, p. 398. *Regesta*, 1467). 'Officialis curie' of the Patriarch in Acre is also mentioned in 1273 (*Regesta*, no. 1388).

[33] Delaville, no. 483; *Regesta*, no. 528.

[34] Rozière, no. 168; *Regesta*, no. 543.

the chaplain, a cleric, and a *crucifer*, who wrote the deed on the order of the chancellor, *magister* Monachus. More often the signatures of the *testes* are divided between *de clericis*, followed by another set of witnesses called 'de laicis.'[35] A similar procedure was followed, as we saw, in the royal court of Jerusalem. The fact that the documents emanated from the Patriarch or the prior of the Holy Sepulchre, and also the possibility of locating the properties in the 'quarterium patriarchae', make their legal standing clear. In some deeds the signatures do not indicate social rank or any connection with the Church of the Holy Sepulchre,[36] but the witnesses are known to us as burgesses of Jerusalem. In a special case such as, for example, an arbitration by Patriarch William I (1142–5) between the abbey of St. Mary of Josaphat and the church of the Mount of Olives, the signatures of the high prelates are followed by monks of St. Mary and then by 'testimonium laicorum', from which was distinguished the *testimonium burgensium*.[37] The burgesses of the Patriarch are introduced at least once after the signatures of the canons of the Holy Sepulchre, as 'de patriarchali curia'.[38] Leaving the problem of clergymen, we shall concentrate on its lay members. Most conspicuous is the apparent absence of knights and certainly of nobles of any standing from the *curia*. Conversely, we always find burgesses. Some of them belonged to the Patriarch's household, where they served, together with clergymen, in filling domestic offices. Some examples are worth quoting.

A charter of March 1167 is signed among others by a Gaufridus *dapifer*, Audebartus *pincerna*, and Arnaldus *marescalcus*.[39] In 1169 Gaufridus is still the Patriarch's seneschal,[40] as he is in 1175, and Aldebert still the *pincerna*.[41] They are still attested in their respective offices in 1177.[42] The seneschal Gaufridus signed in 1161 as 'senescalcus domini Amalrici patriarchae', with the cognomen 'Turonensis', Geoffrey of Tours.[43] After his first appearance in 1153 we do not lose sight of him for thirty years, just before the débâcle of Hittin. The last time he signs a document is in 1186. Geoffrey of Tours belonged to the higher class of Jerusalem's

[35] Delaville, nos. 375–6; *Regesta*, no. 430–431.
[36] Delaborde, no. 23. p. 55–6; *Regesta*, no. 213.
[37] Delaville, *Archives*, no. 19; *Regesta*, no. 379.
[38] Delaville, *Archives*, no. 5; *Regesta*, no. 170.
[39] Delaville, *Archives*, no. 26; *Regesta*, no. 431.
[40] Rozière, no. 167; *Regesta*, no. 469.
[41] Delaville, no. 483; *Regesta*, no. 528.
[42] Rozière, no. 168; *Regesta*, no. 543.
[43] *Regesta*, no. 369. Possibly 'de Tour' as he also signs 'Galfridus de Turonia' in 1153. See next note.

burgesses. He is usually to be found either in the entourage of the king of Jerusalem or that of the Patriarch and the canons of the Holy Sepulchre. For the first seven years (from 1153 to 1161) he is associated with the Holy Sepulchre, and then in 1161 he appears as the Patriarch's seneschal. During this time Geoffrey signed deeds which dealt with the Holy Sepulchre's property in St. Lazarus[44] and in Mahumeria,[45] and at the same time some royal charters of Baldwin III, which he signs proudly from among the *burgenses regis*.[46] After 1161 Geoffrey appears as the Patriarch's seneschal, an office he kept for at least nine years, till 1177. But during the same period he signed a charter of 1161, several documents of the new King Amalric[47] and of the Patriarch,[48] as 'Gofridus de Tors de juratis Jerusalem'.[49] In 1175 when he is witnessing as *dapifer Patriarchae*, he also signs royal deeds among the *burgenses Jherusalem*[50] and *de juratis civitatis*.[51] After this date the title of seneschal is not mentioned, but his standing in the royal court and in that of the viscount did not change even under Baldwin IV,[52] nor did he lose contact with the canons of the Holy Sepulchre.[53] We clearly have here a man of standing among the burgesses of Jerusalem. Despite his connections with the Holy Sepulchre, as a *familiaris* and finally as chief officer of the Patriarch's household, he is at the same time a *iuratus*, a member of the royal Court of Burgesses of Jerusalem.

The Patriarch's butler, Aldebert, is less prominent. As the Patriarch's *pincerna*, he served for some time as the head of the household.[54] His house was near the Temple area,[55] i.e. outside the Patriarch's quarter. Even less is known about Arnaud, the Patriarch's marshal.[56]

Beside these members of the *curia Patriarchae* of burgess origin, who belonged to the Patriarch's household, we find in the *curia* people who held no office in the household. Their signatures could have fulfilled two different functions: as actual members of the *curia*, where a given transaction took place, or as *testes* to a deal. A clear division appears for the

---

[44] Ibid., no. 284 (A.D. 1153).   [45] Ibid., no. 302 (A.D. 1155).

[46] Ibid., nos. 299, 300, 301, 333, 332 (A.D. 1155–8).

[47] Ibid., no. 450 (A.D. 1168). It could have been another man (so Delaborde), but we doubt it. Cf. *Regesta*, nos. 504 (A.D. 1173), 516 (A.D. 1169).

[48] Ibid., nos. 456, 455 (A.D. 1168); *ROL* ix. 187 (A.D. 1169).

[49] *Regesta*, no. 391 (A.D. 1161).   [50] Ibid., no. 531.   [51] Ibid., no. 534.

[52] Ibid., no. 545 (A.D. 1177); no. 643 (A.D. 1185), and in the viscount's court as *juratus*, ibid., no. 561 (A.D. 1178).

[53] He witnessed the renting of land in Mahumeria, which belonged to the Holy Sepulchre (*Regesta*, no. 561 (A.D. 1178)).

[54] *Regesta*, no. 543: 'Aldebertus pincerna, tunc temporis praeceptor domus mee'.

[55] Ibid., no. 535 (A.D. 1175).   [56] Ibid., no. 431, 528 (A.D. 1167).

first time in the middle of the twelfth century, and even then it did not become the general rule. Yet the difficulty is perhaps more apparent than real, as the signatures of the members of the court are basically those of witnesses, though of a more elevated standing. Still, we can assume that if a given property was in the *vicus ecclesiae*, then we are dealing with members of the court of the Church. The same holds true if the property was an *elemosina*, even if outside the *quarterium ecclesiae*.

It may be impossible to identify all the burgesses mentioned, but we can do it for some who often appear in the deeds connected with the Holy Sepulchre. Such an outstanding burgess was Gaufridus Acus whom we can follow for the long span of twenty-seven years, from his first signature on a royal ordinance of Baldwin II abolishing some customs at the gates of Jerusalem[57] until the eve of the Second Crusade, when in 1147 he countersigned a charter of Baldwin III.[58] The man was of non-noble and probably very humble origin. About 1125 a knight 'Radulf de Fontanellis', who was often found in the king's entourage,[59] gave him a vineyard on the road leading from Jerusalem to Bethlehem: 'quia diu bene ac familiariter michi servivit.'[60] We could imagine our Godfrey Acus as a sergeant of Raoul de Fontaines, who possibly came to the Holy Land with the First Crusade. When he received this vineyard, the man must have been around thirty or forty years old.[61] Between *c.* 1125 and 1141 we see him signing documents on behalf of the Patriarch and the canons of the Holy Sepulchre,[62] in the entourage of the Knights of St. John,[63] and signing a royal charter of Fulk.[64] But whereas in 1136 he signs distinctly as *de burgensibus*, in 1141 he signs as *dominus*[65] and in 1144 and 1147 he already belonged to the *barones regis*, signing charters of Baldwin III among his noblemen.[66] At this time the man was around sixty or seventy and this is the last we hear of him. As to his special connection with the

---

[57] Ibid., no. 91.   [58] Ibid., no. 244 (A.D. 1147).

[59] Attested from 1108 in the court of Baldwin I (*Regesta*, no. 52), then under Baldwin II up to 1127. Seems to have gone to Antioch where he signed a deed in 1134 (*Regesta*, no. 148) and then to Tripoli, 1142–5 (ibid., nos. 212, 236).

[60] Rozière, 121; *Regesta*, no. 111.

[61] He must have been twenty to twenty-five years old when he signed a royal charter, perhaps even older.

[62] *Regesta*, nos. 128, 129 (A.D. 1129); no. 141 (A.D. 1132). Rozière, 105 (A.D. 1134–5); *Regesta*, no. 343.

[63] It concerned a non-noble (*Regesta*, no. 130 (A.D. 1129)).   [64] Ibid., no. 164.

[65] This title does not indicate the rank, as it was used indifferently for knights, burgesses, and clergy. But in our document the *burgenses* sign after the *domini*, who included the canons of the Holy Sepulchre.   [66] *Regesta*, nos. 226, 244.

Holy Sepulchre, we might point out that the charter by which Radulf de Fontanellis conceded a vineyard to Gaufridus Acus is found in the Cartulary of the Holy Sepulchre, the only explanation being that at some time this property came into the possession of the canons. Another point of interest is a village in the vicinity of Emmaus ('Amwas), which in 1141 belonged to the Knights of St. John. It is called 'casale de Gaufrido Agule'.[67] Röhricht's identification of this with 'castrum Gauafridi de Agolt' is out of the question, [68] but it tallies well with our Gaufridus, who signs in 1129 as Goffridus de Acula.[69] In this vicinity several members of the higher class of Jerusalemite burgesses possessed villages.[70]

Another interesting personality is Pierre de Perigueux (Petrus Petragoricus), who appears on the deeds of the Holy Sepulchre between 1133 and 1160,[71] and whose original occupation was that of a goldsmith.[72] He never reached the rank of a Gaufidus Acus, but he was connected with the same institutions and the same people. Up to 1141 he signs several documents belonging to the Holy Sepulchre,[73] then he reappears in the court of Queen Melissenda[74] and later in that of Baldwin III.[75] Yet even during this time he remains constantly in the entourage of the canons of the Holy Sepulchre, where he signs documents until 1160.

Another category of people may be represented by Robertus Cocus, a contemporary of those already mentioned, attested between 1133 and 1160. Not much is known of him, except for his permanent presence with the canons of the holy Sepulchre for almost thirty years.[76] As far as we can see he never was a *iuratus*,[77] and we never see him among the attendants of the royal court.

This list could be enlarged to include dozens of the *burgenses* of Jerusalem connected with the Holy Sepulchre. But this will not advance us any more in our knowledge of the Patriarch's *curia*. The examples chosen prove that all these burgesses belonged to a kind of city professional

[67] Ibid., no. 205.
[68] The place was in the principality of Tripoli (*Regesta*, no. 78).   [69] Ibid., no. 130.
[70] In the same vicinity several villages were called by the name of their holders, who were burgesses: '. . . Casale de Porcel et de Gaufrido Agule . . . et de Bacheler et de Girardo Bocher' (Delaville, no. 140). On Porcel cf. *Regesta*, nos. 91, 111, 130, 164, 166, 205, 430–1, Delaville iv. 248–9, n. 372; on Bacheler cf. *Regesta*, nos. 91, 111, 205, 173; on Girardus Bocher, cf. *Regesta*, 111, 205. We are less sure about the social rank of the last one.
[71] *Regesta*, nos. 146, 365.   [72] Cf. ibid., no. 154.
[73] Ibid., nos. 146, 154, 158, 204 (A.D. 1133–41).
[74] Ibid., nos. 259, 268 (A.D. 1150–1).   [75] Ibid., no. 299.
[76] In 1155 he signs with other burgesses but not among the *iurati*, ibid., no. 310.
[77] Ibid., nos. 146, 223, 310, 335, 343.

officialdom. We do not know much about their economic position, but even supposing they were not wealthy, they certainly formed a special group characterized by its close connections with the ruling circles in the city and in the kingdom. Whereas their position in the city of Jerusalem was the result of natural development, their position in the kingdom was an accidental outcome of the fact that Jerusalem was a royal city, a capital, and the seat of the king. A rather unexpected but prominent feature of this group was its simultaneous connection with the royal and ecclesiastical administrations of the city. The same people served in the Court of Burgesses and in the Court of the Patriarch, a fact which probably made for the smooth running of the whole machinery. This probably also facilitated the transaction of business where both jurisdictions were concerned. The matters that came before the Court of the Patriarch were those connected with his standing as the *seigneur justicier* of the quarter, but it is our impression that there were attempts to extend it also over property of the Holy Sepulchre, usually *elemosinae*, outside the *quarterium Patriarchae*, that is into the royal part of the city.

It is impossible to say when this Court of the Patriarch came into being. Still, it seems to us that the Court of the Patriarch already existed *c.* 1135. Two charters which emanate from the canons of the Holy Sepulchre seem to point in that direction. The first, of 1135, records the sale of a house in Jerusalem to the prior and canons of the Holy Sepulchre. It is witnessed by seven people, all of them goldsmiths, headed by one 'Seybertus iudex'.[78] The other a year later, 1136, gives permission to a couple, Andrew and Hosanna, to build a house on a plot of land which belonged to the Holy Sepulchre 'in parte regis'[79] for a rent of 2 besants, with the stipulation that the house will go to the Church after their death. This is witnessed by eight people, some known burgesses, one official of the Church ('magister clientum Sancti Sepulcri'), headed by one 'Huldredus iudex'.[80] It seems plausible to see in these *iudices* a part, or even the heads, of the Holy Sepulchre's lay court. The title *iudex* does not appear later on, but it may be recalled that in the thirteenth century the *iurati* of the Court of Burgesses are called *iudices*. This is only hypothesis, but it seems to fit in point of time and procedure with the parallel development of the royal Court of Burgesses.

The Court of the Patriarch was a record office and a court of law. In all

[78] Rozière, no. 82; *Regesta*, no. 154.
[79] Rozière, no. 107; *Regesta*, no. 166. See below, p. 309.
[80] Rozière, no. 107; *Regesta*, no. 166.

probability it dealt also with administration, though this can be only assumed, not proved. The court as record office dealt with property alienations and possessory relations (e.g. leasing in all forms of land parcels, houses, shops, etc.). In this aspect it also recorded possessory relations in its tenures-in-alms outside its own quarter. As far as can be seen the possessory relations did not differ from those generally valid in the kingdom, and known to us from the *Livre des Assises des Bourgeois* and the more recent *Livres du plédéant et du plaidoyer*.

Being the *dominus* of the quarter, the Patriarch was responsible for the upkeep and for traffic in squares and streets of his quarter. Thus we see him laying down building rules. In 1137 Patriarch William permits one Robertus Medicus, who bought land in his quarter, 'firmam voltam edificandi super viam que est inter ipsam domum et campum meum, super quam domus fabricam sine timore casus, posset erigere'.[81] Needless to say, building in the Patriarch's quarter needed his confirmation. In August 1175, when the Patriarch Amalric of Nesle authorized the Knights of St. John to buy several houses in his quarter,[82] 'licet eis libere et inibi pro libito suo edificare absque alique mei vel successorum meorum contradictione.' In such cases it is difficult to know whether the Patriarch acts as *seigneur justicier* or *seigneur foncier*. Permission to build will be asked of him in both cases. This is proved by two other documents emanating from his *curia* and dealing with building on his property, but not in his quarter—one in November 1136, when Andrew and Hosanna were given permission to build their house 'de proprio super terram sancti Sepulcri, quae est in Jherusalem in parte regis'.[83] A similar case is attested by an authorization given to a Syrian, Arnulf son of Beruald, to build a third and fourth floor on top of houses belonging to the canons and built over arches (beneath which were the Hospitallers' money-exchange), where there was an oven belonging to the Holy Sepulchre.[84] As the property was in the ecclesiastical lordship, the canons' permission, which meant the creation of a burgage-tenure in their lordship, put several

---

[81] Delaville, *Archives*, no. 5, cf. charter of 1235 in Delaville, no. 2127 (ii. 494); *Regesta*, no. 170. The land was near the 'lacus Balnearum', that is near the Patriarch's palace.

[82] 'In vico qui descendit a porta David ex parte domus Hospitalis', Delaville, no. 483 (A.D. 1175); *Regesta*, no. 528. There is no doubt that the Hospitallers, whose buildings were in the Patriarch's quarter (above, p. 301 n. 26) tried to create for themselves, if not a lordship, at least an *immunitas*.   [83] See above, p. 308 and n. 79.

[84] Rozière, no. 80; *Regesta*, no. 223. Such high buildings were rather exceptional in Jerusalem. This was different in Tyre even in the eleventh century and in Acre in the thirteenth. See above, Ch. 8, p. 236 and *passim*.

conditions upon the new tenant: he was allowed to sell his new property to burgesses and Syrians; the canons were to have a pre-emption right, paying 1 mark of silver less than any prospective buyer. The eventual new tenant would continue to pay the *cens* of 9 besants a year. This, as we see, follows precisely the customs ruling burgage-tenures in the kingdom.

The *juridiction gracieuse*, alienation of property or exchanges of property, naturally came before the Patriarch or the prior and his *curia*. In July 1137 the prior allows one Galteriùs de Lucia to sell his house—a burgage-tenure paying a *cens* of 1 besant to the Holy Sepulchre—to Robertus Medicus.[85] We can follow up the history of this house, which was bought by the Hospitallers thirty years later. Giving his consent to an alienation in March 1167, the Patriarch stipulated the safeguarding of his rights.[86] The tangible sign of dependence between the lord and the tenant was the *cens*, which, as in this case, was only a token payment and does not represent its real rent value.[87] If our interpretation is correct, the Patriarch's authorization is that of the lord of the quarter. We would like to know whether the consent carried with it the payment to the lord of *lods et ventes*, but the document is silent on this point. A similar procedure can be gleaned again from a deed of 1144, where a man rented a house before the *curia* of the Patriarch, receiving permission of alienation as long as the payment of the *cens* to the Holy Sepulchre was assured and the legal status of the buyer was the same as the seller's.[88] In a deed of 1154 from the *curia*, the same privilege is granted with the common limitation of alienation to Military Orders.[89] Besides alienation of tenures, the court dealt with one of the more current transactions, such as renting of property, buying and selling of *cens*,[90] with the usual conditions of pre-emption options and a lower price than that of the best offered.

[85] Delaville, *Archives*, no. 5; *Regesta*, no. 170: 'prebui Galtero de Lucia ut domum . . . Roberto medico . . . jure hereditario habendam et libere ac quiete possidendam pro LXXX bisantiis venderet et traderet.'
[86] Delaville, *Archives*, no. 25; *Regesta*, no. 430: 'laudo et concedo Hospitali . . . quasdam domos . . . quas Robertus Medicus . . . assensu et voluntate nostra eidem vendiderunt, ut libere eas habeat et quiete in perpetuum possideat . . . Quicumque domos illas habeat ab ipso [Hospitali] tenebit nobis . . . unum bizantium censualiter reddet.'
[87] 1 besant per year, as compared with the value of the house, 80 besants in 1136.
[88] Rozière, no. 80; *Regesta*, no. 223: 'cui voluerit burgensium vel Suryanorum vendendi potestatem obtineat.' Cf. ibid., nos. 136–9.
[89] Cf. Rozière, no. 110; *Regesta*, no. 295: 'quibus voluerint eam vendant aut donant exceptis Templariis et Hospitalaribus et aliis quibuscumque monasteriis.'
[90] Delaville, *Archives*, nos. 5, 25, 26; *Regesta*, nos. 170, 430, 431; Rozière, nos. 107, 110, 105; *Regesta*, nos. 166, 295, 343; Delaville, no. 483; *Regesta*, 528.

In all these cases the *curia Patriarchae* is a record office. There is no doubt that it is better developed than the Viscount's Court, because the chancery of the Holy Sepulchre can furnish the written deeds. Though these had no legal standing in the Viscount's Court, they would certainly have full force in the *curia* where they were written.

The *curia* was also a court of litigation. Unfortunately, its decisions are not preserved, as the Cartulary of the Holy Sepulchre was not a court register and kept only deeds connected with the possessions of the establishment (besides papal and royal privileges). But there is no doubt that *burgenses* of the ecclesiastical lordship were judged in the Patriarch's court. Only one document survives to witness this function and the picture is rather blurred, because some legal features make the case an exceptional one. This is a protocol of proceedings, a 'Breve recordationis, conventionis et donationis' of litigation between one Maria, widow of Petrus and wife of Roger, 'cliens Sancti Sepulcri' from the village of St. Lazarus, and her son-in-law Bernard, a 'cliens patriarchae', about the dowry of her daughter, wife of the aforesaid Bernard. The question was debated and 'postea diffinita est in capitulo Sancti Sepulcri coram domino Willelmo patriarcha et Petro subpriore et Anselmo cantore et Goffrido thesaurario et magistro Roberto, canonicis Sancti Sepulcri, et coram Anschetino, quondam vicecomite Jerusalem et Rainaldo de Pontibus et Goiffrido Acu.'[91]

Why should such a case come before the Court of the Patriarch? The bone of contention was a house, part of which was assigned as dowry to Maria's daughter. It was located near the Temple area and did not belong to the Holy Sepulchre.[92] Consequently it was not *ratione materiae* that the case was brought before the chapter of the Holy Sepulchre. The reason was in the legal position of those concerned, namely as *clientes*[93] of the Holy Sepulchre, which created a patron–client relation. In some cases, like that under discussion, we can see the canons' attempts to settle their *clientes* in their own quarter; they would abandon their former property to the canons or sell it and move to their new quarters. Obviously as long as they did not live in the Patriarch's quarter or as long as they held property elsewhere, they remained the king's burgesses. It is therefore understandable

---

[91] Rozière, no. 109; *Regesta*, no. 158.

[92] In June 1135 Roger and Mary promised the canons of the Holy Sepulchre: 'domum quam habebant in Jerusalem venderent, et omnes res quascumque et ubicumque haberent, cum consilio canonicorum *super terram Sancti Sepulchri* vel ad sanctum Lazarum vel in Jerusalem reducerent' (Rozière, 111; *Regesta*, no. 156).

[93] Discussed below, pp. 312–13.

that we see among the men who took part in the consultation and arbitration a former viscount of the city and two men who were *jurati* of the court of the viscount. The burgesses appear again, as *testes* to the *Breve*. This fits well with the rules of the *Livre des Assises des Bourgeois*, that in mixed cases the viscount should appear in the court of the Church.[94] The case just mentioned could serve as proof that this court held jurisdiction over the burgess inhabitants of its quarter but the people involved were *clientes*, and consequently had a particular type of relation with the Church of the Holy Sepulchre. Even if the burgesses of the Patriarch's lordship were judged in civil cases by his court, it does not seem that grave criminal cases were in its competence. The executive power of this *curia* seems also to have been limited. In a deed of 1135 a house was sold to the canons of the Holy Sepulchre, near the church of St. Karitot (location unknown) but probably in the Patriarch's quarter. The seller invokes an anathema on the violator of this transaction 'et in fiscum regium auri libram persolvat.'[95]

Generally speaking, we can imagine the relations between the Patriarch and the inhabitants of the Patriarch's quarter as that of a *dominus terrae* with his subjects, though in serious cases they would be judged by the royal, i.e. the viscount's court of the city; in some cases, namely where their personal status and the legal status of their property did not correspond, they would be judged by a mixed ecclesiastical and lay court.[96] From the mass of inhabitants of the quarter the canons created a special group connected with them and dependent on them in a more direct way. There are two expressions in our documents to describe their special status, *confratres* or *fratres*, and *clientes*. It seems that no clear difference existed between the two groups and the use of the one or other expression was accidental.[97]

What did *cliens* mean? No doubt it expressed a relation of dependence. So in mid-thirteenth century Acre *clientes* were groups of men who

---

[94] *LdAdB*, ch. 181. *Livre du plédéant*, ed. Beugnot, ch. 72.

[95] Rozière, no. 82; *Regesta*, no. 154.

[96] e.g. Frankish inhabitants who lived in the Patriarch's quarter but whose property was outside its boundaries.

[97] The problem was studied by A. Couret, *Notice historique sur l'Ordre du Saint Sépulcre, 1099–1905*[2] (Paris, 1905), but his conclusions were prejudiced by assuming that the Military Order of the Holy Sepulchre was founded at the beginning of the twelfth century. Cf. W. Hotzelt, 'Die Chorherren vom Heiligen Grabe in Jerusalem' and 'Kirchliche Organisation und religiöses Leben in Palästina während der Kreuzzugszeit', *Das Heilige Land* ii (1940), 43–173.

enjoyed special protection from powerful factors such as the Military Orders.[98] The connotation of dependence is also proved for twelfth-century Jerusalem. In the case brought before the court of the Patriarch in 1134–5,[99] Maria, her husband Roger, and her daughter's husband Bernard, were all clients of the Patriarch, Bernard being a man of some standing, brother to the prior of the Holy Sepulchre. Their dependence on the church of the Holy Sepulchre is created by a *feudum* held from the church.[100] In this document the couple promised to settle in the Patriarch's quarter or the church's village of St. Lazarus. The canons threaten that otherwise 'et fraternitatem et amititiam domus irrecuperabiliter perderent.' In a deed of 1129 we have another *confrater* from St. Lazarus who holds a *feudum* of the Holy Sepulchre, and a *nutritus famulus* who has to marry the daughter of the holder of this *feudum*.[101]

These people who held *feuda* from the Holy Sepulchre were certainly not knights. They were small people and their 'fiefs' were certainly not fiefs of the knightly class. In all probability this was one of the ways by which the Holy Sepulchre recruited its contingent of sergeants, which it owed as military service to the kingdom.[102] The word *clientes* denoted perhaps a kind of vassalic relationship of people who did not belong to the knightly class. The canons had a special official to deal with these *clientes*; in a document of November 1136 he is called *magister clientum Sancti Sepulcri*.[103]

Confratres seems to point to a greater dependence. They were not lay brothers, but a kind of *nutriti* of the Church. The following declaration from a deed of 1129 seems to be typical. A married couple promised to resign their fief (held from the Holy Sepulchre) to the canons at their death, but with the stipulation that their son 'post patris et matris obitum in ecclesia Sancti Sepulcri victum et vestimentum habiturum'.[104] In another case in 1132 the widow Mabilia sold a garden to the canons for the large sum of 170 besants. After her death her house would go to the canons, but during her lifetime they promised to give her 'cotidie panem

---

[98] Cf. Prawer, *Histoire* ii. 359–60; *Latin Kingdom*, p. 225 n.

[99] See above, p. 311.

[100] Rozière, no. 111; *Regesta*, no. 156.   [101] Rozière, no. 77; *Regesta*, no. 128.

[102] Two different contingents were due from the city of Jerusalem. The city owed the service of 500 sergeants and the Patriarch and the canons of the Holy Sepulchre owed the same number. (John of Ibelin, pp. 426–7. Cf. Smail, *Crusading Warfare*, pp. 90 ff.).

[103] Rozière, no. 107; *Regesta*, no. 166.

[104] Rozière, no. 77; *Regesta*, no. 128. On this type of association with the Hospitallers, see Riley-Smith, *Knights of St. John*, pp. 244 ff.

unum canonicorum et dimidiam litram vini temperati et scutellam de coquinato, in die vero dominica et magnis sollempnitatibus recentis frustum carnis vel de cibo, quem domini comederent'. This was promised to the couple by the 'canonici Sancti Sepulcri, confratres et domini mei'.[105] In 1133 one Bernard and his wife are 'in fraternitate nostra suscepti', say the canons, and promise to leave their house after their death to the canons: 'si autem ipsi propria relinquere et cum omnibus suis ad nos venire voluerint, deinde victus et vestimenti necessaria eis impendemus.'[106] Similar dispositions are to be found in a transaction of *c.* 1135. Bernardus of Bourges (Bituricensis) and his wife promised two-thirds of their house after their death to the canons and were accepted on this condition into the *confraternitas*. If one party died, the survivor could resign his third and go to the canons to receive 'victum et vestitum'.[107] This list of examples could be enlarged by documents from outside Jerusalem. The entrance into the *confraternitas* is always connected with granting of spiritual privileges together with economic advantages, so in the case of Bernardus Bituricensis, he and his wife were promised that they would be 'participes omnium bonorum suorum spiritualium . . . in perpetuum'.[108] The people mentioned all seem to have been in economic difficulties, possibly older men and couples who assured their economic and spiritual future by resigning parts of their property immediately and promising the rest after their death.[109] It seems plausible to suppose that people who were *clientes* or *fratres* of the Church came under the jurisdiction of the Patriarch's Court. In any case the Cartulary of the Holy Sepulchre contains a large number of charters dealing with them. But were all *clientes* judged by this court? We are inclined to answer this question positively, because all these *clientes* or *confratres* held property from the canons, and such property being *frankalmoigns* came under the jurisdiction of the Patriarch's Court. Thus they were under the jurisdiction of the Church; if not *ratione personae* (though even this might have been justified) they were so *ratione materiae*.

[105] Rozière, no. 106; *Regesta*, no. 141.
[106] Rozière, no. 104; *Regesta*, no. 146. This seems to be the same as one Bernardus de Castro Radulfi, who bought this house in Jerusalem eight years earlier (1125) from some Syrians (Rozière, 103; *Regesta*, no. 110).
[107] Rozière, no. 102; *Regesta*, no. 160.
[108] Rozière, no. 101; *Regesta*, no. 183.
[109] In some circumstances they also assure their successors by leaving to them one-third of their property; e.g. Rozière, no. 102; *Regesta*, no. 160.

12 Burgage-tenures of the Communes and Ecclesiastical Establishments

When dealing with the development of the Court of Burgesses, we came across a curious group of documents which proves that even in this domain, the kingdom, never too strongly administered, witnessed a usurpation of royal power. We refer to the creation of seignorial rights over city property by lay and ecclesiastical institutions. This has to be distinguished from city areas in which seignorial rights were legally bestowed on ecclesiastical or lay establishments, such as the Patriarch's lordship in Jerusalem or particular city quarters that belonged to the Italian communes. The process also reflects some little-known aspects of interaction between competing and centrifugal factors in the Crusader state fabric.

In this context it is superfluous to review the privileges bestowed on the communes during or after the conquest. Generally speaking, royal and later lordly privileges established communal enclaves in some cities, in which the communes might have been regarded as lords of their quarters. Their jurisdiction, though not everywhere the same, claimed as a rule that mixed cases came before the court of the defendant, whereas litigation between nationals of a given commune (usually excluding criminal cases) was judged by their own courts. Yet some privileges conferred on the communes far larger competences—for example seignorial rights over the inhabitants of their quarters. Whereas all nationals of the commune were under its jurisdiction in their own quarter, this did not automatically include *all* the inhabitants of the quarter. Thus privileges often stipulated that subjects of the king or lord of the city, who happened to live in a communal quarter, would be judged by the royal or lordly court. This was almost self-evident in the case of knights and nobles, but less so as far as burgesses were concerned. Only in special cases do privileges stress the right to judge *all* the inhabitants of a communal quarter.

This naturally posed a problem as to the legal position of property inside the communal quarter. We do know that in some cases the communes enfeoffed their property and created fiefs dependent on the commune, but this was certainly not the rule. Normally we have to envisage the communal authorities as conceding plots of land or houses to the inhabitants of their quarter on condition of paying recognition or quit-rents.

The most detailed of the early privileges, that of the Venetians in Tyre, the *Pactum Warmundi* of 1123, stipulated explicitly: 'super cuiusque gentis burgenses in uico et domibus Venetorum habitantes eandem iustitiam et consuetudines quas rex super suos Venetici habeant.'[1] This was the foundation stone of the Venetian power in Tyre. We have already explained the legal position of this quarter, as that of an independent lordship. The Venetians, looking for a definition, described it as corresponding to the king's own lordship in the remaining two-thirds of the city.[2] They were the *seigneur justicier* of the *vicus*, who had a right to quit-rents (*cens*) from the land and property in the quarter (the possession of *superficies* was not identical with the possession of a house built on it). This also meant that, theoretically, they should approve any type of alienation of property held from the commune. As to the type of holding, there cannot be the slightest doubt that it was burgage-tenure, which the commune called *burgisia*.

The legal status of property and its relation to the legal standing of people began to cause problems by the middle of the twelfth century.[3] The Pisans, who had at that time some modest possessions in Acre, had by 1168 to face serious limitations.

I concede [ran a privilege of King Amalric] to them a court against all people, excepting myself, and [the right] to judge all people of Pisa, excepting those who are my men (*homines mei*) and have houses, or income or real estate (*possessiones stabiles*) in my kingdom. They will be judged by me and my judges.[4]

But in times of stress the commune's bargaining power grew and the privilege of 1187 granted by Conrad of Montferrat to Tyre sounds a different note:[5]

In addition, I grant that all Pisans, and those who are thought of by the name of Pisans, sailors as well as burgesses[6] and even knights and counts or laymen of whatever condition, should be judged in the court of the Pisans in all cases and deeds and trespasses that we can say or think of, but excluding fiefs and *assises*[7] and

---

[1] Tafel–Thomas i. 88.   [2] See above, Ch. 8, pp. 222 ff.   [3] Above, pp. 239, 244.
[4] Müller, no. 11, p. 14. The possessions of Pisa in Acre were later (1182) enlarged by Baldwin IV (ibid., no. 19, p. 23).
[5] Ibid., no. 23.   [6] *Scapuli vel burgenses*. See above, Ch. 8, p. 246 n. 88.
[7] 'Assisia' here means an amount of money or income assigned on a lord's monopoly, like market or gate-customs or port revenue.

what is connected with them. In the latter they should be judged in the court of the lords.

Clearly, *burgenses* meant Pisans who were permanent inhabitants of the kingdom or had possessions therein. Their property consisted of burgage-tenures as opposed to fiefs or rent-fiefs which were judged by baronial or royal courts. But whereas there was a convenient solution for legal questions connected with the Pisans and their property inside their own quarter, the problem became complicated if a Pisan left and settled outside its boundaries. His property there was not held from the commune but from the lord of the city, unless—an additional complication—the quarter in which he settled belonged to another commune. Did the Pisan carry his status with him and could he impose it on his possessions outside his national quarter? Even the more than generous privilege of 1187 put a restraining clause, stating: 'from the houses of the Pisan burgesses outside the lordship (*extra honorem*) of the Pisan commune, the king will be allowed to receive a *taille*, if he receives it for the commune of the city of Tyre.'[8]

The privileges and properties held by Pisans in Tyre were drastically curtailed a few years later (1193) by Henry of Champagne, the ruler of the kingdom. A harsh order limited the number of Pisans allowed to stay in Tyre to thirty and implicitly abolished the privileges granted by Conrad of Montferrat. In addition, Henry of Champagne created a direct link between property and the legal standing of the Pisan nationals. 'If any Pisan should hold from me a *burgesia*, either he will renounce the *burgesia* which he holds from me and henceforth will be as free (*liber*) as other Pisans, or, if he wants to hold the *burgesia*, he will be obliged to me like other burgesses.'[9] Pisans should accordingly abandon their possessions outside their quarter or they would henceforth be held from the lord of the city, as that of other Frankish inhabitants. The Pisans would not carry their privileged status outside their own quarter.

Complications also arose the other way round. Such was, for example, the case of the Pisan parish church in Acre. After lengthy litigation Bishop Theobald agreed and confirmed its ecclesiastical privileges, safeguarding his property rights to the land on which the Pisan church of St. Peter was built, as well as to the land on which they built the tower of their *vicus*. For

[8] On the Commune of Tyre see H. E. Mayer, 'On the Beginnings of the Communal Movement in the Holy Land: The Commune of Tyre', *Traditio* 24 (1968), 443 ff.

[9] Müller, no. 37, p. 60.

the former the consuls were to pay a recognition quit-rent (*nomine censu*) of 4 besants, for the latter 12 besants a year.[10]

The problem of mixed litigation about property continued to occupy even the rulers of Cyprus. Henry II's Lusignan privilege of 1291 which accorded tax exemptions to the Pisans, despite the rather pompous announcement that the consuls had the right 'far portare bastone', contained a limiting jurisdiction clause which stated 'salvo di facto di giustitia et di borgesia'.[11] Of the Pisans' organization of their administration little is known except the fact that in 1286 they kept registers of their court proceedings.[12]

Far more can be learned from other communes. An excellent example of the difficulties created by the differences between the legal status of person and their properties is exemplified in the lawsuit of the Genoese against the Lady Agnes Gastaldi in 1212.[13]

Whereas there is little material for Genoa and Venice in the twelfth century, we are in a better position for the thirteenth. The most remarkable document in our context is the treaty between Genoa and the lord of Tyre, Philip of Montfort, dated 1264, after the expulsion of the Genoese from Acre.[14] Their rights of jurisdiction were clearly expressed in the following terms: 'quod commune Ianue habeat in Tyro de suis predictis Ianuensibus et *burgesiis* infra suos confines curiam liberam criminaliter et pecunialiter.'[15] In the extensive territory now given to the Genoese they had complete freedom to build, but not more than two-storey buildings and no fortifications.[16] As the new treaty had to ensure the monopolistic standing of Genoa in Tyre, thereby replacing the former position of the Venetians, the lord of the city obliged himself not to create enemy or competing territory in the city: 'Et quod dominus Tyri non possit dare hoc, quod sibi remanet de *barrigisia*, communitatibus, nec frareriis pro hospitando, neque pro alia re facere.' *Barrigisia* is a strange expression but from the context it refers to city land, as burgage-tenure was its legal particularity. To prevent complications resulting from the difference between the position of men and land, the lord of Tyre stipulated: 'Et

[10] Ibid., no. 52, p. 82–3.
[11] Ibid., no. 73, p. 108.
[12] Ibid., p. 105: 'prout in actis curie Pisane in Accon dicitur plenius contineri'.
[13] See above, Ch. 8, p. 239.
[14] See Prawer, *Histoire* ii. 371 ff.
[15] *AOL* ii. 225 ff.
[16] Ibid. 227: 'usque in duobus solariis tali modo, quod ipsi non possint facere turrim nec aliud quod petineat ad fortalicium'. All the following quotations are from the same text.

quod si commune Ianue, vel aliquis de predictis Ianuensium vult extra ruam predictam emere aliquod edificium, vel aliquid ubi possit edificari, quod ipsi non possint facere sine voluntate domini Tyri.'

How the communal administration dealt with its city property is clear from the Genoese inventories in Acre of 1249.[17] In addition to the property held for the use of the commune or leased for the time of the *passagium*, the commune had a special register, which clearly indicated its contents: 'Incipiuntur census qui annuatim redduntur et solvuntur ... de domibus et haedeficiis positis et hedeficatis super *burgensiam* et in rugam communis Ianue et etiam *rocognoscimenta*, quae redduntur communi de hedificiis.' *Burgensia* obviously corresponds to the *barrigisia* of the Genoese privilege in Tyre of 1264. The payments differed appreciably from house to house, but we are not clear whether this was the result of the difference between real rent and recognition payments. Only in two cases does the inventory state clearly: 'pro recognoscimento annuatim'. This refers to 7 and 4 besants, small payments, but even smaller ones (1, 2, and 3 besants) were paid in other cases. A special item is houses: 'quae solitae erant reddere censum et modo liberae sunt',[18] because they are used by the commune. But there was also a strange enclave of four houses, which 'quamvis sint in burgensia et ruga Ianuensi, liberae sunt et nihil dant, nec sunt de communi.' These should probably be classified as *francs borgesies* once bestowed by the lord of the city, or by the commune.

Even more detailed is the information from the Commune of Venice. Here we find procedures with which we are familiar from Crusader lordships.

If anybody wants to buy a house in our third of the city, he should, and there is a custom that he should buy in our court. And in the purchase of a house there should be given by the buyer to our court 3 besants. The notary who drafts the act of sale, will have a quarter of a besant and a similar quarter will be for the *plazarius* from the buyer.[19]

At that time the Venetians, asserting their standing, went one step further and imposed on everyone who lived in their quarter, or simply bought a house there, a regular oath of fealty to the commune.[20]

Whereas the jurisdiction of the communes over property in their quarters was in many cases justified by their privileges (as some of these could have been interpreted as creating lordships), this was different for

---

[17] *AOL* ii. 213 ff. Cf. above, Ch. 8, p. 237.   [18] *AOL* ii. 221.
[19] Tafel-Thomas ii. 361. Cf. above, p. 280.   [20] Ibid. ii. 360–1.

other powerful factors in the kingdom, especially the Military Orders. The Orders acquired large landed estates, which also included property, parcels of land, gardens, and homes in cities.[21] This created a complex problem as to the legal status of their property, and indirectly as to the legal nexus between these powerful ecclesiastical corporations and the kingdom.

As far as we have been able to ascertain, apart from the earlier oath of the Orders to the Patriarchs of Jerusalem which may be open to a different interpretation as to its practical implications, there was no feudal or other oath that legally linked the Orders to the suzerainty of the king of Jerusalem.[22] This obviously created, theoretically at least, a problem as to the rights of the Orders over the land in their possession and its inhabitants. There is not much doubt about their landed estate in the countryside. The villages and villagers that belonged to the Orders were under their jurisdiction, as they were under the jurisdiction of the lay lords of the kingdom. When an ecclesiastical establishment settled new villages with Frankish inhabitants, the process went one state further. In a well-attested case, like that of Mahumeria[23] (el-Bira), the new settlers took a formal oath of fealty to the canons of the Holy Sepulchre. To all intents and purposes the canons were the *seigneurs justiciers* of the settlement and its inhabitants.

The rights of the canons of the Holy Sepulchre over the settlers of their villages can give us a clue to the solution of our problem. Theoretically, property of ecclesiastical establishments was held in *frankalmoign*. Free as *frankalmoigns* were, they were still tenures held of the Crown or of lay lords. Had the overlord any rights in such property? The large number of alienations, leasing, renting, and parcelling of these properties, would point to complete and unrestricted freedom. Whatever the legality of such transactions, once an estate was given to a Frankish lay lord or to an ecclesiastical establishment, the Crown or overlord accepted the fact of having created a kind of lordship, unless the estate retained the status of a fief in the *mouvance* of the lordship. Notwithstanding, many lordships which should have been in the *mouvance* of the Crown became actually independent lordships.[24]

---

[21] Riley-Smith, *Knights of St. John*, pp. 421 ff.; H. Prutz, *Die Besitzungen des Deutschen Ordens im Heiligen Lande* (Leipzig, 1877).

[22] Prawer, *Latin Kingdom*, p. 269. My colleagues J. Riley-Smith and J. Richard have kindly confirmed this assumption.

[23] See above, Ch. 5, pp. 126–7.   [24] Prawer, *Latin Kingdom*, p. 129.

The problem was different in the cities. The physical factor of compactness, the ease with which the lord and his administration could supervise city property, and finally the presence of the High Court or baronial court, if the city property was part of a fief, or of the Court of Burgesses competent in burgage-tenures, created different conditions. Yet, despite such obvious restraints, we can actually witness a process of evolution, or rather of usurpation. This was probably the result of the growth and the increasing importance of city properties possessed by ecclesiastical establishments. Through royal gifts (in the three main cities Jerusalem, Acre, and Tyre), or through donations of individuals, their property grew enormously. Moreover, the revenue from their landed estates and, no doubt, money gifts of rich pilgrims, allowed them to buy up city land. One even has the impression that some preferred city property and the income from it to the administration of estates in the countryside.[25]

In time the purchase of city land took a particular turn. The ecclesiastical establishments, especially the Military Orders—and for that matter also the Italian communes—tried to concentrate their possessions in compact areas. This was certainly convenient for administration, but it brought with it other results. Though we are best informed about thirteenth-century Acre, this situation already existed in the twelfth century. We refer to the existence of *vici* or quarters, which belonged to the Military Orders. A compound such as that of the Order of St. John in Jerusalem, and even more the quarters of St. John, the Templars, and the Teutons in Acre, were to all purposes independent ecclesiastical lordships, though this was never officially expressed.

It seems, then, that the situation was different in the early period of the kingdom. The kings of Jerusalem and lords of the capital were emphatic when making their donations to churches. We saw King Fulk of Anjou in 1138 insisting on the 'iustitia regali, quam rex debet habere in helemosina, quam ipse dat sanctae ecclesiae' and this was respected as late as 1155.[26] We do not find any similar utterances in the later period, unless we refer to a general rule prohibiting the holding of burgages by ecclesiastical

---

[25] Delaville, no. 422; *Regesta*, no. 492. On the Hospitallers' attempt to acquire land in the vicinity of St. Stephen's Gate (near the church of St. Anne) in Jerusalem, see above, Ch. 10, p. 274.

[26] Rozière, nos. 32 and 53; *Regesta*, nos. 181 and 309. Cf. above, Ch. 11, p. 299, with a similar stipulation of Baldwin III for Acre.

establishments.[27] On the contrary, all goes to show that things moved in the opposite direction.

One of the characteristic features of a burgage-tenure was that its tenant, though he could lease it even in perpetuity, was not allowed to become its *seigneur justicier*. 'Cens sur cens n'a pas lieu' was the sacrosanct axiom; hence the creation of *bail à rente*, which assured to the original tenant income, but no seignorial rights. The latter remained with the authority which theoretically created the burgage-tenure.

This left a legal loop-hole for one type of property, the *frankalmoign* or tenure-in-alms. Ecclesiastical establishments created fiefs without opposition, as this did not diminish the non-existent rights or revenues of the overlord. Would such a procedure be tolerated in city land? We have already seen that this was not so until the middle of the twelfth century. The lord of the city, making gifts to a church from his city land, explicitly safeguarded his rights as overlord. At what point a change occurred is not clear. It might have been as early as the seventies of the twelfth century, when central power was declining,[28] or at the beginning of the thirteenth century, when the capital moved from Jerusalem to Acre and the compounds of the Military Orders (and in their wake other ecclesiastical establishments) became so many independent lordships inside the city, vying with the Italian and Provençal communes and even creating autonomous markets inside their compounds, like the Templars and Hospitallers.[29]

An analysis of the relevant documents reveals that the earliest dates back to 1178 in Jerusalem.[30] The property in question belonged to the Order of St. John, near the New Gate in the quarter of Beaucaire[31] on Mt. Zion inside the walls. In this area, near the Armenian quarter, the Hospital

[27] *Livre au Roi*, ch. 43: 'nules borgesies . . . qui soyent ès devises dou roy, ce est en sa terre ni en la terre des ces homes, ne peut etre doné à yglise ne à religion.'

[28] See above, Ch. 2, pp. 35 ff.

[29] Prawer, *Latin Kingdom*, p. 412, n. 144.

[30] Delaville, *Archives*, no. 47, pp. 136–7; *Regesta*, no. 558. Cf. also above, Ch. 10, p. 281 n. 70.

[31] Delaville, loc. cit., pp. 136–7: 'in vico qui dicitur Belcarii, juxta muros civitatis prope Portam Novam'. We follow here the commonly accepted identification of F. M. Abel, *Jérusalem nouvelle* ii. 945. Accordingly this was a Provençal quarter of Beaucaire, corresponding to the Zion Gate (the medieval one was more to the south). Abel explains the presence of the Provençals as the result of the capture of Jerusalem in 1099 by Raymond of St. Gilles, who actually attacked and penetrated the city in that part of the walls. The archeological excavations of this area conducted during 1976–7 have changed our views considerably on this area in the Crusader period. Unfortunately, the results are not yet published.

owned considerable property.[32] Several houses, we learn, were held here—no doubt as burgage-tenures from the Hospitallers—by one John son of Fulk. He sold them for 97 besants to one William 'Baptizatus' of Blanchguard. The Hospitallers sanctioned the transaction, keeping for themselves the pre-emption right (paying 1 besant less), but above all: 'Vendant vel invadient cui voluerint, salvo *iure et censu* Hospitalis, exceptis militibus et ecclesiis'. Clearly enough, the Hospitallers regard themselves as *seigneur justicier* over this property. This is even more clearly corroborated by the statement: 'De hac autem vendicione recepimus bisancios II et solidos II.' The payment of 2 besants and 2 *sous* is precisely the *ius regis* for *saizine* in transactions in *borgesies* in Jerusalem in 1175.[33]

Nine years later we face a more complicated situation, this time in Acre. A deed of 1184 connected with the Court of Burgesses in that city[34] confronted the rights of the king, of the Order, and of the tenants. A house, held as a *censive* from the Hospital, was pledged by its tenant to another burgess. The debtor died and the creditor recompensed himself, after receiving the agreement of the deceased's family, by formally buying the house for the sum owed to him by the deceased. This did not yet warrant his coming into his new possession and he had to ask for the consent of the Hospitallers. The Order agreed, but limited the buyer's rights (or liberty) of alienation[35] by assuring to itself the former *cens* and guarding its pre-emption right for 1 mark less. The liquidation of the debt and the confirmation of the new tenant are included in the same charter of Roger des Moulins, Master of the Order. The sequestration of the house for the debt of 223 besants was confirmed by the Order 'necnon eciam regalis curie judicio'. The deceased's relatives, his wife, and children agreed to it 'in regali assidens curia'. As to the whole transaction, which also included the Order's agreement to receive the new tenant, our document is the most explicit for the twelfth century: 'Hoc autem est actum . . . apud Accon, in curia regis, in presentia et testimonio Giliberti de Florio, vicecomitis Acconensis, Guillelmi de Furchis, Rainaldi de Trechis, Anselmi Lucensis, Reimundi camerarii, Bernardi de Templo, Odonis de Conchis juratorum curie regis.'

---

[32] Delaville, loc. cit., pp. 136–7, 'et ipsas domos eis datas a nobis dividit via quedam'. Cf. also Hospitaller property in this area in 1175 (*Regesta*, no. 534).

[33] Delaville, *Archives*, no. 34, p. 120; *Regesta*, no. 534: 'et rex inde habuit de jure suo II bisancios et II solidos'. Cf. above, pp. 280 and 319.

[34] Delaville, no. 663 (i. 445–6); *Regesta*, no. 640. Cf. also deeds of 1179, above, Ch. 10, pp. 283 f.

[35] Delaville, loc. cit., 'exceptis viris militantibus et religiosis'.

There is a similar document of Hospitaller origin.[36] It deals with a burgage-tenure in Jerusalem which paid 3½ besants *de censu* a year to the Order.[37] The original act recording the sale is not extant, but the charter of the Hospitallers confirms it as well as the new tenant. The latter is entirely free to dispose of his tenancy, safeguarding the pre-emption right of the Order (for 1 besant less), the annual *cens*, and the rights of the Order. For the authorization of the sale ('ex hoc empcione et concessione') the Order received 2 besants and 2 *sous*. The list of witnesses begins with six from the Order followed by the signatures of nine burgesses, introduced as 'de juratis'. The payment is received by the Hospitallers, who are the *seigneurs justiciers* and this time they stress it by saying: 'domus autem predicta est in vico S. Johannis Evangelisti *in territorio Hospitalis*'. It is the Order that authorizes the sale and accordingly receives the payment.[38]

But not only powerful factors such as the Order of St. John used its *frankalmoign* holdings to become, in some respects at least, *seigneurs justiciers*. The famous monastery of St. Mary Latin, which lost its original establishment in Jerusalem with Saladin's conquest, and like many others tried to continue its existence based on its possessions in Acre, is a good example of such development. A charter given in 1235 by the abbot of St. Mary Latin to the Teutonic Order enables us to reconstruct the legal and procedural situation.[39] The charter stated that the abbot agreed to the sale to the Teutonic Order of a plot of land near Acre, held from the monastery by a knight John Griffus. This sale, clearly of a burgage-tenure, was transacted in 'curia Acconensi'. The details of the transaction are interesting. John Griffus paid an annual quit-rent (*cens*) of 5 besants to the monastery. Henceforth this was to be paid by the Teutonic Order 'secundum usus at consuetudines regni Hierosolymitani'. One would expect that as the sale was transacted in court, the viscount or jurors would intervene, or at least would be found among the witnesses. But none appears and it is the abbot who states: 'investivimus praeceptorem [Ordinis] de pecia terre memorata, salvis Ve bisanciis'. The explanation we suggest is that the property in case was a *frankalmoign* of the monastery and the abbot regarded himself as *seigneur justicier*, who created from the property a burgage-tenure held

[36] Delaville, no. 803, p. 502–3; *Regesta*, no. 651.

[37] This was obviously a quit-rent only as the house was worth 200 besants.

[38] It is worth noting the prohibition of selling: 'ecclesiis, militibus, Surianis et aliis gentibus Romane ecclesie non hobedientibus, salvo tamen jure et censu Hospitalis'. It seems that this *vicus* was actually in the Patriarch's quarter.

[39] Strehlke, n. 80, pp. 63–4; *Regesta*, n. 1067.

from the monastery. Hence his right of *vest–devest*. The sale was transacted in the court only in order to make it public.

The same procedure is again illustrated by a deed of 1239 from the same abbot of St. Mary Latin. One John held from the abbot a vineyard paying an annual *cens* of 13 besants. With the abbot's permission the vineyard was sold for 700 besants to the Teutonic Order. The Order would henceforth pay the *cens* and the abbot excluded knights, Military Orders, and members of communes from any possible future alienation. He also safeguarded for himself the pre-emption right of 1 mark of silver less. Moreover in all cases of alienation: 'solvetis nobis de venditione bisantios III sarracenatos Syrie'.[40]

Complications in city real property reached their peak in the middle of the thirteenth century. Tenures, *cens, encensives* in the narrow streets and crowded cities of the kingdom created situations in which ecclesiastical establishments such as the Military Orders were involved in an almost insoluble situation of servitudes to each other. Moreover, the general privileges of exemption might actually diminish their income, as in a case in which a former burgage-tenure or *censive* held by one of the Orders from a secular person was given as *elemosina*—that is, free from any payment to another Order. This brought the three Military Orders, Hospitallers, Templars, and the Teutonic Order, in 1258 to draw up a lengthy agreement to extricate themselves from the legal knots.[41] Two paragraphs of this agreement are of utmost interest. The Orders agreed that if one of them decided to buy real property the value of which exceeded 1,000 besants, he would make it known to the other Orders, and if they wanted it, the property would be common: 'exceptis feudalibus et *censivis* et dominio sue domus, in quibus alie domus nihil habere possint nec requirere'.[42] Another paragraph complements the previous one. If one of the Orders were to receive in *elemosina* the rights of *censives*, burgage-tenure, or any kind of domination from property held by another Order, the grantee would sell it to a secular person[43] and consequently no servitudes would be created between the Orders.

---

[40] Strehlke, n. 88, p. 70; *Regesta*, n. 1092.

[41] Strehlke, n. 116, pp. 98–103; *Regesta*, n. 1269.

[42] 'Feudalibus' can only mean fiefs.

[43] Strehlke, n. 116, p. 101: 'si contigat aliquam elemosinam vel donationem fieri alicui de tribus domibus super *censivis, burgesiis* vel signoria aliarum domorum et aliis bonis descendentibus ab eisdem, preceptor domus cui elemosina seu donatio facta fuerit, teneatur vendere infra annum seculari persone de dominio domus, a qua descendunt predicta, ita quod domus, cui servicium debetur non possit de hoc servicio sibi debito defraudari.'

Another example of difficulties that arose between ecclesiastical establishments is attested by the deed of arbitration of Thomas, Patriarch of Jerusalem, in litigation between the Teutonic Order and the Dominican Godfrey, nominal bishop of Hebron, in 1273. In this case the house was held as a *censive*, paying a quit-rent of 2 besants a year to the church of Hebron. The arbitration decision gave the house in Mont Musard in Acre to the Teutons, who paid 500 besants for it, but who would continue to pay the yearly *cens* of 2 besants 'eodem modo, prout alie *censure* tenentur eidem episcopo'.[44]

A similar transaction took place in the episcopal palace in Acre in 1273, when the Hospitallers bought two houses from an Englishman, one Richard, for 1,700 besants. The houses were obviously burgage-tenures held from the bishop, each paying 1 besant as annual *cens*. This was to continue to be paid by the Hospitallers. Moreover, the act of selling was carried out in the legal way of a *vest–devest* when the seller handed over a ring to the bishop who gave it to the Hospitallers' treasurer.[45]

It seems quite clear, then, that the grip of the lords of the cities over tenures-in-alms, which they had in the twelfth century, disappeared some time in the last quarter of that century. Corporative bodies such as the Military Orders, and occasionally also less important establishments, parcelled out from their possessions properties—in our case burgage-tenures—over which they retained not only landlords' rights but the rights of overlordship. Yet, as far as we can ascertain, this did not include rights of jurisdiction and herein lies the main difference between them and the Italian communes. Whatever their claims to autonomy, they did not create lordships whose outer sign of independence were their own courts. In fact, in all the documents we have reviewed there was constant recourse to the Court of Burgesses in the different cities.

---

[44] Strehlke, no. 126, p. 117.
[45] Delaville, no. 3514 (iii. 296–7); *Regesta*, no. 1389.

We have followed the development of the Court of Burgesses from its obscure beginnings to the end of the kingdom, seeing how its composition crystallized, how its competence was reasserted, and how its procedure became more defined. But the Court of Burgesses as a body, and even more often some of its members, appear not only as a branch of the judiciary so to speak, but as part of a larger body, connected either with the king or with the lord of their cities. We have to keep in mind that the Court of Burgesses in a royal city is a *curia regis* and in a seignorial city a *curia domini*. The king or lord of the city can use the Courts of Burgesses for purposes other than the judiciary branch of their administration only.

Moreover, the standing of some burgesses as *iurati* not only influenced their position in their own social class, but in their city community, inhabited by nobles and non-nobles, as a whole. Though the Court of Burgesses was not competent to judge cases which did not concern burgesses and burgage-tenures, it could and did co-operate occasionally with the High Court or with a lordly baronial court. Moreover, some burgesses achieved such expertise in legal matters that they often attended meetings of the High Court.

Crusader law has it that the lord and two of his vassals were enough to constitute a legally functioning feudal court. The addition of burgesses or even of jurors of the Court of Burgesses did not then enhance the legality of its proceedings, but made its actions public and added to its solemnity. Such considerations account for a great number of acts of a purely feudal nature, such as enfeoffments or confirmations of alienations of fiefs in which burgesses figure as witnesses. We shall find them signing these privileges as individuals, sometimes as a group distinctly marked as *de burgensibus*, or even as a corporate body when they sign as *de juratis*. In the majority of cases they are simply part of the *curia regis*. The signatures of the king's officers and his nobles are followed by signatures of his burgesses. In some of these cases it is the solemnity of the act that accounts for their presence; in others it is plausible to suppose that though they were thought of as part of the *curia regis*, their presence had a specific purpose. The presence of the king in any court's proceedings (even in that of a baron) made it a *curia regis*. If the problem at hand concerned burgesses only, the court dealt with it in its particular competence, but this did not preclude the possibility that a question regarding fiefs transacted in the High Court should be witnessed by members of the Court of Burgesses. This seems to us to be a peculiar feature of the Latin kingdom, hardly paralleled in contemporary Europe.

Another aspect of the intervention of the Court of Burgesses or of some of its members is in city administration. This point, logical as it seems, deserves special stress because of the particular character of the cities in the kingdom. A Crusader city was not a burgesses' city, it was as much the usual habitat of nobles as of burgesses. Consequently city regulations concerned nobles and burgesses alike. Yet, notwithstanding the differences in their political standing, it was not the nobles, but the burgesses who participated, sometimes even took a preponderant part, in city administration.

The intervention of burgesses in some cases was the consequence of the crystallization of a notion of territorial jurisdiction. The burgesses' jurisdiction comprised the whole territory under the jurisdiction of the lord of the city, nobles and clergy and their particular property excepted. Not all houses in the city were burgage-tenures, some belonged to knights and were part of fiefs, some were *franc-borgesies*—that is, actually city allods. Both were outside the scope of the burgesses' jurisdiction, but the Court of Burgesses could have been and was used as an instance of *juridiction gracieuse*, and consequently non-burgesses were in contact with burgesses. In these conditions it was only normal that burgesses appeared as individuals on knights' charters, dealing with their city property. Where one wanted to make the transactions public and witnessed by *vicini*, burgesses could be expected. Moreover the legal barrier between the two classes was being broken not only in cases of city property. We find burgesses witnessing private charters regarding landed property outside the cities. This is quite often done, because the burgesses of a lord or king are part of the *curia domini* or *curia regis*. But perhaps another consideration should be taken into account—the special structure of Frankish society, whose area of settlement, but for few exceptions, was identical with the city area. The city was always the *caput honoris* of its lord, and quite often its houses were, so to speak, *capita honoris* of his vassals. It is our impression that the Court of Burgesses was technically the judicial instance not only for the city, but for the whole lordship, and its members were sought after to witness charters where lands dependent on a city dwelling were concerned. Obviously this did not apply to a lordship with a number of urban centres, but such cases were exceptional.

The last aspect of the intervention of the Court of Burgesses outside its strict competence, refers to the political life of the kingdom. The Latin Kingdom never reached the degree of development at which its feudal organization, except during revolutionary periods, gave place to a system of 'estates'. Its specific social structure and political organization and its political circumstances brought about a fossilization of its organization. Its central institution was the High Court. The meetings of the High Court developed into what might be called Crusader embryonic parliaments in which the king's tenants-in-chief and his sub-vassals came together; where the members of the clergy, and not only prelates who held fiefs, took part in the deliberations and where the Grand Masters of the Military Orders were present and where finally, in the thirteenth century, the burgess fraternities and the Italian communes took part in its discussions. These facts are hidden, and we venture to assert, are deliberately hidden by the jurists of the thirteenth century, but they transpire from charters and chronicles. By the twelfth century such meetings of the High Court were attended by burgesses. They had hardly any official standing here and they certainly did not represent an 'estate'. It is the burgesses of Jerusalem who often appear on such occasions and our supposition is that this may be explained by their position as the king's burgesses. It is not impossible that their standing as a part of the *curia regis* played some role in according them a place, no doubt a passive one, in the deliberations of these meetings. Under the same heading should be added their participation in deliberations connected with military expeditions. Though their voice on such occasions was not strong, we get glimpses of their presence. In such cases there might have been an underlying feeling of consideration, and perhaps some practical needs, which contributed to their presence.

The frequency and degree of participation of burgesses in all these different political and administrative activities is not the same during the whole of the twelfth century. It is our impression, though this may be an accident of documentation, that around the middle of the century, during the reigns of Melissenda, Baldwin III, and Amalric, their participation reached its peak and then became rarer and less accentuated. In the thirteenth century new political circumstances, among them a long absentee kingship put their participation in the life of the kingdom on a different level and gives the impression of a radical change in their status in the kingdom. We concentrate here on the twelfth century.[1]

We shall first analyse documents in which the burgesses appear as taking part in the administrative and political life of the kingdom. A typical instance of such intervention is a privilege of Baldwin II for the city of Jerusalem in 1120,[2] which abolished customs paid at the city gates on foodstuff brought in. This was done expressly to further the development of the capital.[3] The reform, we are told, was suggested by the Patriarch and clergy of the city and the privilege was given to the church of the Holy Sepulchre and attested by *idonei viri*. After a long list of prelates, which included the Patriarch, some nobles, and officers of the king's household, we find the signature of the viscount of Jerusalem followed by six signatures of people who are without any doubt burgesses. None of them appears later officially as *juratus*, but we see them for a long period in the Court of the Patriarch and often signing documents where burgesses or their property were concerned.[4] Though this early document does not (as will be the custom later) mark the *burgenses* distinctly, there is no doubt about the social status of the signatories. The fact that they sign together at the end of the list proves that they are here to sign as a body representative of, if not representing, the burgesses of Jerusalem. It would be academic to argue whether their signatures are here because of the solemnity of the act or because it concerned their city, and certainly it is out of the question to suppose that their signatures were necessary for the validity of the privilege. Their signatures, though, testify to the consciousness that a solemn privilege from a king to the population of his capital should also be witnessed by some of them—in all probability the most important among them. It was under one of the Baldwins that the burgesses of his capital declared a kind of non-co-operation policy. The

---

[1] For the thirteenth century, see above, Ch. 3.

[2] Rozière, no. 45.

[3] See above, Ch. 4. p. 94.

[4] Rainaldus de Pont (also de Pontibus) witnesses *c.* 1125 a grant to Gaufridus Acus (*Regesta*, no. 111); he also witnessed a donation by a burgess to the Hospitallers in 1129 (ibid., no. 140); a sale of city land in 1132 (ibid., no. 141); with the viscount of Jerusalem he signs an alienation of property by the canons of the Holy Sepulchre in 1132 (ibid., no. 160), and, again with the viscount, a dispute regarding *clientes* of the Holy Sepulchre in 1134–5 (ibid., no. 109). On another signatory Gaufridus Acus, see above, Ch. 11, pp. 306–7. Porcellus, Petrus Porcellus, or Porchet, signs the same type of charter until 1136 (*Regesta*, no. 164). If he is identical with Petrus Porcellus, then his last signature appears in 1167 (ibid., nos. 430–1). Bachelerius signed a grant to the above-mentioned Gaufridus Acus *c.* 1125 (ibid., no. 111). Willelmus Strabo (perhaps not a burgess) signs a donation of King Fulk to the Hospitallers in 1136 (ibid., no. 164). Bertinus' name appears only in our privilege.

story goes that the king imposed a fine on burgesses who would not keep their city tidy.[5] This wise measure was unfortunately taken 'sans le conseill de ses homes et de ses borgeis de la cité.' Consequently if the 'ban' of a cleaning day was announced and some people did not comply, the viscount has to be compassionate and impose the slightest punishment, 'et deit souvent pardouner ces vij sos et demy'. The 'counsel of his men', the typical feudal expression comes here to remind us that the city, like the lordship, was governed by the consent of the ruled, and, that it was as much the burgesses' business to participate in the administration of their city. The 'patriarchal' relations between the viscount, the governor of the city, and the burgesses are reflected in his position as the presiding officer over the burgesses' court.

The position of the burgesses and more exactly of the Court of Burgesses in the administration of their city also explains that they witness privileges connected with duties and customs paid at the city-gates. One such privilege has already been discussed and we may add to it a privilege of King Amalric, in which he absolved the villagers of Turchum from paying an annual payment on grapes ('de racemis suis') at the Jaffa Gate in Jerusalem.[6] This privilege of 1171 was witnessed by the constable, a *grand seigneur* Milo of Plancy, knights always found in the king's retinue, and then by the castellan and viscount of Jerusalem and four of the best-known burgesses of the city.[7]

Another aspect of city administration was the building regulations. The *Livre des Assises des Bourgeois* mentions rules allowing buildings to be erected without embarrassing city traffic by intruding into or building up the streets.[8] A privilege of King Amalric of 1174 shows him in this capacity as city administrator.[9] He defines the building rights of the Hospitallers and of the church of Sancta Maria Maior over a public road. This privilege is done: 'consilio et voluntate et laude *tocius* mee curie' and the witnesses include, besides the Hospitallers and the nuns, 'de viris Jherusalem', where we find the viscount of the city followed by a dozen of the burgesses of Jerusalem. To judge by the list of witnesses, it seems that the *curia* was really the Court of Burgesses and the 'viri Jherusalem', were the jurors of the court. There was nothing to prevent the lord of the city

---

[5] *LdAdB*, ch. 296. This episode is discussed at length in another context. See Ch. 16, pp. 425 ff.

[6] Rozière, no. 184; *Regesta*, no. 488.

[7] Robertus de Pinkeni, Willelmus Normannus, Herbertus Tortus, Willelmus Patronus.

[8] *LdAdB*, ch. 225.

[9] Delaville, no. 464 (i. 318–19); *Regesta*, no. 516.

from deciding on such matters in his baronial court, the latter being not only a court which dealt with fiefs and nobles, but the sovereign instance in the lordship. Nevertheless, the burgesses were present in such cases, and in all probability their court had a say in the decisions.

Under Fulk of Anjou we first witness the appearance of burgesses in documents that have nothing to do with cities, burgesses, or their property. A good example is furnished by a privilege of Fulk to the Hospitallers in 1136. The king confirmed the Order's possession near Beit-Jibrin given by Hugo of St. Abraham (Hebron) and himself added several villages in the area.[10] The privilege was a solemn one, perhaps because of the future plans of the Hospitallers to settle here European Franks. The charter is very detailed and stresses that the grant was given with the consent of Queen Melissenda, the Patriarch William, 'ac tocius regni tam cleri quam populi hortatu'. But this time it is not a simple phrase, because in the eschatocol, after mentioning the sealing of the charter, the king adds: 'ad prenominatorum enim donorum liberam concessionem plures, tam cleri quam *regni testes legitimi* affuerunt.' The list of clergy is then followed by that of 'de baronibus' and winds up with *de burgensibus*, which lists six signatories, 'cum aliis non paucis'. The desire to make the privilege public and solemn is also apparent in the unusual way in which it was confirmed in Nablus, where it was publicly recited.

On other occasions the burgesses are not distinguished from other signatories, but appear at the end of the list of witnesses, often immediately after the name of the viscount of Jerusalem. This can be seen in Fulk's privilege of 1138. The king received from the canons of the Holy Sepulchre the church of St. Lazarus in Bethany, to build a nunnery, and conceded instead some other landed property.[11] This royal privilege has the extremely large number of sixty-eight witnesses, enough to prove that the king and the parties concerned intended solemnity and publicity. It is interesting to note how this mammoth list of witnesses is arranged. After the prelates and clergy are listed the great lords of Tiberias, Caesarea, and Beirut, then lesser nobles and simple knights including Rohard, the viscount of Jerusalem, and Ulric, viscount of Nablus. Then: '*de Jerusalem*: Alardus miles, Hildredus, Sigerius, Humbertus cum barba, Milo camerarius, Bachelarius; *de Accon*: Meinardus de Portu, Nicolaus Dorez, Albricus, Aurentius, Rotlandus [Rollandus] Lucensis'; and finally a list headed 'de peregrinis'. But for Alardus 'miles' and Milo 'camerarius', it is

[10] Delaville, no. 116 (i. 97–8); *Regesta*, no. 164.
[11] Rozière, no. 33; *Regesta*, no. 174.

almost certain that the Jerusalemites and Acconenses are all burgesses, whom we know as witnessing many documents in their respective cities. No other reason can be given for their appearance here, than the solemnity of the privilege. Jerusalem and Acre were both royal cities and their burgesses the king's men. Besides, it seems that the granting of privileges must have been done on a special occasion, as so many people were present in Jerusalem, among them burgesses of Acre. The privilege was written on 5 February 1138 and it is plausible to suppose that this coincided with the fortification of Beit-Jibrin by the king and the Patriarch of Jerusalem.[12] On such an occasion it would be possible to mobilize so many people to witness the king's privilege. In the confirmation of the privilege in 1144 by Baldwin III we shall again find burgesses of Jerusalem.[13] The part taken by the burgesses of Jerusalem in royal administration increased during the reigns of Melissenda and Baldwin III. They sign privileges of every nature. A lawsuit in 1140, brought against a knight who exchanged his fief for land belonging to the canons of the Holy Sepulchre, gave rise to litigation which was settled by Queen Melissenda, who established peace and confirmed the former transaction.[14] Her sealed confirmation was witnessed by members of the clergy and nobility and then *burgenses*: Tosetus, Umbertus de Bar, Petrus de Perregort, Symon Rufus, Albertus Lombardus.

Baldwin III used his Jerusalem burgesses also for purely feudal matters. When Hugh of Ibelin sold several villages held as fief from Amalric, count of Ascalon, to the canons of the Holy Sepulchre, the transaction gave rise to a number of documents: the act of sale, the confirmation by Hugh's overlord, Amalric, and finally the confirmation by Baldwin III. All three documents[15] were written in Acre by the king's chancellor Rudolf in January 1155 (or 1156) and each is accompanied by a long list of witnesses. All three lists have the same structure: after the prelates, the Templars, then 'de baronibus regis' (in Baldwin's III charter with a subdivision 'de hominibus regis'), and finally 'de burgensibus' headed by Arnuf, viscount of Jerusalem, followed by the names of several burgesses. The names of the burgesses are not the same in all three charters, though some names are

---

[12] Röhricht, *GKJ*, p. 206.

[13] In Baldwin III's confirmation of this privilege in 1144 the burgesses appear, strangely enough, under the heading 'de baronibus'. After the signature of the Viscount Rohard and Sado the marshal, we find Bernardus Vacher who was a knight, and also three burgesses of Jerusalem: Gaufridus Acu, Tosetus, and Imbertus de Bar.

[14] Rozière, no. 120 (A.D. 1140) and no. 49 (A.D. 1151); *Regesta*, nos. 200 and 268.

[15] Rozière, nos. 62, 59, 56; *Regesta*, nos. 301, 300, 299.

repeated. A similar case is that of another sale of a fief by the same Hugh of Ibelin in 1158 and the confirmation thereof by Baldwin III in 1160.[16] The act of sale and the agreement of Amalric of Ascalon are signed, among others, 'de burgensibus regis'. These documents seem to have been passed in Jerusalem, as an oath was taken in the chapter of the Holy Sepulchre, but this was the only connection, as far as we can see, between the whole transaction and Jerusalem. The presence of the Jerusalem burgesses in these documents can be only explained on the basis of their growing prestige in their own city. There was certainly no legal reason for their presence. One has almost the impression that the fact of their being *burgenses regis* did enhance the legality and formality of this purely feudal transaction.

How can we otherwise explain their presence at the sale of a fief by a king's vassal, John Gotman, in 1161? To pay his ransom Gotman sold his fief to the canons of the Holy Sepulchre. On 21 November 1161 Baldwin III, as overlord of the fief, agreed in Acre to the sale.[17] The sale then took place in Jerusalem on 3 December 1161 and a charter thus dated gives the details of the transaction. But the witnesses to this charter are somewhat unexpected: the castellan of Jerusalem, Odo of St. Amand, seven knights who belonged to the small nobility of the royal household, and eight well-known burgesses of Jerusalem.[18] We have naturally to assume that the actual sale took place simultaneously with Baldwin's III confirmation in Acre. Moreover it must have been done before a feudal court, the only legal instance for alienations of fiefs. The fact remains that the charter of sale saw valid reasons to invoke its witnessing by the burgesses of the royal city.

The tight connection between the lord and his burgesses, which finds its expression in such an adjective as *idonei viri*, can be seen in an extraordinary charter by which Baldwin of Mirabel, with the consent of his overlord and brother Hugh of Ibelin, rented his village to the Hospitallers. The list of witnesses is composed of three knights and then by two sets of witnesses called: four witnesses de 'burgensibus Ramarum' and eleven called 'de burgensibus Jerusalem'. As in the former case, the transaction must have taken place in the feudal court of Hugh of Ibelin. The charter, probably written some time later, preserved few traces of this court, but added a considerable number of burgesses. Moreover, if the presence of the burgesses of Ramle can be explained on the ground that

[16] Rozière, nos. 63, 60, 57; *Regesta*, nos. 333, 332, 352.

[17] Rozière, no. 99; *Regesta*, no. 368.

[18] Rozière, no. 100; *Regesta*, no. 369.

they were burgesses of the Ibelin family, lords of Ramle and Mirabel, the presence of the witnesses from Jerusalem cannot be accounted for except by virtue of their prestige as the king's burgesses witnessing a deed passed in their city.

But there is more to be said about our deed. It is our impression that about this time (1167) the word *burgensis* began to change its primary meaning in normal usage, if not in legal language. Among the four *burgenses* of Ramle, one at least, Guillelmus Arnaldi, appears two years later as 'miles Ramatensis'.[19] This could be interpreted to mean that he was really knighted, or succeeded in being thought of as a knight, a fact not unique in the annals of the kingdom. But we hesitate to interpret it this way, because among the *burgenses Jerusalem* we find one 'Petrus Magnus de Calenzone', who can be identified with 'Petrus de Fossato', only one year earlier viscount of Kalansua,[20] 'Luvellus miles de Serre', who is certainly not a burgess, and a 'Fulco Niger', who is well attested as a knight in attendance on the king.[21] If the presence of these knights under the heading 'burgenses' is not due to a clerk's carelessness, then we would be inclined to read into the name *burgensis* a new meaning: inhabitant of a city, citizen. Such a usage became current in the kingdom at the end of the twelfth century and was continued in the thirteenth, although this seems to have been limited to nationals of Italian communes settled in the country.[22] It still remains an open question as to whether our document is an early example of this semantic change.

A series of documents passed in 1177 again show burgesses of Jerusalem participating in the king's confirmation of purely feudal privileges.[23] When John Arrabit, a sub-vassal of Balian of Ibelin sold his fief to Constance, countess of St. Gilles, the sale was confirmed by Baldwin of Ramle, his overlord, and also, in two different charters, by Baldwin IV

---

[19] *Regesta*, no. 472. Another signatory Bernardus Parmenterius signs a charter of the viscount of Nablus in 1178 (*Regesta*, no. 566). His cognomen points to a burgess origin.

[20] *Regesta* no. 426.

[21] Cf. *Regesta*, index, s.v. Niger, Fulco.

[22] In 1185 Bohemond III of Antioch confirms privileges to the Genoese in his principality: 'exceptis meis burgensibus Ianuensibus de Antiochia, Laodicea et Gabulo, quos in eorum communione recipi non permitto' (C. Imperiale di Sant' Angelo, *Codice diplomatico* ii. 184; *Regesta*, no. 659). The same in a verbatim confirmation of 1191 (*Liber iurium* i. 432–3). Cf. a privilege to the Genoese of 1205 (ibid. 522). In a privilege for the Genoese in Tyre in 1264: 'universi Januenses, filii Januensium, sive *burgenses* vel alii'. *AOL* ii. 225. In the famous report of Marsiglio Zorzi of 1243 he explains the capture of Tyre by the barons of the kingdom from the 'Lombards': 'occasione nostrorum Venetorum, qui ibi sunt burgenses' (Tafel–Thomas ii. 356). *Burgenses* can thus mean 'subjects' or 'nationals' Cf. above Ch. 8, pp. 246 f., and Ch. 12, pp. 316–17.

[23] Delaville, nos. 516–18 (i. 341 ff.); *Regesta*, no. 545.

and by Sybille, heiress to the kingdom. These two confirmations list, in addition to the noble witnesses of Baldwin of Ramle's charter, two burgesses: Robert of Pinquigni and Geoffrey of Tours. In another grant of Baldwin IV to one of his knights, Petrus Creseca, he gave him 30 quintars of wine from some of his villages (April 1178). The charter was written by William of Tyre, the king's chancellor, and witnessed by the abbot of Mt. Zion, Balian, the castellan of Jerusalem, followed by seven people of the city (the charter does not mention their rank), four of whom are certainly burgesses, and other may be assumed to be so.[24]

In one instance we see the burgesses of Jerusalem signing a royal document under the special circumstances of a military expedition. During the winter of 1178–9 Baldwin IV and the Templars were busy building Castelletum (Qasr al-'Atra), a fort to guard the Jordan crossing through the 'Bridge of Jacob'. It was here (2 April 1179) that administrative matters were dealt with by the king. He authorized a sale of the 'fief of the chamberlain' to Joscelin, son of Joscelin of Edessa.[25] Among the eighteen signatories we find the viscount of Jerusalem and burgesses of that city.

Another example of the close connection between the king and his Jerusalem burgesses is seen in a charter of Baldwin V given in Acre in 1185.[26] The king confirmed the sale of half a *gastina* held from him by a Syrian Guido Raicius[27] to the abbot of Notre-Dame of Josaphat. The sale was done 'per assisiam terre in presentia curie mee'. This privilege written by Peter, archdeacon of Lydda, the king's chancellor, was signed by the lords Rainald of Montréal-Hebron, Joscelin the seneschal, Hugh, lord of Tiberias, the chamberlain, two knights, then by Gilbert de Flori, viscount of Acre, and three or four well-known burgesses from Jerusalem.[28] It will be remembered that Baldwin V was at that time a child of six or seven and was brought to Acre (at the death of Baldwin IV earlier in the year) by Joscelin, the kingdom being actually ruled by Raymond of Tripoli. The

---

[24] Paoli, *Codice diplomatico*, no. 208 (i. 24); *Regesta*, no. 556.

[25] Strehlke, no. 10, pp. 10–11; *Regesta*, no. 579.

[26] Delaborde, no. 43, pp. 91–2; *Regesta*, no. 643.

[27] Guido Raicius of Nablus received it from Amalric in 1174 (Kohler, no. 399, pp. 40–1). He participated in a 'vue de terres' in Aschar (near Nablus) ordered by Balian of Nablus (Kohler, no. 46). He sold half his property (the other belonged to Gilbert of Nablus) to the abbey of Notre-Dame of Josaphat 'eo quod Neapolis redditus quos comparaverat Baliano Neapolis et assissiis solvere non poterat.'

[28] Robert de Pinkeni, Gaufrid de Tour, Radulf Iterii de Jerusalem, and Gautier Malpinus. The last was perhaps a knight of the king's household, cf. *Regesta*, nos. 367 and 556. As to the family name Pinkeni (many varieties) there was, it seems, a noble and a burgess family bearing that name.

Jerusalem burgesses must have come with their young king from Jerusalem to Acre. When the royal privilege was granted they were in attendance at court and witnessed the charter, though it dealt with a purely feudal matter.

These unexpected links between the king of Jerusalem and the burgesses of his capital go far to show that the legal separation of nobles and non-nobles was not as formal as the thirteenth century jurists would like us to believe. The court of Jerusalem, the feudal court, often saw in its midst the burgess inhabitants of the capital. Let us not forget that this was the *curia regis* and the king had some liberty to decide on its composition—not that the burgesses were *ex officio* members of the court, but they were members of the 'lower' royal court. They were in the king's household, in his capital's militia, and generally speaking in his entourage. In Jerusalem, where the working of the chancery was quite rudimentary, their presence in witnessing documents was accepted as normal. In time their connection with the court made their signatures a 'royal element' in charters not passed by the king, but by other lords. Feudal law was very reluctant to give them a standing in the High Court, but their testimony was accepted even by that law in several cases.[29]

The example of the royal court of Jerusalem found its counterpart in the smaller courts of other lordships. Few privileges connected with these courts are extant and do not always enable the identification of the different people who witnessed these documents. As typical we might think of a charter of 1164 granted by Gautier Brisbarre of Beirut, which, in listing some witnesses, says: 'et omnes milites et *burgenses* civitati Beriti'.[30]

If we leave the kingdom proper and look to its northern neighbours, we find similar practices. In the restitution of a property to the canons of the Holy Sepulchre in 1135, Fulk of Anjou, as regent of the principality of Antioch, says that their claim was brought 'in curia Antiochie'. The restitution was made 'habito consilio domini patriarche et episcoporum, et baronum *simulque burgensium*'. This privilege is then witnessed by prelates, nobles, Thomas the viscount of Antioch, and finally 'de burgensibus' followed by three signatures.[31] In this case we would go further than assigning to the burgesses a passive role of witnessing only.

---

[29] John of Ibelin, ch. 160, *Lois* i. 244.

[30] *AOL* ii B, no. 21, p. 139; *Regesta*, no. 395. In a parallel charter, *AOL* ii B, no. 23 we read: 'et alii complures, quorum nomina hic non sunt scripta'!

[31] Rozière, no. 86; *Regesta*, no. 157.

The *consilium burgensium* may have been sometimes devoid of any exact meaning, but we think that it was different in this case. The charter states that the claim caused an inquiry, 'quod nos diligenter perscrutantes, comperimus per secretarios et fideles testes domini Antiocheni et patriarche' and then 'reddimus eis, sicut inventum est a secretariis nostris'. As the canons possessed city property, it seems quite obvious that burgesses took part in this inquiry to establish claims to the property. It is possible that the *curia* in which this was transacted was the High Court, with the attendance of burgesses.

The principality of Tripoli furnishes another interesting case for the presence of burgesses in the *curia* of the principality. In 1142 Raymond of Tripoli bestowed on the Hospitallers a complex of properties which included, among others, Rafaniyah, Barin, Mardabech, and Crac des Chevaliers. This was done 'coram universa curia mea', 'assensu et voluntate baronum meorum et hominum', 'coram universa mea curia tam clericorum vel laicorum'. This transfer of property created a huge enclave of immunity because the Order received 'ligietatem omnium hominum, tam militum quam *burgensium*, ibi terras habentium et possessiones'. It would thus have been normal in these circumstances for the burgesses to take part in the proceedings. Their standing is described in the eschatocol: 'Hoc autem donum ... concessi ... assensu et voluntate ... testium subscriptorum', followed by thirty-eight signatures of clergy and nobility. And then: 'Interfuerunt etiam huic dono et isti *de burgensibus* testes', followed by ten names, 'et ceteri omnes quorum nomina tedium esset magis quam proficium enarrare.'[32] In a verbatim ¢onfirmation three years later, in 1145,[33] the *de burgensibus* list comprised some seventeen names. Some clauses follow the above list and the document ends: 'his omnibus donis supranominatis existunt testes barones mei et *burgenses* prescripti et insuper Petrus [chancellor] qui hanc cartam composuit.' The two eschatocols apparently differ in assigning a place to our burgesses. Whereas in the first they are clearly put as bystanders present, whose names our chancellor regards as tedious to list, in the second deed they are put on the same footing as the barons present. Legally their presence was perhaps superfluous, but on the other hand, the prince and the Hospitallers were interested in making the donation public, especially as the knights and burgesses of the ceded territories would in future be the subjects of the Hospitallers. The assent, says Raymond, was that of the barons, the

32 Delaville, no. 144; i. 116–18. *Regesta*, no. 212.
33 Delaville, no. 160; *Regesta*, no. 455.

burgesses were simply present. This was a formal distinction. The presence which did not voice contradiction was in itself a consent, even if not asked for.

In both principalities then in the twelfth century the burgesses had a larger place in political life than their official status would have warranted. Their economic standing, which was not lower than that of the simple knights (and sometimes certainly higher), the lack of an unsurmountable social barrier between classes of the same conquering minority, would go far in explaining this phenomenon. But we would suggest that the main reason lay somewhere else. The fact that Crusader society was an urban society, and the city the place of cohabitation of nobles and burgesses must have played an important role in the relative standing of burgesses in the centres of royal and seignorial administration.

Legal Sources and Legal History

14 The Evolution of Landed Property in the Latin Kingdom: the *Assise de Teneure* and the *Assise de Vente*[1]

The *Livres des Assises de Jérusalem*, the famous collection of juridical writings composed in the Latin Kingdom and in its sister state, Cyprus, deal with the different aspects of everyday life as reflected in the laws of the kingdom. Unfortunately they tell us relatively little about twelfth-century customs. The treatises were written during the thirteenth century.[2] Several *assises*, those that mention their royal promulgator or sponsor, can be proved to belong to the twelfth century, but *assises* of this kind are extraordinarily few. And from the point of view of historical research the uncertainty as to the birth-date of the different laws makes the writings of the thirteenth-century jurists almost useless as sources of the twelfth-century kingdom. It is, however, possible to reconstruct from them the customs of the twelfth century. This task has never been undertaken, and yet our whole conception of the structure of the kingdom and our picture of the life of the kingdom in its early stages depend on such evidence of the twelfth century as can be distilled from the *assises*.[3]

---

[1] This chapter first appeared as '*The Assise de Teneure* and the *Assise de Vente*: A Study of landed property in the Latin Kingdom', *Economic History Review* 4 (1951), 77–87.

[2] M. Grandclaude, *Étude critique sur les Livres des Assises de Jérusalem* (Paris, 1923), proved that the *Assises des Bourgeois* belong to the thirteenth century and that the earliest juridical treatise is the *Livre au Roi*, written between 1197 and 1205. Cf. a summary of Grandclaude's detailed study by G. Recoura, 'Les Assises de Jérusalem. A propos d'un livre récent', *Moyen-Âge*, 2nd ser. (1924–5) xxvi. 151 f. All further references as to the time of composition of the different treatises and the respective values of manuscripts are based on Grandclaude's revolutionary thesis.

[3] D. Hayek, *Le Droit franc en Syrie pendant les Croisades. Institutions judiciaires* (Paris, 1925), is quite inadequate and uncritical. Even more uncritical is N. Zygadinos, *Zur Frage des Assisenrechts (1099–1517)* (Athens, 1928). Some problems have been dealt with in Beugnot's introductions to the two volumes, but he was concerned rather with the books as a whole than with the particular *assises*. On the other hand, his *Mémoire sur le régime des terres dans les principautés fondées en Syrie par les Francs à la suite des Croisades*, Extrait de la Bibl. de l'École des Chartes, 3rd ser. iv–v (Paris, 1854), (quoted further as Beugnot, *Mémoire*) contains several important remarks which will be discussed later. There is a critical study of the *assises* as sources of constitutional history in La Monte, *Feudal Monarchy*; cf. idem, 'Three questions concerning the Assises de Jérusalem', *Byzantina-Metabyzantinica* i (1946), 201–13. On *assises* of the twelfth century see M. Grandclaude, 'Liste d'assises remontant au premier royaume de Jérusalem (1099–1187)', *Mélanges Paul Fournier* (Paris, 1929), pp. 329–45.

The scarcity of documents and the relative scarcity of chronicles written by Latins living in the East and acquainted with its everyday problems make this work of distillation all the more important.

One of the chapters of the *Assises de la Cour des Bourgeois* deals with the relations between owner and tenant. After stating that a man who is not paying his *cens* can be evicted from his tenancy, the author continues that the lord of the property can, if necessary, repair the building or put the garden to the plough. The evicted tenant will have to pay the rent due and also the cost of repairs or expenses before he can recover his tenancy. Then the document goes on to say: 'Mais se le sire dou cens esteit un an et un jor que il ne preigne son cens de celui qui la tient, la raison coumande qu'il a perdue la chose don il pernet celui sens, par dreit, ce autre couvenant il n'en orent ensemble.'[4]

This custom was, to say the least, exceedingly prejudicial to the proprietor. If he did not collect his *cens* for a year he would not only lose the *cens* but the property itself. An annual prescription was indeed well known in the Middle Ages, but it never went as far as here. In some territories (and we have to look to France for analogies) even the *cens* could not be lost through an annual prescription, and certainly not the property itself.[5]

The strangeness of this law caused the editor, Beugnot, to suggest a correction in the reading of the text. He proposed to read: *la raison coumande qu'il a perdue celui sens.* But are we warranted in changing the text in this manner? The question has to be answered first of all on the basis of the different manuscripts. In the best manuscript, that of Munich,

---

[4] *LdAdB*, ch. 105 (*Lois* ii. 76): 'but if the lord of the *cens* will not take during a year-and-day his *cens*, the reason commands that he will lose by right the object from which he takes this *cens*, if there is no other agreement between the two parties'.

[5] Cf. Beugnot's note on contemporary French customs: *Lois* ii. 76, n. *b*, and 276, n. *a*. He contradicts himself in a note to John of Ibelin, i. 63, n. *b*, where he states according to the *Grand Coutumier*, i. ii, ch. xxi and Laurière, *Institutes coutumières* ii. 266: 'il était reçu en principe, que quiconque avait joui pendant un an et un jour d'une chose réelle ou d'un droit immobilier, par soi même ou par ses auteurs "non vi, non clam, non precario", en avait par cela seul acquis la saisine et possession.' Unfortunately he did not quote the whole phrase, which runs as follows (*Institutes coutumières d'Antoine Loysel* (Paris, 1846), ed. Laurière ii. 138; ed. L. Charondas le Caron (Paris, 1598), p. 138): 'Item à ce qu'occupation suffise pour acquérir possession, trois choses sont nécessaires, c'est à savoir que la chose ne soit mie occupée par force, ni clandestinement, ni par prière, mais paisiblement, publiquement, et non à titre de louage ni de prêt.' These last words are naturally of paramount importance. The annual prescription existed in the Salic law, and later on in the Carolingian capitularies as far as church property was concerned. Cf. V. Foucher, *Assises du Royaume de Jérusalem* (Rennes, 1839) i. 162 n., and Beugnot, *Mémoire*, p. 50. See also Maitland, 'Possession for Year and Day', *Collected Papers* ii. 61 f.

we read: *la raison coumande qu'il a perdue la chose don il pernet celui cens.*[6] The MS. Venice has: *la raizon coumande que il a perdue la chose dont il en pernoit selui sens.*[7] And the same is said by the official Italian translation: 'la rason comanda chel perda la ditta casa, de la quele li perveniva censo de iure'.[8] All the manuscripts then are unanimous in describing the law. It can also be proved that the law in this form was actually applied in the fourteenth century, as is shown by the fourteenth-century *Livre du plédéant*.[9] A century later the same text, which was preserved in the *Livres des Assises des Bourgeois*, was in use in Cyprus, and the courts of Cyprus decided several questions of land tenure according to this law. Nevertheless, it seems that there were some doubts about the law and the jurist's conclusions are not as explicit and precise as we have a right to expect in a legal treatise.[10]

As nothing for the moment warrants a correction of the text, an attempt must be made to explain the emergence of the law. The only juridical opus antedating the *Assises de Bourgeois*, the *Livre au Roi*, does not mention the problem at all, and a statement of the unknown jurist of Acre written *c.* 1240 is the date of its first appearance in sources.[11] But, at about the same time that the jurist of the *burgenses* from Acre wrote his chapter on the *cens*, the feudal council of the kingdom in its capacity as a court of

[6] MS. Munich. Cod. Gall., 51, ed. E.-H. Kausler, *Les Livres des Assises et des usages dou reaume de Jérusalem* (Stuttgart, 1839) i. ch. 102.

[7] Ed. E. H. Kausler, ibid., ch. 94.

[8] The Italian translation was done from the Venice MS. and at this point is very explicit. Canciani, *Barbarorum leges antiquae* (Venice, 1783), ii. ch. xciv, and Foucher, op. cit., p. 161.

[9] *Livre du plédéant*, ch. xlvii; *Lois* ii. 276. Cf. the Italian text in Canciani, ch. xxxiii; Foucher, pp. 179 f.

[10] It would be of importance to know what manuscript was before the eyes of this Nicosian jurist. In the Munich MS. a Latin sentence finishing the chapter makes the whole paragraph incomprehensible. After stating the possibility of losing the property through not receiving the *cens*, we find 'se autre couvenant il n en orent ensemble, ou il ne le paia dedens l an et le ior: car puis peut recouvrer la chose, par dreit et par l'assise de Jerusalem'. This is clear and logical: a special stipulation or the payment of the *cens* during the year-and-day term prevents the loss of the property. But then we read: 'Quia penitencie termino transacto ius suum debet penitus restitui'. It is evident that the author of this Latin sentence misunderstood the meaning of the last French sentence and added a bizarre comment. Strange Latin sentences of this kind, as proved by Grandclaude for several chapters of the *Assises des Bourgeois*, are marginal remarks of a reader or a copyist, which Beugnot unfortunately printed in the text. The Venice MS. is free of these additions and the Italian translation here gives the very clear meaning: 'ma s'el possessor de la casa, ó giardin paga il censo al patron del censo tra l'anno et giorno, el ditto patron potrà recuperar la sua casa, etc.'

[11] Grandclaude fixed the time of the composition of the *Assises des Bourgeois* between 1229 and 1244 or, more accurately but with some hesitation, between 1243 and 1244. A large number of his proofs are uncritical but the date is correct. Cf. J. Prawer, *RHDFE* 29 (1951), 348–51.

law, the High Court, was making use of an *assise* called *L'Assise de la teneure*. That there was some connection between the *Assise de la teneure* and the law under discussion is evident from the chapter of the *Livre du plédéant* quoted above. The *Assise de la teneure* was described in detail by the two eminent lawyers of the kingdom, Philip of Novara and John of Ibelin. Ibelin, writing some ten years after Philip of Novara, said that a man whose property rights were challenged could answer in court 'que il a celui heritage eu et tenu quitement et en pais an et jor et plus et por tant en viaut demorer quittes et en pais par l'assise de la teneure'.[12] Then he went on to discuss a case in which the property was part of a *feudum* and another case in which the challenger was absent from the country during the debatable year-and-day period. In this last case the jurists did not agree among themselves, but some still said that the rights of the tenant should be confirmed because the term of a year-and-day was long enough for the return of the challenger from Europe.[13]

This last point was taken up by John of Ibelin. He remembered having heard ('et je oi dire') that this law was specially established to punish those who, having heritages in the kingdom, ran away when the kingdom was in danger and there was nobody to defend it, but on receiving good news from the kingdom came back to revindicate their abandoned property. Therefore the year-and-day restriction was established to make their claims void. What the jurist probably had in mind were events described by William of Tyre in his history of the first years of the kingdom. He complained of the general trend to re-emigrate from the country, a real flight which left the kingdom defenceless. And he concluded: 'Hi causam edicto dederunt ut annua praescriptio locum haberet, et eorum foveret partes, qui in tribulatione perseverantes, per annum et diem tranquille et sine quaestione aliquid possederant. Quod introductum est ... odio illorum qui timoris causa, suas reliquerant possessiones, ne, post annum redeuntes, ad earum admitterentur vendicationem'.[14]

---

[12] John of Ibelin, ch. 38: 'that he had and possessed the heritage quit and in peace a year-and-day and more, and therefore he should remain quit and in peace by the *assise de la teneure*'. The same comment in a slightly different arrangement, is to be found in Philip of Novara, ch. 11.

[13] 'The *Assise de la teneure* is not forced upon him, as he was outside the country and the other party was not holding the *heritage* when he saw and heard it.'

[14] W.T. ix. 19. This chapter has been unlucky with its modern translators. D. Hayek, op. cit. p. 18, understood it as decreed against those who 'left the land to fight in the ranks of the enemies of the Kingdom'. In the translation of E. A. Babcock and A. C. Krey, *A History of Deeds done beyond the Sea by Wm Archbp. of Tyre*, i. 409, the sentence runs: 'an edict providing that an annual accounting should be held'. Their conclusion on the strength of this

According to William of Tyre, this law was published during the reign of Godfrey of Bouillon. If we care to trust his chronology, it was before the attempted siege of Arsuf in 1100. But even if we do not accept this statement literally, we shall have to conclude that the *assise* belongs to the earliest *assises* of the kingdom and that it was published in the early years of its existence.[15] Later, when the position of the kingdom was strengthened, there was no need to promulgate a law of this kind.

Let us now try to explain what possible connection there is between the *Assise de teneure* and our *assise* on the *cens* as described in the *Assises des Bourgeois*. The law as stated by William of Tyre was clear, but the actual application of the law raised several questions. Generally two variants could occur. One was that the proprietor went to Europe. In the meantime somebody else settled in the place, or put it to the plough. In this case the law was explicit enough: when the first proprietor returned after a year-and-day he could not reclaim his former property and would thus be punished for abandoning the state in time of peril. The second variant was that the proprietor leased his possession. Now what would happen if the tenant would not pay his rent? It is only logical to suppose that if the proprietor was in the kingdom he would summon the recalcitrant lessee before a court and get his money or the eviction of the lessee. But if the proprietor actually went to Europe, or for some special reason did not summon the tenant before a court, the *cens* would remain unpaid. Now, let us suppose that the man who left Jerusalem came back and, after a period of a year and a day, tried to convince the court that he was the real proprietor and that he only temporarily leased his property. What should the court decide?

This is the case dealt with by the anonymous jurist of Acre. As letting property for rent could be used to circumvent the *Assise de teneure*, the courts put a stop to it by ruling that the non-collection of the *cens* during a year-and-day was a proof of, and therefore equivalent to, its

translation that a more 'businesslike basis' of administration existed in the Latin States in the East than in the feudal principalities of the West (ibid., n. 47) is inadmissible.

[15] The appearance of this law in the Christian East in different places and periods is remarkable. We know of its existence in the kingdom of Jerusalem in the twelfth and thirteenth centuries and in Cyprus in the fourteenth century. We find it also in the *Assises d'Antioche* of the beginning of the thirteenth century, from there it was exported to the kingdom of Armenia. Alishan, *Les Assises d'Antioche reproduits en français et publiées par la Société Mekhitariste de Saint-Lazare* (Venice, 1876), chs. 5 and 8, and ibid., *Les Assises des Bourgeois d'Antioche*, ch. 8. Also it seems that an *assise* existing in the Frankish Archipelago is a development of the same *Assise de teneure* (see further) G. Recoura, *Les Assises de Romanie*, Bibl. de l'École des Haute Études (1930), ch. 128.

abandonment,[16] and accordingly the *Assise de teneure* should have taken its course. The role of the *cens* in our case was more important as a symbolic payment in recognition of the tenure than a source of income.[17] The application of the law understood in this way was not only in letter, but even in spirit, in accordance with the *assise* and no doubt fulfilled the purpose for which it was established. This explains the strange custom described in the *Assises des Bourgeois*. The original law was the *Assise de teneure*, but its application in a special case when there was reason enough to suppose a circumvention of the law—leasing property to cover up the flight of its proprietor from the country—gave rise to the procedure described above.

The development of the kingdom doubtless created problems which did not occur to the first legislators. In the first place the influx of new immigrants after the kingdom had proved its viability minimized in great measure the necessity for the law. On the contrary, the law could even have hampered the development of the state. The Frankish merchant who had to go on a voyage could find himself on his return deprived of his possessions in the kingdom. This, no doubt, was prevented by allowing the signing of contracts containing clauses stipulating a two-year payment or some other guarantee for the preservation of the property of the absentee. This is probably the meaning of the words which close the chapter on the non-payment of the *cens*: 'ce autre couvenant il n'en orent ensemble', a clause which probably originated in a later period.

We have so far traced the development of an *assise* established in the infancy of the kingdom to its application in the thirteenth century. Let us

---

[16] It is relevant to quote here an interesting procedure practised in the Frankish Archipelago, *Assises de Romanie*, ch. 128: 'Nesun baron over altro: legio puo dar terra feudal over villano alguno senza alguno servixio, over recognoscimento. Et se lo dara senza servixio over senza recognition, non sera de algun valor; ma quello donator non pora revocar quella donation in vita soa.' No doubt this law aimed not only at preventing the diminution of state services but also preventing the escape of feudal lands from the princely *mouvance* by freeing them from any recognition services or payments.

[17] The cognizance role of the *cens* is pointedly expressed by Philip of Novara and John of Ibelin: 'il a heu et tenu celuy heritage quitement en pais, come le sien, an et jor et plus.' It is expressed most clearly in the *Livre du plédéant*, ch. xlvii: 'heust tenu et uzé ledit heritage ... franchement et quitement, sans nulle encensive paier, ne nulle autre reconoissance ne redevance douner ne paier au seignor de l'encensive ne à autre persoune pour luy, ne à autre nulle chose faire qui à la dite encensive atient et come de l'usage.' The possibility of paying the *cens* to the representative of the proprietor would, in the beginning, I suppose, not be accepted by the court, as it would be actually a circumvention of the law. And the same goes in the beginning for special contracts stipulating ways of preserving the rights of an absentee proprietor.

now look at the *assise* from another point of view. Its establishment was a means for the preservation of the strength of the kingdom. As such its chief bearing was not, strictly speaking, juridical; it was first of all political, and it had certain social and economic consequences. But then, say at about the middle of the twelfth century, when the *assise* had already fulfilled its purpose the state could be expected to lose all interest in it. Yet the law was not abolished. Are we to suppose that it was allowed to live on through negligence? This can hardly be the case. When we find a law discussed by lawyers in the way this one was, it can only mean that the law was alive. We have therefore to look elsewhere for an explanation. We shall come nearer to an understanding of the problem after discussing the working of another *assise*, the *Assise de vente*. The connection between these two will become apparent if we first examine certain limitations which were set to the working of the *Assise de teneure*. The relevant legal argument was as follows. When a claim based on the *Assise de teneure* came before a court, the plaintiff did not deny the year-and-day ruling, but claimed that in his case the *assise* could not be invoked. He based his rights to the property in question on another *assise* ruling the procedure of alienating fiefs. According to this, a fief, *feudum*, or a part of it, could be neither sold nor otherwise alienated except in the feudal court (*Haute Court*), and the selling thereof was conditioned by the consent of the overlord. In this way a new factor now came into play: the *feudum*. But if the property was part of a *feudum* how far was the *Assise de teneure* applicable to it? Philip of Novara said: 'Et l'en dit que aucun feis le faisoit on des fiés meismes; et après demora et torna l'assise as heritages; et se celui qui forpaisa en viaut aver esgart, avoir l'en peut'.[18] This means that the law once was valid also for *feuda*, but later it was restricted to *heritages* only, and the man who claimed that the property in question was a part of his *feudum* might ask the court to inquire into the matter.

This change in the application of the *Assise de teneure* is remarkable. No doubt some special circumstances must have caused the exemption of almost all landed property outside the cities from the operation of the law. In order to discover the cause of the change we have to go back again to the time of its origin.

According to William of Tyre the *Assise de teneure* was decreed at a time when three cities only, Jerusalem, Ramle, and Jaffa, were in the

---

[18] In John of Ibelin the last sentence reads: 'et après demora [des fiés] et torna as heritages, etc.' (the words in brackets are only in three out of six manuscripts), which probably mean the same.

possession of the Crusaders. We know from other sources that but for the small Christian garrison the last two places were almost uninhabited. At this time the property the Crusaders actually held was mostly city property. The property they held outside the cities was at best an overlordship *de jure* which the Crusaders could only hope might someday also become a possession *de facto*. Consequently, when promulgating the *assise*, the Crusaders' lawgivers could have had only urban property in mind.

Let us then consider the only kind of property available at the time, the property inside the city walls or very close by.[19] We might also hazard the guess, though we cannot insist upon it, that the name given by the law-giver to all these possessions was *heritages*, which by a process of differentiation later acquired the more definite meaning of a completely free, non-noble property: *borgesie*. These properties, according to the 'Law of Conquest' as described by Fulk of Chartres and Raymond of Aguilers, had been created incidentally. A man took as property any object he could put a sign on, thereby marking that it belonged to him.[20] The

[19] There is no document left from the time of Godfrey of Bouillon to prove a distribution of feudal lands to his followers. In some measure the scarcity of contemporary documents could account for it. But it seems that we are safe in supposing that a regular distribution of lands never occurred at this time and generally that investiture with feudal holdings was rather exceptional. In this connection we can quote Albertus Aquensis describing the accession of Baldwin I to the throne: 'Quarta denique die postquam ascendit Hierosolymam, convocatis universis, parvis et magnis de omni coetu Christianorum, requisivit de suppellectili fratris sui Godefridi, de armatura et pecunia ejus, de beneficiis cujusque militis ac praepotentis. Qui nichil se de rebus fratris ejus habere attestati sunt, sed eas in elemosinas pauperum et solvendis debitis esse dispersas; beneficia vero prout cuique statuta erant de redditibus civitatum, protulerunt' (Alb. Aqu., vii. 37). It has already been pointed out by Beugnot (*Mémoire*, p. 24) that Godfrey divided between his followers only the revenues of the cities and no landed property. The only property, as far as is known, which could be thought of as given away by Godfrey is the well-known promise of Godfrey to give to the Church several cities in the kingdom, a promise which was never executed. But in this case we cannot forget that the real, basic problem was the official standing of the ruler of the kingdom to the Papacy. Another case of investiture was the confirmation of Tancred as prince of Galilee and this case is rather typical. It was Tancred who captured the country, Godfrey simply confirming him in his possessions. Cases like this were probably the order of the day, though more frequent after the death of Godfrey than during his lifetime when the conquest of the interior was being organized. What kind of relations between king and vassal were created through such confirmations is for the moment a matter of hypothesis. We do not believe that the relations described 150 years later by the jurists of the kingdom were the original ones. We suggest that the relations could probably be likened to the relations created during the *Reconquista* in the non-feudal kingdom of Castile, and that a more definite organization was given to the kingdom only in the second or third decade of its existence.

[20] Fulk of Chartres, I. i, ch. 29: 'Et post stragem tantam ingressi sunt domos civium,

differentiation between feudal and non-feudal property, the first being held from an overlord, the other being property not burdened by any duties or payments, belongs to a later period. When the differences emerged several types of tenure became possible. In the first place, there was land held as feudal tenure with military obligations; in the second place, there was land called *borgesie*—a perfectly free property ordinarily held by burgesses. It was held of a lord and paid a *cens* or was entirely free as *franc-borgesie*.[21] In the third place, there was land held by feudatories without military obligations or any other state-service obligation. This was a completely free property, but not *borgesie*. The nearest analogy would be the European *allodia*. This kind of property completely puzzled Beugnot the editor of the *Assises*.[22] But the difficulty disappears if we rid ourselves of the notion that the Crusaders' state was a perfectly feudal state, whatever that may mean. On the contrary, it is only logical to suppose that this kind of property should have existed in the kingdom. The conquest was the work of *conquistadores* (some on a large scale like Tancred, but some also were small people, *conquistadores* of houses and vineyards) and in the early period their conquests did not need any special seignorial or kingly sanction, and no military services were attached to them. Naturally the larger conquests of later periods were brought into the general feudal framework of the kingdom; but nobody cared very much about small properties, and in this way there remained from the early period a special group of properties, held by persons of knight's rank, free from any service to the state and, nevertheless, not *borgesie*. This absence of a feudal link in land tenure, as an outcome of a conquest, could be compared, it seems to me, to the situation in the kingdom of Castile.[23] In

rapientes quaecumque in eis reppererunt; ita sane, ut quicumque primus domum introisset (ver. domum quamvis aut palatium ingressus fuisset), sive dives sive pauper esset, nullatenus ab aliquo alio fieret iniuria (ver. fieret illi iniuria), quin domum ipsam aut palatium, et quodcumque in ea repperisset, ac si omnino propria, sibi assumeret haberet et possideret. Hoc itaque ius invicem tenendum stabilierant. Unde multi inopes effecti sunt locupletes.' Raimund d'Aguilers, 275 B and 292 E. These sources have been used for other statements. Cf. Alb. Aqu. vi. 43, W.T. viii, chs. 20–1, and others.

[21] Cf. above, Ch. 9, p. 251 n. 9.

[22] The European *allodia*, he remarks (*Mémoire*, p. 38), were created 'sur des circonstances particulières . . . qui avait permis à certaines terres d'acquérir et de conserver une immunité complète. . . . Ce qu'on ne peut expliquer aussi aisément, c'est que les Francs aient transporté cette exception dans un pays nouveau pour eux, où ils etaient libres d'etablir les institutions les plus conformes à leur besoins.'

[23] In a later period it was probably the class interest of the knights that was decisive: 'et la vente meismes qui est dou fié franc, qui ne doit point de servise ne d'omage ne de redevance, est contre l'assise' John of Ibelin, ch. 249. As the state did not get any services from these

(continued)

the fourth place, there were the *borgesies* that were held by knights, but were part of a *feudum*, to distinguish them from *borgesies* held by knights, that were not part of their *feudum*.[24] In the fifth place, there were the tenures-in-alms, the *francalmoigns* found all over Christendom.

This diversity in the kinds of property and holdings will give us some idea of the development in land law from its uniformity at the time of the conquest to its heterogeneity at the time of the lawyers. This differentiation, and especially the emergence of a clear picture of feudal tenure, obstructed the working of the *Assise de teneure*. In the beginning the *assise* applied, as was logical, to everybody and to all kinds of property. But now it faced feudal opposition. The feudatories demanded exemption from the working of the law for their class of property. In law their opposition rested on another *assise*, not less important than the one discussed above. It was the *assise* known as *Assise de vente*. According to it a *feudum* could not be alienated, except through the honorial court. If, therefore, a man could not prove that he became proprietor of a *feudum* through the mediation of the High Court, or for that matter any other honorial court, and the transfer lacked the approval of the lord, the property was not considered to have been alienated and could be reclaimed. It is to this period that Philip of Novara and John of Ibelin allude when saying that the *Assise de teneure* applied in the beginning also to *feuda*, but that later on the *feuda* were exempted from the implications of the *Assise de teneure*, and the *assise* was applied to *heritages* only.[25]

The interesting point is that although the feudal claims were acknowledged, no amendment was published. The Nicosian jurist made use of this omission to defend the year-and-day holder. He stated that no

---

properties the only explanation which could account for this arrangement was the interest of the class in preserving its properties intact.

[24] *Livre du plédéant*, ch. 21: 'Borgezies qui sont esté faites par la Haute Court, si come sont pluzors maizons et jardins et chans qui sont joins as fiés; et encement rentes qui sont donées et aliénées en la Haute Court, qui se apellent de borgesie, lesquels bourgesies sont franches ou en aucune redevance au chief seignor.'

[25] We have not succeeded in establishing the time of this change, but it is probable that it happened in the middle of the twelfth century, in the period of the strongest growth of the kingdom. Beugnot (*Mémoire*, p. 38) says that when, half a century after the Conquest, there was no reason to fear that the *seigneurs* would abandon their property, and after a native aristocracy crystallized in the kingdom, the working of the *Assise de la teneure* was restricted to the *borgesie* only. I am not so positive as to the time of this restriction, but it is probable that Beugnot is correct. On the other hand, it was not the state that was interested in restricting the working of the *assise* (in this case the state could have officially promulgated the restriction, which it did not) it was the aristocracy that was interested in the limitation of the application of the law. On the state interest see further.

exception was ever published exempting specific kinds of property from the working of the law.[26] And, if an argument of this kind is voiced in Cyprus in the fourteenth century, we have to assume that the same could have happened in the Latin Kingdom.

Thus the parallel developments of two *assises* in some measure contradict each other. Both underwent a similar development, both were established in the interest of the state: one to prevent an *exodus* from the country, the other to uphold a feudal aristocracy, the mainstay of the kingdom. But, with the passing of time, the *Assise de teneure* lost its *raison d'être* and became more and more a part of the law of property. On the other hand, the *Assise de vente*, according to the social structure of the kingdom, remained an integral and decisive part of the state constitution. Why then did not the state abolish the *Assise de teneure*, or at least why did it not limit officially its application? The reason has to be sought in the interest of the state, different from the interest of its burgesses and knightly subjects.

The power of the state depended entirely on its ability to realize the services assessed on the lands of its subjects. It is true that the chief burden was placed on the shoulders of the knights, but they were not the only ones to fear state services. The burgesses were also bearing some state burdens. The *burgenses* of the cities were taxed in order to mobilize and keep up an army of *pedites* or *sergenz*.[27] Now we do not know exactly how the taxation to keep up an army of *sergenz* was organized, but no doubt the basis of taxation was first of all landed property and often other sources of income.[28] And here probably lies the reason for not abolishing the early law of tenure. The state sometimes preferred an unjust holding *de facto*, which could be taxed in any moment of need, to a legal, but absentee, holder. It was this typically medieval interdependence of state organization and landholding, the same in the Latin Kingdom as in Europe, that left its mark on the development of the law. To understand the organization of the kingdom we have to start from property relations.

---

[26] *Livre du plaidoier*, ch. 16: 'En ladite assize [de teneure] le teil n'entent que il est desevré ne excepté nulle manière de gent ne nul héritage, ne de fié ne d'autre; et se les héritages qui sont des fiés fussent en aucune manière exceptés, ou les vozissent avoir dessevrés, lorsque tant de sages furent, quant les assizes furent faites et ordonées et proprement ceste, il l'eussent especifiée l'estat desdis héritages qui estoient et seroient de lor fiés.'

[27] The list of the services of the burgesses of the cities is preserved in John of Ibelin, ch. cclxii.

[28] The only actual document about taxation is the copy of an ordinance to be found in W.T. xx. 23.

The development of the two *assises* which we have tried to reconstruct is an example of this basic fact, that property relations are not only private law but are first and foremost a part of the medieval public law.

The limitation of the application of the *Assise de teneure* thus remained an unsolved legal problem in the kingdom. The feudal jurists could argue that the *assise* did not run in feudal tenures, but the *burgenses'* lawyers could justly claim that it was never officially limited. But let us accept the point of view of the feudal jurists, let us agree with them and assume that the *assise* was not valid in *feuda*. Even in this case we shall find new difficulties typical of the organization of the Kingdom of the Crusaders. When the defendant argued in court he could demand proof that the specific plot of land was part of a *feudum* and not property with full proprietary rights. The defendant's answer relates to a very simple but significant fact that should a *quo warranto* inquest demand proofs of feudal ownership it would not be easy to find them. In some cases there might be written grants of the *feudum* to an ancestor, but this was not common in the thirteenth century. Let us not forget that even the so-called *Lettres de Sépulcre* were lost in the thirteenth century. On the other hand, from the very beginning knights and nobles owned property not held in feudal tenure, and yet submitted to the jurisdiction of the feudal court and not to the Court of Burgesses.[29] Moreover, through intermarriage with *burgenses* they could acquire *heritages* and their heirs received the whole possession, feudal lands and *borgesies* alike, without any discrimination. They had to do homage, indeed, for their feudal holdings, but homage and investiture did not enumerate their possessions. Generally only the name of the former possessor was mentioned, into whose rights the new vassal was entering through the ceremony of investiture. The transmission of entire properties obliterated the differences between the two kinds of title to land held by the same family. Moreover by infeudation an *heritage* could become feudally held property.[30]

Thus, to ascertain whether a specific plot of land was a part of a *feudum*,

---

[29] See above, p. 352 n. 24. The same existed in the principality of Antioch (*Assises d'Antioche*, ch. 8).

[30] It seems that in the Frankish Archipelago the arrangements were different. The knights could not turn part of their *feudum* into a *borgesie*, as they could not give away any part of their *feudum* without service. (*Assises de Romanie*, ch. 128; cf. 31.) But this is a prerogative of the ruler: 'Et si lo Principo far puo borgesia de feo, over parte de feo' (ibid., ch. 142). On the other hand, the ruler it seems, could not turn *borgesies* into feudal holdings. If a *burgensis* should die intestate, say the *Assises*, the prince will hold his property for a year waiting for an heir. If nobody claims the property 'sera distribuido per l'anema soa' (ibid., ch. 118; cf. 38).

or not, was a difficult and complicated matter. If there was no written privilege the feudal land could be proved by a record of the court, but records of this kind were established only in the middle of the thirteenth century. Another possibility would have been to check the claim by a land register. But here we come to the crucial fact that a land register of this kind did not exist in the Latin Kingdom of the twelfth century. There existed something which could more or less fulfil the same role, a list of feudal and non-feudal services, preserved in the book of John of Ibelin, belonging to the twelfth century.[31] It is a curious list, which needs a detailed study to establish the time of its composition and contents. Here it will suffice to point out that the list enumerates the chief seignories and the smaller *feuda* in the kingdom and their respective services. This was, on the face of it, enough to assure the services of the kingdom, but was not enough to ascertain the landholdings in the kingdom.[32] The state got its services and did not care very much about the actual state of tenures. But here it seems to us, the state made a cardinal mistake. The absence of a real land register sapped the foundations of the state: the actual size of the feudal tenures.

The difficulties of proving feudal tenure had consequences which were not only juridical. The confusion in titles of possession left a loop-hole for machinations of dishonest knights aiming at the circumvention of the law. A knight could evade the law by declaring all parts of his property as feudal tenures. As this did not involve any extra services, he did not thereby incur any disadvantage. On the other hand, all his property was now immune from the working of the *Assise de teneure*, and thus would not be lost through protracted absence. And there was another danger graver still. The kingdom, through the *Assise de vente*, tried to prevent the exhaustion of its resources by limiting the possibilities of alienating *feuda*

---

[31] See above, p. 353 n. 27.

[32] It is a matter of conjecture if a register of this kind existed in the principality of Antioch. The important chapter which dealt probably with some kind of a register is undoubtedly mistranslated from the Armenian original. It is difficult to understand what a *Carte statistique* could possibly mean in the thirteenth century. Recoura states that a land register existed in the Frankish Archipelago. This is proved by several narrative sources, but the general arrangement of this register could be learned from a case related in the *Assises de Romanie*, ch. 91. When a man loses his privilege of infeudation, his oath is sufficient to prove his possession, 'veramente s'el non se pora provar lo servixio, per lo signor so e per li suo legii li sera imponudo lo servixio segondo la qualitade del feo. Lo registro etiamdio antigo è sufficiente pruova' (*Assises de Romanie*, ch. 91). Cf. ch. 90: 'Se terra sera conceduta ad alguno, et ello non habia letere de la concession, et habia testimonii degni de fede, la donation valera a la vita del donatario. Me se par li testimonii sera provado lo servisio, la donation valera ferma a ello et a li suo heriedi de so corpo legitimamentre.'

outside the knightly class owing military services. The same result was aimed at by checking the possibilities of subinfeudation. Subinfeudation of part of a fief was possible only with the assent of the overlord and of his court. But even in this case the *fié por son cors*[33] could not be enfeoffed and the whole fief, even after its infeudation, had to continue the original services due to the overlord.[34] But a knight in financial distress could evade the restriction on the part of the seller by declaring a part of his fief as *heritage*, and he could quite legally sell his *heritage* without asking anybody's consent. Moreover, the alienation, if done in the Court of Burgesses, would give a quasi-legal standing to the transaction and a quasi-legal seal to the character of the property. The only argument the thirteenth-century jurist could advance was: 'cil qui le vent ou aliene s'en deit garder par la fei qu'il deit au seignor', which could not prevent a man intent on raising money illegally from using a ruse to sell part of his fief.

In this case again the ultimate loser was the state and the king. The property which, as feudal tenure, depended on them, suddenly disappeared from their *mouvance*. Another possibility of circumventing the law was by voluntarily letting the *Assise de teneure* take its course. Under a secret pact the seller could simply promise that he would not challenge for a specific time (year-and-day) the tenure of the land intended to be sold— for example, by not asking for the *cens*. When the time passed witnesses would be found to prove that the man held the land unchallenged, although its proprietor, being in the country, could have challenged it. This way could have been used when there was reason to suppose that somebody in the Court of Burgesses would know that it was feudal land, and, as such, unalienable in that Court. In both cases it was the state that was the chief and ultimate loser and was being impoverished.

From the point of view of the state the only radical solution could have been found by compiling a *cadastre* of fiefs. A Crusaders' Domesday book could have solved the question. But the Latin Kingdom never established such a *cadastre*. At best there was a register in the High Court which was not very effective in checking unlawful machinations, and there was a list

---

[33] The *fié por son cors* seems to correspond to the *servitium unius militis* and describes in our case a part of landed property, or a percentage of income, sufficient to entertain the military services of one man. Similar arrangements are to be found in the Frankish Archipelago (*Assises de Romanie*; chs. 41 and 31). A sub-vassal cannot infeudate at all and a vassal not more than one-third of his *feudum*. This arrangement seems to presuppose that two-thirds of the property will be enough to render the services of one knight.

[34] Cf. *Livre au Roi*, ch. xliv.

of services owed to the kingdom. In the thirteenth century there was probably a list of payments and services in the *Secrète*.[35] But the services could have been performed and the eventual payments paid while the might of the kingdom based on feudal property was being hollowed from within. Naturally the consequences were not seen at once. The knight who sold a part of his fief and got liquid capital could, for some time, quite easily perform his obligatory duties. But some while after the transaction, or a generation later when his heirs had received a diminished patrimony but were obliged to perform the same duties, the damage done to the property would become apparent.

Up to the present landed property in the Crusader Kingdom has not been adequately studied.[36] We cannot, therefore, estimate the extent of the damage done to the kingdom through the disintegration of fiefs. But that the process made rapid and far-reaching progress we can learn from the kingdom of Cyprus, some years after the fall of Acre.

The kingdom of Cyprus was the heir to the Latin Kingdom in its institutions and organization. Therefore some of the problems confronting the Latin Kingdom could also be found on the island kingdom. One of its problems we have described. But in Cyprus they found a radical solution. It was Henry II Lusignan who apparently took an unusual interest in the conditions of property in his kingdom and in the situation of his subjects. An inquest of *borgesies* held by the clergy deprived the owners of their possessions. This was an attempt to apply a law disregarded in the Latin Kingdom. Rules as to alienation of the *borgesies* were re-established; and, in 1297, we are told by the anonymous jurist from Nicosia, that King Henry, the son of Hugh,

coumanda que tous les heritages qui estoient de fiés fussent especefiés et par preveliges et par Segrete et par toute autre maniere, et furent mis par escrit. Lesqués se troverent pluisours desdis heritages, que tout l'eritage estoit dou fié; et autre que la moité estoit dou fié et l'autre moité de la bourgesie. Et fu doné à la court, à ce que la court ce deust prendre bien garde de non soufrir que teil heritage de fié ce puisse aliener que en la Haute Court.[37]

It was only this radical solution, the exact specification of the composition of fiefs, a measure which must have looked like a revolution, that stopped their potential decomposition. And this measure accomplished also the amendment in the procedure of an old law of 200 years standing, the old *Assise de teneure.*

---

[35] The *Secrète* had in fact larger competences, See above Ch. 6, pp. 190–2.
[36] See Riley-Smith, *Feudal Nobility, passim.*
[37] *Livre du plédéant,* ch. xvi.

15 The Sources and Composition of the *Livre des Assises des Bourgeois*[1]

The *Livre des Assises des Bourgeois* has existed in print in an Italian translation rendered by order of the Republic of Venice since 1535. Despite its early printing, it never reached the fame or popularity of other books of jurisprudence produced in the Latin Orient. Other legal treatises created in the Latin Orient and regarded as an expression of 'pure feudalism' or as representatives of French law between the eleventh and thirteenth centuries were often quoted and commented on by savants, scholars, and even by law practitioners of the *ancien régime*. It was only at the end of the eighteenth century, just a few years before the French revolution, that the manuscripts of the *LdAdB*, that is to say the French manuscripts of the text, were found in the archives of Venice and some time later, in the Munich archives. Their publication was delayed for a curious reason—the publication of the *Code Napoléon*. The jurist Agier, future president of the court of appeal in Paris, who proposed, as early as 1788, to publish the *LdAdB* together with other books of jurisprudence of the Latin Orient, wrote in 1806: 'By now these books have no other use but for history; and from this point of view I do not find it interesting enough to devote my time to a work which in itself is not very attractive.'

When the law practitioners' interest was waning, historians found it immensely interesting, partly in order to study the law of the Latin Kingdom in itself, and partly as a source of the customary law of France. And thus, all of a sudden, a text, which had been neglected for many centuries, became the subject of three almost simultaneous publications. In 1839 Victor Foucher, published the Venice MS. accompanied by the official Italian translation; in 1840 E. H. Kausler published the text of the Munich MS. together with that of the Venice MS. and in 1843, on behalf of the French Academy, Beugnot published an edition which was regarded as a definitive and critical edition. The latter was based on the Venice MS. which was 'corrected' by the Munich MS. This edition was used during the whole of the nineteenth century, and a good part of the twentieth, as

---

[1] An earlier version of this chapter appeared as 'Étude préliminaire sur les sources et la composition du *Livre des Assises des Bourgeois*', RHDFE (1954), 198–227, 358–82.

the basis for dealing with the Latin Orient or with French customary law. It was only in 1923 that Maurice Grandclaude, in a thesis which became a classic, proved the poor quality of Beugnot's edition. At the same time he proved that the accepted dating of the *LdAdB* was mistaken.

We can summarize the different opinions and evaluations of the *LdAdB* as follows. For the ancient historians it represented the official collection of the *Assises des Bourgeois* promulgated by Godfrey of Bouillon and his successors. Later on it was regarded as the reconstitution of the original *assises*, which became necessary when the famous *Letters of the Holy Sepulchre* were lost with the fall of Jerusalem into the hands of Saladin. Finally, the *LdAdB* was divested of its official dignity and relegated to the modest rank of a private law treatise written by a jurist in Acre between 1240 and 1244. Nevertheless, its historical importance is not diminished. The *LdAdB* is the only legal treatise on the judicial practice of the courts of the viscounts. It is also the only one from which we can learn the law and procedure which ruled the burgesses of the kingdom in the thirteenth and, no doubt, also during the twelfth century.

From the beginning, the basic question which faced historians, and especially historians of law, was to find which European sources, or more exactly French sources, were used in the composition of the *LdAdB*. This question actually has two different aspects which were not immediately distinct and even today are not clearly established. On the one hand we have to know (a) what were the sources of the *law* of burgesses and, on the other, (b) what were the sources used by the author of the *LdAdB* when he wrote his treatise in the middle of the thirteenth century. It is not surprising that the two questions were confused, considering traditional opinion, which regarded the *LdAdB* as an official or a semi-official collection of the laws of the kingdom. But once the *LdAdB* was recognized as a private treatise of law, it was only natural to split the problem of sources into two different questions. This does not mean that there should be a basic difference between the laws current in the kingdom and the laws presented by our treatise. This is a problem which still needs to be studied. The problem was to find out whether the author of the *LdAdB* was inspired by a literary model for his treatise. As far as we know, only H. Prutz, M. Grandclaude, and more explicitly H. Mitteis have approached the problem in this particular way.

The question of the origin of the law of burgesses gave rise to a large number of answers. One can find the *Leitmotiv* of these answers summarized in the title of Foucher's edition, 'The Assises of the Kingdom of Jerusalem compared with each other, as well as with the laws of France, the Capitularies, the Établissements of St. Louis, and the Roman Laws'. Crusader society, Beugnot maintained, 'offered, in a restricted frame, the image of the whole of Europe, because every region contributed to its formation', and the French preponderance in the Crusader armies exactly reflected the position of France in European culture at the end of the eleventh century. Consequently, studies of the *LdAdB* attempted to distinguish the various contributions which came from different European customs and more precisely from French customary law. The references to the customary law in Beugnot's edition were with Foucher a real flood of extracts and quotations from Roman law, the *Leges barbarorum*, and French customary law.

The idea of French customary law ruling the kingdom, an idea based on the accepted image of Crusader society, overshadowed the whole study of the law of burgesses and directed research into a blind path. One has the impression that historians felt the necessity to find a unique source for the *LdAdB*, but failing that, they consoled themselves by accumulating examples and analogies, which were sometimes very far fetched indeed. There were two exceptions to this general line of research: H. Prutz, who found Roman elements in the *LdAdB*, and wanted to explain them by assuming the reception of Byzantine-Roman law still in force among the native population of the country conquered by the Crusaders, and L. A. Warnkönig, who was perhaps the first to have some inkling of the truth when he declared this Roman law to have been imported from Europe, although he could not point to any definite source or to the ways and means of the transmission. Beugnot, who finally influenced all the research, was never very positive or decisive in the opinions he pronounced. In his introduction to the *LdAdB* the problem was lost in a cloud of natural law in which almost any opinion could find satisfaction.

As for the *LdAdB* seen as a literary treatise, distinct from the law it purposed to describe, the difficulties were even greater. Since the treatise was assigned to the twelfth century (before Grandclaude assigned its composition to 1229–44), no one thought to compare it with contemporary legal treatises. It is true that it was only after Beugnot's publication that many of the twelfth-century treatises, until then entirely unknown or known only from the monumental work of Savigny, were printed and became accessible to scholars. And yet the true source of the *LdAdB* was already in the hands of C. Giraud in 1835, eight years before Beugnot's publication. In 1838 Giraud even published a single chapter from that source. Unfortunately this was published in a book in which one would hardly look for medieval law—*Recherches sur le droit de propriété chez les Romains* (Aix, 1838). And it was Giraud, again in a study published in 1843, who affirmed a connection of this source with the *LdAdB*, but like many of his contemporaries, he honoured the Crusader jurists, who, as representatives of progress had 'influenced the French law of the continent'.[2] Somehow Giraud did not see that the source from which he published a single chapter contained almost 60 per cent of all the materials included in the *LdAdB*. Giraud's brief remarks passed unnoticed and when, at the beginning of the twentieth century, two German scholars published the translation of the text known to Giraud, the latter's study was unknown to them, as it remained unknown to the historians of law who commented on the new publication.

These brief remarks suffice to summarize the main lines of research of the *LdAdB*. If we now return to this problem, adding thereby to the very long list of studies which has dealt with the *LdAdB* since 1806, it is because we believe we have found the major source which served the author of the *LdAdB*.[3]

While preparing a study of the burgesses of the Latin Orient, we found some obscurities in the *LdAdB* regarding the laws of marriage. A former study of this problem had already pointed to difficulties in the interpretation of the twenty-five chapters of the *LdAdB* devoted to this problem. These chapters, which form a kind of *opusculum: De pactis de matrimonio*, are interpolated by a chapter written in Latin and taken from canon law. To this *opusculum* have to be added some other chapters (*de testamentis*), which deal with relevant subject matter. Whereas the first part of the *opusculum* basically presents a *régime dotal*, the second part is that of community of property (*régime de communauté*). The two parts are not contradictory, and except for some ambivalent expressions, the two systems seem to have coexisted. In other words, we are facing a specific legal situation in which the system of the Roman dowry was overlaid by a system of partial community of property. Such a phenomenon is quite well known in the *pays de droit écrit* in France, as well as in some regions of Spain and Italy. The *LdAdB* also noted the liberty of alienation of the *dos* by the husband with his wife's consent. As we have never found a

---

[2] The text was discovered by Raynouard who used it in his *Dictionnaire de la langue des troubadours*. He drew Giraud's attention to this text. Cf. *Revue de législation* iii (Oct. 1835), 52, and C. Giraud, *Recherches* i (Aix, 1838), 142 ff.

[3] See the bibliography of the *LdAdB* in Appendix B, below, pp. 408–9.

renunciation of the *Senatus consultum Velleianum* in Crusader documentation, we conclude that the *lex Julia* was in force in the Latin Kingdom, that is to say that here we are dealing with ante-Justinian legislation, in all probability with Theodosian legislation. Such a situation existed in southern France before the thirteenth century, that is before the renaissance and the growing reception of Justinian law.

These two conclusions, drawn from the analysis of the *LdAdB*, are corroborated by a special expression: *creissement de douaire* used by the author of the *LdAdB* to describe the *dos ex marito*. This expression cannot be anything but a translation of the Latin *augmentum dotis*, so frequent in the customary law of the *pays de droit écrit* or its equivalents *excreyx, screyx, etc.*, which we find in the region of Provençal and Catalan dialects. Having narrowed down the field of our investigation we found not only a source from which the author of the *LdAdB* could have drawn inspiration and a few chapters on marriage, but a source from which he took over entire chapters and doubtless used as the model of his treatise. This source is: *Lo Codi. La somme du Code en provençal de la première moitié du XIIe siècle.*

The LdAdB *and* Lo Codi

Lo Codi, a treatise of Roman law, a *Summa* of the Code in Provençal, was written, according to its editors, *c.* 1149 in Arles. This treatise, whose influence spread over southern France and part of Spain, thus reached the utmost limits of Christian Europe, namely the Latin Kingdom of Jerusalem. *Lo Codi*, which was translated into Latin, French, Dauphinois, Catalan, and Castilian, can rightly boast that with the exception of Gratian, no other book of jurisprudence enjoyed such diffusion.

The numerous translations prove, if not its use, at least the constant interest of theoreticians of law in *Lo Codi*. We may add that on the practical level its undoubted influence is attested for the *Charte d'Arles*, the *Coutumes de Tortose*, the *Fors de Béarn*, and the *Fors de Morlaas*. Finally, there are translations and extracts in some more recent treatises of the fifteenth century, such as the *Coutumes d'Anjou et du Maine* or the curious *Lois de l'Empereur* of Bearnaise origin. Now the *LdAdB* should be added to the long list of the conquests of *Lo Codi*.[4]

We shall try to establish the correspondence between the respective chapters of the *LdAdB* and the Latin translation of *Lo Codi* as follows. As not all the manuscripts of *Lo Codi* are divided into books and chapters, we shall follow the divisions of the printed Latin text, where the editors also

---

[4] See the bibliography of *Lo Codi* in Appendix C, below, pp. 410–11.

introduced the subdivision into *leges*. The numbers of books, chapters, and *leges* of *Lo Codi* opposite the numbered chapters of the *LdAdB* point to a direct translation, even if the translation is only partial, that is if it includes only a part of the chapter, the rest being an addition of the author of the *LdAdB*. 'Cf.' marks chapters of the *LdAdB* influenced by *Lo Codi*, although there is no direct translation.

LdAdB	Lo Codi	LdAdB	Lo Codi
xi	cf. ii. 5. 1	xlii	cf. iv. 35
xiii–xiv	cf. i. 2	xliv	cf. iv. 10
xv	ii. 2. 2		iv. 69. 10
xvi	ii. 2. 3–4	xlv	vii. 26. 2
xvii	ii. 5	l	cf. viii. 41. 1
xviii	ii. 5. 2	li	iv. 3. 2
	ii. 5. 4	liv	cf. iv. 28. 6
xix	ii. 5. 3	lv	cf. iv. 35
xx	ii. 5. 5		viii. 25. 1–2
	ii. 6. 1	lvi	cf. viii. 14
xxi	ii. 6. 4–5		iv. 38
	ii. 6. 9	lxv–lxvi	viii. 38
xxii–xxiii	cf. iii. 4. 1	lxviii	viii. 25. 2
xxiv	iii. 4. 1	lxx	viii. 38. 4
xxv	cf. iii. 1	lxxii	cf. viii. 38. 3
xxvii	iv. 58. 7	lxxiii	cf. viii. 38. 4
xxviii	cf. iv. 58. 4	lxxiv	viii. 24. 1
xxix	cf. iv. 58. 4		cf. viii. 26
xxx	cf. iv. 59	lxxv	cf. viii. 25. 5
xxxi	viii. 13. 2		cf. viii. 25. 3
xxxii	viii. 25. 4	lxxvi	cf. viii. 38. 4
xxxiii	cf. iv. 61		cf. viii. 37. 2
	cf. iv. 62. 6	lxxviii	cf. iv. 64. 2–4
	iv. 62. 9	lxxxii	cf. viii. 39. 2–3
	cf. iv. 68. 1–2	lxxxv	iv. 69. 1–2
xxxiv	cf. iv. 68. 2	lxxxvi	cf. iv. 69. 15
xxxv	cf. iv. 68	lxxxvii	cf. iv. 45. 3
xxxvi	cf. iv. 68	xcii	cf. iv. 69. 11
xxxvii	cf. iv. 64. 5		iv. 69. 13
	cf. viii. 25	xciv	cf. iv. 69. 11
xxxviii	cf. i. 2. 12		iv. 69. 21

LdAdB	Lo Codi	LdAdB	Lo Codi
xcv	cf. iv. 69. 10	cliii	cf. iii. 39. 5
xcvi	cf. iv. 69. 7	cliv	iii. 31. 3
	cf. iv. 69. 9	clv–clvi	v. 1. 2–3
xcix	cf. iv. 69. 19	clvii	v. 1. 4
c	cf. iv. 69. 13	clxi	v. 2. 5
cii	cf. iv. 70. 5	clxii	v. 2. 6
	cf. iv. 70. 14	clxiii	v. 5. 3
ciii–civ	cf. iv. 55. 1	clxiv	v. 5. 4
	cf. iv. 55. 3	clxv	v. 5. 5–7
cix	iv. 57. 1; 7; 8; 3; 4; 6	clxvi	v. 5. 9–10
cx	cf. iv. 57. 6	clxvii	v. 11. 1
cxiii–cxiv	viii. 36. 2	clxviii	v. 11. 2
	iv. 12. 2	clxix	v. 14. 1
	cf. ii. 3. 5	clxx	v. 16. 1–2
	cf. ii. 3. 10	clxxi	v. 16. 13
cxvi–cxvii	cf. iii. 5. 1–2	clxxii	cf. v. 17
	cf. iii. 12	clxxiv	v. 18. 1–2
cxviii	cf. iii. 5. 1–2	clxxiv	v. 18. 2
cxix	cf. iii. 5. 2	clxxv	v. 20. 1–2
	cf. iii. 5. 12	clxxx	cf. v. 21. 1; 4
cxxi	iii. 5. 2	clxxxiii	vi. 25. 1
cxxviii	cf. iii. 12. 3	clxxxvi	cf. vi. 29. 1–2
cxxix	cf. iv. 48. 2	clxxxviii	cf. vi. 63
cxxxiii	cf. ii. 5. 5	clxxxix	vi. 34
cxxxiv–cxxxv	cf. iv. 30. 4–5	cxc	vi. 48. 1–2
cxxxvi	iv. 30. 9		cf. vi. 63
	cf. iv. 32. 3	cxcii	cf. vi. 75. 4
cxxxix	cf. iv. 32	cxciii	cf. vi. 68. 4
cxl	cf. iv. 33	cxciv	vi. 79. 1–2
cxli	cf. iv. 33. 4	cxcv	vi. 82. 1–6
	cf. iv. 33. 6	cxcvi	vi. 85
cxlii	cf. iv. 33. 1; 3		cf. vi. 80
cxliii	cf. iv. 33. 4	cxcvii	vi. 91
cxlv	cf. iv. 30. 3	cxcviii	vi. 37
cxlvii	cf. viii. 34. 2	cxcix	vi. 31. 1
cxlviii	iv. 30. 5	cc	vi. 19. 1–2
cxlix	cf. iv. 30. 3		vi. 21. 1
cl–cli	cf. iii. 39. 5	cci	vi. 20. 1

LdAdB	Lo Codi	LdAdB	Lo Codi
cci	cf. vi. 22	ccxxiii	cf. iv. 69. 5
ccii	vi. 24. 1–3	ccxxiv	iii. 11
cciii	vi. 55. 2	ccxxv	cf. vi. 4
	vi. 56	ccxxvi	cf. vi, viii
cciv	vii. 1. 1–2	ccxxx	cf. ii. 18
ccv	vii. 4. 1–4		ii. 25
ccvi	vii. 5. 1–4		cf. ii. 19
ccvii	vi. 1. 4	ccxxxiii	cf. iii. 31. 3–7
ccviii	iv. 23. 5–6	ccxxxiv	iii. 19
	iii. 40. 2–5	ccxxxv	iii. 17
ccx–ccxi	viii. 51. 1	ccxxxix	vi. 12. 2
	cf. viii. 57		vi. 11. 1–3
	cf. vi. 75. 1	ccxl–ccxli	vi. 12
	vi. 92. 3–5	ccxlix	cf. vii. 11. 2
ccxii	vi. 97	ccli	vii. 9
	cf. vi. 98–9	cclii	vii. 11. 1
ccxiii	viii. 28		vii. 10
	viii. 33	ccliv	cf. vii. 16
	cf. viii. 51. 4–5		cf. vii. 15. 1–2.
ccxv	iv. 47. 2		cf. vii. 16. 1–2
	iv. 40. 4–5	cclvi	ix. 7
	cf. iv. 41	cclvii	cf. ix. 15
	cf. iv. 42. 1–2	cclx	cf. 9. 19
ccxvi	cf. iv. 56	cclxiv	cf. ix. 16. 1–2
ccxvii	iv. 13. 4–5	cclxxvi	vii. 20–1
ccxviii–ccxix	iii. 23. 1–2	cclxxvii	ix. 4. 1–2
ccxxii	cf. vi. 26	cclxxviii	cf. ix. 24

This list clarifies the influence exercised by *Lo Codi* on the *LdAdB*, but it can be used only as a point of departure for a more detailed study of the relations between the two treatises; this is no substitute for such a study. In fact, many chapters of the *LdAdB* which we have not indicated as dependent on *Lo Codi*, because they do not represent a translation or a direct dependence, are actually developments or variations of ideas expressed in *Lo Codi*. Conversely, in chapters indicated as corresponding, the author of the *LdAdB* often has not used more than a single phrase or a single paragraph from *Lo Codi*. Obviously, the variety of relations cannot be expressed by two columns of numbers. Pending a more detailed study, it simply permits an understanding of the relations between the two treatises and the division of the subject matter in the *LdAdB*. With *Lo Codi* as a model it will also permit us to draw some conclusions as to the author and original text of the *LdAdB*.

The Author and Structure of the Livre des Assises des Bourgeois

The author of the *LdAdB* is unknown and there is no indication as to his name or origin. Moreover, the two basic manuscripts at our disposal are only copies and their particular characteristics reflect their respective copyists rather than the author of the original. Consequently, what can be attempted is more in the nature of characterization than an identification.

The author lived in Acre and wrote between 1229 and 1244, though this period can probably be narrowed down to 1240–4. There is no doubt that he belonged to the burgesses of the city, and we would postulate that he did not belong to the patriciate of this social stratum. Knowing the way in which he worked and thought, we are almost sure that he would have indicated his patrician origin if this were the case. He belonged to the middle class of the burgesses, more precisely to a group which would be classified today as a professional class. This was a class of law practitioners or people connected with the functioning of the Court of Burgesses in the city. For some time he might even have been a *iuratus* or *juré* of the court, though in mid-thirteenth century Acre the *iurati* seem to have belonged to a class of burgesses with some standing in the community; they already belonged to a class in which, as in the case of the Antiaumes, state service ran in the family, without making its members salaried functionaries. The author probably belonged to the same class of people as his epitomizer, who lived three generations later in Cyprus. The latter described his career as follows: 'Je os compli soixante dix ans d'aage, et avoye uzé en la court de la visconté quarante ans, c'est assaver onze ans juré de la court, et onze ans escrivains et le remanant de son aage estoit avantparlier.'[5] At seventy he had forty years of service in the court. He probably started out as a *scriba* of the court, before moving to the group of *jurés* and finally ended as advocate, *avantparlier,* or counsel who made his living from this profession.[6] The author of the *LdAdB* probably belonged to a similar social class in Acre.

It is not easy to say much about the man's education, or about his age when he decided to write the *LdAdB*. He must have been of mature age

---

[5] 'Abrégé du Livre des Assises de la Cour des Bourgeois', *Lois* ii. 319.
[6] On the *avantparlier*, ibid. 245.

with a long career behind him in the judicial administration of Acre. If his book was written *c.* 1240, he was probably born during the last two decades of the twelfth century. As he never mentioned any such event as the fall of Acre to Saladin, perhaps he was born after the reconquest of the city, that is after 1191. If he was ever abroad, there is no allusion to it, although he mentions a young man 'who went to schools to acquire some science'.[7] There is no doubt that he knew Latin, but his knowledge was not that of a scholar. He had hardly any of the formal legal education dispensed in the first half of the thirteenth century in any of the great centres of law study, whether in Italy or across the Alps, and his knowledge of any *droit savant* was basically that of a curious layman.

His knowledge of the Scriptures was cursory and his quotations are of *loci communes,* phrases which are didactic or moralizing, or which added, according to his lights, an element of decorum to a treatise of law. He probably learnt Latin in one of the city's ecclesiastical schools; he was possibly destined in his youth for the Church, but never ordained. His attitude to the Church and ecclesiastical jurisdiction was that of utmost reverence. In a period in which lay and ecclesiastical jurisdictions were clashing all over Europe, he was meticulous in safeguarding the rights of the Church.[8]

He knew some canon law, at least in the realm in which its decisions were binding, namely marital law. But even in this case, he was not up to date or interested in what went on in the schools.[9]

His knowledge of the customary law, of the current law of the kingdom, was that of a practitioner and not of a man with legal training. His knowledge came from many years of assistance in the functioning of the court, which was composed of law practitioners, and their knowledge of customary law. This is evident from his predilection for the minutiae of procedural law on the one hand, and from his utter inability to formulate general rules, or principles of law, on the other. He almost always deals with specific cases; lengthy dissertations on the same subject matter were split up into many chapters devoted to the accidental and hypothetical.[10] It fits in with this type of knowledge and mental make-up, that, although he had a general idea of how to organize his subject matter by following *Lo Codi,* he always strayed from the general plan and wrote in what one would call an associative track.

---

[7] *LdAdB*, ch. 215.   [8] *LdAdB*, ch. 178.
[9] See below, Appendix A, notes to chs. 176–7.
[10] e.g. *LdAdB*, chs. 33–6, 58–63, 71, 105–6, 216.

His knowledge of Roman law was superficial, but he tried hard to impress his readers with this knowledge, as he did with his Latin. Thus we find such phrases as: 'Let the *judge* know that *actor* is clamant and *reus* is respondent' (ch. 9), or about a man 'ut amicus veritatis fiat' (ch. 7). Typical again are: 'Le chose ... pecuniaires, si come est *aurum et argentum* ...; chose criminels, si com est *homicidium, periurium, furtum, rapiam*' (ch. 22), or Latin expressions which do not add much to the understanding of the law, but introduce *termini technici,* which might have impressed a layman. In one place he quotes Azo without mentioning the name of that great luminary of the legal science.[11] We doubt if he knew his *Summa* or *Brocarda.* He probably heard the expression and was struck by its comprehensiveness and simplicity and thus included it in his treatise.

There must have been a streak of vanity in our author, who shows off his knowledge of another profession, that of medicine. A lengthy chapter furnishes us with the whole lore of medical knowledge. He is somewhat suspicious of the professional *miege,* but he himself has a lot to say about diagnosis and medications. Good and bad surgery, hot and cold places in the human anatomy, diets, doctor's excuses, were reviewed in connection with a breach of contract.[12]

He had the highest regard, as might have been expected, for the judicial administration of the kingdom and took a highly moralizing tone in describing the virtues demanded of its officers. As a member of the profession, his attitude was to look askance at any infringement of the competence of the court or its jurors. Thus at a time when the Italian communes became a major factor in Crusader internal politics, he categorically states that their autonomy was limited to minor internal affairs. His attitude to the Military Orders is quite ludicrous.[13] In relation to both, his attitude is anachronistic and reflects a kind of wishful thinking on the part of a minor representative of the Crusader establishment.

This anachronistic attitude or traditionalism is also perceived where legal innovations came in to undermine his own convictions. Such a case was that of the ordeals. Officially abolished in 1215 by the Fourth Lateran council, they lingered on in Crusader procedure. For the author of the *LdAdB* the ordeal, 'porter iuise', is 'garantie de Dieu' (ch. 132) and 'dreituriere chose a toutes gens qui dreit quierent' (ch. 261). The implementation of the new prohibitions of the Church enacted by the lay authority of the kingdom is met with a fulminating protest. A royal

---

[11] See below, Appendix A, notes to ch. 156.
[12] *LdAdB,* ch. 231.   [13] *LdAdB,* ch. 144.

prohibition of the ordeal was an act against God and against the oath taken by the king.[14]

Certainly, there can be no comparison between the author of the *LdAdB* and the great legal minds of the kingdom, such as John of Ibelin or Philip of Novara, who could easily compete with a Beaumanoir. At one point, however, he was true to the legal tradition—in advising people how to advance their interests even if this did not contribute to the objectivity of law.

The original text of the *LdAdB* was not preserved: its copies are from the beginning and the middle of the fourteenth century. Grandclaude suggested that the Cod. gall. 51 of Munich, which is the older copy, was written by one André, a clerk of the court of the viscount of Nicosia in Cyprus between 1315 and 1317. This means that the copyist worked some three generations after the composition of the original text. It is therefore impossible to surmise how many links intervened between the original and the copies in our possession.

Although only a new discovery may bring us nearer to the original text of the *LdAdB,* it does not seem beyond our powers to reconstruct the original pattern of the treatise. M. Grandclaude has already suggested that the original was divided *à la romaine,* into books, titles, and laws; he saw in the Latin phrases (some of them so badly mauled that it took all the acumen and erudition of an H. Kausler to bring them back to some semblance of Latin) indications of the original structure.[15] We are less positive as to these opening Latin phrases. They may well have been the additions of a later proprietor, who, for the sake of convenience, added these phrases to make the treatise easier to use. Yet Grandclaude seems to have been quite right, that the author organized his subject matter into divisions, which roughly corresponded to some divisions in the Roman codification. Strangely enough, although we now know he used *Lo Codi,* he did not follow its nine divisions, which according to twelfth-century usage corresponded to the first nine books of the Code. In fact one has the clear impression that the author tried, and we may add very successfully so, to conceal his model. The result was, that the *LdAdB* was divided into *tituli,* but the larger divisions are not clear, and we doubt if it was ever divided into *libri.*

[14] *LdAdB*, ch. 26: 'le roi ou la rayne de cuy est la terre ne le veut laisser desfaire au iuise ou il est iuge par droit, il fait tort, et si vait contre Dieu et contre son sairement, et il meysmes se fauce, et ne peut ce faire par droit.'

[15] L. A. Warnkönig has noted (ii. 524): 'Each new subject begins with a misunderstood fragment from Justinian's legal collections.'

Although we are not sure as to the authenticity of the Latin phrases at the head of the chapters, we think that it is possible to arrive at a fairly clear idea as to the structure of the treatise by paying attention to the rubrics and the text. There are two very specific phrases in the rubrics and sometimes in the text, where the author indicates the subject matter, sometimes of the previous and sometimes of the following chapters and often of both. One such phrase is: 'Si coumencerons hui mais de dire les jugemens et tout premier coumencerons etc.'[16] 'Hui mais', more commonly 'maishui', meaning 'henceforth', indicates the end of a division and the beginning of another. The other phrase is: 'Puis que vos aves oy desus des autres raisons, drois est que vos ores la raison des... etc.',[17] or a similar expression.[18] In some other cases, instead of these two expressions, the rubric announces the matter to be treated not only in the next chapter, but in a number of chapters.[19] Following these indications, we think that the original text was not divided into *libri,* but into twenty-six parts, conceived as *tituli,* subdivided into chapters, which can be regarded as *leges.*[20] These divisions are more or less clear, although a better trained legal mind would probably have organized the material in a more systematic way. One of the reasons for the not always thorough organization of the material was the insertion of royal *assises* and other pieces of legislation, but not always at the appropriate place. Thus two chapters on the communes (chs. 142; 144) are inserted into a *titulus* on pledges; a version of the *Lex Aquilia* (chs. 231–3), an *Assise* on Disinheritance of Baldwin III, the customs of Acre (chs. 236–8), are inserted between chapters dealing with lost property, run-away serfs, and theft. Another cause of obscurities in the structure of the treatise is that matters of procedure are interwoven with the main subject matter of law.

We suggest that the original division of the *LdAdB* into *tituli* was as follows:

I.   De iustitia et iure, chs. 1–24.

II.   De iudiciis, chs. 25–7.

III.   De conventionibus inter venditorem et emptorem, chs. 28–41.

IV.   De bonae fidei contractu, id est de commodato, chs. 42–9.

---

[16] *LdAdB*, chs. 25, 27, 134, 239.

[17] *LdAdB*, chs. 42, 116, 155, 181, 210, 233, 270, 286.

[18] *LdAdB*, ch. 103.

[19] *LdAdB*, chs. 225, 231, 234, 236.

[20] A. Warnkönig in *Gelehrte Anzeigen,* x. 973 suggested six major divisions, but he was referring to the subject matter rather than the actual divisions of the treatise.

V.   De solutionibus, chs. 50–4.
VI.   De pignoribus, chs. 55–64.
VII.   De fideiussoribus, chs. 65–84.
VIII.   De locatione et conductione (rerum et operarum), chs. 85–102.
IX.   De deposito, chs. 103–7.
X.   De societate, chs. 108–10.
XI.   De conventionibus, chs. 111–15.
XII.   De induciis, chs. 116–33.
XIII.   De testibus, chs. 134–43.
XIV.   De communi dividundo, chs. 150–4.
XV.   De pactis de matrimonio, chs. 155–80.
XVI.   De testamentis, chs. 181–203.
XVII.   De franchitate, chs. 204–9.
XVIII. De donationibus, chs. 210–24.
XIX.   De rebus perditis et servo fugitivo, chs. 225–30.
XX.   (Lex Aquilia), chs. 231–3.
XXI.   Exhereditation, chs. 234–5.
XXII.   Tariffs of the *Fonde* and of the *Chaine*, chs. 236–8.
XXIII. De furtis, chs. 239–55.
XXIV.   De iniuriis et insultu et verberibus, chs. 256–69.
XXV.   De maleficiis, chs. 270–85.
XXVI.   Droit des mesfais (fines), chs. 286–97.

For the sake of clarity, we use Roman titles for the divisions of the *LdAdB*, but this should not be construed in any way as meaning that it was a treatise of Roman or even of Roman customary law. It is Crusader law in Roman garb.

Obviously the *LdAdB* is an extremely precious source for our knowledge of the laws and procedure in the courts of the kingdom. But the treatise should also be evaluated from the point of view of the legal literature of the period. The date of its composition and the way in which its author organized his material assures it, if not a place of honour, at least a remarkable place in the legal annals of Europe. Chronologically, it should be placed between the time of the composition of the second part of the *Très-ancien coutumier de Normandie* (*c.* 1223) and the *Summa de legibus Normanniae* (1254–8). More important, it antedates the three great French *coutumiers*, the *Conseil à un ami* of Pierre de Fontaines (*c.* 1254–9), the *Livre de jostice et de plet* (*c.* 1260), and the great Beaumanoir's *Coutumes de Beauvaisis* (1283). Proceeding in the manner of the anonymous author of the *Livre de jostice et de plet*, who wanted to put into writing the Customs of the Orléanais, but fell under the spell of Roman law (almost two-thirds of the treatise follows the Pandects), the author of the *LdAdB*, though, or perhaps because, less learned, preserved the laws of the Latin Kingdom better. The same is true if he is compared with Pierre de Fontaines, who put into writing the customs of Vermandois, but in reality extensively paraphrased the Code. Writing some ten years earlier in Acre, the author of the *LdAdB* could have said with more right than Pierre de Fontaines: 'Nus n'entreprit onques devant moi ceste chose' (i. 3). Our author's attempt is thus in point of time a remarkable feat in itself. Perhaps the fact that the kingdom was an entity *sui generis* made him more conscious of its particularity.

Attention should also be drawn to a no less remarkable feature of the treatise. In the thirteenth century and for many centuries to come, it is the only treatise that specifically dealt with one strata of society, the burgesses. The custumals of Europe dealt basically with the nobility and its specific possessions, the fiefs. Even in cases in which they recorded the position of other strata of society or their property, this was done from the point of view of the nobility. To study manorial law, one has to have recourse to manorial records and for city law, particular city charters are necessary.

The *LdAdB* is the earliest legal treatise which specifically deals with the class of burgesses and as such it is unique in the legal annals of the thirteenth century. The reasons can only be surmised. The most important was probably the fact that there were no local urban customs, and consequently the author could deal with the whole stratum of burgesses of the kingdom. Another, that the consciousness of difference was far more acute because of the permanent coexistence of nobility and burgesses inside the same confines of city walls. The author of the *LdAdB* who must have attended the Court of the Viscount for many years, a court held only a short distance from the royal, feudal court in Acre, must have felt some sort of vindication when confiding to writing the laws of his own estate.

The model and the Livre des Assises des Bourgeois

Let us begin with a numerical summary of the relations between the *LdAdB* and *Lo Codi*. The *LdAdB* in the Munich MS., which is the basis of our study, has 297 chapters (the Venice MS. has 267 only). Of the 297 chapters, we found 63 directly translated from *Lo Codi* and 59 dependent upon it, and so we can prove the influence of *Lo Codi* upon 122 chapters out of 297. But actually the dependence is greater. The Munich MS. has

19 chapters in Latin (absent from the Venice MS.), which were then repeated in French; consequently we have double chapters. We think that these chapters did not belong to the original text and in any case they do not add anything new to the subject matter of the *LdAdB*. In addition, 12 chapters dealt with the judicial organization of the kingdom; 12 chapters with royal fines; 6 chapters were variations on the same subject, namely the oath of witnesses who belonged to different religious denominations. All these chapters, which dealt with public and penal law, were not in *Lo Codi*. In addition, 11 chapters referred to *assises* promulgated by the different kings of Jerusalem. If we deduct these 60 chapters from the 297 chapters we can see that of the remaining 237 chapters, 122 were influenced by *Lo Codi*.[21] But this is not enough to give an exact idea of the influence of *Lo Codi* on the *LdAdB*.

In an analysis of our author's use of *Lo Codi*, we observe that he started out by dealing with the judicial organization of the kingdom and thus followed either the example of the *Digesta* or of books of customs from different cities. Beginning with ch. xv, he followed *Lo Codi* (Books ii to vi) until ch. ccix. The only exceptions were chs. lxv–lxxxiv, where, in a rather unexpected way, we find material which he took from Book viii of *Lo Codi*. This is a problem which we shall explain later on. Beginning with ch. ccx, the borrowing from *Lo Codi* is less frequent and is not taken from Books vi–ix only; we find material here which he took from Books iii and iv. This change in the order of material can be explained by the way in which the author of the *LdAdB* used *Lo Codi*. Ch. lv of the *LdAdB* dealt with *gages* (securities or pawns) for debts. It lists a limited number of examples, but after ch. lxv it returns to securities in detail, this time not securities of debtors, but securities of *pleges* (pledges) for the debtors. *Lo Codi* did not deal specifically with this problem, but devoted a large part of Book viii to securities of debtors. The author of the *LdAdB* drew from this part of *Lo Codi*, but applied the material to the securities of pledges.

In the last part (beginning with ch. ccx) the borrowings are less frequent and the order of *Lo Codi* is not preserved. The *LdAdB* ends with twelve chapters dealing with fines and payments due to the royal justice for diverse trespasses. In relegating these chapters to the end the author of the

---

[21] We count only the *assises* whose royal author is known. On the *assises* of Baldwin, see below, Ch. 17. According to M. Grandclaude the twelfth-century *assises* are included in thirty-five chapters of *LdAdB*. In this case 122 chapters out of a total of 213 were influenced by *Lo Codi*.

LdAdB followed the example of the last part of the Code of Justinian. It is also in this last part that we mainly find the legislation of the Latin Kingdom: the establishment of the Court of the Market (*Cour de la Fonde*), the port customs and those of the market of Acre, the 'nostrification' of foreign medical doctors etc., as well as particular *assises* promulgated by Baldwin III (1143–62), Fulk of Anjou (1131–44), and Amalric (1163–73).

To what extent does the discovery of the relation between *Lo Codi* and the *LdAdB* solve the problem of the original text of the Crusader treatise? Beugnot, as we know, followed or agreed with V. Foucher and gave preference to the Venice MS. against E. H. Kausler who preferred the Munich MS. Kausler's choice was later accepted by H. L. Zeller and vindicated by M. Grandclaude. Note that even before Kausler's publication Pardessus underlined the importance of the Munich MS. This opinion was also shared by Warnkönig and Giraud. But though the Munich MS. is closer to the original, it had already undergone changes at the hands of not very skilful copyists, who included in the text the marginal notes of some readers. Linked with the problem of the authenticity of the text is that of chapters found in one of the two manuscripts only. Were they part of the original, now lost, text of the *LdAdB*, or are they simply additions made by later copyists? It seems that this question can be partially solved now by a comparison with *Lo Codi*. Thus chs. ccxii–ccxvii, ccxxii, ccxxiv, and ccxxxi, which are in the Munich MS. only are either translated or influenced by *Lo Codi*. On the other hand we have not been able to establish any specific relation between the chapters that are in the Venice MS. only and *Lo Codi*, although perhaps ch. cxcvii of the *LdAdB* (as edited by Foucher) might have been influenced by *Lo Codi* iv. 52. 3. This observation, although not conclusive, as to the 'legitimacy' of the five chapters in the Venice MS. only,[22] proves in any case that fourteen chapters, found in the Munich MS. only, belonged to the original text of the *LdAdB*.[23]

We cannot here solve the numerous questions that arise from the discovery of the close relation between *Lo Codi* and the *LdAdB*, but it is not out of place to point out problems which now seem to be of fundamental importance for a new and better evaluation of the

[22] Chs. 195, 197, 212, 235, 265, ed. V. Foucher.

[23] Chs. 100, 212–17, 222, 224, 229–32, 272. This list does not include the nineteen Latin chapters already mentioned: 13, 22, 42, 65, 85, 103, 108, 111, 116, 134, 150, 155, 176, 181, 210, 225, 239, 256, 270. This is a slightly different list from that printed by M. Grandclaude.

LdAdB, as well as for a different appreciation of the population to which it related.

A major problem is that of the relation between the *LdAdB* and the different texts, original and translations, of *Lo Codi*. Until now only the Latin and the Dauphinois texts of *Lo Codi* have been published. A critical edition of the Provençal texts and the publication of other translations remain a *desideratum*. On the basis of the material at our disposal, by a process of elimination, we may still try to draw some conclusions.

In our opinion, the *LdAdB* had nothing to do with the French translation of *Lo Codi*. As for the Dauphinois translation, which was based on the Latin translation, it belongs to the fifteenth century, and consequently could not have any relation to the *LdAdB*. We have not seen the Castilian Madrid MS., and we have not been able to find any decisive proof that the text of the *LdAdB* depended upon the original Provençal. Our tentative conclusions are as follows: 1. The author of the *LdAdB* did not know the French versions of *Lo Codi*, otherwise he would simply have copied the text when writing his own French treatise; in this case entire phrases, found in *Lo Codi* and in the *LdAdB* would have been identical. This, as far as we have been able to establish, never happened. 2. The same is true for the Dauphinois text, even if it were of more ancient date than that to which it is usually assigned. 3. As far as the original Provençal text is concerned, the question is far more complicated. The comparison we were able to make between the Provençal texts in the Bibliothèque Nationale in Paris and the *LdAdB* does not prove any direct connection. No translation was ever able to hide the original, especially if the original and the translations were as close as the French and the Provençal, the Catalan and the Castilian languages. Our examination of the *LdAdB* did not prove any foreign linguistic influence.[24]

Having in a sense negative proofs, we would like to draw attention to an expression which seems to corroborate our conclusions, and perhaps to lead to a positive solution. Treating *De pactis de matrimonio*, the author of the *LdAdB* called the Roman *dos* (*dos ex uxore*) 'douaire'; and what was called in the customs of France *douaire* (*dos ex marito*), the author called 'creissement de douaire'.[25] Yet in the *pays de coutumes* of France the

---

[24] We wonder if the word *bounasse* in ch. 46 of Venice MS. (missing in Munich MS.) is not of Provençal origin: *bounace*, French *bonace*—good weather. But this chapter itself, being a part of the maritime legislation of King Amalric, has nothing to do with *Lo Codi*. Cf. also the Provençal texts printed below, Ch. 17, pp. 442 ff.

[25] See ch. 164, Appendix A below, pp. 397 ff.

376 Legal Sources and Legal History

expression *croissement de douaire* was not used to define the *dos ex marito*. It was in the Midi and in parts of Spain that this was the normal usage. It is in Gascony, Bearn, Navarra, Roussillon, Gerona, Languedoc, Forez, Lyonnais, Beaujolais, and even in the Dauphiné, that we find an institution called *augmentum dotis, agenciamentum*, or in the spoken language *screix, creix, excreix*, all expressing the same idea.[26] No doubt, the *creissement de douaire* was an equivalent of one of these terms. Consequently, it would be obvious to look for this expression in the Provençal text of *Lo Codi*, as the expression belonged to the linguistic region of the treatise. But the Provençal *Lo Codi* employed the expression *espolisizi* [sic]. This form *esposalizi*[27] derived from the Latin *sponsalitium*,[28] like the *espousailles* of the French manuscripts of *Lo Codi*. Consequently, the expression *creissement de douaire* certainly did not derive from one of the existing Latin or Provençal texts of *Lo Codi*.[29] We are inclined, then, to believe that the author of the *LdAdB* had a Latin translation, perhaps based on the Provençal text under his hand, which is not in our possession.

This last point can also be confirmed by another significant fact. Indicating the cases of disinheritance of children and of parents, the author of the *LdAdB* followed the enumeration of the original Provençal and not that of the Latin translation which we know.[30] As we do not believe that the author of the *LdAdB* used the Provençal text of *Lo Codi*, we are inclined to believe that he used a Latin text which was more faithful to the Provençal original than the surviving Latin translation. A similar question was raised for the Bearnais text of the *Lois de l'Empereur*. Enumerating the cases of disinheritance, the Bearnais text was the only one among the

---

[26] P. Viollet, *Histoire du droit civil français* (Paris, 1905), p. 865; L. A. and T. H. Warnkönig, *Geschichte der Rechtsquellen und des Privatrechts* (Basel, 1848), p. 261, and cf. bibliography in the notes to *LdAdB*, ch. 164 in Appendix A below.

[27] The rubrics of v. 3 and v. 4 of the Provençal text published by J. Tardif in *Annales du Midi* 5 (1893), 34–70.

[28] The Latin rubrics of *Lo Codi* have *antefactum* another typical expression of the *pays de droit écrit*, Spain and Italy. For Italy: F. Brandileone, 'Studi preliminari sullo svolgimento storico dei rapporti patrimoniali fra coniugi in Italia', *Archivio giuridico* 67 (1904), 201–84. But the Customs of Tortosa v. 5. § 3, which depend on *Lo Codi* v.11.2: 'Et omnes gaudimentum quod potest mulier habere de dote et de donatione propter nuptias id est de *antifacto*, debet mulier expendere in se et in marito et in filiis quos habuerit de illo marito' translate: 'Pere la muyller del fruits del dot e del *creyx* deu fer ses necèssaris a si e a ses fills e a son marit.' In the same text again the *donatio propter nuptias* is translated *escreyx*. The *LdAdB* which took ch. 168 from the same text, speaks only of *douaire*, that is *dos ex uxore*, and does not mention the *creissement de douaire*.

[29] Should we then think about the Castilian texts, which were not preserved.

[30] See Ch. 17 below, pp. 442 ff.

translations of *Lo Codi* that followed the order of the Provençal text.[31] But it is not proven that it was really the Provençal original that he followed and not another Latin translation.

The proof that *Lo Codi* was used as a model by the author of the *LdAdB* stresses, in a sense, the value of the *LdAdB* as an authentic source, which described laws that actually ruled the *burgenses* of the Latin Kingdom. Even in cases in which a chapter of the *LdAdB* is no more than a translation from *Lo Codi*, there are usually differences in important aspects of law and procedure. If *Lo Codi* were simply the source of a piece of literary plagiarism, the author of the *LdAdB* would never have tried (as he actually did) to change its dispositions. All these changes, additions, and omissions, often enigmatic changes, cannot be explained otherwise than by the intention of the author of the *LdAdB* to adapt the treatise which served him as a model for the redaction of the usages of the Latin Kingdom. Consequently, we can say with assurance that the law which was represented in the *LdAdB* did correspond to the judicial realities of the kingdom.

How can we explain that *Lo Codi* was used in preference to other possible treatises of law? In a country ruled by dynasties from Lorraine, Anjou, and Poitou, how can it be explained that a jurist from Acre chose a Provençal treatise of law as his model? The presence of a dynasty from Toulouse in Tripoli (we do not know anything about the *assises* of this county, apart from the fact that they existed), does not seem to be sufficient explanation. To see in the use of *Lo Codi* a fortuitous event—that the author simply cast about for a treaty on Roman law—is not satisfactory either. When he composed his treatise between 1229 and 1244, he had a vast range at his disposal—a choice including the *Summa Trecensis*, the *Summa* of Rogerius, the *Summa* of Placentin, and even the *Summa* of the famous Azo. These were sufficiently diffused at that time to support the theory of a fortuitous choice of *Lo Codi* by the Palestinian author. He himself was a practitioner of law, in a country where nobles were jurists and advocates, and kings were *iurisperiti* and protagonists of jurisprudence.[32] We believe that the choice of *Lo Codi*, although it may have been

---

[31] Namely the sixteen *raisons* for disinheritance.

[32] The famous Johannes Andreas thus described Hugh IV Lusignan (1324–59), king of Cyprus and Jerusalem: 'quem sine hyperbola constat omni scientia theologica, iuris utriusque et septem artium liberarium editum' (quoted by J. F. Schulte, *Die Geschichte der Quellen und Literatur des Canonischen Rechts* ii (Stuttgart, 1875), 210, no. 30). Some knowledge of law was part of the royal image of the kings of Jerusalem. This can be seen in the characterization of almost every king by William of Tyre.

partly due to the character of the book, as a popular manual of Roman law, was even more influenced by its practical character. *Lo Codi* was not a pure exposition of Roman law, it was more an interpretation with an eye toward practical use. The laws of Justinian were not simply stated, but rather their application in Provence. This might have been decisive in the choice of *Lo Codi* by the author of the *LdAdB*. Whether or not this last point is accepted, we still have to admit that our author chose *Lo Codi* as his model because in many domains it described practices similar to those that existed in the kingdom. It would have been illogical to choose a legal *répertoire* bearing no relation to the usages of the kingdom. The current notion that the author of the *LdAdB* knew Roman law and introduced it into his treatise should be differently formulated. The reason for the use of *Lo Codi* as a model was partly due to the fact that the laws of the Latin Kingdom were in some respects similar, or came very close to, those presented in *Lo Codi*.

At first view this seems less plausible than the accepted opinion, according to which the customary law of the kingdom developed spontaneously,[33] and then the author of the *LdAdB* tried to describe it in Roman terms. This opinion fits the current idea of the Crusader feudal organization—that is, by definition, the customary organization of the kingdom.[34] But when we want to size up this 'spontaneous evolution', when we look for its origins and the factors that determined its development, we fall into a vacuum. If we dismiss, once and for all, the image of a 'perfectly feudal state',[35] we shall certainly gain much in

[33] This was argued by H. Mitteis, 'Zum Schuld- und Handelsrecht der Kreuzfahrerstaaten', *Beiträge zum Wirtschaftsrecht*, i (Marburg 1931), 229–88.

[34] Cf. J. La Monte, 'Three questions concerning the Assizes of Jerusalem', *Byzantina– Metabyzantina* 1946. Cf. above, Ch. 1, pp. 6 ff. This gives rise to another question, namely how far do the treatises of John of Ibelin and his *confrères* reflect the kingdom's real organization? See J. Richard, 'Pairie d'Orient Latin: les quatres baronnies des royaume de Jérusalem et de Chypre', *RHDFE* 1950, pp. 67–8. Cf. also above, Ch. 14, p. 351. On Frankish feudalism in Greece, see P. W. Topping, *Feudal institutions as revealed in the Assises of Romania* (Philadelphia, 1949). Cf. the reviews of C. Verlinden in *Revue belge de philologie et d'históire* 30 (1952) and J. Prawer in *RHDFE* 1954, fasc. 1.

[35] Many of these definitions were influenced by Beugnot's introduction to the *Lois*, which reflected ideas current among historians *c.* 1840. In his study on the Crusader rural system Beugnot assigned to the Crusaders ideas quite close to those of the Manchester economists (*Bibl. de l'École des Chartes*, 3rd ser., vols. iv–v) and explained the customary law of Crusader burgesses thus: 'Les coutumes syriennes prenaient leur origine dans les codes de Justinien reproduits par les Basiliques et dans les constitutions isolées des empereurs grecs; or, ces lois, qui étaient connues et étudiées en Europe, provenaient précisément de ces principes de droit naturel vers lesquels le droit coutumier cherchait à s'élever, en dépit des liens qui le tenaient attaché aux idées conventionnelles créées par la féodalité... En leur [aux bourgeois et aux

clarity; instead of trying to construct formulas which obscure more than clarify, we shall approach the realities of the kingdom.

In what follows we shall try to suggest what could have been the basis of the customary law of the burgesses and propose a tentative explanation of the reasons that prompted the author of the *LdAdB* to take *Le Codi*, a treatise of practical Roman law, as a model for his work.

The Burgesses of the Latin Kingdom and their Customary Law

Customary law was closely linked with the populations in which it originated and then progressively transformed and adapted to changing needs and conditions. Finally, as in the Middle Ages, it ousted personal law, and as territorial law it ruled a territory mainly inhabited by the population which created it. These definitions, commonly accepted, become less clear in dealing with a state recently created and even less so in dealing with a population newly formed.

If the Crusades are thought of as a migration—as in fact they were—how can one describe the creation of a customary law? We know that Crusader society was composed of two main classes, the nobility and the burgesses. From the beginning both classes probably lived under different jurisdictions, each with its own laws. But what kind of laws were they? 'Customary law' is the normal answer, 'French customary law' is the more precise answer. Some historians prefer to be more prudent and speak of French customary law, in which one also finds the customs of other European countries.[36] All these definitions, one more vague than the other, are rationalizing historical reconstructions, accepted because they fit the image of the populations of the Crusader states. They do not bring us any nearer to tangible results.

We know the ethnic composition of the armies of the First Crusade, but we know less about the ethnic structure of the waves of migration that followed. No doubt there was an overwhelming majority of settlers from France, but they hailed from all corners of the country. Consequently, the question of the geographical origins of that customary law is not easily solved and even less so as far as the burgesses are concerned. For a law to become the customary law of the kingdom it had to be a law common to

Syriens] imposant le même code de lois, le législateur rendit hommage à deux grandes vérités, à savoir que le droit naturel est la loi commune des hommes, et que l'expression la plus pure de ce droit se trouve renfermée dans le code des Romains' (*Lois* ii., p. xxvi).

[36] Such vague notions were common in the studies of Brodeau, De Lalande, Dupin, Taillander, and others. For Beugnot's view see the previous note; J. M. Pardessus, *Mémoire* 1829, pp. 15–16 had a clearer notion of the problem.

a large number of members of the class it ruled, or it had to be accepted as such. But this was more feasible for the nobility than for the burgesses.

Land possession, the dominant type of property and the base of seignorial rights, was in the Middle Ages the intersection point of public and private law. The Latin Kingdom, like its European counterparts, knew of an institution which was common to the whole noble class, whatever its origin—the *feudum*. After the first wave of conquest, lands that were in the hands of nobles or simple knights became fiefs, and as such the base of the political structure of the kingdom. Around this institution, imported by the conquerors, was formed a whole set of customary law on the basis of acquired experience and new circumstances.

The question of a common law of the burgesses was entirely different. The point of departure should naturally be sought in the ethnic composition of this class. Unfortunately, until now there has been no study of this problem—which would necessitate a kind of *enquête* or *dépouillement* of the sources of the different regions of France.[37] However it is our view that a rough outline of the picture can be drawn with some certainty. The preponderance of Frenchmen from the north in the class of nobility does not necessarily mean that the same was true for the burgesses. It can be affirmed with certainty that the composition of that class was different. No doubt in the First Crusade the nobles from northern France dominated the social ladder. But, and this is a point to which we should draw attention, only a small number of *pedites* from northern France, who left before the armies of the First Crusade, ever reached Jerusalem. The army of Peter the Hermite, as well as other peasant armies—all these wandering bands were exterminated in Hungary or in Asia Minor. Those who survived were the *pedites* who accompanied the Crusade of the nobility. They were the initial nucleus from which the class of burgesses grew. They counted no more than several thousands and even this is probably an overestimate. But at the time of Saladin, in 1187, we can evaluate the Crusader population of the country at something like 120,000 souls.[38]

[37] Du Cange's *Familles d'Outremer* (ed. E. Rey), complemented by a large number of monographs (cf. J. La Monte, 'Chronologie de l'Orient latin', *Bulletin of the International Committee of Historical Sciences* (1943), pp. 141–202 (and see above, Ch. 2, pp. 23–4) furnishes an impressive, though not exhaustive, picture of the different houses of nobility which participated in the Crusades. There is nothing of this kind for the burgesses or serfs who left Europe for the Holy Land. R. Fawtier, *Les Capétiens et la France* (Paris, 1942), pp. 193–6, suggested such a study, but this still remains a *desideratum*.

[38] At the time of the capitulation to Saladin Jerusalem counted some 30,000 inhabitants.

Where did they come from? We know that the great Crusades included a relatively small number of non-nobles. In these military expeditions the *pedites* from the peasant class did not count for much; the commanders of the armies, and even the Papacy, discouraged their departure. No doubt they participated in the Crusades, accompanying the knightly forces, but they were relatively few and a great number came back to Europe with the leaders with whom they departed. The class of burgesses was not created as a result of these military expeditions. It was rather the outcome of waves of peaceful immigration which came from Europe.

There is no need to discuss the motives of the Crusades, multiple and varying according to social class, although religious sentiments prevailed. But the constant, peaceful immigration to the Latin Kingdom in between the great military expeditions, was little, if at all, influenced by religious zeal. Religious propaganda was important for the short periods of the great expeditions, but it lost much of its significance in times of peace. It is rather in the social and economic situation that one should look for motives behind the peaceful immigrations into the Latin Kingdom.

These observations suggest in what social milieu and in what geo-demographic framework one has to look for the populations that migrated to the Holy Land and contributed to the creation of the class of burgesses. Northern France, Normandy, Flanders, and Lorraine, which furnished the knights and commanders of the First Crusade, could scarcely have played the same role in the creation of the non-noble class of the Crusader Kingdom. The earliest Crusades coincided with the great outbreak of urbanization. The newly founded or resurrected cities opened their gates to the surplus of rural population, which was easily integrated in the urban economy. During the whole of the twelfth and thirteenth centuries, the great period of urban expansion, they continued to do so. In these circumstances it is impossible to regard the newly created cities, with individual exceptions, as centres of emigration. There was nothing in their social or economic structure to induce their inhabitants to emigrate. No such change as that supposed to have taken place in the lordly castle has been proved for the cities. Moreover the population of the cities, though permanently growing, was negligible compared with the inhabitants of

Similar, or slightly higher, numbers can be assigned to Tyre and Acre. This brings the population of the three great cities to *c.* 100,000. The population of smaller cities was well below that of the great centres. Still, we know of more than forty settlements with a Court of Burgesses. Consequently the Latin population could be estimated at some 120,000 inhabitants at the time of the collapse of the First Kingdom. Cf. above, Ch. 6, p. 182, and Prawer, *Latin Kingdom*, p. 146.

the rural areas. Consequently if there was any emigration from these areas, it must have been in its great majority—the peasants. In the twelfth century the Crusades, agricultural colonization, and urban settlement were the three main channels that drained the rural areas. We do not deny the existence of any urban immigration, but numerically it must have been quite insignificant.[39]

The situation was entirely different in the south of France. Here city life was never extinguished. If an urban population emigrated to the Holy Land, it was rather from the cities of the Midi and Italy. In these areas situated near the sea and in contact with the Holy Land, the idea of emigration to Outremer was more attractive. There was also the relative ease of communication. The shores of the Holy Land which the northerner could reach only by crossing the whole of France, were far more accessible to the Provençals, the people from Languedoc, Catalonia, and Sicily. Consequently, although in the cities of the south there were no more reasons to induce people to migrate to the Holy Land than in the cities of the north, it is certain that the southern peasant and city inhabitant, particularly the latter, had more facilities for migrating. And so it seems to us rather natural to regard the south as the cradle of the class of burgesses, and the southern peasant and city inhabitant as its principal element.[40]

There are no statistics to corroborate our views. Only a study such as that envisaged by the late R. Fawtier for the nobility, enlarged in such a way as to include the other classes, could furnish us with more precise data.

Though we lack direct proofs of European origin, the Holy Land seems to furnish some indications. Two documents relating to Crusader burgesses of the twelfth century may be regarded as symptomatic and offer a kind

[39] French and German cities are often mentioned in Crusader sources, but this should not mislead us as to their role in the movement. Crusader propaganda was the work of the Church and it was only normal that the cathedral or city church should be the centre of this activity. In the twelfth century one would hardly expect a preaching of the Crusade in isolated villages. It is in this light that one has to understand Bernard of Clairvaux boasting that he emptied the cities by sending their inhabitants on the Crusade. The demographic changes and the movement of colonization were succinctly summarized by M. L. Génicot, 'Sur les témoignages d'accroissement de la population en Occident du XIe au XIIIe siècles', *Cahiers d'histoire mondiale* i. (Paris, 1953), 446–62.

[40] The fact that the burgesses of the kingdom were free men, though often of servile origin, is explained by the fact that every individual who joined a Crusade or came to the Holy Land became automatically free. Pardessus and Beugnot wanted to explain the liberty of burgesses by assuming that they were of free, that is urban, origin (Pardessus, 'Mémoires', p. 15). This point of view was rightly abandoned by later historians. The preponderance of southern population was noted by H. Prutz, *Kulturgeschichte*, pp. 111 ff.

of circumstantial evidence. Both are linked to colonization activities in the Holy Land and their particular interest resides in the fact that they supply most important indications of the geographical provenance of the burgesses. The first document includes forty names. Twenty-six carry *cognomina* which indicate the origin of their bearers. The names we have been able to identify can be classified as follows: six Palestinians; and from the remaining twenty: one from Flanders, twelve from southern France, two Gascons, one Lombard, one or two Poitevins, one Catalan, one from Burgundy, one from Carcassonne, two, it seems, from Forez, and one, not very certain, from Perigord. In the second document, also from the middle of the twelfth century, which relates to a newly founded village, we find forty names with geographical *cognomina*, which can be identified with certainty. Along with ten burgesses of Palestinian origin, the rest can be classified as follows: four Provençals, four from Berry, four from Poitou, three Lombards, two Auvergnats, two Gascons, two Catalans, three Burgundians, one from Venice, one from Tours, one from Limoges, and finally three burgesses called *Francigenae*.[41]

According to these two documents, it is tempting to believe that the north of the Loire was not represented, unless exceptionally, among the burgesses. Such examples could be multiplied, but this would not be very helpful, as we would never know if a given list was 'typical' or not. Consequently, although we shall not overemphasize the lists, it seems impossible not to take them into account.

What could have been the common law of this class of burgesses? What tradition, comparable to that of the fief among nobles, could this class have brought over to the Latin Kingdom? We doubt if any single institution was common to all the burgesses in the way that the institution of fiefs was common to the nobility.[42] There were at least two different traditions, one more consistent, the other more heterogeneous. The first was the customary tradition of southern France, of Catalonia, of Italy, the surviving old Roman tradition, though deformed by abuse, ignorance, foreign influences, and its adaptation to the changing circumstances during the 600 years that separated the legislation of Theodosius from the establishment of the Latin Kingdom. The addition of non-Roman elements

---

[41] The two documents were analysed in detail in Ch. 5 above, pp. 127 ff.

[42] E. D. Glasson, *Histoire du droit et des institutions de la France* iv, (Paris, 1891), 244–5, conscious of the problem, argued that because the Crusaders came from all corners of Europe it was impossible to accept one binding customary law. Consequently, to prevent legal confusion and chaos until a customary law crystallized the kings undertook an active legislative programme.

of Germanic origin and the creation of local elements were certainly important. Still, the basic notions of Roman law survived, awaiting the twelfth and thirteenth centuries when the renaissance of Roman law infused them with a new lease on life.

Side by side with this southern tradition (although it does not take into account local variations), we have the tradition of northern France. This was customary law, varying from one place to another, almost from one estate to another. Its heterogeneous elements were brought to the Latin Kingdom by the earliest immigrants. The merits of one or the other tradition are beyond the scope and competence of our study. We do not insist on the preponderance of the *méridionaux*, which favoured the customs of their region; we pass over the fact that in cases of opposition between these two traditions, the customs of the south, more homogeneous and solid, were better adapted for survival. What is important first of all is the great change in the social and economic life of the European immigrants when they reached the shores of the Latin Kingdom.

We have already stressed that the majority of new immigrants, certainly those from the north, were peasants. It was their mode of life that was radically changed—one may say, revolutionized. It is true that there were attempts to create a Frankish agriculture in the kingdom, but from beginning to end the Crusaders remained an urban society. The peasants had to become artisans and small merchants in order to live. Once they departed from their hamlets, they left behind plough and scythe. They had to adapt to a new, more complex, framework of life, that of the cities. The ancient social links were broken. The *stirps*, the village, the family, were abandoned and a new social mould surrounded them on every side.

In these conditions, what custom could they invoke? These people came from hundreds of different manors, where not only customs were different, but, more important, the customs were those of a rural society, fitting the rhythm of life in a rural economy, based on self-production more than on exchange. Their customs belonged to an early phase of society, the pre-urban society of the early Middle Ages. Only here and there were they adapted to the new circumstances that accompanied the development of cities, such as the *Très-ancien coutumier de Normandie*, which devoted a special section to the status of burgesses, or the urban charters of the new city agglomerations. City life must have been a permanent problem for these new immigrants, not prepared by their earlier experience for their new circumstances.

The situation was quite different for those who came from the *pays de droit écrit.* They were better prepared for the conditions of their new existence, because city life never ceased to exist in their own country. Moreover the arts and crafts of the classical world, the ancient habits of life partly survived invasions. For them urban crafts, and even commerce, were not entirely new. Finally, their legal traditions—of Roman origin— were better adapted to the new exigencies. Altered as they were, they could still answer the problems of city life. Even if they provided no ready-made answer they were better equipped for adaptation than the rural traditions of the north. And even if we imagine the immigrants from the Midi as of peasant origin (although we are rather inclined to believe that a large number came from the cities), let us not forget that the customs of the rural areas of the Midi were also Roman.[43]

Comparing both judicial traditions in the light of changes in social structure and economic activities created by the Latin Kingdom, we do not hesitate to say that it was Roman customary law that became the basis of the common law of the burgesses of the kingdom. This does not imply that Roman customary law was universally prevalent. Public law, the court of the viscount, the procedure followed in the courts, were definitely not Roman, but replicas of northern institutions, particularly linked, in our view, with Normandy and Flanders.[44] But those sections of law that dealt with marriages, contracts, commerce, etc., were marked by customary Roman law as it was exercised in the eleventh and twelfth centuries in the Midi and neighbouring countries.

[43] The survival of Roman law in the Early Middle Ages was for a long time a bone of contention between two schools. One led by Fitting argued for its continuity and tried to corroborate it by the different *Epitomae* and *Exceptiones*; another school led by J. Flach, and in some measure by Max Cohen, did not regard these *opuscula* as anything but academic or even grammatical exercises. We note the basic studies only: H. Fitting, 'Le scuole di diritto in Francia durante l' XI secolo', *Bolletino dell'Istituto di diritto romano*, iv (Rome, 1891), 166–96; A. Tardif, *Histoire des sources de droit romain* (Paris, 1890); C. Lefebvre, 'Le droit des gens mariés en pays de droit écrit', *RHDFE* 1911. In our context the important studies are: E. de Hinojosa, 'La reception du droit romain en Catalogne', *Mélanges Fitting* ii (Montpellier, 1908), 391–408; E. Meynial, 'De l'application du droit romain dans la région de Montpellier aux XIIe et XIIIe s.' *Atti del Congresso Internazionale di Scienze Storiche* 9 (1904), 147–69; H. Kantorowicz, op. cit., n. 5; R. Caillemer, *Les débuts de la science du droit en Provence* (Valence, 1907); P. Vinogradoff, *Roman Law in Medieval Europe* (Oxford, 1929). A large number of studies is being published in the *Recueil de mémoires et travaux*, pub. par la Société d'histoire du droit et des institutions des anciens pays de droit écrit (Toulouse–Montpellier) 1948 ff. and H. Coing (ed.), *Hdb. d. Quellen und Literatur d. neueren europäischen Privatrechtsgeschichte* i (Munich, 1973): P. Weimar, 'Die legistische Literatur der Glossatorenzeit', pp. 129–260. Cf. the excellent summary and study of A. Gouron, *La Science juridique française aux XIe et XIIe siècles. Ius Romanum Medii Aevi*, part I, 4 d–e (Milan 1978).

[44] This view differs from that of La Monte, *Feudal Monarchy*. See below, Chs. 16 and 17.

If the author of the *LdAdB* took *Lo Codi* as a model for his treatise, it was because he found affinity there with the customs practised in the kingdom. *Lo Codi* was written around the middle of the twelfth century and meant as a practical treatise. Thus its author, having expounded a rule of Roman law, often states that the rule is no longer in use or that current practice is different. But despite these efforts at adaptation *Lo Codi* was 'more Roman' than the law exercised in Provence at the same period.[45] If *Lo Codi* was modified by the author of the *LdAdB*, it was for the same reason. The Roman law he found in *Lo Codi* was already transformed in the judicial practice of the kingdom.

It would have been inconceivable that customary law of Roman origin brought over in the period that immediately followed the conquest, should have remained unchanged, without being influenced or adapted. When it is presented to us in the middle of the thirteenth century, it appears as a mixture of Roman law and customs of French origin. These customs influenced some well-defined aspects of judicial life. Note also that some of the usages which appear to have come from customary France, did not come from there directly. It is possible (and we have proof of it, for example, in marital law), that they were established in the *pays de droit écrit* before the establishment of the Latin Kingdom. Consequently they came, in all probability, with the Roman customary law of the Midi. One of the studies remaining to be done on the *LdAdB* is to show how this Roman customary law was influenced by French customs.

The non-Frankish Population of the Kingdom and its Laws

We have tried to show the existence of conditions which made the 'reception' of Roman customary law in the kingdom possible. The starting-point of our analysis was the Frankish population. Let us now examine other elements of the kingdom's population. Below the nobles and alongside the burgesses were the Italian communes, and on the lowest rung of the social ladder came the native population. It is only plausible to suppose that these strata of society influenced the laws and customs of the kingdom.

As far as the Italian communes were concerned, it is evident that in some of the most vital aspects of their activities it was Roman law that was the basis of their particular laws. Moreover, they were better placed than anyone else to draw upon the benefits accruing from the revival of the

[45] Cf. R. Caillemer, 'Lo Codi et le droit provençal au XIIe siècle', *Annales du Midi* 18 (1906), 496 ff. and esp. p. 503.

study of Roman law in Ravenna or Bologna. Their contacts with the burgesses—mainly commercial—could not but strengthen the Roman element in the customary laws of the burgesses. Although autonomous, the laws of the Italian courts had numerous opportunities for infiltration into the usages of the kingdom. Cases—probably everyday occurrences— in which the plaintiff was a burgess and the accused a national of an Italian commune, would come before the court of the accused, that is before the court of the Italian commune. In these circumstances, mutual influence was inevitable. But even without considering litigation, it seems obvious that the Italian merchants influenced the customary laws of the country. For example, the Italians used contracts in their commercial operations. But written contracts were not recognized in the Courts of the Burgesses. The consequence of such divergence of procedure was remarkable. The *LdAdB* declared formally:'If it happens that a man or a woman bring to court a charter as proof, the jurors of the court should by law neither receive nor hear nor believe it if it is not a sealed privilege of the lord of the city, or of another place, because this [i.e. the sealed privilege] should be upheld and believed.'[46] But how to proceed if one of the parties to a contract was a member of a commune? If the parties concluded the agreement by a 'charter written by the hand of a notary and guaranteed by other jurors', then

this charter is as valid between them and has to be held as firm, as if it were a sealed privilege; and the consul of the commune from which it is claimed, should enforce the payment or the restoration to the other party of everything that is said in the charter, by law and *assise*. But in the royal court it should not be valid and no judgment should be pronounced upon it by any juror whoever he may be, on any charter, if it is not as stated before.[47]

This, if literally interpreted, means that there was a moral obligation to fulfil the terms of the contract. The consul—the head of the commune— should enforce the observation of the agreement, but no royal—no seignorial court for that matter—accepted a legal contract as proof! This was an unthinkable situation in regular commerce, and in time a different procedure was envisaged by the author of the *LdAdB*, as follows: 'If it happens that a sale is transacted in the court . . . of land, etc. and a charter is made thereof in the presence of viscount and jurors, and later on there is a litigation about what the charter, which was made in court, says, reason commands that whatever is said in the charter should be maintained and be valid in court.'[48]

---

[46] *LdAdB*, ch. 140.   [47] *LdAdB*, ch. 142.   [48] *LdAdB*, ch. 141.

Thus solicited by two different legal systems, the Roman contract on the one hand, and the typical German system, suspicious of written documents, with a preference for living witnesses on the other, the law of the Latin Kingdom chose to sanction a charter which dealt with property, but on condition that it should be delivered in a court of justice, where viscount and jurors were some sort of glorified witnesses.[49]

A large number of Italians, called *Lombardi*—probably Italians from the south and Sicilians—mingled with the burgesses without being separated from them by autonomous communal organizations. Their own legal traditions are quite well known from the surviving customs of Sicilian and south-Italian cities under the rule of the Normans. Their Romano-Byzantine basis cannot be doubted and we can follow their introduction into the kingdom, as Cahen has shown for the principality of Antioch. The romanizing tendencies of these customs cannot be doubted.

Turning to the overwhelming majority of the inhabitants of the country, we see the kaleidoscopic mixture of races and faiths which composed the local population. In cities, where most of the Crusaders lived, the burgesses mixed with Oriental Christians of every denomination, whereas the Muslim population though partly urban, remained, in its overwhelming majority, in the countryside. In what sense could the 'Syrians'—the Oriental Christians—influence the customs of the country? The answer cannot be doubted. These communities lived under the *jus graeco-romanum*. Less than a generation before the arrival of the Crusaders, the northern part of their future states, like the district of Antioch, was still held by Byzantium and ruled by Byzantine law. More to the south (in parts of Lebanon and in Palestine) Byzantine law was in force until the Arab conquest at the beginning of the seventh century. But despite the foreign conquest, people continued to live and to be ruled by their original law, which now became part of the national heritage of the 'Syrians'.

In the market-place and the port area, the centres of local and international commercial activity, Roman law as a kind of *lingua franca* of legal relations, was used in everyday business. In this constant meeting of heterogenous elements there was no better instrument of collaboration. Each community could preserve its proper customs when business deals were transacted among its own members. But in relations with members

---

[49] It is worth indicating the appearance of *notarii*, sometimes *iudices*, who expedited legal instruments during the thirteenth century. They were overwhelmingly Italians. Their probable influence on the legal customs of the kingdom deserves a special study. Cf. above, p. 292 n. 129.

of other communities it had to renounce its own judicial customs to some extent or commercial, and in some measure social, relations would have been impossible. At the same time, it was necessary for the rules not to be entirely foreign or contrary to current practices. The customary Roman law, preserved in the *pays de droit écrit*, could easily fulfil this task.[50]

This is not a simple hypothesis. If, for example, we examine the working of the Court of the Market, the *Cour de la Fonde*, we see it composed of 'VI legal jurors, IIII Syrians, and II Franks', presided over by a *bailli*, who represented the viscount. This court was competent in cases of 'debts and securities, which had been lost or damaged, or cases such as renting of houses', 'buying or renting', 'leasing, lending, delivering, donating, recognizing what was claimed, concluding business, giving arrhes or payments, etc.'[51]

From what sources could the court have drawn its decision for the *lex dicenda*? Can we imagine the Crusaders imposing an entirely new law in commercial matters, in contracts, sales, renting, associations, donations, obligations of every type, on a population which had its own traditions in all such matters, age-old traditions, far superior to the rudimentary customs brought over from castles and manors of northern France? The answer cannot be in doubt. This court, competent to try cases between people of different communities could not have laid down any other but its own traditional law—the traditions of Rome and Byzantium as they survived in the country. From this point of view let us now analyse what is said by the *LdAdB* about the law applied in the Court of the Market.

Let it be known that the jurors of the Market should judge those people who do wrong one against another as in cases of selling and buying, of renting and of other things; and *they should judge them as it is established in this book* what has to be done by the jurors of the Court of Burgesses and not otherwise. Because be they Syrians or Greeks or Jews or Samaritans or Nestorians or Saracens, they are people like the Franks, to pay and to restore what will be adjudicated, precisely as it is established in the Court of the Burgesses in this book in which are established all the rules for all the people.

This chapter practically implied that the law that applied to the local population in commercial matters and which we cannot imagine to be much different from the traditional Roman-Syrian law, corresponded to

[50] Ten years before Beugnot's vague explanations (above, p. 378 n. 35), L. A. Warnkönig had clearer ideas on the subject. 'The reviewer [i.e. Warnkönig] is of the opinion, that the numerous decisions of the Roman law are not taken from the *Basilicae* or from the still valid legal books of Justinian, but migrated there from France' (*Gelehrte Anzeigen* x (1840), 962).

[51] *LdAdB*, ch. 236.

that of the burgesses. This was possible—in a sense normal—because the burgesses and the local population had a common denominator for their legal affairs—Roman customary law. This does not mean that the customary law of the *pays de droit écrit* was the same as Roman-Syrian law. Far from it; but it would be difficult to contest a common basis for both. Their encounter in the Holy Land drew them even nearer, until a uniform legislation crystallized, acceptable to the burgesses as well as to the native population.

We have tried to prove that the private law of the burgesses in the kingdom rested upon the basis of Roman customary law. But let us not forget that this situation existed only in the first period of the kingdom, in the period of the crystallization of its judicial organization. For the later period we can surmise its evolution from the way in which the *LdAdB* presents the law of the burgesses. It is doubtful that the renaissance of Roman law, which had such a tremendous influence on Mediterranean countries, was felt in the Latin Kingdom. The legal tradition, once cystallized—a phase which did not extend beyond the middle of the twelfth century—closed itself to foreign influences. It became conservative and a thirteenth-century author could quite well have used ancient terms and reproduced it according to twelfth-century models. How far this law became conservative can be shown by the example of the canon law. In the middle of the thirteenth century, marriage impediments were ruled in Europe—by the decrees of the Fourth Council of Lateran. But the law proclaimed by the *LdAdB* was not that of 1214 but of the previous period.[52] Philip of Novara also proved that at his time the decrees of the Fourth Council of Lateran were not observed in the kingdom, despite efforts to introduce them. Crusader law, being conservative, or, in Grandclaude's phrase, 'regressive', underwent the only influence possible, that of the feudal law of the nobility.

The law reproduced in the *LdAdB* is a composite picture of two great factors in the legal life of the burgesses: Roman customary law brought over from the *pay de droit écrit*, modified, perhaps, by the current practice of 'Syrian' tradition and Italian practices, and the customary law of northern France.

---

[52] Cf. J. Prawer, 'L'établissement des coutumes du marché à Saint-Jean d'Acre et la date de la composition du *LdAdB*', *RHDFE* 1951, pp. 329 ff.

Appendix A
De pactis de matrimonio

To visualize the relationship between the *LdAdB* and *Lo Codi* we print chs. 156–80 of the *LdAdB* and the corresponding chapters from *Lo Codi*. They form an *opusculum: De pactis de matrimonio.*

LdAdB clvi

Item de eodem. Ce est, yci orres et entendres dou mariage c on fait, et de quel aage deit estre l oume et la feme avant que il se puissent espouser en sainte yglise.

Bien pevent saver tous homes que le bon mariage est mout chier a Dieu et mout profitable as homes et as femes, car ce dit l escriture de la lei: *saluantur enim uir infidelis per mulierem fidelem, et mulier infidelis per uirum fidelem.*[1] Ce est, que le baron qui n en a fei se sauve par sa feme qui a fei, et la feme qui n en a fei se sauve par son baron qui a fei. Donc deivent bien tous homes saveir et toutes femes et chevaliers et borgeis que par la lei dou ciel et par les decres et par l asisse est mestier que el mariage seit III choses esgardees. Tout premierement, ce est premiers i deit estre esgarde *etas* au mariage, ce est l aage, apres i deit estre esgarde *consensus personarum*, ce est que la volonte i soit de l un et de l autre, et *remotio parentele*, ce est que l oume n aparteigne a la feme. Mais bien coumande la raison que l aage i deit estre tout premier, car le baron deit aveir tout premier XIII ans au mains, et la feme auci deit aver XIII ans au mains,[2] quant il c espousent.

Lo Codi v. 1. 2

Si aliquis uult accipere uxorem, multa debent considerari. Prius debet considerari etas utriusque, et ipsius qui accipit uxorem et mulieris que accepit uirum.

Lo Codi v. 1. 3

Similiter nullus potest eam ducere, quamuis possit eam firmare, si sit minor xiiij annis. Femina quoque non potest accipere maritum, si est minor xij annis, quamuis possit ipsa firmare maritum.

---

[1] I Cor. 7: 14: 'Sanctificatus est enim vir infidelis per mulierem fidelem et sanctificata est mulier infidelis per virum fidelem.'

[2] MS. Venice: 'la feme doit ausi avoir XII ans'. This seems the better reading but *ausi* prevents a definitive correction.

LdAdB clvi (cont.)

Et ce il avient que l ome et la feme ne sont de tel aage con deit estre et il se prenent, ne deit valer celuy mariage par dreit, por ce qu il est contre Dieu et contre sainte yglise et contre l assise. Encores seit ce qu il n apartiegnent a la feme ne la feme a l ome, car ce dient les sains decres: *quia parentela collateralis extenditur usque ad septimum gradum.* Ce est, la lignee qui vient a l oume ou a la feme ci c estent iusque au VII degre. Mais la dreite lignee, qui vient et descent, si est dou pere au fis et dou fis a ces nevous et des nevous[3] a leur enfans, et enci s estent iusques atant com nous avons desus dit, et non por tant se dit l escripture de la lei: *si Adam uiueret, nullam sibi in uxorem conpulare non posset.* Ce est, ce Adam vesquist encores, il ne poreit prendre par dreit nule feme por moillier, por ce que nous tous et toutes soumes fis et filles de Adam et d Eve sa moillier. Car se fu nostre premerain pere et nostre premiere mere.[4] *Matrimonium est uiri et mulieris coniunctio, indiuiduam uite consuetudinem retinens.*[5] Ce est, la lei et l asise coumande et dit que le mariage est si bon que puis que l ome et la feme se sont pris par mariage il ne se pevent partir mais ior de lor vie ce par la mort non. Car ce dit l apostle missires sai[n]t Pol: *mulier sui corporis potestatem non [h]abet set uir.*[6] Ce est, la feme n a mie poier de son cors, mais ces maris, encement ne l oume n a mie poier de son cors, mais sa moillier.

LdAdB clvii

Ici orres par quel raison ce peut partir le mariage qui n est fait si com il deit.

S il avient que aucuns hom prent moillier et il est maindre de XIII ans, et la feme de XIII ans,[7] si com dit est dessus: la raison coumande qu il se deit partir celuy mariage par dreit sans nule paine et sans peche, se andui le veullent, ou soit que l un le veille. Et se le prestre qui les espousa sot qu il estoient maindre de l aage que establi estoit, et il les espousa sur ce par sa malice ou par priere qui li en fu faite d aucun ou por aveir qui li en fu dones: la lei et l asize coumande que celuy prestre ne deit puis messe chanter iusque ciaus qu il espousa malement seient d aage, et qu il en ait este a nostre pere l apostoille qui licence li doigne de chanter, car ce est dreit et raison. Mais ce il ont este ensemble charnaument le marit et la moillier, ne se det

---

[3] In the Roman sense of *nepos*.

[4] Cf. Azon, *Summa Codicis* (Lyons, 1540), i. v, f. CXXI[v]: 'Prohibentur autem nuptie multis modis et in primis ratione sanguinis in infinitum inter ascendentem et descendentem adeo ut si Adam hodie viveret cum nulla posset contrahere ut. j.e.l. nemini. Inter collaterales autem prohibentur ut inter frates et sorores. Inter consobrinos autem non prohibentur iure poli (usque) ad vij gradum.' In this edition there is a cross-reference: 'Prohibent, vid. plene de ista materia per do. io. lupū hispanū, in tractato de matrimonio, i. vj. col. j.' I have not been able to identify this Johannes Lupus Hispanus. Among the numerous Johannes Hispani who commented on canon law, there is one Johannes de Deo, called Hispanus (Portuguese by birth), author of a lost *Summa de sponsalibus*. He was in Bologna between 1247 and 1253 (cf. Schulte, op. cit., ii. 94 ff. and esp. 106). The phrase reappears in the Glosses of Accursius on the *Institutes* i. 10 to *in infinitum*: 'adeo ut si hodie Adam viveret, non posset habere uxorem, secundum Jo. vt. ff. de ritu nup. 1. nuptiae consistere.' Kantorowicz, op. cit., p. 94, attributed it to Johannes Bassianus.

[5] *Instit.* I. 1. 9. This quotation does not fit the following French text, which begins with an explanation 'ce est'. In the Venice MS. there is no quotation from the *Institutes* and the phrase begins: 'Car la lei', which does not make sense.

[6] I Cor. 7:4.

[7] MS. Venice indicates the age of the woman ('XIII ains'), but not that of the man.

puis partir celuy mariage par dreit, encores soit ce que andeus le voississent, ce il
n en y aveit autre iuste raison, si com est s il si s apartenissent par parente.[8]

Lo Codi v. 1. 4

*Si ille qui firmauit uxorem est minor xiiij annis et femina minor xij annis, possunt se
diuidere absque omni pena et sine peccato, si ambo hoc uolunt uel solum modo unus, licet
sit inde factum sacramentum, et licet sit inde promissa fides.*

LdAdB clviii

Ici orres la raison de celuy qui espouse feme qui est sa parente, et dou prestre qui
l espouse et de ceaus qui furent a oyr cele messe, quel pene en devent aver.

S il avient que aucuns hom, ou chevalier ou borgeis qui que il soit, prent por
feme sa cousine ou sa parente el tiers degre ou au cart:[9] la raison et la lei coumande
que celuy mariage se det partir par ce que la feme et l oume se devent andeus rendre
en religion, et tout can que ils ont si com fies ou terres ou casaus, seit de par la feme
ou de par le baron, ou seit de servise celui fie ou soit sans servise, si det estre tout
dou seignor par dreit. Car se il ont eu enfans de celui mariage tant com il ont este
ensemble ou soit par force ou par ce que l iglise et le seignor le soufreit : le dreit et
la raison coumande que ceaus enfans ne sont pas heirs, ni ne devent posseir ni tenir
nul des biens qui furent de leur pere ne de leur mere, par dreit ne par l assise, ains
deivent estre tous dou seignor.[10] Et le chapelein qui les espousa et sot qu il
s aparteneent si det souspendu a tous iors d office et de benefice, et le clerc auci ce
il le sot, et tuit cil et toutes celes qui furent a l espouser et sorent qu il s aparteneent
si sont escoumnies, si qui il n en ont part en nul des biens de sainte yglise ni entrer
dedens l iglise iusque il soient asot pas l evesque de la vile ou par le patriarche. Mais
se celuy ou cele qui s aparteneent, si com est dit dessus, et se prirent par mariage
aveent aucun prochein parent, si com est de par la feme ou de par le baron de par
qui celuy fie meut, et il ait este tel presoune qui se seit portes leaument vers le roi
ou vers le seignorage de la terre, et il soit d aage de deservir se que ses parens ou sa
parente tenoit que la seignorie a saizi par dreite : le roi ou le seignor de la terre ou
la dame est tenus par dreit de rendre li ce que ceaus ne pevent mais posseir ne tenir
ne estre nent plus heir. Et se celui ou cele qui aparteneit a ceaus ne vint ce requerre
dedens l an et le ior que li rois ou la rayne aura saisi celuy fie ou celuy casau, li rois
n est puis tenus de rendre ce qu il a saisi a nuluy, puis que l an et le ior est passe, par
dreit ne par l assise, mais tout est dou seignor.[11] Et c il n ia nul parent si com est dit
desus, le dreit et l asise coumande que tout deit estre dou seignor de la terre, car ce
est le dreit heir de ceste defaute et de ce peche et de tort qui a este fait contre Dieu
et contre les bons us et les bones coustumes dou reaume de Jerusalem qui establirent

---

[8] This whole chapter deals with matters under ecclesiastical jurisdiction which
consequently did not come before the Court of Burgesses.

[9] Cf. J. Prawer, 'L'établissement des coutumes du marché à Saint-Jean d'Acre', *RHDFE*
1951, appendix.

[10] This again belonged to ecclesiastical jurisdiction. The author probably drew his material
from either a collection of canon law or a feudal custumal. Attention should be drawn to the
fact that the author mentions apparently feudal and not burgess property.

[11] The year-and-day prescription dominates the whole system of Crusader jurisprudence.
See above, Ch. 14, pp. 343 ff.

les proudes homes ou les bons reis qui furent. Et se il rendre ne ce voleent, mais s en ci fussent[12] de la terre et estraiassent tous lor biens, l assize coumande que tout deit estre dou seignor par dreit. Et se le chappelein qui l espousa ne sot qu il furent parent, ne dit ne li fu par quei il ne les deust espouser, le dreis comande qu il n en deit aveir nule paine de celui espousement par dreit, et autel raison doit estre de ceaus qui furent a l espouser et ne sorent qu il s aparteneent, qu il n en devent pas estre entredis.

LdAdB clix

Ici orres en quel maniere on deit afier et espouser en l iglise, et quel mariage vaut, et quel paine devent paier a l iglise celuy ou cele par qui remaint que le mariage ne se fait.[13]

S il avient que aucuns hom veille prendre feme, qui que il soit ou chevalier [ou] borgeis, la raison coumande que l iglise ne les deit espouser c il ne sont premiers afies en tel maniere, ce est que celuy qui veut prendre feme si deit iurer sur Sains que il n a feme vive ne autre iuree ne afiee ne plevie ne fait nul vou par quei il ne puisse bien et leaument prendre ceste feme que il veut ores prendre, et apres ce sairement puis qu il l aura fait deveint auci II homes iurer por luy en tel maniere com est dit desus. Et auci est tenue [la feme] de faire et II femes o luy come est dit desus, et enci deit estre et det valer l afier. Et puis deit l iglise metre termine en l espouser, et por quei? por ce que dedens celuy termine deit estre cries par III iors a la premiere messe, et deit dire en ceste maniere le prestre: 'a vous, seignors et dames, fait assaver sainte yglise que le tel home deit prendre ytel feme iusque a tel ior, et se nul ou nulle y sait riens que dire por quei ce mariage ne det estre, si veigne avant et le die ains qu il soient espouses,' et qui ni venra dedens celuy terme, il ne det puis estre creus de rien que il die, nule persoune qui seit este en la terre et ne le dist dedens celuy termine ains qu il fussent espouses. Et ce mariage deit valer par dreit, par ce qu il ne s apartienent d aucun parente, si com est dit desus. Et ce est raison par dreit et par l asise dou reaume de Jerusalem.

LdAdB clx

Item de eodem, qui debet penam dare pro matrimonio. Ce est, yci ores la raison des afiailles et des repentailles c on paie.

Se un home [a] afiéé une feme si comes est dit desus, et repentailles en sont mises a l afier, et il avient puis que aucun se repente de celuy mariage faire: la raison coumande que bien se pevent repentir le quel que se veut ou l oume ou la feme, par ce que il paie celuy ou cele qui se repentira les repentailles que mises y sont, et atant en est quite par dreit et par l asise, et peut puis bien prendre autre feme, et la feme autre baron sans ce que nul cet de riens tenus a l autre por ceaus afiailles.[14]

---

[12] MS. Venice: 'mais s'en fuissent de la tere'.

[13] The contents of this chapter do not correspond to the matter announced in the rubric. There is nothing about fines to be paid to the Church. MS. Venice: 'Ci ores raizon coument l'on doit feme afier, et coment l'on doit espouzer en sainte iglise'.

[14] MS. Venice: 'sans se que l'un soit de riens tenu a l'autre par seaus afiailles'.

LdAdB clxi

Ici orres la raison de celuy qui a afiee feme et ne la prent et li a doune aucune chose, si la peut recouvrer ou non puis.

S il avient que aucuns home [a] afiéé feme et puis ne la prent, et il li a donee aucune chose: bien coumande la raison que il peut bien demander ce qu il i a mande, et li deit rendre la feme par dreit, c il n en aveit tel volente quant il li manda ce que il a demande qu il li eust ausi ce doune ia n l eust il afiee.[15] Et se est raison que il peut recouvrer ce que il a done a cele qu il volet espouser, puis qu il ne remaint en luy ne en la soue partie qu il ne la preigne a la feme, mais remaint dever partie de la feme ou par aucun des siens.[16] Mais [s] il remaint en celuy qu il ne là preigne, la raison coumande que celuy ne det pas recouvrer ce que il a baille a la feme, par dreit ne par la lei[17] ne par l asise. Et tout autel raison com est dit de l oume de ce que il done, tout autel raison est de ce que la feme, ce elle avet riens done ou mande a celuy qui la devet prendre et l avet afiee.

Lo Codi v. 2. 5

Si ille qui securauit uxorem non accepit eam, bene potest ei petere illud quod donauit, nisi habebat talem uoluntatem quando dederit ei, quod donasset ei quamuis non securasset eam. Hoc quod dictum est quia sponsus potest petere et recuperare donum quod fecit sponse sue si non accepit eam, hoc uerum est quando non remanet pro eo quia non accepit eam nec ex sua parte, set remanet ex parte femine uel pro alia iusta causa.

Set si remanet in marito uel in illo in cuius potestate est, non potest recuperare illud quod dedit: immo femina potest illud retinere et recuperare illud quod dedit ei. Illa eadem racio que dicta est ex parte uiri, eadem est ex parte mulieris que fecit donum illi qui firmauit eam.

LdAdB clxii

Ici orres la raison de celuy ou de cele qui a afie baron, et meurt ou l un ou l autre avant qu il ce preignent, et quel dreit det estre de leur choses qui remainent a leur parens.

S il avient que aucuns hom ait afiéé feme et il li a done ou fait doner aucune chose si com est dit desus, et il avient que l un des II meurt avant que l autre, ce est qu il seient pris:[18] la raison coumande que il ne ses hairs dou mort ne pueent demander de ce qu il ont baille a feme ou la feme au baron qui morte est, se non la mite de ce que il baille fu. Mais s il l avet baisee a l afier, n en pevent riens demander les hairs dou mort a celuy ni a cele a cuy fu li dons doune, ne ce li dons avoit este fait ains que il eust afiee, n en pevent riens demander ni aveir par dreit

---

[15] MS. Venice: 'ce il n'avoit telle volente quant il li manda la choze que il demande, que ia ne leust il afiée si l'eust il donne.' Both texts were obscure enough to be omitted by the Venetian committee charged with the Italian translation. The text is easily understood on the basis of the corresponding text of *Lo Codi.*

[16] *Remaint = remanet,* i.e. if it is not by his fault that the marriage did not take place.

[17] Quite often the word *loi* (= *lex Romana*) indicates the influence of *Lo Codi.*

[18] The end of the phrase should be understood as: 'ains qu'il seient pris'. MS. Venice: 'avant que il se soient pris par mariage'.

li hairs dou mort ni de la morte de celui don,[19] par dreit ne par la lei ne par lassise dou roiaume de Jerusalem.

Lo Codi v. 2. 6

Si aliquis firmauit uxorem et dedit ei aliquam rem mobilem sicut supra dictum est, et aliquis ex eis moritur antequam accipiat eam: si ipse basiauerit eam, nec ipse nec heres ipsius potest petere nisi medietatem de hoc quod donauit ei. Set si non fuerat eam osculatus, totum potest petere, si ideo donauit quia firmauerat eam. Set si donasset ei quamuis non firmaret eam, nichil potest petere. Alia racio est ex parte femine, si ipsa donauit marito quem firmauerat, et moritur unus de illis duobus ante quam uir ducat eam quia ipsa uel heres ipsius, si ipsa est mortua, totum potest petere.

LdAdB clxiii

Ici orres la raison de la feme veve qui prent autre baron dedens celuy an que l autre est mors.[20]

　　S il avient que une feme prent baron dedens celuy an que ces premiers maris est mors, la raison coumande qu elle ne le puet faire par dreit, et c elle l aveit fait, ce est que elle eust pris autre mari ains que l an et le ior fust passes de la mort de l autre maris, tel paine li est establie que, c il aveneit que aucuns hom estrange venist a mort et li laisset aucune chose en sa devise, qu elle n en peut point aver, ou seit qu il soit ces parens ou non, ne ne li devent point douner cil ou celes qui ont les choses dou mort en garde, et ce elle l aveit receu, si coumande la raison qu elle nel peut retenir, ains le det rendre as hairs de celuy qui le li aveit laisse, et ce elle nel veut rendre as hairs dou mort, l iglise ou la cort reau les li deit faire rendre, par dreit.

Lo Codi v. 5. 3

Similiter hanc aliam penam debet habere mulier que accipit maritum ante quam transeat annus post mortem alterius, quia si aliquis extraneus qui nichil pertineat mulieri uel aliquis parens mulieris ultra tercium gradum dimittit in morte sua aliquid mulieri, ipsa mulier non potest petere illud, et si acceperit inde aliquid, non potest aliquid retinere set debet reddere illis personis quibus lex precipit, quia heres illius persone que dimisit potest illam rem petere, siue succedat defuncto ex testamento siue ab intestato.

---

[19] *Lo Codi* depends on *Cod. Theod.* iii. 5, 6, or b. 16, c.v.5. The author of the *LdAdB* changed the conditions, obviously according to the custom of the kingdom. In the *pays de droit écrit* Roman law was usually followed, but at least one analogy can be found with Crusader law and this in the *Fuero Viejo* of Castile, ch. V, t. III. 4. The *adelentado* of Castile, Don Diego Lopez de Faro, concluded: 'if it was established that the young lady accorded to her fiancé the favour of *osculum* after the promise was made, she will keep all her presents; but, if on the contrary, she did not bestow upon him this favour when the engagement was made, she should render all that she received' (E. Stocquart, 'Le régime matrimonial au Moyen-Âge en Espagne', *Rev. de droit internat. et de législation comparée*, 2nd ser. xi (1909), 698–9.

[20] *Lo Codi* v. 3. 1–4 and v. 4. 1–4 defines the *sponsalicium*, which should be equal to the *dos*, and the prohibition to alienate the *dos* and the *sponsalicium*. As the customs of the Latin Kingdom were different, as indicated below, the author of the *LdAdB* did not translate these chapters.

LdAdB clxiv

Ici orres la raison de l autre paine qui det aver cele feme qui prent marit avant que l an et le ior soit passe de la mort de l autre baron, ou c ele engroisse dedens celuy an meysmes d autre.

Encement c il avient que aucune feme qui est veve prent autre mary dedens celuy an que le premier mary fu mors, si li est tel paine establie que se ses maris li laissa aucune chose a sa mort elle n en deit point aver, et se elle l a nel peut retenir, ne se autre le tient n en est tenus de riens rendre li, ains le det aver tout ce, que celui li avet laisse, le pere ou la mere dou mort ou son frere ou sa sœur ou ses nevous ou ces niesses ou ses cousins germains iusques au segont degre,[21] et ce le mort n a nule de ses persounes qui sont dites desus, la raison coumande que tout det estre dou seignor de la terre, par dreit, a qui eschiet tout. Et si deit aver auci autre paine cele feme veve qui prist mary dedens celuy an que l autre fu mors, que celuy creissement de douaire que le mort li fist ou autre por luy, quant il la prist, par desus ce qu elle li donet,[22] elle ne det riens aver, ia soit ce que ces maris li eust dit que, c il morust avant le luy, qu elle l eust, n en aura elle ia riens, por ce que dreit n en est.

Lo Codi v. 5. 4

Adhuc debet sustinere aliam penam mulier que infra annum in quo primus maritus mortuus est accepit alium maritum, quia si primus maritus dimisit et aliquid in morte, ipsa non debet illud habere: nec potest illud petere, si alii homines teneant, nec potest retinere, si ipsa habet, id est non debet habere dominium neque usumfructum, immo debent habere ille persone quibus lex precipit, id est pater mariti et mater et auus et auia et filii sui usque ad secundum gradum, id est filius et filia et nepotes, et fratres. Et si non est ibi aliqua istarum personarum, debet redire ad fiscum. Similiter sponsalicium quod dedit maritus uxori sue quando accepit eam, uel alius pro co, non debet mulier habere, quamuis fecisset ei talem conuencionem quod ipsa haberet, si prius ipse moreretur quam mulier.

[21] The *LdAdB* failed to translate the sons and daughters of the deceased. *Nepos*, 'grandchild', was understood as 'nephew', son of brother or sister. Consequently they were relegated to a position after the brothers and sisters. First cousins are related, in the Roman computation, in the fourth degree and consequently go beyond the second degree prescribed by Roman law, but they are related in the second degree according to the canon computation, followed by the *LdAdB*. MS. Venice: 'iusque au septième degré'. This is certainly influenced by the seventh-degree (parentage) recognized by the *LdAdB* as the limit of legal marriage and consequently the limit of parentage.

[22] *Creissement de douaire* is equivalent to *sponsalicium*. This is the result of the way the *LdAdB* uses the word *douaire*, viz. as *dos ex uxore*. The expression *creissement de douaire* is doubtless of meridional origin. Failing a translation of the Latin *augmentum dotis* (cf. E. de Laurière, *Glossaire*, s.v. *augmentum*), we have to relate it to *crex, creix, screyx, excreyx* from Gascony, Languedoc, Navarre, and Catalonia. Cf. A. G. Boucher d'Argis, *Traité des gains nuptiaux et de survie qui sont en usage dans les païs de droit écrit* (Paris, 1785, 2nd edn. 1856), p. 420; C. Ginoulhiac, *Histoire du régime dotal et de la communauté en France* (Paris, 1842), p. 152; G. Desdevises du Dezert, *De conditione mulierum iuxta Forum Navarrensium* (Caen, 1888), p. 27; Salvador Minguijón Adrian, *Historia del derecho español* (Barcelona, 1933), p. 243; Bienvenido Oliver, *Historia del derecho en Cataluña, Mallorca y Valencia. Codigo de las Costumbres de Tortosa*, ii (Madrid, 1876). The nearest expression to *creissement de douaire* is *creissement de maridage* quoted by F. Mistral, *Dictionnaire provençal-français*, as a Gascon expression (no source indicated).

LdAdB clxv

Item de eodem pena altera. Encement cele meysme feme qui prist mari avant qu elle ne deust si li est estably une autre paine, ce est que:

C il avient que aucuns sien parent meurt sans devise, elle ne peut ni ne det aver ce que li en avereit[23] par parente, ce elle n en eust pris baron avant qu elle ne deust. Et autel meysme paine deit aver cele feme qui engroissa dedens celuy an meysmes que ces maris fu mors, ou seit de ces maris ou seit d autre que ses maris,[24] et ce est raison par dreit et par la lei et par l asise de Jerusalem, ni ne peut par dreit aver son douaire[25] par ce qu elle vende les heritages ou les terres ou les vignes ou autres choses en meubles, ne qu elle les puisse prendre a son heus par pris. Mais coumande la raison que elle det aver les rentes des biens et les harnois de l ostel celuy qu elle aporta a celuy maris que mors est, ou que celuy fist faire por luy, et tout le remanant deit estre des enfans dou mort ou de ces parens. Et de celes rentes deit traire son douaire, et si tost com elle l aura pris, si ne deit puis rien aver es choses de celuy sien premier mary, por ce que elle prist mary avant qu elle ne dut.

Lo Codi v. 5. 5–7.

(5) *Similiter hanc penam patitur mulier supra dicta, quod non potest succedere alicui suo parenti, si moritur sine testamento, postquam transit tercium gradum parentum.* (6) *Similem penam debet habere mulier que inpregnata est infra unm annum in quo maritus mortuus est.* (7) *Pena illius femine supra dicte est, quia nec potest nec debet aliquid habere de rebus ipsius mariti qui mortuus est, quamuis dedisset ei in sponsalicium uel alio modo donasset ei in uita sua, uel dimisisset ei in morte sua aliquo modo: set fructus, id est gaudimentum, illarum rerum potest retinere in uita sua, et dominium debet esse filiorum quos habuit de illo marito qui dimisit ei rem.*

---

[23] MS. Venice: 'avenroit'.

[24] The copyist of MS. Munich obviously mistranslated *inpregnata est infra unum annum* by *engroissa*. The Latin text meant to say: 'if she becomes pregnant during the year which followed the death of her husband'. The copyist of MS. Venice, aware of the strange consequences of such a conclusion, ended the phrase by: 'ou soit de mariage ou d'autre' in the sense that it is not important if she remarried or not. Perhaps MS. Munich should read: 'ou seit de ses [instead of: *de ces*] maris ou soit d'autre que ses maris'.

[25] Despite the equivalence *sponsalicium – douaire* the *LdAdB* here uses the expression *douaire* in the sense of *dos ex uxore*, as also proved in the text which follows; cf. also ch. 162. Moreover we think that the phrase here is mutilated and should read as follows: 'Et si deit aver auci autre paine cele feme [as in ch. 164] que de celuy creissement de douaire que le mort li fist elle ne det riens aver par lei, ni ne peut par dreit aver son douaire.' This seems justified not only from the legal point of view, but also on the grounds of style and grammar. The expression: 'ce est raison par dreit et par la lei' etc. is always put at the end of an *assise*, law, or custom, and it has the same function in our text. On the other hand the expression *ni ne* is a double negative (cf. the first phrase: *ne peut, ni ne det*). We suggest then, that after 'par l'assise de Jerusalem', which finished the phrase and 'ni ne peut' some words are missing and we have tried to fill the lacuna. Cf. below, p. 399 n. 28.

LdAdB clxvi

Ici orres la raison des choses dou fis dou p remier mary qui vient a mort, s il en peut rien laisser a sa mere.[26]

Si il avient que le fis dou premier marit vient a mort et il fait sa devise, et il laisse aucune de ces choses a cele sa mere: la raison coumande que bien le peut faire, et vaut celuy dont tot auci com c il eust doune aucune persone estrange, ia soit ce que elle eust pris autre marit si com est desus dit, et ci en peut faire sa volente, ia soit ce que son fis eust fait testament ou non testament,[27] mais que done li ait devant bones gens. Et ce est dreit et raison par l'assise. Et ce est raison de ce que dit en l autre chapistle la ou il parole de ce qu elle ne peut vendre ni engager les choses dou premier marit por son douaire, mais que soulement prendre les rentes, ce est veir ce les choses murent de par la feme, la raison coumande qu elle en peut faire sa volente, et c est dreit et raison par l assise.[28]

Lo Codi v. 5. 9–10

Filius prioris mariti bene potest dimittere omnes res suas matri, sicut posset dimittere alii, quamuis mater accepisset alium maritum uel postea accipiat. Et poterit mater habere illud quod filius ei dimisit, sicut posset alius homo cui dimisisset, quamuis non potuisset ita totum habere, si filius suus non fecisset testamentum, id est si mortuus esset ab intestato. Mater non potest uendere neque donare neque pignorare neque aliter alienare neque in uita neque in morte res illas de quibus supra diximus quod ipsa debet habere solum modo gaudimentum, id est si maritus dimittit ei uel si fuerunt filii ex parte patris tantum, nisi hoc faciat illis filiis qui fuerunt prioris mariti quem maritum prius habuit quam illum quem nunc habet.

LdAdB clxvii

Ici orres la raison de celuy qui est tenus de paier le douaire por le mort a sa feme.

S il avient que les mariages se partent par la mort dou marit, la raison coumande que I sien hair dou mort ou cil qui averont ces choses devent rendre le douaire a sa feme. Mais ce les mariages fu dounes au pere dou mort ou [a] sa mere ou a aucun

---

[26] *Lo Codi* v. 5. 8 which was not translated by the *LdAdB*, states that a mother who remarried has no right to any part of the property of her predeceased son, if the latter received anything from his father, even if the son died without leaving children; but she has a life-interest in the part she would have received as property if she remained a widow. Moreover she has a right to a brother's share in the property which belonged to her son but which was not part of his (father's) patrimony.

[27] This does not mean that he died intestate, but that instead of a written testament he made an oral will in the presence of lawful witnesses.

[28] The definition of property which 'murent de par le baron' and property which 'murent par la feme' corroborate our suggestion for the correction of ch. clxv. If the reference was actually to a *dos* and *augmentum dotis*, then the practice indicated here is quite clear. Note also that the official Italian translation, which follows the Venice MS. deviates here and translates: 'si se tal beni sonno di esso marito, ma se sonno de la donna, li suoi dotali, la puol disponer d'essi ad libitum'.

des siens, dreis est que cil que resurent le mariage[29] si deivent rendre le douaire,[30] et c il sont mors, si le devent rendre leurs hairs par tel partie com chacun a eu des choses dou mort, car ce est dreit et raison par l asise.

Lo Codi v. 11. 1

Si matrimonium finitur morte mariti uel uxoris uel alia iusta causa uel alia causa que non sit iusta, solum modo non sit culpa mulieris, maritus debet mulieri reddere dotem, si fuit uiuus, et si fuit mortuus, debent ei reddere heredes sui, si maritus habuerit dotem uel alius pro eo. Set si dos illa fuit data patri mariti, pater debet reddere et si pater est mortuus, heredes ipsius tenentur, unusquisque pro ea parte quam habet de hereditate.

LdAdB clxviii

Ici orres la raison par quel chose peut la feme demander son douaire et le det aver en la vie de son baron.

Bien saches que c il avient que uns homs qui ait feme coumence a guier et a bevre et au manger et a destruire can que il a si qu il coumence a apovrir: la raison coumande que la feme peut bien demander son douaire, et est tenus ces maris, par dreit, de metre son douaire ou le vaillant en la main de proudes homes ou en tel leuc, que see sauf a celuy ou a cele qui aveir le devra, car ce est dreit et raison par l asise et par la lei de Jerusalem.

Lo Codi v. 11. 2

Donec matrimonium durat inter maritum et uxorem non potest mulier petere dotem suam, nisi maritus factus est pauper uel quod facit aliquid unde apareat quod debeat esse pauper. Set si hoc apparet, femina potest petere dotem et donacionem propter nupcias, et maritus debet ei reddere, et mulier debet tenere et custodire res illas sicuti maritus facerat, si teneret eas. Et omne gaudimentum quod potest mulier habere de dote et de donacione propter nupcias, id est de antifaito, debet mulier expendere in se et in marito et in filiis quos habuerit de illo marito, et in illis in quibus maritus expenderet, si haberet dotem et antifaitum, et non alio modo.

LdAdB clxix

Ici orres la raison de celuy qui n a de quei paier le douaire de sa feme, et c il en deit aver nul mau.

S il avient que aucuns hons seit mis en plait de rendre le douaire de sa moullier, et il est tant povres que il n en a de quei rendre: la raison et la lei coumande que

---

[29] This expression is equivalent to *maritagium*, which is known from the Frankish period and later in the *pays de droit coutumier*. Usually it denotes the *dos ex uxore*. The same expression with the same meaning is also known from the Midi, cf. p. 403 n. 35.

[30] *Maritagium* should not be understood as 'qui ont reçu la dote doivent payer le douaire' (in the customary sense), but 'qui ont reçu la dot doivent le rendre'. MS. Venice: 'S'il qui resurent le mariage, si doivent rendre leur hairs par tel partie come chascun avera des chozes dou mort'. This is followed by the Italian translation: 'ma se la dote fusse stà datta al padre, ò al madre, ò ad alcun parente del morto, è iusto che loro, ò suoi heredi, e quelli che haueranno di suoi benni, la paghino'.

celuy ou cele, qui rendre devoit celuy douaire et n a de quei paier que il ne doit mie por ce estre mis en prison ne condampnes dou cors, mais det paier tant com il a,[31] et dou remanant det iurer sur Sains que il li donra can que il li guaaignera traiant sa vie escharsement, et qu il ne se partira de la vile sans son conge iusques il l ait paiee, et atant en deit estre quite par dreit et par la lei et par l assise dou reaume de Jerusalem.

Lo Codi v. 14. 1

Si maritus mittitur in placito ut dotem reddat uxoris sue, et ipse est ita pauper quod non possit illam reddere, ipse non debet condempnari nisi in quantum ipse facere potest, uel nisi in quantum ipse fecit suo malo ingenio quod non posset pagare. Set debet promittere quod paget illud quod remanet, si ipse lucratus fuerit de quo possit pagare.

LdAdB clxx

Ici orres quel raison det estre des dons que le mari fait a sa moillier puis que il l a prise, et quel don vaut et quel don n en vaut.

Bien saches que nus hons ne peut faire don a sa moillier puis que il l a prise, si ne le fait a sa mort ou en son testament, et c il le fait en autre maniere, ne vaut celuy don, por ce que la choses est auci soue com c il ne l eust ia dounee, et la pevent recouvrer les heirs dou mort par dreit de tos ceaus qui tenreeint la chose, se ceaus qui tienent la chose ne l ont tenue an et ior sans ce que nus hom en ait fait clain ne riens demande, il n en devent riens respondre par dreit ne par l assise a nul heirs qui soit en celuy ior d aage.

Lo Codi v. 16. 1, 2

Rub. *Si maritus donat aliquid uxori sue uel uxor marito uel pater filio uel filius patri.*

Modo dicamus que racio est de donacione quam fecit maritus uxori sue post quam accipit eam, uel quam fecit uxor marito suo, uel pater filio, uel filius patri. Nullus homo potest facere donacionem uxori sue post quam duxit eam, si ipse non facit in morte uel in testamento. Et si ipse fecerit alio modo, non ualebit donacio, et res illa quam ei donat remanet sua, sicuti si nichil donasset ei, et potest rem illam dimandare et ipse et heres ipsius omnibus hominibus qui tenent rem ipsam, si ipse non tenuerit eam tanto tempore quod possit se defendere.

LdAdB clxxi

Ici orres la raison dou don que l on peut faire a sa moillier, et det valer par dreit.

Tel fes avient que le marit si peut bien faire don a sa moillier, si com est c il establis que sa moillier ait chacun mes I besanz ou II marc d argent ou plus ou mains por son vivre ou por nourir ces anfans et sa maisnee. La raison et le dreit coumande que bien le peut bien faire ce don, et det estre ferme et le det aver sa moillier tant come ses maris li aura establly, et tenus sont cil qui averont les choses de son marit

---

[31] *LdAdB* deviates here from the Latin text of *Lo Codi*, but conforms to the Provençal original, which reads: 'de tant cum el pot pager', quoted by Fitting, op. cit., introduction, p. 53.

en garde de douner ly se que ces maris li a done por son vivre et por ces enfans. Car ce est dreit et raison par l'asise de Jerusalem.

Lo Codi v. 16. 13

Aliquando est quod maritus potest donare uxori sue, sicuti est si donat ei per unum quemque annum, uel per singulos menses, ideo ut ipsa nutriat se uel filios suos uel familiam suam.

LdAdB clxxii

Ici orres la raison dou mariage, par cantes choses ce peut puis partir le mariage puis qu il est fait, ce est puis qu il se sont pris encemble.[32]

Si il avient que uns hons ait prise une feme, et cele feme devient puis mezele, ou chiet dou mauvais mau trop laidement, ou li put trop fierement la bouche et le nes, ou pisce aucune nuit au lit si que tout ce gastent ces dras: la raison commande que, se le marit s en claime a l iglise et ne veut plus estre o luy por ce mahaing qu il i a, que l iglise les det despartir par dreit,[33] mais l iglise det tout premier avant qui les parte prendre la feme et metre en un hotel o III autres bounes femes qui soient o elles XV iors ou I mes por veyr se ce est verite que ses maris dit, et c il veent et counoissent par celes femes que elle ait la tache que ces maris dit, dreis est qu il seient partis et que celuy ou cele qui avera la tache que dite est desus soit rendus en religion,[34] et le maris peut puis bien prendre autre moullier, par droit, puis que il sera partis de l autre feme qui se cera rendue en ordre de religion. Et tout autel raison est dou marit c il avoit le mahaing que dit est desus et sa moillier n en eust point dou mahaing, et tout en autele maniere deit estre iuges com est dite la raison devant de sa feme, et ce est dreit et raison par l asise.

Lo Codi v. 17

Rub. *Per quas causas maritus potest se diuidere ab uxore sua uel uxor a marito.*

LdAdB clxxiii

Ici orres la raison de celuy mariage qui se partent par acun essoigne.

---

[32] This chapter is not taken from *Lo Codi*. The problems of divorce belonged to ecclesiastical jurisdiction and the 'civilists' did not deal with it. *Lo Codi* v. 17 reads: 'Sicuti homines possunt accipere uxores et femine possunt accipere maritos, similiter sunt quedam iuste et certe causae per quas maritus potest dimittere uxorem suam sine pena, quamuis non uelit hoc femina . . . sed quia non est in consuetudine hodie quod matrimonium diuidatur nisi per canones, sicuti propter parentelam uel per adulterium quod facit femina, ideo non est necessarium ut inde aliquid dicamus.'

[33] The reasons listed here were not accepted by canon law as sufficient for a divorce. Cf. V. Foucher, op. cit., pp. 324–5. *Las Siete Partidas* iv. 1. 8 did count them as valid for a dissolution of an engagement: 'si alguno dellos se ficiese gafo, ò contrecho, ò perdiesse les narices ol aveniese alcuna otra casa mas desaguisada que alguna destas sobredichas', but not sufficient for a divorce, cf. ibid. iv. 2, 7. But there is a good analogy in the *Fors de Morlaas*, § 357: 'Si ere fevide meserarie et sa lect ave pudente', quoted by F. Laferrière, *Histoire du droit français* v (Paris, 1858), 437.

[34] A similar case is once mentioned in the *Livre au Roi*.

S il avient que une feme se parte de son baron par aucune de ces teches qui sont dites desus, la raison comande que son marit est tenus de douner atant a l abaye ou elle se rendera come sa moillier li aporta en mariage,[35] et se l abaye ne la veut por tant receivre, il est tenus de tant douner leur par quei il la receivent. Et ce il n a tant come elle li dona en mariage, la raison coumande que il n en est tenus de douner li se non tant come il porra douner et non de plus, par dreit et par l asise.

LdAdB clxxiv

Ici dit la raison de celuy mariage qui est partis et il ont enfans, qui les deit nourir.

S il avient que uns hons se soit partis de sa moillier par aucune iuste raison, et il ont enfans eu: la raison coumande que ce les enfans sont menors de III ans, il les deit nourir la mere iusque il aient VII ans, et le pere lor deit douner dou cien a manger et a bevre et a vestir et a chausser et tous lors estouviers. Mais se lor mere est malade de meselerie ou dou grant mau, la raison coumande qu elle ne deit nul nourir des enfans, mais le pere, por ce que tost poret ocirre ou mahaigner aucun de ces enfans ou par la maladie ou par la meselerie qui mout tost cort. Mais ce elle n en a nule de cestes choses si com est mezele ni dou mauvais mau, bien les peut nourir iusques as VII ans, si come est dit desus, o les despences dou pere segont se que il porra, et puis se le pere les voisist prendre a ces enfans, et il ne voisissent aler au pere, ou la mere ne les li vost baillier, por ce qu il avet pris autre feme ou par autre iuste raison: le dreit comande que les iures devent esgarder et entendre le fait dou pere et de la mere, et la ou il vorront que les enfans seront miaus, la les deivent laisser iusque il aient XII ans, et puis ont poer d aler estre o le pere ou a la mere ou o qui que il vorront, par dreit et par l asise.

Lo Codi v. 18. 1–2

Si maritus dispartitus est ab uxore sua aliquo modo et ipse habet filios ex ea qui sunt minores tribus annis, mater debet eos nutrire donec sint tres anni transacti. Sed si ipsi sunt maiores tribus annis, pater debet eos nutrire.

Etiam iudex debet inquirere cum quo possint melius stare, uel cum patre uel cum matre, et ipse debet precipere ut ille teneat infantes cum quo melius poterunt manere, siue sint minores tribus annis siue sint maiores.

LdAdB clxxv

Ici dit la raison de ceaus anfans qui sont bastars, ques dreis il deivent aver es heritages de leur pere et de leur mere et en lor choses.

S il avient que uns homs tient une feme qui n a point de baron en son hostel, ne il n a point de feme et gist o luy et ont enfans, bien comande la raison et l asise que ces anfans peut il bien laisser et en sa vie et a sa mort ces heritages et son aver par dreit, par ce qu il n en ait autres anfans leaus ni pere ni mere. Mais c il a autres

---

[35] *Maritagium* in the sense of *dos ex uxore*. The erratic vocabulary of the *LdAdB* has its counterpart in the *termini* of Bearn: *dot et eydes, maridagi, doari, doage* (P. Luc, *Vie rurale et pratique juridique au Béarn aux XIVe et XVe siècle* (Toulouse, 1943), p. 82).

anfans leaus ou pere ou mere[36] ne le peut faire c il ne les veillent acuillir par leur bone volente, mais c il les ia acuille[n]t en le frerage,[37] bien pevent puis atant aver l un frere come l autre, par dreit et par l asise.

Lo Codi v. 20. 1–2

Contingit aliquando quod illi filii qui non sunt nati de uxore possunt habere hereditatem patris sui. Si aliquis homo qui non habet uxorem iacet cum aliqua femina quam posset ducere in uxorem rationabiliter si ambo uoluissent, et ipse tenet eam solam in domo sua et habet filios ex ea, bene potest donare illis filiis quos habet ex ea in uita sua et in morte omnes res suas, hoc est totam pecuniam et possessiones, si ipse non habet legitimos filios neque habet patrem uel matrem uel aliam superiorem personam. Set si ipse habet aliquam de superioribus et ipse non habet filios legitimos, potest similiter dare omnes res suas filiis supradictis preter falcidiam quam debet relinquere superioribus parentibus, scilicet illis qui sunt proximiores.

LdAdB clxxvi

De matrimonio. Ce est yci orres conbien coumande la lei et l'assise con deit estre esposer.[38]   A Septuagesima[39] usque in octauam Pasche et in Letania maiori et in diebus Rogacionum et in tribus hebdomadibus ante festiuitatem Sancti Johannis Baptiste et in Aduentum Domini usque post octavam Epifanie et in Omnibus

---

[36] Roman law awarded the *falcidia* to ascendants, but for *LdAdB*, which did not follow Roman law, *Lo Codi* presented many difficulties. Although the author of the *LdAdB* faithfully followed *Lo Codi* he tried to give it another meaning. This explains the clumsiness with which he introduced *père* and *mère*.

[37] This is not the *frérage* known from customary law. V. Foucher, op. cit., p. 320, n. 1, quotes an interesting analogy from Lombard law (b. ii, t. 8, l. 6). This *frérage* may be linked with the Byzantine practice of *adelphopoiia*, which, however, had no legal standing in law. Cf. Zachariae v. Lingenthal, *Geschichte des griech.-römischen Rechts* (Berlin, 1892), pp. 118–19.

[38] The rubric is obscure and a better reading is in MS. Venice: 'Ci ores raizon conbien de tens hom doit laisser de non faire espousailles mais bien pevent fere affialez.' The following chapter (in Latin) does not exist in MS. Venice, but there is a corresponding French chapter in MS. Munich. The much mutilated text is printed here with H. Kausler's corrections.

[39] The text of Gratian, *Decret*, c. 9. c. xxxiii, qu. 4, is different from that of the *LdAdB*. *LdAdB* must have taken it from a collection of canon law which I cannot identify. The *Rogationes*, usually translated as *Roaisons* or *Rouvoisons* are referred to in this context in a letter of Clemens III or Celestin III, where the diversity of procedure is indicated (*Decret. Gregorii*, l. ii, t. ix, c. iv). Generally speaking the canonists modified the severity of the custom. Magister Rufinus (+c. 1192) understood *separentur*: 'ita tamen ut, si ecclesia postea eis coniugia invicem consenserit, restaurari possit matrimonium ratumque effici' (*Summa decretorum*, ed. H. Singer, p. 504). Similarly Mag. Gandulphus Bononiensis (+c. 1185), *Sententiarum lib. quatuor*, ed. I. Watter (1924), p. 608: 'intelligitur a cohabitatione, usque dum praedictum tempus compleatur et satisfactio peragatur'. Cf. also Alexander de Hales, *Glossa in IV Libros Sentent. Petri Lombardi* iv (Florence, 1957), 513–14. But cf. Petrus Lombardus, *Sententiae*, l. iv, dist. 32. PL 192, col. 924.

Sanctorum vigiliis nupcias celebrare prohibemus, quod si factae fuerunt, separentur.[40]

LdAdB clxxvii

Item hec est de eodem

Bien saches que des le dimanche de Careme prenant des moines en iusques a VIII iors apres la Pasque ne doit ni ne peut nus hons espouser ni es iors des grans Litanies ni en les iors des Preeres ni en les III semaines devant la feste de Saint Johan Baptiste ni as Avens de nostre Seignor en iusque a VIII iors apres le Baptesme ne doit nus hom espouser, ni en toutes les vegiles de Sains ne deit hon espouser, por ce que la lei et les sains decres le defendent. Et c il avenist par aucune aventure aucun houme espousast en ces iors qui sont defendus et par la lei et par sainte yglise : la raison coumande que celuy mariage ne vaut, ni les enfans qu il auront ne seront mie dreit heir d aver ce que eschier lor devret, et est tenue sainte yglise par dreit de partir celuy mariage. Mais en tous les iors de l an pueent bien les homes faire afiailles, et si devent valer, mais ne pevent confermer le mariage, ce est espouser, se non es iors que commandes sont. Et encores par les saintes coustumes est defendu c on ne preigne por feme la feme qu il a tenue au fons en sainte yglise a baptiser, ne que son fis ne preigne por moillier la fille de sa fille esperitau qui puis est nee qu il la tint au fons, mais ce ses anfans furent avant nes qu il la tenist au fons, bien ce pevent prendre par dreit.[41] Et par la sainte fei est desfendu que mariage ne soit entre Crestiene et Sarasin, por ce que bien deivent tous homes saver-que par la sainte assise de Jerusalem ait la feme la mite de tous les biens que son baron gaaigne o luy despuis que il la prent :[42] car ce est droit et raison par lasise, *quia ex quo uir et mulier fiunt una caro, merito quicquid uir acquirit uxore uiuente iure cedit uxori medietatem.*

LdAdB clxxviii

Ici orres la raison dou marit et de la moillier, et en quel cort il se deivent clamer la moillier se ses maris li mesfait ou la bate.

[40] In *Lo Codi* this is followed by two chapters respectively entitled : 'Quomodo possunt uendi et inpignorari res illorum qui sunt minores XXV annis' and 'Quomodo minor XXV annis potest alienare res suas' (v. 21 and 22). These chapters were of no interest to the author of the *LdAdB*. Having used all the material of *Lo Codi* referring to marriage, he adds some dispositions of the canon law and customary laws of the kingdom, which he did not find in *Lo Codi*. Note the strange rubric *De matrimonio* in the middle of an *opusculum* : *De pactis de matrimonio.*

[41] Marriage impediment in the case of spiritual parentage is that between the son of a godfather and his god-daughter. But if the son was born before the baptism of the daughter, he can marry his father's god-daughter. But this was changed by a decree of Alexander III: 'Et licet primus canon exinde editus natos post compaternitatem adinvicem copulari prohibeat, alter tamen canon posterius editus primum videtur corrigere, per quem statuitur, ut sive ante, sive post compaternitatem geniti sunt, simul possunt coniungi, excepta ille persona duntaxat per quam ad comparnitatem venitur' (x, l. iv, tit. ix, c. 1).

[42] This strange passage (perhaps some sort of *continuatio titulorum*) introduces ch. 180, which deals in detail with the rights of women in *gains de survie*. The Latin end-phrase did not belong to the original text.

Se il avient que clamour se face en la cort, si com est la feme de son baron de bature ou le baron de sa feme en la cort reau, la raison coumande que ceste clamour ne deit mie estre oye ne iugee par cort reau, mais le det mander le vesconte et les iures a sainte yglise, et iqui se peut plaindre l un de l autre et sainte yglise est tenue de chastier les et d adrecer les en pais. Car se le baron ou la feme se clamoit de son baron en la cort reau de la bateure, et il avient que le baron gaaigne le plait contre sa feme de ce don elle c est clames de luy, ou la feme desraigne ce dont elle c est clamee de luy : dreis est que celuy, qui sera vencus de celuy clain, que il paie le dreit de la cort, et don paiera la feme le dreit de la cort se non de ce de son baron, car elle n en a riens qui ne soit de son baron, ne le baron n a riens qui ne soit de sa feme ausi. Et por ce que le baron ni la feme ne peut riens perdre que atant ni ait de damage li uns coume li autres, car toutes leurs choses sont coumunaus, a estably la raison et l asise que nule clamour que face la feme de son baron ni le baron de sa feme ne doit estre faite se non en sainte yglise qui est choses de misericorde. Ne nule cort ne se det entremetre dou fait de matrimoine se non sainte yglise, ce ce ne fust clamor de murtre ou de trayson enver la reaute. Car ce le clain est de ce, la raison coumande que celuy clain deit venir par dreit en la cort reau. *Quia Christi ecclesie sacramentum in se continet matrimonium ideo coniugatos decet in ecclesia purgari. Et unum alteri in eadem reconsiliari, nisi forte omicidii uel criminis majestatis reatur alter eorum accusetur.*

LdAdB clxxix

Ici orres la raison de celuy qui prent une feme o tous ces dreis en mariage.

S il avient que un home prent une feme en mariage o tous ces dreis, et puis que il l ot prise si vint avant aucun home ou aucune feme et le mete en plait de ce qu il a pris o luy, ou de ce que la feme prist o son baron li met l on plait, et c il avient que le baron mete celuy plait sur sa feme ou la feme sur son baron : la raison coumande que puis que l on l avera mis sur l autre ne peut puis riens recouvrer n amender de ce que fait en cera, mais couvient que teigne ce que celuy ou cele en aura fait. Car ce est dreit et raison par l asise, et por ce se gart bien celuy home qui metra sa feme en son leuc por pladier, qu il la coumise a tel qu elle ne die riens sans son conceill, car ce elle diseit riens qui li deust torner a damage, elle ni ces maris ni poret riens puis amender en cele dit qu elle a dit, *quia maiora presumsit mulier fatiori*.

LdAdB clxxx

Ici orres la raison de ce, se la feme et le baron guaaignent et conquierent encemble.

S il avient que un home et sa feme ont ensemble conquis vignes on terres ou maisons ou iardins, le dreit dit que la feme doit aver la moitie de tout par dreit et par l assise dou reaume de Jerusalem. El se la feme et le baron ont enfans, ia ne lairont por leurs anfans de vendre ni de douner leur biens a qui que il voront, ni de beivre ni de manger leurs biens tant coume il vivront. Et ce le baron vient a mort, il peut douner sa part ou il vora ou a ces anfans ou a autre. Et puis que le marit de la feme est mort, la feme peut puis faire de sa part sa volente, por ce qu ele la conquis encemble o luy. Mais la raison coumande que tant come le baron vive, la feme n a nul poier de douner sa part a nuluy, par dreit ne par l asise.[43] Mais se le baron et la feme estoient mors et il aveent laisse leur maisons a leur enfans, se il sont d aage bien pevent vendre et douner ceaus eritages a qui que il voront, chascun sa part. Mais se il ne sont d aage, il ne pevent vendre ni doner leur heritage a nuluy. Mais se leur pere ou leur mere leur laisserent chose meuble si com est aver ou iuiaus ou robe, et l un des anfans est d aage et les autres non: la raison comande que celuy qui est d aage peut bien prendre sa part de celuy aver et faire sa volonte et deit estuier le remanant et sauver as autres freres qui ne sont d'aage, car ce est dreit et raison. *Quia adulte et perfecte etatis fratres et fratribus impuberibus et minoribus legitimi tutores et curatores esse debent.*

Cf. *Lo Codi* v.21.1;4

[43] The chapter refers to a *régime de la communauté de conquêts* which is superimposed on the *régime dotal* already exposed. The whole system is not dealt with here (additional material in ch. 183). This combination of both systems existed in many regions of the *pays de droit écrit*, although the system of the *LdAdB* does not seem to have existed in its entirety in other places. Similar systems however existed in Toulouse, Bearn, Pays Basque, Basse Navarre, Catalonia, and Tortosa. We cannot accept the conclusions of J. J. Raikem in his observations on *Li Paweilhars. Rec. des coutumes de Liège* i (Brussels, 1870), 247–53, where he attempted to find the source of Crusader marital law in the customs of Liège. Cf. F. Bomerson, 'La mainplévie dans le droit coutumier liègeois', *RHDFE*, 1930, pp. 294 ff., esp. pp. 316–21.

Appendix B
Bibliographical Note on the
Livre des Assises des Bourgeois

There is no complete bibliography of the *Livre des Assises des Bourgeois*. We shall try to fill this gap to a certain extent by the following list.

On the different manuscripts, editions, and translations cf. M. Grandclaude, *Étude critique sur les Livres des Assises de Jérusalem* (Paris, 1923). Idem, 'Classement sommaire des mss. des principaux Livres des Assises de Jérusalem', *RHDFE* 1926, pp. 418–74.

The full text has been published by V. Foucher, *Assises du Royaume de Jérusalem* (from a manuscript in the Bibl. de Saint-Marc de Venise), i. 1 (Rennes, 1839); E. H. Kausler, *Les Livres des assises et des usages du reaume de Jérusalem*, i (Stuttgart, 1839); Comte Beugnot, 'Assises de la Cour des Bourgeois', *Lois* ii (Paris, 1843).

We note the following studies: B. J. Docen, 'Die "Assises dou Reaume de Chipre" handschriftlich noch in der Münchener Bibliothek befindlich', *Beyträge zur Geschichte und Literatur,* ed. I. Ch. von Aretin ix (Munich, 1807), 1278–86. Camus–Dupin, *Lettres sur la profession d'avocat et bibliothèque choisie des livres de droit* ii (Paris, 1820), 4–5; A. Taillandier, 'Dissertation sur les Assises de Jérusalem', *Thémis ou Bibl. des jurisconsultes* vii, 10 (1826); K. E. Schmid, 'Über die Assisen von Jerusalem', *Hermes* xxx (Leipzig, 1828), 315–41; J. M. Pardessus, *Collection de lois maritimes antérieures au XVIIIe siècle*, i, ch. VII: 'Droit maritime des pays conquis par les Croisés en Orient' (Paris, 1828), pp. 261–82; J. M. Pardessus, 'Mémoire sur l'origine du droit coutumier en France et sur son état jusqu'au XIIIe siècle', *Mémoires de l'Institut royal de France*, Acad. des Inscriptions et Belles-Lettres (29 May 1829), x (1833), 666–765; J. M. Pardessus, 'Mémoire sur un monument de l'ancien droit coutumier de la France, connu sous le nom d'Assises du Royaume de Jérusalem', Acad. des Inscriptions et Belles-Lettres (31 July 1829), *Thémis*, 1829, pp. 1–17; C. Laferrière, *Histoire du droit français* i (Paris, 1836), 473–535; E. H. Kausler, 'Des assises de Jérusalem et des diverses éditions de ce recueil qui se préparent en ce moment', *Revue française et étrangère de législation et d'économie politique*, ed. M. Foelix, vi (1839), 386–400; V. Foucher, 'Réponse à E. H. Kausler', ibid. 460–470; V. Foucher, 'Lettre à M. Foelix a l'occasion de quelques critiques sur la publication des Assises de Jérusalem', *Revue de législation et de jurisprudence*, ed. par Wolowski, ix (1839); M. Foelix, 'Compte rendu de l'édition d'E. H. Kausler', *Revue franç. et étrangère*, vii (1840), 152–3; J. M. Pardessus, 'Rapport fait à l'Acad. des Inscriptiones et Belles-Lettres au nom de la Commission des travaux littéraires, sur la publication des Assises de Jérusalem' (16 Feb. and 2 Mar. 1838); L. A. Warnkoenig, 'Compte rendu de l'édition d'E. H. Kausler', *Gelehrte Anzeigen, hrsg. v. Mitgliedern d. Kön.-bayrischen Akad. d. Wissenschaften*, x (Munich, 1890), nos. 116–23, pp. 929–92; Comte Beugnot, 'Introduction aux Assises de la Cour des Bourgeois', *Lois* ii (Paris, 1843); H. G. 'Compte rendu de l'édition des Assises par

Beugnot', *BEC* ii (1840–1), 289–95; T. Smith, *The Assize of Jerusalem, read before the Leicestershire Literary Society*, 7 Jan. 1842 (Leicester, 1842); F. Lajard, 'Compte rendu de l'édition des Assises par Beugnot', *Histoire littéraire de la France* xxi (1847), 433–67, esp. 459 ff.; P. Paris, 'Compte rendu de l'édition des Assises par Beugnot', *Journal des savants* (1841), p. 292; ibid. (1844), p. 248; C. Giraud, 'Du droit français dans l'Orient au Moyen Âge et de la traduction grecque des Assisses de Jérusalem', *Revue de législation et de jurisprudence* xvii (Jan.–June 1843), 22–44; also published in *Séances et travaux de l'Acad. des sciences morales et politiques* (12 Nov. 1842), ii (1842), 261–84; P. Viollet, 'La Cour du vicomte dans l'Orient latin'. Positions de thèses de l'École des Chartes, 1863 (unpublished); F. Monnier, 'Godefroi de Bouillon et les Assises de Jérusalem', *Acad. des sciences morales et politiques*, Séances et travaux, 100 (1873), 73 ff. and 101 (1874); Fauconneau–Dufresne, *Les Assises du Royaume de Jérusalem* (Colmar, 1869), mainly based on Pardessus, 'Mémoire sur l'origine'); T. Twiss, *The Black Book of the Admiralty* iv (London, 1876), pp. xvi ff.; E. G. Rey, *Les Colonies franques de Syrie aux XIIe et XIIIe siècles* (Paris, 1883); G. Dodu, *Histoire des institutions monarchiques dans le royaume latin de Jérusalem* (Paris, 1894), esp. pp. 36–8; H. Prutz, *Kulturgeschichte der Kreuzzüge* (Berlin, 1883), esp. pp. 344 ff.; E. Glasson, *Histoire du droit et des institutions de la France* iv (Paris, 1891), 243–54; A. Teichman, 'Ueber die Assisen von Jerusalem und von Antiochia', *Festgabe der jurist. Fakultät d. Univ. Basel zum 70en Geburtstag von A. Heusler* (Basel, 1904), pp. 35–8; H. L. Zeller, *Die Assisen von Jerusalem nach der Hs. München, Cod. gall. 51* (Berlin, 1910); idem, 'Das Seerecht in den Assisen von Jerusalem nach der Handschrift Venedig', *Sitzungsberichte der Heidelberger Akad. d. Wissen, Phil.-hist. Klasse*, XVIte Abhandlung (Heidelberg, 1916); E. Derazé, *Le Mariage d'après les Assises de Jérusalem* (Poitiers, 1910); P. Christin, *Étude des classes inférieures d'après les Assises de Jérusalem* (Poitiers, 1912); R. Marque, *Les Successions testamentaires d'après les Assises de Jérusalem* (Poiters, 1912); M. Grandclaude, *Étude critique sur les Livres des Assises de Jérusalem* (Paris, 1923); cf. F. L. Ganshof in *Byzantion* ii (1925), 479–81, and G. Recoura, 'Les Assises de Jérusalem. A propos d'un livre récent', *Moyen-Âge* 26 (1924–5); M. Grandclaude, 'Classement sommaire des mss. des principaux Livres des Assises', *RHDFE* 1926, pp. 418–75; D. Hayek, *Le Droit franc en Syrie pendant les Croisades. Institutions judiciaires* (Paris, 1925); N. Zygadinos, *Zur Frage des Assisenrechts, 1099–1517* (Athens, 1928); M. Grandclaude, 'Liste d'Assises remontant au premier Royaume de Jérusalem (1099–1187)', *Mélanges Paul Fournier* (Paris, 1929), pp. 329 ff.; H. Mitteis, 'Zur Schuld und Handelsgeschichte der Kreuzfahrerstaaten', *Festschrift für Ernst Heymann* (Marburg, 1931), pp. 229–88; John L. La Monte, *Feudal Monarchy in the Latin Kingdom of Jerusalem, 1100–1291* (Cambr., Mass., 1932), esp. pp. 281–2; idem, 'Three questions concerning the Assises of Jerusalem', *Byzantina–Metabyzantina* i (New York, 1946); J. Prawer, 'L'établissement des coutumes du marché à Saint-Jean-d'Acre et la date de composition du *Livre des Assises des Bourgeois*', *RHDFE* 1951, pp. 329–51; J. Richard, 'Colonies marchandes privilegiées et marché seigneurial. La Fonde d'Acre et ses "droitures"', *Moyen Âge* 59 (1953), 325–40; P. Zepos, 'Quelques remarques sur les rapports entre le droit byzantin et le droit des latins en Orient', *Festschrift H. Lewald* (1953), pp. 209–15; J. Prawer, 'Étude préliminaire sur les sources et la composition du *LdAdB*', *RHDFE* (1954), pp. 198–227, 358–82.

16 Crusader Penal Law and its European Antecedents

The main argument of the previous chapter was that the anonymous Crusader law practitioner, author of the *Livre des Assises des Bourgeois*, who lived around the middle of the thirteenth century in Acre, used a Latin version of the Provençal law manual *Lo Codi* as the model for his own work. This poses an obvious question: to what extent does the *LdAdB* contain or reflect actual Crusader practice? Though the *LdAdB* often used Roman terms, Roman law, or Roman 'popular' law, it does not necessarily follow that Roman law was 'received' in the Latin Kingdom. A glance at the legal procedure of the Crusader courts proves the contrary. Our Crusader lawyer used *Lo Codi* as a model, a framework in which to mould current Crusader law. The latter, no doubt, included elements of Roman law, but its basic contents were of medieval European origin.

Several attempts have been made to connect Crusader law with its European cradle, but so far, no conclusive results have been reached. Victor Foucher, whose edition of the *LdAdB* was cut short by Kausler's vastly superior edition,[1] tackled the problem but never reached any conclusions, and his voluble annotations were a sad example of perfect chaos. Beugnot did not fare much better.[2] Excellent scholar that he was, he started out with the general idea that Crusader law reflected the cosmopolitan composition of the Crusader population.[3] Consequently, his illustrations and explanations, though often illuminating, roam freely over the vast sources of legal practice and jurisprudence of Western Europe. The texts quoted by Beugnot, though often helpful to the understanding of Crusader practice, hardly ever point to any defined European area in which it may have originated. Other historians started out from the proposition that one should look for the cradle of Crusader institutions in the birth-place of Godfrey of Bouillon and his successors.[4] Apart from some generalities, the point was never proven.

---

[1] See above, Ch. 15, Appendix B, pp. 408–9.

[2] *Lois* ii. 1–226.

[3] In fact this was the way in which Crusader thirteenth-century jurisprudence liked to view its own customary law.

[4] M. Bernardi, 'Mémoire sur l'origine de la pairie en France et en Angleterre', *Mém. de*

Note also the following studies: F. Litten, 'Ueber *Lo Codi* und seine Stellung in der Entwicklungsgeschichte des Culpa-Problems', *Mélanges Fitting* ii (Montpellier, 1908), 609–34; Otto Wesemann, *Ueber die Sprache der altprovenzalischen Handschrift nouv. acq. fr. 4138 der B.N. zu Paris* (Halle, 1891). The influence of *Lo Codi* on the *Charte d'Arles* was pointed out by H. Fitting, op. cit., p. 60; on the *Coutume de Tortose* v. 5, § 3, cf. E. de Hinojosa. 'La réception du droit romain en Catalogne', *Mélanges Fitting* ii (Montpellier, 1908), 399; on Anjou, H. Fitting, op. cit., p. 60; cf. C. J. Beautemps-Beaupré, 'Cy sont les Coutumes d'Anjou et du Maine intitulées selon les rubriches de Code, dont les aucunes sont concordées de droit escript (1437)', *Coutumes et Institutions d'Anjou et du Maine antérieures au XIVᵉ siècle*, i, pt. II (Paris, 1878); *Les Lois de l'Empereur* were published by J. Brissaud and P. Rogé, *Textes additionnels aux anciens Fors de Béarn* (Toulouse, 1905). The influence of *Lo Codi* was first pointed out by Meynial, 'Le Codi et les Fors de Béarn', *RHDFE* 30 (1906), 382 ff., and the study was completed by P. Rogé, *Les Anciens Fors de Béarn* (Toulouse, 1907), pp. 397 ff.

A Latin text related to *Lo Codi* and preserved in Venetian legislation was published by B. Pitzorno, 'Il "Liber romanae legis" della "Ratio de lege Romana"', *Rivista italiana per le sc. giur.*, 43 (1907), 101–34, and idem, 'Il "Liber romanae legis" degli "Judicia a probis iudicibus promulgata"', ibid. 44 (1908), 269–92. Cf. idem, 'Il diritto romano come diritto consuetudinario', *Per il XIV centenario della codificazione giustinianea*, ed. P. Ciapessoni (Pavia, 1934), pp. 743–91.

Since before the First World War there have been no particular studies of *Lo Codi* excepting our own, published in 1954. This was followed by two important discoveries by R. Feenstra (Latin version MS. Lucca, Bibl. Feliniana 437): 'A propos d'un nouveau manuscrit de la version latine du Codi', *Rec. droit écrit* vi (1967), 37–45; *Collectanea Stephan Kuttner* iii (*Studia Gratiana* xiii) (Bologna, 1967), 57–81, and two pages discovered by P. Ourliac of an unknown provençal manuscript assigned to *c.* 1250–70; P. Ourliac, 'Sur deux feuilletes du Codi', *Mélanges Roger Aubenas* (*Rec. droit écrit* ix) (Montpellier, 1975), 595–612. More recently a Provençal text of *Lo Codi* was published by F. Derrer, *Lo Codi. Eine Summa Codicis in provenzalischer Sprache aus dem XII Jahrhundert. Die provenzalische Fassung der Handschrift A* (Sorbonne 632) (Zurich, 1974) This is based on one manuscript only and needs to be collated with the other Provençal manuscripts. The problem is summarized by A. Gouron 'Du nouveau sur Lo Codi', *Revue d'histoire de droit*, 43 (1975), 271–7, and P. Ourliac in *RDH* 53 (1974), 56–9. Cf. H. Kantorowicz, *Studies in the Glossators of Roman Law*, 2nd edn. (Aalen, 1969), pp. 170 ff. and 343, and the studies of P. Weimar and A. Gouron, above, p. 385 n. 43 (*in fine*).

Appendix C
Bibliographical Note on *Lo Codi*

The texts so far published are a Latin and dauphinois translation and one of the Provençal versions. H. Fitting and H. Suchier, *Lo Codi, Eine Summa Codicis in provenzalischer Sprache aus der Mitte des zwölften Jahrhunderts*: i, H. Fitting, *Lo Codi in der lateinischen Uebersetzung des Ricardus Pisanus* (Halle, 1906). For the dauphinois translation, see L. Royer and A. Thomas, *La Somme du Code. Texte dauphinois de la région de Grenoble. Notices et extraits des mss. de la B.N. et autres bibliothèques*, xlii (Paris, 1932). The provençal texts are in Paris: MS. Bibl. de la Sorbonne 632; B.N. nouv, acq. fr. 4138, 4504, fr. 1932. The edition prepared by H. Suchier was never published. Extracts were published by K. Bartsch, *Chrestomathie provençale* (4th edn. 1880), pp. 299–303, and J. Tardif, 'Une version provençale d'une Somme du Code', *Annales du Midi* 5 (1893), 34–70. Two French translations are in the B.N. MSS. fr. 1069, 1070, 1933.

The Castilian manuscripts are in the Bibliotheca Nacional in Madrid (R. 393 and Ii 72); their edition prepared by two Spanish scholars, Rafael de Ureña y Smenjaud and Adolfo Bonilla was never published. Cf. G. M. Broca 'Juristes y jurisconsults catalans del segles XI–XIII, fonts dels seus coneixements y transcendencia que exerciren', *Annuari d'Institut d'Estudis Catalans* (Barcelona, 1908), pp. 429–40, and H. Suchier, *Die Handschriften der Castilianischen Uebersetzung des Codi* (Halle, 1900). The Catalan manuscripts which belonged to the Templars of Daroca at the beginning of the fourteenth century and were confiscated by the king of Aragon, disappeared. Cf. R. Baer, 'Handschriftenschätze Spaniens', *Sitzungsberichte der philosophisch-historischen Klasse der Kaiserlichen Akademie der Wissenschaften*, 125 (Vienna, 1892), 69–71; H. Suchier, 'Manuscrits perdus de la Somme provençale du Code de Justinien', *Annales du Midi*, 6 (1894), 186 ff.

The publication of *Lo Codi* gave rise to reviews and discussions. The most important were the following: H. Fitting, 'Vorläufige Mittheilungen über eine Summa Codicis in provenzalischer Sprache', *Sitzungsberichte der phil.-hist. Klasse der Berliner Akademie* 37 (1891), 763–6; idem, 'Die Summa Codicis und die Questiones des Irnerius', *Zeitschrift der Savignystiftung für Rechtsgeschichte* 17 (1896), 26–9; H. Suchier, *Fünf neue Hss. des Provenzalischen Rechtsbuches Lo Codi* (Halle, 1899); J. Tardif 'Une version provençale d'une Somme du Code', *Annales du Midi* 5 (1893), 34–70, and 'La version provençale de la Somme du Code de Justinien', ibid. 8 (1896), 470–4; A. Thomas, ibid. 12 (1900), 138 ff. and 14 (1902), 121 ff.; R. Caillemer, 'Lo Codi et le droit provençal au XIIe siècle', ibid. 18 (1906), 494 ff.; E. Bonduard, 'Lo Codi, ancien livre de droit provençal', *Revue du Midi* 13 (Nîmes, 1899), 458–66. Cf. H. Kantorowicz, *Studies in the Glossators of the Roman Law* (Cambridge, 1938), pp. 164 and 173.

We propose to approach this thorny problem by analysing a limited group of Crusader laws in the *LdAdB*. We have already indicated that its closing chapters contain an *opusculum* of Crusader penal law.[5] This part also includes some of the official acts of royal legislation, the *assises* of the kings of Jerusalem, as well as the custom tariffs of the port and markets of Acre. In placing penal law at the end of the *LdAdB*, its author followed the order of Justinian's Code, but there was no resemblance whatsoever between Roman and Crusader penal practice.

The penal law of the *LdAdB* is contained in chs. 270–97 of Kausler's edition (Beugnot, chs. 277–304).[6] It is introduced by a banal chapter, 270, full of pious legal and biblical clichés, and then continues with an enumeration of different offences and their respective penalties, mainly the loss of life and limb. It also lists minor law infractions which were punished by fines. Despite the variety of cases, we shall try to prove that the latter had a common denominator. Moreover, the fines are expressed in terms of currency which hardly ever appear in the hundreds of legal deeds and commercial contracts connected with the Latin Kingdom.

Crusader numismatics prove a bi-metal system of currency, doubtless taken over from the previous Muslim period. The basic gold coin was the *bisantinus sarracenatus*, composed of 24 *carroubles* or carats. Additionally, there was the silver coin, the *denarius*, or *denier*, and its smaller units: the *obolus* and *pougeois*. The silver coins, though certainly in circulation, very rarely appear in our documents; possibly, because the value of landed property, which is the main object of transactions in extant Crusader deeds, usually dealt with higher sums and consequently paid in gold currency. However, the list of custom dues from Acre included a number of taxable objects whose dues were paid in *deniers* or *drahans*.[7] Where *deniers* are found, one would expect *solidi*, the normal money of account, and the *libra*, the unit of weight from which the *deniers* derived. Strangely enough, neither appears in our relatively abundant documentation, with

l'Acad. des Inscriptions et Belles Lettres 10 (1833), 606–8. J. Britz, *Mém. sur l'ancien droit de Belgique* i (Bruxelles, 1846), 37–40. E. Poullet, *Essai sur l'histoire du droit criminel dans l'ancienne principauté de Liège* (Bruxelles, 1871), p. 102. French origin is also advocated by Pardessus, 'Mém. sur l'origine du droit coutumier en France et sur son état jusqu'au XIIIe siècle', *Mém. de l'Acad. des Inscriptions et Belles Lettres* 10 (1833), 731.

[5] See above, Ch. 15, pp. 371–4.

[6] All further quotations refer to Kausler and those in brackets to Beugnot's edition.

[7] *LdAdB*, chs. 237–8: e.g. wine brought from Nazareth, Saforie, and Shfar'am will fetch XII *drahans* from each camel-load (p. 280). These payments are common in the market (ch. 238), pp. 283 ff. Here often the *drahan* of the Munich MS. appears in that of Venice as *denier*.

the exception of the penal *opusculum* of the *LdAdB*, as well as a few other instances of Crusader law which deal with fines or payment for court services. Here we find *solidi* or *sous* in particular quantities, foremost in the traditional form of the fine of *sexaginta solidi*. This is a clear reversion to the European tradition, that of the royal 'ban', which originated in the early Middle Ages and was diffused during the Carolingian period. This traditional fine henceforth dominated European penal law, a descendant of that tradition, for almost 500 years, despite the tremendous changes in the value of money and the evolution of economy over the centuries. Its appearance then in Crusader legislation, brings us back to Europe, more precisely to Western Europe, which exported its conquerors, settlers, and laws to the Holy Land. Together with the 60s. fine, Crusader law knew of another fine, also expressed in *solidi*, namely that of 7½s. This is a strange and unusual amount, and before attempting to gauge its meaning, we shall list the cases in which it appeared in the *LdAdB*.

There could be no claim against the assailant who came to an agreement with his victim through intermediaries or by directly settling with him for a sum of money, even if the victim died afterwards. Still, the relatives of the victim could *lever par bataille* the pledges or witnesses of the agreement. But, if the original defendant could prove that the agreement with the victim was made before a court and he paid *sept sous et demy de la clamor qu'il (le naffré) avoit faite sur luy*, then the plaintiffs (relatives) had not even the right of *lever l'un garans par bataille*.[8]

Clearly, the defendant paid the court 7½s. for what is called *clamor*, accusation. This rather obscure payment becomes clearer when compared with other cases. Thus, in a dispute which came before the court, the losing party, whether claimant or defendant, had to pay to the court 7½s. and that not later than seven days after the judgment.[9]

The same fine was paid by a man who declared that his property had disappeared from his lodging. In such a case, the landlord and all other lodgers took an oath, that they had neither stolen nor known who had stolen them. 'From these oaths,' continues the *LdAdB*, 'the court should not take any of the 7½ *sous*, which are established to be taken *en tous les faus*

---

[8] Ch. 274. MS. Venice, ed. Beugnot, ch. 281, is more explicit than the Munich MS. edited by Kausler, but there is no difference as to the basic contents.

[9] Ch. 286. Beugnot misunderstood the meaning of this chapter (in his edition ch. 293) by explaining the fine of 7½s. as the damages to be paid by the losing party. It is clear that whereas the losing party owes damages which equal the amount of money of the claim, a rule established as early as the Council of Nablus in 1120 (Mansi, *Concilia* xxi, col. 264), the fine announced here is clearly indicated as being paid: 'si deit douner *a la iustise* VII sos et demy'.

clains.' 'Et por ce que cestuy n'est mie clain, ains deit enci estre fait, ne doit la iustise nule riens aver.'[10] Here payment is again defined as a fine for false claim. If the claimant did not pay the $7\frac{1}{2}s$. fine, it was because there was no formal accusation by any person, rather a simple complaint.

The payment of $7\frac{1}{2}s$. appeared again in a form, which can hardly be classified as a fine, viz. a case in which the plaintiff won his case because he had two good *garens*, witnesses, whose testimony was accepted by the court.[11] In such a case, the winning plaintiff 'had to give to the court *XV sos* for the two witnesses, who disproved the claim (*por ces deux garans qui desrainerent le clain*).' This obviously means a payment of $7\frac{1}{2}s$. for each witness.[12]

The next three cases in which the $7\frac{1}{2}s$. fine appeared were different from the others. Their common denominator is the infringement of the royal ban. Thus, a culprit who infringed the ban imposed by the lord of the city was condemned to pay to the court $67\frac{1}{2}s$.[13] This general rule was followed by a particular case, of a merchant who used false measures or false weights. Here again, the fine to be paid the court was $67\frac{1}{2}s$.[14] In the last two cases, we therefore seem to have a compound fine of 60s. and $7\frac{1}{2}s$. A final case, not devoid of humour, was that of an *establissemens* of one of the Baldwins, proclaimed by the city crier, ordering the inhabitants to clean the streets of the city. The citizens who failed to comply with the order, were condemned to a fine of $7\frac{1}{2}s$. But, adds the *LdAdB*, as King Baldwin did not consult the vassals and burgesses of the city in this matter, the viscount should have pity and take as little as possible, or even forgo the fine entirely.[15]

The last three cases were concerned with an infringement of a *ban*, in two cases of a major *ban* and a compound fine, in the last case a 'small *ban*' and the $7\frac{1}{2}s$. fine.

[10] Ch. 297, ed. Beugnot 304.

[11] Ch. 287, ed. Beugnot 294. The heading of MS. Venice: 'Ici ores la raisson que l'on doit paier a seluy qui guaaigne en court son plait par ses garens' is obviously wrong and does not correspond to the contents of the chapter. The Munich MS. has the correct heading: 'Ici dit que det paier celuy qui a guaaigne son plait par ces garans.' The Venice copyist must have found the contents of this practice very strange and interpreted it as damages to be paid to the winning party.

[12] *LdAdB* does not mention in this case the challenging of the witnesses by battle. As the challenge of the witnesses, *garens*, was a normal part of the procedure, we assume that the case was such that the challenge was not acceptable—e.g. if the case involved property of less than I mark value. See below, p. 427 n. 59.

[13] Ch. 293; Beugnot 300: 'Qui enfraindra le banc.'

[14] Ch. 294; Beugnot 301.

[15] Ch. 296; Beugnot 303.

The perseverance of these traditional—one is almost inclined to say ritual—fines, is really astonishing as we find them re-emerging in the kingdom of the Lusignans in Cyprus, two generations after the loss of the Latin Kingdom (1291).

The direct link between the two legal traditions, of Jerusalem and of Cyprus, is not in doubt. The anonymous author of the Cypriot book of jurisprudence, *Abrégé du Livre des Assises des Bourgeois* (or *Livres du plédéant et du plaidoyer*), mentioned the great legal deeds of the Antiaume family of Acre in the second half of the thirteenth century. He glorified the subtlety of those famous lawyers who even found a loop-hole in the law which enabled them to let free a man who committed murder.[16] To analyse the long-winded explanation is outside the scope of our study, but the gist of the matter is: a false accusation was launched against a third party, the hypocritical claimant then alleged remorse, took back the accusation 'and was ready to pay *la fauce clamour vii sous et demi*'. The continuity of the 'false claim' and its 7½s. fine was paralleled by the continuity of the fine for ban-infringement. A long list of surviving ordinances of the kings of Cyprus repeated the traditional fine time and again. As these are actual ordinances, the vocabulary is clearer than in the books of jurisprudence. There was a basic distinction between the 'great ban' and the 'small ban' subject to fines of 60s. and 7½s. respectively. In addition there was the compound fine of 67½s.

The compound ban of 67½s. appeared in Cyprus, in 1295, in a curious variation. Hazard players paid a fine according to their social standing: nobles and knights paid 500 besants, the landlord 1,000 besants, others paid the double ban of 67½s. each. Three years later, in 1298, an ordinance regulated the size of cloth fabricated on the island. Transgressors were threatened *paier le petit banc qui est vii sos et demi*. The same ordinance

---

[16] Beugnot, *Lois* ii. 229–352; ch. 28 (p. 339) under discussion points perhaps to the fact that the anonymous author of the *Abrégé* was a member of the Antiaume family established in Cyprus, or, more plausibly, a close *familiaris* of the family. We know that the anonymous author lived in the middle of the fourteenth century in Cyprus during the reign of Hugh IV (1324–59) and wrote his book at the age of around seventy (Beugnot, *Lois* ii, Introduction, p. LX. M. Grandclaude, *Étude critique*, p. 92). He indicates his age as seventy in ch. 20 (p. 319), forty years of which he spent in different capacities in the court (ibid.). The way in which a murderer may be set free is indicated in ch. 28 (p. 339). This secret was known to Raymond, the father of Nicolas Antiaume, who lived at the time of King Aimery (1192–1205). The secret was then confined to Nicolas's son Balian, as well as to three nobles, the lords of Arsuf, Tyre, and Jaffa. Our author seems to have known it from Nicolas Antiaume, who lived in the middle of the thirteenth century. Nicolas Antiaume is known in 1243 (Röhricht, *GKJ*, p. 858). On the Antiaumes, see above, Ch. 10, pp. 289–90.

imposed the punishment of *grant banc* on people who bought property from slaves; again the selling of poor-quality silk was punished by a fine of 67½*s*.[17]

Another ordinance of 1300 regulated the quality of fabric on the island and imposed a fine of 67½*s*. on transgressors. A year later, in 1301, the selling of spices and syrups of dubious quality was threatened by a fine of 67½*s*.[18] An ordinance of Hugh of Lusignan, which regulated city cleaning, imposed a fine of 67½*s*. on whoever threw debris into the river or into the streets; the same ordinance regulated the upkeep of rivers and streets *en paine dou petit banc, qui est vii sos et demy*.[19]

We have already pointed out that the use of *solidi* or *sous* in the kingdom was virtually restricted to the penalties of Crusader law and was particularly linked to the amounts of fines. *Sous* are also to be found in some other cases, but always connected with court payments.[20] They appear in juxtaposition and are also quite well known from Europe, where the penalty differed according to the social standing of the victim. It was expressed by the same figure, but in different currency. For example in Beauvaisis, in the second half of the thirteenth century, assault upon a noble was punished by a fine of £60, but in the case of a villein, by 60*s*.[21] In Crusader legal tradition, it would be besants and *sous*. An assault upon a knight by a knight incurred the *amende* of 100 besants to the lord and 100*s*. to the victim;[22] whereas the assaulted knight received 100 besants, an assaulted burgess received 100*s*.[23] Non-Franks and women paid and received half that amount, that is, their lord received 50 besants and the victim 50*s*.[24]

Besides these few cases where *sous* appear in a group of fines of 100 and

[17] 'Bans et Ordonances des rois de Chypre', no. IX, *Lois* ii. 362.

[18] Ibid., no. XV, §§2–3; no. XVII. *Lois* ii. 365–6.

[19] 'Bans et Ordonances', no. XXIX, §2. *Lois* ii. 373.

[20] *Sous* and *deniers* are also mentioned as payment to subaltern court officials in Cyprus (*Abrégé du LdAdB*, chs. IX, XXII). As to the actual value of the *sous*, see above, Ch. 15, p. 280.

[21] L. A. and T. A. Warnkönig, *Französische Staats- und Rechtsgeschichte* iii (Basel, 1848), 184. Cf. Beaumanoir, ch. 30: 'Gentilhomme—60 livres; l'oume de pooté—60 sols,' quoted by Beugnot, *Lois* I. 546, n. b.

[22] Philip of Novara, ch. 75 (*Lois* i. 546). Cf. John of Ibelin, ch. 114 (ibid. i. 187). *LdAdB*, ch. 269 (*Lois* ii. 204).

[23] *Livre au Roi*, ch. 17 (*Lois* i. 617–18), as compared with ch. 19, p. 619 and John of Ibelin, ch. 114 (*Lois* i. 187).

[24] Philip of Novara, ch. 75 (*Lois* i. 548). John of Ibelin, ch. 114 (ibid. 187). *LdAdB*, chs. 289–97 (*Lois* ii. 222). The rule is explicit: 'por ce que le Surien ne paie de bateure que demie lei, ni ne refeit que demie lei.' Exactly the same rule relates to women.

50, modelled on that of 100 and 50 besants, *sous* appear in the sums of 7½s., 60s., and 67½s. only.[25]

The Crusader 60s. fine was clearly the old traditional fine for infringing the royal ban, the 'great ban', the usual, common ban or ban for great misdeeds,[26] whereas the 7½s. fine was a small ban. Doubtless, the 67½s. was a compound ban of 60s. and 7½s. In addition, the payment of 7½s. appeared as a specific payment due to the court, as a part of the litigation procedure, either in a case of false claim (ch. 293), or as payment due to the court if an accusation was made but the case was not actually judged by the court because the parties had come to a voluntary agreement.

It is quite clear that the fines under discussion had nothing to do with any local, native fines. The 60s. had a venerable European ancestry and can be traced back to the Merovingians and Carolingians. Thus it is clear that the amount, as well as the units of currency in which they were counted, came to Syria and the Holy Land with the Crusaders.

The question to be discussed now is whether these traditional fines can be related to any specific European territory. The 'great ban' of 60s. definitely cannot be related to any particular European area, since all countries that inherited from the Carolingian Empire accepted the sacrosanct ban of 60s. The situation cannot be better described than as stated in a classic study of Maurice Prou:

This fine [*amende*] of 60 *sous* already appeared in Merovingian times . . . This was the royal fine *par excellence*. It also preserved this character in the Capitularies where it was called by the king, *bannum nostrum*. Despite the changes in the value of money over the centuries, the amount of 60 *sous* persisted after the Carolingian period. It was the same fine which would be transmitted from century to century, as even as late as the fourteenth century the word *compositio* was often used to describe it.[27]

Thus, whereas the 60s. fine is no indicator as to the origins of the

[25] Modelled on this sum is the heavy fine imposed on a man who claims that justice was miscarried ('fauce les jugemens de la cort'). The man is condemned to a fine of £67 to be paid to the jurors of the court and twice as much (£135) to the lord (*LdAdB*, ch. 268 (232), *Lois* ii. 203). It seems that the penalty of infringing the prince's ban was fixed in Antioch at another 'traditional' sum of 36s. Remarkably enough, wherever this sum is mentioned it appears in the form: '36 sous, qui font 44 dirhems nouveaux'. 'Assise des Bourgeois', *Assises d'Antioche* (Venice, 1876), ch. vi, xiv, xv, xix.

[26] E. Brinckmeier, *Glossarium diplomaticum* (Gotha, 1856), p. 265: *bannum consuetum* or *assuetem*. Cf. the basic division in the 'Cap. de partibus Saxoniae', ed. Boretius, *Capitularia* i, no. 26, par. 31: '. . . bannum . . . de faida vel maioribus causis in solidos LX; de minoribus vero causis . . . bannum in solidos XV constituimus.'

[27] M. Prou, *Les Coutumes de Lorris et leur propagation aux XIIe et XIIIe siècles* (Paris, 1884), pp. 59–60.

Crusader penal law, the situation is different for the fine of 7½*s.* which, as far as we have been able to establish, was absolutely unknown until the beginning of the twelfth century.[28] It is true that in addition to the 60*s.* fine, the Capitularies mention a smaller fine, but this one amounted to 15*s.* It was only at the beginning of the twelfth century, in an area quite well defined that we witness the appearance of an *amende* of 7½*s.* Its appearance was invariably linked with the great contemporary social and economic changes in the wake of rural and urban colonization. As such, it marked the beginning of a long process of change in the legal framework of the older settlements, still living under the customary legal traditions of the feudal system. Conversely, it coincided with the fixing of the initial organization of new settlements. The changes in procedure henceforth followed in the old and new courts, as well as a drastic change in the tariffs of fines, was common to the whole movement of inner colonization once happily described by von Below as *Städtegründungsfieber.* But, there were variations in different areas. The differences followed some sort of pattern, influenced by the fact that privileges accorded to a given locality were bestowed by the same authority on other localities in its own domain, or imitated in neighbouring areas by other authorities. It is precisely in one of such 'family' of privileges that we find not only affinity, but identity with Crusader fines.

The earliest examples we have been able to find come from the French royal domain at the time of Louis VI. In two royal cities of the Capetian domain, Bourges and a new settlement area inside the city of Étampes, royal privileges reduced the traditional ban from 60*s.* to 5*s.* and 4*s.* The same reduction would then be found extended progressively to almost the whole royal domain. But in both cases there was an additional clause on fines. The privilege bestowed on settlers in the New Market (St. Gilles) of Étampes in 1123 stated: 'De districto et forisfacto VII solidorum et dimidii pro XVI nummis omnibus diebus condonamus.'[29] Similarly, a privilege for Bourges, accorded by the same king, between 1121 and 1136, dealt with the reduction of fines. The fine of 60*s.* remained valid but a small fine to be paid to the *vicarius* by the losing party was fixed at 2½*s.* In addition,

---

[28] It has been argued, mistakenly, that it existed in the Salic Law (H. Brunner, 'Duodecimalsystem und Decimalsystem in den Busszahlen der fränkischen Volkrechte', *Forschungen zur Geschichte des deutschen und französischen Rechtes* (Stuttgart, 1894) pp. 482–487). But cf. E. Glasson, *Histoire du droit et des institutions de la France* iii (Paris, 1889), 542.

[29] A. Luchaire, *Louis VI le Gros. Annales de sa vie et de son règne, 1081–1137* (Paris, 1890); Catalogue, no. 333 (quoted below as *Cat. Louis VI*); *Ordonances des rois de France* XI (Paris, 1769), p. 183 (quoted below as *Ordonances*).

'si despexerit vicarium, habebit vicarius *VII solidos et dimidium*, et iterum quatuor denarios.' And again, 'homo non capiet vadimonium sine vicario, quod si fecerit, habebit ex eo vicarius *VII solidos et dimidium*.'[30]

These two early privileges prove that *c.* 1120–30 the fine of 7½*s.* was already practised in the royal Capetian domain. It was imposed for an infringement of law in the larger sense of the expression, including what might be called contempt of judge and court, by the exercise of a *saizie extrajudiciaire*. Moreover, in Étampes, the fine of 7½*s.* was already being reduced to 16 *nummi* (possibly 1*s.* 4*d.*). The privilege bestowed on the New Market in Étampes was bestowed twenty years later, with some modifications, on other quarters of the city, viz. the domain of the churches of Notre-Dame and St. Martin.[31] In 1141 Louis VII reduced the *forifactum* of 7½*s.* to 12*d.*

These cases show the existence of the *forifactum* of 7½*s.* or, as it was later called, the *amende*, in Bourges and in Étampes, and even its reduction to 16*s.* or 12*d.* A new departure was taken in the most famous *charte-lois* of medieval history, the privilege of Lorris-en-Gâtinais. The original charter of Louis VI is lost, but its contents are known from the extant privilege of Louis VII. Consequently no exact date can be fixed for the original except that it fell within the reign of Louis VI, 1108–37.[32] The confirmation of Louis VII dates from 1155.[33] The customs of Lorris had already spread before this confirmation. When the customs of the New Market of Étampes of 1123 were bestowed on Boissi-le-Sec and Forêt-le-Roi by Louis VI, [34] the customs of Lorris had already been conferred upon Le Moulinet (Gien) and Chapelle-la-Reine (Fontainebleau.)[35]

In the customs of Lorris-en-Gâtinais, among the various reductions in fines our attention is drawn to §14 which reads: 'Et si homines de Lorriaco vadia duelli temere dederint, et, praepositi assensu, assensum antequam

---

[30] G. Thaumas de la Thaumassière, *Histoire de Berry*, new edn. 1865, pp. 80–3; idem, *Coutumes locales de Berry* (Bourges, 1579), p. 62; *Cat. Louis VI*, no. 578. The charter is known from a confirmation of Louis VII in 1144–5 (*Ordonances* i. 9); A Luchaire, *Études sur les actes de Louis VII* (Paris, 1885), Cat. no. 140 (quoted below as *Cat. Louis VII*).

[31] Teulet, *Layettes du trésor des Chartes* i. 52–6, no. 74. *Cat. Louis VII*, no. 80.

[32] *Cat. Louis VI*, no. 607. The authorship of Louis VI is based on the charter of confirmation of Philip II Augustus. L. Delisle, *Catalogue des actes de Philippe-Auguste* (Paris, 1856), no. 187 and see next note.

[33] *Cat. Louis VII*, no. 351.

[34] *Cat. Louis VI*, no. 601. *Ordonances* vii. 34.

[35] Le Moulinet: *Cat. Louise VI*, no. 618, known from a confirmation of 1159, *Cat. Louis VII*, no. 424. Chapelle-la-Reine: *Cat. Louis VI*, no. 608; *Cat. Louis VII*, no. 795, confirmed by Philip II Augustus, *Cat. Philippe-Auguste*, no. 171. See next note.

tribuantur obsides, concordaverint, II solidos et VI denarios persolvat uterque; et, si obsides dati fuerint, *VII solidos et VI denarios persolvat uterque*.'[36] Whereas we already had an existing fine of 7½s. in Bourges and Étampes at the beginning of the twelfth century, the same fine in Lorris-en-Gâtinais is obviously a new franchise bestowed upon its inhabitants. Paragraph seven of the same privilege also lowered the tariff of other fines: 'Et forisfactum de LX solidis ad V solidos, et forisfactum de V solidos ad XII denarios veniat, et *clamor praepositi* ad IV denarios.' M. Prou, who made the most thorough study of our *charte-lois*, commented that the *clamor praepositi*, here reduced to 4d. corresponded to the *districtum* of other *chartes-lois* which derived from Lorris, like those of Chaumont-en-Bassigny and Sceaux-en-Gâtinais (A.D. 1153, §4). This had to be distinguished from §14 of Lorris, with its 7½s. fine, which was that of a *falsus clamor* or *fause clamor*.[37]

M. Prou understood this trespass as follows: 'In the primitive feudal law, to refuse battle was to avow one's culpability. But, it was barbarous to compel the accused to run the danger of the outcome of single combat, and the Crown tried to mitigate the severity of this procedure.' The payment of the 7½s. paid to the prévôt was an indemnity 'quite justified for the inconvenience caused the royal officers by this unnecessary beginning of the process'.[38]

Actually, things were probably more complex. Together with the general reduction of the 60s. ban, which we find in very many charters—no doubt a great bonus to the population—the paragraph under discussion relates to another aspect of royal policy, the earliest attempts to abolish, or at least to curb, single combat as part of legal procedure. There were basically three stages in this type of procedure: the accusation and the pledging (*vadium*) of an object (such as the throwing of a glove) of claimant and plaintiff; the appearance of pledges (*obsides*) and their oath (they will suffer with the losing party); and finally, the combat, itself divided into a first stage in which the first blows were exchanged and then the continuation of the combat.[39] The voluntary agreement between the contending parties was understood as proof of remorse on the part of

---

[36] M. Prou, *Les Coutumes de Lorris*, p. 52. The division into numbered paragraphs is that of Prou.

[37] Prou, op. cit., p. 41.

[38] Ibid., p. 52.

[39] A. Coulin, *Verfall des offiziellen und Entstehung des privaten Zweikampfes in Frankreich* (Berlin, 1909), pp. 3 ff.

claimant or defendant. One claiming and the other negating, one was obviously asserting a false claim. The authorities, eager to avoid combat, induced the parties, by imposing a small fine of 2½s. only, to compose the quarrel. This was the case when a claim was made but not pledged. If the parties had already presented their pledges, the fine was higher, 7½s. This was still more reasonable than the hazardous result of a combat. In the later development of this process, there would also be a fine which would allow a combat, already joined, to be interrupted by agreement.[40]

The diffusion of the charter of Lorris and its derivatives is well known. We have already mentioned its spreading during the reign of Louis VI. Under his successor, Louis VII, who confirmed the original privilege, we find it bestowed on Yèvre-le-Chalet (Pithiviers), Sceaux-en-Gâtinais (1153), Villeneuve-le-Roi (Joigny, 1163). The custom then spread to Champagne, the Orléanais, and so on. M. Prou counted no less than eighty-five localities, which enjoyed the *charte-lois* of Lorris by 1300.[41]

But Lorris was not the only mother of a large legal *progenies*. At least two other charters vied with it in popularity, the charter conferred on Prisches in Hainault in 1158 and that conferred upon Beaumont-en-Argonne 1182, which played a similar role in the northern and eastern parts of France.[42] We should also mention the Norman Breteuil with its Anglo-Norman descendants.[43] All these charters conferred judicial privileges upon their recipients and among them, the reduction of the *amendes*. Yet, *none* mentions the 7½s. fine. Moreover, the charters which derived from Lorris-en-Gâtinais, even those that are supposedly identical, did not always contain the 14th paragraph of the original privilege. They often contained a similar paragraph but with a different tariff of *amende*.

It is outside the scope of this study to follow up the variations of our paragraph beyond the twelfth century, as this obviously has no connection with our main argument. But the twelfth-century variation may be of some importance. The closest copy of the charter of Lorris of 1153, which was conferred upon Sceaux-en-Gâtinais, does not contain the paragraph under discussion,[44] although we find the lowering of the *forisfacta* from

---

[40] A. Coulin, *Der gerichtliche Zweikampf im altfranzösischen Prozess und sein Übergang zum modernen Privatzweikampf* (Berlin, 1906), pp. 165 ff.

[41] M. Prou, op. cit., p. 105.

[42] L. Verriest, 'La fameuse charte-lois de Prisches', *Revue belge de philologie et d'histoire* 2 (1923), 327 ff. E. Bonvalot, *Le Tiers-État d'après la charte de Beaumont et ses filiales* (Paris, 1884).

[43] M. Bateson, 'The laws of Breteuil', *EHR* 15 (1900), 73 ff.; 16 (1901), 92 ff.

[44] *Ordonances* xi. 199.

60*s*. to 5*s*., from 5*s*. to 12*d*., and the *districta* to 4*d*. However, we do find our *amende* in Le Moulinet, which received its charter from Louis VI and then a confirmation from Louis VII in 1159.[45] A verbatim repetition of our paragraph is also found in the privilege of Louis VII (sometimes assigned to Louis VI), for Bois-commun-en-Gâtinais, known from a confirmation of Philip II Augustus in 1186.[46]

At the time that the charter of Lorris was propagated throughout the royal domain and soon spread to the domains of Courtenay, Sancerre, and Champagne,[47] some variation seems to have developed in other places. Such was the fortified locality of Chambli (Oise). Its first charter dates from 1173 and a new one was conferred on it by Philip II in 1222. In §11 we read: 'Duella vero nostra sunt tali modo. De datis vadiis habebimus XV solidos; de obsidibus datis propter hoc plus XXX solidos; *de duello victo LXVII et dimidium* si duellum fuerit de fundo terre vel pecunia.'[48] Similarly, a contemporary charter granted by Philip II to Beaumont-sur-Oise established fines on merchants who used false measures. In addition (§21): 'Nobis inde solvet VII solidos et dimidium pro emenda', and also (§8), as in Chambli: 'Duella nostra sunt. De vadiis duelli datis, habebimus XV solidos tantum; de hostagiis XXX solidos; *de duello victo LXVII solidos et dimidium*, si duellum fuerit de fundo terre vel pecunia.'[49] This was confirmed by Louis VIII in 1223, who granted the same customs in the same year, to Asnière near Beaumont-sur-Oise.[50]

---

[45] Ibid., p. 200.

[46] *Cat. Louis VII*, no. 790. *Cat. Philip II*, no. 174. *Ordonances*, IV. 732

[47] A verbatim, or almost verbatim, repetition of §14 of Lorris is to be found in the following charters: Montargis (§17) conferred by Pierre de Courtenay, brother of Louis VII in 1170, *Ordonances* xi. 472; Voisines (Berry) charter of Philip II in 1187, Delisle, *Cat.* no. 208, *Ordonances* vi. 455–6. An interesting variation in Philip II's privilege for Villeneuve-Saint-Melon (Senlis) in 1196, §3: 'Forisfactum LX solid. erit ad VII solidos et dimidium, et forefactum VII solid. et dimidium erit ad duodecim denarios.' Delisle, *Cat.* no. 531, *Ordonances* vi. 637. Charter of Theobald of Champagne to Evry, §11, 1199, *Ordonances* v. 201. Charter of John of Châlons for Auxerre, in 1223, §7, *Ordonances* v. 421; charter of Guy de Nevers for Mailly-le-Château, in 1229, §12, *Ordonances* v. 716; charter of Guy de Clermont for Clermont-en-Bassigny in 1248, *Ordonances* v, sub 1327, cf. ibid. vii. 33. Later on the fine of 7½*s*. will spread widely over the provinces of France. V. Foucher, *Les Assises*, p. 756, wanted to connect it with the Salic *dilatura* (where the amount is not stated) which is certainly wrong. See C. Boutems, 'Les dommages et intérêts dans les lois barbares', *RHDF* 47 (1969), 454–73. The sources quoted by V. Foucher following A. Loysel, *Institutions coutumières avec notes d'Eusèbe de Laurière*, ed. M. Dupin et E. Laboulaye (Paris, 1846), l. VI, tit, II, §35, no. 855, date from the end of the thirteenth and later centuries.

[48] *Ordonances*, xii. 304.

[49] Ibid., 298.

[50] Ibid., 308, 313.

The fines in this group of privileges were certainly related to those of the previous period. The basic units were 7½s. and 60s. The whole group of fines (and this was common to many other regions and privileges) was called by the king, *duella, duella nostra.* The fine for the *vadium* was of 7½s. paid by both litigants. Both sides were fined 15s. (obviously cases in which the parties came to an agreement), if pledges had already been produced. But if the combat took place, and this was limited to property and money (a sum of money in which judicial combat still survived), the loser paid the compound fine of 60s. and the small *ban* of 7½s.

The review of the 7½s. fine leads, in our context, to two general conclusions. The fine arose, or at least appeared in our sources, at the beginning of the second quarter of the twelfth century, *c.* 1120–30. Its appearance was limited to the royal Capetian domain, in and to the south of the Île-de-France, to Bourges, Étampes, and the Gâtinais. Later on we find it in the north-eastern part of the Capetian domain, on the Oise near Senlis. It is difficult to be specific as to the circumstances in which the fine of 7½s., unknown to the *Leges barbarorum* and to the Capitularies, became part of the penal procedure in the Capetian domain. In all probability it derived from a 15s. fine in the Salic Law. Although there were already two places, in the second quarter of the twelfth century, in which the fine of 7½s. was well established and was actually being reduced, it was during this period, generally speaking, that higher fines were reduced to the level of 7½s. There can be little doubt that the privileges of Louis VI and Louis VII played a major role in the extension of the reduced fine, which later became a standard fine in the process of the waning judicial combat.

The 7½s. fine was invariably imposed in two cases: for a 'false claim', and the infringement of a lower *ban.* The former derived from the notion that the claimant or defendant, by coming to an agreement at any stage of the process, thereby proved that the claim or the defence was false. At the same time, the fine allowed the curbing of the combat procedure.

These two cases correspond to those found in the Latin Kingdom and in the kingdom of Cyprus of the Lusignans.[51] The correspondence cannot be a chance coincidence. It is more than plausible to assume that the fine of 7½s., which was such a remarkable feature of the Crusader law of

---

[51] Although the payment of 7½s. is not mentioned explicitly, it seems that it was also implied in some other chapters of the *LdAdB*, in cases in which one of the parties was declared 'home desleau'. Thus, when a man denied a debt and later avowed it, he would lose the 'response' of the court and in addition: 'si est encheus enver la seignorie con deit douner home desleau' (ch. 52). Similar cases are in chs. 67, 78, and 110. This is perhaps different in the case of a man who 'mentie sa fei', who was to be branded by a hot iron, ch. 86.

Burgesses, was brought to the Levant from the Capetian domain in France. Can more be said as to the reception of this fine from the Capetian domain? Our sources do not warrant definite conclusions, but it seems to us that some suggestions are possible. It is tempting to link the introduction of the fine with two Crusader names connected with two places in the Capetian domain—Arpin (or Harpin) of Bourges, who, having sold his fief to Philip I, joined the Crusade and died in 1102 in the Holy Land[52] or Bernard of Étampes, who must have been a personality of standing under Baldwin II (1118–30) or Baldwin III (1143–62); his name was given to the fortified place of Edrei in Transjordan: *Civitas Bernardi de Stampis, Cité Bernart d'Estampes*. The place was captured by Baldwin II *c.* 1118, but the name of this Frankish noble, a native of the Capetian domain does not appear before the Transjordanian expedition of Baldwin III in 1147 (W.T. xvi. 10). It remains then, an open question as to when the city got its new Frankish name. It is unfortunate that we do not know anything about the eponymous Frankish lord. However, there is little actual proof of any connection between these nobles and the Crusader fines apart from the fact that nobles from these places settled in the Latin Kingdom.

A possible clue, may be found in the *establissemens* of King Baldwin regulating the cleaning of the streets of the city. The royal ordinance threatened the neglecting citizens with a fine of 7½s. Alas, the Latin Kingdom had five kings by the name of Baldwin. What can be said with certainty is that the ordinance belonged to the twelfth century, for no Baldwin ruled in the thirteenth century. This can probably be narrowed down, as Baldwin V, who died in his childhood, could hardly have promulgated the *establissemens*, and we doubt if Baldwin I (1100–18) would have promulgated such an *establissemens* for the still empty city of Jerusalem. This leaves us with Baldwin II (1118–30), Baldwin III (1146–60), or the leper King Baldwin IV (1173–82). We are inclined to assign the *establissemens* to Baldwin II or Baldwin III, but rather to the latter. Though there is no direct proof, we may induce some circumstantial evidence. We remember that the author of the *Livre des Assises des Bourgeois* asked the viscount to be charitable towards those who infringe this ban, because: 'li rois Bauduins y mist ces establissemens sans le conseille de ses homes et de ses borgeis de la cite.'[53] This statement assumes a given stage of development of state and city organization, with which we can hardly credit the early period of the kingdom. It fits a more advanced

---

[52] See above, Ch. 2, p. 24 n. 19. [53] Ch. 296 (Beugnot 303).

stage of institutional organization more easily, in which the king, lord of the city, took some kind of consent on the part of the governed into consideration.[54] This points to an established and well-functioning Court of Burgesses, which was, and remained until the revolutionary movements of the thirteenth century, the sole instrument of city rule as well as the only channel for voicing city sentiments.

The Court of Burgesses was not created by a single legislative act—as alleged by thirteenth-century jurists—but came into being through an evolutionary process in which witnesses of standing became the *jurés* or *iurati* of the court. The title *regalis curia*, presided over by the viscount of the city appeared in 1149 for the first time[55] and the *regie maiestatis iurati*, appeared in 1155 only,[56] although burgesses witnessed property transactions as early as the last year of Baldwin I, 1118. We are inclined to think that the Court of Burgesses began to function not earlier, and possibly later, than the reign of Baldwin II. It then took some time until it could voice the resistance sentiments of the citizen. Thus, we could suggest that the Street Ordinance with its fine of $7\frac{1}{2}s$. was promulgated under Baldwin II or more plausibly under Baldwin III.

Perhaps additional indications may also be found in the legislative activity of the kings of Jerusalem. One of the factors in reducing the tariff of fines during the twelfth and thirteenth centuries, as we have already indicated, was the striving of the authorities to introduce a wiser and juster legal procedure, and the elimination, wherever possible, of the judicial combat. Such attempts first arose, naturally enough, in the newly created or resuscitated urban settlements.[57] The Latin Kingdom was certainly not among those in the first ranks of this movement. The overwhelming influence of the nobility, even in the cities, would have been a major obstacle to a general movement in this direction. And yet, the kingdom did not remain entirely outside the movement of legal reforms, as it did not remain outside the attempts to abolish the ordeal by water and fire.[58]

One of the expressions of this legal movement was a royal *assise*, luckily preserved, because often invoked in the courts. According to Crusader

---

[54] It can hardly be argued that the plea for mitigation was made by the mid-thirteenth-century author of the *LdAdB*. Surely a simple ordinance promulgated in the twelfth century, and probably for Jerusalem, was hardly in force a hundred years later in Acre or Tyre. Clearly the ordinance and the comment were taken from an earlier source.

[55] Rozière, no. 112.

[56] Rozière, no. 108.

[57] Coulin, above, p. 421 n. 39.

[58] *LdAdB* 261 (Beugnot 267).

legal practice, the claimant in a criminal lawsuit made his accusation with two witnesses, who were also pledges of his veracity. The defendant, after denying the claim in a strict and formalistic way, word for word, could disprove the claim by what was called *lever les garens*, that is, by accusing the pledges of perjury. At that point, the defendant had the right to join combat with one of the pledges and the result decided the issue.

At an early stage in the history of the kingdom it was established that in litigation in which the amount of money involved was higher than 1 mark of silver, there was a *tornes de bataille*.[59] So much the more, if life and limb were concerned: clearly, a man who could not find 'pledges', could not accuse, and if he were accused and could not produce pledges, he automatically lost his case.

Some time later, these harsh general rules were somewhat tempered by the distinction between serious and less serious criminal offences; light injuries—for example when a man was beaten up, kicked, or lost his teeth—or a more serious offence, when the beating involved *arme esmolue ou mace de fer* (sharp instrument or mace).[60] In all such cases, if the accused avowed his responsibility or the claimant could produce witnesses, an *assise* abolished judicial combat, imposing an *amende* which went to the lord and an indemnity payment to the assaulted.[61] But even this procedure was found to be inadequate. Not only did it favour the stronger, but in a land of immigration it was prejudicial and discriminated against pilgrims and new immigrants who could not easily find pledges when assaulted by a local Frank. This was reformed by a famous *assise* known as *l'Assise dou rei Baudoin de cop aparant*.[62] The new *assise* dispensed with pledges altogether. A simple oath of the accused, that he was innocent, acquitted him from the accusation. In practice, we hear from Philip of Novara, the *seigneur justicier* would very often make a private and extra legal inquiry

---

[59] e.g. Philip of Novara, ch. 75 (*Lois* i. 546): 'de toute querele d'un marc d'argent ou de plus y a tornes de bataille contre un des garens.' Cf. ibid., ch. 9 (*Lois* i. 482). Cf. M. Grandclaude, 'Liste d'assises remontant au premier royaume de Jérusalem', p. 336. The payment of 1 mark of silver is mentioned again in connection with *lods et ventes* paid by the seller to the Court (ch. 31). The rule of battle in cases above 1 mark of silver is also found in the *Assises d'Antioche* (Venice, 1876), p. 58.

[60] Philip of Novara, ch. 75 (*Lois* i. 546).

[61] If the litigants were knights: 1,000 besants to the lord, and the harness of the knight (probably without the horse) to the assaulted; if among burgesses: 100 besants to the lord and 100s. to the assaulted; if between non-Franks: 50 besants to the lord, 50s. to the assaulted (ibid.). In cases of assault by mace and sharp instrument, the combat remained in force, ibid. 536.

[62] Ibid. 547.

so that the powerful should not escape punishment by an easy oath.[63] Here we witness three stages in the development of the legal procedure: compulsory combat, procedure without combat replaced by testimony of witnesses, the *Assise du coup apparent*, which accepted the oath of the defendant as a basis for acquittal without witnesses. Even in the earliest phase of this procedure, there was already a limitation of combat by the sum of 1 mark of silver. This was an important limitation and surely an imported one, as this unit of weight or account, as far as we could ascertain, appears very seldom in the rich Crusader documentation, and even then, in a transaction with a foreigner.[64] As a legal norm, it seems to point to north-eastern France, possibly Flanders,[65] and may have been brought over with Godfrey of Bouillon or his brother Baldwin I. Like all such tariffs, it remained unchanged as part of the legal system, survived the Latin kingdom, and reappeared in Cyprus. This traditional amount, we are told, was counted in Cyprus as corresponding to 25 local besants.[66] We cannot establish when the second phase—that is the testimony of witnesses—was substituted for judicial combat, but we can almost with certainty assign the *Assise du coup apparent* to Baldwin III. A late abbreviation of the *Lignages d'Outremer* reads: 'Apres la mort du Roy Foulq fu roy de Jherusalem Bauduin son fis et fist l'assise de nouplesse et *celle dou coup, come s'en claime par l'assize de Roi Bauduin.'*[67]

We are quite aware that the *assise* of Baldwin III is in itself no proof that the introduction of the $7\frac{1}{2}$s. fine should also be assigned to the same king of Jerusalem. But if we take into account that this type of fine was an aspect of the process of abolishing judicial combat, such a possibility seems

---

[63] Ibid. 548, last phrase.

[64] e.g. *Regesta*, no. 93.

[65] A fine of 10 marks was a standard fine in Liège at the end of the thirteenth century. See 'La loi muée (1287)', *Coutumes du pays de Liège* i (Bruxelles, 1870). But it is also found in Bourges at a later date (G. Thaumas de la Thaumassière, *Histoire de Berry*, p. 336).

[66] In a pre-emption right of the lord to a heritage, he pays: 'I marc d'argent, qui a esté esclerzi et prizé et uzé, c'est assever XXV besans en Chipre' (*Abrégé du LdAdB*, ch. 29, *Lois* ii. 258). It is difficult to specify the 'legal' equivalent of 1 mark of silver in besants or silver currency. It seems that it was above 10 besants, if we correctly interpret ch. 43, or above 20 besants if we correctly interpret ch. 80. We are rather inclined to the latter, seeing that in Cyprus it was evaluated at 25 besants. As to the real value of 1 mark of silver, it can be calculated for 1173, following an agreement between Constance, Countess of St. Gilles, and the Grand Master of the Hospital. For a village in the plain of Ascalon the Order promised to pay her 500 besants a year in Outremer or, should she go back to Europe: 'pro illis D bisantiis XII marcas et dimidiam argenti meri ad pondus Troie' (Delaville, no. 551; i. 374). Consequently, 1 mark of silver was actually equivalent to 40 besants.

[67] MS. Munich, Cod. Gallus 771, fo. 246^r. See below, Ch. 17, pp. 464–7 with notes.

very plausible. The reign of Baldwin III also coincided with the great diffusion of the *charte-lois* of Lorris in the Capetian domain and its introduction at the same period in the Latin kingdom seems a near probability. It is superfluous to insist on the strong connections between the Latin Kingdom and France in general, and the Capetian court in particular. The presence of the king of France, Louis VII, in the Holy Land during the Second Crusade, might have been a factor in the introduction of the new Capetian fine into the kingdom. This is not impossible but hardly demonstrable. It suffices to note that for a given section of Crusader penal law we have been able to demonstrate the possibility of direct transfer of usages from the Capetian domain into the kingdom.

17 Roman Law and Crusader Legislation: The *Assises* on Confiscation and Disinheritance[1]

One of the more controversial questions of Crusader historiography is that of royal legislation. As early as the middle of the thirteenth century, a new chapter was added to the already well-developed legend of Godfrey of Bouillon, namely that of Godfrey the Legislator, the author of a considerable amount of legislation, codification, and the architect of the judicial organization of the kingdom.

Modern historians are almost unanimous[2] as to his legislative activity, but they differ as to its importance and scope. It is certain that laws or *assises* were solemnly promulgated by Godfrey, in the presence of clergy and nobles, and then the enacted laws were deposited in the church of the Holy Sepulchre.[3] This is in substance what John of Ibelin reports and there is no reason to disbelieve him. But when he mentions *inquisitiones* which were allegedly conducted among newcomers in Acre to ascertain the best laws governing their lands of origin, or the sending of commissions to Europe[4] for the same purpose, he is probably following a literary tradition, perhaps that of Titus Livius, about the redaction of the first laws of Rome.[5] Laws and customs were certainly introduced into the kingdom, but not in this way. Some imported laws and customs of this kind are in fact known to us but they belong to a later period.[6]

Little is known about the legislation of the Latin Kingdom. Only a few *assises* bear the name of their legislator. For others, all that can be conjectured is their date.[7] Usually their aim was to give a more permanent form to the fluctuating practices of an immigrant society. The legislation

---

[1] This chapter appeared as 'Étude sur le droit des *Assises de Jérusalem*: droit de confiscation et droit d'exhérédation, *RHDFE* 1961, pp. 520–51; 1962, pp. 29–42.

[2] See above, Ch. 15, p. 359. On Godfrey's of Bouillon alleged legislation, see above, Ch. 10, p. 263 and Ch. 14, p. 347.

[3] M. Grandclaude, *Étude critique sur les Livres des Assises de Jérusalem* (Paris, 1923).

[4] John of Ibelin, chs. 1–3.

[5] Titus Livius, iii. 31. 8; Pomponius, *Dig.* i. 2. 2. 4.

[6] Cf. e.g. J. Richard, 'Pairie d'Orient latin', *RHDFE* 28 (1950), 67 ff.

[7] M. Grandclaude, 'Liste d'Assises remontant au premier royaume de Jérusalem', *Mélanges P. Fournier* (Paris, 1929), pp. 329 ff. These and other *assises* were studied in their historical context by Richard, *Royaume latin*.

did not follow any pre-established plan and did not aim to create a homogeneous code of law. It responded to the challenge of particular needs and circumstances. We catch a glimpse of that process when we examine, for example, the enactments of the Council of Nablus (1120). Twenty-four enactments were promulgated by king, clergy, and nobility, regulating problems characteristic of a state in the process of organization after a conquest (for example rights of jurisdiction and of tithes), or characteristic of an immigrant, mixed society (bigamy, litigations, illicit relations with Muslim women, etc.).[8]

These premises underlie consideration of two *assises* assigned to Baldwin II. Although not unknown, they have never been studied in detail. They are, however, very important, because they contribute to the understanding of the earliest organization of the kingdom. Moreover, they bear witness to current legal influences and, as we shall try to prove, they are an unknown chapter in the expansion of the reborn study of Roman Law in the Middle Ages. This will also bring us to consider contemporary centres of legal culture during that great century of the renaissance of Roman law in Europe. Finally the later vicissitudes of this early legislation will illustrate important constitutional changes in the history of the kingdom.

a. *The* Assise *on Confiscation*

The first of these *assises*, that on confiscation, is preserved in the *Livre au Roi*,[9] an anonymous treaty composed after the fall of Jerusalem, *c.* 1197–1205;[10] the second, preserved in the *Livre des Assises des Bourgeois* (*c.* 1240–4),[11] deals with disinheritance of children by parents and parents by their descendants. In both cases we know the name of the royal legislator through one source only. If we take into consideration the apparent contradiction between the *assises* and the customary procedure which was followed in the middle of the thirteenth century, we may

[8] Mansi, *Concilia* xxi. 262 ff.

[9] Ed. Beugnot, ch. 16.

[10] Cf. p. 430 n. 3. We do not agree with M. Grandclaude's view as to the, 'Caractère du Livre au Roi', *RHDFE* 1926 (1952), 308 ff.

[11] For an attempt to date the *LdAdB* see J. Prawer, 'Établissement des coutumes du marché à Saint-Jean d'Acre', *RHDFE* 25 (1951), 329–50. Some of this list of tariffs have been better interpreted by J. Richard, 'Colonies marchandes privilegiées et marché seigneurial. La Fonde d'Acre et ses "droitures"', *Moyen-Âge*, 59 (1953), 325–40, but we agree as to the date. The date proposed by Riley-Smith, *Feudal Nobility*, p. 85 and n. 188, *c.* 1260, seems hardly acceptable, if only on the grounds that it is impossible to assume that the author of the *LdAdB* writing *c.* 1260 did not know of the reform of the court registers in 1251. This we learn from the *Livre du plédéant*, written three generations later.

justly ask whether one lone testimony is acceptable. Involuntarily, we think of that well-known practice of attributing recent law to the Ancients, in order to give it more authority, and present it as *altes Recht*, the importance of which was so brilliantly described by F. Kern. There is, however, no reason that the author of the *Livre au Roi* should have included in his treatise a law in flagrant contradiction with contemporary usage if the *assise* were not authentic. He would have suppressed the one or the other.

The author of the *Livre au Roi* calls the *assise* on Confiscation of fiefs *Etablissement* and it consists of twelve 'reasons' listing cases in which the king has the right to confiscate a vassal's fief. The list ends: 'Et tout ce est raison par dreit et par l'assise et par l'establissement dou roi Bauduin segont, a cuy Dés pardoint. Amen.' In every case, the penalty is the same: 'si deit estre deserités a tousjors.'

This *assise* concerns only royal vassals, called *homes liges, home lige ou terrier ou baron, terrier ou autre*. Before the time of King Amalric (1163–74), who elevated all royal vassals of the kingdom to the rank of *hommes liges*, the title 'liegeman' *stricto sensu* was applied to the royal tenants-in-chief only.[12] The *assise* then clearly refers to royal vassals, and this is well stressed in the title: 'peut li rois deseriter ses homes liges sans esgart de cort'. The most revered law and practice of the kingdom, the one that comes back again and again under the pen of the jurists, is the rule that a lord cannot confiscate his vassal's fief without his court's judgment. But according to our *assise*, even the great vassals of the Crown can lose their fiefs without judgment of their peers.[13] This is an archaic situation, then, which doubtless antedates the time of King Amalric. It fits well with the time of the first Baldwins, when royal power, following the period of conquests, was strong and the authority of the Crown was paramount against particularistic and centrifugal tendencies in the feudal nobility.[14] Our *assise*, which determined the relations between the king and his vassals, strengthened the king's position, although to some extent it also safeguarded vassals from too arbitrary decisions from their lord.

[12] The feudal vocabulary of the kingdom was fairly fluid, especially in its early period. Cf. J. Richard, op. cit., p. 430 n. 6. 'Baron' seems to have denoted a knight in royal service, a member of his retinue, or an officer of the Crown before it described an actual holder of a barony.

[13] We are aware that this is said in the title and not in the text of the chapter. Yet it is unthinkable that the author did not find anything in the text to prompt the phrasing of his title, especially when contemporary customs were diametrically opposed to the *assise*.

[14] See above, Ch. 1, pp. 15ff.

Consequently, it seems to us that there is no reason to question Baldwin's authorship of the *Assise* on Confiscations.[15] This will be corroborated by the study of the *Assise* on Disinheritance.

Let us now analyse the *Assise* on Confiscation. The penalty that is constantly found—to be 'deserités a tousjors'—emphasized confiscation and perpetual forfeiture, a penalty characteristic in this form of a period prior to that of the learned law. Then confiscation, 'commise', and legal seizure, which were punishments for feudal offences or complementary to capital punishment, would be differentiated, sometimes benefiting the lord of the fief, sometimes the lord who held high justice.[16] Our *assise* is poor in legal distinctions but clear and efficient in the framework of state organization.

To facilitate an analysis we print below the text of the *Livre au Roi*, ch. xvi:

Ici orrés par quantes raisons peut li rois deseriter ses homes liges sans esgart de cort, se il font ver luy nules de ces choses qui sont si devisées. La premiere raison si est, s'il avient que aucun home lige lieve armes contre son seignor, si deit estre deserités à tousjors. La segonde raison si est, s'il avient que aucun home lige fait justice contre son seignor ou contre sa terre, si juge la raison qu'il det estre deserités à tousjorsmais. La tierce raison si est, se aucun houme lige fait ou fait faire fauce monée ou faus besans en son casau ou en sa maison, si juge la raison que il det estre deserités a tousjors mais. La carte raison si est, s'il avient que aucun home lige veut empoisouner son seignor ou sa moillier ou aucun de ses anfans, si juge la raison qu'il det estre deserités à tousjors. La quinte raison si est, se aucun home lige ou terrier our baron dou reaume faiseit faire port en sa terre, de naves et de vaisseaus, et chemin en paienime, por amender sa terre et por amermer les droitures dou roi, si juge la raison qu'il det estre deserités à tosjorsmais. La siste raison si est, si aucun home lige, qui que il fust ou terrier our autre, faiset faire et labourer et batre monée en sa terre, si juge la raison qu'il det estre deserités à tousjorsmais, por ce que nul hom ne deit aver port, euvreneour ou monée labourant, fors li rois, par droit ne par l'assise. La septime raison est, se aucun home lige entre, par force des Sarasins, contre la volenté de son seignor, et sans esgart de cort, en saisine de ces casaus et de sa terre don il det servise et homage au roi, si juge la raison qu'il det estre deserités à tousjorsmais. La huitime raison si est, se aucun home lige fait relever ses vileins par son comandement et par s'ayde et par son conceill contre son seignor et venir vers luy as armes leveés, si juge la raison qu'il det estre deserités à tousjorsmais. La

---

[15] To be exact we would rather say one of the Baldwins. We shall try in the last part of this chapter to assign both *assises* to Baldwin III. Here and elsewhere we use Baldwin II to avoid repeating Baldwin II or Baldwin III.

[16] E. Blum, 'La commise féodale', *Revue historique du droit* 4 (1923), 31–102, and P. Timbal, 'La confiscation dans le droit français du XIIIe siècle', *RHDFE* 21 (1943), 47–79. Cf. J. Goebel, *Felony and Misdemeanor* (New York, 1937), pp. 250 ff. F. Joüon de Longrais, 'Le droit criminel anglais au moyen-âge', *RHDFE*, 34 (1956), esp. 403–6.

nouvime raison si est, se aucun home lige grepist son fié et se renée et devient Sarasin, si juge la raison qu'il det estre deserités à tousjorsmais. La disime raison si est, se aucun home lige y a qui ait guerpi son seignor en sa besoigne, en la bataille as Sarasins, et s'enfuirent et le laisserent prendre; et c'il ne fussent fuis et ce fucent tenus adès o luy, il ne fusse entrepris li rois ne mors: si juge la raison qu'il det estre deserités à tosjors. La onsime raison si est, s'il avient que aucun home lige ne veut faire le comandement de son seignor de faire se qui est reisnable chose de faire, si juge la raison qu'il det estre deserités à tosjorsmais. La dousime raison si est, que c'il avient que aucun home lige vent ou baille por aucun aver son hostel ou sa vile qu'il teneit, as Sarasins, sans congé de son seignor, si juge la raison qu'il det estre deserités à tousjorsmais. Et tout ce est raison par dreit et par l'assise et par l'establissement dou roi Bauduin segont, à cuy Dès pardoint. Amen.

One group of 'reasons' for confiscation is that of typical feudal cases, such as a vassal having 'abandoned his lord in his need when fighting the Saracens and the king was taken prisoner or killed', or 'when a vassal refused to obey the order of his lord when the demand is reasonable', or again 'when someone raised his villeins against his lord and comes against him in arms', or finally in cases that could be regarded as disavowing (although the circumstances make it rather a case of treason), namely 'if a vassal seized against the will of his lord and without judgment of court with the help of Saracens such villages and such land for which he owes service and homage to the king.'[17] All other cases can scarcely be considered simply feudal offences. Indeed, although they do not infringe the feudal or vassalic nexus, they offend the king's sovereign rights. They are committed 'por amermer les droitures dou roi', they are diminishing the king's rights as we have it in the *assise*. These are the cases in which 'one made or caused that false coinage should be made or false besants', or again 'when one ordered a port to be made in his land for vessels and ships and roads to paynim', or 'made money in his land . . . because nobody has the right to have a port or make money but the king.'[18] These are simply regalian rights, the violation of which was punished by the confiscation of the fief. A third group of offences comprised attacks on the king's person, his family, or possessions.[19] Finally, there were offences which despite their appearance could hardly be considered feudal offences: 'when a man abandoned his fief, apostasized, and became a Saracen', or 'when a vassal

---

[17] Following the order of the *Livre au Roi*, reasons 10, 11, 8, and 7. The last one is interesting, showing a vassal whose fief was confiscated and who seizes his possession without court order, by force, or even by treason, as he relies on Muslim help against Christians.

[18] *Raisons* 3, 5, and 6.

[19] *Raisons* 1, 2, and 4.

sells or pledges for money his home or city which he held to the Saracens without the permission of his lord.'[20] These were actually cases of treason against the state or against Christendom.

It was normal for feudal offences to be punished by confiscation. Since the fief was an integral part of the feudal relation,[21] its confiscation was the logical consequence of its infringement. Parallel examples are easily found in the Frankish, Anglo-Saxon, and Visigothic kingdoms.[22]

But the infringement of regalian rights is in a different category. In Europe in the 1130s it would have been hard to find confiscation as the punishment for the violation of the regalian right of *monategium*, for the simple reason that in almost every state which evolved from the Carolingian empire, the mint was no longer a royal monopoly. We have to wait until the thirteenth century to see its reappearance. The situation was different in a few great principalities, but with some exceptions it would be difficult to find any legal effort to establish this regalian or ducal monopoly. How then did the Crusader legislator establish such a monopoly? The starting-point obviously was the political reality of the kingdom, where the royal power was strong enough to safeguard its right to mint, to collect port revenues, and to impose duties on the great caravan routes leading to and from Islam. We do not doubt, however, that the form, as well as the subject matter of that legislation, was directly influenced by the renascent Roman Law.

The regalian rights safeguarded by the fifth and sixth *raisons* of the *assise*, were modelled on Roman law. In the latter, the counterfeiting of coinage was a *crimen laesae maiestatis*[23] punishable by the confiscation of property. The same law also conceived apostasy a sacrilege, a *crimen laesae maiestatis*.[24] Treason, included in Roman law under the notion of apostasy, was considered in our *assise* in the special case of surrendering a town or manor to the Saracens. These offences, as already remarked, can scarcely be classified as typical feudal offences. Betrayal was a crime of treason against a sovereign who personified the state, and not the betrayal of the

---

[20] *Raisons* 9 and 12. What is stressed in the ninth reason is not the *guerpissement* of the fief, but apostasy. The twelfth reason is not clear. We can with some difficulty imagine a vassal selling his 'ville', which can be a 'casale', village, to a Saracen, but it is more difficult to imagine the sale of a hostel in a city against the will of the lord. Perhaps 'hostel' has here a different meaning, like 'hospitium', land colonized by 'hospites', settlers.

[21] Cf. E. Blum, op. cit., pp. 45 ff.

[22] e.g. Sanchez Albornoz, *En torno a los origenes del feudalismo* i (Mendoza, 1942), 194.

[23] *Cod.* ix. 24. 2.

[24] Pauly–Wissowa, s.v. *maiestas*, and cf. P. Timbal, op. cit., pp. 44–6.

lord by his vassal. The surrender of a town or of a manor followed the rule: 'Lex autem Julia maiestatis praecipit eum, qui maiestatem publicam laeserit, teneri, qualis est ille, qui in bellis cesserit aut arcem tenuerit ['tradiderit', following Mommsen] aut castra concesserit.'[25] And is not the offence by which a liegeman raised his villeins against his lord, as in Roman law: 'is, cuius opera dolo malo consilium initum erit ... quo armati homines cum telis lapidibusve in urbe sint convaniantve adversus rem publicam, locave occupentur vel templa, quove coetus conventusve fiat hominesve ad seditionem convocentur', or 'quive hostibus populi Romani nuntium litterasve miserit signumve dederit feceritve dolo malo, quo hostes populi Romani consilio iuventur adversus rem publicam, quive milites sollicitaverit concitaveritve, quo seditio tumultusve adversus rem publicam fiat.'[26] Was there any reason to specify that the rebellion should have been aided by the Saracens, if the very fact of taking up arms against the lord was stigmatized in the first *raison* of the assize, and the offender condemned to confiscation? The explanation is obvious: this first *raison* was concerned with an offence of the feudal order, whereas the present one was a case of state treason. Finally we would like to emphasize the importance of the fourth *raison*, the case of poisoning the lord or the members of his family. Was there a special reason to mention this kind of murder? Poisoning was a foul (*laid*) offence—a felony. This may perhaps explain why it was included in the *assise*, but we would rather look for its inclusion in the Roman reasons of 'ingratitude', which allowed the parents to disinherit their children. We shall return to this question later.

Thus Baldwin II's *Assise* on Confiscation reviews different types of offences: feudal on the one hand, and those that could be qualified as offences against the state, personified by the king, on the other. About 1130 the latter were innovations, even unexpected innovations.

The novelty of that legislation is put into relief if compared with contemporary European legislation. The oldest was the *Usualia*, that is to say the primitive core of the *Usatges de Barcelona*,[27] composed *c.* 1058. A few customs (§§ 30–48) dealt with the relations between lord and vassals. However the offences mentioned (refusal of service, abandoning of the lord in case of need, attempt upon the life of the lord and of his family) are typically feudal only. In 1047 a *Constitutio de causis feudi amittendi*,

---

[25] *Dig.* xlviii. 4. 3.

[26] *Dig.* xlviii, 4. 1.

[27] Cf. Valls y Taberner, 'Els "Usualia" de Curialibus Barchinonae essaig de reconstruccio', *Estudis universitatis Catalans*, 19 (1934), 270–80.

attributed to the Emperor Henry III, dealt only with an attempt upon the Emperor's life and honour.[28] It is not before 1140 that analogies with Baldwin's *assise* appear in the Ariano legislation for Norman Sicily. And the Ariano legislation was directly modelled on Roman Law, and its §§ 4, 18, 20–2 dealt with regalian rights, like the Crusader *assise*.[29] Finally it was to be the *Libri Feudorum*, a treaty of *droit savant*, that would influence the legislation and customs of Europe.[30] But with the Ariano legislation, we are already ten years after the promulgation of our *assise*. When we admire the legal work of the Normans of Sicily who, to quote H. Niese: 'als literarisches Unternehmen standen die Assisen im damaligen Europa wohl einzig da', we should not forget that other Frenchmen in much more difficult circumstances were following the same path at the eastern end of the Mediterranean. To both, Roman law was the beacon in the turbulent sea of a newly created state.

If in legal practice Baldwin II's legislation and that of the Normans of Sicily, have a place of their own, another country, Norman England, offers striking analogies in legal theory. Contemporary with Baldwin II, the anonymous author of the *Leges Henrici I* quoted almost the same cases of confiscation that we encounter in the legislation of the two Mediterranean states.[31] Glanvill (*c.* 1190) followed later[32] but we have to to wait for Bracton to find among the offences of *lèse majesté*, an attempt upon the king's life, rebellion, advice given to the prejudice of the king, counterfeit of seals and coins, these offences being punished by death and confiscation.[33]

Did the Norman traditions influence the Latin Kingdom? Although

---

[28] *MGH Constitutiones* i, no. 55. This 'constitutio' is often assigned to Henry VI in 1196.

[29] Brandileone, *Il diritto Romano nelle leggi normanne e sueve di regno de Sicilia* (Turin, 1884). The Italian school of law history which stresses the Norman origins of Sicilian legislation assigns to Roman Law a preponderant influence on the decrees of Ariano. Cf. H. Niese, *Die Gesetzgebung der normannischen Dynastie im Regnum Siciliae* (Halle, 1910), p. 100.

[30] On the *Libri Feudorum*, cf. below, p. 440 n. 43. A hundred years later, the major part of these felonies would be sanctioned in Bordeaux by the loss of the rights of bourgeoisie (*Livre des coutumes de Bordeaux*, ed. Barckhausen (Bordeaux, 1890), pp. 27, 37–8). The new concept of the state enabled the burgesses to enter the framework reserved until now to the nobility.

[31] Leges Henrici I (1114–18), ed. F. Liebermann, *Gesetze der Angelsachsen*, i (Halle, 1903), 43, 3; 43, 7; 55.

[32] Glanvill, *De legibus*, ed. G. E. Woodbine, ix. 1.

[33] Bracton, *De legibus*, ed. T. Twiss, 1. 3, trac. 2, c. 3 (fo. 1186), influenced Britton and Fleta and the anonymous *Mirror of Justices*, ed. W. J. Whittaker and F. W. Maitland, i. 15. Judicial practice of the middle of the fourteenth century brought forth the Treason Act of 1351 (25 Edw. III, s. 5), which is reminiscent of the *assise* of Baldwin II. See Pollock and Maitland, *History of English Law* ii. 505.

not impossible, it is unlikely in the case of the *Assise* on Confiscation, which, as we shall try to prove, was directly influenced by Roman law, which came to the kingdom from southern Europe.

How did the *Assise* on Confiscation evolve in the Latin Kingdom during the twelfth century? It was originally intended for the king's tenants-in-chief. What we do not know is whether it was also applicable between the lords and their vassals. Obviously, cases of infringement of regalian rights had no place in relations between lords and vassals, at least as long as the great lords did not usurp minting rights. In other cases we may suppose that penalties established by Baldwin II were followed in seignorial courts. But does it mean that the lords could seize their vassals' fiefs, without judgment of their court? Once again, there is no answer to this question. The two revolts which occurred in the kingdom, that of Romain of Le Puy and of Hugh of Le Puiset (confused by William of Tyre who placed both in the reign of Fulk of Anjou) ended in the confiscation of the rebels' fiefs. We do not know the details concerning Romain of Le Puy, lord of Transjordan, but we possess a full account concerning Hugh of Le Puiset, lord of Jaffa.[34] He was publicly accused in the High Court of having 'jurée et porchaciée la mort son seigneur le roi, comme traitres qu'il est.'[35] One of his relatives charged him with having constantly refused to obey the king. This, writes William of Tyre, was contrary to the *mores* and laws of the kingdom. Hugh was formally accused in the king's court and, as he did not appear in court, he lost his case by default. But finally, through the mediation of nobles, peace was established. Hugh was banished for three years, his fiefs were legally seized, and their revenue used to pay his debts.[36] All this happened less than ten years after the promulgation of the *assise* of Baldwin II! Naturally one could invoke the particular circumstances: the accused was suspected of being the queen's lover. In Europe this would have been enough for confiscation, as it would have been regarded as an attack on the honour of the lord's wife. But Fulk was in a difficult position. He could not confiscate the fief arbitrarily without being accused of prejudice. To safeguard his prestige he needed

---

[34] Richard, *Royaume latin*, pp. 69 and 90, and see above, p. 27 n. 32. Cf. H. E. Mayer, 'Studies in the History of Queen Melisende of Jerusalem', *Dumbarton Oaks Papers* 26 (1972), 104 ff.

[35] W. T. xiv. 16: 'Exsurgens ... Galterus Caesariensis ... in coetu procerum ... publice, et more accusatoris objicit comiti, quod majestatis crimine reus erat, et quod contra domini regis salutem, cum quibusdam factionis ejusdem complicibus, contra bonos mores et contra nostrorum disciplinam temporum conspirasset.'

[36] Ibid. xiv. 17.

the Court's judgment even if he could have formally punished Hugh of Le Puiset without it. The only clear deduction from these events is that the High Court could pronounce the confiscation and that this procedure was certainly the ordinary one. But was it possible to bypass it?

Whatever the case, at the end of the twelfth century, when the author of the *Livre Au Roi* was composing his work, it was absolutely impossible to imagine any confiscation without the court's judgment. Thus there is a change, an almost revolutionary change between *c.* 1130 and *c.* 1190.

This revolutionary modification of the procedure reflects a change in the balance of power between Crown and magnates. This took place during the reign of King Amalric (1163–74).[37] It was the famous *Assise sur la ligece* that expressed the new reality in the political life of the kingdom. We have suggested that in order to make his barons accept the *Assise sur la ligece*, King Amalric compromised with them by offering a reform of the *Assise* on Confiscation.[38] Henceforth, neither the king nor his tenants-in-chief were allowed to dispossess of their vassals fiefs without a judgment of court.

The confiscation cases listed in Baldwin II's *Etablissement* evolved during the twelfth and thirteenth centuries until they found a new and totally different theory in the work of John of Ibelin. This evolution has been outlined, though without details, by J. L. La Monte.[39] But before discussing this evolution, let us turn to the second *assise* of Baldwin II, that on Disinheritance. We shall try to prove that it was this *assise* that influenced the evolution of the Law of Confiscation in the kingdom.

b. *The Assise on Disinheritance*

Baldwin II's *Assise* on Disinheritance is preserved in the *Livre des Assises des Bourgeois*.[40] It deals with the right of disinheriting successors by ancestors and vice versa. It thus forms a link in the long chain of legislation beginning with Justinian's famous *Novella* 115 of 1 Feb. 542, until its last survivors in the eighteenth century.[41] The fact that Baldwin II had promulgated such an *assise* throws some light on the internal conditions in the early Latin Kingdom. Taken together with the contemporary

[37] See above, Ch. 2, pp. 35 ff.

[38] Ibid., p. 37.

[39] 'Note on the law of treason in the Assises of Jerusalem', *Feudal Monarchy*, Appendix E, pp. 276–80.

[40] Chs. 234–5.

[41] On the evolution of this *Novella*, see J. Merkel, *Die justinianischen Enterbungsgründe. Untersuchungen zur deutschen Staats- und Rechtsgeschichte*, ed. O. Gierke, 94 Heft (Breslau, 1908).

decree of Nablus, the whole reflects an unattractive situation, even though it is difficult to gauge reality by the contents of penal law.

It is not a pure coincidence that Baldwin II was the author of the *assise*. Confiscation of fiefs and disinheritance were both the result of the violation of the same deep-rooted feeling, of close union based on affection, loyalty, and cohesion as between members of a family or members of the seignorial family, the *maisnie*. The vassal, although no more a *nurritus*,[42] belonged to the seignorial family, in the larger sense of the word. In both cases of family or feudal nexus, it was ingratitude that was considered the most vile vice. The similarity is so close that the Lombard *Libri Feudorum* will say:

Praedictis modis beneficium debere amitti tam naturalis quam civilis ratio suadet, quod colligi potest, si quis novam constitutionem [*Novellam* 115] justas exheredationis causas enumerantem et alias constitutiones veteras justas repudii et ingratitudinis causas, quibus et matrimonia recte contracta solvuntur et donationes jure perfectae revocantur, subtiliter scrutatus fuerit.[43]

Thus the association between the idea of confiscation and disinheritance is so clear that if we admit Baldwin II's authorship of one of these two *assises*, we shall attribute the second one to him also without hesitation. Moreover, both manuscripts of the *Livre des Assises des Bourgeois*, those of Munich and Venice, attribute the same *assise* to a Baldwin. The qualification 'li rois Baudouin dou Borc a qui Dieus pardoint' explicitly indicates Baldwin II, king of Jerusalem between 1118 and 1130.

The most striking feature of this *assise* was the fact that the legislation of Baldwin II broke with the Germanic traditions known to us from the different *Leges Barbarorum*. The starting-point of the *Leges* was the inalienability of patrimonial possessions. This almost entirely precludes the possibility of children's disinheritance. And since wills were little known and rarely used, the parents' power to dispossess their progeny was singularly reduced.

Thus Baldwin II's *assise*, compared with the customary traditions of northern France, represented a sudden change in the judicial concepts of the time. Its origins date back to the Roman tradition—more exactly to that of Justinian. As to the source of its inspiration, Baldwin's legislation closely followed the *Novella* 115. It presupposed the existence of wills and permitted disinheritance.

[42] A large number of texts illustrating such relations was printed by J. Flach, *Les Origines de l'ancienne France* ii (Paris, 1893).

[43] *Consuetudines feudorum*, ed. C. Lehmann (Göttingen, 1892), tit. X, c. 2 § 8.

We do not know what customs existed in the Crusader Kingdom before the promulgation of the *assise* by Baldwin II, but it can be said with some certainty that they were not entirely different. It is inconceivable that Baldwin II should have wanted to revolutionize the existing customs. It is more likely that he tried to fix the causes of disinheritance, causes which were certainly not entirely indeterminate, but probably fluctuating. What was their origin? They will certainly have come from European countries where Roman law was still alive: Mediterranean Spain, Italy, and more probably, Languedoc or Provence. Baldwin II's *assise* did not apply to feudal law which rule fiefs and nobility. It was preserved in the *LdAdB* only, and we find no trace of it in the works of the feudal jurists. This would fit with the fact that the twelfth-century burgesses were of southern origin.[44]

If the contents of the *assise* are easily linked with Justinian's legislation, its form and actual text pose a number of questions. As to the form, it paralleled the *assise* on Confiscations.[45] This is not surprising, because both *assises* issued from the same royal chancery.

But the actual text, the form in which the *assise* has come down to us, poses problems which, as we shall see, transcend Crusader legislation in importance. They bring us into close touch with the renaissance of the Roman law in the twelfth century. Our discovery of the connection between the *LdAdB* and the Provençal manual of Roman law is also valid in the case of the *Assise* on Disinheritance. Indeed chs. 234–5 of the *LdAdB* which contain it, correspond to chs. 17 and 19 of the third book of *Lo Codi*. We print four related texts here to make the comparison easier: 1. A text related to *Lo Codi* and taken from the *Ratio de lege romana* (see below, p. 450 n. 49). 2. The Provençal original of *Lo Codi*.[46] 3. The text of *LdAdB*. 4. The Latin translation of *Lo Codi* by Richard of Pisa (Ricardus Pisanus). The numbers added indicate the order of the *raisons* or *causae* in the respective texts. We have changed the order to facilitate comparison.

---

[44] See above, Ch. 15, pp. 382 ff.

[45] The order of the *raisons* is the same in both *assises*.

[46] We would like to express our thanks to Mme Yves Mulon who copied for us the MS. Sorbonne 632, fo. 23 ss. and collated it with B.N. MS. fr. 1932 and MS. fr. nouv. acq. 4138.

Ratio de lege romana, ed. Pitzorno, ch. 35.

Lo Codi (Provençal text) Sorbonne MS. 632, fo. 23 ᵒ a, 23 ᵛᵒ b) (Coll. with B.N. MS. fr. 1932 and B.N. MS. n. a. fr. 4138).

Sed propter legem romanam sunt xiiij cause quod pater vel mater, avius vel avia possunt exhereditare filios suos.

Aquellas causas per que pot lo paire. e la maire e li avis. e li avia deseretar sos effanz sunt xiv.

Prima. Si filius misit manum in patre ad malum faciendum.

(1) Si cum es si l fillz mes sas mas esson paire per mal a faire (i).

(2) Si fecit patri suo magnam contumeliam vel opprobium.

(2) O si el i fei gran contumelia. zo es gran antan (ii).

(3) Si accusaverit patrem de crimine, nisi fecisset contra imperatorem vel commune terre.

(3) O si el acuset son paire de crim. Isters si ill l acuset de crim que el avia fait contra l'emperador, o contra lo comun de la terra qu adonc non pot esser per aizo deseretar (iii).

(5) Si filius facit ingenia cum quibus velit occidere patrem.

(5) O si lo filz fara engeing ab que el volia aucire son paire (v).

(6) Si filius iacet cum matrigua sua vel concubina patris.

(6) O si el iaira ab sa mairastra. o ab la concoa de son paire (vi).

(7) Si filius misit in placito patrem suum per calumniam id est pro torto com sua scientia, et pro induciis et longamento que querit filius in illo placito pater recipiat grande dampnum.

(7) O si lo fillz met em plait son paire per calumpnia zo es a tort son ecient e per alongament que l filz demanda en aquel plait lo paire en recept gran dan (vii).

Livre des Assises des Bourgeois, ed. Kausler, ch. 234.

Lo Codi, Latin trans. by Richard of Pisa, ed. Fitting, 1. III. 17.

Ici orres la raison par quantes choses peut deseriter le pere et la mere ses anfans par dreit et par raison et par l asise de Jerusalem et par la lei meysme.

Que sunt ille cause per quas filius et filia possunt exhereditari. Cause ille pro quibus pater et mater et auus et auia possunt exheredare filios sunt xiiij.

Cil avient par aucune mesaventure que le fis ou la fille mete main sur son pere ou sur sa mere et la bate: la raison iuge qu il est deserites, par dreit, celuy enfant qui ce aura fait, se le pere et la mere veullent.

(1) sicuti si filius misit manus suas in patrem et offenderet patrem.

La segonde raison por quei le pere et la mere pevent deseriter leur anfans si est se les anfans font grant honte a lor pere ou a leur mere, car ce est raison et dreit.

(2) uel si fecit ei grandem contumeliam id est grande uituperium.

La tierce raison par quei il sont deserites si est, se il metent mensonge d aucun crim de mauvaistie sur leur pere ou sur leur mere et les acusent a cort, si que per iaus ne remaint que li peres ou la mere n ait grant mal et grant honte.

(3) uel si ipse accusauit patrem in crimine nisi accusauit eum in crimine maiestatis, id est in offensione quam fecit contra imperatorem. uel contra communem tocius ciuitatis in qua ipse manet, quia tunc non poterit ideo exheredari.

La carte raison par quei il pevent estre deserites si est, se lis fis ou la fille fist aucune chose ou la quel chose il vost ocirre son pere ou sa mere.

(5) uel si filius faciet aliquod ingenium ad occidendum patrem suum.

La quinte raison si est que deserites devent estre, se les fis gist o sa marastre, ou se la fille gise o son parastre, charnaument.

La siste raison si est, se le fils ou la fille mete en plait son pere ou sa mere d'aucune question a tort, a son essient, et par l aloignement que li fis ou la fille font de celuy plait li peres reseit grant damage.

(6) uel si filius mittat patrem suum in placito per calumpniam, id est tortuose et par elongamentum quod filius peciit in illo placito pater sustinuit maximum dampnum.

(8) *Si pater est in captione pro pecunia quam debet et rogat filium ut intret et faciat firmantiam pro se et ipse non vult intrare. Verum est de filio masculo in isto casu.*

(8) O si lo paire es em prison per auer que el deu. e el preia son fill que el intre e fermanza per el e el non i vol intrar en aquella fermanza per lo paire. de tant con om lo vol penre e fermanza. mas aco es vers solament del filz mascles (viii).

(13) *Si pater est captus a saracenis et filius non vult eum recuperare; si pater moritur, hereditas illa debet esse ecclesie.*

(13) O si lo paire es pres de serradis. e lo filz no l vol donar redempzo: e adons si l paire mor em poder de serradis. la heretaz que seria del fillz si agues donada la redempzo: deu esser de la gleisa (xiii).

(9) *Si interdicit patri suo ut non fatiat testamentum.*

(9) O si el uedet a son paire que el non dones son gatge (ix).

(10) *Si ipse stat cum ioculatoribus sine voluntate patris, nisi pater sit ioculator.* (11) *Filia si fuerit minor XXV annorum et pater vult ei dare maritum qualem decet et ipsa non vult accipere sed ducit malam vitam cum alio homine.*

(10) O si el ista ab ioglars ses voluntat del paire. mas zo es vers. si l paire non es ioglars. eussament que el en pot deseretar son fill. x. (11) O si ella es filia que sia menre de XXV. anz e l paire li vol donar tal marit cum li taing. e ella non li vol penre. mas ten mal segle ab altre ome (xi).

(12) *Si pater est furiosus et filius non vult eum vestire nec pascere.*

(12) O si lo paire es furiosus. e lo fillz non lo vol conrear ni vestir. e adonc si om len somon e el non e vol faire: peret la heretat del paire ancara no l l deseretaes lo paire (xii).

(14) *Si pater est christianus et filius ereticus.*

(14) O si lo paire es de dreita fe. e lo fillz es eretgues (xiv).

la septime raison si est, se le pere ou la mere est en prison de Sarasins por aver et on le veut prendre en gage en leuc de son pere ou de sa mere iusque il aient porchassee leur raenson, et li fis ne veut entrer por luy.

(7) uel si pater est in carcere pro pecunia quam debebat et rogat filium suum ut faciat firmanciam pro se, [et filius non uult facere firmanciam pro se] in quantum homines volunt illum filium recipere propter firmanciam: set hoc verum est de filiis masculis.

La huitisme raison par coi pevent estre deserites les anfans des biens de leur pere ou de leur mere si est, se le pere ou la mere est en prison de Sarasins, et les anfans ont bien de quei rechater le et nel veullent rechater ne traire de prison.

(12) uel si pater captus est a sarracenis et filius non uult ei dare redempcionem, tunc si pater moritur in potestate sarracenorum, illa hereditas que deberet esse filii, si ipse dedisset redempcionem pro patre, debet esse ecclesie.

La IXᵉ raison si est, c il deffendy a son pere ou a sa mere a sa mort qu (il) ne fist testament ni por Des ni a nul autre.

(8) uel si filius contradixit patri suo, ut non faceret testamentum.

La Xᵉ raison si est, se les fis ou la fille maugre son pere ou de sa mere use o iugleors, et devient iuglier, et la fille fait puterie et devient coumunau, et ses peres la veut marier et elle ne vost.

(10) uel si ipse manet cum ioculatoribus contra uoluntatem patris: set hoc uerum est, nisi pater sit ioculator. (10) uel si est filia que sit minor XXV annis, et pater uult ei dare bonum maritum, et ipsa non vult accipere illum maritum, set plus uult facere uoluntatem suam cum luxuriosis hominibus.

La XIᵉ raison si est, se le pere est hors de son sens, ou la mere, et ces anfans ne le gardent ne ne li font ce que faire li devent et par ce celuy vait et chet et se brise le col ou se fait aucun autre mau: la raison iuge que celles choses dou pere ou de la mere qui devent estre de ces anfans s il eussent fait ver yaus se qu il deussent, si deivent estre dou seignor, par dreit.

(11) uel si pater est furiosus et filius non uult eum pascere uel uestire et aliquis admonet filium ut hoc faciat et facere non uult, perdit hereditatem patris, quamuis pater non exheredauit filium.

La dousime raison si est, se li peres est de dreite fei, et li fis ou la fille est hereges ou Patalin, et li peres et la meres est de dreite fei.

(13) uel si pater est bone fidei et catholice et filius est hereticus.

(4) *Si filius stat cum maleficis sicut maleficus, idest cum omnibus qui fatiunt malas artes.*

(4) O si el estara li fillz ab maleficis a guisa de maleficio. zo es ab homes qui fazunt mala art lo pot deseretar sos paire (iv).

Ratio de lege romana, ed. Pitzorno, c. 35.

Lo Codi (Provençal text) Sorbonne MS. 632, fo. 23 ^{vo} b.-24 ^{ro} a (Coll. with BN. MS. fr. 1932 and BN. MS. n. a. fr. 4138).

Aquellas causas per que podunt li fill deesretar lor paires e lor maires. o lor avis. o lor avias. o las autras sobiranas personas sunt (vii).

(1) *si pater vult occidere filium sine crimine maiestatis.*

(1) si lo paire liura lo fill a mort isters si lo fillz avian ren fait contra la maiestat del emperador. zo es que l volges aucire o un de sos cosseillers.

(2) *si voluerit eum tosicare et cognoscitur verum esse.*

(2) si lo paire apareillet verens o alcun malefici contra la vida del fill.

(4) *si vult occidere matrem filii sui.*

(5) si l mariz dona a ssa moiller o li moiller a son marit medinas per aucire o per tolre lo sen o en autra guisa volra aucire l us l autre. per aquest forfaig pot lo fillz deseretar aquel que o aura faig.

(3) *si negaverit filio suo ut non faceret testamentum de hoc quod facere potest.*

(4) si lo paire vedet a son fill que non fedes testament en aquellas causas en que el lo podia faire.

(4) *uel si filius manet cum maleficis, id est cum illis qui faciunt malam artem.*

Livre des Assises des Bourgeois, ed. Kausler, ch. 235.	**Lo Codi**, Latin trans. by Richard of Pisa, ed. Fitting, 1. III. 19.

Ici orres per quantes choses peut li fis deseriter par dreit son pere et sa mere de tout ce que que il ont.

Celes raisons par quei les anfans pevent deseriter leur peres et leur meres si sont VII choses.

Per quas causas filius et filia possunt exheredare patrem et matrem de omnibus que habent.

Ille cause per quas filii possunt exheredare patrem uel matrem uel auum uel auiam uel alias personas superiores sunt VII.

La premier si est, se li peres ou la mere vost ocire son anfant sans nul forfait.

(1) *Si pater tradit filium ad mortem, nisi filius fecisset aliquid contra maiestatem imperatoris, id est quod uoluisset imperatorem occidere uel aliquem de consiliariis suis.*

La segonde raison si est, se li peres ou la mere vost enpoisouner son anfant por prendre ce qu il avet.

(2)

La tierce raison si est, se le pere vost ocirre la mere de ces anfans ou se la mere vost ocirre le pere de ces anfans.

(5) *si maritus dat uxori sue uel uxor marito medicinas ad perdendum sensum uel ad occidendum unus alium, uel alio modo uolet occidere unus alium: per istud forfactum poterit filius exheredare illum qui hoc fecerit.*

La carte raison si est, se le peres ou la mere deffendy a son enfant qu il ne se coumniast por ce que testament ne feist dou sien propre et per ce moruth desconfes et sans receivre son Creator a sa mort.

(4) *si pater uetavit filio, ut non faceret testamentum in illis rebus in quibus filius posset facere testamentum.*

(6) *si filius fuerit in captivitate et pater noluerit eum redimere.*

(7) si lo filz sera catius antre sarradis: e lo paire no l volra vedemer si mor l ai: pert lo paire totas las causas de que lo fillz pot testament faire. e aquestas causas zo es del fill qui est morz en caitivitat: deurant esser donadas a la gleisa. oa caitius redemer. E si lo fillz entorna pot deseretar son paire car no l volg redemer.

(7) *si filius est vere fidei et pater fuit hereticus.*

(8) si lo fillz es catholicus e conois que lo paire es eretges pot l en lo fillz deseretar.

(5) *si iacuerit cum nora, vel cum concubina filii sui.*

(3) si l paire s aiostet a la moiller o a la concoa del fill.

(8) *si filius est furiosus et pater noluisset eum adiuvare.*

(6) si lo fillz aura perdut son sen e lo paire no l volgat gardar ni faire metgar si pois lo filz garis: pot deseretar son paire de son testament.

Atrestals es de la maire. e deus autres sobires parenz. E si non i es alcuna d aquestas causas: deu li totas oras laissar la terza part de tot lo seu.

La quinte raison si est, se li fis ou la fille est en prison de Sarasins por son pere ou por sa mere, et il nel veulent rechater de chaitivete.

(7) *si filius fuerit captus a sarracenis et pater noluit eum redimere, pater perdit omnia bona filii de quibus filius poterat facere testamentum, et res iste que sunt filii qui mortuus est in captiuitate debent esse ecclesie, uel debent dari ad redempcionem captiuorum, et si filius reuertitur poterit exheredare patrem, propterea quia pater noluit eum redimere.*

La VIᵉ raison si est, se les anfans sont de droit fei et le pere ou la mere sont Patalins (MS. Venice adds: ou hereges).

(8) *si filius est catholicus et pater est hereticus, filius potest exheredare patrem.*

La septime raison si est, se li peres ou la mere se vont reneer en terre de Sarasins ou deviennent Juis ou Sarasins [MS. Venice ou Samaritans].

(3) *a si pater miscet se cum uxore uel cum bagascia filii.*

(6) *uel si perdiderit filius sensum suum et pater noluit eum medicare neque custodire: si postea filius liberatur, potest exheredare patrem.*

Idem est de matre et de aliis superioribus personis. Et si non est aliqua de predictis causis, filius semper debet ad minus terciam partem omnium bonorum relinquere patri et matri el aliis superioribus.

A comparison of the different texts brings us to the following conclusions. There is a slight difference in the order of the *raisons* for disinheriting children, and there is also a difference in their number. The Latin translation of *Lo Codi* mentions fourteen titles, but in the actual text there are only thirteen. The Latin translator omitted one, since the original Provençal text actually contains fourteen. The omission is significant and we shall return to it later on. The *LdAdB* lists twelve *raisons*, but they correspond to the thirteen of *Lo Codi*, the ninth and tenth of *Lo Codi* being summarized in one in the *LdAdB*. In the first part then, which treats the reasons permitting parents to disinherit their children, the real difference consists in the omission of §4 of *Lo Codi* by the *assise* of Baldwin II (printed at the end of the text: 'Si filius manet cum maleficis id est cum illis qui faciunt malam artem').

In the second part, which enumerates the reasons for which children can disinherit their parents, the differences are more important. *Lo Codi*, having announced seven reasons, actually lists eight. The title of the *LdAdB* announces seven reasons, the text enumerates the same number but the reasons are different from those of *Lo Codi*. The seventh reason of the *LdAdB*: 'se li peres ou la mere se vont reneer en terre de Sarasins ou deviennent Juis ou Sarasins' (MS. Venice: 'ou Samaritans') is not mentioned in *Lo Codi*. On the other hand the two paragraphs of *Lo Codi*, 'Si pater miscet se cum uxore uel cum bagascia filii' and 'si perdiderit filius sensum suum et pater noluit eum medicare neque custodire, si postea filius liberatur potest exheredare patrem', are not to be found in the text of Baldwin II's *assise*.

The text of the *assise*, in the form that has reached us, has some particularities. Among the reasons for which parents can disinherit their children, we find (§7) a case in which a son refused to enter a Saracen prison for his father. We know that the Munich MS. has the better version of the *LdAdB*, but here it seems that we would do better to follow that of the Venice MS., which omits the word 'Sarasins', since it is really not plausible to assume that the *assise* referred to a Muslim prison. We simply cannot imagine a situation in which a Frank would be put in a Muslim gaol for debts due to a Muslim in the Latin Kingdom (remembering that it would have been a private gaol). We think that the original text (and the nearest to the text of *Lo Codi*) read originally: 'se le pere ou la mere est en prison par aver et on le veut prendre en guagiere pour la delivranse dou pere ou de la mere et li fis ne veut entrer [en guagiere] por luy.' The word *prison* can mean 'gaol' or 'captivity' and this is probably the reason the text was misunderstood and the word *Sarasins* was added. Following the 'corrected' text, instead of 'prendre [le fis] en guagiere pour la delivranse dou pere', which stated the obligation of a son to be *garens* of paternal debts,[47] or to go to gaol as a pledge to a Christian creditor, it was explained that the son should actually replace his father in a Muslim gaol. Thus, it became natural to speak of *raenson*. Therefore, the Venice MS. has the better reading, and it may have been corrected by the copyist himself.

Having introduced the word *Sarasins* into the preceding 'reason' the author of the *LdAdB* certainly modified the order of the paragraphs presented in *Lo Codi*. It now seemed natural to him to follow the seventh *raison* by a paragraph also dealing with Muslims. This explains why the thirteenth paragraph of *Lo Codi* became the eighth in the *LdAdB*. Another difference: in the *LdAdB* it is not the Church but (and this is in conformity with the customs of the Latin Kingdom) the overlord to whom a succession without heir escheats. It is incumbent on the lord, as a moral obligation, to give part of the property to the Church for the salvation of the deceased's soul.

In spite of some differences, the analogy between the Baldwin II's *assise* and the text of *Lo Codi* is so clear that there is no doubt of the close relation between the two.[48] Yet the problem is more complex than it seems at first sight. The Provençal *Lo Codi* was written, according to its editors Suchier and Fitting, *c.* 1144, and its Latin translation was made, according to Fitting, by Richard of Pisa *c.* 1152, or according to Patteta, Besta, and Kantorowicz, in the second half of the twelfth century, or between 1176 and 1196 according to Pitzorno.[49] Even if we admit the earliest possible date for the composition of the original Provençal *Lo Codi*, *c.* 1144 or

---

[47] An actual case of a Jew whose son was pledged by his father for the ransom money due to the Franks in Ascalon is known from a Geniza letter (1154–87), published by S. D. Goitein in *Tarbiz* 31 (1962), 287–90, and commented on by J. Prawer in *Shalem* 2 (1976), 103–5 (both in Hebrew, English summary in *Immanuel* 9 (1979), 81–7).

[48] The similarity of texts was observed by J. Merkel (above, p. 439 n. 41), but since he did not know the close relations of *Lo Codi* and the *LdAdB* (which for some reason he assigned to Cyprus), he wrote: 'Ebenso errinnert die Fassung in den Assisen mehrfach an Lo Codi, ohne das jedoch eine direkte Beeinflussung sich nachweisen liesse.'

[49] The dating of the text of *Lo Codi* and its different versions and translations is complicated. The proofs of the date of the original are based on the siege of Fraga in Spain and the date of composition of the *Summa Trecensis*. In the Provençal text an example of a gift given on a condition reads as follows: 'se Fraga sera presa entro ad un an o entro a dos', whereas the example of the Latin text is that of the siege of Milan by the Emperor. Fitting, consequently, suggested 1144 for the Provençal text, that being the date of the siege of Fraga (but actually there was another siege in 1133) and 1158–62 for the Latin translation made by Richard of Pisa. But there are difficulties in this chronology, seeing that the author or authors

(continued)

even *c.* 1133,[50] we come across a chronological impossibility: Baldwin II died in 1130. It is therefore obvious that *Lo Codi* could not have been the direct source of Baldwin's *assise*.[51]

Thus we have to refer to sources of *Lo Codi* that could also have been those of Baldwin. It was the opinion of so competent a scholar as Fitting that the causes of disinheriting the parents in *Lo Codi* were drawn from the *Epitome Juliani*, cvii. 3, whereas the causes of disinheriting descendants were drawn from the *Authenticum* cxv. 4 (and not from the *Epitome Juliani* cv. 5). He added:

So ensteht die Vermuthung die Rechtfertigunsgründe der Enterbung von Kindern seien gar nicht unmittelbar aus dem *Corpus iuris*, sondern aus einem (uns nicht bekannten) anderen Werke entnommen, das aus dem Julian geschöpft hatte. Wahrscheinlich zählte dieser, ebenso wie die *Exceptiones Petri* (I, 15), die indessen hier keinesfalls die Quelle gewesen sind, bloss eine Gruppe der Enterbungsgründe auf, und die Verfasser unserer Summe waren daher genötigt, die zweite unmittelbar aus dem *Corpus iuris* zu nehmen, wass dann aus dem *Authenticum* geschah.[52]

But J. Merkel, who made a thorough study of the history of disinheritance, was less positive on this point: 'Die Gestaltung entfernt sich überhaupt im einzelnen ebensosehr vom Julian wie vom *Authentikum*, so dass mann, wenn nicht eigene Bearbeitung durch den Verfasser, eine Vorlage vermuten müsste die von beiden sich ebenfalls unabhänging machte.'[53] Moreover, fragments of another Latin version of *Lo Codi* were found in an *opusculum* called *Liber romanae legis*. On its basis, Pitzorno suggested that the list of disinheriting parents depends on the *Epitome Juliani* and not on the *Authenticum*. This proves, he argued, its chronological precedence

---

of *Lo Codi* knew the *Summa Trecensis*, which was composed in the middle of the twelfth century. F. Patteta, 'La *Summa Codicis* et les *Questiones* falsamente attribuite ad Irnerio', *Studi Senesi* 14 (1897), 87 ff.; E. Besta, *L'opera d'Irnerio* i (Turin, 1896), 223, n. 3; H. Kantorowicz, *Studies in the Glossators of the Roman Law*², (Aalen, 1969); B. Pitzorno, 'Il *Liber romanae legis*' della *Ratio de lege romana*, Per la storia del c.d. *Codi* in Italia', *Rivista italiana per le scienze giuridiche*, 43 (1907), 101–34; idem, 'Le consuetudini giudiziari Veneziane anteriori al 1229', *Miscell. di storia Veneta*, ser. III, 2 (1910), 297–347; idem, 'Il diritto romano come diritto consuetudinario', *Per il XIV centenario della codificazione giustinianea*, ed. P. Ciapessoni (Pavia, 1934), pp. 743–91. See A. Gouron (above, p. 385 n. 43) and p. 451 n. 54.

[50] i.e. if the siege of Fraga in 1133 is regarded as decisive in establishing the date of the composition of the Provençal text. Fitting's argument that this refers to the siege of Fraga in 1144 is not entirely convincing.

[51] But see below, pp. 465–8.

[52] Fitting, op. cit., introduction, pp. 12–13.

[53] Merkel, op. cit., p. 39.

to the translation of Richard of Pisa.[54] The problem is therefore complex, and textual comparisons are not conclusive.

Some of the problems to be investigated are whether the text of the *LdAdB* is closer to the Latin version or to the Provençal original of *Lo Codi*. We have already compared Baldwin's *assise* to the translation of Richard of Pisa. It is obvious that despite very close similarities, the text of the *assise* was not a translation of the other (apart from the chronological difficulties which we have already discussed).

Let us now compare the *assise* with the Provençal text of *Lo Codi*. One paragraph is conspicuous. The fifth *raison* in the *LdAdB*, 'se le fis gist a sa marastre ou se la fille gise o son parastre charnaument',[55] does not appear in the Latin text of Richard of Pisa, but is found in the *Epitome Juliani*, as the sixth *causa*, 'si novercae auae vel concubinae patris, se turpiter miscuerit'; and in the Provençal original of *Lo Codi*, 'o si el iaira ab sa mairastra, o ab la concoa de son paire', and in the Latin version given by the *Liber romanae legis*, 'si filius iacet cum matrigua sua vel concubina patris'.

Contumelia is commented on in the Provençal 'zo es gran aunta', which corresponds to the *LdAdB*; 'font grant honte', but is not found in any of the Latin versions.[56] The sixth *raison* of the *LdAdB*, 'se le fils ou la fille mete en plait son pere ou sa mere d'aucune question a tort a son essient et par l'aloignement que le fis ou la fille font de celuy plait li peres reseit grant damage', corresponds to the Provençal 'o si lo fillz met em plait son paire per calumpnia zo es a tort son ecient e per alongament que l filz demanda

---

[54] According to B. Pitzorno, 'Il diritto romano', pp. 781–2, a law treatise was written in Tuscany at the beginning of the twelfth century. The treatise is lost, but fragments of its last version were preserved in the Venetian treatises *Liber romanae legis* and *Judicia a probis hominibus promulgata*. The Provençal *Lo Codi* and the text of Richard of Pisa, allegedly a canon of Sta Maria Maggiore in Pisa, are based on these treatises. Although it is outside the scope of this study to deal with that problem, it seems to us that the fragments are not sufficient to draw definite conclusions. Pitzorno's philological comparisons made in order to prove that the *Liber romanae legis* is nearer the Provençal text of *Lo Codi* than the Latin translation of Richard of Pisa, or that the causes of disinheritance of descendants in the *Liber* are taken from the *Epitome Juliani* rather than from the *Authenticum* are hardly convincing. Pitzorno gives the impression that this line of reasoning was somewhat biased by his belief in the priority of jurisprudence which originated in Italy. Cf. below, p. 454 n. 59.

[55] The end of that *raison*, 'se la fille gise o son parastre' is unexpected. One would rather expect: 'se le fils gise o . . . [concubine] son pere'. Still this is not impossible. The *assise* actually deals with the right of the mother to disinherit her daughter, if she had illicit relations with her father-in-law.

[56] *Epitome Juliani*: 'si gravem atque inhonestam contumeliam eis faciat'. Richard of Pisa: 'contumelia, id est grande vituperium'. *Liber romanae legis*: 'magna contumelia vel opprobium'.

en aquel plait lo paire en recept gran dan', but in this case the Latin versions are slightly different.[57] The seventh *raison* which was certainly in the original 'se le pere ou la mere est en prison por aver et on le veut prendre en gage en leuc de son pere ou de sa mere et li fis ne veut entrer por luy', follows the Provençal closely: 'o si lo paire es em prison per auer que el deu, e el preia son fill que el intra en fermanza per el, e el non i uol intrar en aquella fermanza per lo paire—de tant con om lo uol penre e fermanza'; but it differs from the Latin versions. We come to the same conclusions as to the twelfth *raison*, 'se li peres est de dreite fei et li fis ou la fille est hereges ou Patalin', which closely follows 'o si lo paire es de dreita fe, e lo fillz es eretgues'.

When we examine the causes for disinheritance of descendants, the case is quite different. Although the *LdAdB* contains almost all the contents of *Lo Codi*, it follows neither the Provençal original nor the Latin translation of Richard of Pisa, nor that of the *Liber romanae legis*. In the fifth *raison* the *LdAdB*, the Provençal original, and Richard's translation all have the noun *Sarrazeni* (*Sarasins*, *Saradis*), which does not appear in the *Liber romanae legis*, but we doubt if this is conclusive because it could have been introduced here by simple analogy with one of the *raisons* of the disinheritance of parents.[58]

The comparison of our texts leads to the conclusion that the first part of our *assise* closely corresponds to the Provençal text of *Lo Codi* and slightly less to the Latin translations of the *Liber romanae legis* and of Richard of Pisa. On the other hand, the second part of the *assise* has no direct relation to any known version of *Lo Codi*. It was suggested that the Provençal text used the *Epitome Juliani* in its first part, and an unknown source which derived from the *Epitome Juliani*, and was perhaps related to the *Exceptiones Petri*, in the second part.[59]

---

[57] *Liber romanae legis*: 'Si filius mittit in placito patrem suum per calumpniam id est pro torto cum sua scientia, et pro induciis et longamento que quaerit filius in illo placito, pater recipiat grande dampnum.' This phrase seems to be a translation from Provençal rather than an original Latin text. The *alongamentum* derives from a mistranslation of the Latin *delatio* in the *Epitome Juliani*, where it actually means informing. The author of the *Liber romanae legis* had certainly before him this translation, which he retranslated into Latin as *induciae* and *longamenta*. The same is true for: 'malefici . . . id est omnes qui fatiunt malas artes'. Here the 'explanation' was certainly superfluous, but it becomes comprehensible if it was translated from the Provençal: 'malefici . . . zo est . . . homes qui fazunt mala art'.

[58] It is precisely the text of the *Epitome Juliani*: 'si unus ex liberis in captivitate sit, eumque parens non redimerit, eadem teneant, quae de parentibus captivis supra constituimus', which could have influenced this reason for disinheriting descendants.

[59] Fitting, introduction to *Lo Codi*, p. 12.

Before reaching any conclusions as to that unknown source, we have to examine the relation between the text of Baldwin II's *assise* and the text in *Lo Codi*. We do not doubt that Baldwin II promulgated this *assise*, we are almost certain that its contents were preserved in the *LdAdB* (especially seeing that the parallel *assise* of Baldwin II is preserved in the *Livre au Roi*). It is clear, however, that there is no guarantee as to the accuracy, phraseology, and above all the language, of the transmitted text.

There cannot be any doubt that the language of the *assise* was Latin and not French, the language of the *LdAdB*. Although the Latin Kingdom used French in its legal documents (even before France did) in the first part of the thirteenth century, legislative acts could hardly have been written *c.* 1130 in any language but Latin. Consequently, the text furnished by *LdAdB*, is in the best of cases a translation of the original. This in itself precludes any conclusion based on philological grounds. Notwithstanding this difficulty, other conclusions are possible. We have demonstrated that the author of the *LdAdB* used *Lo Codi* as a model for his own work.[60] Thus the author of the *LdAdB* (in the middle of the thirteenth century) is certain to have found Baldwin II's *assise* in his Roman guide. We think that a distant echo of his astonishment can be detected in the title of the chapter, where we read: 'Ici orres la raison par quantes choses peut deseriter le pere et la mere ses anfans par dreit et par raison et par l'assise de Jerusalem et par la lei meysme.' The *lei* as used at that time is usually Roman law, but this adds a new difficulty to our problem. Did not the text of *Lo Codi* influence the French version of the Latin original of the *assise*?

We can only guess what happened. Basically, we think that Baldwin II's *assise* is well preserved in the *LdAdB*, but that the text of *Lo Codi* influenced the French translation which came down to us. Let us briefly recall the differences between the text of the *LdAdB* and that of *Lo Codi*, beginning with the change in the order of the *raisons*. Obviously, this change is the result of the fact that the *raisons* of the original *assise* of Baldwin II were listed differently. Likewise, in the eleventh *raison* for parents' disinheriting their children we see that the meaning of the *Novella* of Justinian has been changed. Whereas in the *Novella*, the disinheritance of children can profit other members of the family, the *LdAdB* says that the parents' possessions: 'si deivent estre dou seignor par dreit'.

Moreover, we think that the *Assises* of Confiscation and Disinheritance influenced each other, which might be expected if they were promulgated

[60] See above, Ch. 15.

at the same time. This might explain why in the disinheritance of parents (§ 2), poisoning (corresponding to § 4 of the Confiscation), was distinct from the attempt on the life of children (§ 1). Similarly, apostasy of parents (§ 7) may have paralleled apostasy as a cause of confiscation (§ 9).

On the other hand, as we saw, in these two chapters the *LdAdB* was doubtless closer to the Provençal *Lo Codi* than to its Latin translation by Richard of Pisa. But this was more of an exception. We have suggested that the anonymous author of the *LdAdB* followed a Latin text, that of Richard of Pisa or another Latin version of *Lo Codi*. Now, if the text of our *assise* is closer to the Provençal text, the reason must lie in the fact that Baldwin II's *assise* was in itself closer to it. But evidently Baldwin II did not know the Provençal text of *Lo Codi*, as it did not yet exist at that time. Consequently, his legislation was inspired by a similar text, which twenty years later would inspire the authors of *Lo Codi*.

We do not know what text it was, but we can try to locate it in time and place. The text must have already existed between 1118 and 1130, when it served as a model for Baldwin II. It was written in Latin, which left its traces even in the Provençal text in expressions like: *malefici, contumelia, calumpnia, furiosus*, later commented on in Provençal.

There is another point to be considered. If we compare the *Authenticum*, the *Epitome Juliani*, and the *Exceptiones Petri* with Baldwin II's *assise* and the whole cycle of *Lo Codi* and its translations, we see the introduction of *Sarraceni, Sarasins, Sarredis* into the *Novella* of Justinian. Whereas the *Novella* and the *Epitome* speak of *captivitas*, the *LdAdB* has *prisons de Sarasins*; the *Liber Romanae legis* has 'captus a Saracenis'; *Lo Codi* has 'pres de Sarredis', and Richard of Pisa has 'captus est a Sarrecenis'. The conclusion one could suggest is that a Muslim captivity would be more likely to occur after than before the First Crusade. What is more certain is the locating of this source in the area of the Mediterranean, the only one where Muslim captivity was a reality.

One more point has to be discussed. The last *raison* for disinheritance of parents is heresy. This is differently stated in the *LdAdB*: 'se li peres ou la mere se vont reneer en terre de Sarasin ou deviennent Juis ou Sarasins.'[61] It is understandable that such a law was promulgated in the Latin Kingdom, and indeed, there are sources bearing witness to such occurrences. However, we have to observe that the *Usatges* of Barcelona present the same version as our *assise* and in this they differ from the

<hr/>

[61] The Venice MS. reads: 'Juis ou Samaritans'. The reading of the Munich MS. is preferable.

Exceptiones Petri from which the whole chapter was taken. The last case in the *Usatges* of Barcelona as the reason for disinheriting parents reads as follows: 'Si filii se Sarracenos fecerint et penitere noluerint.'[62] It would be too early to conclude a direct influence or link between the two legislations, but it strengthens our belief that the Languedoc, Provençal, and Catalan areas (which were often politically connected at the beginning of the twelfth century), are possible places of origin of that unknown source, which influenced Baldwin II's legislation. This is even more plausible, since the majority of the so-called bourgeois population of the Latin Kingdom came from southern Europe, carrying with it Roman traditions, which were still alive, as attested by the *Usatges* of Barcelona and the *Petri Exceptiones*.[63]

c. The Law of Treason from Baldwin II to John of Ibelin

In this part of our study we shall attempt to define the place of the legislative work of Baldwin II, as expressed in his *assises*, in the legal evolution of the Latin Kingdom. To that end we shall follow the evolution of both *assises* in the kingdom. Our documentation of the Law of Confiscation is by far the richer. Still it is possible to draw an approximate picture of the general trend of the evolution of both *assises*.

J. L. La Monte, dealing with the Law of Treason, has already sketched the development of the Law of Confiscation, but by a singular inadvertence he did not take into account the *Livre au Roi* from the end of the twelfth century, which fills the gap to some extent between the time of Baldwin II and the middle of the thirteenth century with its two famous jurists, Philip of Novara and John of Ibelin.

Baldwin II's *Assise* on Confiscation is the earliest, but not the sole source for the twelfth century. We can actually witness the augmentation of the

---

[62] 'Usatici Barchinone Patrie' in Giraud, *Essai sur l'histoire du droit français au moyen-âge* ii (Paris, 1846), 480 ff. The text of the *Livre de Tübingue*, c. 63 (later *Exceptiones Petri* i, 15), influenced the most recent part of *Usatici*, c. 77. The controversy on the relationship between these two texts which began with a famous study of J. Ficker and continued by Max Cohn (Conrat), G. Mor, and others was partly summarized by Valls i Taberner' 'Les descobertas de Ficker sobre els "Usatges de Barcelona" i llurs afinitats amb les "Exceptiones Legum Romanorum" and 'El problema de la formaciô dels Usatges de Barcelona', *Estudis d'historia juridica catalana* (Barcelona, 1929), pp. 46–9.

[63] The question of the origin of *Livre de Tübingue* and the *Exceptiones* has been the subject of lively discussion. Cf. M. G. Mor, 'L'introduction du droit Justinien en France', *Recueil de mém. et travaux de l'Université de Montpellier*, 3 (1955), 47–53. A different approach was suggested by E. Meyer, 'Zum Petrus der Exceptiones Legum Romanorum', *Zeitschrift für Rechtsgeschichte*, Roman. Abt. 71 (1954), 274–318.

number of cases punished by confiscation, and at the same time the introduction of gradations in the sanction: confiscation and perpetual forfeiture were sometimes transformed into temporary sequestration or feudal *commise*. By these intervening steps we arrive at the middle of the thirteenth century, to a full-fledged theory, though one not very well defined, which is set beneath three main headings: *traison, foi mentie*, and *défaut de service*. This is the theory presented by Philip of Novara and more particularly by John of Ibelin.

The decisive point in this evolution, if our interpretation is correct, took place at the time of King Amalric, since it was then that the decisions of the High Court regarding confiscations definitely replaced any possible arbitrary judgments of the Crown. On the other hand, judgments in the baronial courts replaced arbitrary decisions of the lords. It was during this period that the revolutionary change occurred, if not *de facto*, at least *de jure*. Its repercussions would be felt not only in matters of confiscations, but in fact in the whole structure of the Crusader feudal system. From the legal point of view, it is enough to mention that this change in procedure had already brought the author of the *Livre au Roi* to pronounce the following principle: 'Mais tant come l'ome lige est desaisi n'est il tenus de repondre a son seigneur de riens que il li die, por ce que la raison iuge que hom desaisi n'est de rien tenus a son seignor.'[64] This is probably how the legal evolution progressed, introducing legal distinctions and subtleties, which will not shed a very flattering light on the jurists of the Latin East.[65]

The *Livre au Roi* mentions cases of confiscation which we do not meet in Baldwin II's *assise*. They are the outcome of certain breaches of the feudo-vassalic nexus:[66] the refusal of the vassal to enter as a hostage for his lord, or to serve as a pledge for his debts.[67] In addition to the confiscation of all his possessions, the offender lost the 'reponse de cort'.[68] He was considered to have 'menti son homage et sa fei au besoign a son droituryer

[64] Ch. 22.

[65] H. Brunner went so far as to call them 'Silbenstecher', hair-splitters, 'Wort und Form im altfranzösischen Prozess', *Forschungen zur Geschichte des deutschen und französischen Rechts* (Stuttgart, 1894), p. 274.

[66] We use the happy expression of M. Bloch and F. L. Ganshof, as the felony is in this case an infringement of the nexus between the lord and his vassals, an infringement of vassalic relations as well as the mutually binding contract which derived from the fief tenure.

[67] *Livre au Roi*, chs. 7–8. At the time of Amalric or Aimery, this obligation was extended even to fiefs held by a vassal by the right of his wife (John of Ibelin, ch. 249 *Lois* i. 398; cf. Richard, *Royaume latin*, p. 203).

[68] This addition may perhaps prove that the confiscation was the principal punishment and not a complementary punishment of loss of life or banishment.

seignor en terre'. What was the legal origin of these obligations and the harsh punishment which followed their infringement? It may be that the case in the *assises* of Baldwin II of the vassals' obligations to do what is *reisnable* already included these duties; it probably included other obligations which were, so to speak, self-evident and there was no need to name them. Whether such cases were implicit in the *assise*, or were later introduced explicitly, we shall probably not go wrong if we assume that the well-defined obligations arose from the fact that vassalic relationship became coloured by that existing in the framework of a family. The sacred character given to these obligations derived from the idea that refusal to accomplish them would be a case of flagrant ingratitude. Ingratitude was the common denominator of all the cases of children being disinherited by their parents and the cases of confiscation by the lord. Indeed, the child who was not ready to be a pledge for his parents, or would not ransom them from captivity, could be disinherited as the vassal could lose his fief. This was a punishment well rooted in the *Novella* of Justinian as it was in the Latin Kingdom, since Baldwin II promulgated it in his legislation.[69] The fact that the legislation concerning these two aspects of life was promulgated at the same time, or almost at the same time by the same king,[70] made the task of the jurists who sat as royal vassals in the High Court of the kingdom easier. This can be corroborated by another case, also included in the *Livre au Roi*, which showed how purely family notions were transplanted into vassalic relations. The *Livre au Roi*, dealing with an unmarried heiress who leads a scandalous life, says: 'det estre deséritee a tous iors, ia soit que sa mere qui remese est, ne l'en veille deseriter por ce, si la peut desériter le seignor', and the fief will be

---

[69] It is interesting to note that for Innocent III (A.D. 1199) a vassal's refusal to pay his lord's ransom and even to enter for him as a hostage was a *crimen laesae maiestatis*: 'si rex aliquis temporalis de terra suae dominationis ejectus, in captivitatem forsitan deveniret, nisi vasalli ejus pro liberatione regia non solum res suas exponerent sed personas, nonne cum restitueretur, pristinae libertati et acciperet tempus justitiam judicandi, infideles eos et proditores regios et velut laesae majestatis reos damnabiles reputaret et quosdam eorum damnaret suspendio, quosdam mucrone feriret et excogitaret etiam mortis hactenus inexcogitata tormenta quibus malos male perderet et in bona eorum fideles aliquos subrogaret?' (*PL* 214, coll. 809–10).

[70] We suggested above a different reading of the *assise* on disinheritance of children: 'se le pere ou la mere est en prison de Sarasins por aver et on le veut prendre en gage en leuc de son pere ou de sa mere iusque il aient porchassee leur raenson, et le fis ne veut entrer por luy.' We think that in the original the noun 'Sarasins' did not exist. Still one may ask if the copyist's addition was not the result of a current assimilation of disinheritance and confiscation? Here it were the causes of confiscation (to enter as hostage for one's lord), which influenced the causes of disinheritance.

given to one of her sisters.[71] From the legal point of view her behaviour was: 'la traison et la honte qu'elle a faite a son pere et a sa mere et a tous les siens'; 'la fornication et . . . péché qu'elle a fait', and finally 'la honte qu'elle a fait a luy meysme de gaster l'onour de sa virginité en puterie don elle estoit tenue dou garder au marit que son seignor ou sa dame li eust doune.' Here, as we see, family notions invaded the framework of the seignorial *maisnie*. Fornication was considered a case of *traison* committed by the girl towards the members of her family. However, it is the lord's role that is the most interesting. Fornication was a misdeed which was followed by punishment in the family, and parents could disinherit their daughter. But what right had the lord to intervene and to seize the fief and even compel recalcitrant parents to disinherit their daughter? If there were no other daughters, such disinheritance could readily become a case of escheat to the lord. The only possible explanation was that the lord was considered, in this connection, the protector of virtue: a *pater familias*, who safeguarded the morality of his family. His intervention, which might be followed by confiscation, could not be justified on the basis of a feudal offence or a breach of common law.[72] These were concepts of Roman law which infiltrated feudal customs, ready to receive them, because of family concepts of the vassalic nexus. This made possible the evolution that we are tracing for the Latin Kingdom.

The right of confiscation also evolved in another direction. Besides purely feudal offences, the *Livre au Roi* included non-feudal or not entirely feudal offences, which were also punished by confiscation. Such was the case of a vassal who refused to be the king's ambassador or as the author says, who refused to go *en message*.[73] We would have regarded it as a feudal default but the *Livre au Roi* carefully informs us that the lord cannot require this service if it is for 'nul besoing de luy qu'il en ait'. He can only ask it 'por le proufit dou reaume ou par le besoing de la terre'. The lord paid the expenses, but he could confiscate his vassal's fief, if the latter refused this kind of service. This distinction between the same service, which for the lord was not requisite, but if asked *pro publico bono* and not performed, was followed by confiscation, is rather curious. It is tempting

---

[71] Ch. 33.

[72] It is different in a case of fornication with a woman of one's own family. In the thirteenth century this was punished by confiscation of the fief, because it was regarded as an offence against the lord's honour. In practice at the beginning of the twelfth century (Council of Nablus in 1120) fornication, or rather adultery, was punished by banishment from the Kingdom.

[73] Ch. 29.

to think that perhaps the notions of state and the service due to the Crown as distinct from the king's position as a feudal suzerain were already emerging in the kingdom of the twelfth century. There is also an echo of the strong royal power which existed in the kingdom until the middle of the twelfth century.

So far we have discussed cases in which confiscation was the main penalty. However, cases were known in the *Livre au Roi* in which confiscation was a complementary penalty, as it was in Rome and in all early Germanic states. Thus, in cases punished by death or banishment, cases of murder,[74] or if the vassal lost a trial by battle,[75] or was sentenced for forgery of a privilege, the main penalty was banishment followed by the confiscation of his fief.[76] If a vassal refused to advise litigants in the High Court, he was banished and his fief confiscated. This last case is considered a typical feudal infringement, as it was a breach of the obligations devolving from the feudal oath.[77] If the vassal refused to appear before the High Court after three summonses, he was also accused of a breach of feudal obligations. He committed 'fait contre sa fei et renée Dieu par ce qu'il a promis de faire tous ces coumandemens et ne les fait.'[78] In these two cases, we are dealing with *déloyauté*, which was a breach of the law, a perjury, and consequently the culprit has 'renée Dieu'.[79]

The last offence punished by confiscation was heresy. Actually, the *Assise* on Confiscation deals with apostasy. We believe, however, that confiscation also punished heresy properly speaking, though it was not explicitly mentioned. We recall that Baldwin II's *assise* disinherited heretical parents or children. At the end of the twelfth century apostasy was still judged according to that *assise* and the apostate's fief was confiscated.[80] It seems, however, that a need was felt to make some change

---

[74] Ibid., ch. 20.   [75] Ibid., ch. 20 *in fine*.

[76] Ibid., ch. 46. This offence should be assigned to the influence of the Roman law. It is actually found in Germanic law which was influenced by Roman law. Cf. *Chindasvinth* vii. 5. 2, quoted by Sanchez Albornoz, op. cit., p. 194.

[77] *Livre au Roi*, ch. 24: 'et est celuy escheus de douner tel dreit au seignor c'on doit douner home desleaus; car bien est esprovée chose qu'il soit desleaus, puisqu'il, a neé conceil de dire verité à son essient à celuy ou à cele à cui il est tenus par sa fei de conceillyer.'

[78] Ibid., ch. 52.

[79] 'Desleau' was a legal expression often used in the Crusader jurisprudence of the Latin Kingdom. Among other punishments inflicted on him was always the loss of 'reponse de cour', that is that he would not be able to testify before the court and would not be accepted as judge or juror.

[80] *Livre au Roi*, chs. 22–3. The Council of Nablus (A.D. 1120) also dealt with apostasy, but only of members of the clergy.

in the law concerning heretics, though the reason for this decision is not very clear. In a case of apostasy the man would normally abandon his country and run away into Muslim territory. His fief was then abandoned (*guerpi*) and in a case of *guerpissement des fiefs*, the fief escheated to the lord. On the other hand in a case of heresy the offender did not always abandon his country; he became a menace because he remained there and could propagate his heresy. Such questions (including that of the family of the heretic) were settled by an *assise* of King Amalric, whose legislation was decisive in the history of the kingdom.[81] Heresy was henceforth punished by the stake and by confiscation of property.[82] However, if the fief was held by a heretic husband, the widow had a right to her dowry and furniture; if the fief was held through the woman, she held half the fief as long as she lived. In both cases, we suppose, the children were deprived of their inheritance, which after their mother's death, escheated to the lord. If it was the woman who was guilty, she would be burnt at the stake and her husband would lose her dowry ('se qu'il prist o luy en mariage').

This was the Law of Confiscation as it appeared in the *Livre au Roi* at the end of the twelfth century, and it represented a transition period in legislation which became more detailed, but not more systematic, by the middle of the thirteenth century. John of Ibelin was the exponent of this later stage of Crusader legislation. Although the technical expressions *saisie, commise,* and *confiscation* were not used, all three were practised. John of Ibelin wrote: 'l'on peut par l'assise ou l'usage dou reiaume de Jerusalem, perdre son fié en trois manieres: l'une, est an et jor, l'autre, tote sa vie; la tierce, lui et ces heirs.'[83] Naturally, such cases were judged by the High Court and John of Ibelin did not even remember that there was a time when things were different. Nor did he mention Baldwin II's *Assise* on Confiscation. That could have been embarrassing in the middle of the thirteenth century. Indeed, the jurists often voluntarily forgot the 'monarchic' past of their constitution. And yet the core of Baldwin II's *assise* was well preserved by John of Ibelin. Punishment by absolute confiscation ('lui et ces heirs') was for the same offences as those listed by Baldwin II and Amalric:

Qui est herege; qui se renée; qui met main sur le cors de son seignor; qui vient as armes contre son seignor en champ; qui rent, sanz congié de son seignor, sa cité ou

---

[81] Richard, *Royaume latin*, pp. 203–4, prefers to assign this *assise* to King Aimery at the end of the twelfth century, because heresy became at that time a menacing problem. But as we saw already there was a legislation against the *Patarins* at the time of Baldwin II.

[82] *Livre au Roi*, ch. 21.   [83] John of Ibelin, chs. 184 and 190.

son chasteau ou sa forterece à son ennemi, tant come il ait à mangier et a boivre tant ne quant; qui traïst son seignor et livre à ces ennemis; qui porchasce la mort et le deseritement de son seignor et est de ce ataint ou prové; qui vent son fié contre l'assise; qui est appelé de trayson et vencu en champ, ou defaillant de venir sei defendre en la court de son seignor de la trayson que l'on li met sus, se il en est semons si come il deit.[84]

They were, however, the same in theory, but not in practice. The most striking fact was the disappearance of the regalian rights whose infringement was sanctioned by confiscation: the right to mint money, the right to establish custom stations, the right to open harbours. When the *Livre au Roi* was composed, these rights were already beginning to be out-dated. John of Ibelin did not even remember them.

The jurists of the Latin East did not succeed in establishing a coherent theory of the Law of Confiscation. The most reliable, Philip of Novara, was very discreet on the problem.[85] John of Ibelin, theorist and scholar, tried to summarize the practice of his time, but did not arrive at a coherent system. He seems to have distinguished three types of offences: *trahison, foi mentie, défaut de service.* (The first was subdivided into *trahison apparente* and *trahison non apparente.*) These were sanctioned respectively by (a) absolute confiscation; (b) confiscation for life; (c) confiscation (*saisie*) for a year and a day. But these distinctions were not always referred to, and the reasons for assigning an offence to one or other category were often obscure. Thus the same offence was at one time *trahison* and at another *foie mentie.* In all probability the circumstances of the offence influenced its classification.[86]

When John of Ibelin wrote in the middle of the thirteenth century, the political regime of the kingdom differed from that of the 'thirties of the twelfth century. Consequently, the whole legal practice changed its character and pursued different aims. Baldwin II's *assise* aimed at

---

[84] John of Ibelin, ch. 190. [85] Philip of Novara, ch, 14, *Lois* i. 487–8.
[86] The problem is outside the scope of this study. We shall only indicate the sources: John of Ibelin, chs. 81, 95–8, 190, 192, 195. Note also that John of Ibelin knew the notion of *crimen laesae maiestatis.* It is interesting to note that the only case in which John of Ibelin mentions Roman law was in association with cases of confiscation. Absolute confiscation which deprived descendants and collateral relatives was the same: 'par l'assise ou l'usage dou reiaume de Jerusalem et par droit escrit' (ch. 92). Beugnot's suggestion that John of Ibelin knew the law from hearsay only is inadmissible. In the same chapter John not only eulogized the Code but explicitly mentions the *Lex Julia* (C. IX, t. 8. 1. 5) and an edict of Arcadius. This is certainly more than hearsay, but it is true that the influence of the Roman law is not conspicuous.

strengthening royal power and safeguarding the young state. A hundred and fifty years later the *assise* became a kind of tariff for offences, safeguarding the interests of the barons rather than those of the king and of the kingdom. The jurists even found a subterfuge to evade an accusation of self-evident treason. Even more characteristic, the abandoning of the lord in need, the refusal to fight or to serve in a garrison, were not more than offences of *foi mentie*, and, as such, punished by confiscation for life only.[87]

Let us return to the *Assise* on Disinheritance. We find no sources from the twelfth century, but the *LdAdB* furnishes us with information about the middle of the thirteenth century. By then, the *assise* had become a striking anachronism. Its reasons for disinheritance were part and parcel of a legal system in which wills were common and descendants had the right to claim part of their parents' possessions, and vice versa, parents had the right to claim part of their descendants' possessions. The laws of disinheritance could be used only in a system in which there was a *legitima* or *quarta Falcidia* as it was called in the Middle Ages (the quantity is not important). But in the thirteenth century that *legitima* did not exist in the kingdom. In the sphere of matrimonial law, in a case of an intestate death, the widow had a right to her dowry (*dot*) and during her lifetime to her husband's estate (*propres*) and her dower (*douaire*), and finally to half the acquired property (*conquêts*) in full ownership. Thus, in practice, the descendants had only a claim to their part in the 'conquêts'. Moreover, as the father could freely dispose of his acquisitions, and the mother enjoyed the revenues of the estate of her husband during her lifetime there was no room for a *legitima*. Although some points should be further explained, we have the rules clearly set out in the *LdAdB*. The *LdAdB* consciously rejected all the chapters that asserted the right of descendants and direct ancestors to a *legitima*, which were set out in detail in the model he was copying, *Lo Codi*. It was only by pure coincidence that a phrase from *Lo Codi* found its way into the *LdAdB*. The theory of the *LdAdB* was summed up in two chapters. The first, having proclaimed the widow's right to half of the *conquêts*, says: 'Et se la feme et le baron ont enfans ia ne lairont por leur anfans de vendre ne de douner leur biens a qui que il voront, ni de beivre ni de manger leurs biens tant coume il vivront.'[88] The other, dealing with a deceased intestate, said:

[87] John of Ibelin, ch. 191.   [88] *LdAdB*, ch. 180.

S'il avient que uns hons ait conquis eritages ou autre aver avant qu'il preigne feme, et puis prent feme et avient par la volonté de nostre Seignor que il chiet malade et meurt sans devise qu'il face de nule riens: la raison coumande et iuge que tout can que il avet deit estre de sa feme par dreit, encores seit ce que celuy . . . ait pere et mere et fis et filles et seur et freres.[89]

This latter quotation clearly shows the conscious and absolute rejection of all claims admitted by Roman law.

The *Assise* on Disinheritance was outdated by the middle of the thirteenth century, when the *LdAdB* was written, and probably even earlier. The stages in this evolution are missing, but we can clearly see the general trend. Family cohesion, considered as an economic unit, was loosened or even broken. Children had little legal claim on their parents' possessions. Parents naturally safeguarded their children's interests. In the class of *burgenses* we notice an evolution which tended to free possession from family claims. They are freely disposed without any control or limitation. This seems to correspond to a similar phenomenon in Europe, witnessed for example by the weakening of the *retrait lignager* among commoners.

d. *Baldwin II or Baldwin III—the Legislator King.*

An interesting problem arises in the dating of the promulgation of a well-known *assise*, the *Assise du coup apparent.* Two *Assises du coup apparent* were promulgated during the twelfth century. The date of the first is nowhere stated, but Philip of Novara pointed out that it was established 'au commencement quand les premières assises furent faites'. The second was promulgated by a king 'Baudouin', and was known as the *Assise dou rei Baudoyn de cop aparant.*[90] The intrinsic importance of this *assise* has escaped the attention of historians, who usually prefer to follow John of Ibelin than Philip of Novara. The historical interest of the first *assise* lies in the procedure and the list of fines, which reveals an interesting picture of the kingdom's society. But the *assise* of Baldwin is far more interesting since it shows us a typical social problem in a kingdom based on immigration, the first of its kind created by Europeans. Philip of Novara reveals that following complaints from pilgrims and poor people, it was necessary to reform the procedure. According to custom, proof of a transgression was established by the confession of the offender or the testimony of two witnesses, coreligionists of the accused. But poor people

---

[89] *LdAdB*, ch. 183.
[90] Philip of Novara, *Lois* i. 547. Cf. John of Ibelin, chs. 113–14, *Lois* i. 185 ff.; *Livre de Geoffroi le Tort*, ch. 22, *Lois* i. 440; Jacques d'Ibelin, ch. 51, *Lois* i. 465.

and pilgrims, strangers in the land, had great difficulty in finding witnesses ready to testify against their compatriots, or against powerful men in the land. This is all the more plausible to assume, if we remember that the accused could challenge the witness by battle (*lever les garens*). Therefore: 'quant les pellerins se clamoient et l'en lor faisoit maintenant droit, il s'en partoient tous laidis et se plangoient partout là où il aloient.[91] To improve relations between the inhabitants of the country and the newcomers[92] Baldwin promulgated a new *assise*. Prima facie it seems to be a strange piece of legislation. The accused now had, it declared, the possibility of confessing or simply of swearing that he was not guilty. How this new *assise* could have benefited pilgrims is not self-evident. In fact, it could help in cases when pilgrims were falsely accused by the inhabitants of the country. By a simple oath the pilgrim could now absolve himself of an accusation. However, this could hardly have profited the pilgrim in a case in which he was the plaintiff. In a roundabout way the new *assise* also benefited the poor people of the country. If the plaintiff was a knight accusing a non-noble of *coup apparent*, the latter 'en sera quite celui qui que il seit, se il veaut neier le cop par son serement.[93]

Now our problem is to determine when this popular *assise* was promulgated. The name of the king is 'Baudouin', but there were five of them in the Latin Kingdom. Beugnot attributed it to Baldwin I (1100–1118). But there is no other proof for this than the fact that Baldwin I was first destined to the Church and consequently 'un prince eclairé et dont l'éducation avait été littéraire'.[94] This was also Grandclaude's opinion, who wrote: 'c'est généralement lui, en effet, que les textes visent quand ils parlent du rou Baudouin sans indication du surnom ou du numéro de règne.'[95] La Monte preferred to attribute it to Baldwin IV, thus dating this *assise c.* 1180.[96] La Monte was certainly right when he pointed out that if the *assise* was promulgated by Baldwin I, Philip of Novara could hardly have said that a former *assise* was: 'lonc tens usées'. Of Baldwin III and Baldwin IV, La Monte preferred the latter, since in Crusader tradition he enjoyed the reputation of a legislator. When the kings of Jerusalem and

---

[91] Philip of Novara, loc. cit. The whole explanation was glossed over by John of Ibelin.

[92] It is superfluous to quote the numerous sources on that question from the *Itineraria* as well as the poems of troubadours and *Minnesänger*.

[93] Philip of Novara, loc. cit. Beugnot seems not to have really understood the meaning of this *assise*. See his Introduction to *Lois* i, p. XXIII.

[94] Beugnot, loc. cit.

[95] Grandclaude, op. cit., p. 338.

[96] La Monte, *Feudal Monarchy*, p. 30.

Cyprus took their coronation oaths they promised: 'Les assises dou royaume et dou rei Amauri et dou rei Baudoyn son fiz . . . garderai.'[97]

None of these proofs is conclusive. But a manuscript mentioned by Grandclaude, Munich MS., Cod. Gall. 771, and as far as we know, never since consulted, throws a new light on the problem. This manuscript contains, between fos. 245 and 250, a partially unpublished text[98] of the *Lignages d'Outremer*. It is a curious summary of the *Lignages*, which deals with the kings of Jerusalem and Cyprus only. It dates from 1458–60. Here we find the following text: 'Après la mort du Roy Foulq fu roy de Jherusalem Bauduin son fis et fist *l'assise de noupless (de) et celle dou coup*, come s'en claime par l'assise du Rou Bauduin. Et mourut sans hoirs et se fu le cart Roy de Jherusalem et reigna XXI ans.'[99]

Without any doubt, the anonymous author of the *Lignages* attributed the promulgation of two *assises* to Baldwin, son of Fulk of Anjou—that is, Baldwin III (1143–62): the *Assise du coup apparent* and the *Assise de la noblesse*. There is no other source to corroborate this statement. However, if we (like La Monte) dismiss the possibility of attributing the *Assise du coup apparent* to Baldwin I, there is nothing[100] to preclude the possibility of assigning it to Baldwin III.

What about the *Assise sur la noblesse*? There are in fact two *assises* that could be named *Assise sur la noblesse*: the *Assise sur la ligece* of Amalric and that on Confiscation of Fiefs of Baldwin. We do not see any other important *assise* that could be named *Assise sur la noblesse*. Moreover, the anonymous author of the *Lignages* attributed the *Assise sur la noblesse* to a Baldwin, but to Baldwin III. We must then reconsider the authorship of the *assise* on Confiscation.

In the description of Baldwin III by William of Tyre he emerges as remarkably knowledgeable about the customary law of the country. Indeed, the prince knew it better than the members of his feudal court.[101] This fits quite well with an inclination to legislation, but it is not conclusive (other kings merited similar characteristics, although none of them received such eloquent praise). We would like however to draw attention to a particular paragraph in the *Assise* on Confiscation—the

[97] John of Ibelin, ch. 7, *Lois* i. 30.

[98] M. Grandclaude, 'Classement sommaire des mss. des principaux livres des Assises de Jérusalem'. *RHDFE*, 1926, pp. 419 ff.

[99] fo. 246[r]. I would like to express my thanks to my friend H. E. Mayer of Kiel University, who kindly checked my reading of the manuscript.

[100] La Monte gave no reason to eliminate Baldwin II.

[101] W. T. xvi. 2.

reference to an armed revolt against the king, a revolt all the more dangerous because supported by Saracens. J. Richard has already conjectured[102] that this could refer to the revolt of Hugh of Le Puiset. But this revolt broke out in 1132, after the death of Baldwin II, under his successor Fulk. Richard suggested that there might have been a later addition to the *Etablissement* of Baldwin II. However, if we attribute the *assise* to Baldwin III, there will be no chronological difficulty.

There is another reason for the corroboration of this new hypothesis. We have seen how difficult it is to clear up the relationship between the Provençal text of *Lo Codi* and the *Etablissement* of King Baldwin. The earliest possible date of the redaction of the Provençal *Lo Codi* was that of the siege of Fraga in 1133. But even this earliest date does not correspond to the possible date of the *Etablissement*, since Baldwin II died in 1130. This is of course also true of the later date of 1144 or the middle of the twelfth century, if we admit that the *Summa Trecensis* was known to the author of *Lo Codi*.[103] However, if we assume that the *Etablissement* was the work of Baldwin III (1143–1162) as the manuscript of the *Lignages* seems to indicate, we can dispense with this difficulty.

In conclusion, although it is impossible to be certain as to the royal authorship of the *Etablissement*, it seems plausible to attribute it to Baldwin III. If this is so, we can also conclude that royal power was still strong in the Latin Kingdom in the middle of the twelfth century.[104]

---

[102] Richard, *Royaume latin*, p. 69.

[103] See above, p. 451 n. 49, and next note.

[104] The eventual results of this solution obviously influence the dating of *Lo Codi*. Cf. A. Gouron, 'Du nouveau sur *Lo Codi*', *Revue d'histoire du droit* 48 (1975), 271 and cf. idem, above, p. 385 n. 43.

Military History

18. Crusader Security and the Red Sea

The security of their kingdom was one that must have preoccupied the Latin rulers in the East. Despite the often adventurous behaviour of Crusader warriors and the erratic decisions of their rulers, it is impossible to argue that they were not conscious of larger political problems and did not respond to their challenge in terms of political and military thought and action. For relatively long periods the march of events was dictated by the Crusaders and not by their Muslim antagonists. This in itself postulates that political aims were fixed by the Crusaders themselves. This is not to suggest that they always followed master plans. Heedless reactions, thoughtless initiatives, and simple fits of rage were everyday occurrences, but only occasionally did they dictate the decisive evolution of political events and consequently of military actions. Crusader leadership was not merely a collection of swaggering warriors, and some kind of political thinking, though it has not come down to us in the shape of formulated plans, must have existed. Here and there, though unfortunately very seldom, we get glimpses of such political consciousness. The kingdom's historian, William of Tyre, refers to it in some memorable passages.[1] Not only as a historian, but also because he was a *familiaris* of the royal court of Jerusalem, he reflects ideas current in circles of Crusader leadership. This did not blind him to political and military actions which in his judgment were detrimental to the kingdom or contradicted normative rules of conduct in what we would call today international relations.[2] Yet our study will have to rely on different proofs than the sporadic utterances of a great historian. Our ultimate resort will be to the Crusaders in action, pursuing a given policy for longer stretches of time and changing this line of conduct when different aims were fixed, a conscious change caused by newly opened opportunities in the surrounding area.

The earliest period in the history of the kingdom was that of conquest. Its immediate aims are clear but there is an obvious abyss between the hopes and aspirations of the rulers and the tangible results. Knowing better than the Crusaders, as we do, the Islamic world which surrounded

---

[1] W.T. xxi, 6, 8; xxii. 1.   [2] W.T. xx, 5 and 16.

the tiny European colonies, we hesitate to assign to their rulers wishful thinking, a belief that they could conjure the future, or pure megalomania. Perhaps the nearest answer will be that they felt unmitigated confidence in their superiority and were also ignorant of the foe they were facing.

The epitaphs of the earliest rulers of the kingdom described their *res gestae* and their political programme in most glowing terms. Godfrey of Bouillon whose tomb had, it seems, two inscriptions, is described in the shorter as 'qui totam istam terram aquisivit cultui Christiano', and in the second the Franks are described as a nation, 'Sion loca sancta petens', and their leader as 'Egypti terror, Arabum fuga, Persidis horror'. His aim was, according to this inscription: 'Syon sua reddere iura, catholiceque sequi sacra dogmata iuris et aequi'.[3] The epitaph of his successor Baldwin I is far more flamboyant: 'quem formidabant, cui dona tributa ferebant Cedar, Egyptus et Dan ac homicida Damascus'.[4] Cedar are the Bedouin, Dan can only mean the northernmost reaches of the kingdom[5]—Damascus. Fulk of Chartres, chaplain to the deceased king, described him in even more flamboyant terms. A catalogue of captured cities (Acre, Caesarea, Beirut, Sidon, Tripoli, and Arsuf) is followed by: 'Terras Arabum vel quae tangunt mare Rubrum, addidit imperio'. Such glaring exaggerations, which one might expect in epitaphs, reappear unexpectedly in more serious sources. Baldwin I is described in one charter as 'Duci Godefrido in regnum Asiae successit',[6] and in another charter 'Regnum Babilonie atque Asie disponente'.[7] The same Baldwin I, 'Rex Judee et Iherusalem', in the earliest privilege to the Genoese, promised them, if they participated in the capture of Babylon—that is of Cairo—'tertiam partem civitatis Babyloniae cum tribus casalibus melioribus'.[8]

Whatever the origin of such claims, the immediate aims of the conquest were far more practical. There were clearly three frontiers to be established, most important by far being that of the sea coast. Ten years (1100–10) of fighting assured Crusader domination of the coast from Beirut to the Sinai desert, with the exception of Tyre (captured in 1124)

[3] Sabino de Sandoli, *Corpus Inscriptionum Crucesignatorum Terrae Sanctae, 1099–1291* (Jerusalem, 1974), p. 54.

[4] Ibid., p. 57.

[5] 'A Dan usque Bersabee', e.g. 1 Kgs. 3:20, is the classical biblical description of the frontiers of the Holy Land.

[6] Delaville ii, no. 1, p. 897.

[7] Rozière, no. 36, p. 71.

[8] C. Imperiale di Sant'Angelo, *Codice diplomatico della republica di Genova* I (Rome, 1936), no. 15, p. 21; *Regesta*, no. 43.

and Ascalon (1153). The second was the frontier facing Damascus, whence the interior and mountainous part of Palestine was ruled. Here the first thrust of Tancred (1099), through Judaea and Samaria, brought him to Galilee and its capital Tiberias, and across the Jordan to the Golan Heights (al-Sawād). The earliest result was the establishment of a sphere of influence rather than a demarcated frontier line, a problem which was to be solved in a particular way before the end of the first decade of Crusader rule. The third was the southern frontiers, where Crusader control of Jerusalem and Bethlehem staked out claims but did not assure any permanence of possession.

The continuous and unrelenting attacks on the coastal cities were certainly not a haphazard policy. The abandoning of Jaffa, which fell without a blow during the march on Jerusalem and proved to be one of the most fatal mistakes on the part of the Egyptians, showed to the Crusaders the importance of a port which, in the circumstances, was the umbilical cord connecting them with Europe. The land-routes through Asia Minor were definitely barred with the tragic end of the Crusades of 1102–3, and only the Syro-Palestinian harbours could assure the arrival of reinforcements and even of simple, badly needed provisions. The thrust to the north, through Judaea and Samaria, in the direction of Damascus, pointed to opportunities, but also to immediate difficulties. The fortified places of Galilee, Safed, Tiberias, Mt. Tabor were captured without resistance, and once across the Jordan the Crusaders faced the high plateau of the Golan. No fortified places barred the road to Damascus. Obviously its emirs had not felt menaced in this area. Strongpoints, if they ever existed, were probably administrative centres of little or no military importance. Theoretically this left the Crusaders with two options: the erection of a line of fortifications, such as they were to build later on to contain Ascalon, or a direct assault on the great capital of Syria, such as was to be attempted by the ill-fated expedition of the Second Crusade. Neither option was at that point feasible. The kingdom lacked manpower and resources either for direct attack or for an elaborate line of fortifications. This created a kind of no man's land, an unfixed frontier facing Damascus, the choicest area of mutual razzias, which devastated the land on both sides of the Jordan and the Lake of Galilee. The need to establish a southern frontier brought the Crusaders to Hebron, but the main efforts of the first decade were concentrated elsewhere and the problem was not tackled until the second decade of Crusader rule. The first decade, a time of turmoil not always related military efforts, still showed a pattern of priorities. It ended in the domination of the coast and the conquest of the Saljuq-held interior of the country. In the north, moreover, beyond the radius of Crusader-held fortresses, it created a no man's land area which faced Damascus.

It was, however, the second decade of Crusader domination which seems to have been the formative age of security thinking. Following some earlier expansionist attempts, as well as Muslim incursions into their territory, the Crusaders came to the conclusion, or so it seems, that secure boundaries must coincide with natural frontiers. The expressions should not be taken in any strict sense, as medieval notions of frontiers were nowhere clear demarcation lines. In favourable circumstances major routes and approaches were fortified by strongpoints to control strategic areas. In between, columns of light cavalry could easily penetrate the frontier lines. The most secure frontier was a combination of natural boundaries with fortifications here and there to strengthen them. The Crusaders identified natural frontiers with the desert. Therein lies the main difference between the Latin Kingdom proper and its northern principalities. The latter hardly succeeded even in establishing themselves to the east of the deep valleys and the great rivers of the Syro-African rift. Though attempts of this kind were made in Antioch and Tripoli, their results proved ephemeral and time and again the Crusaders were thrown back across the rivers, trying desperately to keep to some strongholds on their eastern banks. It was only in the southernmost Latin Kingdom that the Crusaders effectively dominated the territories across the Jordan, the *Oultre Jourdain*. Here the eastern frontier was established on the demarcation line dividing the more or less cultivated areas from the desert.

This frontier and security concept found two different solutions in the vast spaces of Transjordan between Damascus and the Red Sea. In the northern part, between Mt. Hermon in the north and the Yarmuk river in the south, the Crusaders created a political and strategic situation which, under the existing demographic circumstances, was the best possible solution. This Damascene territory was permanently exposed to Crusader attacks from Galilee, either by way of the Jordan crossing at the 'Bridge of the Daughters of Jacob' (Jisr Banāt Ya'qūb) in the north or through Sinnabra to the south of the Lake of Galilee. Invaded time and again for a whole decade,[9] undefended by any strongpoints, and too far away to be

---

[9] The first invasion led by Tancred in 1100 was followed by attacks by the prince of Galilee in 1104. At that time the Crusaders seem to have built fortifications at 'Al'āl and

effectively protected by Damascus, it was an easy prey for Crusader razzias. On the other hand the Crusaders were in no position to implant themselves here by fortifying the high plateau, as any such attempt would have been interrupted by Damascene expeditions. This led to a curious agreement between the Crusaders and Damascus, concluded as early as 1108: the whole area was declared to be what might be called today a demilitarized zone, both parties consenting not to build any fortifications there. In the context of sovereignty, there was a kind of 'condominium' in the sense that the revenues of the area were shared between the princes of Galilee and the emirs of Damascus, each receiving one-third, the remaining third left to the local peasantry.[10] Demilitarization did not assure non-belligerency. This was too much to ask. Expeditions and razzias were launched from time to time by the Crusaders as well as by the Damascenes, each accusing the other of breaking the agreement. Yet, despite these infractions, the agreement remained in force until the eve of the battle of Hattin (1187), and this despite the fact that Damascus changed rulers, falling into the hands of Zengi and then Saladin, the two official leaders of the Jihad against the Crusader Kingdom.[11]

Once a *modus vivendi* was created on the north-eastern frontiers the Crusaders tried to buttress their hold on this sensitive area by implantation on its southern perimeter. It was the Yarmuk river that the Crusaders regarded as the southern frontier of the demilitarized zone, although according to Arab sources the area should have extended far more to the south.[12] Here in the Yarmuk depression between Muzeirib and Edrei, in the plain of Maidan, the famous desert fair took place, where twice yearly camels, horses, mules, and cattle were sold and bought by the fellahin and Bedouin. In the middle course of the Yarmuk the Crusaders fortified an almost inaccessible place, a cave called Habis Jeldak (Cave de Sueth),[13] and

---

Qasr-Bardawil which were destroyed in 1105–7 by the emir of Tyre and the ruler of Damascus. In a Muslim invasion in 1108 even Tiberias was temporarily captured. In 1110 Baldwin I attacked the Damascene territory of the Biquā', the deep valley between Lebanon and Anti-Lebanon.

[10] This earliest agreement of 1108 included the Sawād and Jebel 'Awf. In 1110 a similar agreement regarding the valley of Lebanon was suggested by the Damascenes. Ibn al-Qalānisi, *The Damascus Chronicle*, transl. H. A. R. Gibb, p. 92.

[11] Prawer, *Histoire* i. 434, cf. Kemal al-Din, transl. Blochet, *ROL* iii. 541.

[12] In 1106 or 1107 the ruler of Damascus staked out his claim to Balka, between al-Salt and the Arnon river at the northern shore of the Dead Sea. The Turkish commander was expelled by Baldwin I in co-operation with the local Christians. By 1119 the Crusaders ruled effectively Jebel-'Awf, Aljabania, al-Salt, and the Ghur; Ibn al-Athir in *RHC HOr*. i. 314–16. Cf. ibid. iv. 277.

[13] In 1111 the place was already in the hands of the Crusaders and was captured from

(*continued*)

tried to establish themselves at Muzeirib and Edrei.[14] Moreover, though the documentation is rather scanty, we see Crusader ecclesiastical institutions receiving villages in this area.[15] At the same time the local Bedouin, though even successfully resisting the Crusaders, had finally to submit to an annual payment for pasture rights.[16] Even further to the east the Crusaders attempted to create protectorates at Basra and Salkha by helping, and perhaps even fomenting, revolts of the local emirs against their Damascene overlords.[17]

The areas to the south of the Yarmuk, the biblical Gilead (Arabic: Jebel 'Awf), and its southern barrier at Jebel 'Ajlun, and Yabbok or Zerqa river, were thinly populated. The only major settlement, Jerash (Gerasa) was rased and burned to the ground by the Crusaders as early as 1119. The Crusaders, according to William of Tyre, had not sufficient manpower to keep it.[18] Crusader attempts to dominate the Yarmuk river suggest that the Crusaders excluded this area from the 'condominium' agreement with Damascus and regarded it as their own domain.[19] It is not clear whether the Damascenes or the Egyptians dominated this area before the arrival of the Crusaders, who began to implant themselves there in the middle of the second decade of the kingdom. In 1115 they reconstructed mighty Shaubaq, henceforth Montreal, and at the same time, or a year later, implanted themselves some 350 km more to the south at 'Aqaba on the Red Sea.[20] From Montreal they dominated the area to the north and, far more important, the main highway of Transjordan, which led to Hijjaz,

them by the Damascenes. In 1119 it was recaptured by the Crusaders. Nur al-Din unsuccessfully attacked the place in 1158. It was captured by Farrukh-Shah, Saladin's lieutenant in Damascus in the summer of 1182, but recaptured by the Crusaders in October 1182.

[14] In 1119 the Crusaders captured Edrei, called in 1146 Cité Bernard d'Étampes. W.T. xxi. 10.

[15] Delaborde, nos. 14 and 18.

[16] Alb. Aqu. xii. 30.; Ibn al-Athir, pp. 315–16.

[17] The earliest attempt was that of 1104, when the emir of Basra, in revolt against the rulers of Damascus, sought Crusader help. Ibn al-Athir, *RHC HOr.* i. 223–4; Alb. Aqu. *RHC HOcc.* iv. 622. In 1147 the military commander of the Hauran asked for Crusader help against Damascus. The Crusaders tried to establish a protectorate, and attacked Damascus unsuccessfully (W.T. xvi. 8). In 1151 another attempt was made, this time by Sirkhol, commander of Basra, who sought Crusader help in his rebellion against Damascus. He surrendered a year later. Ibn al-Qalānisi, p. 310; Abu Shama, *RHC HOr.* iv. 74.

[18] *Eracles* xii. 16.

[19] It is not impossible that this was the result of a fluctuating geographical vocabulary of this area. We witness this phenomenon since biblical times. Cf. *Encyclopaedia Biblica* ii (Hebrew, Jerusalem, 1973), 513.

[20] Alb. Aqu. xii. 21; W.T. xi. 31.

branching off at Ma'an to 'Aqaba and therefrom to Sinai and Egypt. Crusader castles or strongpoints at al-Salt, Crac, Taphila, Shaubaq, Hurmuz, Celle, Vaux Moïse, and 'Aqaba dotted the main highway. Though not easily patrolled because of the great distances, this highway dominated the water sources and was the main artery of communication. There was nothing to the east of this line that could have endangered the Crusader hold on the area: no cites, castles, or even strongpoints, that could serve as mobilization points for an enemy based either on Damascus or on Egypt. Thus the strategy of secure frontiers in the north-east and in the east was based on the same idea: to push the frontier across the Jordan, whose many fords made the shallow river a doubtful natural frontier, to the limit of the desert.[21] In the north, where the propinquity of Damascus could have endangered the principality of Galilee, the area was demilitarized; more to the south the Crusaders strengthened the natural barrier of the transversal Yarmuk and Judair rivers. In this region we hear of villages actually dominated by the Crusaders: Elgor, Maidan, Arthe, and Cedar; Betaras, Zaar, Avera up to Edrei (parallel to Judair). Gerasa was destroyed, but single villages, Seecip, Bessura, Elale to the north of the Dead Sea, were dominated by the Crusaders, as were Hable and Cansir on the road at the southern end of the Dead Sea which linked Cisjordan with Transjordan.[22] The desert road to the Red Sea or Hijjaz was dominated by Crusader strongholds, which at times, and for remuneration, supplied military convoys to the caravans moving to and from Mecca, and obviously claimed tolls and customs on their merchandise.

The same policy to reach the desert and make it a natural frontier was also pursued on the south-western approaches of the kingdom. The probing expeditions of Tancred across the Jordan in the first year of the kingdom were paralleled by Baldwin I's expeditions into Transjordan and along the main northern road which crossed the Sinai peninsula and reached the easternmost branches of the Delta of the Nile. This road across the desert, five to seven days' distance in forced rides for a light-armed

---

[21] The Jordan can be crossed at many places, but only fords linked to roads were important. The following are known from Crusader sources: The Bridge of the Daughters of Jacob, Sinn el-Nabra, al-Ma'ajami, the Bridge of Hussein, the Bridge of Damiya, the ford of St. John. Cf. J. Prawer and M. Benvenisti, *Map of the Crusader Kingdom of Jerusalem* (with index), *Atlas Israel* IX/12.

[22] Seecip (Seetip), Elgor, Arthe, Betaras (Petaras), Zera, and Avarazaar (Avara-Haar) are mentioned in a confirmation by Pascal II (29 July 1103) to the Archbishop of Mt. Tabor. *Regesta*, no. 39. Bessura and La (Elale) in a privilege (1130) of Baldwin II to St. Mary Josaphat. *Regesta*, no. 133; Canzil and Hable in a privilege of Maurice, lord of Montreal (1152), to the Order of St. John. *Regesta*, no. 279 and cf. no. 551.

cavalry detachment,[23] had one major oasis, al-'Arish, and a number of smaller oases or water holes.[24] In 1118 Baldwin I crossed the desert and appeared in Egypt before the walls of Farama, which was abandoned by its surprised inhabitants and burned. He pushed on, it seems, even to Tanis, where he fell ill and died. His body was brought to Jerusalem by his companions.[25] This was a probing expedition. Chronologically following Crusader penetration into southern Transjordan and 'Aqaba, it shows a pattern: the appreciation of the desert as a secure border. This could not have been completed before the conquest of the Ascalon strip, strongly held by the Egyptians, who rightly appreciated its importance. Provisioned by sea and by land, it was Egypt's outpost across the desert on the unmarked frontier of the Latin Kingdom. With a garrison that changed four times a year, and a population which was actually on the payroll of the Egyptian army, it was a permanent menace to the kingdom, endangering the road between Jerusalem and Jaffa at the height of the plain of Ramle; it also endangered Hebron and Bethlehem. This situation lasted for almost two generations, until the fall of the city of Ascalon in 1153. But during the last twenty years of that period the Crusaders, unable to capture the city, neutralized it by building a ring of fortresses which barred all the main roads leading to the kingdom.[26] But already before Ascalon had fallen, the Crusaders had pushed their frontier beyond the city, along the main road to Egypt. Gaza was fortified in 1149/50 and Deir al-Balah, the Darom of Crusader and Arabic sources, shortly before 1170. It was Darom that became the Crusader desert outpost, supervising the northern road to Sinai.[27] By the middle of the twelfth century the Crusaders could look with some satisfaction at their desert *cordon sanitaire*.

The third period in what we would like to call Crusader strategic thinking began in the middle of the century and lasted for one generation. Possibly as a result of King Amalric's personal involvement who, as a former count of Jaffa and Ascalon, was sensitive to the frontier area of his old county, the kingdom was plunged into a grandiose plan for the

[23] It took ten days for a fully fledged military expedition to reach Egypt. Prawer, *Histoire* i. 299 and 440.

[24] 'La Devise des Chemins de Babiloine, 1289–91,' ed. H. Michelant and G. Raynaud, *Itinéraires à Jérusalem* (Geneva, 1882), pp. 241–3.

[25] Alb. Aqu. xxi. 25–6; W.T. xi 31.

[26] Bethgibelin was erected in 1136 (W.T. xiv. 22); Ibelin in 1141 (W.T. xv. 24); Blanche-Garde in 1142 (W.T. xv. 25); Gaza in 1149–50 (W.T. xvii. 12). Cf. J. Prawer, 'Ascalon and the Ascalon Strip in Crusader politics', (Heb.) *Eretz-Israel* 4 (1956), 231–48.

[27] Prawer, *Histoire* i. 447.

domination of Egypt, a political move opposed in some quarters of Crusader leadership.[28] The growing strength of Zengi in Syria limited military action in the north, but political unrest in Egypt opened possibilities in the south. For almost ten years the Crusaders, allied to one of the contending parties, invaded Egypt, with the sporadic co-operation of Byzantium. Victorious, the Crusader flag was hoisted for some time in Cairo and their armies besieged Alexandria.[29] But the great enterprise ended in a tremendous fiasco. Even an Egyptian party contending for power could not base its rule for any length of time on Crusader lances. There were rich spoils from the campaigns, and even greater expenses. By the end the coffers were empty and Crusader manpower certainly no stronger. Moreover, the direct result of the invasion was the creation of a new geo-political configuration. Egypt was saved from the Crusaders by a Syrian army commanded by Shirkuh and then by Saladin. After 1169, when the last Crusader troops left Egypt, Saladin ruled Egypt, formally as lieutenant of Nur al-Din in Damascus. We do not need to follow here their ambivalent relations from the murder of the last Fatimid Caliph of Egypt in 1169 until the death of Nur al-Din in 1174. All attempts at co-operation were thwarted by Saladin,[30] and the Crusader fortresses in Transjordan were never seriously threatened by a combined attack launched simultaneously from Cairo and Damascus.

It is during the last ten years before Hattin that we see a change in Crusader strategic thinking. After 1174 Saladin embarked upon the subjugation of Zengid Syria in the name of the Jihad, claiming that he was in no position to attack the Crusaders effectively until the Muslim forces had been unified and mobilized. The 'Abbasid Caliph in Baghdad was sceptical of this policy despite Saladin's protestations,[31] but this did not prevent Saladin from pursuing the policy vigorously. The creation of a Saladin dominion in Egypt and in Syria put the finger on the sorest spot of the Near Eastern Muslim areas. Crusader rule of the desert roads in Transjordan brought into relief the Christian wedge between the now united Syria and Egypt. What had been until now more in the nature of a nuisance and a commercial burden, became a major emotional, political, and to some extent, even military problem. Not that militarily the

---

[28] There were five Crusader invasions of Egypt: September 1163, summer of 1164, the beginning of 1167, October 1168, and the last in October 1169.

[29] Prawer, *Histoire* i. 436.

[30] So in 1171 and in 1173. Cf. Prawer, *Histoire* i. 450–4.

[31] Ibid. 541.

obstacles were unsurmountable. Armies from Damascus and Egypt could converge on Transjordan, but it took another ten years before Saladin was strongly established in both areas, and not even then without sporadic opposition.[32] Politically things looked more serious. With Syria and Egypt united, the Jihad proclaimed, one could hardly justify the payment of tributes by the Mecca caravans to the Crusaders. One easy victory had a propaganda effect. In 1171, two years after becoming the lord of Egypt, Saladin attacked and easily captured 'Aqaba after fifty-five years of Crusader domination. He could now proclaim the liberation of a Hajj road, though not the most frequented one, from Egypt to the Holy Cities of Arabia.

The Crusaders' sensitivity to security problems thus became more acute and gave rise to a new trend in strategic thought, which can be formulated as follows: the security of the kingdom could not be assured by simply guarding the ends of the military and commercial routes that reached it from across the desert. The new strategic thinking postulated the transfer of the frontiers and the establishment of Crusader strongpoints across the desert at its western entrance. In this new perspective the domination or mastery of the Sinai peninsula became of paramount importance. The *cordon sanitaire* of the north-eastern frontiers had to find a corollary in the south-west. It was not the official leadership of the kingdom that was the architect of this new strategy. We can credit it to the lord of Transjordan, obviously more sensitive because more threatened by the new developments. The first attempts in this direction can already be seen in 1172,[33] but it was four years later, in 1177, that this strategy became more pronounced. Renaud of Châtillon, at that time lord of Transjordan, is one of the most picturesque personalities in the Crusader Levant. In historiography he is the embodiment of a glorious adventurer, a pirate of the seas of sand, if not the man responsible for the outbreak of hostilities, which led to the disaster of Hattin.[34] This is partly due to his famous, or infamous capture of a Muslim caravan in Transjordan in peacetime, and partly to exploits which, taken in isolation, look like pure razzias into

---

[32] In 1169 the Sudanese palace guards rebelled against Saladin. In 1173 the survivors of the Fatimid regime tried to co-operate with the Crusaders and the Normans of Sicily to overthrow him. In April 1174, Saladin discovered the plot and the conspirators were executed. In September 1177 Sudanese troops from Aswan threatened Cairo, but were slaughtered by al-Malik al-'Adel. In that year the Crusaders attacked Qal'at Gindi in Ras Sudar in western Sinai: cf. Prawer, *Histoire* i. 610–11.

[33] Prawer, *Histoire* i. 610 and 613–15.

[34] See G. Schlumberger, *Renaud de Châtillon* (Paris, 1898); Prawer, *Histoire* i. 594–5.

Muslim territory with no other end than spoils and robbery. Yet, an over-all view of his activities leads us to a different interpretation. Renaud was not a simple scheming robber lord. To start with, his knowledge of the Levant was excellent. A former prince of Antioch he made a name for himself as the Devil ('Shaitan') of Muslim Syria; fifteen years of captivity in Aleppo waiting to be ransomed was a hard school in the East; he knew Arabic and probably Turkish; he easily found common languages with the Bedouin of his territories as well as with those of nothern Hijjaz; his marriage to the heiress of Transjordan put him, at the time of Saladin, in charge of the most sensitive Crusader frontier. Nobody will put beyond him high-handed strikes to replenish his coffers with the spoils of rich caravans, but his normal revenues came from tolls, customs, and protection money exacted from caravans on the highway of his lordship. He organized a Crusader spy service in Transjordan manned by Bedouin tribes and a similar one deep in the south, in northern Hijjaz. His relations with the nomadic tribes must have been excellent, if Saladin was forced to crush the spy ring and later on even to expel the Bedouin.

For five years (1177–82) Renaud's activities clearly pointed to his main aim, to control the Muslim entrance points to the desert. The Crusader frontier was no longer to rely on the defences of its outlying fortifications. Rather these would turn into bases and springboards for the control of desert routes, deep into enemy territory. In 1177 or 1178 the first expedition of this kind was launched. Starting, it seems, from Montreal, a Crusader cavalry detachment moved south, bypassed ʿAqaba, and then turning west moved along the middle road across Sinai (to the south of Nakhl) stopping at Wadi Sudar on the north-west coast of Sinai and finally halting at Fāqūs, between Bilbais and Tanis, on the eastern branch of the Nile. At that point our documentation leaves us in the dark and we do not know of any tangible results of the expedition. Yet its purpose seems to have been clear: it was the eastern Egyptian defences that had become vulnerable to Crusader attacks, and the Sinai caravans had now more to fear than Bedouin razzias. Control of the desert routes meant control of the oases. The most important was al-ʿArish on the main northern road of Sinai. In 1182 the Crusaders raided the place. There were no fortifications and the local population ran away. The Crusaders cut down the palm trees on which the livelihood of the oasis inhabitants depended. These exploits and what was behind them could hardly have escaped the vigilance of Saladin and they explain why he fortified Qalʿat Guindi, a fortress in the Wadi Sudar, which led to the western coast of

Sinai, and from which a road led to Wadi al-Ahtha, 'Uyun Musa in the eastern part of Suez, and then over Jisr 'Ajrud on the road to Cairo.[35] What was done in the western part of Sinai found its complement in the eastern part. In 1182 Renaud invaded northern Hijjaz as far as Taima. The expedition took place in the spring when there was enough fodder on the desert roads. Taima was a main halting point in Hijjaz on the road to Medina and the expedition was accomplished with the help of the local Bedouin tribes.

The attacks across Sinai and in Sinai make a pattern which is confirmed by Crusader sources. Ecclesiastically, probably following the preceding Byzantine period, the abbot of the monastery of St. Catherine in the heart of Sinai was the Bishop of Paran (=Firan), a suffragan of the archbishop of Transjordan.[36] But now we find a clear territorial claim: 'Mt. Sinai was in the territory of the lord of Crac', says a Crusader source written in this period.[37] The frontiers of the kingdom did not end at Darom in the north and around Petra in Transjordan in the south. Sinai belonged to the kingdom. It was therefore in the nature of things that its southern key-point, 'Aqaba, should be recaptured. At the end of 1182 or beginning of 1183, a Crusader expedition started out from Crac, its camels carrying parts of ships which were reassembled at the Gulf of 'Aqaba. 'Aqaba was captured, and the small fortified island off the coast, Jazirat Far'un, put under siege. A Crusader squadron of three ships (two besieged the island) moved through the Red Sea pillaging merchant and pilgrims' vessels, 'Aidhab on the coast of Egypt, opposite Jedda, then Hawra and Rabbij in Hijjaz. Here the Crusaders disembarked and made their way in the direction of Mecca, guided by Bedouin who also probably supplied camels or horses. When a Muslim army finally caught up with them, they were one day's march from Mecca. According to one of the Arab sources the great threat from the expedition, apart from its obvious reverberation throughout the world of Islam, was that from it the Franks would learn the direction of the winds in the Red Sea. This brings us to think that Renaud's ships wanted to reach Bab al-Mandeb at the outlet to the Indian Ocean and its fabulous spices.

The attempt to control Sinai and the desert failed and the strategic

[35] G. Wiet, 'Les inscriptions de la Qal'ah Gindi', *Syria* 3 (1922), 58–65. It is possible that even Jisr 'Ajrud was attacked on this occasion. Prawer, *Histoire* i. 611, n. 26.

[36] John of Ibelin, *Lois* i. 417: 'L'arceveque dou Babbat (-Rabbat), qui est dit de la Pierre dou Desert, a un suffragant, l'evesque dou Faran qui ores est au Mont Synay.'

[37] Ibid. 417 and *Chronique d'Ernoul et de Bernard le Trésorier*, ed. L. de Mas Latrie (Paris, 1871), p. 68.

blunder of Hattin put an end to this phase of Crusader strategy. The Third Crusade and its scanty results created borders which were hardly defendable. In fact, the notion of frontiers lost some of its meaning. Crusader domination extended as far as it could actually be exercised from the maritime cities and some inland castles, which now became frontier fortifications. No less decisive was the fact that Saladin inaugurated a new policy, which was to be very effectively followed by al-Malik al-Mu'azzam, ruler of Damascus. This was a scorched-earth policy. Castles and city citadels, once captured, were razed to the ground. Saladin put his finger on the main weakness of the kingdom, its failure actually to colonize the captured lands. There was not enough manpower to master them effectively, let alone to settle them. Now, after the battle of Hattin and the tremendous loss of life and after Saladin's systematic destruction of castles and cities, there was neither manpower nor resources for reconstruction. Crusader sporadic military expeditions from the maritime cities could roam the country, not always even encountering Muslim armies, but such expeditions brought no tangible results. These could have been accomplished only by rebuilding and repopulating the cities and castles, a gigantic enterprise of restoration beyond the power of the Crusaders. They themselves were obviously conscious of the new situation. The answer to the challenge gave rise to a new strategy based on a single premiss: the domination of the Holy Land could only be achieved by the neutralization or domination of Egypt. The restored kingdom had to be won on the battlegrounds of Egypt.

The Fifth Crusade, in 1218, was directed against Egypt, and so was that of St. Louis in 1248. Both tried to wring out of the Sultans of Egypt, menaced in Cairo, the return of the Holy Land, and at most succeeded in doing so. In both cases the Sultans offered to comply, but in both cases there was strong opposition among the Crusaders to the cession of Cisjordan alone and an obstinate demand was voiced for the restoration of Transjordan and its fortifications.[38] The expeditions against Egypt, on the point of victory, ended in military disasters. The appearance of the Mongols and the simultaneous creation of the Mameluke kingdom in Egypt, which quickly made itself master of Syria, put an end to this last phase of Crusader strategic thinking. Its legacy was pursued in the *De Recuperatione Terrae Sanctae* treatises, in which the conquest of Egypt became the key-point of Crusader *reconquista* strategy.

---

[38] Cf. Prawer, *Histoire* ii. 156, 340, and 346.

19. The Battle of Hattin[1]

One of the most decisive battles of the Middle Ages was the battle of Hattin (1187). Although fought in the remote Galilean Mountains, it reverberated through the Near East and, by putting an end to the Latin Kingdom, triggered off the Third Crusade, one of the greatest military enterprises of the Middle Ages. No wonder, then, that the battle left its mark on historiography—more particularly on military historiography.[2] If we now try to reconsider its military aspects, this is because few studies have used all the sources available—rich but often obscure—and even fewer have related them to topographical facts.

Detailed descriptions of the battle are preserved in a number of chronicles and letters, some written soon after the event. But only one description, and that related to a single and strange episode, was written by an actual eyewitness. The chronicles and letters were by people who during the battle had stayed in Jerusalem, Acre, or Tyre, or by writers still more removed in space and time, who gathered evidence from those who had taken an active part in the battle. Among the Western sources, we have three important chronicles which furnish the Frankish version of the campaign. The most remarkable is an anonymous narrative, written in the kingdom, whose author gathered information from eyewitnesses he

---

[1] This chapter was published in a slightly shorter form in French in *Israel Exploration Journal* 7 (1964), 117–24.

[2] Among studies dealing with the battle from the military point of view, we note: H. Delpech, *La Tactique au XIIIe siècle* i (Paris, 1886), 360–75; G. Kohler, *Die Entwicklung des Kriegswesens und der Kriegsführung in der Ritterzeit von der Mitte des 11 Jahrhunderts bis zu den Hussitenkriegen* iii (Breslau, 1890), 216–24; C. Oman, *A History of the Art of War in the Middle Ages* i (London, 1924), 324–33; H. Delbrück, *Geschichte der Kriegskunst im Rahmen der politischen Geschichte* iii (Berlin, 1929), 427; Smail, *Crusading Warfare, 1097–1193*, pp. 189–203. In addition: Röhricht, *GKJ*, pp. 430–9; R. Grousset, *Histoire des Croisades* ii (Paris, 1935), 788–99; M.W. Baldwin, *Raymond III of Tripoli and the Fall of Jerusalem, 1140–1187* (Princeton, 1936), pp. 96–135, 151–5; F. Groh, *Der Zusammenbruch des Reiches Jerusalem, 1187–1189* (Jena, 1909); J. Richard, 'An Account of the Battle of Hattin referring to the Frankish Mercenaries in Oriental Moslem States', *Speculum* 27 (1952), 168–77; E. Blyth, 'The Battle of Hattin', *Pal. Expl. Fund, Quart. Statement*, 54 (1922), 32–8; G. Dalman, 'Schlacht von Hattin', *Palästina-Jahrbuch* (1914), pp. 41 ff., and since the earlier publication of the present chapter, P. Herde, 'Die Kämpfe bei den Hörnern von Hittin', *Römische Quartalschrift* 61. 1–50.

met in all probability after the fall of Jerusalem, i.e. about four months after Hattin. This is the *De expugnatione Terrae Sanctae per Saladinum Libellus*.[3] Valuable also are the *Continuations* of William of Tyre, whose own narrative ended in 1184. The Latin one is of little concern,[4] but those written in French—four in number—are of considerable interest. These can be reduced to two main versions, one very detailed,[5] the other more concise.[6] The relation between them is somewhat complicated,[7] but the authors of the two versions, or of their sources, were well acquainted with the region. Another source, which seems to be of Frankish origin, is preserved in the chronicle of Robert of Auxerre[8] and, with some variations, in a Universal Chronicle preserved in a Vatican manuscript.[9]

To these chronicles we have to add four letters sent from the Holy Land to Europe, which included descriptions of the events. They are: a 'Letter from the Genoese consuls to Pope Urban III', written by the city's authorities and based on an account of a Genoese merchant who returned from the Holy Land and who apparently brought to Europe the first news of the disaster;[10] a letter from the princes of the Holy Land to the Emperor Frederick I (end of July);[11] a letter from the Hospitallers to Archimbald in Italy (end of August);[12] and the letter from the Templar Terricus to Pope Urban III (August).[13]

---

[3] *De expugnatione Terrae Sanctae per Saladinum Libellus* (henceforth *Libellus*), ed. J. Stevenson, *Rolls Series*, 66 (London, 1875) in the appendix to *Radulphi de Coggeshall Chronicon Anglicanum*; cf. also H. Prutz, *Quellenbeiträge zur Geschichte der Kreuzzüge* (Danzig, 1876). There are valid reasons for assuming that his informer was a member of the contingent of Raymond of Tripoli.

[4] *Die lateinische Fortsetzung Wilhelms von Tyrus*, ed. M. Salloch (Berlin, 1934).

[5] The most detailed is that given in the manuscripts of Colbert and Fontainebleau, printed as version A–B of *Eracles, RHC HOcc*. ii. 52 ff.

[6] Ibid, versions C–G, published also as *Chronique d'Ernoul et de Bernard le Trésorier*, ed. M.L. de Mas Latrie (Paris, 1871).

[7] This complicated question has not yet found a unanimous answer. Cf. Mas Latrie in the preface to his edition and in the appendix. Cf. M.R. Morgan, *The Chronicle of Ernoul and the Continuation of William of Tyre* (Oxford, 1973).

[8] *MGH SS*, 26, pp. 249 ff.

[9] *Reg. Lat.* no. 598, published by Richard, op. cit., pp. 175–6.

[10] This letter (end of September 1187) was published by K. Hampe in *Neues Archiv der Gesellschaft für ältere deutsche Geschichtskunde* 22 (1897), 278–80. Cf. *Regesta*, no. 664a.

[11] 'Principes transmarinae Ecclesiae ad Fridericum I', *MGH SS* 21. 475. Cf. *Regesta*, no. 658.

[12]. 'Fratres Hospitalis ultramarini Archumbaldo' in Ansbert, *Historia de expeditione Friderici I imperatoris*, ed. A. Chroust in *Quellen zur Geschichte des Kreuzzuges Kaiser Friedrichs I* (Berlin, 1928), pp. 2–4. This letter was also preserved in other sources, cf. *Regesta*, nos. 661 and 661a.

[13]. 'Terricus magnus praeceptor Templi Urbano III', cf. *Regesta*, no. 660.

Among Arab sources, the most important is Imad al-Din al-Isfahani. He relied chiefly on Saladin's own testimony or on that of Saladin's companions. The campaign of Hattin was recorded in his *al-Barq al-Shāmī*. Unfortunately the volume concerning the year of the battle is lost, but the battle is also described in his *al-Fath al-Qūsī fī al-Fath al-Qūdsī*, and in Saladin's dispatch, written by Imad al-Din, to his brother in Yemen.[14] Excerpts from the dispatches inserted in Abu-Shama's chronicle[15] replace the normally voluble correspondence of the Qadi al-Fadil, Saladin's vizier, who was ill and bed-ridden during the campaign. During the summer of 1187 Saladin's famous biographer, Beha al-Din ibn Shadad, went on pilgrimage to Mecca and did not resume his duties until about a year after the battle of Hattin (1188). His account,[16] therefore, though near the events, is not exactly that of an eye-witness. The great Arab chronicler, Ibn al-Athir, was not with the armies of Saladin until later, but he recorded in his chronicle an episode of the battle told him by Saladin's son, al-Malik al-Afdal, who fought there with his father.[17] Finally we should mention a letter of a contemporary, 'Abd Allah ben Ahmed al-Muqaddasi, written at Ascalon on 20 August 1187, preserved by Muhammed ibn el-Qadsi[18] and reproduced by Abu Shama.[19]

Since the description of the events has come to us from many different sources, there are obvious difficulties in reconstructing them. But, in addition to the normal historical method of confronting different and often contradictory sources, there is another criterion which enables us to evaluate the truth and exactness of our sources—namely the topography of the area, which as recently as a hundred years ago did not differ very much from what it was during the Crusades.

Mobilization of the Armed Forces

Towards the end of May 1187, Guy of Lusignan, king of Jerusalem,

---

[14]. The part of *al-Barq al-Shāmī*, which deals with the events of A.H. 573–5 and A.H. 578–80 was preserved. Imad ed-Din el-Katib el-Isfahani, *The Conquest of Syria and of Palestine by Saladin*, ed. C. de Landberg, 1888. The editor included the famous *Rissāla* (= missive). German translation and detailed explanations by J. Kraemer, *Der Sturz des Königreichs Jerusalem (583/1187) in der Darstellung des 'Imād ed-Dīn al-Kātib al-Isfahāni* (Wiesbaden, 1952). Some of the more important passages were used by Abu-Shama.

[15]   Abu-Shama, *Le Livre des deux jardins, RHC HOr.* iv. 260 ff.

[16]   Beha ed-Din ibn Shadad, *Anecdotes et beaux traits de la vie du Sultan Yousouf, RHC HOr.* iii. 92 ff.

[17]   Ibn al-Athir, *Kamel Altevarykh, RCH HOr.* i. 677 ff.

[18]   Abu-Shama, pp. 286 ff.

[19]   The Syriac and Armenian sources do not furnish any important data. European sources

ordered a general mobilization. The assembly point, as was usual for campaigns in Galilee or on the frontiers of Damascus, was the springs near Saforie.[20] By the end of June an army, one of the largest ever mobilized by the Crusaders, was encamped there. According to various sources, it numbered no fewer than 1,200 knights and 15,000 to 18,000 foot-soldiers. These figures included the light cavalry of the 'Turcoples' and the troops of the Military Orders, in addition to contingents from the County of Tripoli and the Principality of Antioch. Ironically enough, it was the thorough success of mobilization, an urgent response to the menacing danger, that facilitated Saladin's task and caused the collapse of the kingdom after the defeat of Hattin. When the Frankish hosts gathered in Saforie, Muslim armies from Iraq, Syria, and Egypt, hastily summoned by Saladin's proclamation of the Jihad, mustered on the eastern banks of the Jordan. A detachment led by Saladin immediately attacked the lordship of Transjordan and besieged Crac and Montreal, while the rest of the army waited for reinforcements at Tell 'Ashtara. At the end of May Saladin, after a campaign in Frankish Transjordan, where he marauded and plundered the countryside but did not succeed in taking the Crusader strongholds, returned to Tell 'Ashtara. The Muslim military strength concentrated in Transjordan comprised, it seems, about 12,000 horsemen and a very large number of foot soldiers. The latter were of little importance in the Turco–Arab tactics. From Tell 'Ashtara the army moved to the south of the Sea of Galilee by way of Khisfin and arrived at el-Qahwani (Crusader: *Cavan*), near the bridge of Sinn al-Nabra (Crusader, *Senabra*). Here the army encamped, except for some detachments sent westward, until 1 July 1187. It was obvious that any decisive encounter, if one were to take place, would be in the region between Saforie and Tiberias in the north or Sinn al-Nabra in the south.

Not everybody in the Christian camp favoured a military operation, particularly a decisive battle. Raymond of Tripoli, prince of Galilee through his marriage to Eschive, heiress to Tiberias, was definitely opposed. Relying upon knowledge acquired during the long years of war against Muslim armies in the Holy Land and in Syria, he argued that, during the hot summer months, whoever was able to get an adequate water supply for troops and horses held the advantage. For the time being, the situation was the same for both camps: the Muslim camp on the shores

of the Third Crusade mention the battle of Hattin from second- and third-hand accounts.
    [20] 'Şippori' in Hebrew, 'Saffūriye' in Arabic, 'Sepphoris' in Greek, 'Saforie' in Crusader sources.

of the Sea of Galilee, the Christians around the rich springs of Saforie. If the Crusaders were to move eastward, they would be almost wholly cut off from water supplies in the arid and desolate region between Saforie and Tiberias. True, there were some water supplies south of the Beth-Netofah valley (Arabic: *Sahel al-Baṭṭôf*), but not enough for an army such as the Crusader army. Raymond's second argument was founded on an excellent appreciation of Saladin's army: the Muslims who came from distant countries were ready for immediate action, but would not remain long enough to pursue a long campaign. Sooner or later Saladin's army would disintegrate, and not even Saladin would be able to prevent this. (The actual events of the Third Crusade confirm the accuracy of this argument in detail.) So Tiberias would finally be evacuated and liberated.

On 2 July, leaving al-Qahwani, Saladin crossed the Jordan at Sinn al-Nabra and approached Tiberias. He did not attack the town immediately, but took up quarters on the hills overlooking the city from the west, thus isolating it and creating a barrier between Tiberias and the Crusaders at Saforie. Protected by the main Muslim forces on the hills, some picked detachments descended to the shore of the lake and besieged the city. That same night, they had already breached the walls and penetrated the abandoned lower town, as the garrison and part of the population took shelter in the citadel, which was in the northern part of the city. The news of the siege reached Saforie on the same day (2 July). At first the opinion of Raymond of Tripoli prevailed but, after a council of war which took place during the night of 2 and 3 July, and urged on by the Grand Master of the Templars, Gerard of Ridefort, King Guy decided to attack. When the Crusaders' camp awoke to hear the king's new decision, Saladin was moving his heavy equipment and provisions from the Sea of Galilee to Kafr Sabt.

The Road Network between Saforie and Tiberias

What really deserves re-examination, is the topography of the region and in particular of the road network. The region between Saforie and Tiberias is a mountainous plateau, crossed by shallow valleys and wadis. This permits an easy passage from west to east through Lower Galilee, from the Mediterranean to Tiberias and the Jordan River, a passage paralleled in the south by the Valley of Jezreel. The main road begins at Acre and, proceeding south-east, reaches the south-west point of the Valley of Beth-Netofah (Crusader: *Vallée Batof*), close to Khirbet al-Bedeiwiyah. Two kilometres to the east it meets with a road leading to Saforie in the south.

After that the main road, proceeding east–south–east, enters the Wadi Rummanah (Talmudic: *Rimmôn*) at the foot of the impressive massif of Mt. Tur'an. The mountain rises 300 m above the plateau, 500–550 m above sea level. In one of its folds nestles the village of Tu'ran. Between the road and the mountain is a flat area later to be called Marj al-Sunbul (the Plateau of Ears of Corn). The road, emerging from Wadi Rummanah, runs eastward to Wadi Jaraban (Wadi of Plantations) and Sahel el-'Atl (Vacant Plain). Leaving Wadi Jaraban, the ancient road divides: the first route leads north-east towards the plain between Meskenah (Talmudic: *Mashkena*) to the north and Lubiyah (Talmudic: *Lavi*) to the south, and continues as far as Hajarat al-Nasara (The Stones of the Christians), west of Tiberias. The other, east-south-east, passes north of Shejerah and Kafr Sabt (Talmudic: *Kfar Shûbtay*) and, following the course of Wadi Mu'allaqa (Suspended Wadi), turns north-east and, passing through Damiyah (Talmudic: *Damîn*) and Tell Ma'un (Talmudic: *Beth Ma'ôn*), reaches Tiberias. Another path leads to the southern Wadi Fejjas, through Khirbet Basum.

This description roughly corresponds to the network of roads as they existed at the end of the twelfth century. Since it is the clue to the battle, some additional remarks are necessary. The main west–east road is essentially the Darb al-Hawarnah, 'The Road of the Inhabitants of Hauran' which links the Jordan fords and the Sea of Galilee, with the Mediterranean coast in the west. We do not know when it was built, but we may assume that it was built by the Romans. Hebrew sources of the Talmudic (Byzantine) and Arab periods enable us to complete our outline of the road-system. The road named 'Roman road' in the *Survey of Western Palestine* and on the map of the Palestine Exploration Fund printed at the end of the last century, generally corresponds to the Talmudic information. It has been described by S. Klein, to whom we are indebted for important contributions to the study of Talmudic and post-Talmudic Galilee.[21] Klein's work has been complemented by the studies of M. Avi-Yonah, especially in an excellent map of the Holy Land during the Roman and Byzantine period, and in his commentary in the *Historical Geography of*

---

[21] The Roman roads were studied by P. Thompson, 'Die römischen Meilensteine', *ZDPV* 40 (1917), 68; A. Saarisalo, 'Topographical Researches in Galilee', *Journal of the Palestine Oriental Soc.* 9 (1929), 33. Cf. S. Klein, *The Galilee* (Hebrew), which summarizes his many studies of the subject. The Roman road is indicated on the *Map of Palestine*, Sheets V–VI, published by the Palestine Exploration Fund. The various localities in the Byzantine period are indicated in *Sefer ha-Yishuv* i (Heb., Jerusalem, 1939).

Palestine.[22] These studies and twelfth-century evidence bring us to revise our understanding of the road network in certain places.

The main road from Acre eastwards bifurcated after passing through the massif of Mt. Tur'an at the height of Kafr Sabt.[23] The main bifurcation was not here, however, but several kilometres to the west. The road joined the exit from Wadi Jaraban, and turned at an obtuse angle east–north–east, towards the area between Meskenah and Lubiyah. This road, which also led to Tiberias, must have been the main road between Tur'an and Tiberias in the Talmudic and post-Talmudic period. This is indicated by the fact that the Talmudic sources insist on 'Mashkena' (Meskenah) rather than Kafr Sabt as the middle of the road between Tiberias and Saforie, and therefore as the usual meeting place of travellers going from Saforie to Tiberias or vice versa. Indeed we read in the Talmud: 'Like the two travellers who depart, one from Tiberias and one from Sepphoris and meet each other at the place called Mashkena'.[24] The 'Hospice of Lubiyah'[25] was not the actual site of Khan Lubiyah, but a place located near the point of bifurcation. The proposed correction is corroborated by medieval sources (see below). G. Dalman indicated this road in an account of a journey of exploration in 1909:

'The road to Tiberias separates south of Kefr Tur'an into two branches. One leads straight to the east and then bends southward in the direction of Kefr Sabt (the ancient Kefar Shubtay) and Tiberias. It is indicated as the main road, but at present it is abandoned for the more northerly road through Lubiye, which, strangely enough, was omitted from the English map [*PEF*]. No doubt the surveyors were not conscious of its importance. In the middle of a col (*Einsattelung*), it crosses a plateau which extends from Lubiye (280 m) to Kh. Meskene (233 m) ... Following this road, the traveller coming from the Lake of Tiberias is spared the need to climb mountains, and continues travelling on an easy road leading on the plain, westward. This crossroad is however also the place where the traveller, proceeding eastwards to the Sea of Galilee, can turn and proceed north-east. It is also here that basalt begins to appear, so important in the vicinity of the Lake ... Close to Nimrin, a town of priests and carpet manufacturers on a hill, the road turns steeply beneath Qarn Hattin first reaching Hattin's spring and then, at 133 m above sea-level, the village of the same name.

---

[22] M. Avi-Yonah, 'Map of Roman Palestine', *Quarterly of the Dept. of Antiquities of Palestine* 5 (1936), 179. Idem, *The Holy Land from the Persian to the Arab conquests (536 B.C. to A.D. 640). A Historical Geography* (Grand Rapids, Michigan, 1966).

[23] Taking into account the topography of the region the bifurcation should be to the east of Wadi Mu'allaqa.

[24] *Talmud Yerushalmi, Berakhot* 13d, and cf. ibid., *Sanhedrin*, 21a, where 'Mashkena' is indicated as being 9 miles from Sippori (Saforie) and 7 miles from Tiberias.

[25] *Pûndaqà* (from *pandokion*) *de Lubyah*. Cf. S. Klein, *The Galilee*, pp. 95 and 120.

Without being aware of it, Dalman followed the precise route taken by the Crusaders when they set out for the battle of Hattin.[26] This inadvertent omission of a bifurcation and of a road from the map of the Palestine Exploration Fund, a map used by all historians of the Crusades, has misled many, as is evident from the uncertainties of the descriptions of the route followed by the Crusaders to the fatal battle-ground.

With this revision of the road network, we now turn to Crusader sources to follow the movements of the Christian and Muslim hosts leading to the battle.

The March on Qarn Hattin

On Friday, 3 July, the Crusaders moved from the rich springs of Saforie, the al-Qastal springs (Spring of the Castle 1·5 km south of the village of Saforie). The time of breaking camp is nowhere recorded but, since the king gave the new orders about midnight, after the last meal of the day, we can assume that the hasty departure took place just before sunrise, probably about 4 a.m.[27]

The Crusaders were confronted by two roads: one led from Saforie (where one can still see the small Crusader fortress with built-in Roman sarcophagi and the remarkable Crusader church) to the north to meet Acre's main road at Kh. Bedeiwiyah; the other led to the east through an easily passable wadi to Mash-had some 4·8 km further on. The Crusaders took the latter road.[28] The army marched in three columns: the vanguard commanded by Raymond of Tripoli; the centre by the king; and the rearguard by Balian of Ibelin. The mounted knights were preceded and probably flanked also by archers and crossbowmen, as well as by units of

---

[26] G. Dalman, *Orte und Wege Jesu* (Gütersloh, 1919), pp. 110 ff. Cf. his study in *Palästina-Jahrbuch* 10 (1914), 41.

[27] *Eracles*, pp. 52–3, states in both versions that the war council took place during the king's supper, near midnight. Even if the order to break camp was given immediately, it is hardly possible to assume that an army of some 15,000 men could have actually moved before 4 a.m. *Eracles*, p. 62, states: 'dou matin'. At this time of year it means around 4 a.m.

[28] All versions of *Eracles* state that the Crusaders captured a Muslim witch, a slave of a Syrian Christian from Nazareth, 2 leagues from Nazareth. The road we have indicated crosses precisely 2 leagues to the north of Nazareth the road leading from Nazareth to Kafr Kanna. This excludes the possibility that the Crusaders took the route which leads from Saforie to Kh. Bedeiwiyah to the north. This seems corroborated by Raymond of Tripoli, who argued that between Saforie and Tiberias there is only one source which could supply such a large army. He certainly referred to 'Ain Jozeh ('Spring of Nutts'), 1 km south of Kafr Kanna, not far from the road taken by the Crusaders from Mash-had, which passes Kafr Kanna and continues to Mt. Tur'an. Moreover, this was shorter than the road through Kh. Bedeiwiyah to Wadi Rummanah.

Turcoples, mounted archers who fought like the Saljuq or Turkish contingents. The heavy cavalry were the weakest point of the army when faced with Muslim troops far more mobile than their own. The enemy's mounted archers could shoot from well outside the range of Crusader spears and lances and thus avoid a frontal encounter with the Frankish cavalry. Once a Frankish horse was hit, the Crusader was at the mercy of the Muslim bowmen.[29] Against their dense rain of arrows there were only the Crusader foot-archers. Since they preceded and flanked the cavalry, they prescribed the rhythm of the march and, by slowing it down, made the Franks an easier target. For these reasons the Crusaders, and especially the Military Orders, who were the permanent nucleus of the kingdom's army, introduced the light mounted bowmen, the Turcoples.[30]

No sooner did the first Crusader units leave the springs of Saforie than they were attacked by Saladin's cavalry based on Kafr Sabt. Saladin himself commanded the central column, while the right and left wings were commanded by Taqi al-Din 'Amr and Muzaffar al-Din respectively.[31] The Frankish army was harassed on all sides but managed to preserve its unity. Vulnerable to the attackers' arrows, it did not break up into small units, which would have been easily destroyed by the Muslims. Many horses were hit by the enemy, who got within shooting distance. Time and again the same tactic was repeated. The Muslims shot and emptied their quivers from far outside the range of the Crusader weapons; then they disappeared on their light horses, only to reappear with new supplies of arrows.

During the morning the Crusader columns ventured into the Wadi Rummanah, their left wing partially sheltered by the massif of Mt. Tur'an, which rises some 200–300 m above the wadi.[32] After five or six hours of

---

[29] In this connection it is worth while quoting Abu-Shama, pp. 271–2: 'A Frankish knight (*fāris*), as long as his horse was in good condition, could not be knocked down. Covered by a cotte-de-mailles (*zaraja*) from head to foot, which made him look like a block of iron, the most violent blows made no impression on him. But once his horse was killed, the knight was thrown and taken prisoner. Consequently, though we counted them [Frankish prisoners] by the thousands, there were no horses among the spoils, whereas the knights were intact. The mount had to be felled by spear or sword, to bring down the knight from his saddle.'

[30] The basic problem was analysed by Smail, *Crusading Warfare*, pp. 111–12. Cf. Prawer, *Latin Kingdom*, pp. 340–1.

[31] The disposition of the Muslim troops is indicated by Muhammed ibn al-Qadsi in Abu Shama, p. 286.

[32] The two summits of the massif of Mt. Tur'an are 548 and 503 m high. The southern slope rises to 400 m, i.e. 200 m above the Wadi Rummanah.

difficult progress, at about 10 a.m.,[33] the Crusaders bypassed Kafr Tur'an, in the folds of Mount Tur'an. There, invisible and at some distance from the main road, was an important spring. The distance, or the presence of Muslim bowmen on the flank, ruled out the possibility of reaching the spring, and the Crusaders continued eastward. They had covered by then a distance of 12 km from Saforie. They continued for another two hours until noon, when Raymond, who commanded the vanguard, was informed that the continuous harassment had slowed down the march of the columns behind him and finally brought them to a standstill.[34] The vanguard was by then near the junction of the Meskenah and Lubiyah roads, and since early morning had covered some 18 km, a little more than half the distance between Saforie and Tiberias. Raymond, seeing that there was no hope to cover the remaining 17 km and to reach the sea of Galilee, made a bold decision and modified the plan of the march. Instead of moving a tired army eastwards through Lubiyah and Tell Ma'un—a dangerous plan, as the Crusaders would enter a region barred by Muslim troops in the south at Kafr Sabt and by Muslim detachments besieging the citadel of Tiberias—he decided to cross the rising ground to the north,[35] and to reach the abundant spring of Kafr Hattin.

A Crusader chronicler, well acquainted with the region, described this dramatic moment: 'There was no water at all where they stood, and therefore to pitch tents on this spot was impossible; but not far from there, beyond that mountain on the left, was a village named Hattin where there was plenty of water from the springs. There it was possible to bivouac for the night, and to resume in good form the march to Tiberias the following day.'[36] Raymond's decision was basically sound. Even if the Crusaders had continued their march with the same speed as during the first half of the day, they needed five or six hours before reaching Tiberias. Given the heat and their exhaustion, there was little chance of success. On the other hand,

---

[33] The time-table suggested here is based on an average march of 2–3 km per hour.

[34] *Eracles*, p. 62: 'A hore de midi' and again 'a mijor', and in another version, p. 59: 'il fu bien none', that is at noon. *Eracles*, p. 62: 'Chevaucherent a grant meschef contre mont la valée qui est apelée le Barof'. Barof or Batof is the Talmudic 'Biq'at Beit Netōfa', Arabic 'Sahl al-Battof'. This dry valley parallels Wadi Rummanah behind the massif of Mt. Tur'an. The ground of Wadi Rummanah begins to rise in the east, which explains the 'contre mont'.

[35] The road south of the Mt Tur'an massif rises from 200 to 220 m to the east, reaches 250 m at Kh. Meskenah and some 300 m further north-east. This explains *Eracles*, p. 62: 'torna contre mont la costiere'.

[36] *Eracles*, p. 62: 'la ou il estoient n'avoit point d'eve... mais iqui pres, outre cele montaigne a senestre, avoit un casal qui a nom Habatin [= Hattin], ou il a eve de fonteines à grant planté, ou l'en porroit herberger la nuit et lendemain aler a Tabarie a grant loisir.'

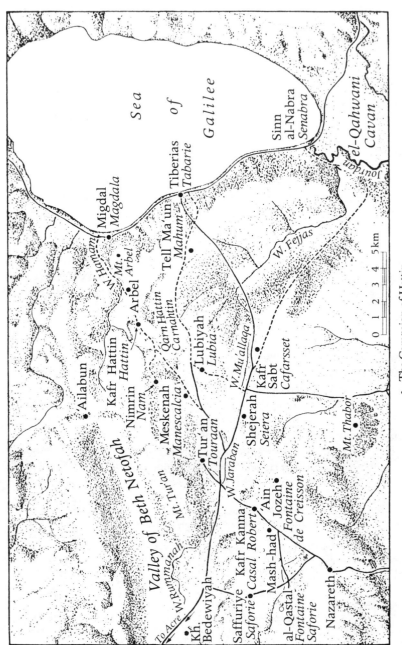

3. The Campaign of Hattin

the Crusader army was only about 5 km from the springs of Hattin, a distance that could have been covered the same day.[37] For this decision Raymond was severely censored. The Christians, it was argued, should have pushed forward and attacked the Muslims, who could have been defeated.[38] The king followed Raymond's advice: the route they had followed so far was abandoned, and the host turned left, around the slope of the Mt. Tur'an massif.

Since the region is now familiar, we can easily reconstruct the Crusaders' manoeuvre. The troops were at the Meskenah bifurcation leading north to Hattin and east to Lubiyah, Tell Ma'un, and Tiberias. Close to Meskenah, the army turned left, i.e. north-east. Kafr Nimrin on Mt. Nimrin was now to its left, Qarn Hattin to its right, and in front of it, 5 km distant, at the bottom of the deep gorge (a descent from *c.* 300 m to 120 m in space of 1 km), at the foot of Qarn Hattin were the springs of Kafr Hattin.[39] Raymond's plan to reach these springs was a reasonable one.

When the Crusaders were ordered to leave the main road, however, their formation began to disintegrate.[40] The contact between the knights, who spurred their horses in order to reach water quickly, and the foot bowmen, the only ones able to keep back the mounted Muslim archers, was broken. The Muslims, who correctly interpreted the Crusader manoeuvre to reach the springs, advanced quickly and barred the entrance to the path to Kafr Hattin and established themselves at the springs.[41] At the same time the Crusaders' rearguard came under heavy attack. The Templars who composed that column tried to charge but did not succeed. The king, now convinced that it was no longer possible to reach even the springs, ordered the Crusaders to pitch camp where they were.[42] While they were pitching their tents at Meskenah,[43] Muslim assaults continued

---

[37] Even this was not easy as there was a steep rise from 185 to 300 m in a space of 2 km.

[38] *Eracles*, p. 63: 'Car se li Crestien eussent lors point esforceement, li Turc eussent esté desconfit.'

[39] Cf. *Libellus*, p. 223.

[40] *Eracles*, p. 63: 'en celui torner li Crestien se desayverent por covoitise d'aler a l'eve.'

[41] Ibid.: 'li Turc pristrent cuer et lor corurent sus de toutes pars, et s'avancerent si que il pristrent l'eve.'

[42] Contrary to *Eracles*, p. 63, and its versions, where the advice was allegedly given by Raymond. This is hardly plausible, because Raymond, as we indicated, wanted at all cost to reach the sources of Hattin. We should rather follow the author of the *Libellus*, p. 223, who indicates that the order was issued by the king *ex improviso* and despite Raymond's opposition. The latter, hearing the order, exclaimed: 'Heu, heu, Domine Deus, finita est guerra, traditi sumus ad mortem et terra destructa est.'.

[43] There are different spellings of the name, among them *Manescleia*, which seems to be

(*continued*)

without respite, and did not cease until nightfall. The assailants now reorganized. The right wing under Taqi al-Din 'Amr seized the entrance to the gorge which led to Hattin.[44] His troops spread over the plateau between Nimrin and Qarn Hattin, a space of about 4 kilometres, closing the entrance to the two steep paths which run from the plateau to the springs. At the same time the main body of the Muslim army commanded by Saladin, at the heels of the Crusaders' rearguard during the march along Mt. Tur'an, pitched its tents near Kafr Lubiyah, thus facing the main Crusader troops encamped at Meskenah. According to the testimony of a Frankish chronicle, the two enemy camps were so close that the soldiers of the two camps could speak to each other. The Muslims surrounded the Crusaders so tightly, says another chronicler, that not even a cat could make its way out of the camp. The situation and the morale in the two camps were very different. The Crusaders were tormented by thirst, for neither they nor their horses had had any water since leaving Saforie. Moreover, the Muslims knew that the Crusaders were trapped. Throughout the night cries of 'Allāh akbar' and 'la ilāha illā Allāh' were heard from the Muslim camp. Meanwhile Saladin gave orders for moving military equipment from this main base at Kafr Sabt and assuring water supplies from the Sea of Galilee. Camels carried water-filled goatskins, which were emptied into cisterns or makeshift reservoirs specially dug for this purpose in the camp. Other caravans brought military equipment: 400 loads of arrows were distributed among the various Muslim contingents, and seventy dromedaries carrying arrow reserves were stationed among the troops.[45]

The Day of the Battle

On Saturday, 4 July 1187, at dawn, after a sleepless night, the Crusaders set out towards their destiny. It was already too late to retreat. The fate of the army was to be determined in the fight for access to the springs at Kafr Hattin. The Muslims let the Crusaders break camp and leave. The attack was launched after 9 a.m.[46] when the oppressive sun in this arid mountainous region was high in the east, directly in the faces of the

---

the nearest to Meskanah. It was finally *Marescalcia* which won the day, probably because of its familiarity to European ears.

[44] This was his position on the following day. Beha al-Din, p. 94; al-Qadsi, p. 284.

[45] Abu Shama, p. 266.

[46] Archumbald's letter: 'circa horam tertiam.' *Eracles*, p. 64: 'haute tierce'. 'Haute tierce' points rather to a later hour, the end of the third hour, i.e. near noon.

Crusaders. The Crusaders moved from Meskenah, over a rising plateau, to Hattin. Once again the main attack, possibly led by Saladin in person, was directed against the Crusader rearguard, the Templars. They fought back vigorously, but since other Frankish contingents could not support them, their counter-attack failed.[47] Meanwhile, the bulk of the Crusader army moved to the rising ground between Nimrin,[48] and the Horns of Hattin. This mountainous plain,[49] facing what is now the kibbutz Lavi, slopes gently to the north, but from Qarn Hattin in the north-east the slope is extremely steep. Only two or three paths abruptly descend to the funnel-like gorge of Kafr Hattin at the bottom.[50] The Crusaders' goal was to force the Muslim barrier at the brink of the plain leading to Kafr Hattin.[51] But the Muslims resumed their attack and fell simultaneously on the rearguard and on the right wing. The Crusaders reorganized their troops. The most detailed description gives the following picture:

> When they were ranged and divided into columns, the foot soldiers were ordered to defend the army by shooting arrows, so that the knights could more easily resist the enemy. The knights were to be protected by foot-soldiers from enemy archers, and the foot soldiers helped by the lances of the knights against the inroads of the enemy. Thus by mutual help both would be protected and saved.[52]

The tactic was correct, but at the critical moment the foot archers failed and scattered under the impact of the Muslim attack. In despair, the king gave the order to encamp, hoping to rally his troops, but the rallying

---

[47] The Genoese letter to Pope Urban III (above, n. 10, p. 279), seems to refer to this episode. Cf. *Libellus*, p. 223.

[48] Archumbald indicated in his letter (p. 2, 1. 25–8), that the king marched one league more to 'Naim'; another manuscript has 'Anam', obviously, as already suggested by Chroust, 'Nam'. This cannot refer to either the biblical Na'im, near Mt. Tabor, or Tell al-Naam some 10 km south-east of Hattin. The only possibility is the village of Nimrin, which topographically corresponds to our data. It is worth noting that on the famous map of Jacotin, the cartographer of Napoleon's expedition to the Levant, Nimrin is indicated as the place of General Junot's victory (April 1799) over the troops of Damascus. The French name on the map is Ne'men, the printed Arabic name 'Nemen' or 'Naman', is quite close to the spelling of Archumbald.'

[49] The battlefield is an irregular quadrangle, 2 km by 2 km. The ground rises in the east leading to the Horns of Hattin and in the west to the outcrops of Mt. Nimrin.

[50] From 300 m above sea level at the foot of the Horns to 120 m at the level of the sources of the village of Hattin.

[51] *Libellus*, p. 224: 'Processit denique comes [Tripoli] ut obtineret locum quem Turci jam incoeperant appropinquare.'

[52] *Libellus*, p. 224: 'Cum autem ordinati essent, et per acies distincti, praeceperunt peditibus ut sagittando munirent exercitum, quatinus milites levius hostibus obstarent, ut milites muniti per pedites a sagittariis hostibus, et pedites per lanceas militum ab incursu hostium essent adjuti, et ita utrique mutuo adjutorio defensi salutem obtinerent.'

turned into confusion. 'The columns became loose and, gathered around the Holy Cross they were thrown into disorder, running hither and thither.'[53] The Muslim attacks intensified, and the Crusaders succeeded, in pitching three tents only, at the foot of Qarn Hattin.[54] Moreover, the Muslims started brushwood fires, and since at that time there was a western wind blowing from the Beth Netofah Valley,[55] the Crusaders were suddenly surrounded by flames and dense smoke. The Muslim army was now hidden from the Crusaders by an opaque smoke-screen, while the Crusaders were cornered in a narrow, rocky plain, their masses an easy target for enemy arrows. Raymond in the vanguard was cut off from the main body of the army. According to the author of the *Libellus*, which was very favourable to Raymond, the count decided that all was lost. Ordering 'qui potest transire transeat', the ancestor of *sauve qui peut*, he tried to break the Muslim hold on the entrance to the steep path which led to the village of Hattin. Here there was water in abundance, and beyond the way was open through the Valley of Arbel and the Wadi Hamam to the Sea of Tiberias, north of Migdal (al-Majdal; Magdala).

Raymond's action is differently described in the various Crusader sources. Though the action itself is not in doubt, the chronological sequence is not clear. The author of the *Libellus*, as we saw, insists on an independent decision of Raymond. On the other hand the author of *Eracles* placed the action in another context—that of the king's order. The Muslims let the thirsty Crusaders' army move from Meskenah. They waited until the heat of the day became unbearable. Some knights from Raymond's contingent, unable to resist, left the army and went over to Saladin, and so did the foot soldiers. At that point: 'When the king saw the distress and anxiety of our people, and that the foot soldiers were going to surrender to the Saracens, he ordered the count of Tripoli to pounce on the Saracens, because the battle was on his land and he had the right of first attack.'[56] It is impossible to decide which version to follow. The *Libellus* seems to be more realistic and exonerates Raymond on grounds of stringent circumstances; *Eracles* exonerates him even more by ascribing his action to the king's order. Neither was sufficient to vindicate

[53] *Libellus*, p. 225: 'Igitur diffusae sunt acies, et descenderunt circa sanctam crucem confusi et intermixti huc atque illuc.'

[54] Letter of Archumbald, p. 4: 'The count of Tripoli came to the king and told him to pitch his tents (*attentare*) near a mountain, a kind of fortress, and there was no possibility of pitching more than three tents only there.'

[55] *Eracles*, p. 64.

[56] Ibid. and in all versions.

Raymond's good faith. The fact that he saved himself, in conjunction with his agreement with Saladin some years earlier—an agreement which, if not an actual act of treason, came dangerously near it—labelled him as a traitor.

In whatever circumstances the decision was taken, we can follow Raymond's movements. The Muslim commander who faced Raymond was Taqi al-Din, Saladin's beloved nephew. Like every Muslim commander, he knew that no force could stop the charge of the swiftly moving block of an iron-clad Crusader column. This was especially true in the present case, when Raymond's knights were to charge down the steep slope leading to Kafr Hattin. Taqi al-Din took the right decisions. When Raymond and his troops charged he ordered his troops to open ranks. The Crusaders rushed through the Muslim array without coming in contact with the enemy. Then the Muslims closed ranks again, facing the bulk of the Crusader army, which had lost contact with its former vanguard.[57] The Crusaders' morale was broken by the failure of a breakthrough. Foot soldiers and even knights began to surrender. Yet the army was still intact and defended itself. Unfortunately at that critical moment the foot soldiers failed. They abandoned the battle-field, and in complete disorder began to climb the steep slope leading to the northern summit of Qarn Hattin, some 30 m above the surrounding plateau. This massive desertion of the infantry marked the beginning of the end. Repeated royal orders were of no avail. The foot soldiers who reached the summit no longer thought of battle. Nothing, not even death, could bring them back into the whirlwind of Muslim and Christian horsemen at their feet. The Crusader knights, though no longer protected from enemy arrows, because their own bowmen had abandoned them, fought heroically. They repelled numerous Muslim attacks, which continuously thinned their ranks. At the end, those who were still able climbed the hill and entrenched themselves on the summit, probably on the southern side of the hill. The king's red tent was pitched beside the True Cross, carried from Saforie. Here the knights regrouped. From the saddle between the two peaks they charged twice.[58] One of these charges even endangered

---

[57] *Libellus*, p. 226 has a dramatic description of Raymond's flight or attack. Although the text is not too clear, the topographical data are well indicated. Raymond 'et ceteri Pullani, qui adhuc erant equitantes, videntes hoc dedere terga, atque supradictum locum angustum vi (*vers. in*) equorum concalcando Christianos et pontem faciendo, quasi per planum iter, ita per angusta loca et scopulosa super suos et Turcos et crucem fugiendo transierunt.'

[58] Ibn al-Athir, pp. 685 ff.

Saladin's life. Exhausted and thirsty, the Crusaders continued to spread death around them. It was only when the True Cross was captured and the red tent of the king of Jerusalem overthrown, that the battle was over. The Muslims, who by now had reached the top of the hill, found Frankish soldiers lying motionless on its two peaks. They had no strength left to fight. The Crusaders lost the battle, and with it a kingdom which had existed for eighty-eight years, since the conquest of Jerusalem in July 1099.

Index